Communications
in Computer and Information Science   762

Commenced Publication in 2007
Founding and Former Series Editors:
Alfredo Cuzzocrea, Orhun Kara, Dominik Ślęzak, and Xiaokang Yang

More information about this series at http://www.springer.com/series/7899

Dong Yue · Chen Peng
Dajun Du · Tengfei Zhang
Min Zheng · Qinglong Han (Eds.)

Intelligent Computing, Networked Control, and Their Engineering Applications

International Conference on Life System Modeling
and Simulation, LSMS 2017
and International Conference on Intelligent Computing
for Sustainable Energy and Environment, ICSEE 2017
Nanjing, China, September 22–24, 2017
Proceedings, Part II

 Springer

Editors

Dong Yue
Nanjing University of Posts
 and Telecommunications
Nanjing
China

Chen Peng
Shanghai University
Shanghai
China

Dajun Du
Shanghai University
Shanghai
China

Tengfei Zhang
Nanjing University of Posts
 and Telecommunications
Nanjing
China

Min Zheng
Shanghai University
Shanghai
China

Qinglong Han
Swinburne University of Technology
Melbourne, VIC
Australia

ISSN 1865-0929   ISSN 1865-0937 (electronic)
Communications in Computer and Information Science
ISBN 978-981-10-6372-5   ISBN 978-981-10-6373-2   (eBook)
DOI 10.1007/978-981-10-6373-2

Library of Congress Control Number: 2017951426

Printed on acid-free paper

This Springer imprint is published by Springer Nature
The registered company is Springer Nature Singapore Pte Ltd.
The registered company address is: 152 Beach Road, #21-01/04 Gateway East, Singapore 189721, Singapore

Preface

This book constitutes the proceedings of the 2017 International Conference on Life System Modeling and Simulation (LSMS 2017) and the 2017 International Conference on Intelligent Computing for Sustainable Energy and Environment (ICSEE 2017), which were held during September 22–24, in Nanjing, China. These two international conference series aim to bring together international researchers and practitioners in the fields of advanced methods for life system modeling and simulation as well as advanced intelligent computing theory and methodologies and engineering applications for sustainable energy and environment. The two conferences held this year were built on the success of previous LSMS and ICSEE conferences held in Shanghai and Wuxi, respectively. The success of the LSMS and ICSEE conference series were also based on several large-scale RCUK/NSFC funded UK–China collaborative projects on sustainable energy and environment, as well as a recent government funded project on the establishment of the UK-China University Consortium in Engineering Education and Research, with an initial focus on sustainable energy and intelligent manufacturing.

At LSMS 2017 and ICSEE 2017, technical exchanges within the research community took the form of keynote speeches, panel discussions, as well as oral and poster presentations. In particular, two workshops, namely, the Workshop on Smart Grid and Electric Vehicles and the Workshop on Communication and Control for Distributed Networked Systems, were held in parallel with LSMS 2017 and ICSEE 2017, focusing on the two recent hot topics on green and sustainable energy systems and electric vehicles and distributed networked systems for the Internet of Things.

The LSMS 2017 and ICSEE 2017 conferences received over 625 submissions from 14 countries and regions. All papers went through a rigorous peer review procedure and each paper received at least three review reports. Based on the review reports, the Program Committee finally selected 208 high-quality papers for presentation at LSMS 2017 and ICSEE 2017. These papers cover 22 topics, and are included in three volumes of CCIS proceedings published by Springer. This volume of CCIS includes 70 papers covering 8 relevant topics.

Located at the heartland of the wealthy lower Yangtze River region in China and being the capital of several dynasties, kingdoms, and republican governments dating back to the 3rd century, Nanjing has long been a major center of culture, education, research, politics, economy, transport networks, and tourism. In addition to academic exchanges, participants were treated to a series of social events, including receptions and networking sessions, which served to build new connections, foster friendships, and forge collaborations. The organizers of LSMS 2017 and ICSEE 2017 would like to acknowledge the enormous contribution of the Advisory Committee, who provided guidance and advice, the Program Committee and the numerous referees for their efforts in reviewing and soliciting the papers, and the Publication Committee for their editorial work. We would also like to thank the editorial team from Springer for their support and guidance. Particular thanks are of course due to all the authors, as without their high-quality submissions and presentations the conferences would not have been successful.

Finally, we would like to express our gratitude to our sponsors and organizers, listed on the following pages.

September 2017

Bo Hu Li
Sarah Spurgeon
Mitsuo Umezu
Minrui Fei
Kang Li
Dong Yue
Qinglong Han
Shiwei Ma
Luonan Chen
Sean McLoone

Organization

Sponsors

China Simulation Federation (CSF), China
Chinese Association for Artificial Intelligence (CAAI), China
IEEE Systems, Man & Cybernetics Society Technical Committee on Systems Biology, USA
IEEE CC Ireland Chapter, Ireland

Technical Support Organization

National Natural Science Foundation of China (NSFC), China

Organizers

Shanghai University, China
Queen's University Belfast, UK
Nanjing University of Posts and Telecommunications, China
Southeast University, China
Life System Modeling and Simulation Technical Committee of CSF, China
Embedded Instrument and System Technical Committee of China Instrument and Control Society, China
Intelligent Control and Intelligent Management Technical Committee of CAAI, China

Co-sponsors

Shanghai Association for System Simulation, China
Shanghai Association of Automation, China
Shanghai Instrument and Control Society, China
Jiangsu Association of Automation, China

Co-organizers

Swinburne University of Technology, Australia
Queensland University of Technology, Australia
Tsinghua University, China
Harbin Institute of Technology, China
China State Grid Electric Power Research Institute, China
Chongqing University, China
University of Essex, UK
Cranfield University, UK
Peking University, China

Nantong University, China
Shanghai Dianji University, China
Jiangsu Engineering Laboratory of Big Data Analysis and Control for Active
   Distribution Network, China
Shanghai Key Laboratory of Power Station Automation Technology, China

Honorary Chairs

Li, Bo Hu, China
Spurgeon, Sarah, UK
Umezu, Mitsuo, Japan

Advisory Committee Members

Bai, Erwei, USA
Ge, Shuzhi, Singapore
He, Haibo, USA
Hu, Huosheng, UK
Huang, Biao, Canada
Hussain, Amir, UK
Liu, Derong, USA
Mi, Chris, USA

Nikolopoulos,
   Dimitrios S., UK
Pardalos, Panos M., USA
Pedrycz, Witold, Canada
Polycarpou, Marios M.,
   Cyprus
Qin, Joe, HK
Scott, Stan, UK

Tan, KC, Singapore
Tassou, Savvas, UK
Thompson, Stephen, UK
Wang, Jun, HK
Wang, Zidong, UK
Wu, Qinghua, China
Xue, Yusheng, China
Zhang, Lin, China

General Chairs

Fei, Minrui, China
Li, Kang, UK
Yue, Dong, China

International Program Committee

Chairs

Chen, Luonan, Japan
Han, Qinglong, Australia
Ma, Shiwei, China
McLoone, Sean, UK

Local Chairs

Chiu, Min-Sen, Singapore
Cui, Shumei, China
Deng, Mingcong, Japan
Ding, Yongsheng, China
Ding, Zhengtao, UK
Fang, Qing, Japan

Fridman, Emilia, Israel
Gao, Furong, HK
Gu, Xingsheng, China
Guerrero, Josep M.,
   Demark
Gupta, Madan M., Canada

Hunger, Axel, Germany
Lam, Hak-Keung, UK
Liu, Wanquan, Australia
Luk, Patrick, UK
Maione, Guido, Italy
Park, Jessie, Korea

Peng, Chen, China
Su, Zhou, China
Tian, Yuchu, Australia
Xu, Peter, New Zealand

Yang, Taicheng, UK
Yu, Wen, Mexico
Zeng, Xiaojun, UK
Zhang, Huaguang, China

Zhang, Jianhua, China
Zhang, Wenjun, Canada
Zhao, Dongbin, China

Members

Andreasson, Stefan, UK
Adamatzky, Andy, UK
Altrock, Philipp, USA
Asirvadam, Vijay S.,
    Malaysia
Baig, Hasan, UK
Baker, Lucy, UK
Barry, John, UK
Best, Robert, UK
Bu, Xiongzhu, China
Cao, Jun, UK
Cao, Yi, UK
Chang, Xiaoming, China
Chen, Jing, China
Chen, Ling, China
Chen, Qigong, China
Chen, Rongbao, China
Chen, Wenhua, UK
Cotton, Matthew, UK
Deng, Jing, UK
Deng, Li, China
Deng, Shuai, China
Deng, Song, China
Deng, Weihua, China
Ding, Yate, UK
Ding, Zhigang, China
Du, Dajun, China
Du, Xiangyang, China
Ellis, Geraint, UK
Fang, Dongfeng, USA
Feng, Dongqing, China
Feng, Zhiguo, China
Foley, Aoife, UK
Fu, Jingqi, China
Gao, Shouwei, China
Gu, Dongbin, UK
Gu, Juping, China
Gu, Zhou, China
Guo, Lingzhong, UK

Han, Bo, China
Han, Xuezheng, China
Heiland, Jan, Germany
Hong, Xia, UK
Hou, Weiyan, China
Hu, Liangjian, China
Hu, Qingxi, China
Hu, Sideng, China
Huang, Sunan, Singapore
Huang, Wenjun, China
Hwang, Tan Teng,
    Malaysia
Jia, Dongyao, UK
Jiang, Lin, UK
Jiang, Ming, China
Jiang, Ping, China
Jiang, Yucheng, China
Kuo, Youngwook, UK
Laverty, David, UK
Li, Chuanfeng, China
Li, Chuanjiang, China
Li, Dewei, China
Li, Donghai, China
Li, Guozheng, China
Li, Jingzhao, China
Li, Ning, China
Li, Tao, China
Li, Tongtao, China
Li, Weixing, China
Li, Xin, China
Li, Xinghua, China
Li, Yunze, China
Li, Zhengping, China
Lin, Zhihao, China
Lino, Paolo, Italy
Liu, Chao, France
Liu, Guoqiang, China
Liu, Mandan, China
Liu, Shirong, China

Liu, Shujun, China
Liu, Tingzhang, China
Liu, Xianzhong, China
Liu, Yang, China
Liu, Yunhuai, China
Liu, Zhen, China
Ljubo, Vlacic, Australia
Lu, Ning, Canada
Luan, Tom, Australia
Luo, Jianfei, China
Ma, Hongjun, China
McAfee, Marion, Ireland
Menary, Gary, UK
Meng, Xianhai, UK
Menhas, Muhammad
    Ilyas, Pakistan
Menzies, Gillian, UK
Naeem, Wasif, UK
Nie, Shengdong, China
Niu, Yuguang, China
Nyugen, Bao Kha, UK
Ouyang, Mingsan, China
Oyinlola, Muyiwa, UK
Pan, Hui, China
Pan, Ying, China
Phan, Anh, UK
Qadrdan, Meysam, UK
Qian, Hua, China
Qu, Yanbin, China
Raszewski, Slawomir, UK
Ren, Wei, China
Rivotti, Pedro, UK
Rong, Qiguo, China
Shao, Chenxi, China
Shi, Yuntao, China
Smyth, Beatrice, UK
Song, Shiji, China
Song, Yang, China
Su, Hongye, China

Sun, Guangming, China
Sun, Xin, China
Sun, Zhiqiang, China
Tang, Xiaoqing, UK
Teng, Fei, UK
Teng, Huaqiang, China
Trung, Dong, UK
Tu, Xiaowei, China
Vlacic, Ljubo, UK
Wang, Gang, China
Wang, Jianzhong, China
Wang, Jihong, UK
Wang, Ling, China
Wang, Mingshun, China
Wang, Shuangxin, China
Wang, Songyan, China
Wang, Yaonan, China
Wei, Kaixia, China
Wei, Lisheng, China
Wei, Mingshan, China
Wen, Guihua, China
Wu, Jianguo, China
Wu, Jianzhong, UK

Wu, Lingyun, China
Wu, Zhongcheng, China
Xie, Hui, China
Xu, Sheng, China
Xu, Wei, China
Xu, Xiandong, UK
Yan, Huaicheng, China
Yan, Jin, UK
Yang, Aolei, China
Yang, Kan, USA
Yang, Shuanghua, UK
Yang, Wankou, China
Yang, Wenqiang, China
Yang, Zhile, UK
Yang, Zhixin, Macau
Ye, Dan, China
You, Keyou, China
Yu, Ansheng, China
Yu, Dingli, UK
Yu, Hongnian, UK
Yu, Xin, China
Yuan, Jin, China
Yuan, Jingqi, China

Yue, Hong, UK
Zeng, Xiaojun, UK
Zhang, Dengfeng, China
Zhang, Hongguang, China
Zhang, Jian, China
Zhang, Jingjing, UK
Zhang, Lidong, China
Zhang, Long, UK
Zhang, Qianfan, China
Zhang, Xiaolei, UK
Zhang, Yunong, China
Zhao, Dongya, China
Zhao, jun, China
Zhao, Wanqing, UK
Zhao, Xiaodong, UK
Zhao, Xingang, China
Zheng, Xiaojun, UK
Zhou, Huiyu, UK
Zhou, Wenju, China
Zhou, Yu, China
Zhu, Yunpu, China
Zong, Yi, Demark
Zuo, Kaizhong, China

Organization Committee

Chairs

Li, Xin, China
Wu, Yunjie, China
Naeem, Wasif, UK
Zhang, Tengfei, China
Cao, Xianghui, China

Members

Chen, Ling, China
Deng, Li, China
Du, Dajun, China
Jia, Li, China
Song, Yang, China
Sun, Xin, China
Xu, Xiandong, China
Yang, Aolei, China
Yang, Banghua, China
Zheng, Min, China
Zhou, Peng, China

Special Session Chairs

Wang, Ling, China
Meng, Fanlin, UK

Publication Chairs

Zhou, Huiyu, UK
Niu, Qun, China

Publicity Chairs

Jia, Li, China
Yang, Erfu, UK

Registration Chairs

Song, Yang, China
Deng, Li, China

Secretary-General

Sun, Xin, China
Wu, Songsong, China
Yang, Zhile, UK

Contents

Intelligent Modeling, Monitoring, and Control of Complex Nonlinear Systems

Advanced Methods for Networked Systems

Control and Analysis of Transportation Systems

Advanced Sliding Mode Control and Applications

Advanced Analysis of New Materials and Devices

Advanced Fuzzy and Neural Network Theory and Algorithms

A Robust Fuzzy c-Means Clustering Algorithm for Incomplete Data

Jinhua Li[1], Shiji Song[1(✉)], Yuli Zhang[1,2(✉)], and Kang Li[3]

[1] Department of Automation, TNList, Tsinghua University,
Beijing 100084, People's Republic of China
lijinhua11@mails.tsinghua.edu.cn, {shijis,zhangyuli}@mail.tsinghua.edu.cn
[2] Department of Industrial Engineering, Tsinghua University,
Beijing 100084, People's Republic of China
[3] School of Electronics, Electrical Engineering and Computer Science,
Queens University Belfast, Belfast, UK
k.li@qub.ac.uk

Abstract. Date sets with missing feature values are prevalent in clustering analysis. Most existing clustering methods for incomplete data rely on imputations of missing feature values. However, accurate imputations are usually hard to obtain especially for small-size or highly corrupted data sets. To address this issue, this paper proposes a robust fuzzy c-means (RFCM) clustering algorithm, which does not require imputations. The proposed RFCM represents the missing feature values by intervals, which can be easily constructed using the K-nearest neighbors method, and adopts a min-max optimization model to reduce the impact of noises on clustering performance. We give an equivalent tractable reformulation of the min-max optimization problem and propose an efficient solution method based on smoothing and gradient projection techniques. Experiments on UCI data sets validate the effectiveness of the proposed RFCM algorithm by comparison with existing clustering methods for incomplete data.

Keywords: Robust FCM · Interval data · Robust clustering algorithm

1 Introduction

Clustering analysis is a common technique in machine learning and data mining and has wide applications. Traditional clustering methods only tackle "complete" data sets, where no missing feature values exist. However, missing data are common occurrences in practice due to various reasons, such as missing replies in

S. Song—This work was supported by the Major Program of the National Natural Science Foundation of China under Grant 41427806, the National Natural Science Foundation of China under Grants 61503211 and 9152002, and the Project of China Ocean Association under Grant DYXM-125-25-02.

© Springer Nature Singapore Pte Ltd. 2017
D. Yue et al. (Eds.): LSMS/ICSEE 2017, Part II, CCIS 762, pp. 3–12, 2017.
DOI: 10.1007/978-981-10-6373-2_1

questionnaire, high cost to acquire some feature values and improper collection procedure of data.

To address incomplete data clustering problems, a direct method is to use the two-step approach, which first estimates the missing feature values by imputation [16] and then applies the traditional clustering methods for complete data. Besides the imputation-based approaches, four strategies are proposed by [3] to tailor the FCM algorithm to handle incomplete data, including the whole data strategy (WDS), the partial distance strategy (PDS), the optimal completion strategy (OCS) and the nearest prototype strategy (NPS). In addition to these strategies, principal component analysis (PCA) [9] and local PCA [4] have also been used to capture incomplete data structure.

The limitations of these direct and iterative imputation methods are two-fold. First, these methods require an accurate estimation of the missing feature values, which is difficult to obtain in practice. To address this issue, interval data structures have been developed to represent the missing feature values in [6,7,12,17]. Specifically, [6] define new distance function for interval data and extend the classical FCM to handle missing data. [7] also express missing values by interval data, but use the genetic algorithm to search for proper imputations of missing feature values. [12] estimate interval data by an enhanced back-propagation neural network. [17] design an improved interval construction approach using pre-classified cluster results and search for the optimal cluster by particle swarm optimization. Another limitation of existing clustering methods for missing data is that the cluster results are usually sensitive to the estimation of the missing feature values specifically for small-size and highly corrupted data sets [8].

The aim of this paper is to present a robust FCM clustering algorithm for incomplete data based on interval data representation. To guarantee the clustering performance, we introduce the concept of robust cluster objective function, which is the maximum of the traditional cluster objective function when the missing feature values vary in the considered intervals. Different from the existing algorithms based on interval distance function or optimal imputation [6,7,17], we formulate the clustering problem as a min-max optimization problem based on the idea of robust optimization, which has been successfully used in the field of operations research [18,19], and machine learning, including the minimax probability machine [5,10,13], robust support vector machines [11,15] and robust quadratic regression [14].

To solve the proposed min-max optimization problem, we design an efficient iterative solution method. We first give an equivalent reformulation of our robust optimization problem and analyze its relationship with the classical FCM. Then, we show how to update the cluster prototype and membership matrices separately by solving convex optimization problems. Since both problems are non-smooth, we propose a smoothing method to speed up solution process. To tackle the constrained optimization problem in the process of updating the membership matrix, we present an improved gradient projection method. Numerical experiments on UCI data sets validate the effectiveness of the proposed RFCM algorithm by comparison with other algorithms.

The remainder of this paper is organized as follows. Section 2 presents our RFCM model. In Sects. 3, we give an equivalent reformulation and give the solution method. In Sect. 4, numerical experiments are implemented and discussed. Finally, we conclude this research in Sect. 5.

2   RFCM Clustering Algorithm

Consider a set of n objects $I = \{1, \cdots, n\}$ and each object has m features $\{x_{ij} : j \in J\}$, where x_{ij} describes the j-th feature of the i-th object quantitatively. Let $x_i = (x_{i1}, \cdots, x_{im})^{\mathrm{T}}$ be the feature vector of the i-th object and $X = (x_1, \cdots, x_n)$ be the feature matrix or data set. The task of clustering problems is to assign these objects to K clusters.

In practice, due to various reasons, the data set X may contain missing components. A data set X is referred to as an incomplete data set if it contains at least one missing feature value for some objects, that is, there exists at least one $i \in I$ and $j \in J$, such that $x_{ij} = ?$. For an incomplete data set X, we further partition the feature set of the i-th object into two subsets: $J_i^0 = \{j : x_{ij} = ?, \forall j \in J\}$ and $J_i^1 = J \setminus J_i^0$.

Since it is usually difficult to obtain accurate estimation of missing feature values. This paper represents missing feature values by intervals. Specifically, for any $i \in I$, we use an interval $[x_{ij}^-, x_{ij}^+]$ to represent unknown missing feature value where $j \in J_i^0$, and use $\bar{x}_{ij}$ to represent known feature value where $j \in J_i^1$. To simply notations, in the following, let $\bar{x}_{ij} = \frac{x_{ij}^- + x_{ij}^1}{2}$, $\delta_{ij} = \frac{x_{ij}^+ - x_{ij}^-}{2}$ for any $j \in J_i^0$, and $\delta_{ij} = 0$ for any $j \in J_i^1$. For details on how to construct these intervals for missing feature values, see [6,17].

To reduce the impact of inaccurate estimation of the missing feature values, this paper considers the following robust cluster objective function:

$$\min \max \left\{ \sum_{k=1}^{K} \sum_{i \in I} u_{ik}^p \|\bar{x}_i + y_i - v_k\|^2 : y_i \in [-\delta_i, \delta_i], \forall i \in I \right\}$$

$$\text{s.t.} \sum_{k=1}^{K} u_{ik} = 1, \ u_{ik} \in [0,1], \ \forall \, i \in I, k = 1, \cdots, K, \tag{1}$$

The Eq. (1) is a difficult nonlinear optimization problem, and it is hard to solve (1) directly. However, by exploiting the structural properties of (1), we will design an efficient algorithm in next section.

3   Solution Method

3.1   Equivalent Reformulation of (1)

The following Proposition 1 simplifies the two-level min-max optimization problem (1) into a single level minimization problem, and provides the basis of designing effective solution methods for (1).

Proposition 1. *Problem (1) is equivalent to the following problem:*

$$\min_{U,V} \sum_{i \in I} \sum_{j \in J} \left\{ \sum_{k=1}^{K} u_{ik}^p (\bar{x}_{ij} - v_{kj})^2 + 2\delta_{ij} \left| \sum_{k=1}^{K} u_{ik}^p (\bar{x}_{ij} - v_{kj}) \right| + \sum_{k=1}^{K} u_{ik}^p \delta_{ij}^2 \right\} \tag{2}$$

$$s.t. \sum_{k=1}^{K} u_{ik} = 1, \ u_{ik} \in [0,1], \qquad \forall \ i \in I, k = 1, \cdots, K.$$

Proof. We simplify the robust cluster objective function for given U and V as follows:

$$J^R(U,V) = \sum_{i \in I} \sum_{j \in J} \max_{y_{ij} \in [-\delta_{ij}, \delta_{ij}]} \sum_{k=1}^{K} u_{ik}^p (\bar{x}_{ij} + y_{ij} - v_{kj})^2$$

$$= \sum_{i \in I} \sum_{j \in J} \max \left\{ \sum_{k=1}^{K} u_{ik}^p (\bar{x}_{ij} + \delta_{ij} - v_{kj})^2, \sum_{k=1}^{K} u_{ik}^p (\bar{x}_{ij} - \delta_{ij} - v_{kj})^2 \right\}$$

where the last equation uses the fact that $f(y_{ij}) = (\bar{x}_{ij} + y_{ij} - v_{kj})^2$ is a convex function and attains its maximum over $[-\delta_{ij}, \delta_{ij}]$ at the endpoints. For given $i \in I$ and $j \in J$, we have

$$\max \left\{ \sum_{k=1}^{K} u_{ik}^p (\bar{x}_{ij} + \delta_{ij} - v_{kj})^2, \sum_{k=1}^{K} u_{ik}^p (\bar{x}_{ij} - \delta_{ij} - v_{kj})^2 \right\}$$

$$= \sum_{k=1}^{K} u_{ik}^p (\bar{x}_{ij} - v_{kj})^2 + 2\delta_{ij} \left| \sum_{k=1}^{K} u_{ik}^p (\bar{x}_{ij} - v_{kj}) \right| + \sum_{k=1}^{K} u_{ik}^p \delta_{ij}^2,$$

which completes the proof.

Proposition 1 also shows that when $\delta_{ij} = 0$ for any $i \in I$ and $j \in J$, our RFCM reduces to the classical FCM.

Let $h(U, V)$ be the objective function of (2). The following proposition analyzes properties of $h(U, V)$.

Proposition 2. *For any given $U \geq 0$, $h(U, V)$ is convex in V and for any given V, $h(U, V)$ is convex in U.*

Proof. First, for any $U \geq 0$, it is easy to see that the first term of $h(U, V)$ is convex in V. Note that the absolute function is convex; thus, the second term of $h(U, V)$ is also convex in V. Since the last term of $h(U, V)$ is constant for given value of U, we have that $h(U, V)$ is convex in V.

Second, from the proof of Proposition 1, we have that

$$h(U, V) = \sum_{i \in I} \sum_{j \in J} \max \left\{ \sum_{k=1}^{K} u_{ik}^p (\bar{x}_{ij} + \delta_{ij} - v_{kj})^2, \sum_{k=1}^{K} u_{ik}^p (\bar{x}_{ij} - \delta_{ij} - v_{kj})^2 \right\}.$$

Since $f(x) = ax^p$ is convex in x when $a \geq 0$ and $p \geq 1$, we have both $\sum_{k=1}^{K} u_{ik}^p (\bar{x}_{ij} + \delta_{ij} - v_{kj})^2$ and $\sum_{k=1}^{K} u_{ik}^p (\bar{x}_{ij} - \delta_{ij} - v_{kj})^2$ are convex in U for any given V. Note that the maximum of two convex function is still convex; thus, we complete the proof.

Proposition 2 shows that although (2) is a complex non-convex minimization problem, when either the value of U or that of V is fixed, we only need to solve convex minimization subproblems. The next two subsection focuses on designing efficient solution methods to these two subproblems.

3.2 Optimizing V for a Fixed Value of U

For a fixed value of U, we need to solve the following convex piecewise quadratic problem:

$$\min_{V} \sum_{j \in J} \sum_{i \in I} \left\{ \sum_{k=1}^{K} u_{ik}^p (\bar{x}_{ij} - v_{kj})^2 + 2\delta_{ij} \left| \sum_{k=1}^{K} u_{ik}^p (\bar{x}_{ij} - v_{kj}) \right| \right\}. \tag{3}$$

Note that (3) is decomposable in index j. Let $v_j = \{v_{1j}, \cdots, v_{Kj}\}$. Therefore, it is sufficient to solve the following subproblem separately for each $j \in J$:

$$\min_{v_j} \sum_{i \in I} \sum_{k=1}^{K} u_{ik}^p (\bar{x}_{ij} - v_{kj})^2 + 2 \sum_{i \in I} \delta_{ij} \left| \sum_{k-1}^{K} u_{ik}^p (\bar{x}_{ij} - v_{kj}) \right|. \tag{4}$$

Due to the non-differentiability of the absolute function $g(x) = |x|$, (4) is a non-smooth convex minimization problem. Although the sub-gradient method can be used to solve such non-smooth optimization problems, its search direction may oscillate around non-smooth points. To improve computation efficiency, we introduce the following smoothing upper bound estimation (SUBE) function of g:

$$g_\epsilon(x) = \begin{cases} x, & \text{if } x \geq \epsilon, \\ \frac{x^2}{2\epsilon} + \frac{\epsilon}{2}, & \text{if } |x| < \epsilon, \\ -x, & \text{if } x \leq -\epsilon, \end{cases}$$

where $\epsilon > 0$. It is easy to see that for any $\epsilon > 0$, $g_\epsilon(x)$ is a smooth function and $0 \leq g_\epsilon(x) - g(x) \leq \epsilon/2$, and

$$g_\epsilon'(x) = \begin{cases} 1, & \text{if } x \geq \epsilon, \\ \frac{x}{\epsilon} + \frac{\epsilon}{2}, & \text{if } |x| < \epsilon, \\ -1, & \text{if } x \leq -\epsilon. \end{cases}$$

By introducing the SUBE function $g_\epsilon(x)$, instead of directly solving the non-smooth optimization problem (4), we only need to consider the following smooth optimization problem:

$$\min_{v_j} \phi(v_j) = \sum_{i \in I} \sum_{k=1}^{K} u_{ik}^p (\bar{x}_{ij} - v_{kj})^2 + 2 \sum_{i \in I} \delta_{ij} g_\epsilon \left(\sum_{k=1}^{K} u_{ik}^p (\bar{x}_{ij} - v_{kj}) \right) \tag{5}$$

The gradient of the objective function ϕ is given as follows:

$$\frac{\partial \phi(v_j)}{\partial v_{kj}} = 2\sum_{i \in I} u_{ik}^p (v_{kj} - \bar{x}_{ij}) - 2\sum_{i \in I} \delta_{ij} g_\epsilon' \left(\sum_{k=1}^{K} u_{ik}^p (\bar{x}_{ij} - v_{kj}) \right).$$

Therefore, for a fixed value of U, we design the following smoothing gradient descent method to solve (5).

Algorithm 1. Smoothing Gradient Descent Algorithm (SGDA)

---

0 Input U, $j \in J$, the maximum iteration number N_{max} and error bound $Err > 0$.

1 Initialization: $v_{kj}^0 = \frac{\sum_{i \in I} u_{ik}^p \bar{x}_{ij}}{\sum_{i \in I} \sum_{i \in I} u_{ik}^p}$ for $k = 1, \cdots, K$. Let $n = 1$.

2 Update: set $\epsilon = \frac{Err}{n}$, $v_{kj}^n = v_{kj}^{n-1} - s_n \frac{\partial \phi(v_j^{n-1})}{\partial v_{kj}}$ for $k = 1, \cdots, K$ and $n = n + 1$.

3 Stop criteria: if $n \geq N_{max}$ or $|\phi(v_j^n) - \phi(v_j^{n-1})| \leq Err$, goto step 4; else goto step 2.

4 Output solution $v_j^* = v_j^n$.

During the solution process, SGDA decreases the approximation error ϵ repeatedly. In the SGDA, the step size can be either set as $s_n = a/(b + n)$ with $a, b > 0$ or selected by the Armijo rule [1].

3.3   Optimizing U for a Fixed Value of V

For a fixed value of V, we need to solve the following constrained convex minimization problem:

$$\min_{U} \sum_{i \in I} \sum_{j \in J} \left\{ \sum_{k=1}^{K} u_{ik}^p \left((\bar{x}_{ij} - v_{kj})^2 + \delta_{ij}^2 \right) + 2\delta_{ij} \left| \sum_{k=1}^{K} u_{ik}^p (\bar{x}_{ij} - v_{kj}) \right| \right\} \tag{6}$$

$$\text{s.t.} \ \sum_{k=1}^{K} u_{ik} = 1, \ u_{ik} \in [0,1], \qquad \forall \, i \in I, k = 1, \cdots, K.$$

Note that (6) is decomposable in index i. Let $u_i = \{u_{i1}, \cdots, u_{iK}\}$. Using the SUBE function as in the last subsection, we consider the following smooth subproblem separately for each $i \in I$.

$$\min_{u_i} \psi(u_i) = \sum_{j \in J} \left\{ \sum_{k=1}^{K} u_{ik}^p \left((\bar{x}_{ij} - v_{kj})^2 + \delta_{ij}^2 \right) + 2\delta_{ij} g_\epsilon \left(\sum_{k=1}^{K} u_{ik}^p (\bar{x}_{ij} - v_{kj}) \right) \right\}$$

$$\text{s.t.} \ \sum_{k=1}^{K} u_{ik} = 1, \ u_{ik} \in [0,1], \qquad \forall \, k = 1, \cdots, K.$$

$$\tag{7}$$

The gradient of the objective function ψ is given as follows:

$$\frac{\partial \psi(u_i)}{\partial u_{ki}} = 2p\sum_{j \in J} u_{ik}^{p-1} \left((\bar{x}_{ij} - v_{kj})^2 + \delta_{ij}^2 \right) + 2\sum_{j \in J} \delta_{ij} p u_{ik}^{p-1} (\bar{x}_{ij} - v_{kj}) g_\epsilon' \left(\sum_{k=1}^{K} u_{ik}^p (\bar{x}_{ij} - v_{kj}) \right).$$

To solve (7), we design the following smoothing gradient projection descent algorithm.

Algorithm 2. Smoothing Gradient Projection Descent Algorithm (SGPDA)

0 Input V, $i \in I$, the maximum iteration number N_{max} and error bound $Err > 0$.

1 Initialization: $u_{ik}^0 = \left(\sum_{t=1}^{K} \left(\frac{\|\bar{x}_i - v_k\|^2}{\|\bar{x}_i - v_t\|^2} \right)^{\frac{1}{m-1}} \right)^{-1}$ for $k = 1, \cdots, K$. Let $n = 1$.

2 Update: set $c = \frac{Err}{n}$, $\bar{u}_{ik}^n - u_{ik}^{n-1} - s_n \frac{\partial \psi(u_i^{n-1})}{\partial u_{ik}}$ for $k = 1, \cdots, K$ and $u_i^n = \text{Proj}_\Delta \left(\bar{u}_i^n \right)$. Let $n = n + 1$.

3 Stop criteria: if $n \geq N_{max}$ or $|\psi(u_i^n) - \psi(u_i^{n-1})| \leq Err$, goto step 4; else goto step 2.

4 Output solution $u_i^* = u_i^n$.

In SGPDA, the projection operator Proj_Δ denotes the projection onto the simplex $\Delta = \{x \in R^K : \sum_{k=1}^{K} x_k = 1, x_k \geq 0, \ \forall k = 1, \cdots, K\}$. [2] has shown that Proj_Δ can be computed in $\mathcal{O}(K \log K)$ time.

Based on the solution methods for subproblems $(\tilde{P}_U^j)$ and $(\tilde{P}_V^i)$, our RFCM algorithm can be summarized as follows.

Algorithm 3. RFCM Algorithm

0 Input data: estimated data $\bar{X}$, interval size data δ, the number of clustering K, the maximum iteration numbers N_{fcm} and N_{sub}, and the error bounds Err_{fcm} and Err_{sub}.

1 Initialization: Initialize the clustering centers V^0 by randomly choose K samples, and set $k = 1$.

2 Update U when V is fixed as $V = V^{k-1}$:

   For $i \in I$

        Sovle $(\tilde{P}_V^i)$ by SGPDA with the input: $V = V^{k-1}$, i, N_{sub} and Err_{sub}.

   End

      Set $U^k = \{u_i^* : i \in I\}$.

3 Update V when U is fixed as $U = U^k$:

   For $j \in J$

        Sovle $(\tilde{P}_U^j)$ by GPDA with the input: $U = U^k$, j, N_{sub} and Err_{sub}.

   End

      Set $V^k = \{v_j^* : j \in J\}$.

4 Calculate objective function value $h^k = h(U^k, V^k)$.

5 Stop criteria: if $k \geq N_{fcm}$ or $|h^k - h^{k-1}| \leq Err_{fcm}$, then return $(U^*, V^*) = (U^k, V^k)$; otherwise, let $k = k + 1$ and goto step 2.

6 Output U^* and V^*.

---

4   Numerical Experiments

4.1   Data Sets

We conduct experiments on two data sets of the UCI database: Wine and Seeds. All these data sets are complete data sets. To generate the incomplete data sets, we adopt the method used in [3,6]. Specifically, we use the missing completely at random (MCAR) mechanism to generate the missing feature values. We randomly select a specified percentage of components and designate them as missing. We further make sure the following constraints are satisfied:

1. Each object retains at least one feature;
2. Each feature has at least one value present in the incomplete data set.

4.2   Experimental Results and Discussion

We compare the proposed RFCM algorithm with the classical FCM using the WDS, PDS and NPS strategies on Wine and Seeds data sets. The missing rates of these data sets vary from 0% to 20%. We report the number of misclassification and misclassification rate of these algorithms on test data sets.

We generate 100 incomplete data instances of Wine and Seeds data sets and report the averaged performance of different algorithms in Tables 1 and 2, respectively. Results given by the proposed RFCM, the classical FCM using the WDS, PDS and NPS strategies are labeled as "RFCM", "WDS", "PDS", and "NPS", respectively.

Table 1. Performance of different FCM algorithms on the incomplete Wine data set

%	Number of misclassification				Misclassification rate			
	WDS	PDS	NPS	RFCM	WDS	PDS	NPS	RFCM
0	16.2	16.2	16.2	16.2	9.1	9.1	9.1	9.1
5	18.0	21.0	18.8	17.4	10.13	11.82	10.56	9.77
10	19.7	24.1	21.7	18.5	11.05	13.54	12.18	10.37
15	22.4	27.0	23.7	19.6	12.61	15.17	13.29	11.02
20	25.4	32.6	25.1	22.4	14.28	18.33	14.12	12.58

From Tables 1 and 2, we have the following observations.

(1) For all the test data sets, the proposed RFCM algorithm provides the best clustering performance in terms of misclassification rate. For example, when the missing rate of the Wine data set is 20%, the misclassification rate of RFCM is only 12.58% while the misclassification rate of WDS, PDS and NPS are 14.28%, 18.33% and 14.12%, respectively.

Table 2. Performance of different FCM algorithms on the incomplete Seeds data set

%	Number of misclassification				Misclassification rate			
	WDS	PDS	NPS	RFCM	WDS	PDS	NPS	RFCM
0	22.3	22.3	22.3	22.3	10.62	10.62	10.62	10.62
5	22.2	25.4	23.5	19.3	10.58	12.13	11.18	9.17
10	23.6	45.8	31.4	23.1	11.24	21.81	14.95	11.01
15	25.3	42.8	32.2	24.2	12.04	20.40	15.34	11.53
20	33.7	61.4	30.3	27.1	16.07	29.23	14.44	12.94

(2) When the missing rate is small, missing data have little adverse effect on the performance of the proposed RFCM and missing data even help RFCM to give better performance.
(3) The cluster prototypes given by RFCM also have smaller cluster prototype errors compared with cluster prototypes given by WDS, PDS and NPS.

5   Conclusion

This paper proposes a robust FCM algorithm to cluster data sets with missing feature values. The RFCM algorithm represents the missing feature values by intervals. Different existing interval-based clustering algorithms, which only replace the traditional Euclidean distance with a modified distance function for interval data, the RFCM algorithm adopts the idea of robust optimization and aims to find an optimal cluster with the minimum wort-case cluster objective function value. Therefore, it can guarantee the worst-case performance of the resulted cluster output and minimizes the adverse effect of missing feature values. This paper formulates the robust clustering problem as a two-level min-max optimization problem and provides an equivalent reformulation. An efficient solution method is further designed based on smoothing and gradient projection techniques. Experiments on UCI data sets also validate the effectiveness and robustness of the RFCM algorithm by comparison with existing clustering algorithms.

References

1. Bertsekas, D.P.: Nonlinear Programming. Athena Scientific, Belmont (1999)
2. Condat, L.: Fast projection onto the simplex and the l-1 ball. Preprint HAL, 1056171 (2014)
3. Hathaway, R.J., Bezdek, J.C.: Fuzzy c-means clustering of incomplete data. IEEE Trans. Syst. Man Cybern. Part B Cybern. **31**(5), 735–744 (2001)
4. Honda, K., Ichihashi, H.: Linear fuzzy clustering techniques with missing values and their application to local principal component analysis. IEEE Trans. Fuzzy Syst. **12**(2), 183–193 (2004)

5. Lanckriet, G.R.G., Ghaoui, L.E., Bhattacharyya, C., Jordan, M.I.: Minimax probability machine. Adv. Neural Inf. Process. Syst. **1**, 801–808 (2002)
6. Li, D., Hong, G., Zhang, L.: A fuzzy c-means clustering algorithm based on nearest-neighbor intervals for incomplete data. Expert Syst. Appl. **37**(10), 6942–6947 (2010)
7. Li, D., Hong, G., Zhang, L.: A hybrid genetic algorithm–fuzzy c-means approach for incomplete data clustering based on nearest-neighbor intervals. Soft. Comput. **17**(10), 1787–1796 (2013)
8. Li, J., Song, S., Zhang, Y., Zhou, Z.: Robust k-median and k-means clustering algorithms for incomplete data. Math. Prob. Eng. **2016**, 1–8 (2016)
9. Shibayama, T.: A PCA-like method for multivariate data with missing values. Japan. J. Educ. Psychol. **40**(2), 257–265 (1992)
10. Song, S., Gong, Y., Zhang, Y., Huang, G., Huang, G.-B.: Dimension reduction by minimum error minimax probability machine. IEEE Trans. Syst. Man Cybern.: Syst. **47**(1), 58–69 (2017)
11. Trafalis, T., Gilbert, R.: Robust support vector machines for classification and computational issues. Optim. Methods Softw. **22**(1), 187–198 (2007)
12. Wang, B.L., Zhang, L.Y., Zhang, L., Bing, Z.H., Xu, X.H.: Missing data imputation by nearest-neighbor trained bp for fuzzy clustering. J. Inf. Comput. Sci. **11**(15), 5367–5375 (2014)
13. Wang, Y., Zhang, Y., Yi, J., Qu, H., Miu, J.: A robust probability classifier based on the modified-distance. Math. Probl. Eng. **2014**, 1–13 (2014)
14. Wang, Y., Zhang, Y., Zhang, F., Yi, J.: Robust quadratic regression and its application to energy-growth consumption problem. Math. Probl. Eng. **2013**, 1–10 (2013)
15. Huan, X., Caramanis, C., Mannor, S.: Robustness and regularization of support vector machines. J. Mach. Learn. Res. **10**, 1485–1510 (2009)
16. Yao, L., Weng, K.-S.: Imputation of incomplete data using adaptive ellipsoids with linear regression. J. Intell. Fuzzy Syst. **29**(1), 253–265 (2015)
17. Zhang, L., Bing, Z., Zhang, L.: A hybrid clustering algorithm based on missing attribute interval estimation for incomplete data. Pattern Anal. Appl. **18**(2), 377–384 (2015)
18. Zhang, Y., Shen, Z.-J.M., Song, S.: Distributionally robust optimization of two-stage lot-sizing problems. Prod. Oper. Manag. **25**(12), 2116–2131 (2016)
19. Zhang, Y., Song, S., Shen, Z.-J.M., Wu, C.: Data-driven robust shortest path problem with distributional uncertainty. IEEE Trans. Intell. Transp. Syst. (2017). doi:10.1109/TITS.2017.2709798

Multi-objective Optimization Improved GA Algorithm and Fuzzy PID Control of ATO System for Train Operation

Longda Wang[✉], Xingcheng Wang, Dawei Sun, and Hua Hao

School of Information Science and Technology,
University of Dalian Maritime Dalian, Liaoning 116026, China
wanglongda@dlmu.edu.cn

Abstract. In order to solve the problem that automatic train operation control system considering the single factor and control is not easy to be accurate, a multi-objective optimization (MO) based on improved genetic algorithm (GA) and fuzzy PID control method is proposed in this paper. Firstly, based on train operation characteristics, a multi-objective model of train operation process is established. Secondly, in order to improve the performance of the algorithm, the train operation process is optimized by using linear weight method and multi-objective genetic algorithm. Third, in order to suppress the local convergence of GA, a dual population genetic mechanism is adopted in the iterative process. Finally, a fuzzy PID controller is embedded into the control designer after target curve and control train operation in real time according to the real time running state. The results show that the proposed algorithm can get a reasonable MO result and accurate real-time control.

Keywords: ATO · Multi-objective optimization (MO) · Genetic algorithm (GA) · Fuzzy PID

1 Introduction

Automatic train operation (ATO) control system is the core of speed and energy consumption control. However, the indicators considered by the researches of ATO control strategy are incomplete, and these indicators cannot reflect the multi-objective features of train operation process [1].

Various control schemes have been proposed in recent works on the ATO control strategy [2–8]. In [2], under actuator saturation caused by constraints from serving motors, an on-line approximation based robust adaptive control problem for the ATO system is proposed. An actuator saturation nonlinearity with unknown system parameters and nonlinear dynamics during the whole operational process is considered explicitly. The robustness of the system can be improved. In order to obtain compromises between journey duration and energy saving, an approach for speed tuning in railway management is proposed in [3]. The proposed method can deal with a bi-criteria optimization problem, which consists in designing speed profiles integrating both criteria in order to provide patterns of speed control. Besides, this method integrates the energy consumption as a criterion to optimize. In [4], in order to minimize

© Springer Nature Singapore Pte Ltd. 2017
D. Yue et al. (Eds.): LSMS/ICSEE 2017, Part II, CCIS 762, pp. 13–22, 2017.
DOI: 10.1007/978-981-10-6373-2_2

the net energy at substations, an optimal ATO speed profiles of metro trains taking into account the energy recovered from regenerative brake is designed. Meanwhile, a model of a train with an on-board energy storage device as well as a network model for estimating the energy recovered by the train is presented. In [5], the adaptive optimal control (AOC) method is developed to improve the dual heuristic programming (DHP) design with respect to modeling errors as well as optimality, and an automatic train regulation (ATR) designed was developed and evaluated by using AOC method. The result shows that the AOC method is able to find a near-optimal solution more rapidly and accurately than the DHP method. In [6], a novel online learning control strategy is proposed to solve the train automatic stop control (TASC) problem. Meanwhile, an extensive comparison study on a real-world data set collected in the Beijing subway line is performed. The proposed online learning algorithm can dynamically reduce stopping errors by using the precise location data. In [7], an optimization approach for the speed trajectory of high-speed train in a single section is studied. Besides, a MO model for the speed trajectory is developed by considering the constraints such as safety requirement, track profiles, passenger comfort, and the dynamic performance. It should be noted that numerical examples are given to illustrate the effectiveness of the train operation process optimization. However, there is a little related literature published about the MO based on improved GA and fuzzy PID control method in order to solve ATO control system. The main advantages of the proposed algorithms are summarized as follows:

(i)   For the optimization algorithm of the train operation process applied to the ATO system, it is necessary to establish an optimization model of the train running process. In this paper, a more in-depth analysis of the train running process is carried out to derive a formula for calculating the fitness function with acceleration, distance and velocity as real-time measurements to simplify the calculation.

(ii) It is difficult to find a satisfactory solution in the latter part of the iteration by using genetic algorithm. Therefore, this paper uses a dual population genetic mechanism. It uses two populations to evolve at the same time and exchange the outstanding individuals in genetic information with each other, for obtaining a higher equilibrium state by destroying the former equilibrium state within the population, which breaks down the "dominant" position established in the long process of a single population, thus jumping out of local optimum.

(iii) General researches on optimization of train operation are limited to finding a relatively optimized train trajectory, instead of considering its rationality in practice. It is obviously not enough for ATO control system applied to the actual train operation control system. In this paper, a speed controller based on fuzzy PID control strategy is used to track the target curve after finding an optimized trajectory.

2   Multi-objective Model of Train Operation Process

ATO system of the train is a complex nonlinear system. It includes a plurality of input and output variables, and regards energy consumption, precise parking, punctuality, comfort and other performance index as control targets.

2.1   Constraint Model

Energy consumption of the train is represented by the energy consumed when the train overcomes resistance and operates in the whole running process. The train energy function can be obtained:

$$E = \frac{\int Fvdt}{\xi_M} + At + \xi_B \int Bvdt \tag{2}$$

In (2), F is the train running traction; B is the train running braking force; v is the train running speed; A is the train auxiliary power; t is the train inter-station running time; ξ_M is the product factor of that traction electric energy converting to mechanical energy; ξ_B is the product factor of that braking mechanical energy converting to electric energy.

Because train operation process is the major thing to consider, so the train auxiliary power A can be ignored. Simultaneously, setting the value of product factor ξ_M, ξ_B to 1 and simplifying formula 3 according to integral linearity, and the traction force F and the braking force B are expressed with $m \cdot a - R$, and vdt are expressed with ds, which can be expressed as:

$$E = \int (F + B)vdt = \int (ma - R)ds \tag{3}$$

Therefore, the Eq. (3) above is discretized, then train running energy consumption model can be expressed:

$$K_E = \sum_{i=1}^{n} (ma_{i-1} - R_{i-1})(s_i - s_{i-1}) \tag{4}$$

In (4), s_i is position of running point; R_i is resistance of running point; a_i is accelerated speed of running point; K_E is the energy consumption measurement index.

Comfort reflects the riding quality of passengers, and it is usually expressed by the accumulation of the acceleration difference in the unit time. Therefore, train running comfort model can be expressed:

$$K_C = \sum_{i=1}^{n} |a_i - a_{i-1}| \tag{5}$$

In (5), K_C is the comfort measurement index.

The indicator model of exact parking is the distance difference between running distance of train in the whole running process and the distance of train from running starting point to docking stations. The parking error of the docking station will keep within the range of ± 20 cm, the exact parking model can be expressed as:

$$K_P = |S_z - S'| \tag{6}$$

In (6), K_P is parking accuracy error measurement index; S_Z is the actual driving distance of the train; S' is the distance between two stations.

The punctuality model can be expressed by the difference between the train running time and the given time, and then train punctuality model can be obtained:

$$K_T = \left| \sum_{i=1}^{n} T_i - T \right| \tag{7}$$

s_i and a_i refer to the position and accelerated speed of i-th operation condition.

After gaining s_i and a_i, v_i and t_i can be gained by the following formula:

$$v_i = \sqrt{2a_i(s_i - s_{i-1}) + v_{i-1}^2} \tag{8}$$

$$t_i = \frac{v_i - v_{i-1}}{a_i} \tag{9}$$

For the punctuality index, T is the specified running time of the train in the running interval. The error of actual running time of the train and specific time is not more than 5%.

2.2   Multi-objective Optimization Model

In summary, the multi-objective optimization model is shown as

$$\min\{K_E, K_C, K_P, K_T\} \tag{10}$$

In (8), min represents getting the minimum value of the function, namely, each sub-goal function takes the minimum value as much as possible. This paper presents by linear weight method to gather it as single objective optimization problems. Before the polymerization, each index should be nondimensionalized, and the solution should be obtained by the genetic algorithm.

$$f = w_1 K_E + w_2 K_C + w_3 K_P + w_4 K_T \tag{11}$$

In (11), w_1, w_2, w_3 and w_4 are weight coefficients, the formula is expressed as follows

$$\begin{cases} w_i = w'_{1i} \times w_{2i} \\ w_{2i} = 1/|\Delta f_i(X)| \\ a_i \le f_i(X) \le b_i \\ \Delta f_i(X) = \frac{b_i - a_i}{2} \end{cases} \tag{12}$$

where w'_{1i} represents the principal factor, and satisfy $w_{11} + w_{12} + w_{13} + w_{14} = 1$, which reflects the relative importance of the i-th indicator; w_{2i} represents the correction factor, which is used to adjust the effect of each target on differences in dimension and magnitude; $f_i(X)$ represents the objective function value of the i-th indicator; a_i and b_i represent the upper and lower bounds of the objective function values of the i-th index; $f_i(X)$ is the tolerance of the objective function value of the i-th indicator. The train operation optimization is equivalent to find a train trajectory to take into account the various operational indicators. In (12), X is the trajectory, and $f_i(X)$ is the objective function value of the i-th index.

In the formula (13), $w_i(i - 1, 2, 3, 4)$ expresses weight of each fitness index. The formula (4), (5), (6), (7), (8) and (9) are substituted into formula (11), we can get fitness function:

$$F = 1/f = \left(\begin{array}{l} w_1 \sum_{i=1}^{n} (ma_{i-1} - R_{i-1})(s_i - s_{i-1}) + w_2 \sum_{i=1}^{n} |a_i - a_{i-1}| + w_3|S_Z - S'| \\ + w_4 \left(\sum_{i=1}^{n} \left[\left(\sqrt{2a_i(s_i - s_{i-1}) + v_{i-1}^2} - v_{i-1} \right) / a_i \right] - T \right) \end{array} \right)^{-1}$$

(13)

In (13), F is fitness function. From the formula (13), it is can be seen that this paper designs a fitness calculating function with acceleration, distance and velocity as real-time measurements. This fitness calculating function greatly simplifies the calculation in the iterative process, which can guarantee the accuracy and optimization of the results.

3   Improved Genetic Algorithm and Fuzzy PID Control

The main disadvantages of genetic algorithm are summarized as follows: (1) the local search ability of the algorithm is weak, and it is easy to fall into local optimal solution; (2) The convergence speed of the algorithm is relatively slow [9].

3.1   A Dual Population Genetic Mechanism

Population will constantly evolve as time goes on, thus, it will have more and more excellent quality. However, due to their growth, evolution, environment and the limitations of the initial population, they will gradually evolve to the characteristics of the relative advantage of the state after a substantial amount of time has lapsed. Thus, the character of the population will not greatly change.

Dual population genetic mechanism is a parallel mechanism, and it uses two populations to evolve simultaneously. It exchanges the genetic information carried by the excellent individuals in the population. In order to break the equilibrium state of the population, to achieve a higher equilibrium state, it will jump out of local optimization. The calculating process of the Improved genetic algorithm is shown in Fig. 1.

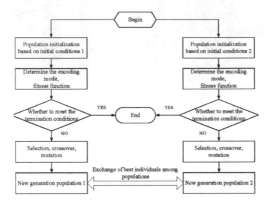

Fig. 1. Flow chart of dual population genetic algorithm mechanism

The schematic diagram of the optimal individual in the exchange population can be shown as follows (Fig. 2):

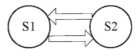

Fig. 2. Exchange of optimal individuals

3.2 Fuzzy PID Method

To verify the tracking effect of controller on target curve, the solved velocity curve shall be tracked by using self-adaptive fuzzy PID speed controller. Self-adaptive fuzzy PID speed controller includes two parts, one is fuzzy controller, and the other is PID controller [10–12]. Its fundamental principle of Self-adaptive fuzzy PID controller is to find out the fuzzy relation between each parameter of PID and deviation e and deviation variation rate ec. The functional block diagram is shown as Fig. 3:

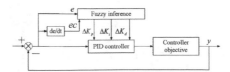

Fig. 3. Principle of self-adaptive fuzzy PID speed controller

In design of fuzzy controller, the PID parameter (K_P, K_I, K_D) should be used in deviation e and deviation variation rate ec to design the controller as shown in Fig. 4.

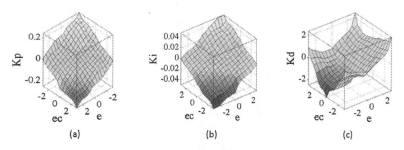

Fig. 4. PID parameter fuzzy control-rule

4   Instance Simulation

4.1   Data Processing in Train Operation Environment

The basic parameters of train are shown in Table 1:

Table 1.   Basic parameters of train

Parameter name	Parameter characteristics
Train weight (t)	332
Maximum running speed/(km/h)	80
Formation scheme	4 motor 2 trail
Mean starting acceleration (m/s^2)	(0–35 km/h) $\geq$ 1.0
Mean acceleration (m/s^2)	(0–80 km/h) $\geq$ 0.6
Mean deceleration frequently used for braking (m/s^2)	(80–0 km/h) $\geq$ 1.0

4.2   Operate Curves of Optimization by Genetic Algorithm

To verify the optimal performance of genetic algorithm, Matlab2010a platform is used to simulate in this paper. It is not advisable to obtain extremely small optimization progress when consuming a huge computational cost in the optimization of the train operation. This article sets the following initialization parameters. The population size is 50, maximum population algebra is 200, crossover probability is 0.8, and mutation probability is 0.02. Operate curves of optimization by genetic algorithm,genetic algorithm iterative convergence curve are shown in Figs. 5 and 6.

The maximum running speed of train follows the speed limit on the line, and the speed of train entering into a station is less than the speed limit in station. It can be seen from Fig. 7 that the fitness function increases with the increase of genetic algebra. When the genetic algebra is greater than 50 generations, the fitness function does not change. At this time, the genetic algorithm has obtained the ideal optimal solution.

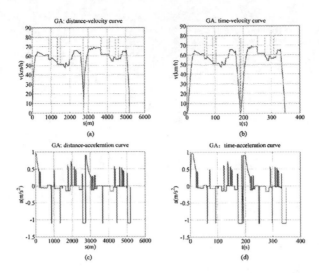

Fig. 5. Operate curves of optimization by genetic algorithm

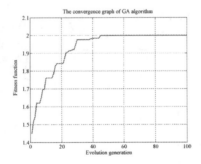

Fig. 6. Genetic algorithm iterative convergence curve

4.3 Tracking Curve of Control by Fuzzy PID

The quality of train tracking target curve directly reflects the feasibility of control algorithm. The tracking simulation results can be gained by velocity controller through tracking and simulating the target curve. Tracking curve of control by fuzzy PID are shown in Fig. 7.

As shown in Fig. 7, there are no large fluctuation in process of train tracking target curve. Meanwhile, the tracking curve and target curve are basically coincident, which shows that the following performance of train for target curve is pretty good. Thus, the proposed algorithm is feasible.

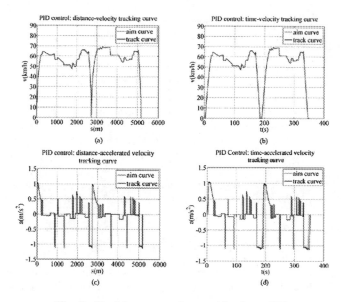

Fig. 7. Tracking curve of control by fuzzy PID

5   Conclusion

In this paper, the multi-objective optimization model of train is presented, and the train operation process is optimized by genetic algorithm. Meanwhile, to obtain a better solution, a dual population genetic mechanism is adopted in the iterative process, so as to improve the performance of genetic algorithm. The optimized result shows that the punctuality, precision parking, comfort, energy saving and other multiple performance requirements of train have been met. Finally, based on generating train running target curve by genetic algorithm, the self-adaptive fuzzy PID control is embedded in the train control system, and the target curve is tracked. The problem of speed controller following target curve can be handled well, the train can operate smoothly and safely, and possess perfect robustness.

Acknowledgments. This work is supported by Nature Science Foundation of China under Grand 60574018.

References

1. Deb, K.: Solving goal programming problems using multi-objective genetic algorithms. In: Evolutionary Computation, CEC 1999 (1999)
2. Gao, S., Dong, H., Chen, Y., et al.: Approximation-based robust adaptive automatic train control: an approach for actuator saturation. IEEE Trans. Intell. Transp. Syst. **14**(4), 1733–1742 (2013)

3. Lejeune, A., Chevrier, R., Rodriguez, J.: Improving an evolutionary multi-objective approach for optimizing railway energy consumption. Procedia - Soc. Behav. Sci. **48**, 3124–3133 (2012)
4. DomíNguez, M., FernáNdez-Cardador, A., Cucala, A.P., et al.: Energy savings in metropolitan railway substations through regenerative energy recovery and optimal design of ATO speed profiles. IEEE Trans. Autom. Sci. Eng. **9**(3), 496–504 (2012)
5. Sheu, J.W., Lin, W.S.: Adaptive optimal control for designing automatic train regulation for metro line. IEEE Trans. Control Syst. Technol. **20**(5), 1319–1327 (2012)
6. Chen, D., Chen, R., Li, Y., et al.: Online learning algorithms for train automatic stop control using precise location data of balises. IEEE Trans. Intell. Transp. Syst. **14**(3), 1526–1535 (2013)
7. Shangguan, W., Yan, X., Cai, B., et al.: Multiobjective optimization for train speed trajectory in CTCS high-speed railway with hybrid evolutionary algorithm. IEEE Trans. Intell. Transp. Syst. **16**(4), 2215–2225 (2015)
8. Gu, Q., Lu, X.Y., Tang, T.: Energy saving for automatic train control in moving block signaling system. In: International IEEE Conference on Intelligent Transportation Systems, pp. 1305–1310. IEEE (2011)
9. Costa, A., Cappadonna, F.A., Fichera, S.: A hybrid genetic algorithm for minimizing makespan in a flow-shop sequence-dependent group scheduling problem. J. Intell. Manuf. **28**(6), 1–15 (2017)
10. Liu, T.: Application of a variable-universe and self-adaptive fuzzy PID controller in DC motor speed control system. J. Chem. Technol. Biotechnol. **79**(79), 486–490 (2011)
11. Control of the Dual-closed Loops Speed Governing System of DC Motor by Self-adaptive Fuzzy PID Controller. Mechatronics (2009)
12. Cui, Y.L., Lu, H.L., Fan, J.B.: Design and simulation of cascade fuzzy self - adaptive PID speed control of a thyristor-driven DC motor, pp. 655–660. IEEE (2006)

Research on AGV Trajectory Tracker Based on Fuzzy Control

Tongqing Feng[1(✉)] and Bin Jiao[2(✉)]

[1] Electrical Engineering College, Shanghai Dian Ji University, Shanghai, China
780862201@qq.com
[2] Shanghai Dian Ji University, Shanghai, China

Abstract. Aiming at the problem of Automated Guided Vehicles (AGV) trajectory tracking, a fuzzy controller is designed by the fuzzy control principle. The distance deviation and the angle deviation of the car are taken as the input variables of the fuzzy variable, and the voltage analog quantity can be used as the output variable. The traditional PID controller and the designed fuzzy controller are simulated by Matlab software. And the simulation results show that the AGV trajectory tracker based on fuzzy control can effectively solve the problem of unsatisfactory control in the case of large deviation.

Keywords: AGV · Fuzzy control · Trajectory tracking · Matlab software simulation

1 Introduction

Trajectory tracking control is one of the most important parts of the automatic navigation system. The level and precision of the controller are related to the safety and reliability of the AGV car. At present, the PID controller is used in the trajectory tracking controller of AGV. When the initial deviation angle is small, the AGV based on PID controller can eliminate the angle and distance error in a short time and the steady-state error is also guaranteed in a small range. However, in the actual use of the factory floor, the AGV is more complex, there may be large curvature of the corner and more complex operation. In this case, the PID controller is difficult to meet the requirements of the AGV track tracking and cannot quickly eliminate the distance error and angle error. It will lead to the AGV off track, so that the system cannot run.

Therefore, the nonlinearity in the actual operation of the AGV makes the trajectory tracking becomes a difficult problem in the control process. The literatures [1–3] is the research of many scholars. In view of the complexity and non-linearity of AGV in practical application, this paper designs a fuzzy controller based on fuzzy theory to track the trajectory of AGV car under large deviation.

2 The Dynamic Model of AGV System

In this paper, we use the method of system identification. According to the statistics of the input and output data and the corresponding rules, we can estimate the corresponding mathematical model. The relationship between the angle deviation a, the

© Springer Nature Singapore Pte Ltd. 2017
D. Yue et al. (Eds.): LSMS/ICSEE 2017, Part II, CCIS 762, pp. 23–32, 2017.
DOI: 10.1007/978-981-10-6373-2_3

distance deviation d of AGV and the speed difference ΔV of the driving wheel can be shown as follows:

$$\begin{bmatrix} \dfrac{da}{dt} \\ \dfrac{dd}{dt} \end{bmatrix} = \begin{pmatrix} 0 & 0 \\ V_0 & a_{22} \end{pmatrix} \begin{bmatrix} a \\ d \end{bmatrix} + \begin{bmatrix} \dfrac{1}{H} \\ 0 \end{bmatrix} \Delta V + \begin{bmatrix} \theta \\ \mu \end{bmatrix} \tag{1}$$

In the formula, H is the driving wheel wheelbase [4], V_0 is the speed of the O time, θ, μ are for the deviation of income.

According to the introduction of the control voltage of the car, the state space equation of the whole system is established. The analog signal of the voltage is regarded as the input variable of the system and the car speed value is regarded as output value. We can obtain Formula (4) by n order difference and differential Eqs. (2) and (3).

$$a_0 y(k+n) + (k+n+1)\ldots + y(k) = b_1 U(k+n+1) + \ldots + b_n U(k) \tag{2}$$

$$\overline{a_0}\frac{d^n y(t)}{dt^n} + \overline{a_1}\frac{d^{n-1} y(t)}{dt^{n-1}} + \ldots + \overline{a_n} y(t) = \overline{b_1}\frac{d^{n-1} U(t)}{dt^{n-1}} + \ldots + \overline{b_n} U(t) \tag{3}$$

$$A = D_{m+1}\overline{A}, B = D_m \overline{B}$$
$$A = [a_0, a_1, a_2, \ldots\ldots, a_n]^T \tag{4}$$
$$B = [b_0, b_1, b_2, \ldots\ldots, b_n]^T$$

According to the literature [5], we choose the best signal period and the adjustment time [6]. Then the system identification is carried out by Matlab software, which can be obtained as follows:

$$y(k) = -1.886y(k-1) - 0.698y(k-2) + 0.0087u(k) + 0.6835u(k-1) + 0.448u(k-2)$$

The transfer function can be obtained as follows:

$$G(s) = \frac{0.0087s^2 + 0.6835s + 0.448}{s^2 + 1.886s + 0.698} \tag{5}$$

Since higher order functions cannot be added to the entire state equation, so we can reduced the order processing:

$$G(s) = \frac{0.4876}{s + 0.7098} \tag{6}$$

Differential equation can be written as follows:

$$\dot{V}(t) = -0.7098V(t) + 0.4876U(t)$$
$$\Delta\dot{V}(t) = -0.7098\Delta V(t) + 0.4876\Delta U(t)$$

(7)

Therefore, the relationship between driving voltage difference and velocity difference is obtained.

According to a series of formulas in front of the paper, we can regard the analog voltage difference of the driving wheel as the input. The speed of the wheel is regarded as state variables and the output are the distance error and angle error. Therefore, the state equation of the whole system is obtained as follows:

$$\begin{bmatrix} \dfrac{d\Delta V}{dt} \\ \dfrac{da}{dt} \\ \dfrac{dd}{dt} \end{bmatrix} = \begin{pmatrix} -a & 0 & 0 \\ \dfrac{1}{H} & 0 & 0 \\ 0 & V_0 & 0 \end{pmatrix} \begin{bmatrix} \Delta V \\ a \\ d \end{bmatrix} + \begin{bmatrix} b \\ 0 \\ 0 \end{bmatrix} \Delta U$$

(8)

The state of the formula is $[\Delta V \ a \ d]$. Based on the above inference, the kinematics model of the whole system can be obtained.

3 The Work of Fuzzy Control Algorithm

3.1 Determination of AGV Fuzzy Variables

The purpose of tracking is to reduce the operation angle and distance errors of the planned trajectory of the AGV. Therefore, the car angle error a and the distance error d are regarded as the input variables of fuzzy variables and the voltage analog U that can change the corresponding error of the car is regarded as output variables. Because we often take the input error and error rate of change as the two input language variables of the controller in the fuzzy controller, so in this paper, an integrated error E is obtained by combining the angle error a and the distance error d. Because of the change of the comprehensive error rate is F, so we take the two variables as input variables of the controller. Among them, the weight of the angle error a is k, the weight of the distance error d is 1−k.

3.2 The Establishment of the Domain of AGV

In this paper, the scope of the variables is proposed by Mamdani. They can be depicted as follows: the input and output variables are all taken [−6 6], the scope of the field [−B B] (unit angle: degree) of angular error is [−25° 25°] and the domain [−K K] (unit: V) of variable U of the system output is [−0.9V 0.9V].

3.3   The Determination of Membership Function

Because the triangular membership function expression is simple and the effect is not much difference, so in this paper, according to the practical considerations, we take the triangular membership function. The membership function of input variables are as shown in Figs. 1 and 2 below and the output variable is shown in Fig. 3 as follows.

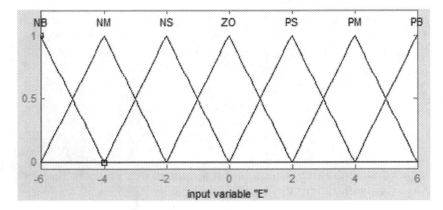

Fig. 1. Membership function of input variable E

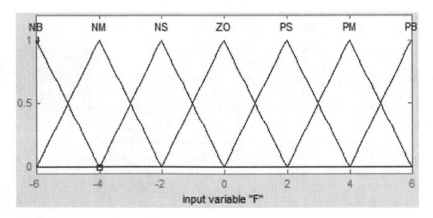

Fig. 2. Membership function of input variable F

3.4   The Defuzzification

We take the center of gravity which is enclosed by the abscissa of the fuzzy set and the curve of membership function as the end result of the algorithm. In this paper, we consider the simple and practical effect, using gravity method [7].

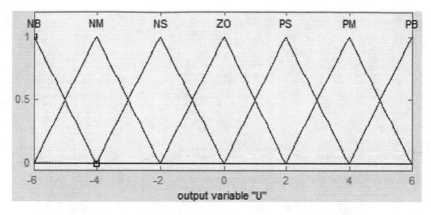

Fig. 3. Membership function of output variable U

3.5 AGV Trajectory Tracking Rules

Trajectory tracking is an important part of fuzzy controller, which is based on the expert experience and control theory. The design of fuzzy controller model statement in this paper is depicted as follow:

$$\text{If } E = A \text{ and } F = B \text{ Then } U = C.$$

In this paper, we use a common fuzzy control rule which is shown in the Table 1 below.

Table 1. Rule parameter of table fuzzy control

E	F						
	NB	NM	NS	ZO	PS	PM	PB
NB	PM	PM	PB	PS	ZO	PS	ZO
NM	PM	PB	NS	NS	ZO	ZO	NM
NS	PB	PB	PB	NS	ZO	NB	NB
ZO	PB	PB	NS	ZO	NB	NS	NS
PS	NB	NS	ZO	NB	NS	NS	NM
PM	NS	ZO	NB	NS	NS	NM	NM
PB	ZO	NB	NM	NB	NM	NM	NM

Using the Matlab software to build a fuzzy controller to get the rule graph of fuzzy controller and the rule surface of fuzzy controller which are shown in Figs. 4 and 5 as follows.

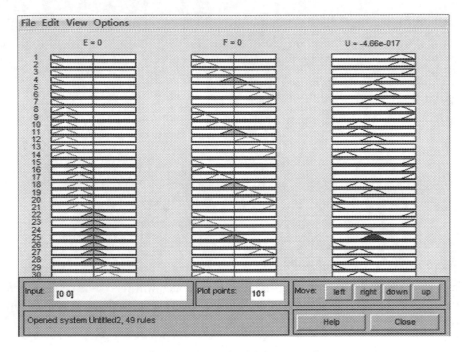

Fig. 4. Rule graph of fuzzy controller

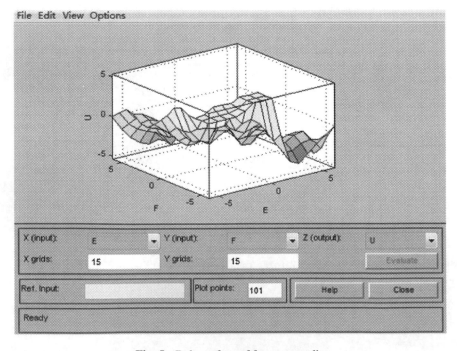

Fig. 5. Rule surface of fuzzy controller

4 The Simulation Results and Analysis

4.1 Simulation and Analysis of PID Controller

In order to reflect the effect of the fuzzy controller in the trajectory tracking of AGV car, this paper firstly uses the PID controller [8] to adjust the AGV car with the same distance deviation d and angle deviation a. According to the state Eq. (8) of the system, the simulation model of AGV car is built and the simulation results are shown in Fig. 6.

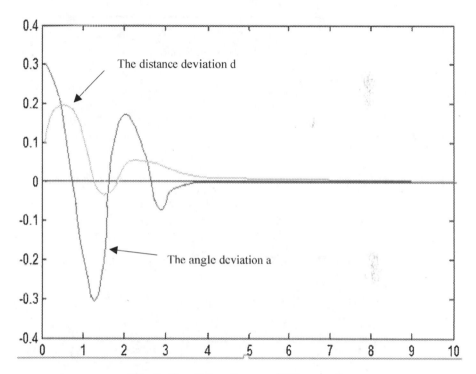

Fig. 6. Simulation diagram of PID controller

As the figure shows, when given the initial trajectory deviation, PID controller can respond in a timely manner and the angle error decreased gradually, but the distance deviation is not immediately reduced. With the slow progress of time, the angle deviation will increase in the opposite direction and the distance deviation is signifi-cantly reduced. However, under the control of the PID controller, if the angle deviation and the distance deviation will eventually stabilize, it will fluctuate more than three to four times. Finally, the AGV car can return to the predetermined trajectory.

4.2 Fuzzy Controller Simulation and Analysis

According to the state space Eq. (8), the fuzzy controller simulation model is built by using the Simulink module [9] of the Matlab simulation software. In this paper, we select that the car's initial angle deviation is a = 0.3°, the distance deviation is d = 0.1 m and the weight is 0.5. The initial speed of the left and right wheels is 0.4 m/s and the initial deviation rate is about 0. The gain of Gain1 is 0.7098 and Gain4 is 0.4876, which are obtained by the Formula (7) of the second chapter. Because the $k_E = 10.1$, $k_F = 25.1$ in the fuzzy controller, so the simulation results of the fuzzy controller are shown in Fig. 7 as follow.

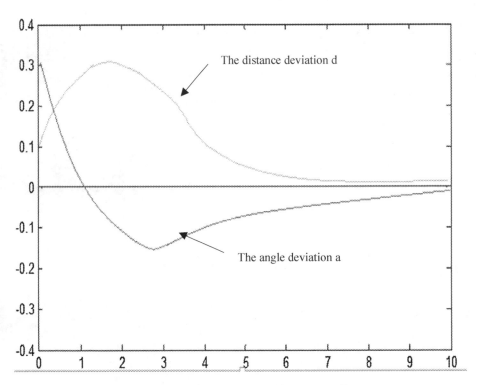

Fig. 7. Simulation diagram of fuzzy controller

As the figure shows, when the trajectory deviation appears in the AGV trajectory, the fuzzy controller can react and the angle deviation will decrease gradually, but the distance deviation does not immediately reduce. In a very short period of time, the car's angular deviation and distance deviation will tend to zero. Therefore, the AGV can achieve the purpose of trajectory tracking. Compared with the deviations of the PID controller, there is a significant improvement in the repeated fluctuations. By changing the parameters of the simulation model and the proportional coefficient of the controller, we can get a more ideal graphics which is as shown in Fig. 8. The distance deviation fluctuation is smaller and the recovery time of the error has been further improved [10].

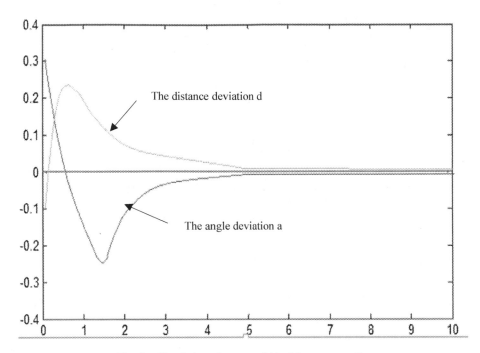

Fig. 8. Simulation diagram of ideal fuzzy controller

5 Conclusion

Using the Matlab software to establish the simulation model of the fuzzy controller by the given initial angle and distance deviation of the AGV. Then we can get the fuzzy control simulation map and can be seen that fuzzy controller is very effective to the error elimination of the AGV. Finally, we can get a more ideal effect diagram by adjusting the parameters correspondingly. By comparing the simulation results of these two controllers, it can be clearly seen that the AGV trajectory controller which is based on fuzzy control theory is more effective and more stable than the conventional PID controller. Therefore, the trajectory tracking based on fuzzy control theory can be applied to the actual operation of AGV.

References

1. Liu, Z.W., Wu, Y.M., Wang, J.X.: Application of Dijkstra algorithm in laser guided AGV scheduling system. Mech. Eng. Autom. **201**, 35–38 (2017)
2. Yang, Y.N., Fang, Q.G.: Study on tracking of AGV trajectory based on fuzzy control. Hoisting Transp. Mach. **02**, 16–18 (2011)
3. Cheng, H.: AGV trajectory tracking control strategy research. Master's thesis of Hefei University of Technology, Hefei. **03**, 1–7 (2016)

4. Wang, H.D.: Dynamic analysis of universal wheel based on AGV. J. Mach. Des. **32**(4), 97–100 (2015)
5. Wu, Q.P., Jin, Y.P., Ren, P.: Key technologies of automatic guided vehicle trends. Manuf. Autom. **35**(5), 106–109, 121 (2013)
6. Tan, C.C.: Experimental AGV control and guidance system research and development. Guangxi University, Guangxi. 05, 2–3 (2012)
7. Wang, B., Hu, B., Wang, C.X.: Automatic guided vehicle control system research and design. Autom. Instrum. **34**(5), 1–4 (2013)
8. Yue, M., Zhang, Y., Tang, F.Y.: Path following control of a two wheeled surveillance vehicle based on sliding mode technology. Trans. Inst. Measur. Control **35**, 212–218 (2013)
9. Zhang, K., Xu, L.H.: Research on magnetic navigation AGV differential steering control algorithm based on fuzzy control. Autom. Instrum. **10**, 01–04 (2016)
10. Chen, W., Cheng, H., Zheng, T.: Research on AGV trajectory tracking based on T-S fuzzy neural network. Chem. Autom. Instrum. **43**(4), 367–369 (2016)

Stability Determination Method of Flame Combustion Based on Improved BP Model with Hierarchical Rate

Rongbao Chen[✉], Zipei Cao, and Benxian Xiao

Hefei University of Technology, Hefei 230000, China
crbwish@163.com, caozipei@163.com, xiaobenxian@163.com

Abstract. For the purpose of automatic monitoring of the boiler combustion stability and quantifying the degree of combustion stability, a determination model for the combustion stability based on BP neural network is proposed. This model, according to the digital image processing technology, captures flame combustion state images, then extracts combustion states. Aimed at shortcomings of BP algorithm – anti-jamming ability, slow learning rate, easy to fall into local minimum, etc., this paper proposes a BP algorithm based on hierarchical dynamic adjustment of different learning rates. The samples are divided into training samples and test samples for training and testing the established model. Experience has shown that the improved model not only has better fault-tolerance and mapping ability but also improves recognition rates and computing speed, which can meet the real time requirement of stability determination.

Keywords: Flame image processing · Improved BP algorithm · Hierarchical dynamic adjustment of different learning rates · Combustion stability

1 Introduction

With the development of IT technology and digital image processing technology, large-scale power plant boiler started to use the image monitoring system of boiler flame. But the current image monitoring system is just automatic detection for combustion and extinguishment of coal. Although this image monitoring system of boiler flame provides a technology platform for automatic monitoring of combustion stability, the combustion stability monitoring still needs operators to observe flame images because the method of judging combustion stability based on flame images is not mature yet. Therefore, the stability judgment is one of key problems to be solved in the automatic monitoring system of combustion state. The solution of this problem has practical significance to realize the automatic monitoring of combustion state and the safe operation of boilers [1].

BP neural network is suitable for this complex process of boiler flame combustion because of its non-linear mapping, self-adaptation, self-learning, network generalization and fault tolerance.

© Springer Nature Singapore Pte Ltd. 2017
D. Yue et al. (Eds.): LSMS/ICSEE 2017, Part II, CCIS 762, pp. 33–43, 2017.
DOI: 10.1007/978-981-10-6373-2_4

However, the existing BP algorithm in the process of model training showed slow convergence, a large number of training steps, easy to fall into local minimum, difficult to determine the network structure and poor generalization ability, which greatly limits the development of judgement model for flame combustion stability [2]. Although some scholars have put forward a lot of improved algorithms, the inherent nature of BP network has not been improved well and many algorithms only improved on one side, then the application range was limited [3].

To solve this problem, this paper, based on analyzing flame images, improves the training method and transfer function, constructs a new composite error function, at the same time, proposes a new method of adjusting different learning rates and an idea of grouping training. This improved BP algorithm greatly improves the model reliability, promotes the research of the combustion stability determination model.

2 Flame Image Preprocessing and Combustion Parameter Selection

2.1 Flame Image Preprocessing

The flame analysis of combustion characteristics is the key to determine the detection algorithm of flame images. Figure 1 shows a furnace flame image. In order to obtain more accurate and more realistic flame characteristics and to obtain more clear flame combustion parameters, the flame image needs to be preprocessed. This paper adopts the existing method of paper [4] to preprocess flame images which includes gray-scale and median filter.

Fig. 1. Furnace flame image

Gray-scale is the process of converting a color image into a gray image. According to the transformation relationship between RGB color space and YUV color space, establishing a corresponding relationship between brightness Y, R (red), G (green) and B (blue): $Y = 0.3R + 0.59G + 0.11B$. Calculating the luminance value Y of each pixel, and the luminance value information is used as the gradation value of the gray scale image.

Median filter can filter out random noise in flame image. Because of its non-linear, median filter do not affect step signal which would not result in image blurring. The digital equation of median filter is expressed as:

$$g(x, y) = med\{f(x - i, y - i)\}, i, j \in S \tag{1}$$

In the equation, g(x,y) and f(x,y) is pixel gray level of the image data matrix, and S is a sliding window.

2.2 Combustion Parameter Selection

Some combustion parameters are mentioned in paper [4–8], including flame average gray, average gray of effective area, high thermal field area, circularity, offset of flame center and flame abundance. As the camera placed in a poor position in this study, the circularity is not ideal. When the combustion parameter is chosen too much, the complexity of fuzzy neural network will be increased. Therefore, this paper selects five combustion parameters, which are flame average gray, average gray of effective area, flame abundance, area ratio of high thermal field and offset of flame center. Those parameters are extracted from preprocessed flame images.

As the pulsation rate of pulverized coal is 10–30 Hz, and the pulsation rate of flame center is 5–10 Hz [9]. In order to eliminate the influence of flame pulsation on the judgement of stability combustion, obtaining the maximum, minimum and average values of the flame parameters which taken by every five frames of flame videos, then obtaining parameter samples, so that each set of sample data contains one flame pulsation at least. A combustion parameter database is obtained.

3 Combustion Stability Judgment Model Based on BP Neural Network

BP algorithm includes two aspects: the forward propagation of signal and the reverse propagation of error, namely when calculating actual outputs, the direction is from inputs to outputs, but when correcting weight and threshold, the direction is from outputs to inputs.

Suppose the number of input layer, hidden layer and output layer is N, M and L respectively. Any input sample vectors are $\zeta^k = (\zeta_1^k, \zeta_2^k, \ldots, \zeta_N^k), 1 \leq k \leq P$, actual output vectors are $C^k = (C_1^k, C_2^k, \ldots, C_L^k)$, expected output vectors are $y^k = (y_1^k, y_2^k, \ldots, y_L^k)$, the weights that connect the input layer and hidden layer are $w_{ij}(1 \leq i \leq N, 1 \leq j \leq M)$, the weights that connect the hidden layer and output layer are $v_{jt}(1 \leq j \leq M, 1 \leq t \leq L)$, the output threshold values for each unit of hidden layer are $\theta_j(1 \leq j \leq M)$, the output threshold values for each unit of output layer are $t_t(1 \leq t \leq L)$, $g(x)$ and $f(x)$ are transfer functions of hidden layer and output layer respectively. Suppose m is iterative number of training network, link weights and actual outputs are all functions of m.

(1) When signal start forward propagation, the propagation direction is from input layer to hidden layer, and then from hidden layer to output layer, there is an influence between two adjacent neurons. If output values of output layer does not reach desired values, the back propagation process is performed. Repeating these two processes alternately until the network error reaches a sufficiently small value [10].

Using the input samples $\xi^k = (\xi_1^k, \xi_2^k, \ldots, \xi_N^k)$, link weights w_{ij} and thresholds θ_j to calculate neuron inputs S_j^k in the hidden layer. Then, neuron outputs O_j^k in the hidden layer are calculated by S_j^k and transfer function $g(x)$:

$$S_j^k(m) = \sum_{i=1}^{N} w_{ij}(m)\xi_i^k - \theta_j(m); i = 1, 2, \ldots, M \tag{2}$$

$$O_j^k(m) = g\left(S_j^k(m)\right); j = 1, 2, \ldots, M \tag{3}$$

Likewise, using outputs b_j^k in the hidden layer, link weights v_{jt} and thresholds r_t to calculate neuron outputs L_t^k in the output layer, and then neuron response C_t^k in the output layer is calculated by L_t^k and transfer function $f(x)$:

$$L_t^k(m) = \sum_{j=1}^{M} v_{jt}(m)O_j^k - r_t(m); t = 1, 2, \ldots, L \tag{4}$$

$$C_t^k(m) = f\left(L_j^k(m)\right); t = 1, 2, \ldots, L \tag{5}$$

(2) The reverse propagation of error, that is, firstly calculating the output error of neurons, layer by layer. Then adjusting all weights and thresholds, according to the error gradient descend method. So that the final outputs of the modified network can be close to desired values.

For all training samples, the global mean square error function between actual output values C_t^k of the neural network and ideal expected values y_t^k is expressed as:

$$\begin{aligned} E(m) &= \frac{1}{2}\sum_{k=1}^{P} E_k(m) = \frac{1}{2}\sum_{k=1}^{P}\sum_{t=1}^{L} \left(e_t^k(m)\right)^2 \\ &= \frac{1}{2}\sum_{k=1}^{P}\sum_{t=1}^{L} (y_t^k - C_t^k(m))^2 \end{aligned} \tag{6}$$

In the equation, $e_t^k(m) = y_t^k - C_t^k(m)$ is error of the t-th neuron at the m-th iteration of network.

For the traditional BP algorithm, generally selecting Sigmoid function (short for s-type function) as the transfer function of BP neural network, that is

$$f(x) = g(x) = \frac{1}{1 + e^{-x}} \tag{7}$$

4 Improved BP Algorithm

4.1 Shortcomings of BP Algorithm

BP algorithm has a solid theoretical basis, rigorous derivation process, beautiful symmetrical formula, clear physical concept, and strong versatility. However, it is found that BP algorithm has some shortcomings with the long-term use process, mainly including the following aspects [11]:

(1) Slow convergence.
(2) Easy to fall into local minimum.
(3) Network structure is difficult to determine.
(4) Poor generalization ability.

4.2 Improved BP Algorithm

In the process of determining combustion stability, due to a large number of network training samples and a certain number of duplicate samples, trying to adopt a training method of packet processing in the improved BP algorithm, which means that P training samples were divided into N groups, the number of samples for each group is $P_i(1 \leq i \leq n)$, then make each group of samples to train network, adjust learning rates after a study of each group [12]. In the training method of packet processing, for training samples $P_i(1 \leq i \leq n)$, the global mean square error function between the actual output values C_t^k of neural network and the ideal output value y_t^k is expressed as:

$$E = \frac{1}{P}\sum\nolimits_{k=1}^{P_i} E_k = \frac{1}{2P}\sum\nolimits_{k=1}^{P_i} \sum\nolimits_{t=1}^{L} \left(e_t^k\right)^2$$
$$= \frac{1}{2P}\sum\nolimits_{k=1}^{P_i} \sum\nolimits_{t=1}^{L} (y_t^k - C_t^k)^2 \tag{8}$$

In the equation, $e_t^k = y_t^k - C_t^k$ is error of the t-th neuron in the output layer.

BP algorithm is based on the squared error sum function as the objective function and uses the gradient descent method to find the minimum algorithm. In the initial stage of the training samples, output values are far from expected values, E is relatively large, and ΔE has a larger space for descent, so E has a greater contribution to accelerate the network's convergence. With training samples and training times increase, output values are gradually close to desired values, E decreases, and the space of decline is also shrinking. At this time, the convergence rate of network will become very slow. Meanwhile, due to the global mean square error function E is a nonlinear function, means that connection space composed of E isn't a paraboloid which only have one minimum point, but a hypersurface with a number of local minimum. Therefore, the convergence process of back propagation networks is easy to fall into local minimum, and cannot converge to the global minimum point. The reason for this problem is that the BP learning rule adopts the gradient descent direction of error function to converge [12]. In order to solve this problem, this paper constructs the composite error function:

$G_\lambda = \lambda E + (1 - \lambda)E_G(m)$, and uses $G_\lambda(m)$ to replace the global mean square error function $E(m)$. The concrete expansion is expressed as:

$$G_\lambda(m) = \lambda E(m) + (1 - \lambda)E_G(m)$$
$$= 0.5\lambda \sum_{k=1}^{P_i} \sum_{t=1}^{L} \left(e_t^k(m)\right)^2 + (1 - \lambda) \sum_{k=1}^{P_i} \sum_{t=1}^{L} \left(y_t^k e_t^k(m)\right)^2 \quad (9)$$

In the equation, $\lambda = \exp(-|\Delta E(m)|/E(m))$, $\Delta E(m) = E(m) - E(m-1)$ are error variations. $|\Delta E(m)|/E(m)$ is error change rate. $E(m)$ is the global mean square error in the m-th cyclic learning.

In the initial stage of training samples, the actual network outputs are different from the expected outputs ($\lambda = 1$). At this time, $G_\lambda(m) = E(m)$ is the global mean square error function, and the network convergence speed accelerates. With training samples and training times increase, E decreases constantly. When λ is from 1 to 0, the part of contribution value for $(1 - \lambda)E_G(m)$ increases, at this time, $G_\lambda(m) = E_G(m)$. The network convergence speed also accelerates, which overcomes the shortcoming of slow convergence speed of the traditional BP algorithm to a certain extent. For the convergence of function $G_\lambda(m)$, when $e_t^k(m) \to 0$, the composite error function can make $E(m)$ and $E_G(m)$ reach the minimum at the same time, and its convergence is consistent with the convergence of $E(m)$.

For the problem of slow convergence speed, this paper adopts a new method to adjust different learning rate, that is, to separately adjust the learning rate η_1 of output layer and the learning rate η_2 of hidden layer, which replaces the fixed learning rate η in the traditional algorithm. According to the Delta learning rule, link weights v_{jt} which are form implicit function to output layer and link weights w_{ij} which are form input layer to hidden layer respectively are:

$$\Delta v_{jt} = \eta_1(m)\left(-\frac{\partial G_\lambda(m)}{\partial v_{jt}(m)}\right)$$
$$= -\eta_1(m)\left[\frac{\partial \lambda E(m)}{\partial e_t^k(m)} + \frac{\partial (1 - \lambda)E_G(m)}{\partial e_t^k(m)}\right] \cdot \frac{\partial e_t^k(m)}{\partial C_t^k(m)} \frac{\partial C_t^k(m)}{\partial L_t^k(m)} \frac{\partial L_t^k(m)}{\partial v_{jt}(m)} \quad (10)$$
$$= \eta_1(m) \sum_{k=1}^{P_i} \delta_t^k(\lambda, m)O_j^k(m)$$

In the equation, $\delta_t^k(\lambda, m) = (y_t^k - \lambda C_t^k(m))C_t^k(m)(1 - C_t^k(m))$.

$$\Delta w_{ij}(m) = \eta_2(m)\left(-\frac{\partial G_\lambda(m)}{\partial w_{ij}(m)}\right)$$
$$= -\eta_2(m)\left[\frac{\partial \lambda E(m)}{\partial e_t^k(m)} + \frac{\partial (1 - \lambda)E_G(m)}{\partial e_t^k(m)}\right] \cdot \frac{\partial e_t^k(m)}{\partial C_t^k(m)} \frac{\partial C_t^k(m)}{\partial L_t^k(m)} \frac{\partial L_t^k(m)}{\partial O_t^k(m)} \frac{\partial O_t^k(m)}{\partial S_t^k(m)} \frac{\partial S_t^k(m)}{\partial w_{ij}(m)}$$
$$= \eta_2(m) \sum_{k=1}^{P_i} \delta_t^k(\alpha, \lambda, m)\xi_j^k$$

$$(11)$$

In the equation, $\delta_t^k(\alpha, \lambda, m) = \alpha(1 + O_j^k(m))(1 - O_j^k(m)) \sum_{t=1}^{L} \delta_t^k(\lambda, m)v_{jt}(m)$.

Besides, in the improved BP algorithm, the learning rate of $\eta_1(m)$ and $\eta_2(m)$ respectively adopt the following corrected equations [13]:

$$\eta_1(m+1) = \eta_1(m) - \tau \frac{\Delta E(m)}{E(m)}, 0 < \tau < 1 \tag{12}$$

$$\eta_2(m+1) = \eta_2(m) - \tau \frac{\Delta E(m)}{E(m)}, 0 < \tau < 1 \tag{13}$$

In the equation, $\eta_1(m+1)$ is the learning rate of output layer of group samples in the $m+1$-th cyclic learning. $\eta_2(m+1)$ is the learning rate of hidden layer in the $m+1$-th cyclic learning. τ is a constant which range from $0 < \tau < 1$, and this paper takes τ as 0.5 [13].

Therefore, the corrected equations of connection weights v_{jt} and w_{ij} respectively are:

$$v_{jt}(m+1) = v_{jt}(m) + \eta_1 \sum_{k-1}^{P_i} \delta_t^k(\lambda, m) O_j^k(m) \tag{14}$$

$$w_{ij}(m+1) = w_{ij}(m) + \eta_2 \sum_{k=1}^{P_i} \delta_t^k(\alpha, \lambda, m) \zeta_j^k \tag{15}$$

5 Simulation of Combustion Stability Determination Based on Improved BP Neural Network

5.1 Improved BP Neural Network Training

In order to test model performances, "1–4" is used to respectively represent 4 kinds of combustion states [5]: "1: very stable", "2: general stability", "3: slightly unstable", "4: very unstable". The decision attribute of samples uses "1", "2", "3" and "4" as four kinds of combustion state, and model outputs are decimals which locate in interval [0, 5]. Therefore, it is necessary to deal with output results, and choosing appropriate method to test model performances. Rounding model outputs, and respectively corresponding to each combustion state. Due to the combustion stability determination of samples is based on the interval partition, coupled with flame pulse and image noise, it is bound to cause some inaccurate. Therefore, when model outputs adjoin samples, they have little influence on the stability determination, such as "1" and "2 denote all stable states, just different extent. However, when the stability differs by two degrees, such as "1" and "3", the two kinds of combustion states differ considerably, at this time, the model outputs are not credible. So defining state difference as ΔS, confidence factor as γ. When the model outputs (rounded) is coincident with samples ($\Delta S = 0$), the result is right, and the confidence factor $\gamma = 1$; When differ by one degree ($\Delta S = 1$), the result is slightly inaccurate, and the confidence factor $\gamma = 0.5$; When differ by two or three degrees ($\Delta S = 2$ or $\Delta S = 3$), the model outputs is wrong, and the confidence factor

$\gamma = 0$. The confidence R is used as one of the performance parameters. Supposing the number of test samples is n, γ_k are confidence factors of k-th sample. The model's confidence can be calculated by:

$$R = \sum_{k=1}^{n} \gamma_k \times 100\%/n \qquad (16)$$

In addition, P is accuracy of model, P = (stability)/(sample total) *100%, which represent the proportion of model outputs that are coincident with samples. When the model confidence R and accuracy P meet requirements, the model can be used to determine combustion stability, otherwise retraining and retesting the model until meeting the requirements.

Algorithm steps:

Step1: Initializing link weights, thresholds and learning rate (η_1 and η_2). Supposing all training samples are divided into n groups, the sample number of each group is $P_i (1 \le i \le n)$, ε is expected error criterion in the group and M is the maximum iteration number.

Step2: Randomly inputting any samples in this group $\xi^k = (\xi_1^k, \xi_2^k, \ldots, \xi_N^k)$;

Step3: Calculating respectively output values of the hidden layer and output layer according to the input samples ξ^k;

Setp4: Calculating the mean square error of samples, judging whether all training samples complete learning or not. If it is, calculating the global mean square error according to Eq. 10, and $m = m + 1$; otherwise, go to Step2;

Setp5: Judging whether cyclic learning times m is greater than the maximum iteration times M or not. If it is, go to Step7. Otherwise, judging whether the global training sample mean square error $|E(m)|$ in this group is less than expected error standard ε. If it is, go to the Step7; otherwise, go to step6;

Step6: Judging ΔE. If $\Delta E > 0.001$, different learning rate $\eta_1(m)$ and $\eta_2(m)$ need to be reset, and returning Step2; if $\Delta E < 0.001$, correcting the learning rate $\eta_1(m)$ and $\eta_2(m)$ of all input samples according to Eqs. 12 and 13, and correcting link weights of the output layer and hidden layer;

Step7: Calculating each confidence factor γ of test samples;

Step8: Calculating the confidence R and accuracy P;

Step9: If the confidence level meets requirements, the model is set up successfully, and the test is over. Otherwise, returns Step2;

5.2 Combustion Stability Output

This paper chooses 4000 test samples in the sample database after processing. In order to verify the validity of improved BP algorithm, using the 200 samples which are selected from the 400 test samples to compare with the result. Transfer functions of the output layer and hidden layer select Sigmoid function. For two combustion stability determination models of the traditional BP algorithm and improved BP algorithm (methods as described in Sect. 5.1), inputting samples, then getting the final results as shown in Figs. 2 and 3. Figure 2 is the combustion stability simulation of traditional BP algorithm. Figure 3 is the combustion stability simulation of improved BP algorithm.

As shown in Figs. 2 and 3, they are "sample decision", "BP network output", "stability interval", "stability error curve" and "sample confidence level" respectively. The X axes are the number of samples. The Y axes of "sample decision", "BP network output" and "stability interval" represent the 4 kinds of combustion states described in Sect. 5.1; the Y axis of "stability error curve" represents error difference; the Y axis of "sample confidence level" is confidence size. The stability is a theoretical continuation of multi-attribute decision making theory in literature [10]. The size of stability reflects the degree of stability.

Contrasting the five parameter comparisons between Figs. 2 and 3, the data in Fig. 2 is relatively rough, Fig. 3 shows more detailed data. This illustrates that compared with the traditional BP algorithm, the improved BP algorithm can more accurately reflect the stability of samples, and more persuasively determinate stability and confidence of samples.

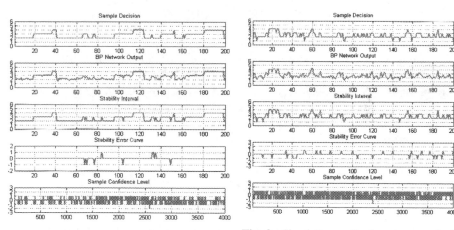

Fig. 2. Simulation of the traditional BP algorithm

Fig. 3. Simulation of the improved BP algorithm

Defining the accuracy and confidence to determine performance parameters of the established combustion determination model (show in Sect. 5.1), the results are as follows by checking (Table 1):

Table 1. Performance parameters of the combustion determination model

Algorithm type	Traditional BP	Traditional BP	Improved BP
Samples	4000	4000	4000
Hidden layer	30	30	30
Training steps	20000	20000	20000
Accuracy	82.56%	82.56%	82.56%
Confidence level	91.25%	91.25%	91.25%
Runtime of single sample	0.0094	0.0094	0.0094

6 Conclusion

BP neural network has strong nonlinear mapping ability. It can approximate the nonlinear function by arbitrary precision, so it is more suitable for the modeling complex problems such as flame combustion. However, due to slow convergence speed, a large number of training steps, easy to fall into local minimum and so on, its application in practice has been confined in some ways. Based on the above considerations, this paper improves the network training method and transfer functions, constructs a new composite error function, at the same time, adopts hierarchical dynamic adjustment of different learning rates, and obtains a new improved BP neural network.

The improved BP neural network model is used to simulate combustion samples. The results show that compared with the traditional BP algorithm, the improved BP algorithm has faster convergence speed, higher accuracy and confidence, and can be used to determine combustion states effectively. The improved algorithm is an effective method for training BP network and determining combustion stability, which further improves performances.

References

1. Zu, C.G., Zhou, H.C., Lou, C.: Diagnosis and analysis of combustion stability based on flame images. In: Hubei Electric Power (2006)
2. Kamarthi, S.V., Pittner, S.: Accelerating neural network training using weight extrapolations. Neural Netw. **12**(9), 1285–1299 (1999)
3. Srinvas, M., Patnaik, L.M.: Adaptive probabilities of crossover and mutation in genetic algorithm. IEEE Trans. Syst. Man Cybernet. **24**(4), 162–167 (2004)
4. Chen, R.B., Fan, W.T., Bian, J.C.: Research on stability criterion of furnace flame combustion based on image processing. In: International Conference on Control Engineering and Communication Technology, pp. 568–572 (2012)
5. Chen, R.B., Bian, J.C., Meng, F.H.: Research on closed-loop control system based on image-signal processing of furnace flame. In: International Conference on Energy, Environment and Sustainable Development, pp. 1095–1100 (2013)
6. Chen, R.B., Meng, F.H., Xiao, B.X.: Research on combustion stability based on interval number and multiple attribute decision making. Yi Qi Yi Biao Xue Bao/Chin. J. Sci. Instrum. **36**(3), 552–559 (2015)

7. Chen, R.B., Ma, W.Y., Xiao, B.X., Cao, Z.P.: Study on the parameter discretization algorithm of furnace flame image based on rough set theory. In: 35th Chinese Control Conference (2016)
8. Xu, B.C., Zhang, D.Y., Cheng, L.: Study on combustion stability based on flame images. Comput. Eng. Appl. **48**(9), 168–171 (2012)
9. Liu, H.: Judging boiler combustion stability based on flame image and fuzzy neural network. Chin. J. Sci. Instrum. **29**(6), 1280–1284 (2008)
10. Qiao, J.F., Han, H.G., Qiao, J.F.: Optimal structure design for RBFNN structure. Acta Automatica Sinica **6**, 865–872 (2010)
11. Wang, Y., Cao, C.X.: Analysis of local minimization for BP algorithm and its avoidance methods. Comput. Eng. **28**(6), 35–36 (2002)
12. Liu, Z.G., Yang, Y., Ji, X.H.: Flame detection algorithm based on a saliency detection technique and the uniform local binary pattern in the YCbCr color space. SIViP **2**, 1–8 (2016)
13. Wong, W.K., Yuen, C.W.M., Fan, D.D.: Stitching defect detection and classification using wavelet transform and BP neural network. Expert Syst. Appl. **36**(2), 3845–3856 (2009)

A Genetic Neural Network Approach for Production Prediction of Trailing Suction Dredge

Zhen Su[1,2], Jingqi Fu[1(✉)], and Jian Sun[2]

[1] Department of Automation, College of Mechatronic
Engineering and Automation, Shanghai University, Shanghai 200072, China
jqfu@staff.shu.edu.cn
[2] Marine Equipment and Technology Institute, Jiangsu University of Science
and Technology, Zhenjiang 212003, China

Abstract. The working efficiency and economic benefit of trailing suction dredge are directly dependent on the earth production, so prediction of earth production is of great significance in the mechanism analysis and efficiency optimization of the trailing suction dredge. Suction dredger dredging process mode is a complex, non-linear dynamic model, and the model is affected by a variety of factors. This paper presents a genetic algorithm to improve the BP neural network model that is used to predict dredger production. In order to overcome the shortcomings of traditional BP neural network training time long and easy to fall into local minimum, this paper uses genetic algorithm to optimize the initial weights and thresholds of BP neural network for dredger production prediction. The simulation results show that the genetic BP neural network has a better fitting ability. Compared with the BP neural network, it has the characteristics of good global search ability and high accuracy. The result shows that genetic BP neural network can accurately predict the production.

Keywords: Trailing suction · Hopper dredger · Genetic algorithm · Neural network · Production prediction

1 Introduction

With the gradual reduction of world fossil fuels and the rising temperatures around the world, there is a growing focus on energy efficient use and low-carbon reductions. The dredger needs to consume a lot of fuel in the process of dredging, so how to get the dredger low energy consumption, high efficiency work has become the focus of dredging industry research direction [1, 2]. In recent years, a large number of studies have been carried out on energy consumption analysis and efficiency optimization of dredging operations for trailing suction dredgers [3, 4]. The dredger production is the most important indicator of the performance of the dredger, so production prediction is an important work in the efficiency optimization process.

The hopper dredger sails to an area with suitable sand that can be excavated from the bottom with a drag head. It starts filling the onboard cargo hold, the so-called

© Springer Nature Singapore Pte Ltd. 2017
D. Yue et al. (Eds.): LSMS/ICSEE 2017, Part II, CCIS 762, pp. 44–52, 2017.
DOI: 10.1007/978-981-10-6373-2_5

hopper. In this hopper, a separation process takes place where the sand settles at the bottom and excess water flows overboard. Once the hopper is full with sediment, the ship sails to the discharge location where the unloading takes place by either opening the bottom doors or pumping the material out of the hopper by the dredge pumps. This is one dredging cycle. Two processes dominate the production of a trailing suction hopper dredger: the incoming production process from the drag head, pump and pipeline and the sedimentation process in the hopper [5].

Suction dredger dredging process mode is a complex, non-linear dynamic model, and the model is affected by a variety of factors, include: ship equipment parameters, soil-type dependent parameters and construction control parameters [6, 7]. Braaksma established a dynamically model of the trailing suction dredger, and used predictive control algorithm to optimize the overall performance of the trailing suction dredger [8]. van Rhee analyzed the sedimentation process in detail and established the overflow loss model [9]. Pei-sheng et al. expounds the major mathematical models that have been developed independently for trailing suction hopper dredgers to optimize their production and improve their working technology according to the changes of seabed [10]. Yang et al. studied the performance of the cutter suction dredger and predicted its production by neural network [11]. In fact, the structure and construction method of the cutter suction dredger and the trailing suction dredge are quite different. Therefore, this paper uses the genetic neural network algorithm to focus on the prediction production of the trailing suction dredge. Our team has completed the density prediction [12], and this paper mainly introduces production prediction on the basis of this technology.

2 Predictive Principle of Dredger Production

In lading stage, instantaneous production m_i (kg/s) of the trailing suction dredge equals flow rate into the hopper Q_i (m³/s) multiplied by flow density into the hopper ρ_i (kg/m³), production is calculated as follows:

$$m_i = Q_i \cdot \rho_i \tag{1}$$

Therefore, production prediction of trailing suction dredge that is flow rate and density prediction. The production of a trailing suction hopper dredger depends on a range of variable, such as the pump speed, the ship's speed, the visor angle or the ship's draught and so on.

In the drag head model, we choose four variables: the ship's speed, the visor angle, drag head depth and wave compensator pressure. We base this choice on the inputs that influence the performance the most, and incoming mixture density as the model output. In the pump pipeline model, we choose four variables: the pump speed, dredging depth, ship's draught and the pressure loss over the drag head as the model input. The flow rate into the hopper as the model output. The model is shown in Fig. 1.

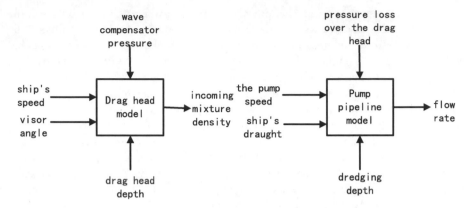

Fig. 1. The drag head model and pump pipeline model

3 Genetic Neural Network Prediction Model

3.1 Construct Production Prediction Model

In view of the accuracy of the mud pump pipeline model affected by a variety of factors, and the interaction between the various factors can not accurately known [13]. Considering that BP neural network has a good nonlinear fitting ability, the structure is not complicated and practical, but it has some shortcomings such as the long training time and the shortcomings of the global search ability, and the genetic algorithm is a kind of global search algorithm which imitates the evolution theory of biology, and the global search ability is very strong. Therefore, the combination of genetic algorithm and BP neural network not only makes the BP neural network have good nonlinear fitting ability, but also has strong global optimization ability. Based on the above analysis, the genetic algorithm is used to improve the neural network to predict production of trailing suction dredge. The structure of the neural network can be determined by the number of input and output of the model. The genetic algorithm is used to optimize the weights and thresholds of the neural network. The connection weights and thresholds are assigned to the BP neural network, and finally the BP neural network is trained and the production is predicted.

3.2 Genetic BP Neural Network

Genetic algorithm is a kind of parallel random search optimal method which is simulated by natural genetic mechanism and biological evolution theory [14]. The basic principle is based on the biological circles in the "natural selection, survival of the fittest" evolutionary rule and get. The genetic algorithm is to encode parameters that need to be optimized, and any one of the codes is called a gene. The string of genes is called chromosomes, and multiple chromosomes are called groups [15]. The number of chromosomes is called population size. The degree to which chromosomes are adapted to a given environment is called fitness. The algorithm is to encode the problem parameters into chromosomes. According to the given fitness function, the new chromosomes are obtained by selecting and crossing, and finally the parameters of fitness are found. Genetic neural network is used to optimize the initial weights and thresholds of neural networks by genetic algorithm. After neural network training and network prediction based on optimized values [16]. This method overcomes the shortcomings of traditional neural network initial weights and threshold stochastic selection, which is easy to fall into local optimization. The process is shown in Fig. 2.

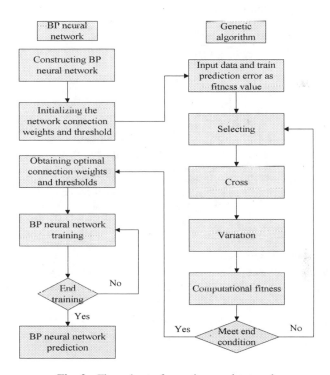

Fig. 2. Flow chart of genetic neural network

The implementation steps of genetic algorithm have initialize the population, determine the fitness function and the selection, cross and other operations. The specific steps are as follows:

(1) Population initialization: genetic algorithm can't directly identify the parameters which need to optimize. So the parameters need to be encoded. The parameters will generally be encoded with binary. Thus, the neural network initial weights and thresholds are encoded, each of which is an individual.

(2) Fitness function: The value used to judge the quality of the individual, the text of the real value and the network prediction of the error as the individual fitness value (F).

$$F = k\left(\sum_{i=1}^{n} abs(y_i - o_i)\right) \qquad (2)$$

In the formula, n is number of network outputs, y_i is expected output, o_i is predict output, k is coefficient.

(3) Choose: From the population, selecting some individuals to multiply the offspring in accordance with the probability. The higher the probability of fitness is greater. The probability of chromosome selection is p_i:

$$f_i = k/F_i \qquad (3)$$

$$p_i = \frac{f_i}{\sum\limits_{j=1}^{N} f_i} \qquad (4)$$

In the formula, F_i is chromosome fitness, N is population size, k is coefficient.

(4) Crossover: Select two individuals from the group, and then cross the operation to produce a better next generation of individuals, a_k and a_l the cross method is:

$$\left.\begin{array}{l} a_{kj} = a_{kj}(1 - b) + a_{lj}b \\ a_{lj} = a_{lj}(1 - b) + a_{kj}b \end{array}\right\} \qquad (5)$$

In the formula, b is any number within [0,1].

(5) Mutation: From the population to take an individual, to which the gene to be changed to produce a new generation of individuals, the variation is:

$$a_{ij} = \begin{cases} a_{ij} + (a_{ij} - a_{max}) * f(g) & r > 0.5 \\ a_{ij} + (a_{min} - a_{ij}) * f(g) & r \leq 0.5 \end{cases} \qquad (6)$$

In the formula, a_{max} is a_{ij}, s upper limit, a_{min} is a_{ij}, s lower limit, $f(g) = r_2(1 - g/G_{max})^2 r_2$ is random number, g is evolution times, G_{max} is maximum number of iterations, r is any number in [0,1].

4 Production Prediction and Result Analysis

4.1 Training Data

The data come from the April 2016 in Xiamen Port construction of the "new tiger 8" rake suction dredger collection. The data contain the ship's speed, the visor angle, drag head depth, wave compensator pressure, the pump speed, dredging depth, ship's draught, the pressure loss over the drag head, incoming mixture density and the flow rate into the hopper. We collected one set of data every 30 s, and there are 180 sets of data. The first 150 sets of data were used to train the network, and the last 30 sets of data were used to predict.

Because the data collected by the sensor may be affected by noise or have abnormal construction data, the data must be preprocessed, and the method of dealing with abnormal data, filter denoising and so on.

4.2   Genetic Algorithm Parameter Selection

That genetic algorithm population number and genetic algebra are too small is difficult to find the optimal solution and too large is to increase the algorithm optimization time. So the paper population size is 40, genetic algebra is 100; That probability and mutation rate are too large will destroy the optimization of the individual, too small will be difficult to produce new individuals. The text of the crossing probability is set to 0.7, the variation rate is set to 0.1.

4.3   BP Neural Network Parameter Selection

The input layer has 4 nodes, the output layer has 1 node, the hidden layer node number is 2 * 4 + 1 = 9, there are 4 * 9 = 36 weights between the input layer and the hidden layer and 1 * 9 = 9 weights between the hidden layer and the output layer. The hidden layer has 9 thresholds and the output layer threshold is 1, so the genetic algorithm optimization parameter is 36 + 9 + 9 + 1 = 55. The number of neural network iterations is set to 100, the learning efficiency is 0.1, and the target error is 0.0001.

4.4   Example Verification and Result Analysis

In order to verify the feasibility and effectiveness of the genetic neural network, this paper uses the two algorithms to predict the training in the environment of Matlab7.0. The BP neural network model is predicted and the neural network is optimized by genetic algorithm. BP neural network prediction of network parameters. The error is calculated as follows.

$$\sigma_{MAPE} = \frac{1}{N} \sum_{i=1}^{N} |p_i - \overline{p}_i|/p_i \tag{7}$$

In the formula, p_i is actual value; $\overline{p}_i$ is predicted value, N is sample size.

(1) Flow density into the hopper prediction

The flow density into the hopper prediction results of BP neural network prediction and genetic neural network prediction are shown in Fig. 3 and their errors are shown in Fig. 4. BP, GA-BP model predictive performance results are shown in Table 1.

It can be seen from figures and table that BP neural network prediction result's relative error is 3.82%. While the genetic neural network error is 1.65%, smaller than

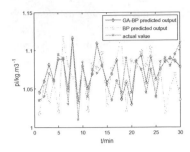

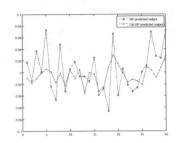

Fig. 4. Error analysis

Fig. 3. Flow density into the hopper prediction results

Table 1. BP, GA-BP model predictive performance results

Prediction model	Relative error	Gradient	Correlation
BP	3.82%	0.022	0.901
GA-BP	1.65%	0.012	0.932

BP. Meanwhile gradient decreased and the correlation increased. It indicates that the optimized neural network prediction accuracy is higher.

(2) Flow rate into the hopper prediction

The flow rate into the hopper prediction results of BP neural network prediction and genetic neural network prediction are shown in Fig. 5 and their errors are shown in Fig. 6. BP, GA-BP model predictive performance results are shown in Table 2.

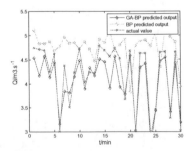

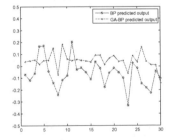

Fig. 6. Error analysis

Fig. 5. Flow rate into the hopper prediction results

It can be seen from figures and table that the BP convergence rate is slow and it is easy to fall into the local minimum point, because of BP's inherent defects. And the prediction effect is improved by the genetic algorithm optimizing the initial weights and thresholds. Relative error drops from 4.62% to 1.8%, gradient drops from 0.03 to 0.014, and correlation increases from 0.892 to 0.938. GA-BP prediction result shows

Table 2. BP, GA-BP model predictive performance results

Prediction model	Relative error	Gradient	Correlation
BP	4.62%	0.030	0.892
GA-BP	1.80%	0.014	0.938

that the curve has a good fit and the prediction error is not large. So it is a effective and reliable method for predicting prediction of trailing suction dredge.

5 Conclusion

BP neural network has the shortcomings of slow convergence and easy to get into the local optimization. In this paper, genetic algorithm is used to optimize it and apply it to the complex nonlinear dredging process model to predict flow density and flow rate. Comparing the experimental results with BP neural network, the results show that the BP neural network prediction model optimized by genetic algorithm has the global optimization ability and has better nonlinear fitting ability. It makes the prediction result more accurate. The algorithm can accurate predict flow density and flow rate of trailing suction dredger according to the current construction conditions, and the result can help operators know the production of the trailing suction dredger. At the same time, it helps to develop an intelligent dredging system for trailing suction dredgers.

Acknowledgment. This work was financially supported by the Science and Technology Commission of Shanghai Municipality of China under Grant (No. 17511107002).

References

1. Aarninkhof, S.G.J., Rosenbrand, W.F., van Rheeand, C., Burt, T.N.: The day after we stop dredging: a world without sediment plumes? In: Proceedings of Dredging Days 2007 Conference, Rotterdam (2007)
2. Braaksma, J., Osnabrugge, J., Babuska, R., Keizer, C., Klaassens, J.B.: Artificial intelligence on board of dredgers for optimal land reclamation. Delft University of Technology (2007)
3. Aarninkhof, S.G.J., Spearman, J., de Heerand, A.F.M., van Koningsveld, M.: Dredging-induced turbidity in a natural context, status and future perspective of the TASS Program. In: Proceedings of the 19th World Dredging Conference (2010)
4. Braaksma, J., Osnabrugge, J., Babuska,R., et al.: Artificial intelligence on board of dredgers for optimal land reclamation. In: CEDA Dredging Days (2007)
5. Braaksma, J., Babuska, R., Klaassens, J.B., de Keizer, C.: Model predictive control for optimizing the overall dredging performance of a trailing suction hopper dredger, pp. 1263–1264. Papers and Presentations (2008)
6. Stano, P.: Nonlinear State and Parameter Estimation for Hopper Dredgers. Delft University of Technology, Holand (2013)
7. Stano, P.M., Tilton, A.K., Babuška, R.: Estimation of the soil-dependent time-varying parameters of the hopper sedimentation model: the FPF versus the BPF. Control Eng. Pract. **24**, 67–78 (2014)

8. Braaksma, J.: Model-Based Control of Hopper Dredgers. Delft University of Technology, Holand (2008)
9. van Rhee, C.: On the sedimentation process in a trailing suction hopper dredger. Ph.D. thesis, TU Delft (2002)
10. Pei-sheng, W., Wan, J., et al.: Principle and method to optimize production of trail ing suction hopper dredgers. China Harbour Eng. 10(5), 8–24 (2004)
11. Yang, J., Ni, F., et al.: Prediction of cutter-suction dredger production based on double hidden layer BP neural network. Comput. Digital Eng. 7, 1234–1237 (2016)
12. Cao, D., Su, Z., Ye, S.: Predicting the drowning boat head density based on genetic BP neural network. China Water Transp. 10, 107–131 (2016)
13. Liouane, Z., Lemlouma, T., Roose, P., Weis, F., Messaoud, H.: A genetic neural network approach for unusual behavior prediction in smart home. In: Madureira, A.M., Abraham, A., Gamboa, D., Novais, P. (eds.) ISDA 2016. AISC, vol. 557, pp. 738–748. Springer, Cham (2017). doi:10.1007/978-3-319-53480-0_73
14. Liu, S.D., Hou, Z.S., Yin, C.K.: Data-driven modeling for UGI gasification processes via an enhanced genetic BP neural network with link switches. IEEE Trans. Neural Netw. Learn. Syst. 27, 2718–2729 (2016)
15. Todd, D.S., Sen P.A.: Multiple criteria genetic algorithm for containership loading. In: Proceedings of the Seventh International Conference on Genetic Algorithms, Michigan State University. Morgan Kaufmann Publishers (2007)
16. Jokar, A., Godarzi, A.A., Saber, M., Shafii, M.B.: Simulation and optimization of a pulsating heat pipe using artificial neural network and genetic algorithm. Heat Mass Transf. 52, 2437–2445 (2016)

Orthogonal Matching Pursuit for Multilayer Perceptions Neural Networks Model Reduction

Xiaoquan Tang[1], Xiaolin Wang[2], and Long Zhang[3(✉)]

[1] School of Automation, Huazhong University of Science and Technology,
Wuhan 430074, China
[2] School of Electronic Information and Electrical Engineering,
Shanghai Jiao Tong University, Shanghai 200240, China
[3] School of Electrical and Electronic Engineering, University of Manchester,
Manchester M13 9PL, UK
long.zhang@manchester.ac.uk

Abstract. Neural networks have drawn much attention in modern machine learning community as they have achieved many successful applications, such as image recognition, speech recognition and system identification. According to the principle of parsimony, simpler neural models are preferable to more complex ones if they have similar generalization performance. However, when building a neural networks model, the neuron number is often determined randomly or by trial-and-error. These methods can often lead to the over-complex networks with many redundant neurons and therefore may result in over-fitting problems. In this paper, a new approach is proposed for obtaining a simplified neural networks with fewer neurons but still keeping a good performance comparing to the initial fully networks. More specifically, the initial neural model with a fixed model size is built using Matlab toolbox. Then, the orthogonal matching pursuit method is employed to select important neurons and drop out redundant neurons, leading to a more compact model with reduced size. Two simulation examples are used to demonstrate the effectiveness of the proposed method.

Keywords: Orthogonal matching pursuit · Neural model reduction

1 Introduction

Neural networks have drawn much attentions from both industrial and academic communities, especially with the development of the proposed deep learning in recent years. Neural networks play an important role in artificial intelligence community. They perform extremely well for many tasks including natural language understanding, question answering, analysing data, etc. [1]. In addition, they win the records in image recognition and speech recognition. It is worth mentioning that deep neural networks is one the most popular learning methods recently. However, deep neural networks are not something new. They have the

© Springer Nature Singapore Pte Ltd. 2017
D. Yue et al. (Eds.): LSMS/ICSEE 2017, Part II, CCIS 762, pp. 53–61, 2017.
DOI: 10.1007/978-981-10-6373-2_6

same structure with the widely used multilayer perceptions (MLP) networks but with more hidden layers.

When building MLP networks and its more complex version, deep neural networks, we often have to manually set number of network layers and number of hidden neurons before employing the parameter optimization methods, such as the widely used gradient method. If we only use three-layer networks with single-hidden-layer, we still have to determine the number of hidden neurons in advance. When setting the neuron numbers, the currently widely used method is the trial-and-error that often requires randomly setting the number of neurons and testing the model accuracy through a learning method. This process is very time-consuming, which often generate a over complex model with large number of neurons. There are two main problems for the over complex models. One is the over-fitting problem with poor generalisation performance, and the other is the large computation problem.

The simple and compact model is often referred as parsimonious model. In practice, if two models perform similarly in terms of their training and test accuracy, the simpler model with fewer neurons is preferable, which is the principle of parsimony. If the neural networks is used for nonlinear system identification or real time control applications, it is high desirable to generate a parsimonious model for the purposes of good generalisation performance and highly computation efficiency [6]. In this paper, we will focus on nonlinear system identification using neural networks.

Many software, such as matlab, have provided neural network toolboxes. These tools have been widely used to build neural networks on a variety of applications. However, most of them do not pay attention to generate a parsimonious model with minimal number of neurons. It is worth mentioning that a scheme of dropping neurons was recently proposed to prevent over-fitting problem [4,5]. This is achieved by integrating random dropping neurons into gradient descent methods using regularization technique. Although this neuron dropout method has attracted significant attractions and the paper was cited more than 2000 times within two years, it requires new training process and may not provide a parsimonious and unique model due to the random dropping scheme.

In this paper, the main objective is to simplify the single hidden layer models produced by Matlab neural network toolbox by deleting unimportant neurons without sacrificing model performance. In other words, the simplified networks with fewer hidden neurons can perform as well as or better than the initial networks with more neurons. This is achieved by shrinking the neurons using Orthogonal matching pursuit (OMP) algorithm. More specifically, the single hidden layer networks, can be formulated as a linear combination of nonlinear neurons. OMP is employed to re-select the neurons and drop unimportant or redundant neurons, leading to an improved model with smaller neuron number. The main difference with the dropout method [4,5] is that the new method does not involve randomness and therefore can produce an unique model. Further, the new method does not require re-training all the parameters and there it can be directly used to improve existing methods performance by deleting unnecessary neurons.

2   Nonlinear System Identification with Neural Networks

A class of nonlinear dynamic systems can be described by the Nonlinear Auto-Regressive with eXogenous inputs (NARX) model, which can be written as [6]:

$$y(t) = f(y(t-1), ..., y(t-n_y), u(t-1), ..., u(t-n_u)) + e(t) \\ = f(x(t)) + e(t) \tag{1}$$

the nonlinear function $f(.)$ is unknown. In this paper, neural networks are used to approximate the nonlinear relationship for the nonlinear dynamic system. $u(t)$, $y(t)$ and $e(t)$ are the system input, output and error at time interval t, $t = 1, 2, ..., N$, N is the length of data. n_u and n_y represent the largest input and output lags. For convenience, $x(t) = [y(t-1), ..., y(t-n_y), u(t-1), ..., u(t-n_u)]$ is rewritten as $x(t) = [x_1(t), ..., x_r(t)]$ where the dimension $r = n_u + n_y$.

Now we use single-hidden-layer neural networks to identify the nonlinear system shown in (1):

$$y(t) = \sum_{i=1}^{M} h_i(w_i x(t) + b_i)\beta_i + e(t) \tag{2}$$

where $y(t)$ is the output, $x(t)$ represents the model input with $t = 1, ..., N$. M is the neuron number of hidden layer. It is worth mentioning that the model input is different with the real system input $u(t)$ and it can include both system input, lagged inputs, system output and lagged outputs. w_i has the same dimension with $x(t)$. b_i is a scale and β_i is the weight between hidden layer and output layer. h_i is neuron function and here it is chosen as Tan-Sigmod transfer function given by

$$h_i(z) = 2/(1 + exp(-2z)) - 1 \tag{3}$$

where z is the input variable (Fig. 1).

Equation (2) can be written as matrix form

$$\mathbf{y} = \mathbf{P\Theta} + \mathbf{E} \tag{4}$$

where

$$\mathbf{y} = \begin{bmatrix} y(1) \\ y(2) \\ \vdots \\ y(N) \end{bmatrix}, \mathbf{\Theta} = \begin{bmatrix} \beta_1 \\ \beta_2 \\ \vdots \\ \beta_M \end{bmatrix}, \mathbf{E} = \begin{bmatrix} e(1) \\ e(2) \\ \vdots \\ e(N) \end{bmatrix} \tag{5}$$

and

$$\mathbf{P} = \begin{bmatrix} h_1(w_1 x(1) + b_1) & h_2(w_2 x(1) + b_2) & \cdots & h_M(w_M x(1) + b_M) \\ h_1(w_1 x(2) + b_1) & h_2(w_2 x(2) + b_2) & \cdots & h_M(w_M x(2) + b_M) \\ \vdots & \vdots & \vdots & \vdots \\ h_1(w_1 x(N) + b_1) & h_2(w_2 x(N) + b_2) & \cdots & h_M(w_M x(N) + b_M) \end{bmatrix} \tag{6}$$

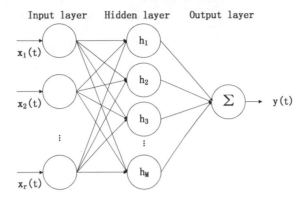

Fig. 1. Architecture of single-layer neural network

Each column in $\mathbf{P}$ is determined by one neuron. In other words, each column has fixed neuron parameters w and b. For convenience, $\mathbf{P}$ is re-written as

$$\mathbf{P} = [\mathbf{p}_1, \cdots, \mathbf{p}_i, \cdots, \mathbf{p}_M] \tag{7}$$

where

$$\mathbf{p}_i = \begin{bmatrix} h_i(w_i x(1) + b_i) \\ h_i(w_i x(2) + b_i) \\ \vdots \\ h_i(w_i x(N) + b_i) \end{bmatrix} \tag{8}$$

According to the approximation theory, neural networks can estimate any nonlinear function by using proper learning methods, even just with single hidden layer. If sufficient hidden neurons are provided which can be equal to the length of training data, it can approach any predetermined accuracy. However, over complex or over-fitted models with large number neurons can not be avoided in practice. The neurons shown in (7) are often redundant. In this paper, OMP is used to select whose important neurons and reduce model complexity in the following section. Figure 2 is used to show the main idea of this paper. The initial neural networks is shown as the top sub-figure and the simplified model is shown the below one with neuron 2 is dropped.

3   OMP for Neural Network Model Reduction

OMP belongs to the general forward selection methods which starts from empty model without neurons and then selects one neuron with largest contribution at a time until a stopping criterion is met. OMP is originally proposed for recovering the sparse vector with a number of measurements in signal processing community and it can be used as a general forward selection method for model reduction. OMP algorithm has been widely used due to the simplicity and competitive performance.

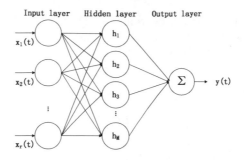

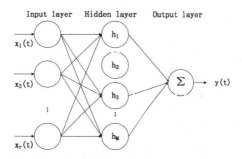

Fig. 2. Neural network shrinkage by dropping neurons

The task of OMP is to select a subset of neurons from the whole neurons candidates $\mathbf{P}$ shown in (7). For simplicity, the indexes of the selected neurons are grouped in an active set Λ. It is initialized to be $\mathbf{0}$ but its size will increase when the neurons are selected. OMP starts from empty model represented by $\hat{\mathbf{y}}_0 = \mathbf{0}$ where $\mathbf{0}$ means no neuron is included into the model and then gradually increase the model size using the following forward selection procedure.

At the beginning, the initial error is

$$\xi_0 = \mathbf{y} - \hat{\mathbf{y}}_0. \tag{9}$$

The neuron that has the largest correlation with the current residual will be included in the active set, i.e.

$$c_0 = max_{i \in \Gamma} |\mathbf{p}_i^T \xi_0| \tag{10}$$

Here, suppose $\mathbf{p}_{i_1}$ is the first selected neuron. Then its weighted coefficient $\boldsymbol{\Theta}_1$ is estimated using least squares method,

$$\boldsymbol{\Theta}_1 = \left(\mathbf{P}_\Lambda^T \mathbf{P}_\Lambda\right)^{-1} \mathbf{P}_\Lambda^T \mathbf{y}. \tag{11}$$

where $\mathbf{P}_\Lambda = \mathbf{p}_{i1}$. The resultant model output with only one neuron is

$$\hat{\mathbf{y}}_1 = \mathbf{P}_\Lambda \boldsymbol{\Theta}_1. \tag{12}$$

and the corresponding model residual is updated by

$$\xi_1 = \mathbf{y} - \hat{\mathbf{y}}_1. \tag{13}$$

At the kth step, find the kth neuron that has the largest correlation value

$$c_k = max_{i \in \Gamma} |\mathbf{p}_i^T \xi_{k-1}|. \tag{14}$$

Suppose $\mathbf{p}_{i_k}$ is selected and the new active set becomes $\Lambda = \{i_1, i_2, ..., i_k\}$. The model neuron weights Θ_k has to be updated using least square methods again, which is given by

$$\Theta_k = \left(\mathbf{P}_\Lambda^T \mathbf{P}_\Lambda\right)^{-1} \mathbf{P}_\Lambda^T \mathbf{y} \tag{15}$$

where $\mathbf{P}_\Lambda = [\mathbf{p}_{i_1}, \mathbf{p}_{i_2}, ..., \mathbf{p}_{i_k}]$. The model output is updated to be

$$\hat{\mathbf{y}}_k = \mathbf{P}_\Lambda \Theta_k. \tag{16}$$

The whole procedure stops when a stopping criterion is satisfied.

Discussions: The reasons why some neurons can be removed are shown as follows. The primary reason is due to the redundancy of neurons. For example, if we have a system that can be perfectly described by one neuron. When we model this system, we do not know how many neurons we need. Here suppose we set up two neurons. Then the modelling methods optimize the parameters of each neuron. The two neurons share same or similar parameters with those of the true neuron. The resultant model is sum of weighted two neurons. Say the weight or coefficient for each neuron is 0.5. Then we can remove any of them and re-tune the coefficient from 0.5 to 1. We can get a simplified model with one neuron. In practices, the redundancy could be very high and the redundant neurons share similar parameters. It is worth pointing out that the redundant neurons could work in a group. For example, the contributions of two neurons, say group one, could be similar to other three neurons, say group two. When simplifying the model, if group one is included into the model and group two will be excluded. Therefore, we can delete some redundant neurons and then just re-tune the weights, leading to a simplified model.

4   Simulation

In this section, the performance of proposed dropping neurons method was investigated using two nonlinear examples.

Example 1: Consider the first sparse nonlinear system

$$y(t) = -0.8y(t-2) + 0.65u(t-1) - 0.05u(t-3)y(t-1) - 0.2u^3(t-1) + e(t) \tag{17}$$

where $u(t)$, $y(t)$, $e(t)$ is system input, output and noise, respectively. The system is excited with a uniformly distributed white noise, $u(t) \in [-1, 1]$. $y(t)$ is polluted by a Gaussian noise $e(t)$ with signal-to-noise 15 dB.

The delayed input and output $\{y(t-1), y(t-2), y(t-3), y(t-4), u(t-1), u(t-2), u(t-3)\}$ from the nonlinear system are used as model input and 1800 samples are used for system identification. 90% of the total samples are used for training data and the remaining 10% is considered as validation data.

The proposed method is tested under three cases that 30, 40 and 50 neurons are predetermined in hidden layer of initial neural network for each example, respectively. The matlab neural network toolbox is used to build the initial model, which is short for NN method.

OMP is used to reduce the model size. For brief, the new method is short for *NN_OMP*. The full results are given in Table 1. It can be seen that the network can be shrinking into a parsimonious structure with half number of initial neurons using the novel method. The training results are given in Fig. 3. Mean Squares Error (MSE) is used to evaluate the model performance. The simulation results show that the simple network has been successfully able to learn the model with a satisfied accuracy. Therefore, the proposed method is demonstrated to be an effective method which can obtain a more parsimonious neural network structure and with high performance as well.

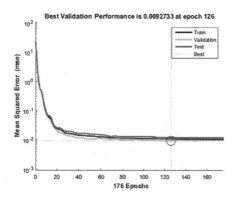

Fig. 3. Example 1: the figure shows the performance of initial neural networks 20 neurons

Table 1. Results for Example 1

	Case 1		Case 2		Case 3	
	Size	Error	Size	Error	Size	Error
NN	30	0.0122	40	0.0100	50	0.0097
NN_OMP	15	0.0155	20	0.0130	25	0.0103

Example 2: Consider another sparse nonlinear system

$$
\begin{aligned}
y(t) = & -0.8y(t-1) + u(t-1) - 0.3u(t-2) - 0.4u(t-3) \\
& + 0.25u(t-1)u(t-2) - 0.3u(t-2)^3 - 0.2u(t-2)u(t-3) \quad (18) \\
& + 0.24u(t-3)^3 + e(t)
\end{aligned}
$$

where $u(t)$, $y(t)$, $e(t)$ is system input, output and noise, respectively. The system is also excited with a uniformly distributed white noise, $u(t) \in [-1, 1]$. $y(t)$ is polluted by a Gaussian noise $e(t)$ with signal-to-noise $15\,dB$. The model input is also selected as $\{y(t-1), y(t-2), y(t-3), y(t-4), u(t-1), u(t-2), u(t-3)\}$ and all the other experiment conditions are the same as the Example 1. Again, three different model sizes are used and all the results are shown in Table 2. The second example has the same conclusion with the first one to confirm the effectiveness of the proposed method.

Table 2. Results for Example 2

	Case 1		Case 2		Case 3	
	Size	Error	Size	Error	Size	Error
NN	30	0.0256	40	0.0155	50	0.0144
NN_OMP	15	0.0194	20	0.0171	25	0.0155

5   Conclusion

Neural networks have been widely used to learn the dynamic behaviors and perform well in various tasks. However, the number of neurons randomly predetermined in the hidden layer is usually large. In other words, the complicated networks may have many redundant neurons which can be dropped out. Generally, a over complex neural networks tend to be over-fitting. The proposed novel approach can simplify neural network using OMP method and produce the parsimonious model that has satisfied performance comparing to the fully connected Neural networks but with fewer neurons in hidden layer. We validate the proposed method with two nonlinear dynamic system examples.

References

1. Lecun, Y., Bengio, Y., Hinton, G.: Deep learning. Nature **521**, 436–444 (2015)
2. Cai, T., Wang, L.: Orthogonal matching pursuit for sparse signal recovery with noise. IEEE Trans. Inf. Theory **57**, 4680–4688 (2011)
3. Zhang, L., Li, K., Bai, E.W., Irwin, G.W.: Two-stage orthogonal least squares methods for neural network construction. IEEE Trans. Neural Netw. Learn. Syst. **26**, 1608–1621 (2014)
4. Pan, W., Dong, H., Guo, Y.: DropNeuron: simplifying the structure of deep neural networks, arXiv preprint arXiv:1606.07326 (2016)
5. Srivastava, N., Hinton, G., Krizhevsky, A., Sutskever, I., Salakhutdinov, R.: Dropout: a simple way to prevent neural networks from overfitting. J. Mach. Learn. Res. **15**, 1929–1958 (2014)
6. Chen, S., Billings, S.A., Luo, W.: Orthogonal least squares methods and their application to non-linear system identification. Int. J. Control **50**, 1873–1986 (1989)

7. Wang, J., Kwon, S., Shim, B.: Generalized orthogonal matching pursuit. IEEE Trans. Sig. Process. **60**, 6202–6216 (2012)
8. Pati, Y., Rezaiifar, R., Krishnapresad, P.: Orthogonal matching pursuit: recursive function approximation with applications to wavelet decomposition. In: Proceeding of 27th Asilomar Conference on Signals, Systems and Computers, pp. 1–5 (1993)

Advanced Evolutionary Methods and Applications

A Fault Diagnosis Method of Gear Based on SVD and Improved EEMD

Mengmeng Song[1] and Shungen Xiao[1,2(✉)]

[1] Department of Physics and Electrical Engineering, Ningde Normal University,
Ningde 352100, China
544824964@qq.com, xiaoshungen022@163.com
[2] School of Mechatronical Engineering and Automation, Shanghai University,
Shanghai 200072, China

Abstract. Considering the random noise and the false IMF component which will led to the decrease of the quality of the EEMD decomposition, a fault diagnosis method is presented based on SVD and improved EEMD. First of all, using the SVD method to denoise fault signals for pretreatment, then using the correlation coefficient norm to eliminate the false IMF components which are gained by EEMD decomposition, then refactor the effective IMF components that are bigger than setting threshold, finally gain fault characteristic frequency of fault signal by using the Hilbert transform envelop demodulation. In rotating machinery fault platform QPZZ-II, fault signals of broken teeth, cracked gear and worn gear are acquired, respectively. Using the method proposed in this paper, finally successfully extract the fault characteristic frequency of different type.

Keywords: SVD · EEMD · Fault diagnosis · Fault gear · Correlation coefficient norm

1 Introduction

Gear is essential part that can transmit power, change the speed and direction in mechanical equipment, with strong carrying capacity, accurate and reliable transmission and gear transmission power and wide speed range, etc. As a result of Its variety and large dosage, lead to frequently gear fault, and even cause serious equipment accident and great economic losses. According to statistics, 80% of mechanical failures are caused by gear, gear faults in rotating machinery are accounted for 10%, gears in the gear box failure are accounted for 60% [1, 2]. So, the gear fault diagnosis technology research is of great significance. The gear failure is usually relatively weak and difficult to identify. Therefore, the extraction of weak gear failure is of great significance. SVD [3, 4] (Singular Value Decomposition) and EEMD [5, 6] (Ensemble Empirical Mode Decomposition) are widely used in fault diagnosis. Xing et al. [7] proposed an intelligent fault diagnosis method based on Intrinsic time-scale decomposition (ITD)-Singular value decomposition (SVD) and Support vector machine (SVM) in their paper. The results showed the proposed approach can accurately diagnose and identify different fault types of gear under variable conditions.

© Springer Nature Singapore Pte Ltd. 2017
D. Yue et al. (Eds.): LSMS/ICSEE 2017, Part II, CCIS 762, pp. 65–74, 2017.
DOI: 10.1007/978-981-10-6373-2_7

Zhang et al. [8] presented Time-varying singular value decomposition for periodic transient identification in bearing fault diagnosis. Results indicated that the proposed method is superior to traditional methods for bearing fault diagnosis. Kui et al. [9] introduced a fault intelligent diagnosis method based on quadratic SVD and Variable Predictive Model-based Class Discriminate (VPMCD), which can adaptively choose effective singular values firstly by using the curvature spectrum of singular values for reconstructing a signal. Experimental results showed that, in the normal and fault condition of bearing, the comprehensive identification precision of this method is 97.5%, and is 8.75% higher than the conventional method based on SVD and Support Vector Machine (SVM). Chen et al. [10] proposed an integrated scheme based on dimensionality reduction method and deep belief networks (DBNs) aiming at improving the accuracy of planetary gearbox fault diagnosis.

In this study, the acquired vibration signals are decomposed through ensemble empirical mode decomposition (EEMD). According to the characteristics of SVD and EEMD, this paper will combine the two ones, play their respective advantages, use SVD method to denoise, subsequently, use EEMD to decompose the noise reduction signal, get multiple intrinsic mode function (IMF), and use the correlation coefficient rule to filtrate effective IMF components to refactor, finally use Hilbert transform to extract the fault frequency of gear.

2   Principle of EEMD

EEMD is an improved method of EMD, which is based on the decomposition of the data itself, does not need to set the basis function in advance, which makes the instantaneous frequency of each component has physical meaning, but also avoid the mode superposition between components. The EEMD decomposition process steps are as follows [11]:

Step 1: The input signal x is added to the white Gaussian noise $\omega_i(t)$ with that the N mean is zero and the standard deviation is constant to construct the initial signal $x_i(t)$, it can be written as

$$x_i(t) = x(t) + \omega_i(t) \tag{1}$$

where the size of $\omega_i(t)$ depends on the white noise standard deviation and the standard deviation of the initial signal Nstd, $i = 1 \sim N$, Nstd is usually set to 0.2.

Step 2: The initial signal $x_i(t)$ is decomposed by EMD to obtain the IMF components and the remainder $r_i(t)$. $x_i(t)$ function is commonly expressed as

$$x_i(t) = \sum_{j=1}^{l} y_{ij}(t) + r_i(t) \tag{2}$$

In which, $y_{ij}(t)$ is the j IMF component generated by EMD decomposition after adding the Gaussian white noise at the i time.

Step 3:   The mean of each IMF component $y_{ij}(t)$ is calculated, and the IMF component $y_j(t)$ and the remainder $r(t)$ are obtained. This step can reduce or eliminate the effects of the addition of $\omega_i(t)$ to IMF. $y_j(t)$ and $r(t)$ are given by

$$y_j(t) = \frac{1}{N} \sum_{i=1}^{N} y_{ij}(t) \tag{3}$$

where $y_j(t)$ is the j IMF component obtained by decomposing the signal $x(t)$ by EEMD.

$$r(t) = \frac{1}{N} \sum_{i=1}^{N} r_i(t) \tag{4}$$

Thus, the signal $x(t)$ decomposed by the EEMD is composed of $y_j(t)$ and $r(t)$, and its function is commonly expressed as

$$x(t) = \sum_{j=1}^{l} y_j(t) + r(t) \tag{5}$$

3   Improved EEMD

The initial signals after EEMD decomposition, due to multiple factors, such as the decomposition error and interpolation error in the decomposition result the IMF components are prone to false. If false components exist characteristic domain, will obviously make the degradation performance of the extraction produce large error. Therefore, it is necessary to eliminate false components. In order to improve the problem that traditional EEMD bring pseudo components because of decomposition, correlation coefficient is introduced to distinguish the false weight. First of all, the noise signals are decomposed by the EEMD to gain multiple IMF components. subsequently, utilizing the correlation coefficient formula as shown in Eq. (6) to filtrate effective IMF components. If the correlation coefficient value calculated by an IMF component is less than the set threshold, the IMF component is treated as a pseudo component, and then the IMF component that is greater than or equal to the threshold is reconstructed to obtain an effective fault signal. The correlation coefficient function is commonly written as

$$\lambda_j = \frac{\sum\limits_{i=1}^{N} (x_i - \bar{x})(y_i - \bar{y})}{\sqrt{\sum\limits_{i=1}^{N} (x_i - \bar{x})^2} \sqrt{\sum\limits_{i=1}^{N} (y_i - \bar{y})^2}} (j = 1, \cdots l) \tag{6}$$

where $\lambda_j (j = 1, \ldots l)$ are the correlation coefficient of all the components and original signal. x and $\bar{x}$ are the original signal and its average, respectively. y and $\bar{y}$ are the IMF component signal and its average, respectively. n is acquisition data sample point of vibration signals.

4 Experimental Analysis

In this experiment, experimental facilities include the QPZZ-II rotating mechanical fault diagnosis workbench, multi-channel data acquisition box, a number of acceleration sensor and so on, as shown in Fig. 1. Through the field experiment, we get four kinds of fault signals that include the normal, cracked, worn and broken gear fault signals, respectively.

Fig. 1. Experimental platform

Diagnostic steps are shown as: First of all, all kinds of fault signals denoised by SVD method are decomposed by EEMD, then gets some IMF components. Calculate the correlation coefficient between each component and denoising signal, eliminate the correlation coefficient which is less than the setting threshold component of the IMF, and refactor the component of correlation coefficient which is greater than threshold value of the fund. Finally, draw the Hilbert spectrum and extract the characteristic frequency of different fault types. The process of gear fault diagnosis displays in Fig. 2.

4.1 Denoising of Fault Signals

In this subsection, Denoising of fault signals are discussed. The original signals of normal, cracked, worn and broken gear are denoised by SVD, respectively. Taking worn gear as an example, there are several singular values before denoising, but it is obvious that these singular values are eliminated after denoising, as shown in Fig. 3. As can be seen from Fig. 3 that these noise signals which represent singular values have been removed. The fault signals of worn gear before and after de-noising are showed in Fig. 4. After computing the signal to noise ratio (SNR) of all kinds of denoising signals, we can see that the SNR of all types of denoising signals is greatly improved after SVD denoising.

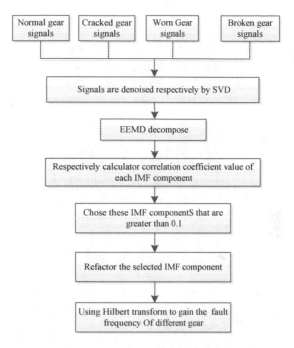

Fig. 2. The process of gear fault diagnosis

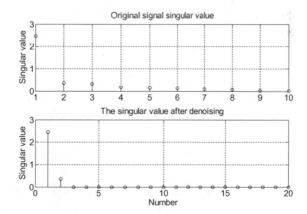

Fig. 3. Singular value of worn gear

4.2 Improved EEMD Decompose

Three gear signals of different fault types denoised by SVD method, subsequently, are decomposed by the EEMD method, respectively gain 10 IMF components, as shown in Fig. 5. In order to eliminate many of the false IMF components, by means of the criterion of correlation coefficient formula, each correlation coefficient value is calculated separately, as shown in Table 1. according to the empirical formula, set up the correlation

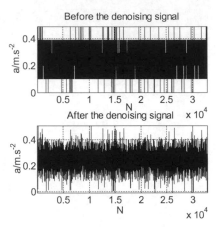

Fig. 4. Denoising of worn gear

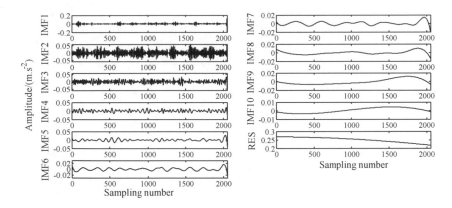

Fig. 5. IMF component signals of worn gear

Table 1. The correlation coefficient value of broken gear fault signals

Fault type	IMF1	IMF2	IMF3	IMF4	IMF5	IMF6	IMF7	IMF8	IMF9	IMF10	RES
Broken gear	0.7073	0.467	0.5618	0.1497	0.062	0.0954	0.0626	0.0054	0.0001	0.0001	0.0051
Crack	0.9288	0.6413	0.2218	0.0566	0.024	0.0099	0.0036	0.0031	0.0014	0.0001	0.0025
Wear	0.555	0.7475	0.5822	0.3252	0.2722	0.1763	0.1459	0.0541	0.0747	0.0784	0.0150

coefficient threshold value is 0.1. Therefore, we believe that if a correlation coefficient value is less than 0.1 is seen as false, and to eliminate it. It is not hard to see IMF1–IMF7 signals of the normal gear can be as the effective component, IMF1–IMF4 signals of broken gear can be as the effective component, IMF1–IMF3 signals of cracked gear can be as the effective component, IMF1–IMF7 signals of the wear fault gear can be as the effective component. Finally, reconstruct the four effective component signals that can be provided subsequently powerful guarantee to extract the fault characteristic frequency.

4.3   Extract Fault Characteristic Frequency

In this section, reconstruct the IMF component signals of broken gear, cracked gear and worn gear, respectively. then using the Hilbert transform for envelope demodulation, finally the spectrums respectively are showed in Figs. 6, 7 and 8.

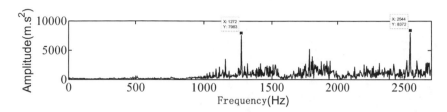

(a) Frequency spectrum of broken gear signals

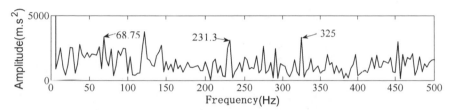

(b) Partial frequency spectrum of broken gear signals

Fig. 6. Frequency spectrum distribution of broken gear signals

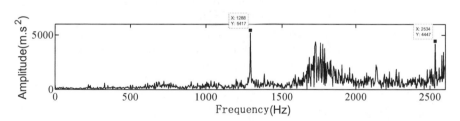

(a) Frequency spectrum of cracked gear signals

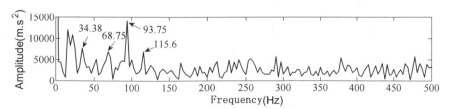

(b) Partial frequency spectrum of cracked gear signals

Fig. 7. Frequency spectrum distribution of cracked gear signals

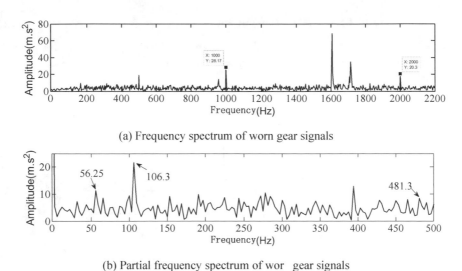

(a) Frequency spectrum of worn gear signals

(b) Partial frequency spectrum of wor gear signals

Fig. 8. Frequency spectrum distribution of worn gear signals

In broken teeth failure experiments, the drive shaft rotation speed is1388 r/min, load current is loaded to 0.1 A, meshing frequency is 1272.3 Hz by the calculation, rotational frequency of the pinion is 23.13 Hz, rotational frequency of big faulted gear is 16.964 Hz. As shown in Fig. 6(a), the spectrum displays fault characteristic frequency of 1272 Hz and fault frequency times of 2544 Hz. As shown in Fig. 6(b), the spectrum of local segmentation illustrates 68.75 Hz frequency that is 4 times of the rotational frequency of the big gear, while 231.3 Hz and 325 Hz are 10 times and 14 times of the pinion rotational frequency, respectively.

In the cracked gear experiment, the drive shaft rotation speed is1405 r/min, meshing frequency is 1287.9 Hz by the calculation, rotational frequency of the faulted pinion is 23.4 Hz, rotational frequency of big driven gear is 17.172 Hz. As shown in Fig. 7(a), the spectrum displays fault characteristic frequency of 1288 Hz and fault frequency times of 2534 Hz. As shown in Fig. 7(b), the spectrum of local segmentation illustrates 34.38 Hz and 68.75 Hz frequency that are 2 times and 4 times of the pinion rotational frequency, respectively. 93.75 Hz and 115.6 Hz are 4 times and 5 times of the big rotational frequency, respectively.

In the worn gear experiment, the drive shaft rotation speed is 1091 r/min, meshing frequency is 1000.08 Hz by the calculation, rotational frequency of the faulted pinion is 18.183 Hz, rotational frequency of big faulted gear is 13.334 Hz. As shown in Fig. 8 (a), the spectrum displays fault characteristic frequency of 1000 Hz and fault characteristic frequency of 2000 Hz. As shown in Fig. 8(b), the spectrum of local segmentation illustrates 56.25 Hz frequency that are 3 times of the pinion rotational frequency. 106.3 Hz and 481.3 Hz are 8 times and 36 times of the big rotational frequency, respectively.

In conclusion, when transmission gears emerge respectively, broken teeth, crack and wear failure, the diagnostic method presented in this paper, various fault types are effective to extract the fault characteristic frequency and multiple of fault characteristic frequency. Therefore, it shows that diagnosis method is feasible and effective.

5 Concluding Remarks

In this paper, a method of fault diagnosis is proposed based on SVD and improve EEMD. First of all, the all kinds of fault signals denoised by the SVD method, are decomposed by EEMD, and get a lot of the IMF components, subsequently, calculate the correlation coefficient value of each IMF component, correlation coefficient value which is less than the given threshold can be as a false component and to give out, and reconstruct the other effective IMF components. Using the Hilbert transform to carry out envelope demodulation, and obtain the fault signal spectrum. In gear transmission experiments with broken teeth, crack and wear, using the diagnosis method proposed in this paper, has successfully diagnosed broken fault characteristic frequency and the multiple of frequency. Therefore, in this paper the diagnosis method proposed is feasible and effective, can also provide a reference for fault diagnosis of rotating machinery parts.

Acknowledgments. This paper was partially supported by the research projects: "Fujian Natural Science Foundation", Grant #2015J01643; "Education Science Project of Young and Middle-aged Teachers of Colleges and Universities in Fujian Province", Grant #JA15545 and #JZ160396; "Ningde City Science and Technology Project", Grant #20150034; "Talents Cultivation Program for Outstanding Young Scientists in Fujian Universities", Grant #MIN Education (2015) 54; "Scientific Innovation Team of Ningde Normal University", Grant #2015T07 and Grant #2015Z03.

References

1. Li, B., Zhang, X.N., Wu, J.L.: New procedure for gear fault detection and diagnosis using instantaneous angular speed. Mech. Syst. Sig. Process. **85**, 415–428 (2017)
2. Zhao, L.J., Liu, X.D., Li, M.: Research progress of methods of gear fault diagnosis. J. Mech. Strength **38**(5), 951–956 (2016)
3. Yang, Z.X., Zhong, J.H.: A hybrid EEMD-based SampEn and SVD for acoustic signal processing and fault diagnosis. Entropy **18**(4), 1–14 (2016)
4. Fu, C.Z., Hasegawa, Y., Tanaka, M.: An Effective gear fault diagnosis method based on singular value decomposition and frequency slice wavelet transform. Int. J. Rotating Mach. **2016**, 1–8 (2016)
5. Jiang, H.K., Cai, Q.S., Zhao, H.W., et al.: Rolling bearing fault feature extraction under variable conditions using hybrid order tracking and EEMD. J. Vibroeng. **18**(7), 4449–4457 (2016)
6. Matej, Z., Samo, Z., Ivan, P.: EEMD-based multiscale ICA method for slewing bearing fault detection and diagnosis. J. Sound Vib. **370**, 394–423 (2016)

7. Xing, Z.Q., Qu, J.F., Chai, J.F., et al.: Gear fault diagnosis under variable conditions with intrinsic time-scale decomposition-singular value decomposition and support vector machine. J. Mech. Sci. Technol. **31**(2), 545–553 (2017)
8. Zhang, S.B., Liu, S.L., He, Q.B., et al.: Time-varying singular value decomposition for periodic transient identification in bearing fault diagnosis. J. Sound Vib. **379**, 213–231 (2016)
9. Kui, L., Fan, Y.G., Wu, J.D.: Fault diagnosis method based on quadratic singular value decomposition and VPMCD. Comput. Eng. **41**(4), 181–186 (2015)
10. Chen, H.Z., Wang, J.X., Tang, B.P., et al.: An integrated approach to planetary gearbox fault diagnosis using deep belief networks. Meas. Sci. Technol. **28**(2), 1–16 (2017)
11. Xiao, S.G., Song, M.M., Kong, Q.G., et al.: A new fault diagnosis method of rolling bearing based on EEMD de-noising and undecimated lifting scheme packet. J. Yanbian Univ. (Nat. Sci. Ed.) **41**(1), 57–63 (2015)

Research on Fault Data Wavelet Threshold Denoising Method Based on CEEMDAN

Zhouqun Liu and Guochu Chen[✉]

Electric Engineering School,
Shanghai DianJi University, Shanghai 201306, China
chengc@sdju.edu.cn

Abstract. In order to carry out fault data denoising effectively, this paper proposes a wavelet threshold denoising method based on Complete Ensemble Empirical Mode Decomposition with the Adaptive Noise (CEEMDAN). This method uses CEEMDAN decomposition to obtain a series of frequency from high to low IMF component and the trend term of the fault data; Using permutation entropy value to determine which containing more noise component; using wavelet threshold denoising method to denoise the IMF component of containing more noise, to retain the effective information in the high frequency IMF component; Finally, reconstruction the signal by adding the high frequency IMF component after denoising, low frequency component and the trend term to obtain the denoised data. In this paper, through simulation and measured data to verify this method. The results shows that the proposed method can suppress the noise interference, retain the useful fault signal, extract fault signal with high accuracy effectively.

Keywords: Fault data · CEEMDAN · Wavelet threshold denoising · Signal noise separation

1 Introduction

In the process of fault diagnosis of gear box, fault data denoising is the key link of fault feature extraction, therefore, fault data noise reduction research is very important. Wavelet threshold denoising [1, 2] method is a mature fault data denoising method, can remove most of the noise in the signal, has been widely used in the field of fault diagnosis. TORRES et al. proposed the CEEMDAN [3] decomposition method which is adding adaptive white noise to the original signal in every stage of decomposition and obtain each IMF component through calculating the only residual signal, which overcomes the modal aliasing phenomenon exists in EMD decomposition [4, 5]; At the same time, compared with the EEMD [6, 7] method, no matter how many times it is integrated, the reconstruction error is almost zero, the decomposition process is integrity, which overcomes the problem of low efficiency of EEMD decomposition.

Given the advantages of wavelet threshold denoising and CEEMDAN decomposition, we put forward a fault data wavelet threshold denoising method based on CEEMDAN in this paper. First, using CEEMDAN decompose the non-stationary time series of fault data into a series of different IMF component. Secondly, considering the

© Springer Nature Singapore Pte Ltd. 2017
D. Yue et al. (Eds.): LSMS/ICSEE 2017, Part II, CCIS 762, pp. 75–83, 2017.
DOI: 10.1007/978-981-10-6373-2_8

permutation entropy algorithm can effectively enlarge the weak variation of the time series [8], calculating the permutation entropy value of each IMF component, according to the arrangement of the permutation entropy value determine the IMF component which need for noise reduction, and then using the wavelet threshold denoising method denoise the selected components. The simulation and case analysis shows that the method can adapt the fault signal processing, suppress random noise and reduce the loss of the effective signal effectively.

2 Basic Principle

2.1 EEMD Method

EEMD is a noise assisted signal decomposition method, through adding different white noise to the original signal and decomposing it by EMD many times. EEMD decomposition overcomes the frequency aliasing problems exists in EMD decomposition, which enhances the thoroughness of denoising.

The implementation of EEMD algorithm is as follows:

(1) Let $s(n)$ denote the original signal sequence, $v^i(n)$ represent the i time test added white noise sequence with standard normal distribution. The i signal sequence denoted by $s^i(n) = s(n) + v^i(n)$, among them, $i = 1, \cdots, I$ said the number of tests.

(2) Decomposing $s^i(n)$ of each experiment signal sequence by EMD, getting $IMF_k^i(n)$, where $k = 1, \ldots, K$ is the number of IMF.

(3) The definition k mode component of $s(n)$ is IMF_k, the average calculating IMF_k^i, getting $\overline{IMF_k}$, that is $\overline{IMF_k} = \frac{1}{I} \sum_{i=1}^{I} IMF_k^i(n)$.

2.2 CEEMDAN Method

In the decomposition of EEMD, including different white noise $s^i(n)$ in each experiment were carried out in different decomposition. Therefore, every time have different residual signal decomposition, that is:

$$r_k^i(n) = r_{k-1}^i(n) - IMF_k^i(n) \tag{1}$$

On the basis of EEMD, CEEMDAN by adding adaptive white noise and calculating the only residual signal obtain IMF, it overcomes the shortcoming of the EEMD, the reconstructed signal are almost identical with the original signal.

The definition of operator $E_k(\cdot)$ is the k mode components generated by EMD method, CEEMDAN produced the k component is denoted as $\widetilde{IMF_k}$, the specific algorithm of CEEMDAN is as follows:

(1) The same with the EEMD decomposition method, CEEMDAN signal do I times experiment for signal $s_n + \varepsilon_0 v^i(n)$, get the first IMF component by EMD decomposition method, calculate:

$$\widetilde{IMF}_1(n) = \frac{1}{I}\sum\nolimits_{i=1}^{I} IMF_1^i(n) = \overline{IMF}_1(n). \tag{2}$$

(2) In the first stage (k = 1), calculating the first only residual signal, that is calculation of $r_1(n) = s(n) - \widetilde{IMF}_1(n)$.

(3) Do i times experiments $(i = 1, \ldots, I)$, in each experiment, decomposing the signal $r_1(n) + \varepsilon_1 E_1(v^i(n))$, until getting the first IMF component. On this basis, the calculation of the second modal components are as follows:

$$\widetilde{IMF}_2(n) = \frac{1}{I}\sum\nolimits_{i=1}^{I} E_1\big(r_1(n) + \varepsilon_1 E_1\big(v^i(n)\big)\big). \tag{3}$$

(4) The rest of each stage, that is $K = 2, \cdots, K$, calculate the K residual signal, and the calculation steps same to process 3, calculating the $k+1$ modal components are as follows:

$$r_k(n) = r_{k-1}(n) - \widetilde{IMF}_K(N). \tag{4}$$

$$\widetilde{IMF}_{k+1}(n) = \frac{1}{I}\sum\nolimits_{i=1}^{I} E_1\big(r_k(n) + \varepsilon_k E_k\big(v^i(n)\big)\big). \tag{5}$$

(5) Implement step 4, until the residual signal is no longer possible to decompose, the standard of judgment for the extremum number margin signal shall not exceed two. In the termination of the algorithm, the number of all modal components is K. The final residue signal is:

$$R(n) = s(n) - \sum\nolimits_{k=1}^{K} \widetilde{IMF}_k. \tag{6}$$

Therefore, the original signal s(n) is decomposed into:

$$s(n) = \sum\nolimits_{k=1}^{K} \widetilde{IMF}_k + R(n). \tag{7}$$

In the decomposition process, I is 10^2 orders of magnitude, ε_1 is 10^{-2} orders of magnitudes.

2.3 Wavelet Threshold Denoising

Wavelet threshold denoising method including hard threshold and soft threshold. The hard threshold function is:

$$\hat{d}_{j,k} = \begin{cases} \hat{d}_{j,k} & |d_{j,k}| > \lambda \\ 0 & |d_{j,k}| \leq \lambda \end{cases} \tag{8}$$

The soft threshold function is:

$$\hat{d}_{j,k} = \begin{cases} sgn(d_{j,k})\left(|d_{j,k}| - \lambda\right) & |d_{j,k}| > \lambda \\ 0 & |d_{j,k}| \leq \lambda \end{cases} \tag{9}$$

where sgn(•) is symbol function; λ represents threshold.

2.4   Wavelet Threshold Denoising Algorithm Based on CEEMDAN

In view of the wavelet threshold denoising method can eliminate most of the noise in fault signal, but also will lose some useful information, The single use of CEEMDAN to reduce noise by decompose the signal, discarding high-frequency noise also abandoned the high frequency information available. This paper puts forward a fault data wavelet threshold denoising method based on CEEMDAN. Fist, the fault signal is decomposed into a series of IMF components by CEEMDAN, and calculate the permutation entropy value of every IMF component, then assessment the random noise in the IMF according to the quantitative of permutation entropy. For the noise with high proportion of IMF component, denoising it by wavelet threshold denoising method, finally, adding the wavelet threshold denoising results, not denoising treatment IMF and residues together to reconstruct the signal after denoising.

The specific implementation steps are:

Step 1: according to the original signal x(t), to select the appropriate threshold;
Step 2: decompose the original signal x(t) by CEEMDAN, obtained a series of IMF components;
Step 3: according to the permutation entropy value select containing more noise IMF components, using the wavelet threshold denoising method denoise it combine the threshold of step 1; the calculation formula of permutation entropy [10] as follows:

$$H_p(m) = \sum_{g=1}^{k} p_g \ln p_g \tag{10}$$

where m is the embedding dimension, Pg is symbol sequence appears probability. Then permutation entropy value to be normalized:

$$H_p = \frac{H_p(m)}{\ln(m!)}. \tag{11}$$

The value of Hp is between [0, 1].

Step 4: according to the wavelet denoising IMF components and other IMF components to reconstruct the signal:

$$x'(t) = \sum_{i=1}^{n} c_i'(t) + \sum_{i=n+1}^{m} c_i(t) + r(t) \tag{12}$$

where $x'(t)$ is the final denoising signal; $c_i'(t)$ is wavelet threshold denoising IMF component; $c_i(t)$ is no need for wavelet denoising processing IMF component.

3 Simulation Experiment

In order to verify the effectiveness of the proposed method, and without loss of generality, design a simulation signal $x(t)$:

$$\left.\begin{array}{l} x_1(t) = 2sin(2\pi15t + \pi/4) \\ x_2(t) = (t+1)(2\pi20t + \pi/2) \\ x_t = x_1(t) + x_2(t) + n(t) \end{array}\right\}. \tag{13}$$

In the formula: $t \in [0,3]$, every 1/1024 s to take a point, n(t) is a random noise signal.

Choose to add the 10 dB Gauss white noise in the original signal, the time-domain waveform of x1, X2, X and s(signal plus noise) as Fig. 1.

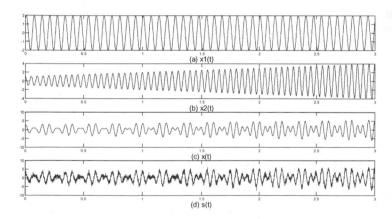

Fig. 1. Simulation signal waveform

According to the simulation signal s(t), using CEEMDAN to decompose it, get 12 IMF components and a residue as Fig. 2.

Calculating the permutation entropy H_p of each IMF component, normalizing them, using H_p value reflecting the degree of randomness of time series, and wavelet threshold denoising processing the IMF which is the H_p value greater than 0.2. According to the definition of signal-to-noise ratio (SNR) to calculate the SNR. The SNR is calculated as:

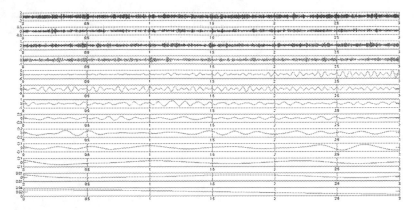

Fig. 2. Simulation signal CEEMD decomposition results

$$\text{SNR} = \frac{\|M\|_2^2}{\|S - M\|_2^2} \tag{14}$$

where SNR is signal-to-noise ratio, $\|\cdot\|_2^2$ is modulus square; M is simulation data without noise; S is simulation data with noise.

Calculation of the permutation entropy value of every IMF component, choosing embed dimension is 3, the time delay is 12, the permutation entropy of IMF1 $\sim$ IMF11 respectively: 0.29852 0.29841 0.29523 0.29144 0.26643 0.23199 0.21279 0.17637 0.14575 0.13400 0.12738 0.11443. The choice of permutation entropy value greater than 0.2 IMF component of wavelet threshold denoising, and then reconstruct the signal. Using wavelet threshold denoising method, CEEMDAN-IMF1 denoising method, CEEMDAN-IMF1-IMF2 denoising method and the method proposed in this paper for noise reduction, when the noise signal's SNR is 10, the standard deviation is 2.3456, after the denoising process, the signal-to-noise ratio of denoising results of four methods respectively: 15.6, 12.8, 12.2, 18.6; the standard deviation is: 0.7669, 0.5417, 0.4321, 0.2522. Four methods of simulation data denoising results as shown in Fig. 3:

Where (a) is the original signal, (b) is the signal after adding noise, (c) is the wavelet threshold denoising result, (d) is CEEMDAN-IMF1 denoising result, (e) is CEEMDAN-IMF1-IMF2 denoising result, (f) is this paper denoising result.

Contrast can be found: wavelet threshold denoising can remove most of the noise, but the signal distortion is very serious; CEEMDAN-IMF1 method in low SNR, and the signal is not smooth; CEEMDAN-IMF1-IMF2 denoising SNR higher than CEEMDAN-IMF1, but local resolution is low; this paper's denoising SNR is highest, the mean square error is minimum, the signal is smooth.

Further comparison of various denoising methods under different noise levels, selecting to join in the original signal SNR is 9, 8, 5, 2,1 dB, comparing the four kinds of denoising methods in denoising effect as indicated in Table 1. Contrast can be found, no matter how much the SNR, in four kinds of noise reduction method, this paper's method can achieve the best effect.

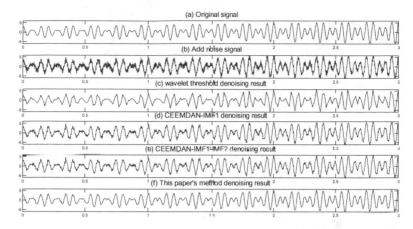

Fig. 3. Comparison of noise reduction results of four methods of simulation data

Table 1. Noise reduction under different noise levels

SNR (dB)	Noise reduction SNR of various methods			
	Wavelet threshold denoising	CEEMDAN-IMF1	CEEMDAN-IMF2	This paper's method
10	15.6	12.8	12.2	18.6
9	9.5	13.2	13.8	18.3
8	8.7	12.0	12.7	16.8
5	6.4	9.4	10.2	14.1
2	4.2	6.2	7.2	10.7
1	4.0	5.2	6.3	9.8

4 Case Analysis

In order to test the method proposed in this paper is effective in the practical application or not, using a wind turbine gearbox bearing fault vibration data verified. Figure 4 is the original fault signal without processing.

Figure 5 shows the denoising results of various denoising methods. It is seen that the wavelet threshold denoising method remove large amounts of noise, but at the same

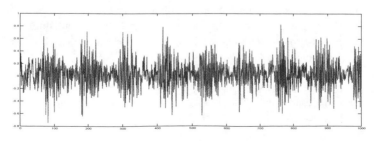

Fig. 4. Original fault signals

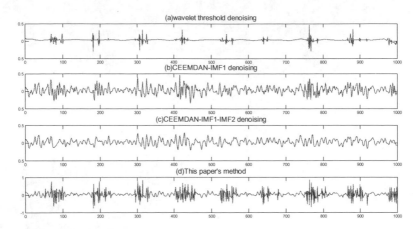

Fig. 5. Results comparison of four kinds of fault signal denoising method

time also lost a lot of useful information, CEEMDAN-IMF1 denoising and CEEMDAN-IMF1-IMF2 denoising by discarded high frequency components, resulting in low signal resolution; this paper's method can reduces the noise, retain the useful fault feature information effectively.

The simulation analysis and the actual application effect indicate that the fault data of wavelet threshold denoising method based on CEEMDAN proposed in this paper overcomes the defect of the wavelet threshold denoising and CEEMDAN, which can eliminate the noise in the fault data, extract useful fault characteristic signal from fault data, get higher precision effectively.

5   Conclusion

Wavelet threshold denoising method can eliminate most of the noise in fault signal, but lose some useful information; CEEMDAN denoising method, discarding high-frequency noise also abandoned the effectively high frequency information, can also lead to the loss of effective information. In order to carry out the fault data denoising effectively, this paper proposes the fault data wavelet threshold denosing method based on CEEMDAN, and verify the method by simulation and measurement data. For the fault data, simulation analysis and experimental results shows that using the denoising method can restrain the noise signal and obtain better denoising effect effectively. Compared with the only use of wavelet threshold denoising and CEEM-DAN denoising, this paper's method presented higher accuracy when the gear box was diagnosed by using these methods.

Acknowledgements. This work was financially supported by Shanghai City Board of education scientific research innovation project (No. 13YZ140) and Ministry of education returned overseas students to start research fund (No. [2014]1685).

References

1. Yang, Z.M., Huang, D.Y.: Application of wavelet transform in improving both signal/noise ratio and resolution of seismic data. Oil Geophys. Prospect. **29**(5), 623–629 (1994)
2. Miao, X.G., Moon, W.M.: Application of wavelet transform in reflection seismic data analysis. Geophysics **3**(9), 171–179 (1993)
3. Donoho, D.L.: De-noising by soft-thresholding. IEEE Trans. IT **41**(3), 613–627 (1995)
4. Torres, M.E., Colominas, M.A., Schlotthauer, G., et al.: A complete ensemble empirical mode decomposition with adaptive noise. In: IEEE International Conference on Acoustics, Speech and Signal Processing (ICASSP), pp. 4144–4147(2011)
5. Huang, N.E., Shen, Z., Long, S.R., et al.: The empirical mode decomposition and the hilbert spectrum for nonlinear and non-stationary time series analysis. In: Proceeding of the Royal Society A: Mathematical, Physical and Engineering Sciences, vol. 454, no. 1971, pp. 903–995 (1998)
6. Tang, B., Dong, S., Song, T.: Method for eliminating mode mixing of empirical mode decomposition based on the revised blind source separation. Sign. Process. **92**(1), 248–258 (2012)
7. Wu, Z., Huang, N.E.: Ensemble empirical mode decomposition: a noise-assisted data analysis method. Adv. Data Sci. Adapt. Anal. **1**(1), 1–41 (2009)
8. Zheng, J.-D., Cheng, J.-S., Yang, Y.: Modified EEMD algorithm and application. J. Vibr. Shock **32**(21), 21–26 (2013)
9. Paya, B.A., Esat, I.I., Badi, M.N.M.: Artifical neural network based fault diagnostics of rotating machinery using wavelet transforms as a preprocessor. Mech. Syst. Sign. Process. **11**(5), 751–765 (1997)
10. Bandt, C., Pompe, B.: Permutation entropy: a natural complexity measure for times series. Phys. Rev. Lett. **17**(88), 21–24 (2002)

Evaluation of K-SVD Embedded with Modified ℓ_1-Norm Sparse Representation Algorithm

Meixi Wang[1], Jingjing Liu[1], Shiwei Ma[1(✉)], and Wanquan Liu[2]

[1] School of Mechatronic Engineering and Automation, Shanghai University,
Shanghai 200072, China
masw@shu.edu.cn
[2] Department of Computer Science, Curtin University, Perth, Australia

Abstract. The K-SVD algorithm aims to find an adaptive dictionary for a set of signals by using the sparse representation optimization and constrained singular value decomposition. In this paper, firstly, the original K-SVD algorithm, as well as some sparse representation algorithms including ℓ_0-norm OMP and ℓ_1-norm Lasso were reviewed. Secondly, the revised Lasso algorithm was embedded into the K-SVD process and a new different K-SVD algorithms with ℓ_1-norm Lasso embedded in (RL-K-SVD algrithm) was established. Finally, extensive experiments had been completed on necessary parameters determination, further on the performance compare of recovery error and recognition for the original K-SVD and RL-K-SVD algorithms. The results indicate that within a certain scope of parameter settings, the RL-K-SVD algorithm performs better on image recognition than K-SVD; the time cost for training sample number is lower for RL-K-SVD in case that the sample number is increased to a certain extend.

Keywords: K-SVD algorithm · Sparse representation · Dictionary · Pursuit methods

1 Introduction

In recent years, a growing interest has been in research of sparse representations of signals. The problem of finding a sparse solution to an image set with linear expression is a popular topic [1]. Technically, with an over-complete dictionary $D \in \mathbb{R}^{n \times K}$, a signal $y \in \mathbb{R}^n$ can be expressed as a sparse linear combination of this dictionary, i.e., there are K prototype signals, $\{d_i\}_{j=1}^{K}$, every of the signal set can be represented as a linear combination of these K signals. The vector $\beta \in \mathbb{R}^K$ is the representation coefficients of the signal. Under mathematical approximation, some typical norms for measuring the offset are the ℓ^p-norms ($p = 1, 2$ and ∞).

Generally, finding a dictionary and its sparse representation coefficients with the minimum number of atoms for signals are usually resolved by using the ℓ_0-norm, which is a NP-hard problem [2]. Some of the popular techniques including OMP, Lasso and so on [3], which will be discussed in Sect. 2. In all those pursuit

© Springer Nature Singapore Pte Ltd. 2017
D. Yue et al. (Eds.): LSMS/ICSEE 2017, Part II, CCIS 762, pp. 84–93, 2017.
DOI: 10.1007/978-981-10-6373-2_9

methods, there is a preliminary concept that the dictionary is known from the beginning. In order to choose an optimal dictionary, the K-SVD [4] is proposed based on the spare representation method OMP and singular value decomposition (SVD). Then, different variants of K-SVD are proposed for different fields [5] but all these K-SVD improved algorithms are based on the OMP method.

The primary destination of this paper is to build a better representation dictionary by embedding K-SVD with different sparse representation pursuit methods. This is different from previous research on the issue of trying to use the original K-SVD with basic method for different applications. Mathematically, the popular technique Lasso with relaxed ℓ_1 penalty will be revised and then embedded into the K-SVD procedure to replace the OMP in alleviating the ℓ_0 norm optimization problem.

The paper is organized as follows. In Sect. 2, the related work of sparse coding was reviewed. In Sect. 3, the original K-SVD algorithm was described. In Sect. 4 a novel dictionary learning algorithms, RL-K-SVD algorithm was proposed. In Sect. 5, some numerical experiments were conducted to evaluate the efficiency on the recovery and recognition of the two K-SVD algorithms. Finally, the conclusions of this paper were drawn in Sect. 6.

2   Sparse Coding: Prior Art

The coefficient vector is a linear expression of few atoms of a dictionary in sparse coding. It has been extensively applied to the field of computer vision problems, such as image recovery [6,7], denoising [8] ,classification [9,10], etc. The most basic and simplest "pursuit methods" are the matching pursuit(MP) [11] and the orthogonal matching pursuit (OMP) algorithms [2,12], which are greedy methods that calculate internal products between the signal and dictionary atoms. For the gaol of efficient learning, a widely accepted pursuit technique is the basis pursuit (BP) [13], which a non-convex problem with ℓ_0-norm are converted into a convex problem with ℓ_1-norm. The focal under determined system solver (FOCUSS) is similar by using the ℓ_p-norm with $p \leq 1$ as a replacement for the ℓ_0-norm [14–17]. Based on maximum a posteriori (MAP) estimation [18], both the FOCUSS and BP can also be motivated, and actually some works can directly apply this reasoning [19].

Another resolution of using the iteration hard thresholding algorithm [21]has drawn much attention, which has the advantage of choosing atoms more accurate in every iteration. Typical algorithms such as [20,21] proposed by Blumensath and Davies. Nevertheless, it is difficult for these algorithms to converge if the spectral norm condition is violated [22]. Since Robert Tibshirani has proposed Lasso algorithm [23]. Because of its nature of constraint and some of the preponderant properties of both subset selection and ridge regression, it tends to produce some coefficients that are exactly 0 and hence gives interpretable models. In this paper, the potential of ℓ_1 penalty Lasso will be excavated when embedded in K-SVD in the application of image process.

3   The K-SVD Algorithm

The K-SVD is a kind of generalization of K-means [24], which finds the best possible code book to represent the data samples $\{y_i\}_{i=1}^N$ by nearest neighbor, by solving $\min_{D,B}\{\| Y - DB \|_F^2\}, B = \{\beta_i\}_{i=1}^N, s.t. \forall i, \| \beta_i \|_0 \leq T_0$,where $D \in \mathbb{R}^{n \times K}$ is the dictionary, $B \in \Re^{K \times N}$ is the coefficient matrix. First stage is sparse coding with a fixed initial dictionary D_0. Second stage is to update the atoms and coefficients. The whole process of K-SVD is as follows in Table 1.

Table 1. The K-SVD algorithm

Step0	Initialize $D_0 \in \mathbb{R}^{n \times K}$
Step1	Sparse coding: using OMP algorithm to compute the representation vectors β_i
Step2	For $J = 1$, loop: dictionary update
Step2.1	Define the group of examples employ the atom of $\omega_k = \{i \mid 1 \leq i \leq N, \beta_T^k(i) \neq 0\}$
Step2.2	Compute the general representation error matrix E_k by $Y - \sum_{j \neq K}^K d_j \beta_T^j$
Step2.3	Restrict E_k by selecting only the columns corresponding to w_k, and acquire E_k^R
Step2.4	Utilize SVD decomposition $E_k^R = U \triangle V^T$ Updated dictionary column $d_k = U(:,1)$ Update the coefficient vector $v_R^k = V(:,1) * \triangle(1,1)$
Step3	$J = J + 1$

For the obtained dictionary, every image will have a specific set of representation coefficients according to this dictionary, which are used to recover the original images or to recognize the test images. So the dictionary learning is critical for the image process. That is why it is imperative to pay attention to evaluations of K-SVD with different sparse representation methods. In this paper, OMP and Lasso are mainly discussed, which are typical spares representation to evaluate the corresponding K-SVD performance in image restoration and image recognition.

4   The Proposed Algorithm

The main improvements during the K-SVD algorithm are in the stage of sparse coding and dictionary update phase. In this section, firstly, the Lasso algorithm was revised by searching the most efficient Sparse Degree(SD) of its coefficients to change the ω_k. Then, the revised Lasso algorithm was embedded into K-SVD for the following experiments.

The Lasso problem is formulated as follows:

$$\min_{\beta \in \mathbb{R}^k} \left\{ \|y - D\beta\|_2^2 + \lambda\|\beta\|_1 \right\}$$

It inflicts a ℓ_1 penalty on the model of traditional least squares estimation. Lasso can compress part of unimportant coefficients to 0, which realize the property of variable selection to embedded into K-SVD.

For β obtained by Lasso, it's not properly to deploy them directly into K-SVD because it's not as sparse as described in the ω_k in the K-SVD algorithm. In order to decrease sparsity index as obtained in OMP, the values β obtained from Lasso need to be simplified: to calculate the index of contribution for different values in β. The following measure of Sparsity Degree (SD) τ is defined as:

$$\tau(\widehat{\beta}) = \| \widehat{\beta} \|_1 \ / \ size(\beta, 1) \in [0, 1]$$

where $\widehat{\beta}$ are the coefficients that discard the unimportant elements to reach better effect. The revise method is demonstrated in Table 2.

Table 2. The revised lasso algorithm

Step0	Input the dictionary D and original signal set $\{y_i\}_{i=1}^N$
Step1	For i = 1:N Use original Lasso algorithm to compute the original coefficients β_i corresponding to the signal y_i
Step2	If $residual = E(:,i) - R*x \leq threshold\ value$ Stop, output the $\widehat{\beta}_i$; Else, leave the top $\tau(\widehat{\beta}) * size(x, 1)$ largest coefficients elements, and set other elements as 0,output the revised coefficient $\widehat{\beta}_i$
Step3	$i = i + 1$
Step4	Output N revised coefficient vectors $\{\widehat{\beta}_i\}_{i=1}^N$ for K-SVD updating dictionary colums

Based on the above algorithm, it can be seen that better performance can be achieved according to both prediction and feature selection. $\widehat{\beta}$ is nonzero and is calculated with SD τ, thus, for i from 0 to T,

$$[value, pos] = max(\widehat{\beta}); \beta_T(pos) = \widehat{\beta}(pos); \widehat{\beta}(pos) = 0$$

Then it has:

$$\omega_k = \{i \mid 1 \leq i \leq k, \|\beta_T\|_1 \neq 0 \bigcap \|\beta_T\|_1 \leq T\}$$

With this symbol, both d_k and β_T are minimized while β_T is stressed to have the same support with β. Then it can be process directly by SVD. It is indispensable that the columns of β_T are normalized and the support of all representations stays the same or gets smaller by possible nulls of terms. It will greatly reduce the data storage and decrease the iteration time of update the dictionary because ω_k represents the most important characteristics of the coefficients.

5   Experiments

The goal of these experiments is comparing the recovery and recognition abilities of RL-K-SVD and K-SVD. Lasso and OMP are standard pursuit methods to obtain sparsity in our case. All the experiments were conducted on a 2.8 GHz and RAM 8.0 GB PC in Matlab. The databases used in this paper are YaleB database and AR face database. YaleB database include 38 subjects,every subject has 64 face samples (sample size is $66*58$). AR database include 100 subjects and every subjects has 16 face samples (sample size is $66*66$).

5.1   Parameters Setting

Before lasso is embedded in the K-SVD algorithm, tuning parameter λ of lasso should be chosen properly for the control of shrinkage amount. Then, lasso is solved and its coefficients are selected according to the parameter τ. More specifically, the choice of $f(\beta)$ is simply $f(\beta) = \| D\beta - y \|^2$, where $D \in \mathbb{R}^{m \times n}$ is a linear measurement matrix satisfying $y = D\beta + \xi$, where $D_{.j}$ denotes the jth column of D, ξ is the recovery error. So our destination is to optimize the λ and τ for 1D and 2D signals to reach the least recovery error.

Optimize λ. For 1D signal, create a 1D signal:

$$y = D * \beta_{orig} + \sigma * randn(m, 1)$$

where $D = randn(600, 550)$, β_{orig} is a sparse coefficient vector.

Input the D and y to original lasso algorithm, and output the β which has minuscule differences with β_{orig}. So the recovery error:

$$Err = \| y - D * \beta \|_2 / \| y \|_2$$

For 2D signals, Samples in YaleB database are all resized to $1024 * 1$. Randomly choose one subject. Use its 63 images as D, and the rest one sample as y. The searching of λ for 1D and 2D is shown in Fig. 1. From the result of λ searching, it can be concluded that choosing $\lambda = 0.01 - 0.05$ ensures relatively less recovery error.

Optimize τ. Also, for 2D signals, define D as the 64 face images of one person in YaleB database(which are resized to $32 * 32 = 1024$). Randomly choose a face image of another person as the 2D signal y for 10 times. Every time, use lasso algorithm to output the coefficients corresponding to the y and calculate

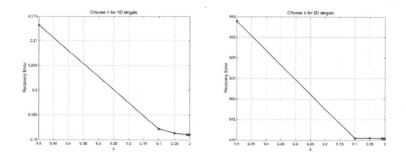

Fig. 1. Choose the best λ for 1D and 2D signals.

the recovery error when change the parameter τ. Then, figure out the mean of recovery errors for 10 times tests. The result of the searching τ is shown in Fig. 2(a). From the result, using the value $\tau = 36/64 = 0.5625$ will get relatively less recovery error. For example, the recovered face image compared to original image are shown in Fig. 2(b), which randomly choose two subject respectively from YaleB and AR database to do recovery test.

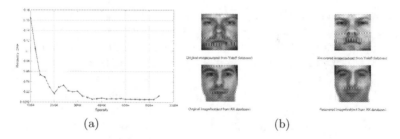

(a)   (b)

Fig. 2. (a) Choose the best τ for the coefficient matrix (64 samples of per subject of YaleB data set is employed) (b) Compare the recovery face with original face (Choose 2 samples respectively from YaleB and AR data set)

5.2 Compare of the Recovery Error

In this section, the compare of the image recovery error ability of two derived K-SVD algorithms will be discussed: RL-K-SVD and K-SVD. Recovery Error is measured by the root mean square error (RMSE).

First, the parameter Dictionary Size (param.K) of K-SVD should be decided to obtain less RMSE. YaleB database is used to search the best dictionary size. Choose 64 samples of one subject. Iteration number is 50. Test 5 times and calculate the average values. The relationship between RMSE and dictionary size is shown in Fig. 3. From the test results, it can be concluded that setting as the max value reaches the least RMSE for RL-K-SVD. The following recognition tests will continue this dictionary setting.

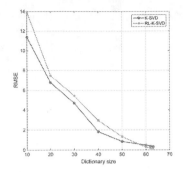

Fig. 3. The relationship between RMSE and dictionary size (test 64 samples of one subject in YaleB database, iteration number is 50)

Second, the convergence of the two derived K-SVD algorithms is tested. Reduce dimension of every AR database image to $n = 500$ by PCA algorithm, where n is defined as sample size. The dictionary size is defined as $param.K$. The convergence result is shown in Fig. 4. The sparsity ratio is represented by $param.K/n$. From the result, RL-K-SVD and K-SVD both converge to stable values.

Finally, the trend of RMSE and training time with the change of sample number is tested. Following the parameter setting of λ, τ and dictionary size as previous experiments. Iteration number is set as 40. All images of YaleB database are resized to $32 * 32 = 1024$. Input samples are randomly chosen from the database. The results are shown in Fig. 5. As the sample number increasing, the RMSE of RL-K-SVD and K-SVD will be stable at some level but K-SVD always has smaller RMSE than RL-S-SVD when the dictionary size is set to max. There is a positive correlation between the training time and sample number but the time cost of RL-K-SVD increase slower than K-SVD when the sample number is big enough.

5.3   Compare of Recognition Rate

First of all, recognition method is introduced in the following:

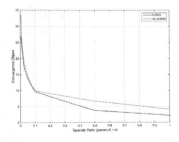

Fig. 4. Convergence analysis of 2D signals

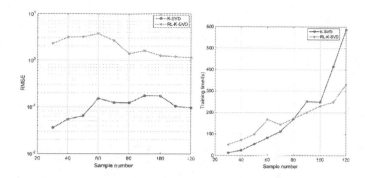

Fig. 5. The relationship between the RMSE and sample number (randomly select samples from the YaleB database, iteration num is 40)

1. Use two derived K-SVD algorithm to train all the images of the 10 persons faces respectively, set dictionary size($param.K$)as different values.
2. Output the Dictionary D from two derived K-SVD algorithm.
3. Half-to-half recognition using SRC algorithm.
4. Output the recognition rate and training time.

The images of Yale B database are resized to $33 * 29 = 957$. Choose 10 subjects' faces samples (64 images per subject) to test. For every param.K, the recognition rate and training time are evaluated for average 5 times. We can see

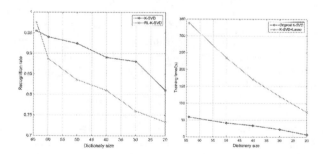

Fig. 6. Compare the recognition rate for the YaleB database with different dictionary size (iteration num is 10).

Table 3. Compare the recognition rate, for every subject, half samples for training and half for testing (YaleB database, $param.K = 64$, $param.L = \tau * 64$, iteration number is 15)

YaleB	Recognition rate	Training time
SRC	83.75%	N/A
K-SVD + SRC	95.48%	58.83s
RL-K-SVD + SRC	97.50%	338.27s

the result form the Fig. 6. When the dictionary size is set as the max number (64), the performance of RL-K-SVD is better than K-SVD, while the training time of it is longer than K-SVD. Setting $param.K = 64$, the compare of recognition rate for two algorithms is shown in Table 3.

6   Conclusions

In this paper, an novel ℓ_1 norm sparse representation algorithm of RL-KSVD is mainly proposed and evaluated. The experiments are indicated based on two data sets: YaleB and AR. As the coefficient vectors of lasso algorithm are not sparse enough, they were firstly be revised by discarding the unimportant coefficient elements. The improvement method is proved by the following experiments. Then, as for the 1D and 2D signals, experiments are designed to search for the better values of the parameters: λ, τ in Lasso algorithm and the dictionary size($param.K$)in the proposed new algorithm RL-K-SVD. It can be archived the conclusion: when the dictionary size is a maximal matrix, the recognition performance of the RL-K-SVD algorithm is better than the K-SVD. When the samples is extended to a certain number, the time cost of RL-K-SVD for training is lower than K-SVD.

Acknowledgments. This work was supported by the National Science Foundation of China (Nos. 61171145, 61671285).

References

1. Mairal, J., Sapiro, G., Elad, M.: Learning multiscale sparse representations for image and video restoration. Multiscale Model. Simul. **7**(1), 214–241 (2008)
2. Davis, G., Mallat, S., Avellaneda, M.: Adaptive greedy approximations. Constr. Approx. **13**(1), 57–98 (1997)
3. Meinshausen, N., Yu, B.: Lasso-type recovery of sparse representations for high-dimensional data. Ann. Stat. **37**, 246–270 (2009)
4. Aharon, M., Elad, M., Bruckstein, A.: rmk-SVD: an algorithm for designing over-complete dictionaries for sparse representation. IEEE Trans. Sig. Process. **54**(11), 4311–4322 (2006)
5. Jiang, Z., Lin, Z., Davis, L.S.: Learning a discriminative dictionary for sparse coding via label consistent K-SVD. In: 2011 IEEE Conference on Computer Vision and Pattern Recognition (CVPR), pp. 1697–1704. IEEE (2011)
6. Zhang, H., Yang, J., Zhang, Y., et al.: Close the loop: joint blind image restoration and recognition with sparse representation prior. In: 2011 IEEE International Conference on Computer Vision (ICCV), pp. 770–777. IEEE (2011)
7. Xie, S., Rahardja, S.: An alternating direction method for frame-based image deblurring with balanced regularization. In: 2012 IEEE International Conference on Acoustics, Speech and Signal Processing (ICASSP), pp. 1061–1064. IEEE (2012)
8. Studer, C., Baraniuk, R.G.: Dictionary learning from sparsely corrupted or compressed signals. In: 2012 IEEE International Conference on Acoustics, Speech and Signal Processing (ICASSP), pp. 3341–3344. IEEE (2012)

9. Wright, J., Yang, A.Y., Ganesh, A., et al.: Robust face recognition via sparse representation. IEEE Trans. Pattern Anal. Mach. Intell. **31**(2), 210–227 (2009)

10. Zhang, Q., Li, B.: Discriminative K-SVD for dictionary learning in face recognition. In: 2010 IEEE Conference on Computer Vision and Pattern Recognition (CVPR), pp. 2691–2698. IEEE (2010)

11. Mallat, S.G., Zhang, Z.: Matching pursuits with time-frequency dictionaries. IEEE Trans. Sig. Process. **41**(12), 3397–3415 (1993)

12. Needell, D., Tropp, J.A.: CoSaMP: iterative signal recovery from incomplete and inaccurate samples. Appl. Comput. Harmon. Anal. **26**(3), 301–321 (2009)

13. Chen, S.S., Donoho, D.L., Saunders, M.A.: Atomic decomposition by basis pursuit. SIAM Rev. **43**(1), 129–159 (2001)

14. Gorodnitsky, I.F., Rao, B.D.: Sparse signal reconstruction from limited data using FOCUSS: a re-weighted minimum norm algorithm. IEEE Trans. Sig. Process. **45**(3), 600–616 (1997)

15. Rao, B.D., Kreutz-Delgado, K.: An affine scaling methodology for best basis selection. IEEE Trans. Sig. Process. **47**(1), 187–200 (1999)

16. Rao, B.D., Engan, K., Cotter, S.F., et al.: Subset selection in noise based on diversity measure minimization. IEEE Trans. Sig. Process. **51**(3), 760–770 (2003)

17. Jung, H., Park, J., Yoo, J., et al.: Radial k-t FOCUSS for high resolution cardiac cine MRI. Magn. Reson. Med. **63**(1), 68–78 (2010)

18. Aad, G., Abat, E., Abbott, B., et al.: Charged-particle multiplicities in pp interactions at measured with the ATLAS detector at the LHC. Phys. Lett. B **688**(1), 21–42 (2010)

19. He, Z., Xie, S., Zhang, L., et al.: A note on Lewicki-Sejnowski gradient for learning overcomplete representations. Neural Comput. **20**(3), 636–643 (2008)

20. Blumensath, T., Davies, M.E.: Iterative hard thresholding for compressed sensing. Appl. Comput. Harmon. Anal. **27**(3), 265–274 (2009)

21. Blumensath, T., Davies, M.E.: Iterative thresholding for sparse approximations. J. Fourier Anal. Appl. **14**(5–6), 629–654 (2008)

22. Blumensath, T., Davies, M.E.: Normalized iterative hard thresholding: guaranteed stability and performance. IEEE J. Sel. Top. Sig. Process. **4**(2), 298–309 (2010)

23. Tibshirani, R.: Regression shrinkage and selection via the lasso. J. R. Stat. Soc. Ser. B (Methodol.) **58**, 267–288 (1996)

24. Jiang, Z., Lin, Z., Davis, L.S.: Label consistent K-SVD: learning a discriminative dictionary for recognition. IEEE Trans. Pattern Anal. Mach. Intell. **35**(11), 2651–2664 (2013)

Study on Path Planning of Unmanned Vehicle Based on Kinematic and Dynamic Constraints

Li Li$^{(\boxtimes)}$, Benshan Zhong, and Ziyan Geng

School of Mechatronics Engineering and Automation, Shanghai University,
Shanghai 200072, People's Republic of China
lili.shu@shu.edu.cn

Abstract. Considering that the conventional A* algorithm does not include vehicle kinematics and dynamics constraints in the unmanned vehicle path planning, methods based on kinematics and dynamics constraints are proposed to solve problems of path planning for unmanned vehicles in this paper, including improved obstacle scanning method, Divide-and-Conquer Method, Greedy Algorithm and so on. Firstly, the kinematics and dynamics constraints of unmanned vehicles path planning are analyzed. Secondly, the corresponding solutions to these constraints are proposed. Thirdly, the Simulink/CarSim united simulation platform is built and the simulation and analysis are carried out under the condition of different obstacles and different speeds. The simulation results show that the proposed algorithm can better solve the problems of unmanned vehicle path planning with kinematics and dynamics constraints, which provides the basic theory and method for the path planning of unmanned vehicle in engineering.

Keywords: Unmanned vehicle · Path planning · A* algorithm · Kinematics and dynamics constraints

1 Introduction

The unmanned vehicle is one of unmanned ground vehicles. It has a broad application prospect in the military field and the intelligent transportation system in the future. Because of this, the unmanned technology is still booming after it has experienced development of decades [1, 2]. As a complex intelligent system, the unmanned vehicle system can be divided into four subsystems: task decision, environment perception, path planning, vehicle control and platform. Path planning is one of the most important parts of unmanned vehicle.

At present, the common path planning algorithms are divided into two categories: Path planning algorithm based on sampling and the path planning algorithm based on the map [3]. Heuristic search algorithm is a kind of path search algorithm based on map. The algorithm can avoid blind search and its search efficiency is high. So heuristic search algorithm is more and more widely used in path planning.

As a classical heuristic algorithm, A* algorithm has been widely used in the path planning of unmanned vehicles. Liu et al. proposes a dynamic multi path planning algorithm based on the A* algorithm [4]. Wang introduces the A* algorithm to the path

© Springer Nature Singapore Pte Ltd. 2017
D. Yue et al. (Eds.): LSMS/ICSEE 2017, Part II, CCIS 762, pp. 94–104, 2017.
DOI: 10.1007/978-981-10-6373-2_10

planning of lunar rover, and formed the path planning technology based on A* algorithm [5]. Ma et al. builds an unmanned vehicle platform for experiment and use A* algorithm to achieve the path planning of unmanned vehicles [6]. To a certain extent, although the traditional A* algorithm can solve the problem of path planning of unmanned vehicles, the vehicle is often regarded as an unconstrained particle or rigid body in these studies. Due to the constraints of the kinematics and dynamics of the vehicle, the path cannot be tracked by unmanned vehicles sometimes.

Some scholars have done some research on the problem of kinematics and dynamics constraints in path planning of unmanned vehicle. Due to the dynamics and kinematics constraints of vehicle are not fully considered in the application of the traditional Artificial Potential Field Algorithm in the local path planning of intelligent vehicles, a local path planning method based on dynamic virtual obstacles is proposed by Wu and Huang [7]. But the Artificial Potential Field Algorithm has the problem of local optimum, and the design of gravitational field is the key to the successful application of the algorithm. Francis et al. uses the kinematics and dynamics constraints to optimize the path planned by D* Lite algorithm [8]. But the optimization method cannot meet the needs of the path tracking under different vehicle speeds. Liu adds the steering angle restriction and curve transition in the Discrete-State A* algorithm and uses the algorithm to plan a path. At the corner, the path can meet the need of driving requirements at a certain speed [9], but it cannot meet the requirements of turning radius of vehicles with different speeds. According to the actual size of the robot, Yang et al. designs a two-dimensional grid plane and the mobile robot is simplified as a moving particle in a two-dimensional grid plane [10]. Thus the robot turning problem is solved. However, this method is not suitable for unmanned vehicles, because unmanned vehicles are big in size and it is impossible that the grid of the environmental map can not be as big as the size of unmanned vehicles.

On the basis of the above research, combing with the advantages of A* algorithm in the path planning of unmanned vehicles, the A* algorithm based on vehicle kinematics and dynamics constraints are used to solve the problem of unmanned vehicle routing in this paper. Firstly, the kinematic and dynamic constraints of path planning are analyzed in this paper, such as turning problem, the problem of access at clearance between obstacles and path tracking problem under different vehicle speeds. Then, the corresponding solutions to these constraints are put forward. Finally, the simulation analysis and verification for the methods proposed in this paper are carried out by Simulink/CarSim united simulation platform.

2   The Description of Unmanned Vehicle Path Planning Problem Based on A* Algorithm

2.1   A* Algorithm Description

The core of the A* algorithm is that it designs an evaluation function for each node, as shown in Eq. (1):

$$f(s) = g(s) + h(s) \tag{1}$$

In Eq. (1), f(s) represents the estimated length of the path from the initial node to the destination node and the Node s is a node of the path. h(s) is the estimated value of the path from the current node to the target node. g(s) is the length of the path from the start node to the current node and its value is known and is shown in Eq. (2):

$$g(s) = \sum_{i=start}^{k-1} cost(s_i, s_{i+1}) \quad k \leq goal \tag{2}$$

In Eq. (2), $cost(s_i, s_{i+1})$ represents the path length from the Node i to the Node i + 1, and goal is the total number of nodes experienced from the start node to the destination node.

2.2   The Problem Description of A* Algorithm in Unmanned Vehicle Path Planning

A* algorithm is a classical heuristic search algorithm which has few nodes, good robustness and fast response to environmental information. However, it ignores the restriction of the vehicle volume and the constraints of kinematics and dynamics, so it has been restricted in the practical application of grid map.

1. The problem of right angle turning and multiple turnings

In real life, we usually hope that the path of the vehicle is smooth and has fewer turns, because that can not only improve the riding comfort, but also improve the security. However, in the application of A* algorithm based on grid map, it is difficult to avoid the right angle turning and multiple turnings. For example, there is a trapezoidal obstacle in the map, then the searched path is likely to be a path with multiple right angles. As shown in Fig. 1, there are multiple right angle turns from the starting point to the end of the path, which reduces comfort and safety. This is clearly not the path we need.

2. The problem of obstacle clearance

In the classical A* algorithm, as long as there is no barrier between the two obstacles grid, the path can pass. However, it does not take into account the volume of

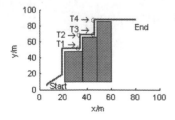

Fig. 1. The path with multiple right

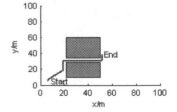

Fig. 2. The path through obstacle angle turnings clearance

the vehicle itself and turning radius of vehicle. In practical applications, if the searched path is narrow, the normal vehicle is unable to pass and turn. As shown in Fig. 2, the path searched by A* passes through the clearance between the two obstacles. If the vehicle volume is taken into account, the road is impassable.

3. The problem of turning in front of obstacles

When the path is being searched, A* algorithm will judge whether the adjacent nodes of the current node is an obstacle. If an adjacent node is an obstacle, the direction of the path will be transferred to other directions. So it will form a turning closed to obstacle. As shown in Fig. 1, the turning points T1 and T3 are very close to obstacles. If the kinematic and dynamic constraints of vehicle are taken into account, the turn is not possible.

3   Model Building Based on A* Algorithm with Kinematic and Dynamic Constraints in Path Planning of Unmanned Vehicle

3.1   The Improved Method of Scanning Obstacle

In order to solve the problem that the distance between the vehicle and obstacles is too short and whether the clearance between obstacles can be through, the improved method of scanning obstacle is proposed in this paper. Before the adjacent nodes of the current node is detected, the circle that its center is a neighbor node and its radius is R is detected. If there is no obstacle in the circle, the current node will be extended, otherwise the node will be ignored and other neighbor nodes will be extended. Assuming that the minimum distance which the vehicle is able to make a normal turn in front of obstacle is L, the path width that allow the vehicle travel normally is H, then R, L and H should meet the following relation:

$$R \geq \max\{L, H\} \tag{3}$$

Not only the path with the constraints can meet the requirements of the normal turning in front of the obstacle, but also the width of the path can make the vehicle running normally.

3.2   Fitting Curve with Divide-and-Conquer Method and Greedy Algorithm

In order to solve these problems of right angle turning and multiple turnings, the fitting curve method is used to deal with the path in this paper. Fitting curve is the main way to deal with discrete points. In order to improve the effect of curve fitting, this paper adopts the idea of Divide-and-Conquer Method [11] to fit segmentally, then the fitting results are combined to fit together. The five polynomial is used to the fitting curve in this paper, as follows:

$$Y = a_0 t^5 + a_1 t^4 + a_2 t^3 + a_3 t^2 + a_4 t^1 + a_5 \tag{4}$$

$$\varphi = b_0 t^5 + b_1 t^4 + b_2 t^3 + b_3 t^2 + b_4 t^1 + b_5 \tag{5}$$

$a_0, a_1, a_2, a_3, a_4, a_5, b_0, b_1, b_2, b_3, b_4, b_5$ are parameters to be solved in Formulas (4) and (5).

In the path searched by the A* algorithm, the change of the longitudinal coordinate of two points is often too large, that is to say there is a local step path. As shown in Fig. 1, the change of the longitudinal coordinate of T1 and T2 and the change of the longitudinal coordinate of T3 and T4 are obviously too large, thus there is a local step path. If the curve is fitted directly according to the points on the path, the result of the curve fitting is not ideal and even through the obstacle, which leads to a wrong path. In this paper, the Greedy Algorithm [12, 13] is used to smooth the path generated by the A* algorithm.

3.3 The Solution of Turning Radius

For problems described in Sect. 2.2, the kinematic and dynamic constraints are added in the path tracking.

1. Control limit constraint and control increment constraint

In the ground fixed coordinate system OXY, the vehicle kinematics equation is:

$$\begin{bmatrix} \dot{x} \\ \dot{y} \\ \dot{\varphi} \end{bmatrix} = \begin{bmatrix} cos\varphi \\ sin\varphi \\ \frac{tan\delta}{l} \end{bmatrix} \cdot v \tag{6}$$

In Eq. (6), (x, y) is the coordinate of rear axle center of vehicle, φ is the heading angle of the car, δ is the front wheel angle, v is the velocity of rear axle of vehicle, and l is wheelbase. The Formula (6) shows that the system can be viewed as a control system that has an input $\vec{u}(v, \delta)$ and quantisty of state $\overline{\chi}(x, y, \varphi)$. The control limit constraint and the control increment constraint are considered in this paper. The expression of control quantisty is as follow:

$$\vec{u}_{min}(t+k) \le \vec{u}(t+k) \le \vec{u}_{max}(t+k) \quad k = 0, 1, 2, 3 \ldots N_c - 1 \tag{7}$$

The expression of control increment constraint is as follows:

$$\Delta \vec{u}_{min}(t+k) \le \Delta \vec{u}(t+k) \le \Delta \vec{u}_{max}(t+k) \quad k = 0, 1, 2, 3 \ldots N_c - 1 \tag{8}$$

The constraint condition appears in the form of the multiplication of the control quantisty and transformation matrix or the multiplication of control increment and transformation matrix. Therefore, it is necessary that get the corresponding transformation matrix of Eq. (8). There is the following relationship:

$$\vec{u}(t+k) = \vec{u}(t+k-1) + \overrightarrow{\Delta u}(t+k) \tag{9}$$

The following formulas are given:

$$\vec{U}_t = \vec{1}_{N_c} \otimes \vec{u}(k-1) \tag{10}$$

$$\vec{A} = B \otimes \vec{I}_m \tag{11}$$

In Eqs. (10) and (11), $\vec{1}_{N_c}$ is a column vector with N_c rows, $\vec{I}_m$ is the unit matrix that its dimension is m, $\otimes$ is Kronecker product, B is a lower triangular matrix that has N_c rows and N_c columns and its nonzero elements are all 1, $\vec{u}(k-1)$ is the actual control quantisty of the last moment. In combination of formulas (9), (10) and (11), the Formula (7) can be converted into the following forms:

$$\vec{U}_{min} \leq \vec{A} \cdot \Delta\vec{U}_t + \vec{U}_t \leq \vec{U}_{max} \tag{12}$$

2. Centroid sideslip angle constraint

Centroid sideslip angle has great effect on the stability of the vehicle, so the centroid sideslip angle must be limited in a reasonable range. The results of the measurement stability study by BOSCH shows: In asphalt pavement with good adhesion, sideslip angle limit β can reach ±12°. On the ice and snow road with low adhesion coefficient, the limit value β is approximately ±2°.

3. The constraint of vehicle attached condition with ground

The dynamic performance of the vehicle is not only restricted by the driving force, but also limited by the condition of the tire and ground attachment. When the vehicle is moving at a constant speed along the longitudinal direction, there is a equation as follows:

$$\vec{a}_{y,min} - \varepsilon \leq \vec{a}_y \leq \vec{a}_{y,max} + \varepsilon \tag{13}$$

$\vec{a}_{y,min}$ and $\vec{a}_{y,max}$ are acceleration limit constraints. ε is dynamic adjustment of acceleration. In the application of A* algorithm, kinematics and dynamics constraints and processing measures of path mentioned in Sects. 3.1, 3.2 and 3.3 are taken into account, so a more perfect path can be obtained. The whole flow chart is shown in Fig. 3.

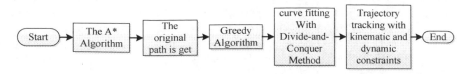

Fig. 3. Flow chart of the application of A* algorithm in unmanned vehicle path planning

4   Simulation and Analysis

In this paper, the united simulation platform is based on CarSim and Matlab/Simulink. In order to fully combine the advantages of the two softwares, an accurate vehicle model with high accuracy need to be established in CarSim and the A* algorithm path search module and path tracking controller based on grid map model also need to be built in Simulink. Finally, the performance of the system is verified by the output and performance indicators. The Simulink and Carsim united simulation platform is shown in Fig. 4.

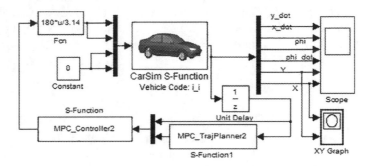

Fig. 4. Simulink/CarSim united simulation platform

In the application of A* algorithm in unmanned vehicle path planning, fitting curve is very basic and important step. All simulations require fitting curve. In this paper. The improved method of scanning obstacle, fitting curve with Divide-and-Conquer Method and Greedy Algorithm and the solution of turning radius are analyzed separately. Then, the comprehensive simulation of these methods is carried out.

4.1   Simulation and Analysis of the Improved Method of Scanning Obstacle

According to the improved method of scanning obstacle described in Sect. 3.1, assume that L = 2.5 m, H = 3 m, so R ≥ 3 m. In order to reduce the amount of calculation, here take R = 3 m.

As shown in Fig. 5, the red rectangle in the coordinate system is obstacles. The quadrilaterals with dotted line are paths searched by traditional A* algorithm. Without considering the size of vehicle, it can be seen that the path will pass through obstacle edges and the clearance between obstacles. The quadrilaterals with real line are paths searched by A* algorithm with the improved method of scanning obstacle. It can be seen that the path no longer passes through the obstacle edge and the clearance of obstacles, which can basically meet the needs of the vehicle driving. However, the path is close to the obstacle at edges of obstacle, which is not safe for driving. This problem will be solved in the following sections.

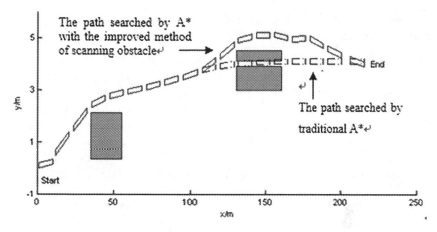

Fig. 5. Simulation of the improved method of scanning obstacle

4.2 Simulation and Analysis of Divide-and-Conquer Method and Greedy Algorithm

In Fig. 5, it appears the problem that the path is too close to obstacles at obstacle corners. The reason is that the curve fitting effect is not good because of local step path at obstacle corners. After the Greedy Algorithm is used to process the path obtained from the traditional A* algorithm, fitting curve with Divide-and-Conquer Method is done and the curve fitting effect will be better. After these methods are applied, the problem is solved, as shown in Fig. 6. It can be seen that the distance between the path and obstacle corners increases greatly. Paths like these are conducive to the safe passage of vehicles.

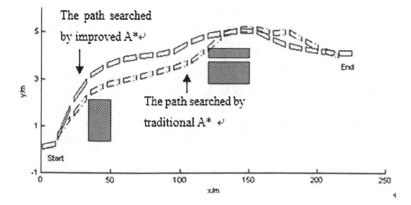

Fig. 6. Simulation of fitting curve with Divide-and-Conquer Method and Greedy Algorithm

4.3   Simulation and Analysis of Path Tracking Based on Kinematics and Dynamics Constraints

After the feasible path is planned, the controller need to track the path. However, due to the different speed of vehicle, the planned path does not necessarily meet the tracking requirements of vehicles at different speeds. As mentioned in Sect. 3.3, the kinematic and dynamic constraints are added to the path tracking, which is a good solution to the problem. As shown in Fig. 7, graphs (a) and (b) are tracking effect graphs at speed of 5 m/s and 15 m/s. It can be seen that the path has a turn at K for avoiding obstacle. The greater the speed, the more smooth the turning at K. So the requirements of the turning radius of the vehicle is met and vehicles can pass safely.

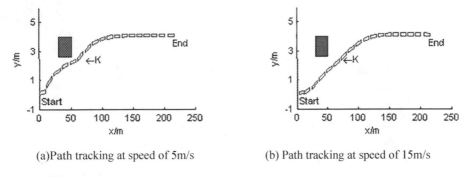

(a)Path tracking at speed of 5m/s   (b) Path tracking at speed of 15m/s

Fig. 7. Effect graphs of path tracking at different vehicle speeds

4.4   Simulation and Analysis of A* Algorithm Based on Kinematics and Dynamics Constraints in Unmanned Vehicle Path Planning

In the Sects. 4.1, 4.2 and 4.3, the improved method of scanning obstacle, fitting curve with Divide-and-Conquer Method and Greedy Algorithm and the solution of turning radius are separately simulated and analyzed. The simulation results show that these methods can solve corresponding problems. For verifying the effectiveness of each method strongly, the comprehensive simulation and analysis are carried out.

In order to verify that methods used in this paper is suitable for complex obstacles, more rectangular and circular obstacles are set up in Fig. 8. It can be seen from Fig. 8 that the path can avoid obstacles better, and will not pass through the clearance between obstacles. By comparing the four graphs in Fig. 8, it can be seen that as the speed of the vehicle increases, the bends where vehicle turns are more and more smooth. So that the vehicle can turn safely.

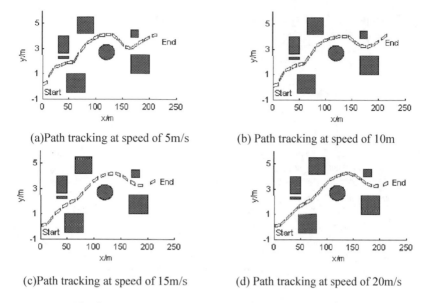

(a)Path tracking at speed of 5m/s   (b) Path tracking at speed of 10m

(c)Path tracking at speed of 15m/s   (d) Path tracking at speed of 20m/s

Fig. 8. Comprehensive simulation with complex obstacles

5 Conclusion

In this paper, the application of A* algorithm with vehicle kinematics and dynamics constraints in the path planning of unmanned vehicles is studied.

(1) The kinematic and dynamic constraints of the A* algorithm in the path planning of unmanned vehicles are analyzed, such as turning problem, the problem of access at clearance between obstacles and path tracking problem under different vehicle speeds.

(2) The corresponding methods of kinematics and dynamics constraints are presented, such as the improved method of scanning obstacle, fitting curve with Divide-and-Conquer Method and Greedy Algorithm and the solution of turning radius.

(3) The separate simulation and integrated simulation of the proposed methods in this paper are carried out, and animation demonstration is showed.

The results of simulation and animation show that the kinematic and dynamic constraints of A* in path planning of unmanned vehicle can be solved effectively by these methods proposed in this paper. These methods can plan a safe and feasible path for unmanned vehicles. So the study provides a theoretical basis for the application of A* algorithm in the path planning of unmanned vehicles. Study on unmanned vehicle path planning covers a wide range of content. The content of this paper is only a small part of them, and there are deficiencies, such as the avoidance problem of arbitrary shape obstacles. In the future, it is necessary to conduct in-depth study of these issues.

Acknowledgments. This work was supported by the National Natural Science Foundation of China (No. 51405280).

References

1. Tan, M., Wang, S.: Research progress on robotics. Acta Automat. Sin. **39**(7), 963–972 (2013)
2. Wang, H.P., Yang, Y., Liu, J.T.: Research and development trend of high-speed mobile robot. Automat. Instrum. **26**(12), 1–4 (2011)
3. Zhang, H.D., Zheng, R., Cen, Y.W.: Present situation and future development of mobile robot path planning technology. Acta Simulata Systematica Sin. **17**(2), 439–443 (2005)
4. Liu, B., Chen, X.F., Cheng, Z.: A dynamic multi-route plan algorithm based on A* algorithm. Microcomput. Appl. **35**(4), 17–19 (2016)
5. Wang, L.M.: Path planning of Lunar Rover based on A star algorithm and B spline function. Jilin University (2016)
6. Ma, J., Wang, J.B., Zhang, X.: Application of A* algorithm in unmanned vehicle path planning. Comput. Technol. Dev. **26**(11), 153–156 (2016)
7. Wu, Y.W., Huang, Z.: Dynamic virtual obstacle based local path planning for intelligent vehicle. J. Hunan Univ. **40**(1), 33–37 (2013)
8. Francis, S.L.X., Anavatti, S.G., Garratt, M.: Dynamic model of autonomous ground vehicle for the path planning module. In: International Conference on Automation, Robotics and Applications, ICARA 2011, Wellington, New Zealand, December, pp. 73–77 (2011)
9. Liu, S.: Research on path planning algorithms for autonomous prospecting vehicle. Jilin University (2016)
10. Yang, X., Zhang, Y., Yang, W., Zhang, H.J., Chang, H.: Research on path planning of indoor mobile robots. Sci. Technol. Eng. **16**(15), 234–238 (2016)
11. Fan, J., Ting, M.A., Zhou, C., Zhou, Y., Tao, X.U.: Application of divide-and-conquer method and efficiency evaluation model in the fast union algorithm of polygons in GIS. J. Geo-Inf. Sci. **16**(2), 158–164 (2014)
12. Zhang, Z., Zhao, Z.: A multiple mobile robots path planning algorithm based on A-star and Dijkstra algorithm. Int. J. Smart Home **8**(3), 75–86 (2014)
13. Li, J., Sun, X.X.: Route planning's method for unmanned aerial vehicles based on improved A-star algorithm. Acta Armamentarii **29**(7), 788–792 (2008)

Hybrid Discrete EDA for the No-Wait Flow Shop Scheduling Problem

Zewen Sun and Xingsheng Gu[✉]

Key Laboratory of Advanced Control and Optimization for Chemical Process,
Ministry of Education, East China University of Science and Technology,
Shanghai 200237, China
xsgu@ecust.edu.cn

Abstract. Flow shop scheduling problem is an important one in the real world production process. As tight constraint condition exits in just-in-time production systems, the no-wait flow shop scheduling problem (NWFSSP) is a typical research topic. In this paper, a hybrid discrete estimation of distribution algorithm (HDEDA) for NWFSSP is proposed to minimize the makespan. The proposed HDEDA utilizes the EDA and bat algorithm (BA). The probability matrix can be a view in the space distribution of the solution well by relying on the knowledge obtained from NWFSSP. The individual generated by sampling has the probability to spread throughout the entire solution space. Then, the designed step-based insertion in the BA stage attains the solution with the best makespan. All of the experiments are performed on the new hard benchmark for flow shop scheduling problems proposed by Ruiz in 2015. Through experimental comparisons, HDEDA shows better effectiveness than other algorithms.

Keywords: EDA · BA · No-wait flow shop · Hybrid algorithm · Makespan

1 Introduction

Production scheduling acts a significant role in the decision making of a manufacturing system [1]. The no-wait flow shop scheduling problem (NWFSSP) can be seen as a vital part of the real-world production system. NWFSSP is widely used in the production and manufacturing industry, steel industry, chemical industry power industry, and food [2–5]. In the past decade, NWFSSP is a popular topic in the area of manufacturing system. Similar to many NP-hard optimization problems, NWFSSP concerns the explosive growth of the dimensional data in manufacturing and service industries [6]. Enhancing availability of data in the manufacturing industry and increasing process requirement in the production efficiency motivate the evolution of effective data-based procedures. For example, the number of new found molecular production every year didn't keep sustainably since the 1970s despite there is a continually increasing input in the research area and thus the urgent need to increase production efficiency [7]. Therefore, numerous scholars are developing effective solution algorithms.

Hall and Sriskandarajah started to focus on NWFSSP in 1996 [8], which is essential for advanced manufacturing systems. Liu *et al.* proposed a hybrid algorithm to minimize makespan, which is based on hybrid particle swarm optimization (PSO) [9].

© Springer Nature Singapore Pte Ltd. 2017
D. Yue et al. (Eds.): LSMS/ICSEE 2017, Part II, CCIS 762, pp. 105–114, 2017.
DOI: 10.1007/978-981-10-6373-2_11

Wang *et al.* [10] focused on the insertion of a new selected job into a former partial sequence. Jolai *et al.* focused on solving bi-objective problem NWFSSP [11]. Ding *et al.* introduced an improved IG algorithm for NWFSSP in the past year [12]. Most scheduling problems, which are proved to be NP-hard combination optimization problems, are difficult to solve using traditional mathematical methods. However, the intelligent optimization algorithm provides a good idea in solving such problems due to their flexible measures. A novel EDA was proposed by Pan and Ruiz for lot streaming FSSP which contains setup times under the situation of the idling and no-idling [13]. Zheng and Wang proposed a Pareto-based EDA for a multi-objective and multi-mode resource-constrained project scheduling (RCPS) model in reducing carbon emission to delay global warming [14]. Meanwhile, the bio-inspired bat algorithm (BA) has been proven efficient in recent years [15, 16]. Each algorithm has its own advantages and limitations. Thus, several researchers are interested in exploring efficient hybrid optimization algorithms. A two stage simulation-based HEDA [17] was proposed for scheduling the flow shop scheduling problem under processing times with stochastic information.

Given the increasing interest in developing many more effective hybrid intelligent algorithms to solve scheduling problems originating from the production process, this study proposes a hybrid discrete EDA (HDEDA) for NWFSSP. The remainder of this paper, how to be organized, is showed as follows. After discussing the assumption and notation, a mathematical model formulation for NWFSSP, as well as an example, is detailed in Sect. 2. Section 3 presents the proposed algorithm for NWFSSP. Section 4 empirically evaluates the effectiveness and efficiency of the proposed algorithm by numerical results and comparisons. In this section, the new hard benchmark for flow shop scheduling, which was proposed by Ruiz in 2015, is used. Finally, the conclusion is provided in Sect. 5.

2 Problem Description

The NWFSSP is a special branch of "zero-buffer" scheduling problems [18]. Each job consists of a series of operations and each operation can only be performed on the specific machine. As the classical permutation flow shop scheduling problem, each job also must be processed sequentially through m machines. Considering the no-wait constraint, each job have to be processed without any interruption between any two consecutive operations. This processing condition expressed that a limited delay for the job starting to be processed on the first machine when it is necessary. In this study, the optimal object of scheduling problem is to minimize the makespan viewed as C_{max} (or $C_{\pi(n),m}$), which is equivalent to the finishing time of the last job leaving the last processing machine. Therefore, the optimization for the NWFSSP minimizes the makespan by choosing a job permutation to determine the job processing sequence on each machine. The mathematic model of the no-wait flow shop scheduling problem (NWFSSP) can be defined as follows:

$$\text{Minimize} \quad C_{\max}(\pi) = C_{\pi(n),m} \tag{1}$$

$$\begin{cases} LD(\pi(1)) = 0, \quad 1 \le i \le n, \quad 1 \le j \le m, \quad i,j \in N \\ S_{\pi(1),1} = 0, C_{\pi(1),1} = S_{\pi(1),1} + T_{\pi(1),1} = T_{\pi(1),1} \\ LD(\pi(j)) = T_{\pi(j-1),1} + \max[0, \max_{2 \le k \le m} \{\sum_{h=2}^{k} T_{\pi(j-1),h} - \sum_{h=1}^{k-1} T_{\pi(j),h}\}](j \ge 2) \\ S_{\pi(i),1} = \sum_{j=1}^{i} LD(\pi(j)) = S_{\pi(i-1),1} + LD(\pi(j)) \\ C_{\pi(i),1} = S_{\pi(i),1} + T_{\pi(i),1} \\ S_{\pi(i),j} = C_{\pi(i),j-1}, j \ge 2 \\ C_{\pi(i),j} = S_{\pi(i),j} + T_{\pi(i),j} \\ C_{\pi(n),m} = S_{\pi(n),m} + T_{\pi(n),m} = S_{\pi(n),1} + \sum_{j=1}^{m} T_{\pi(n),j} \end{cases} \tag{2}$$

where π is the job sequence (i.e., the solution to the NWFSSP); $LD(\pi(j))$ is the limited delay of the job $\pi(j)$ starting at the first machine; $S_{\pi(i),j}$ is the starting time of the $\pi(i)$ at the j-th machine; $C_{\pi(i),j}$ is the completion time of the $\pi(i)$ at the j-th machine. $C_{\max}(\pi)$ is equal to $C_{\pi(n),m}$.

Equation (1) describes the objective function in minimizing the makespan $C_{\max}(\pi)$. Equation (2) provides the method in calculating the makespan $C_{\max}(\pi)$. Time constraints of the processing jobs are also detailed in this equation.

3 Designed HDEDA for NWFSSP

In this paper, the proposed hybrid discrete algorithm is designed based on EDA and BA. For the sake of balance the exploration and exploitation in the proposed hybrid discrete algorithm, EDA and BA were used for global and local searches, respectively. EDA is an intelligent optimization algorithm that describes the solution distribution of the problem through a probability model [13, 14]. During each iteration, the new solution is generated throwing sampling from the probability model. To trace a more promising searching area, the probability model is adjusted by information of some superior solutions in the population. Meanwhile, BA is a bio-inspired meta-heuristic based on the echo-location of bats swarm. It is a simulation of the echo-location behavior of the new swarm intelligence optimization algorithm [19]. Preliminary studies suggest that BA can solve real-world and engineering optimization problems [20]. Each bat from the swarm can achieve the most of "nutritious" destinations by carrying out an individual search, or move toward a "nutritious" area previously discovered by the bat swarm. Thus, a novel algorithm that combines EDA and BA is considered to be designed for solving NWFSSP. In consideration of the discrete characteristics of scheduling problems, a series of discrete strategies in the novel hybrid algorithm is proposed. The details of each step in hybrid discrete algorithm are provided in the following subsections.

3.1   Individual Representation

The original EDA and BA are used for solving continuous problems; thus, they are not ideal to be used for solving discrete scheduling problem. A discrete sequence is used to describe the scheduling solution to NWFSSP for solving this problem better.

$$\pi = [6\ 3\ 5\ 1\ 4\ 2] \tag{3}$$

To decode a given confirmed processing solution into a feasible schedule, the characteristics of the NWFSSP should be considered. Relying on jobs that are processed on all of machines with the same processing order, a permutation sequence of jobs $\pi = \{\pi(1),\ \pi(2),\ ...,\ \pi(n)\}$ is used to describe the processing sequence. An example is shown in Eq. (3). π is a schedule solution that contains six jobs. The processing sequence of the jobs is 6, 3, 5, 1, 4, 2.

3.2   Population Initialization and Probabilistic Model

The initialization naturally used a simple random initialization method to scatter the initial population of individuals in the solution space uniformly. To guarantee the initial quality of some individuals in the population, the NEH heuristic can be used to generate individuals [21].

The traditional probability model describes distribution of searching space as a crucial part of the hybrid EDA. Generally, the probability model can be built relying on the features among superior solutions. Then, EDA can generate new solutions by sampling the probability model. That is to say, a proper probability model and sampling strategy are critical to the performance of HDEDA. Considering the structure of NWFSSP, the probability model is designed as P for describing the probability of the position of the job sequence. In the study, the optimization objective aims minimize the makespan for NWFSSP. P is related to the job sequence (i.e., the solution).

$$P = \begin{bmatrix} p_{11}(l) & p_{12}(l) & \cdots & p_{1n}(l) \\ p_{21}(l) & p_{22}(l) & \cdots & p_{2n}(l) \\ \vdots & \vdots & \ddots & \vdots \\ p_{n1}(l) & p_{n2}(l) & \cdots & p_{nn}(l) \end{bmatrix} \tag{4}$$

Where $p_{ij}(l)$ is the probability, when job J_j appears not behind the i-th position after the $(l-1)$-th iteration. The value of $p_{ij}(l)$ is the important probability of a job when it is decoded into a processing schedule. At the first starting stage of HDEDA, the elements in the probability matrix should be initialized as $p_{ij}(l) = 1/n$ [14]. A random number should be generated between 0 and 1, and compared with the elements in the probability matrix to decide the job permutation. After a series of experiments, the knowledge of process matrix is introduced into the probability matrix. In HDEDA, only half of the individuals are generated (i.e. bats) by sampling the probability matrix.

3.3 Discrete BA Strategy

EDAs focus more on global exploration. Thus, BA is used to lift the restrictions of the exploitation capability in the algorithm. In consideration of the discrete characteristics of the scheduling problems, a series of discrete strategies based on BA are designed to solve NWFSSP.

Vast information can be obtained between individual permutation and process matrixes. Thus, more operations are worth determining. During the echo-location phase, each bat will achieve a selected partial sequence from the current best position. The length is randomly generated ranging from 1 to rounding down the root of job n appended as 1. The starting position is randomly generated. This way, each bat X_i can obtain the most effective location information from X_{new}. Simultaneously, X_i also keeps some information in itself and avoids the large amount of unnecessary computation by comprehensive coverage. If the newly generated bat X_{new} performs better, then the original bat Xi is replaced with X_{new}. Generating X_{new} is detailed in Fig. 1. Performing only a partial sequence substitution of the following steps described above is likely to produce a poor solution. More operations should be performed to find the same job numbers in each bat and repeat them orderly. The entire procedure is presented in Fig. 1.

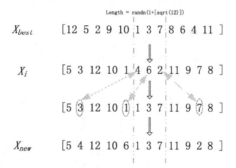

Fig. 1. Steps in generating X_{new} during the echo-location phase

The bat population is sorted by fitness function values (i.e., the makespan) to enhance the searching ability in the proposed discrete algorithm. Then, 10 bats which has the minimum fitness value from all of the population are selected. Further partial greedy search is performed for the 10 bats selected. The 10 best bats will be further optimized rapidly during the search process and be used to guide the probability matrix for updating in Sect. 3.4. The steps of partial greedy search for the 10 selected bats are illustrated in Fig. 2. For each selected bat, the same approach is used to generate a partial sequence randomly and is removed from the original scheduling sequence. Then, the original scheduling sequence becomes incomplete. The removed jobs are orderly inserted into any possible position in the incomplete scheduling sequence. Finally, the best insertion location for generating the new bat X_{new} is retained.

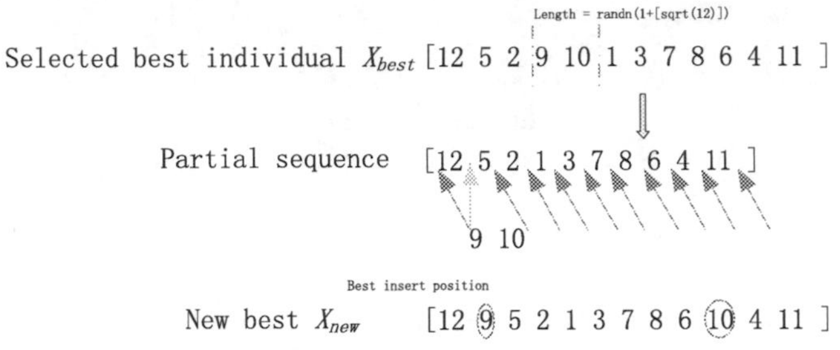

Length = randn(1+[sqrt(12)])

Selected best individual X_{best} [12 5 2 9 10 1 3 7 8 6 4 11]

⇓

Partial sequence   [12 5 2 1 3 7 8 6 4 11]

9 10

Best insert position

New best X_{new} [12 9 5 2 1 3 7 8 6 10 4 11]

Fig. 2. Steps in generating X_{new} for 10 best individuals by random fly

3.4 Updating Mechanism

As an important part of the EDA, the probability matrix needs an update mechanism for sampling better spreading new individuals. The better bats in the population provide a direction in the search space for HDEDA. Thus, after a series of operations, the individuals in the population are updated. Then, better individuals are selected among the individuals in the population for updating the probability model. Equations (5) and (6) describe the details on updating the probability model P. The probability model moves toward the space where contains information of better solutions relying on the ten best bats.

$$p_{ij}(l+1) = (1 - \alpha)p_{ij}(l) + \frac{\alpha}{10 \times i} \sum_{a=1}^{10} I_{ij}^a, \tag{5}$$

$$I_{ij} = \begin{cases} 1, & \text{if job } j \text{ appears before or in position } i \\ 0, & \text{else} \end{cases}, \tag{6}$$

where $\alpha \in (0, 1)$ describes the learning rate; and $I_{i,j}$ represents whether job j exits not behind position i. The probability model is adjusted to represent an effective searching region. Consequently, an updating mechanism should be applied to adjust the problem model during the iteration, which also can be seen as an updating mechanism at each generation.

4 Computational Results

To test the performance of HDEDA, numerical calculation is conducted using the new hard benchmark instances by Ruiz et al. [22]. The whole data can be acquired at http://soa.iti.es. The instances should be widely different, numerous, representative of real-world process. Thus, a good benchmark should have the following desired characteristics: 1. Exhaustive: large number of instances, small and large sized instances; 2. Good responsive for statistical analysis; 3. Have the feature to discriminant analysis.

Benchmark instances describes almost exclusively from all random distributions. Each instance in Ruiz has the same structure of Taillards' instances, which contains information of the job number and the machine number. To evaluate the performance of HDEDA, experiment results will be evaluated by using average relative percentage deviation (ARPD) [20], as shown as follows:

$$ARPD = \frac{avg - G_{best}}{G_{best}} \times 100, \tag{7}$$

where G_{best} represents the makespan acquired by all of the algorithms, and avg is the makespan of the solution which is acquired by a selected algorithm.

HDEDA is coded in C++ (Visual Studio 2012) and runs on a PC with an i7-2600 CPU 3.40 GHz and 2.85 GB available main RAM. The computational results demonstrate the effect of the hybrid discrete algorithm and confirm the effectivity of the proposed hybrid discrete strategy. The following parts present the concept of the parameters settings and computational results.

4.1 Benchmark Description and Parameter Settings

A new hard benchmark of instances for the flow shop scheduling problem was proposed by Ruiz et al. [22]. Considering the actual calculations required and the complexity of the NP-hard NWFSSP, segmental sets are selected from the new hard benchmark. The distribution of the processing time is U(1, 100). The job number of selected benchmark is among [20, 50, 100]. The machine number of selected benchmark is range in [5, 10, 20]. If each instance runs more than 10 times, then the NP-hard instances are more than 700. Thus, the selected benchmarks can meet the demand of a series of factors (Table 1).

Table 1. Factors and levels for the used benchmarks

Factors	Levels
Job's number	20, 50, 100
Machine's number	5, 10, 20
Processing time	U(1, 100)

The 10 additional examples in the benchmarks are used in adjusting certain parameters to improve the performance of HDEDA. Given that other parameters are mostly introduced according to some studies, the parameter Pop_size is given focus. Considering the problems' dimensions, there is a selection from the benchmark instances, which are VFR60_15_1 to VFR60_15_10 with 60 jobs and 15 machines. Six factor levels Pop_size = 10, 30, 60, 100, 150, 200 are set. The convergence curves of the two instances in ten with different Pop_sizes are shown in Fig. 3. From the convergence curves shows that a suitable population size can improve the performance of HDEDA. Thus, population size of HDEDA could be set to 100.

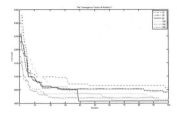 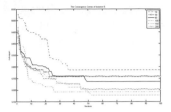

Fig. 3. Performance of HDEDA with different Pop_sizes on VFR60_15_1 and VFR60_15_6

4.2 Performance Assessment

HDEDA is compared with some novel algorithms, such as GA, and discrete BA to further evaluate its performance in solving the NWFSSP. The computational results are processed using ARPD, as shown as follows:

$$\text{ARPD} = \frac{avg - G_{best}}{G_{best}} \times 100, \tag{8}$$

The computational results are overall listed in Table 2.

Table 2. Comparison results of the 10 benchmark problems

Problem Size (n * m)	GA			DBA			HDEDA		
	AVE	Best	Worst	AVE	Best	Worst	AVE	Best	Worst
20 * 5	1.25	0.42	2.15	0.31	0.00	0.45	0.01	0.00	0.03
20 * 10	1.19	0.29	1.87	0.13	0.00	0.48	0.01	0.00	0.04
20 * 20	1.81	0.78	2.81	0.39	0.03	0.71	0.04	0.00	0.08
50 * 5	1.31	1.02	1.52	1.04	0.52	1.66	0.37	0.00	0.85
50 * 10	2.27	1.88	3.86	1.40	0.71	3.05	0.45	0.00	1.01
50 * 20	2.88	2.52	4.34	2.91	0.85	3.59	0.56	0.00	1.24
100 * 20	6.21	3.69	15.97	4.73	1.12	11.27	3.35	0.00	6.97
Average	2.42	1.51	4.65	1.56	0.46	3.03	0.68	0.00	1.46

The algorithms are run 10 times independently for every benchmark problem. The results of the ARPD can effectively demonstrate the effect of all of the compared algorithms. From Table 2, HDEDA acquires the best makespan in the compared algorithms. The average values of each computational ARPD of level benchmarks are mostly minimal. HDEDA is stable in solving the NWFSSP, which indicates robustness. Therefore, HDEDA has a good performance on balance exploration and exploitation. For the same compared standard, the convergence curves of the four algorithms for solving Instance VFR50_10_6 is shown in Fig. 4.

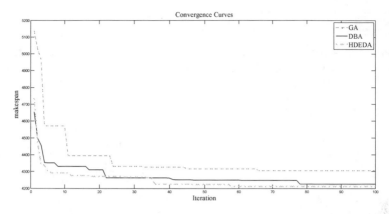

Fig. 4. Convergence curves of instance VFR50_10_6 (n = 50, m = 10)

5 Conclusions

In this paper, a novel hybrid discrete EDA (HDEDA) which contains BA is proposed for the no-wait flow shop scheduling problem (NWFSSP) with makespan minimization. The probability matrix pledges a greater possibility of the generated individuals spreading throughout the entire solution space. Achieving more information about scheduling from the best solution is widely used in BA, which makes it useful in local searches. Therefore, BA can effectively guide the sampling of individuals toward the best one. The numerical comparisons demonstrate the effectiveness and efficiency of the proposed hybrid discrete algorithm.

The contributions of this paper can be summarized as the following:

(1) According to the discrete features of NWFSSPs, a discrete vector encoding method is designed for the proposed hybrid discrete algorithm to optimize in latter operations.
(2) The novel HDEDA is proposed to acquire balance in the exploration and exploitation. The computational results also point out the effectiveness and efficiency of HDEDA.
(3) A series of new hard benchmarks proposed by Ruiz in 2015 are used in the experiment. The new hard benchmark with remarkable discriminant power can effectively reflect the effect of the novel algorithm. The new hard benchmark was easy obtained through a website.

Acknowledgements. This work is supported by the National Natural Science Foundation of China (Grant Nos. 61174040, 61573144, 61673175) and the Fundamental Research Funds for the Central Universities.

References

1. Vasile, M.A., Pop, F., Tutueanu, R.I., et al.: Resource-aware hybrid scheduling algorithm in heterogeneous distributed computing. Future Gener. Comput. Syst. **51**, 61–71 (2015)
2. Yammani, C., Maheswarapu, S., Matam, S.K.: A multi-objective Shuffled Bat algorithm for optimal placement and sizing of multi distributed generations with different load models. Int. J. Electr. Power Energy Syst. **79**(6), 120–131 (2016)
3. Dong, M.G., Li, S.Y., Zhang, H.Y.: Approaches to group decision making with incomplete information based on power geometric operators and triangular fuzzy AHP. Expert Syst. Appl. **42**(21), 7846–7857 (2015)
4. Allahverdi, A.: The third comprehensive survey on scheduling problems with setup times/costs. Eur. J. Oper. Res. **246**(2), 345–378 (2015)
5. Salman, A.A., Ahmad, I., Omran, M.G.H.: A metaheuristic algorithm to solve satellite broadcast scheduling problem. Inf. Sci. **322**(20), 72–91 (2015)
6. Ruiz, R., Vázquez-Rodríguez, J.: The hybrid flow shop scheduling problem. Eur. J. Oper. Res. **205**(1), 1–18 (2010)
7. Eberle, L., Sugiyama, H., Papadokonstantakis, S., et al.: Data-driven tiered procedure for enhancing yield in drug product manufacturing. Comput. Chem. Eng. **87**(6), 82–94 (2016)
8. Hall, N.G., Sriskandarajah, C.: A survey of machine scheduling problems with blocking and no-wait in process. Oper. Res. **44**(3), 510–525 (1996)
9. Liu, B., Wang, L., Jin, Y.H.: An effective hybrid particle swarm optimization for no-wait flow shop scheduling. Int. J. Adv. Manuf. Technol. **31**(9–10), 1001–1011 (2007)
10. Wang, C.Y., Li, X.P., Wang, Q.: Accelerated tabu search for no-wait flowshop scheduling problem with maximum lateness criterion. Eur. J. Oper. Res. **206**(1), 64–72 (2010)
11. Jolai, F., Asefi, H., Rabiee, M., et al.: Bi-objective simulated annealing approaches for no-wait two-stage flexible flow shop scheduling problem. Scientia Iranica **20**(3), 861–872 (2013)
12. Ding, J.Y., Song, S.J., Gupta, J.N.D., et al.: An improved iterated greedy algorithm with a Tabu-based reconstruction strategy for the no-wait flowshop scheduling problem. Appl. Soft Comput. **30**(5), 604–613 (2015)
13. Pan, Q.K., Ruiz, R.: An estimation of distribution algorithm for lot-streaming flow shop problems with setup times. Omega **40**(2), 166–180 (2012)
14. Zheng, H.Y., Wang, L.: Reduction of carbon emissions and project makespan by a Pareto-based estimation of distribution algorithm. Int. J. Prod. Econ. **164**(6), 421–432 (2015)
15. Fister, I., Rauter, S., Yang, X.S., et al.: Planning the sports training sessions with the bat algorithm. Neurocomputing **149**(Part B), 993–1002 (2015)
16. Adarsh, B.R., Raghunathan, T., Jayabarathi, T., Yang, X.S.: Economic dispatch using chaotic bat algorithm. Energy **96**(2), 666–675 (2016)
17. Wang, K., Choi, S.H., Lu, H.: A hybrid estimation of distribution algorithm for simulation-based scheduling in a stochastic permutation flowshop. Comput. Ind. Eng. **90**(12), 186–196 (2015)
18. Qian, B., Wang, L., Hu, R., Huang, D.X., Wang, X.: A DE-based approach to no-wait flow-shop scheduling. Comput. Ind. Eng. **57**(3), 787–805 (2009)
19. Rahmani, M., Ghanbari, A., Ettefagh, M.M.: Robust adaptive control of a bio-inspired robot manipulator using bat algorithm. Expert Syst. Appl. **56**(9), 164–176 (2016)
20. Pan, Q.K., Wang, L., Mao, K., et al.: An effective artificial bee colony algorithm for a real-world hybrid flowshop problem in steelmaking process. IEEE Trans. Autom. Sci. Eng. **10**(2), 307–322 (2013)
21. Fernandez-Viagas, V., Framinan, J.M.: NEH-based heuristics for the permutation flowshop scheduling problem to minimise total tardiness. Comput. Oper. Res. **60**(8), 27–36 (2015)
22. Vallada, E., Ruiz, R., Framinan, J.M.: New hard benchmark for flowshop scheduling problems minimising makespan. Eur. J. Oper. Res. **240**(3), 666–677 (2015)

Design and Optimization of Compliant Revolute Joint Based on Finite Element Method

Li Li[(⊠)], Ziyan Geng, and Benshan Zhong

School of Mechatronics Engineering and Automation of Shanghai University,
Shanghai 200072, People's Republic of China
lili.shu@shu.edu.cn

Abstract. In this paper, compliant revolute joints after topology optimization are reconstructed, and the finite element modeling of the reconstructed geometric models are carried out by ANSYS. A series of optimized compliant revolute joints are applied the boundary constraint to their external circle and tangential force is applied to their inner hollow circle by ANSYS to make the compliant revolute joints spin in the clockwise/counterclockwise direction. Then, displacement and stress of the compliant revolute joints are analyzed respectively. The results show that these structures after being optimized can achieve greater deformation than the initial one, which can meet the demand for large angle in the engineering applications. Simultaneously, the technology of 3D printing is used to fabricate the compliant revolute joints and the designed experimental program is proposed as well. Thus, the models which designed in this paper not only save materials but also improve the performance, which have a certain guiding significance in engineering applications.

Keywords: Compliant revolute joint · Geometric reconstruction · Finite element analysis · Model processing · Design of the experimental program

1 Introduction

Compliant mechanism is a new type of mechanism which utilizes the elastic deformation of itself to transfer or convert forces, motions and energies. The difference between traditional rigid mechanism and compliant mechanism is that the later does not rely on the motion joint to achieve the desired function and it always be produced at once completely. Compared with the rigid mechanism which relies on kinematic pair to transfer energy, the compliant mechanism can avoid some adverse effects such as shock of vibration, friction, wear and so on, which makes it own high precision, free from assembly and no gap in installation. In addition, the technique of manufacture of the normal rigid kinematic joints is complex and a lot of manpower and material resources are required to assemble mechanism, which leads to a higher cost. Nowadays, with the miniaturization of mechanical devices, such as medical devices, robots and other mechanical areas, the size of the mechanism is toward the development of miniaturization. The compliant mechanism is produced at one-time and relies on its

© Springer Nature Singapore Pte Ltd. 2017
D. Yue et al. (Eds.): LSMS/ICSEE 2017, Part II, CCIS 762, pp. 115–124, 2017.
DOI: 10.1007/978-981-10-6373-2_12

flexibility to realize the movement without motion joint, which is very important for the fine operations [1, 2].

The research of compliant mechanism is a hotspot in the field of machinery. There are some main methods about designing compliant hinges: the theoretical formula method; method based on the theory of pseudo-rigid body; the method of topology optimization. (1) Yang designed a new compliant revolute joint based on the theory of elastic deformation, which can realize the requirement for large deformation under macroscopic scale by analyzing its static characteristics [3]. Cao and Jiao achieved the compliance equations for double-axis elliptical flexure hinges by utilizing matrix theory, energy method, Castigliano's displacement theorem and calculus knowledge, the analytical model predictions were confirmed by finite element analysis. The results show the compliance equations for double-axis elliptical flexure hinges are correct and can be used in practical design [4]. However, this method has limitation on the design of compliant hinges and can't be used for the design of universal compliant revolute joint. (2) Wissa et al. designed a compliant spine formulated by a quasi-static design optimization procedure, and finite element analysis was performed on a first generation spine which was then tested by inserting it into an ornithopter's wing leading edge spar. The results show that this passive morphing approach is promising for improved steady level flight performance [5]. Based on pseudo-rigid-body model (PRBM), Feng studied a 2R model which is proposed for the compliant mechanisms with compliant links and a parametric approximation was made to the deflection angle of a compliant link. This model can truly reflect the characteristics of deformation of the terminal of the flexible body which owns large deformation [6]. Tian et al. analyzed compliant guide mechanism which works in micro-nano positioning platform based on pseudo-rigid-body dynamics model. The dynamic characteristics of the pseudo-rigid-body in the micro-nano positioning platform are verified by finite element analysis. The analysis of calculation shows that the pseudo-rigid body model has some guiding significance in the dynamic modeling research [7]. This type of method is only applicable to the mechanism which contain both rigid and compliant components so that it owns lower precision than fully compliant structure. (3) Zhang used the infrastructure method and the homogenization method to do topology optimization design of the compliant mechanism. The extraction of topology and filtering algorithm was given by the relevant optimized model and the material model [8]. Sun et al. analyzed the numerical instabilities in topology optimization such as checkerboards, mesh-dependencies and local minima, which based on the principles of homogenous method and the method of evolutionary structural optimization and the application of topology optimization in the design of micro-flexible mechanism is illustrated by some typical examples [9]. This type of method is general, and the structure of any geometric shape can be designed. With the development of 3D printing and other processing technology, this method has a good prospect of application.

The method adopted in this paper is based on the theory of structural topology optimization. As mentioned above, this type of method is more universal than the others. Additionally, there are a lot of topological optimizations about translational joints and a few revolute joints, let alone compliant revolute joints. However, revolute joint is also essential in some areas such as aerospace, robot, MEMS, medical instruments and so on. Thus, in this paper a series of compliant revolute joints are obtained after topology optimization and ANSYS finite element software was used to analyze and solve the model after geometric reconstruction by UG. In order to avoid the shortcomings of rigid bodies which mentioned in the above, this design used full compliant materials. The results show that these structures can realize larger displacement and turning larger angle on the basis of satisfying the performance of the initial revolute joint, and eliminate the stress concentration which appears in the rigid-flexible structures. Furthermore, the optimized compliant revolute joints also have a certain hardness to meet the demand for rigid in some projects. So the method of this design is feasible completely and more universal than traditional design method.

2 Structural Design of the Compliant Revolute Joint

In this paper, the initial compliant revolute joint is shown in Fig. 1, the ratio of inner and outer circle is 1:4. According to the given load conditions, constraints and performance indicators, MATLAB is used to get the compliant revolute joints after topology optimization and the distribution of the material is optimized in a given area to achieve the sectional view of four flexible rotations, and then model them by UG (interactive CAD system), as shown in Fig. 2. The radius of the outer circle is 55 mm, the radius of inner circle is 14 mm and its thickness is 5 mm.

Fig. 1. The initial compliant revolute joint model.

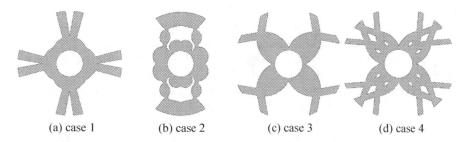

(a) case 1   (b) case 2   (c) case 3   (d) case 4

Fig. 2. The four compliant revolute joints model after topology optimization. (The case1 to the case 4 are the four results after topology optimization by the initial joint.)

3   Finite Element Analysis Based on ANSYS

3.1   Finite Element Modeling

According to the proportion of the optimized models and the main parameters which are given in the above to build the geometric models of finite element which are shown in Fig. 3. In the selection of the unit type, SOLID185 unit is selected, which is an octet element with 8 nodes and 6 degrees of freedom. Thickness of these structures should be small in order to make the angle of them larger and meet the conditions of processing.

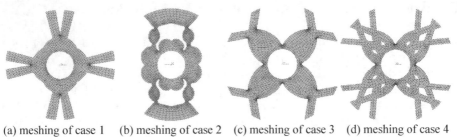

(a) meshing of case 1   (b) meshing of case 2   (c) meshing of case 3   (d) meshing of case 4

Fig. 3. Meshing of compliant revolute joints.

Besides, rubber is selected as the material of this design and its Young's modulus was estimated to be 6.10E + 06Pa, the Poisson's ratio was assumed to be 0.490 and the Mass density was assumed to be 1.00E + 03 kg/m3. Ultimately, the initial meshing was carried out which is shown in Fig. 3.

3.2   Analysis of Displacement

An important structural parameter for measuring the compliant revolute joints is flexibility which reflects the relationship between the deformation of the flexible rotation joint and the generalized force, and it is very important to solve two problems, one is to get deformation with the known force and the other is to get the force with certain deformation [3]. This article is based on the second, it tries to achieve the maximum angle and meet stiffness requirements of the case without exceeding the material yield strength. In the section of define loads, constraint and driving loads are both needed. Boundary constraint is applied to the proposed compliant revolute joints, and then applying 100 N (which can be set according to the demand) to all nodes of the inner surface in clockwise or counterclockwise direction to drive the compliant revolute joints to achieve rotation. After the completion of the four models and applying the load, the initial joint and the four compliant revolute joints after optimization are solved respectively. The displacement of the initial one is shown in Fig. 4 and the displacement of the four groups of structures are shown in Fig. 5. In the two figures, the boundary before deforming is retained in order to observe the deformation after applying the driving load. In Fig. 5(a) and (b), the maximum displacement of

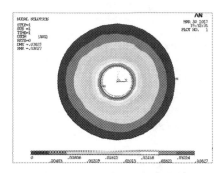

Fig. 4. The displacement distribution of the initial compliant revolute joint

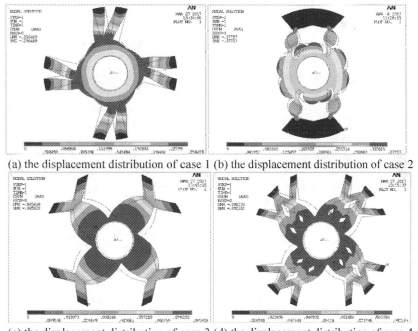

(a) the displacement distribution of case 1 (b) the displacement distribution of case 2

(c) the displacement distribution of case 3 (d) the displacement distribution of case 4

Fig. 5. The displacement distribution of the four compliant revolute joints. (The case1 to the case 4 are the four results after topology optimization by the initial joint.)

optimized compliant revolute joints appear in the circle where exist sharp angle and their value are 0.158695 m and 0.37757 m; In Fig. 5(c) and (d), the maximum displacement of optimized compliant revolute joint appears in the inner circle where applied the driving load and their value is 0.079659 m and 0.082535 m.

The result shows that the optimized compliant revolute joints not only achieve the original performance and they are more likely to achieve large deformation to meet the condition of engineering which is demanded for large angle.

3.3   Analysis of Stress

The compliant material can achieve larger deformation than the rigid material, but there are still some problems that the stiffness of compliant material does not meet the requirements or the stress applied exceed the material yield stress and leads the structure to break. Thus, the stress analysis of the compliant revolute joint is required. According to the analysis of stress, the thickness of the structure where is easy to break need to increase appropriately or change the material of there to maximize its angle of rotation.

In this paper, the dynamic allowable stress of the selected material is ± 0.7 MPa, and the stress distribution of the initial structure and the optimized groups are shown in Figs. 6 and 7. In Fig. 7(a), the value of the maximum stress of case 1 is 0.013194 MPa which mainly focuses on the sharp corner; In Fig. 7(b), the value of the maximum stress of case 2 is 0.042226 MPa which mainly focus on the area where the material is small. In Fig. 7(c) and (d), the value of the maximum stress of case 3 and case 4 are 0.007588 MPa and 0.008673 MPa which mainly focus on the sharp corner and the area where lack of material. However, the two problems about stress concentration mentioned in the above can be avoided properly. Among them, the problem of stress concentration in Fig. 7(a) and (b) is mainly for the structure, which can be avoided by chamfering, smoothing or other structural modification [10, 11]. For example, smoothing the corners with the radius of 1 mm based on Fig. 7(a), as shown in Fig. 8. It can be seen that the stress distribution after modifying is more uniform. If the stress concentration resulted from applying the load such as the cases in Fig. 7(c) and (d), it can be avoided by applying the load to the multi-layer node.

Therefore, this kind of design can achieve larger deformation under the condition of meeting the requirement of strength, and the purpose of designing compliant revolute joint is achieved.

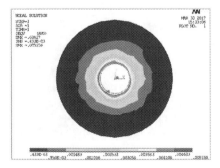

Fig. 6. The stress distribution of the initial compliant revolute joint.

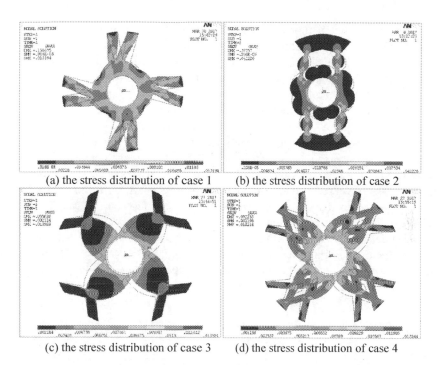

(a) the stress distribution of case 1   (b) the stress distribution of case 2

(c) the stress distribution of case 3   (d) the stress distribution of case 4

Fig. 7. The stress distribution of the four compliant revolute joints. (The case 1 to the case 4 are the four results after topology optimization by the initial joint.)

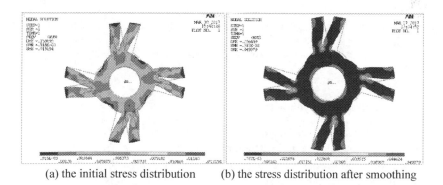

(a) the initial stress distribution   (b) the stress distribution after smoothing

Fig. 8. Comparison of the results of case 1 after modifying.

4   Design of the Experimental Program

4.1   Technology of Process

The processing quality of machine components are basis for ensuring the quality of mechanical products, including the dimensional accuracy and surface quality of machine components in processing. In view of China's mechanical processing status:

On the one hand is the traditional processing technology about cutting and grinding. On the other hand, processing technology based on automation is getting a comprehensive development, which is climbing along the steps of numerical control (NC), flexible manufacturing (FMS) and computer finished manufacturing systems (CMS) [12]. As the structures of the compliant revolute joints designed in this paper are complex and the original processing technology which costs more time and can't achieve the required accuracy. Thus, 3D printing as one of the rapid prototyping technology is chosen to produce the compliant revolute joints which are mentioned in the above and the entities after processing are shown in Fig. 9. However, the structures printed by 3D printing technology own high precision, small error, and short period of process, but 3D printer has not yet reached a mature level currently and it can't support a variety of materials touched in daily life, which has become a major obstacle to 3D printing technology. Due to the limitation of material makes the compliant revolute joints become brittle so that it can't withstand large deformation and it will not achieve the purpose of the experiment. Thus, the compliant revolute joints made by 3D printer will be used to carry out the step of turnover form, and then rubbers will be poured into the model to complete the compliant revolute joints.

(a) the model of case 1 (b) the model of case 2 (c) the model of case 3 (d) the model of case 4

Fig. 9. The entities of compliant revolute joints after printing.

4.2   Measurement of Revolute Angel

The experimental platform was made by numerical control technique which can realize the application of the restraining load and the driving load, and measure the angle of the compliant revolute joint due to the deformation, as shown in Fig. 10(a). Firstly, the compliant revolute joints were inserted into a cylinder respectively whose radius fit their inner circle and the two parts are fixed with glue. Then, a semicircular splint was used to nip the compliant revolute joint to achieve boundary constraint. Finally, using a string to twine the cylinder and hanging a certain weights to achieve the application of the tangential force and add weights according to the law of linear increments. At this time, the revolute angels of the compliant revolute joints can be read directly through the dial in the experimental platform, as shown in Fig. 10(b).

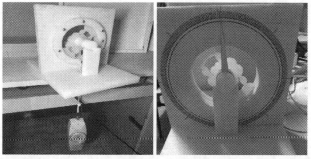

(a) installation of the revolute joint   (b) testing of the revolute angel

Fig. 10. Experimental platform of compliant revolute joint.

5 Conclusions

Compliant mechanism as a new type of mechanism owns high precision, no friction and wear, no assembly and no installation gap, which has much practical significance in some fields such as medical care, aerospace, micro-electromechanical system and so on. In this paper, the model obtained based on the method of topology optimization is universal and can be applied in engineering practice. Firstly, UG (Unigraphics NX) was used to build the optimized compliant revolute joints for geometric reconstruction and then the built models were imported into ANSYS to perform finite element analysis. From the displacement point of view, it is shown that the maximum displacement of the optimized compliant revolute joints are about 2 to 10 times of the initial structure, mainly appear in the circle where exist sharp angles and the inner circle of the compliant revolute joints where applied the driving load. Modifying the structure by chamfering/smoothing and applying the driving load to multi-layer nodes can avoid the problem. And the optimized structures can get larger angle than the initial structure to meet the demand for turning large angles in engineering applications. From the stress point of view, it is shown that the maximum stress of the optimized compliant revolute joints are 3 to 8 times of the initial structure under the condition of satisfying the allowable stress of the material, and mainly occur in the sharp corners and the area lack of materials. Using the method of chamfering/smoothing and increase the thickness of the place where lack of materials to avoid stress concentration. And the feasibility of the method about eliminating stress concentration is proved by an example. In addition, the stress distribution of the optimized structure is more uniform than the initial structure, proving the feasibility of this method again. Finally, the technology of 3D printing was used to make the optimized compliant revolute joints and the initial one. Due to the limit of material, the processed models are relatively brittle which will be re-injection into the rubber by the optimized compliant revolute joints which have been made and then experiment will be carried out to test them.

In the sum, the design can achieve large deformation under the condition of strength, and realize the purpose of designing the compliant revolute joint which is of great significance to engineering application and is instructive for the design of other flexible mechanism.

Acknowledgements. This work was supported by the National Natural Science Foundation of China (No. 51405280).

References

1. Yang, Q.Z., Ma, L.Z., Yin, X.Q.: Type and application of compliant kinematic-pairs in fully compliant mechanisms. J. Jiangsu Univ. Sci. Technol. **24**(4), 9–12 (2003)
2. Hegde, G.S., Vinod, M.S., Shankar, A.: Optimum dynamic design of flexible robotic manipulator. Int. J. Mech. Mater. Des. **5**(4), 315–325 (2009)
3. Yang, Q.Z.: Structural design and flexibility analysis of new compliant revolute pair with macro-scale deformation. Trans. Chin. Soc. Agric. Mach. **43**(9), 209–212 (2012)
4. Cao, F., Jiao, Z.X.: Design of double-axis elliptical flexure hinges. Eng. Mech. **24**(4), 178–182 (2007)
5. Wissa, A.A., Tummala, Y., Hubbard, J.E.J., Frecker, M.I.: Passively morphing ornithopter wings constructed using a novel compliant spine: design and testing. J. Smart Mater. Struct. **21**(9), 1247–1254 (2012)
6. Feng, Z.L.: 2R pseudo-rigid-body model of compliant mechanisms with compliant links to simulate tip characteristic. J. Mech. Eng. **47**(1), 36–42 (2011)
7. Tian, Y.L., Zheng, H.Y., Zhou, M.Y., Ren, Z.: Performance analysis of parallel leaf-spring mechanisms based on pseudo-rigid body model method. Nanoteohnol. Precis. Eng. **10**(1), 6–9 (2012)
8. Zhang, X.M.: Topology optimization of compliant mechanisms. Chin. J. Mech. Eng. **39**(11), 47–51 (2003)
9. Sun, B.Y., Yang, G.Y., Zhen, L.I.: Methods of topology optimization and their applications in design of micro-compliant mechanisms. Nanoteohnol. Precis. Eng. **1**(1), 24–30 (2003)
10. Mahto, S.: Shape optimization of revolute-jointed single link flexible manipulator for vibration suppression. Mech. Mach. Theory **75**(5), 150–160 (2014)
11. Hong, H.Y., Cho, J.E., Chung, J.: Modal analysis and shape optimization of rotating cantilever beams. J. Sound Vib. **290**(1–2), 223–241 (2006)
12. Guo, X.D.: Affection for precision parts processing by machining process technology. Hunan Agric. Mach. **40**(4), 148–149 (2013)

Optimal Sensor Placement Based on Relaxation Sequential Algorithm

Hong Yin[1], Kangli Dong[1], An Pan[1], Zhenrui Peng[1(✉)],
Zhaoyuan Jiang[1], and Shaoyuan Li[2]

[1] School of Mechatronics Engineering, Lanzhou Jiaotong University,
Lanzhou, China
pengzr@mail.lzjtu.cn
[2] School of Electronic Information and Electrical Engineering,
Shanghai Jiao Tong University, Shanghai, China

Abstract. Relaxation sequential algorithm for optimal sensor placement is proposed by introducing the idea of edge relaxation operation of Dijkstra's algorithm. An initial solution set is generated by sequential algorithm, and is improved by relaxation till the relaxation operation terminates. The proposed algorithm takes modal assurance criterion (MAC) matrix as the object fitness function. A truss structure is applied as examples to verify the effectiveness of the new algorithm for optimal sensor placement.

Keywords: Relaxation sequential algorithm · Optimal sensor placement · Modal assurance criterion

1 Introduction

Large-scale complex structures will be damaged during long service period, especially when they are exposed to harsh environment or natural calamities. Modern technologies for structural safety generally require control systems to monitor the structural behavior during the whole operating life. These technologies usually depend on the adoption of increasingly reliable sensors suitable for the monitoring purposes. However, the quality of the obtained information significantly depends on the numbers and positions of corresponding sensors [1]. Owing to the cost limitation, it is difficult and barely to place sensors in all appropriate positions. In this sense, deploying fewer sensors on the structures and acquiring more structure health information is a key issue. Especially, how to place sensors reasonably becomes one of the most importantly problems, which is known as optimal sensor placement (OSP).

Due to the above-mentioned reason, the OSP has received considerable attentions and has been investigated in different areas in the past decade. Generally, there are two possible strategies for OSP: the first one is based on sequential algorithm, and the second one is based on evolutionary algorithm.

As far as the evolutionary algorithm based strategy, the number of sensors is fixed, only the locations of sensors are needed to be adjusted. For example, Yao *et al.* has investigated the GA to place sensors, and the simulation results show better accuracy than EFI method [2]. Guo *et al.* presented some strategies (crossover based on

© Springer Nature Singapore Pte Ltd. 2017
D. Yue et al. (Eds.): LSMS/ICSEE 2017, Part II, CCIS 762, pp. 125–134, 2017.
DOI: 10.1007/978-981-10-6373-2_13

identification code, mutation based on two gene bits) to improve the convergence speed of simple GA [3]. In recent years, the successful application of the new intelligence algorithms in combinatorial optimization problems, such as knapsack problem (KP) [4], bring improved ideas to the problem of OSP. Jung *et al.* presented the application of genetic algorithm to the sensor placement optimization for improving the modal identification quality of flexible structures [5]. He *et al.* proposed a modified modal assurance criterion (MMAC) to improve the modal energy of the selected locations, and used the improved adaptive genetic algorithm to enhance computation efficiency [6]. Yi *et al.* proposed a novel distributed wolf algorithm to improve the optimization performance in identifying the best sensor locations [7].

As far as the sequential algorithm base strategy is concerned, increase (or decrease) iteratively the number of sensors till the termination condition is satisfied. For example, Kammer developed the effective independence method (EFI), which takes Fisher information matrix as math model, evaluates the sensor's contribution for independence between each modal [8]. The EFI method contributes to decrease sensor with lowest contribution for independence. Finally, a subset of sensor positions is selected as the solution of optimal sensor placement problem. Based on a given rank for the system observability matrix, Lim employed an optimal method capable of determining sensor locations by test constraints [9]. Carne and Dohmann used modal assurance criterion (MAC) matrix as a measure of the utility of a sensor configuration [10]. Heo *et al.* presented the modal kinetic energy (MKE) method and optimized the transducer placement of a long span bridge for identification and control purposes [11]. Park *et al.* utilized modal controllability and observability which are defined in balanced coordinate system to select the locations of sensors and actuators [12]. Meo and Zumpano modified the EFI method, and proposed an effective independence driving-point residue (EFI-DPR) method for OSP to identify the vibration characteristics of bridge [13].

From the reviews of the methods based on the afore-mentioned sequential algorithms, it can be concluded that the mathematic models were improved by many researches. However, only few literatures focused on improving the iterative process. Therefore, this paper mainly focuses on improving the iterative process of sequential algorithm for obtaining an improved optimal result.

The purpose of this study is to introduce relaxation technique into traditional sequential algorithm to solve the OSP problem. This new algorithm is termed as relaxation sequential algorithm. That is, relaxation sequential algorithm is inspired by edge relaxation which is the basic operation of Dijkstra's algorithm [14]. It is generally accepted that the shortest path problem of a graph with edge weights can be effectively solved by Dijkstra's algorithm.

This paper is organized as follows: Sect. 2 gives a description of the relaxation sequential algorithm for OSP problem. Section 3 uses relaxation sequential algorithm to solve OSP problem for a steel truss model. Finally, a few concluding remarks are given in Sect. 4.

2   Relaxation Sequential Algorithm

In the OSP problem, a structure is given and the modal matrix $\mathbf{\Phi} \in \Re^{n \times m}$ is obtained by implementing modal analysis algorithm; the input of modal analysis algorithm is the finite element model (FEM) of the structure modeled by commercial ANSYS software. The goal of OSP is to select k rows from the modal matrix $\mathbf{\Phi}$ so that the object fitness function can value as optimal as possible. The maximum off-diagonal element of MAC matrix is selected as the object fitness function, which has been frequently used to measure the correlation between mode shapes [5, 6, 10]. By referring to the idea of edge relaxation, relaxation sequential algorithm is proposed to solve OSP problem. On the other hand, relaxation sequential algorithm can be regarded as an improved version of forward sequential algorithm. Forward sequential algorithm is proposed by Carne and Dohrmann [10].

2.1   Problem Description

The behaviour of a physical system yields the matrix form of the motion equations.

$$\mathbf{M}\ddot{\mathbf{x}}(t) + \mathbf{C}\dot{\mathbf{x}}(t) + \mathbf{K}\mathbf{x}(t) = \mathbf{f}(t) \tag{1}$$

where $\mathbf{M}$, $\mathbf{C}$ and $\mathbf{K}$ are the mass, damping and stiffness matrices respectively; $\ddot{\mathbf{x}}(t), \dot{\mathbf{x}}(t)$ and $\mathbf{x}(t)$ are the corresponding acceleration, velocity and displacement and $\mathbf{f}(t)$ is the force applied to the system. Let $\mathbf{\Phi}$ denote the modal matrix composed of column vectors; the column vectors represent mode shapes (modal vectors), and the elements of column vector correspond to the candidate locations of single axes acceleration sensors. Then

$$\mathbf{x}(t) = \mathbf{\Phi}\mathbf{q}(t) \tag{2}$$

where $\mathbf{q}(t)$ is the vector of target modal coordinates.

In OSP problem, it is necessary to select k rows from $n \times m$ matrix $\mathbf{\Phi}$ so that object fitness function can value as optimal as possible. That is, for $\mathbf{\Phi} \in \Re^{n \times m}$, find a permutation matrix $\mathbf{P} \in \Re^{n \times n}$ so that

$$\mathbf{P}\mathbf{\Phi} = \begin{bmatrix} \mathbf{\Phi}_S \\ \widehat{\mathbf{\Phi}}_S \end{bmatrix}, \quad \mathbf{\Phi}_S \in \Re^{k \times m} \tag{3}$$

where $\mathbf{\Phi}_S$ is the modal sub-matrix which is measured by the selected sensors; k is the number of sensors; sensor means single axes acceleration sensor. Each row of modal matrix $\mathbf{\Phi}$ represents a DOF (degree of freedom), in other words, the row represents a location which can be occupied by a single axis acceleration sensor.

In order to ensure the measured modal vectors being easily distinguished, the maximum off-diagonal element of MAC matrix is applied to evaluate the correlation between measured modal vectors. The object fitness function $f(\mathbf{\Phi}_S)$ is defined as

$$f(\mathbf{\Phi}_S) = \max_{i \neq j} \{MAC_{ij}\},\ 0 \leq f(\mathbf{\Phi}_S) \leq 1 \tag{4}$$

The off-diagonal element MAC_{ij} of MAC matrix is defined as

$$MAC_{ij} = \frac{\left(\varphi_i^T \varphi_j\right)^2}{\left(\varphi_i^T \varphi_i\right)\left(\varphi_j^T \varphi_j\right)} \tag{5}$$

where φ_i and φ_j represent the i-th and j-th column vectors in matrix $\mathbf{\Phi}_S$ respectively; and the φ_i^T denotes the transpose of the vector φ_i. In Formulas (4) and (5), if the off-diagonal elements $MAC_{ij}(i \neq j)$ tend to zero, it means there is small correlation between the modal vector i and the modal vector j; that is to say, the modal vectors can be distinguished easily.

2.2   Principle of Relaxation

The principle of relaxation is on the basis of Dijkstra's algorithm. In Dijkstra's algorithm, an approximation to the correct distance is iteratively replaced by better values until eventually reaching the optimal solution. The approximate distance to each vertex is always an overestimate of the true distance, and is replaced by the minimum of its old value with the length of a newly found path. The notion of "relaxation" comes from an analogy between the estimate of the shortest path and the length of a helical tension spring, which is not designed for compression. Initially, the cost of the shortest path is overestimated, just like a stretched-out spring. As shorter paths are found, the estimated cost is lowered, and the spring is relaxed. Eventually, the shortest path, if one exists, is found and the spring has been relaxed to its resting length. Detailed description can be found in reference [14].

2.3   Description of Forward Sequential Algorithm

For OSP problem, forward sequential algorithm [10] is a greedy algorithm. The input of forward sequential algorithm is modal matrix $\mathbf{\Phi} \in \Re^{n \times m}$; the output is matrix $\mathbf{\Phi}_S \in \Re^{k \times m}$ which can be obtained by Formula (3), but the permutation matrix $\mathbf{P} \in \Re^{n \times n}$ in Formula (3) is unknown. Hence the target of forward sequential algorithm is to iteratively find the permutation matrix $\mathbf{P} \in \Re^{n \times n}$ which will generate the $f(\mathbf{\Phi}_S)$ value via Formulas (3),(4) and (5); of course, the iteration process will be terminated when the $f(\mathbf{\Phi}_S)$ value is less than a preconfigured value.Thus, forward sequential algorithm can be described as follow steps.

Step 1. The m DOFs are obtained from n DOFs through QR decomposition of modal matrix. The Formula of QR decomposition can be expressed as:

$$(\mathbf{P\Phi})^T = \mathbf{QR} = \mathbf{Q} \begin{bmatrix} R_{11} & \cdots & R_{1m} & \cdots & R_{1n} \\ & \ddots & \vdots & \vdots & \vdots \\ 0 & & R_{mm} & \cdots & R_{mn} \end{bmatrix} \tag{6}$$

where $\mathbf{Q} \in \Re^{m \times m}$, $\mathbf{R} \in \Re^{m \times n}$, and $|R_{11}| > |R_{22}| > \cdots > |R_{mm}|$.

Step 2. The best DOF is selected from other DOFs without sensor which can be occupied by a single axis acceleration sensor. Let t represent the current number of DOFs with a single axis acceleration sensor, and then the selected DOF is added to current set of DOFs. Consequently, the placement of $t + 1$ single axes acceleration sensors is determined.

Step 3. If the $f(\mathbf{\Phi}_S)$ of current sensor placement is less than a preconfigured value, then the iteration process will be terminated, otherwise go to step 2.

2.4 Description of Relaxation Sequential Algorithm

For a given OSP problem which has n DOFs and m modal vectors, the edge relaxation operation iteratively updates the current solution by adding a new edge which can improve the solution. Edge relaxation is applied until the value of solution cannot be changed. Based on the above method, the detailed flow chart of relaxation sequential algorithm is shown in Fig. 1.

Like forward sequential algorithm, relaxation sequential algorithm constructs the OSP solution through expanding or reducing a DOF from available DOFs that is seen as row of modal matrix $\mathbf{\Phi} \in \Re^{n \times m}$. However, relaxation sequential algorithm is inspired by edge relaxtion of Dijkstra's algorithm, which has an array **relaxed** to indicate whether OSP solutions is improved.

3 Case Study

To verify the effectiveness of the proposed relaxation sequential algorithm described in Sect. 2, we apply the proposed method and the forward sequential algorithm to the OSP problem for a steel truss model, which is shown in Fig. 2. The weight of steel truss model is 54 kg. The size of the structure is $2800 \times 360 \times 270 (L \times W \times H)$ mm. It is composed of seven sections; each section is 400 mm long. Elastic modulus of steel truss is $E = 1.9 \times 10^{11}$Pa, and Poisson's ratio is 0.30.

A FEM of the steel truss model is established using commercial ANSYS software (Fig. 3). The first 6-order mode shapes of the 96 DOFs FEM of the steel truss model is obtained; the mode shapes (modal vectors) make up a modal matrix $\mathbf{\Phi} \in \Re^{(96 \times 6)}$ as the input of the forward sequential algorithm and relaxation sequential algorithm; the experimental results show that the relaxation sequential algorithm outperforms the forward sequential algorithm in the OSP problem. The natural frequencies and mode shapes (modal vectors) of the steel truss model are shown in Fig. 4.

Apply relaxation sequential algorithm and forward sequential algorithm respectively to select a set of optimal sensor locations for the steel truss model.

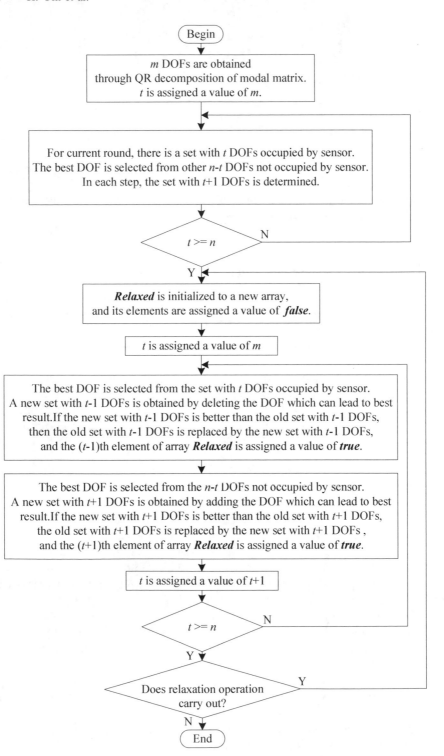

Fig. 1. The flow chart of relaxation sequence algorithm

Fig. 2. Steel truss model

Fig. 3. Finite element model

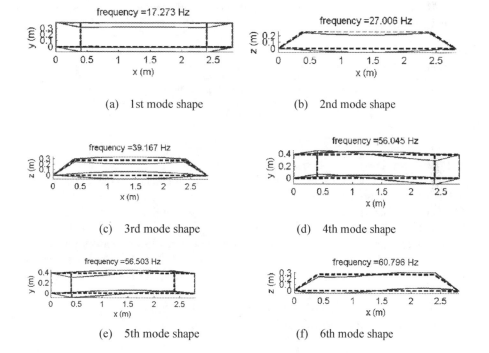

(a)   1st mode shape

(b)   2nd mode shape

(c)   3rd mode shape

(d)   4th mode shape

(e)   5th mode shape

(f)   6th mode shape

Fig. 4. The 1st–6th mode shapes

Figure 5 shows the results of forward sequential algorithm and relaxation sequential algorithm described in Sect. 2. As can be seen, both algorithms have the same input that is modal matrix $\boldsymbol{\Phi} \in \mathfrak{R}^{(96 \times 6)}$ extracted from the FEM of steel truss model. The $f(\boldsymbol{\Phi}_S)$ values of forward sequential algorithm and relaxation sequential algorithm tend to 0. This means that both algorithms are effective in OSP of the steel truss model. On the other hand, the $f(\boldsymbol{\Phi}_S)$ values obtained by relaxation sequential algorithm are lower than that by forward sequential algorithm. This shows that the correlations between modal vectors are weaker.

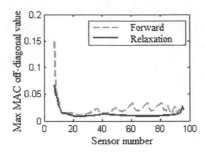

Fig. 5. Results of forward sequential algorithm and relaxation sequential algorithm

Table 1 shows the results obtained by using forward sequential algorithm and relaxation sequential algorithm when the maximum off-diagonal element of MAC is satisfied.

Table 1. Results with the maximum off-diagonal element of MAC being satisfied

$f(\mathbf{\Phi}_S)$	Forward sequential algorithm	Relaxation sequential algorithm
	Number of selected DOFs	
≤ 0.050	9	8
≤ 0.012	21	17

As can be seen, forward sequential algorithm and relaxation sequential algorithm need at least 9 sensors and 8 sensors respectively when the $f(\mathbf{\Phi}_S)$ value is smaller than 0.050. Forward sequential algorithm and relaxation sequential algorithm need at least 21 sensors and 17 sensors respectively while the $f(\mathbf{\Phi}_S)$ value is smaller than 0.012. The results suggest that relaxation sequential algorithm requires fewer sensors for measure vibration of selected DOFs than forward sequential algorithm. The fewer sensors, the fewer data acquisition channels for vibration's data. Thus, the costs of modal testing can be further reduced.

Table 2 shows the results of forward sequential algorithm and relaxation sequential algorithm when the numbers of sensors are the same.

Table 2. Results with the same number of sensors

Number of selected DOFs	Forward sequential algorithm	Relaxation sequential algorithm
	$f(\mathbf{\Phi}_S)$ value	
10	0.040200	0.026000
23	0.011150	0.008416

As can be seen, the $f(\mathbf{\Phi}_S)$ values corresponding to forward sequential algorithm and relaxation sequential algorithm are 0.040200 and 0.026000 respectively when the number of sensors is 10. Moreover, the $f(\mathbf{\Phi}_S)$ values are 0.011150 and 0.008416 respectively while the number of sensors is 23. This shows that relaxation sequential algorithm reaches the better maximum off-diagonal element of MAC than forward sequential algorithm.

4   Conclusions

In this paper, relaxation sequential algorithm is adapted to solve the OSP problem. Steel truss model is employed as the objectives for verifying the proposed approach. The first 6-order modal shapes of steel truss are extracted using ANSYS software. Adopt minimizing the maximum off-diagonal elements of MAC as the object fitness function. The result shows that relaxation sequential algorithm requires fewer sensors for measure vibration of selected DOFs and reaches the better maximum off-diagonal element of MAC matrix in OSP problem.

Acknowledgments. This research is supported by National Natural Science Foundation of China (No. 61463028), and the Young Scholars Science Foundation of Lanzhou Jiaotong University (No. 2013022).

References

1. Vincenzi, L., Simonini, L.: Influence of model errors in optimal sensor placement. J. Sound Vibr. **389**, 119–133 (2017)
2. Yao, L., Sethares, W.A., Kammer, D.C.: Sensor placement for on-orbit modal identification via a genetic algorithm. AIAA J. **1**(10), 1922–1928 (1993)
3. Guo, H.Y., Zhang, L., Zhang, L.L., et al.: Optimal placement of sensors for structural health monitoring using improved genetic algorithms. Smart Mater. Struct. **3**(3), 528–534 (2004)
4. Bansal, J.C., Deep, K.: A modified binary particle swarm optimization for knapsack problems. Appl. Math. Comput. **218**(22), 11042–11061 (2012)
5. Jung, B.K., Cho, J.R., Jeong, W.B.: Sensor placement optimization for structural modal identification of flexible structures using genetic algorithm. J. Mech. Sci. Technol. **29**(7), 2775–2783 (2015)
6. He, C., Xing, J.C., Li, J.L., et al.: A new optimal sensor placement strategy based on modified modal assurance criterion and improved adaptive genetic algorithm for structural health monitoring. Math. Probl. Eng. **2015**, Article ID 626342 (2015)
7. Yi, T.H., Li, H.N., Wang, C.C., et al.: Multiaxial sensor placement optimization in structural health monitoring using distributed wolf algorithm. Struct. Control Health Monit. **23**(4), 719–734 (2016)
8. Kammer, D.C.: Sensor placement for on-orbit modal identification and correlation of large space structures. J. Guid. Control Dyn. **14**(2), 251–259 (1991)
9. Lim, K.B.: Method for optimal actuator and sensor placement for large flexible structures. J. Guid. Control Dyn. **15**(1), 49–57 (1992)
10. Carne, T.G., Dohrmann, C.F.: A modal test design strategy for model correlation. In: Proceedings of the 13th International Modal Analysis Conference, Nashville, TN, pp. 927–927 (1994)

11. Heo, G., Wang, M.L., Satpathi, D.: Optimal transducer placement for health monitoring of long span bridge. Soil Dyn. Earthq. Eng. **16**(7), 495–520 (1997)
12. Park, U.S., Choi, J.W., Yoo, W.S., et al.: Optimal placement of sensors and actuators using measures of modal controllability and observability in a balanced coordinate. KSME Int. J. **17**(1), 11–22 (2003)
13. Meo, M., Zumpano, G.: On the optimal sensor placement techniques for a bridge structure. Eng. Struct. **7**(10), 1488–1497 (2005)
14. Cormen, T.H., Leiserson, C.E., Rivest, R.L., et al.: Introduction to Algorithms, 3rd edn. MIT press, Cambridge (2009)

Temperature and Humidity Compensation for MOS Gas Sensor Based on Random Forests

Peng Xu[1], Kai Song[1(✉)], Xiaodong Xia[2], Yinsheng Chen[3],
Qi Wang[1], and Guo Wei[1]

[1] Department of Automatic Testing and Control, Harbin Institute of Technology,
Harbin 150001, The People's Republic of China
zeroloe@163.com, {kaisong,wangqi,weiguo}@hit.edu.cn
[2] Institute of Aerospace System Engineering Shanghai, Shanghai 201109
The People's Republic of China
xiaxiaodong805@163.com
[3] Department of Measurement and Control Technology and Instrument,
Harbin University of Science and Technology, Harbin 150001
The People's Republic of China
chen_yinsheng@126.com

Abstract. The outputs of Metal Oxide Semiconductor (MOS) gas sensors drift due to the change of temperature and humidity in the environment. This phenomenon leads to additional errors in the measurement and the test precision and measurement stability of gas sensor are greatly affected. A novel strategy for temperature and humidity compensation for MOS Gas Sensor is proposed in this paper. The environmental gas concentrations are measured separately and accurately based Random Forest (RF) method to demonstrate that the proposed strategy is superior at both accuracy and runtime compared with the conventional methods, such as RBF neural network and BP neural network. Results show that the proposed methodology provides a better solution to temperature and humidity drift. The accuracy of the environmental gas sensor array improves about 1%.

Keywords: Random forest · Temperature and humidity compensation · Sensor array · Sensor drift

1 Introduction

With the increasing of the auto possession, the automobile exhaust pollution becomes more and more seriously. It is imperative to detect the concentration the environmental pollutant gases [1]. The concentrations of these automobile exhaust pollution gases (CO, SO2, NO2, O3) are higher, the physical damages are greater. These automobile exhaust pollution gases, however, are harmful to human bodies when exposing for a long period even at extremely low concentrations. The air pollution is inevitable in human survival environment, so it is necessary to detect the pollutants at low concentrations [2]. Gas sensors are particularly vulnerable to the temperature and humidity of the environment. Accordingly, the accuracy of the detection is limited at low

© Springer Nature Singapore Pte Ltd. 2017
D. Yue et al. (Eds.): LSMS/ICSEE 2017, Part II, CCIS 762, pp. 135–145, 2017.
DOI: 10.1007/978-981-10-6373-2_14

precision. Generally speaking, the temperature and humidity of the environment output of the gas sensors are influence by the environment greatly and dramatically.

The reasons for drift are complex, such as the aging of the sensors and the reaction with corrosive gases [3]. Previous studies in sensing technology have suggested that the drift appears randomly and there is no regularity [4]. Therefore, it is difficult to model according to the sensor drift mechanism. There are two methods for sensor temperature and humidity compensation. The traditional method is hardware compensation, such as bridge method, negative temperature coefficient platinum resistance method [5, 6], etc. Hardware compensation method makes compensation by designing the electronic circuit on the whole. After years of hard work and research, the designs on sensors, circuits and temperature compensator have reached the technical limit. Moreover, the humidity compensator cannot be achieved in this way. In order to solve the problem of temperature and humidity compensation, software compensation has become a new research field. This model depends on the output data and avoids the analysis of the internal mechanism. Software compensation divides into two ways: numerical analytic and artificial intelligence [7, 8]. The numerical analytic is approachable in principle and the operating speed is fast. However, the demand of storage space is huge and the acquisition of samples is difficult when facing the three-dimensional space of output voltage, temperature, humidity. Therefore, artificial intelligence predominates in this field. Currently, BP neural network and RBF neural network are widely used for solving compensation methods. These methods can solve this problem to compensate for the various nonlinear errors by the strong ability of function approximation [8]. However, the processing efficiency is low and the calculation speed is slow. As a result, it is difficult to guarantee real time of these methods.

Random forest is a new machine learning model [9]. Breiman invented the classification tree in 1984. The computation is greatly reduced through classified or regressed by binary-tree repeatedly. Breiman evolved random forest from the classification tree by clustering method. Recombine the samples randomly firstly, set up a number of classification trees for each sample and then summarize the results of each classification tree. The prediction accuracy of random forest improves while there is no significant increase in computation. In this thesis, random forest is adopted as method to solve the problem of temperature and humidity drift. The gas concentrations for several gases simultaneously are determined by the sensor array outputs, including the changes of temperature and humidity via this approach. In this way, the temperature and humidity drift is suppressed and the detect accuracy is improved.

2   Random Forest

2.1   Introduction for Random Forest

A random forest, which is a combination of tree predictor using both bagging [10] and randomization, was introduced in 2001 by Breiman and has received considerable attention in biostatistics and other fields in recent years [10]. Random forest is an ensemble of unpruned classification and regression trees (CART), whose samples are created by using bootstrap method from the original samples, and dealt with random feature selection in the CART to induct process. The result of prediction is decision by aggregating (majority vote for classification or averaging for regression) the predictions of the ensemble. Random forest generally presents substantial performance improvement over the CART. The random forest is considered as a strong predictor which aggregating by a numerical of weak predictor (CART). The structure of random forest is shown as Fig. 1

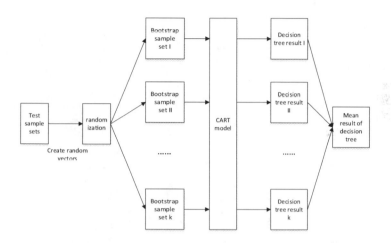

Fig. 1. The structure of random forest

Definition 1. A random forest is a classifier/predictor consisting of a collection of tree-structure classifiers/predictors $\{h(x, \Theta_k), k = 1, \cdots, K\}$ where each tree casts a unit vote for the most popular class (for classification)/an equal valued vote for the prediction (for regression) at input x and Θ_k are independent identically distributed random vectors whose elements are counts on the number of times an input row appears in the bootstrap sample. k is the index of the CART in the forest and K is the total number of CARTs in the forest [10].

For the kth tree, a random vector Θ_k generated in bagging is distributed with the previous vectors $\Theta_1, \cdots, \Theta_{k-1}$ independently and identically. The tree is grown with the training samples and Θ_k, resulting in regression predictor $h(x, \Theta_k)$.

2.2   Random Forests for Regression

The difference between random forest for regression and for classification is the outputs of the tree predictor $h(x, \Theta_k)$ depending on the random vector Θ_k are numerical values instead of class labels [11].

Given the random vector (X, Y) are assumed as independent and identically and the training set is extracted from (X, Y), where X is the input vector and Y is the output vector whose component is numerical. The mean-squared generalization error for the random forest predictor $h(\boldsymbol{x})$ is shown as (1).

$$E_{X,Y}[Y - h(\boldsymbol{X})]^2 \tag{1}$$

The outputs of random forest predictor is formed by averaging the k results of the trees $h(\boldsymbol{x}, \Theta_k)$.

Theorem 1. As $k \to \infty$,

$$E_{X,Y}[Y - \bar{h}_k(\boldsymbol{X}, \Theta_k)]^2 \to E_{X,Y}[Y - E_\Theta(\boldsymbol{X}, \Theta_k)]^2 \tag{2}$$

Denote the right side of (2) as $PE*$(forest), which is the generalization error of random forest. Define the average generalization error of a tree as:

$$PE*(\text{tree}) = E_\Theta E_{X,Y}[Y - \bar{h}_k(\boldsymbol{X}, \Theta_k)]^2 \tag{3}$$

Theorem 2. Assume for all Θ, $EY = E_X h(\boldsymbol{X}, \Theta)$. Then

$$PE*(\text{forest}) \leq \bar{\rho} PE*(\text{tree}) \tag{4}$$

where $\bar{\rho}$ is the weight correlation between the *residuals* $Y - h(\boldsymbol{X}, \Theta)$ and $Y - h(\boldsymbol{X}, \Theta')$, where Θ, Θ' are independent.

The outputs of random forest predictor is formed by averaging the k results of the trees $h(\boldsymbol{x}, \Theta_k)$.

Theorem 2 figures out the circulation for accurate regression forest: low correlation between residuals and low error trees. The average error of the trees is decreased by the factor $\bar{\rho}$. The randomization employed needs to aim at low correlation [12].

2.3 Temperature and Humidity Compensation Method Based on Random Forest

The step of offline temperature and humidity compensation training method based on random forest is described as follow and the training method is shown as Fig. 2:

Step 1: Set the original parameters as default: $n_{\text{tree}} = 1000$ trees and $m_{\text{try}} = 3$, where n_{tree} is the number of CARTs and m_{try} is the number of random features.
Step 2: Compared the regression concentration with the calibration concentration to obtain the relative error.
Step 3: If the relative error is higher, increase and update n_{tree} and m_{try} until the is lower than the threshold;
Step 4: Obtain the optimal parameters and the training method is set.

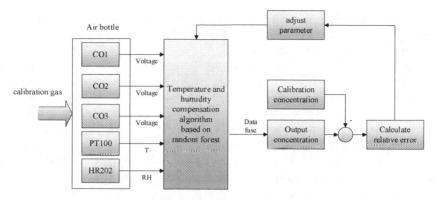

Fig. 2. The offline training method based on random forest

Applying the established compensation method, the drift is suppressed. The online compensation method is shown as Fig. 3 and the step is shown as follows:

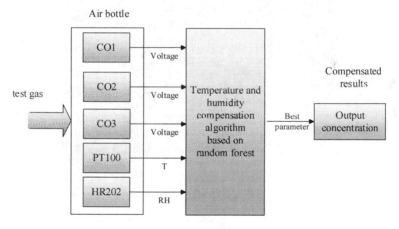

Fig. 3. The online temperature and humidity compensation method based on random forest

Step 1: Collect the environmental gas into the air bottle.
Step 2: Establish a set of 5-value vector as a set of input sample.
Step 3: Obtain the compensated gas concentration after compensation.

3 Experimental Results

3.1 Experimental Set-up

Experiment is established for static concentration measurement. The experiment system was consisted of environmental gas sensor array, gas bottle, environmental gas sources,

5 V power supply, data acquisition card, temperature and humidity chamber, injectors, gas purifier and a computer. The system is shown in Fig. 4. The sensor array consisted of 12 gas-sensitive elements and a temperature-sensitive element (PT100) and a humidity-sensitive element (HR202), was fixed in a sealed organic glass gas bottle whose capacity was 10,000 cm^3. The element in the sensor array is shown in Table 1. The gas temperature and humidity was controlled by the temperature and humidity chamber (CK-150G, Dongguan Kingjo equipments CO., Ltd, its operating temperature scope is − 20–150 °C (± 1.0 °C). Its experiment humidity confine is 20–98% (± 2.5%)). The environmental gases were injected into the gas bottle by injector to control the concentration. Data acquisition device utilized a USB-bus card (USB-6259, National Instruments Inc.) with 32 analog inputs at up to 1 MS/s and a 16-bit A/D conversion accuracy. The computer environment is shown as follow: OS (Win 10), CPU(Intel Core i5-2450), RAM (4G).

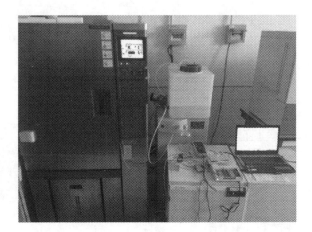

Fig. 4. The experiment platform

Table 1. Elements of sensor array

Sensitive element	Number	Name
CO	3	COA, COB, COC
NO_2	3	NO_2A, NO_2B, NO_2C
O_3	3	O_3A, O_3B, O_3C
SO_2	3	SO_2A, SO_2B, SO_2C
Temperature	1	PT100
Humidity	1	HR202

The software system of concentration measurement developed on the platform LabVIEW is used in gas-sensitive property analysis and calibration experiment of environmental gas sensor array. The software system is composed of the following several functions: gas-sensitive property test, real-time monitoring of gas concentrations, display and save of measurement results, etc. The interface is shown as Fig. 5.

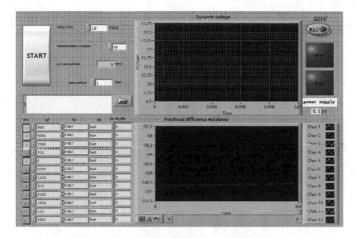

Fig. 5. The interface of software experiment platform

Table 2. Calibation samples of compensation method.

Concentration (ppm)	T (°C)	RH (%)
200	15	60
300	20	65
400	25	70
	30	75
	35	80
	40	85

In order to simulate the low concentration detection under the usual environment. So the condition is shown as follows: measuring range is 200–400 ppm. Operating temperature scope is 15–40 °C. Experiment humidity confine is 60–85%. Table 2 lists the experiment concentration, temperature, humidity. The collect sample points enumerate all combination of the three parameters. Each sample point includes 10 samples. There are $3 \times 6 \times 6 = 108$ sample points and 1080 samples in total.

In order to simplify the calculation, 14 sensitive elements in the sensor array will not be used for the compensation completely. Take CO as an example and the other three kinds of gases are calculated in the same method. So only COA, COB, COC, PT100 and HR202 are used in the experiment.

Firstly, the calibration gas flowed into the air bottle, and the temperature and humidity of the air bottle are controlled by the temperature and humidity chamber. The data collected by the gas sensitive elements COA, COB, COC, the temperature sensitive element PT100 and the humidity sensitive element HR202 are used as a 5-value input.

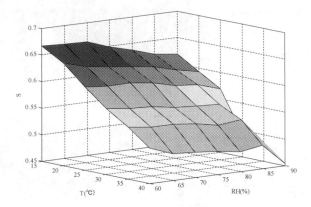

Fig. 6. Temperature vs. humidity vs. sensitivity at 200 ppm for the gas sensitive element COA

3.2 Preparation and Preprocessing of Samples

The input vector X is the outputs of the elements COA, COB, COC, PT100 and HR202 in the sensor array, and the output Y is the CO concentration. The experiment adopt the samples in Sect. 3. Half of them used for training and the others used for test. That is saying the first 540 samples used for training and the others used for testing.

Figure 6 is the sensitive characteristic curve changed with environment temperature and humidity of COA at 200 ppm. It can be seen that the higher the temperature/humidity, the smaller the sensor sensitivity. The output of COA, COB, COC are shown in Fig. 7. S is the sensitive of COA, the value is according to (5).

$$S = \frac{V - V_R}{V_R} \tag{5}$$

To accelerate the training process, the samples need to be dealt by normalization.

$$x_i' = \frac{x_i - x_{\min}}{x_i - x_{\max}} \tag{6}$$

3.3 Result and Analysis

The standard samples were inputted into the procedure to train the random forest model and got a random forest model, which includes 500 tree and 2 features. The test samples were normalized and put into the model. The compensation concentrations were obtained.

Average relative error (ARE) is mainly index to evaluate the method. The formula of average relative error (ARE) is shown as (10):

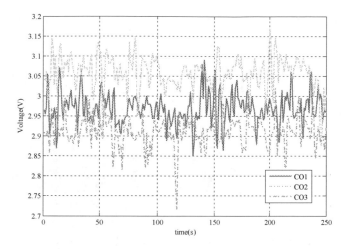

Fig. 7. The characteristic curve of COA, COB, COC at 200 ppm when RH = 70% and T = 30 °C.

Table 3. Performance comparison of BPNN, RBFNN, RF for compensation measurment.

Method	Average relative error (%)	Test time (s)
BPNN	4.81	0.098
RBFNN	4.30	0.431
RF	3.72	0.039

$$ARE = \frac{y' - y}{y} * 100\% \tag{10}$$

where y is the calculate value and y' is the true value. According to (10), the average relative error of random forest is 3.72%.

To further verify the regression performance and convergence speed of random forest, the traditional compensation method such as BPNN, RBFNN was used as the comparison algorithm. The number of BPNN neurons is 20 and number of RBFNN neurons is 5. The comparison results (average relative error and training time) are given in Table 3. The average relative error for each test point is shown in Fig. 8.

The result indicated that random forest is superior to BP network and RBF network at many aspects, such as the approximation capacity, detection speed and detection accuracy. The reason is that the training processes of BPNN, RBFNN take up more computing resources and time consumption. The training samples are insufficient for neural networks to perform a precise concentration estimator. As a result, the random forest method can effectively achieve temperature and humidity compensation.

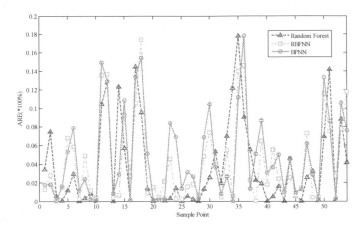

Fig. 8. The ARE of Random Forest, RBFNN, BPNN for the test samples.

4   Conclusion

A novel temperature and humidity compensation method is proposed in this paper. The compensation method is established based on random forest. The detection is real-time and the precision is accurate. The experiment result shows that the average relative error is 3.72%. The experiment shows that the accuracy of temperature and humidity compensation gains compensation effectively by random forest method. It could be further explored to accomplish ross-sensitivity and temperature and humidity compensation directly based on random forest method aimed at four kinds of gas concentrations.

Acknowledgments. This work is supported by the National Natural Science Foundation of China (Nos. 61201306, 61327804 and61271094) and National High-Tech R&D Program of China (No. 2014AA06A505).

References

1. Shigeki, H., Haruhiko, K., Takashi, O.: Dynamic model to estimate the dependence of gas sensor characteristics on temperature and humidity in environment. J. Sens. Actuators B. **60**, 78–82 (1999)
2. Zhang, L., Tian, F.C., Peng, X.W., et al.: Concentration estimation of formaldehyde using metal oxide semiconductor gas sensor array based e-noses. Sens. Rev. **34**(3), 284–290 (2014)
3. Zhang, L., Zhang, D.: Domain adaptation extreme learning machines for drift compensation in E-nose systems. IEEE Trans. Instrum. Measur. **64**(7), 1790–1801 (2015)
4. Haugen, J.E., Tomic, O., Kvaal, K.: A calibration method for handling the temporal drift of solid state gas-sensors. Anal. Chim. Acta **407**, 23–39 (2000)
5. Lee, Y.T., Seo, H.D., Kawamura, A., et al.: Compensation method of offset and its temperature drift in silicon piezoresistive pressure sensor using double wheatstone-bridge

configuration. In: The International Conference on Solid-State Sensors and Actuators, 1995 and Eurosensors IX, Transducers, 570–573. IEEE (1995)

6. Ishikawa, T., Nakayama, A., Niimi, H., et al.: Semiconductor ceramics having negative temperature coefficients of resistance. US20010001205. P (2001)
7. Marinković, Z., Atanasković, A., Xibilia, M.G.: A neural network approach for safety monitoring applications. IEEE Instrum. Measur. (2016)
8. Nenova, Z., Dimchev, G.: Compensation of the impact of disturbing factors on gas sensor characteristics. Acta Polytech. Hung. **10**, 97–113 (2013)
9. Breiman, L.: Random Forest. Mach. Learn. **45**, 5–32 (2001)
10. Breiman, L.: Bagging predictors. Mach. Learn. **24**(2), 123–140 (1996)
11. Chen, C., Breiman, L.: Using random forest to learn imbalanced data. J. (2004)
12. Cui, D., Bo, J.: Comprehensive evaluation of water ecological civilization based on random forests regression algorithm. Adv. Sci. Technol. Water Resour. (2014)

Study on the Magnetic Coupling and Decoupling Algorithm of Electrical Variable Transmission

Qiwei Xu[1(✉)], Jing Sun[1], Yiming Su[1], Weidong Chen[1], Jianshu Huang[1], and Shumei Cui[2]

[1] Chongqing University, Chongqing 400044, China
xuqw@cqu.edu.cn
[2] Harbin Institute of Technology, Harbin 150001, China

Abstract. The Electrical variable transmission (EVT) is an electromechanical energy conversion device, which structure of inner machine (IM) and outer machine (IM) is concentric distribution. The outer rotor of EVT is the common magnetic circuit of IM and OM, which resulting in the serious magnetic coupling between them. In this paper, the internal magnetic field coupling problem of EVT is studied, which based on induction motor principle. Firstly, the finite element method (FEM) simulation is used to study the distribution discipline of the magnetic coupling and its influence on the inductances. The range of the self- and mutual-inductance of IM and OM is calculated quantitatively. Then, the mathematical model of EVT is deduced, then the winding phase current of IM and OM are simulated and analyzed with reference to the variable inductance parameters model. The variable parameter model is reasonable, which consistent with the expected results. Finally, the correctness of the variable parameter decoupling algorithm is verified by the prototype experiment.

Keywords: Electrical variable transmission (EVT) · Serious magnetic coupling · Distribution discipline · Mathematical model · Prototype experiment

1 Introduction

In order to optimize the operating area of internal combustion engine (ICE), improve the fuel economies and reduce emissions, a double rotor electromechanical energy converter is proposed, which is called EVT [1]. The EVT not only can realize the function of step-less variable speed, but also can improve the operating characteristics of ICE and enhance the power performance of hybrid electric vehicle (HEV) [2–4]. At the same time, the EVT can replace the starter and generator, so that the entire powertrain system is greatly simplified [5]. The EVT is a promising application of the electromechanical energy conversion device in the field of electric vehicles, wind power, underwater propulsion and other fields. Currently, it has been extensively studied by the academic world of European, American and Chinese, and different types of prototype are developed initially. Through the study of EVT based on the principle of induction motor, it is found that the most prominent characteristic of EVT compared with other double rotor machines is that the magnetic field of IM and OM has different

© Springer Nature Singapore Pte Ltd. 2017
D. Yue et al. (Eds.): LSMS/ICSEE 2017, Part II, CCIS 762, pp. 146–155, 2017.
DOI: 10.1007/978-981-10-6373-2_15

electromagnetic coupling degrees according to the working states. When IM and OM are working at the same time, the inductor parameters of them are no longer constant, which brings great difficulties to the control practical application of EVT. This paper mainly researches the coupling law and coupling degree of magnetic field in the EVT based on FEM under the different working states, and establishes the EVT model based on the variable parameters to realize the decoupling vector control of EVT.

2   The Structure and Magnetic Coupling Discipline of EVT

2.1   The Structure and Magnetic Field Simulation Analysis of EVT

The specific structure of EVT is shown in Fig. 1, which based on the principle of induction motor.

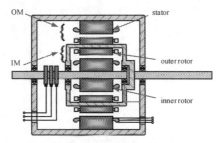

Fig. 1. The specific structure of EVT.

The EVT that shown in Fig. 1 can be seen as two induction motor of radial concentric distribution. The inner rotor and stator have three-phase winding with the same pole pairs (n_p), which can be seen as the stator of IM and OM respectively [6]. The common outer rotor has a separate squirrel-cage in the inner and outer side. Therefore, the EVT cannot be seen the superposition of two induction motors simply [7]. The yoke thickness of the outer rotor yoke should be reduced to accommodate the high power density requirements of the vehicle application. When the two machines work simultaneously, the magnetic field generated by the winding current of inner rotor and stator will pass through the outer rotor and the air-gap more or less, then enter into the stator and inner rotor. Figure 2 shows the quarter FEM model of a 4-pole prototype to verify the distribution of the magnetic field coupling. The EVT with the same excitation current but different phase angles. It can be seen that the magnetic field distribution gradually changes from the series magnetic circuit into the parallel magnetic circuit, and the saturation degree of the outer rotor is gradually increased when the phase angle difference is increased from 0–180°. The parallel magnetic circuit not only reduces the torque properties, but also increases the ripple coefficient of the torque obviously. So it is necessary to avoid the parallel magnetic circuit.

When the excitation current of IM and OM has the same phase angle difference and different amplitudes, the magnetic flux densities and coupling degrees of IM and OM

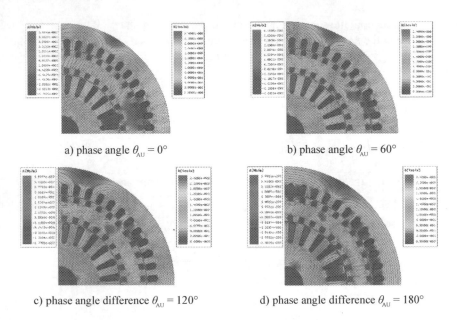

a) phase angle $\theta_{AU} = 0°$ b) phase angle $\theta_{AU} = 60°$

c) phase angle difference $\theta_{AU} = 120°$ d) phase angle difference $\theta_{AU} = 180°$

Fig. 2. Magnetic field distribution diagram of EVT with the same excitation current but different phase angles.

will change on the condition of keeping magnetic field coupling property constant. Figure 3 is the magnetic field distribution of EVT when the excitation current of IM is maintained at the rated value, and the current of OM is gradually increased.

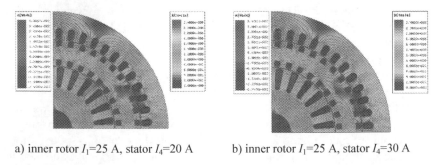

a) inner rotor I_1=25 A, stator I_4=20 A   b) inner rotor I_1=25 A, stator I_4=30 A

Fig. 3. Magnetic field distribution diagram of EVT with the same excitation current but different phase angles.

It can be seen that the excitation current value of OM can affect the operation of IM and vice versa. It is found that the influence of magnetic field coupling on the performance of the machine is mainly manifested in the change of inductance parameter at the different coupling states.

2.2   The Variation Regularity and Analysis of Inductance

The positive sequence of the three-phase symmetrical windings of the inner rotor and stator is A, B, C and U, V, W, respectively. Taking the A, U phase as an example, then the self-inductance and mutual-inductance parameters between the six windings can be obtained by small current method.

$$
\begin{cases}
L_A = \dfrac{\psi_A(i_A+\Delta i_A,i_B,i_C,i_U,i_V,i_W,\theta_{AU})-\psi_A(i_A,i_B,i_C,i_U,i_V,i_W,\theta_{AU})}{\Delta i_A} \\
L_U = \dfrac{\psi_U(i_A,i_B,i_C,i_U+\Delta i_U,i_V,i_W,\theta_{AU})-\psi_U(i_A,i_B,i_C,i_U,i_V,i_W,\theta_{AU})}{\Delta i_U} \\
M_{AU} = \dfrac{\psi_{AU}(i_A,i_B,i_C,i_U+\Delta i_U,i_V,i_W,\theta_{AU})-\psi_{AU}(i_A,i_B,i_C,i_U,i_V,i_W,\theta_{AU})}{\Delta i_U}
\end{cases}
\tag{1}
$$

There are three independent variable and the change range of them are large. Therefore, the FEM software is used to calculate the self-inductance and mutual-inductance of IM and OM at the condition of changing the magnitude of the excitation current (from weak magnetic to over excitation) and the phase angle difference between them (from the series to parallel), respectively. Figure 4 shows the 3D map of the winding inductances of stator and inner rotor by changing the current and phase angle difference of IM and OM.

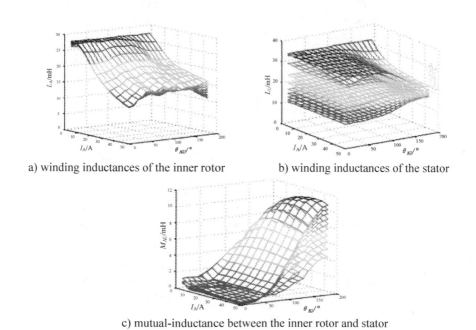

a) winding inductances of the inner rotor   b) winding inductances of the stator

c) mutual-inductance between the inner rotor and stator

Fig. 4. The self-and mutual-inductances of IM and OM.

It can be seen from Fig. 4 that the self-inductance of stator and internal rotor decreases with the increase of the current and phase angle, which results from the decrease of the core's permeability. The inductance is slightly reduced when the excitation current is small due to the initial permeability of the core is small. The mutual-inductance increases with the adding of the A and U phase's angle. However, the reluctance of the outer rotor will become larger, and the inductance will be slightly decreased after saturation.

From the above inductance values, the coupling form and the saturation effect will cause the inductance varying widely. The mutual-inductance value between IM and OM changing can be more than 10 times, which increases the difficulty of precise control of EVT. So the mathematical model of EVT cannot be simply linearized as a conventional motor. That is to say, the inductance parameter in the model must be regarded as the ternary variable function of excitation current and phase angle difference of IM and OM.

3   The Mathematical Model of EVT Under the Coupling Effect

3.1   The Distribution Regularity and State Equations of Magnetic Flux

By analyzing the above magnetic coupling properties, the inductance corresponding to the magnetic flux distribution can be classified according to Fig. 5. In Fig. 5, $L_{\sigma 1}$, $L_{\sigma 2}$, $L_{\sigma 3}$, $L_{\sigma 4}$ is the leakage inductance of the inner rotor windings, inner and outer squirrel-cage windings and stator windings. M_{Aa}, M_{Uu} is the mutual-inductance of IM and OM; MUA is the mutual-inductance between the stator windings and inner rotor windings.

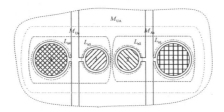

Fig. 5.   The inductance corresponding to the magnetic flux distribution

In order to analyze the electromagnetic torque in the EVT accurately, the virtual displacement method can be utilized, which based on the electromechanical energy conversion principle. Under the linear condition, the magnetic co-energy in the system can be computed as:

$$W'_{\mathrm{m}} = \frac{1}{2}i^T \boldsymbol{\Psi} = \frac{1}{2}i^T \boldsymbol{L}i \tag{2}$$

The electromagnetic torque of the mechanical port (T_e) is equal to the partial derivative of the magnetic co-energy to the rotor angle. Owing to the EVT is a

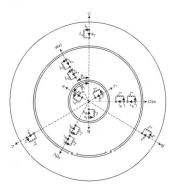

Fig. 6. The model of EVT in the three-phase coordinate system

combination of two three-phase induction motors, the energization situation of three-phase windings in the IM and OM is shown in Fig. 6.

The current vector of the stator windings, outer and inner squirrel-cage windings and inner rotor windings are shown in Eq. (3).

$$
\begin{cases}
\boldsymbol{i}_{s4} = \begin{bmatrix} i_U & i_V & i_W \end{bmatrix}^T \\
\boldsymbol{i}_{r3} = \begin{bmatrix} i_u & i_v & i_w \end{bmatrix}^T \\
\boldsymbol{i}_{r2} = \begin{bmatrix} i_a & i_b & i_c \end{bmatrix}^T \\
\boldsymbol{i}_{r1} = \begin{bmatrix} i_A & i_B & i_C \end{bmatrix}^T
\end{cases}
\tag{3}
$$

The matrix of total magnetic flux can be obtained:

$$
\boldsymbol{\Psi} =
\begin{bmatrix}
\boldsymbol{L}_{s4s4} & \boldsymbol{L}_{s4r3} & \boldsymbol{L}_{s4r2} & \boldsymbol{L}_{s4r1} \\
\boldsymbol{L}_{r3s4} & \boldsymbol{L}_{r3r3} & \boldsymbol{L}_{r3r2} & \boldsymbol{L}_{r3r1} \\
\boldsymbol{L}_{r2s4} & \boldsymbol{L}_{r2r3} & \boldsymbol{L}_{r2r2} & \boldsymbol{L}_{r2r1} \\
\boldsymbol{L}_{r1s4} & \boldsymbol{L}_{r1r3} & \boldsymbol{L}_{r1r2} & \boldsymbol{L}_{r1r1}
\end{bmatrix}
\begin{bmatrix}
\boldsymbol{i}_{s4} \\
\boldsymbol{i}_{r3} \\
\boldsymbol{i}_{r2} \\
\boldsymbol{i}_{r1}
\end{bmatrix}
\tag{4}
$$

It can be seen that the inductance matrix of EVT in the three-phase coordinate system is a 12th high-order square matrix. The coupling effect is strong and the expression of the electromagnetic torque is complicated. According to the vector control of induction motor, the non-singular transformation can be made based on the coordinate transformation under the stator d–q coordinate system. The state variable is i_{s4}–Ψ_{r3}–Ψ_{r2}–i_{r1}; the input variable is u_{s4}–u_{r1}, then the decoupling state equation is established in Eq. (5).

$$
X = AX + Bu
\tag{5}
$$

$$
\begin{aligned}
X &= \begin{bmatrix} i_{s4d} & i_{s4q} & \Psi_{r3d} & \Psi_{r3q} & \Psi_{r2d} & \Psi_{r2q} & i_{r1d} & i_{r1q} \end{bmatrix}^T \\
u &= \begin{bmatrix} u_{s4d} & u_{s4q} & u_{r1d} & u_{r1q} \end{bmatrix}^T
\end{aligned}
\tag{6}
$$

The elements in the matrices A and B are the functions of resistances and inductances in the d–q coordinate system except for 0.

Compared with the ordinary induction motor, the inductance of EVT is a non-linear quantity, so the torque of EVT is still non-linear. The electromagnetic torque of EVT is analyzed by using the mathematical model of it.

3.2   The Motion Equations and Electromagnetic Torque

Figure 7 shows the electromagnetic torque of each component in the EVT.

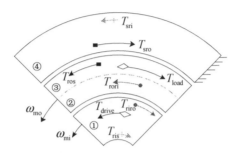

Fig. 7. The electromagnetic torque schematic diagram of EVT

The Fig. 7 regards the counter clockwise as the positive direction. T_{ros} are the electromagnetic force of outer rotor produced by the stator and inner rotor; then the reaction force of the stator generator by outer rotor can be expressed as $T_{sro} = -T_{ros}$; the reaction force of the inner rotor produced by outer rotor is $T_{riro} = -T_{rori}$; the relationship of electromagnetic force between stator and inner rotor is $T_{sri} = -T_{ris}$.

According to the state equation above, the current of the stator, inner rotor, the flux linkages of IM and OM are obtained. The electromagnetic torque of inner rotor (T_{ei}) and outer rotor (T_{eo}) can be deduced based on the d–q axis coordinate system of the stator.

$$
\begin{aligned}
T_{ei} &= T_{ris} - T_{rori} \\
T_{eo} &= T_{ros} + T_{rori}
\end{aligned}
\tag{7}
$$

$$
\begin{aligned}
T_{ros} &= p_n \frac{L_{mo}}{L_{r3}} \left(i_{s4q}\Psi_{r3d} - i_{s4d}\Psi_{r3q}\right) + p_n \frac{L_m}{L_{r2}} \left(i_{s4q}\Psi_{r2d} - i_{s4d}\Psi_{r2q}\right) \\
T_{ros} &= p_n \frac{L_{mo}}{L_{r3}} \left(i_{s4q}\Psi_{r3d} - i_{s4d}\Psi_{r3q}\right) + p_n \frac{L_m}{L_{r2}} \left(i_{s4q}\Psi_{r2d} - i_{s4d}\Psi_{r2q}\right) \\
T_{ris} &= p_n L_m \left(i_{s4q}i_{r1d} - i_{s4d}i_{r1q}\right)
\end{aligned}
\tag{8}
$$

The inner rotor driven by the ICE, and the load driven by the output shaft of outer rotor. The driven torque of inner rotor is T_{drive}, which is linked with the ICE, and the load torque of the outer rotor is T_{load}. Ignoring the frictional resistance, and the motion equation of the inner and outer rotor can be shown as follows:

$$T_{drive} = T_{ICE} = T_{ei} + J_i \frac{d\omega_{mi}}{dt}$$
$$T_{eo} = T_{Load} + J_{ro} \frac{d\omega_{mo}}{dt}$$

(9)

J_{ri} and J_{ro} is the rotational inertia of inner and outer rotor, respectively.

4   Simulation and Experimental Study

4.1   Model and Simulation of Variable Inductance Parameter

Assuming that the speed of IM is zero, the stator and inner rotor windings are at the rated excitation conditions of prototype. A load torque with 40 Nm is applied to the outer rotor. If the inductance parameters of EVT model are obtained by inquiring the 3D numerical values calculated by FEM. The other inputs are the same as above, then the simulation results are shown in Fig. 8.

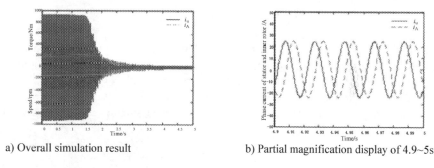

a) Overall simulation result   b) Partial magnification display of 4.9~5s

Fig. 8. Phase winding current waveform of the stator and inner rotor in the EVT with variable inductance parameters.

From the simulation results it can be seen that the EVT can keep stable operation finally. Both of the current (rms) of IM and OM are about 17.33 A, and the phase angle difference is 104.4°.

4.2   Verification of Bench Test

The EVT experimental test platform is built, and the excitations are the same as the simulation models. The load torque of EVT is 40 Nm, which provided by a drag motor. The voltage and current waveforms of inner rotor and stator are shown in Fig. 9.

In Fig. 9, u_A and u_u are the line voltage of the inner rotor and stator windings, i_A and i_u are the current of them. The phase currents rms of IM and OM are 14.8 A and 23.65 A respectively, which windings are triangle connection. The phase angle

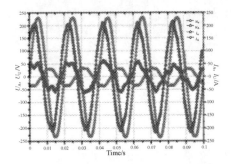

Fig. 9. Voltage and current waveforms of the inner rotor and stator

difference of IM and OM windings is about 152°, which is close to the simulation results of the variable parameters model. However, the current in the stator windings contains harmonic component obviously, which caused by the structure of EVT, i.e., the yoke thickness of outer rotor is too thin to the OM.

According to Fig. 7, the electromagnetic torque of the stator obtained, which shown in Eq. (10).

$$T_{\text{sro}} + T_{\text{sri}} = -(T_{\text{drive}} + T_{\text{load}}) \tag{10}$$

The load torque is −40 Nm, then changing the driven torque of the inner rotor (T_{drive}). The electromagnetic torque of the stator is recorded at different points to compare with the simulation results, which are shown in Table 1. In Table 1, the first row is the driven torque of the input shaft; the second row is the calculation of the stator's electromagnetic torque; and the third row is the simulation value of the stator's electromagnetic torque.

Table 1. Torque results comparison between the measured values and the simulation results.

T_{drive} (Nm)		20 ± 1	10 ± 1	0 ± 1	-10 ± 1	-20 ± 1
Torque of the stator	Calculation value	20 ± 2	30 ± 2	40 ± 2	50 ± 2	60 ± 2
$T_{\text{sro}} + T_{\text{sri}}$ (Nm)	Simulation value	20	32	37	52.5	63

In Table 1, "±" indicates the torque fluctuation range displayed by the torque measuring instrument. There is a certain deviation between the simulated torque values and the actual values according to the comparison between the measured value and the simulation result. However, it is generally consistent with each other, which further verifies the correctness of the decoupling mathematical model with variable inductance parameters.

5   Conclusion

The EVT is an electromechanical energy conversion device, which based on the principle of induction motor. The internal magnetic field of EVT is changing with the working state of IM and OM due to the structural characteristics. Therefore, the distribution of magnetic field and the influence on the inductance parameters of EVT are analyzed. The FEM simulation is used to obtain the 3D numerical table of the changing inductances of IM and OM under the different excitation currents and phase angle differences. The decoupled mathematical model is deduced based on the stator d-q axis coordinate system. However, the inductance matrix was no longer constant, which result from the larger change range of inductance parameters in the EVT. Decoupling simulation models based on the EVT are established. The inductance parameters with variable values that obtained by taking the numerical values into the models. From the simulation results, the properties of EVT with variable inductance parameters can obtain the desired result. Finally, the bench test of the prototype is utilized to verify the correctness of the variable parameters model.

References

1. Hoeijmakers, M.J., Ferreira, J.A.: The electric variable transmission. IEEE Trans. Ind. Appl. **42**(4), 1092–1100 (2006)
2. Miller, J.M.: Hybrid electric vehicle propulsion system architectures of the e-CVT type. IEEE Trans. Power Electron. **21**(3), 756–767 (2006)
3. Cui, S.M., Cheng, Y., Chan, C.C.: A basic study of electrical variable transmission and its application in hybrid electric vehicle. In: Proceedings of IEEE Vehicle Power Propulsion Conference, pp. 1–4 (2006)
4. Xu, L.: A new breed of electric machines-basic analysis and applications of dual mechanical port electric machines. In: Proceedings of 8th International Conference on Electric Machine System, pp. 24–31 (2005)
5. Cui, S.M., Huang, W.X., Cheng, Y., Ning, K.W., Chan, C.C.: Design and experimental research on induction machine based electrical variable transmission. In: Proceedings of IEEE VPPC 2007, Arlington, USA, pp. 231–235 (2007)
6. Kermani, S., Trigui, R., Delprat, S., Jeanneret, B., Guerera, T.M.: PHIL implementation of energy management optimization for a parallel HEV on a predefined route. IEEE Trans. Veh. Technol. **60**(3), 782–792 (2011)
7. Reinbold, V., Vinot, E., Gerbaud, L.: Global optimization of a parallel hybrid vehicle using optimal energy management. In: Proceedings of OIPE Workshop, Ghent, Belgium, pp. 44–45 (2012)

An Improved Dual Grey Wolf Optimization Algorithm for Unit Commitment Problem

Jian Liu[1] and Sanming Liu[2(✉)]

[1] Department of Electrical Engineering,
Shanghai Dianji University, Shanghai 201306, China
494019203@qq.com
[2] Department of Mathematics and Physics, Shanghai Dianji University,
Shanghai 201306, China
liusanmingxyxl@163.com

Abstract. An improved dual grey wolf optimization (GWO) algorithm with binary and dogmatic parts were proposed. The up and down state of units were optimized by binary grey wolf optimization (bGWO), and the exchange velocity was modified by adding two dynamical factors in random number producing. The GWO was used in units' load scheduling during the process of deciding up-down states and after the solution. One examples with 10 units including 24 period of time was simulated, the results showed the proposed algorithm improved convergence rate and accuracy of the solution.

Keywords: Unit commitment · GWO · bGWO · Dynamic weight

1 Introduction

The unit commitment (UC) is one of main problems in power system operation and planning. The basic objective of unit commitment is to schedule the generating unit to meet the load demand at minimum operating cost, while satisfying all equality and inequality constraints. This makes UC a large-scale, non-convex nonlinear mixed-integer programming. In past, many mathematical and different heuristic techniques were given, mainly includes priority list, dynamic programming, branch and bound and Lagrangian relaxation.

Lagrangian relaxation (LR) methodology is one of the conventional techniques, and it adopts Lagrange multiplier to deal with system constraints and modifies objective function with penalty terms [1, 2]. Its computation efficiency is mainly affected by the selection, modification of the multiplier, and also affected by the method of dealing with constraints. Some intelligent optimization algorithms are also used to solve UC problem, Genetic Algorithm(GA) [3], Ants Algorithm [4], Particle Swarm Optimization (PSO) [5] and Tabu Search [6]. These intelligent optimization algorithms are flexible for objective function and constraints, as for UC, they can get ideal suboptimal solutions.

Grey wolf optimization (GWO) [7] is a newly proposed heuristic algorithms which mimics the leadership hierarchy and hunting mechanism of grey wolves in nature. It defines alpha, beta, delta, and omega wolves to build leadership hierarchy in grey

© Springer Nature Singapore Pte Ltd. 2017
D. Yue et al. (Eds.): LSMS/ICSEE 2017, Part II, CCIS 762, pp. 156–163, 2017.
DOI: 10.1007/978-981-10-6373-2_16

wolves and implements search, encircle and attack to simulate the hunting steps. It shows quick convergence rate and precision than PSO, GA. Now it is widely used in engineering project.

Paper [8] adopts GWO in solving the optimal reactive power dispatch (ORPD) problems. The results of this research show that GWO is able to achieve less power loss and voltage deviation than those determined by other techniques. Paper [9] adopts GWO in solving combined economic emission dispatch problems and gets ideal results. As the endeavor of scholars all over the world, it is easy to find that the GWO still exists suboptimum and slow convergence rate problem.

Paper [10] proposes a new version of GWO to solve binary optimum problems and it is used to feature selection. Two approaches are introduced in this paper to perform binary version GWO. The results of benchmarked function show that the bGWO has better fitness than GA and PSO.

According to the predecessor's study, an improved dual grey wolf optimization algorithm for unit commitment problem is proposed in this paper. This paper adopts non-linear convergence factor strategy and dynamic weighting strategies to enhance the ability of GWO in convergence rate and global optimum searching. In order to ensure the population diversity in iteration, two modified factors are added to the bGWO. The GWO and bGWO cooperate in this paper to resolve the UC problem, bGWO optimizes the up and down state of units and GWO optimizes the dispatch of units. A system with 10 thermal units including 24 period of time was simulated, the results proved that the effectiveness of the modification of the algorithm.

2 UC Problem Formulation

2.1 Minimization of Fuel Cost

The generator cost curves are represented by quadratic functions and the total fuel cost can be expressed as follows [11]:

$$\min TC = \sum_{t=1}^{T} \sum_{i=1}^{N} [I_i(t) C_{it}(P_i(t)) + I_i(t)(I_i(t) - I_i(t-1))B_i(t)] \tag{1}$$

This paper neglect the cost of shut down generator. Where N is the number of generators; $I_i(t)$ represents the state of ith generator, 1 is up and 0 is down. $C_{it}(P_i(t))$ is the ith generator fuel cost at time t, can be defined as follows:

$$C_{it}(P_i(t)) = a_i + b_i P_i(t) + c_i P_i^2(t) \tag{2}$$

where a_i, b_i, c_i are the cost coefficients of the ith generator and P_i is the real power output of the ith generator. $B_i(t)$ is startup cost of the ith generator, can be defined as follows:

$$B_i(t) = \partial_{1i} + \partial_{2i}(1 - \exp(-\frac{T_i^{off}(t)}{\tau_i})) \tag{3}$$

where $\partial_{1i}, \partial_{2i}$ are the two coefficients, $T_i^{off}(t)$ is the continues down time of ith generator before time t, τ_i is the time coefficients.

2.2   Constraints

Generation Capacity Constraint. The power generated by each generator should lie between its minimum and maximum limit:

$$P_{Gi}^{min} \leq P_{Gi} \leq P_{Gi}^{max} \tag{4}$$

where P_{Gi}^{min} and P_{Gi}^{max} are the minimum and maximum power generated by the ith generator respectively.

Power Balance Constraint. The total electric power generation must cover the total electric power demand P_D. This is given by limit:

$$\sum_{i=1}^{N} I_i(t)P_i(t) - P_D = 0 \tag{5}$$

Spinning Reserve Constraints. The spinning reserve constraints should meet the grid's demand.

$$\sum_{i=1}^{N} I_i(t)P_{Gi}^{max}(t) \geq P_D(t) + R(t)$$
$$\sum_{i=1}^{N} I_i(t)P_{Gi}^{min}(t) \leq P_D(t) - R(t) \tag{6}$$

where $R(t)$ is the spinning reserve at time t.

The Minimum Up/Down Constraints. The spinning reserve constraints should meet the grid's demand.

$$[I_i(t) - I_i(t-1)][T_i^{off}(t) - T_{imin}^{off}(t)] \geq 0$$
$$[I_i(t-1) - I_i(t)][T_i^{on}(t) - T_{imin}^{on}(t)] \geq 0 \tag{7}$$

where $T_{imin}^{off}(t)$ and $T_{imin}^{on}(t)$ are the minimum down and up time constraints of ith generator respectively; $T_i^{on}(t)$ is the continues up time of ith generator before time t.

The Ramping Constraints.

$$P_{Gi}^{max}(t) \leq P_i(t-1) + r_i^{up}I_i(t-1) + S_i[I_i(t) - I_i(t-1)] + P_{Gi}^{max}[1 - I_i(t)]$$
$$P_{Gi}^{max}(t) \leq P_{Gi}^{max}(t)I_i(t+1) + D_i(I_i(t) - I_i(t+1)) \tag{8}$$
$$P_i(t-1) - P_{Gi}^{min}(t) \leq r_i^d I_i(t) + D_i(I_i(t-1) - I_i(t)) + P_{Gi}^{max}(1 - I_i(t-1))$$

where r_i^{up} and r_i^d are the start-up and shut-down ramp rate of ith generator respectively; S_i and D_i are the ith generator's start-up and shut-down ramp rate.

3 The Grey Wolf Optimization Algorithm

3.1 Dogmatic Grey Wolf Optimization

Social Hierarchy

Wolf alpha (α) is the leader with the highest ranking and responsible for decision making. Wolf beta (β) is the subordinate and help the alpha (α) in decision making. Wolf delta (δ) is the sub-subordinate wolf and with third ranking in the wolves. The lowest ranking grey wolf is omega (ω). The omega plays the role of scapegoat (Fig. 1).

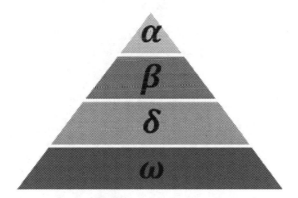

Fig. 1. Social hierarchy structure of wolf

In the mathematical model of the social hierarchy of wolves, alpha (α) is the fittest solution, the second and third best solutions are named beta (β) and delta (δ). Omega (ω) represents the candidate solutions.

Math Model
Encircling Prey

$$D = |C \cdot X_p^d(t) - X^d(t)|$$
$$X^d(t+1) = X_p^d(t) - A \cdot D \tag{9}$$

where A and C are coefficients, $X_p^d(t)$ is the position vector of the prey, and $X^d(t)$ indicates the position vector of a grey wolf. A and C are calculated as follows:

$$
\begin{aligned}
C &= 2 \cdot r_2 \\
a &= 2 - \frac{t}{t_{max}} \\
A &= 2a \cdot r_1 - a
\end{aligned}
\tag{10}
$$

where components of a is linearly decreased from 2 to 0 over the course of iterations and r_1, r_2 are random vectors in [0, 1].

Hunting

$$
\begin{aligned}
D_\alpha &= |C_1 \cdot X_\alpha(t) - X(t)| \\
D_\beta &= |C_2 \cdot X_\beta(t) - X(t)| \\
D_\delta &= |C_3 \cdot X_\delta(t) - X(t)|
\end{aligned}
\tag{11}
$$

$$
\begin{aligned}
X_1 &= X_\alpha - A_1 D_\alpha \\
X_2 &= X_\beta - A_2 D_\beta \\
X_3 &= X_\delta - A_3 D_\delta
\end{aligned}
\tag{12}
$$

$$
X(t+1) = (X_1 + X_2 + X_3)/3
\tag{13}
$$

where $X_\alpha(t), X_\beta(t), X_\delta(t)$ are the positions of alpha, beta, delta respectively. Equation (12) depicts the step of omega to alpha, beta and delta.

3.2   bGWO

The main updating equation as shown as follows:

$$
X_i^{t+1} = \begin{cases} 1 & if \quad sigmoid((x_1 + x_2 + x_3)/3) \geq rand \\ 0 & otherwise \end{cases}
\tag{14}
$$

where rand is a random number drawn from uniform distribution, X_i^{t+1} is the updated binary position in dimension d at iteration t, and $sigmoid(g)$ is defined as follows:

$$
sigmoid(g) = \frac{1}{1 + e^{-10(g-0.5)}}
\tag{15}
$$

3.3   Improved GWO

Non-Linear Convergence Factor Strategy

$$
a = 2 - 2 \cdot \left(\frac{t}{T_{max}}\right)^2 \cdot e^{\left(\frac{t}{T_{max}}\right)}
\tag{16}
$$

In dogmatic GWO, a decreases linearly from 2 to 0, but the convergence of the algorithm is not a linear function. So, a is modified as Eq. (16). Where t is the iteration number, and $T_{\max}$ is the max iteration number.

Dynamic Weighting Strategies. Alpha is not always an optimal point, in the iteration, the other wolves get close to the three wolves, this may result in local optimum. So Eq. (13) are modified as follows:

$$\omega_1 = \frac{|X_1|}{\sqrt{Q_1(X_1)^2 + Q_2(X_2)^2 + Q_3(X_3)^2}}$$
$$\omega_2 = \frac{|X_2|}{\sqrt{Q_1(X_1)^2 + Q_2(X_2)^2 + Q_3(X_3)^2}} \qquad (17)$$
$$\omega_3 = \frac{|X_3|}{\sqrt{Q_1(X_1)^2 + Q_2(X_2)^2 + Q_3(X_3)^2}}$$

$$Q_1 = \frac{|X_1|}{|X_1| + |X_2| + |X_3|}$$
$$Q_2 = \frac{|X_2|}{|X_1| + |X_2| + |X_3|} \qquad (18)$$
$$Q_3 = \frac{|X_3|}{|X_1| + |X_2| + |X_3|}$$

$$X(t+1) = \omega_1 X_1 + \omega_2 X_2 + \omega_3 X_3 \qquad (19)$$

Modified Factors to bGWO. In the updating Eq. (14), the random number rand is between 0 and 1, if rand approaches 1, X_i^{t+1} has high probability to be 0; respectively,

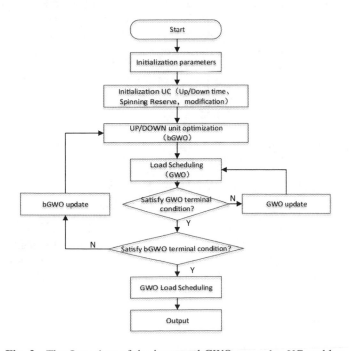

Fig. 2. The flow chart of the improved GWO to resolve UC problem

if rand approaches 0, X_i^{t+1} has high probability to be 1, this restricts the optimization direction. So in this paper, rand is restricted between $[\varphi_1, \varphi_2]$, where $0.1 \leq \varphi_1 \leq 0.4$ and $0.6 \leq \varphi_2 \leq 0.9$.

The steps of the GWO-bGWO for resolving UC (Fig. 2).

4 Results and Discussion

The proposed optimization algorithm is applied to a 10 unit systems to verify its effectiveness. The coefficient of loss matrix and data for 10- unit system has taken from [11]. The result of unit commitment is in Table 1. and the values of generator fuel cost is Table 2.

Table 1. The results of UC problem.

GNO.	Time																							
	1	2	3	4	5	6	7	8	9	10	11	12	13	14	15	16	17	18	19	20	21	22	23	24
1	1	1	1	1	1	1	1	1	1	1	1	1	1	1	1	1	1	1	1	1	1	1	1	1
2	1	1	1	1	1	1	1	1	1	1	1	1	1	1	1	1	1	1	1	1	1	1	1	1
3	1	1	1	1	1	1	1	1	1	1	1	1	1	1	1	1	1	1	1	1	1	1	1	1
4	1	1	1	1	1	1	1	1	1	1	1	1	0	0	0	0	0	0	1	1	1	1	1	1
5	1	1	1	1	1	1	1	1	1	0	0	0	0	0	0	0	0	0	0	0	1	1	1	1
6	1	1	1	1	1	0	0	0	0	0	0	0	0	0	0	0	0	0	0	0	0	1	1	1
7	0	0	0	0	0	0	0	0	0	0	0	0	0	0	0	0	0	0	0	0	0	0	0	0
8	0	0	0	0	0	0	0	0	0	0	0	0	0	0	0	0	0	0	0	0	0	0	0	0
9	0	0	0	0	0	0	0	0	0	0	0	0	0	0	0	0	0	0	0	0	0	0	0	0
10	0	0	0	0	0	0	0	0	0	0	0	0	0	0	0	0	0	0	0	0	0	0	0	0

Table 2. The compare with other techniques

Techniques	Cost	Time
LR [11]	81245.5	–
HPSO [12]	81118.3	33.2 s
GA [13]	79807	–
Modified PSO [14]	79665.8	14.3 s
This paper	79652.1	14.446 s

Compared with other techniques, the algorithm proposed in this paper can corresponding save fuel cost 2.00%, 1.84%, 0.19% from LR, HPSO, GA along with a better time running. It really costs a little longer than Modified PSO but with a better fitness.

5 Conclusion

In this work, the improved dual grey wolf optimization (GWO) algorithm has been successfully applied for solving unit commitment problem. The improved dual grey wolf optimization (GWO) algorithm has been compared to the GA, PSO and LR approach. The results show that the improved dual grey wolf optimization (GWO) algorithm has better convergence characteristics. The results show that the improved dual grey wolf optimization (GWO) is effective tool for handling UC. Numerical examples are considered which show that the proposed algorithm is efficient.

Acknowledgements. This work was financially supported by the Innovation Program of Shanghai Municipal Education Commission (Nos. 15ZZ106, 14YZ157), Shanghai Natural Science Foundation (Nos. 12ZR1411600, 14ZR1417200, 15ZR1417300), Climbing Peak Discipline Project of Shanghai Dianji University (No. 15DFXK01).

References

1. Muckstadt, J.A., Koenig, S.A.: An application of Lagrangian relaxation to scheduling in power-generation systems. J. Oper. Res. **25**(25), 387–403 (1977)
2. Bertsekas, D.P., Lauer, G.S., Sandell, N.R., et al.: Optimal short-term scheduling of large-scale power systems. In: IEEE Conference on Decision and Control Including the Symposium on Adaptive Processes. IEEE Xplore, pp. 432–443 (1982)
3. Chaohao, C., Yuanyu, C.: Optimization of unit commitment by genetic algorithm. J. Power Syst. Technol. **21**, 44–47 (1997)
4. Hao, J., Shi, L., Zhou, J.: An ant colony optimization algorithm with random perturbation behavior for unit commitment problem. J. Autom. Electr. Power Syst. **26**(23), 23–28 (2002)
5. Ting, T.O., Rao, M.V.C., Loo, C.K.: A novel approach for unit commitment problem via an effective hybrid particle swarm optimization. J. IEEE Trans. Power Syst. **21**(1), 411–418 (2006)
6. Victoire, T.A.A., Jeyakumar, A.E.: Unit commitment by a tabu-search-based hybrid-optimisation technique. IEE Proc. – Gener. Transm. Distrib. **152**(4), 563–574 (2005)
7. Mirjalili, S., Mirjalili, S.M., Lewis, A.: Grey Wolf optimizer. J. Adv. Eng. Softw. **69**(3), 46–61 (2014)
8. Sulaiman, M.H., Mustaffa, Z., Mohamed, M.R., et al.: Using the gray wolf optimizer for solving optimal reactive power dispatch problem. J. Appl. Soft Comput. **32**(C), 286–292 (2015)
9. Song, H.M., Sulaiman, M.H., Mohamed, M.R.: An application of Grey Wolf optimizer for solving combined economic emission dispatch problems. J. Int. Rev. Model. Simul. **7**(5), 838–844 (2014)
10. Emary, E., Zawbaa, H.M., Hassanien, A.E.: Binary grey wolf optimization approaches for feature selection. J. Neurocomput. **172**(C), 371–381 (2016)
11. Han, X., Liu, Z.: Optimal unit commitment considering units ramp-rate limits. J. Power Syst. Technol. **18**, 11–16 (1994)
12. Hu, J.S., Guo, C.X., Cao, Y.J.: Hybrid particle swarm optimization method for unit commitment problem. J. Proc. Csee **04**, 004 (2004)
13. Chaohao, C., Yuanyu, C.: Optimization of unit commitment by genetic algorithm. J. Power Syst. Technol. **21**, 44–47 (1997)
14. Zheng, L.I., Tan, W., Qin, J.: An improved dual particle swarm optimization algorithm for unit commitment problem. J. Proc. Csee **32**(25), 189–195 (2012)

A New Quantum-Behaved Particle Swarm Optimization with a Chaotic Operator

Zhenghua Wu[1], Dongmei Wu[1(✉)], Haidong Hu[2], Chuangye Wang[3], and Hao Gao[1]

[1] The College of Automation,
Nanjing University of Posts and Telecommunications, Nanjing, China
dongmei_wul@hotmail.com
[2] Beijing Institute of Control Engineering, Beijing, China
[3] State Grid Guzhen Electric Power Company, Bengbu, China

Abstract. Particle Swarm Optimization has attracted many researcher to do further improvement on many real world problems. The quantum-behaved PSO is tested as an effective improved PSO for getting preferable results on many problems. In this paper, we introduce a chaotic operator into QPSO for further enhancing its global and local searching abilities. The experiments results show that, compared with the other PSOs, our algorithm gets more efficient results. It could be applied in more complex real world problems in our future work.

Keywords: Particle swarm optimization · Quantum-behaved · Chaotic operator

1 Introduction

Optimization methods have been proven as an effective tool for solving many real world problems, such as pattern recognition, industrial manufacture, operational research, and other related fields [1]. They try to find a preferable results to an optimization problem within a reasonable time limit. An acceptable solution that satisfies the constraints and maximizes or minimizes a fitness (objective) function could be solved by an optimization algorithm. The type of a fitness function to optimize is a mathematics model of the solved problem. Recently, evolutionary algorithms (EAs), which is an important component of optimization methods, simulate the evolution of individuals in the nature via the operation of selection, mutation, and reproduction. This evolution is still guided by fitness function which indicates the achievements of the individuals during the evolution processing. Different from traditional optimization methods, EAs use a population of potential solutions, and their direction of evolution are guided by "fitness" information alone. In recent years, several EAs have been proposed for their population-based search strategy, such as Genetic Algorithm (GA) [2], Differential Algorithm (DE) [3], Particle Swarm Optimization (PSO) [4], etc.

In 1998, PSO, which adopts the concept of the emergent motion of swarm birds and fishes searching for food, has been presented by J. Kennedy and R.C. Eberhart. As an important component of Evolutionary Algorithm, the PSO algorithm use the concept of social behavior among individuals to explore a multidimensional solution space, where

© Springer Nature Singapore Pte Ltd. 2017
D. Yue et al. (Eds.): LSMS/ICSEE 2017, Part II, CCIS 762, pp. 164–170, 2017.
DOI: 10.1007/978-981-10-6373-2_17

each particle represents a potential solution at the intersection of all search dimensions. Recently, PSO has been proven as an effective searching algorithm for solving optimization problems in systems, such as power systems [5, 6], image processing [7, 8], fuzzy system control [9, 10], and others [11, 12].

Although PSO has been successfully applied into different real world problems, it still has some shortcomings. Its main drawback is premature phenomenon which dues to showing poor explore search ability especially in the last stage of iteration. Sun et al. [13] proposed a quantum behaved particle swarm optimization (QPSO) for enabling particles has more opportunities to search in global solution space and experimental results proved its effectiveness. Based on this algorithm, we further introduce a chaotic operator into QPSO to improving its global search ability.

This paper introduces PSO in Sect. 2, followed by presentation of the QPSO with a chaotic operator (CQPSO) and the details of its implementations in Sect. 3. The experimental studies of the proposed CQPSO have been presented in Sect. 4. Finally, Sect. 5 concludes the paper.

2 Particle Swarm Optimization and Its Quantum-Behaved Improvement

In PSO [4], the position and velocity vectors of the i th particle in the d-dimensional search space is denoted as $X_i = (x_{i1}, x_{i2}, \ldots, x_{id})$ and $V_i = (v_{i1}, v_{i2}, \ldots, v_{id})$, respectively. A favorable of particle means it gets a smaller fitness value for a minimum problem. The best position of each particle and the population are defined as $P_i = (p_{i1}, p_{i2}, \ldots, p_{id})$ and $P_g = (p_{g1}, p_{g2}, \ldots, p_{gd})$, respectively.

$$v_{id}(t+1) = wv_{id}(t) + c_1 r \, and_1 * (p_{pid} - x_{id}(t)) + c_2 r \, and_2 * (p_{gd} - x_{id}(t)) \tag{1}$$

$$x_{id}(t+1) = x_{id}(t) + v_{id}(t+1) \tag{2}$$

where c_1 and c_2 are two positive constants. $rand_1$ and $rand_2$ are two random values in [0, 1]. The variable w is called inertia weight which controls the convergence of particles.

The traditional PSO algorithm has been tested for showing poor global search ability especially on multimodel functions in the last iteration, which means it can't enable particles have enough velocity to jump out of a local optima. Sun et al. introduced a quantum theory into PSO and presented a quantum-behaved PSO algorithm. As particles in QPSO have chances to search anywhere during their iterations, it shows more power global search ability than PSO.

Through the Monte Carlo stochastic simulation to obtain the particle position equation:

$$x_i(t+1) = p_i(t) \pm \frac{L_i(t)}{2} \cdot \ln(\frac{1}{u}) \tag{3}$$

where, u is random numbers in the interval [0, 1].

For enabling each best position of a particle could contribute to the evolution of population, QPSO uses the concept of average best position *mbest*. Then the evolution of particle equations can be presented as follows:

$$L_i(t) = 2 * \beta \cdot |mbest - x_i(t)| \tag{4}$$

$$mbest = \frac{1}{M} \sum_{i=1}^{M} pbest_i \tag{5}$$

$$p_i = \varphi \times pbest_i + (1 - \varphi) \times gbest \tag{6}$$

$$x_i(t+1) = p_i(t) \pm \beta \cdot |mbest - x_i(t)| \cdot \ln(\frac{1}{u}) \tag{7}$$

where, $L_i(t)$ represents the feature length; the number of particles is denoted as M; β is defined as a contraction - expansion coefficient and linear decreases from 1 to 0.5 generally; φ is a random value in $[0, 1]$; t represents the number of the current iteration; $pbest_i$ represents the personal best position of particle; *gbest* represents the best position of the particles in the whole population.

3   Quantum-Behaved Particle Swarm with an Chaotic Operator (COQPSO)

For finding an effective method to enhance the exploration and maintain the convergence rate of QPSO, we proposed a new QPSO algorithm with a chaotic operator, which enables the proposed algorithm could find a promising optimal value in a short time.

Chaos is the highly unstable phenomenon of deterministic systems in finite phase space with exists in nonlinear system. It has been found as a common concept in different fields including computer science, control system and biology. Research focus on study the chaos on its behavior in dynamic systems. Its achievements highly depends on the initial numbers, an effect which is popularly referred to as the butterfly effect. Kolmogorov [13] proposed a family of dynamical systems on the circle as a simplified model for driven mechanical rotors (specifically, a free-spinning wheel weakly coupled by a spring to a motor). A simplified model of the phase-locked loop in electronics is also a circle map equation.

The circle map is given by iterating the map

$$\theta_{n+1} = \text{mod}(\theta_n + \Omega - (K/2 * pi) * sin(2 * pi * \theta_n), 1)$$

where θ is used as polar angle which values in $[0, 1]$. The coupling strength K and the driving phase Ω are the two important parameters of θ. As a model for phase-locked loops, Ω could be described as a driving frequency. As $K = 0$ and Ω irrational, the circle map is described as an irrational rotation.

For further making progress on the achievements of particles, we replace the μ operator in QPSO by using the circle map operator. For comparing the role of the two operators, we simulate their density distribution. From the 1000 trials given in Fig. 1, we easily find that the density distribution of circle chaos similar with that of quantum operator. But it has more chances to focus on a smaller region in [0, 2] and also could generate bigger values than quantum operator, which means it could search precisely and has more power ability to jump out of the local region.

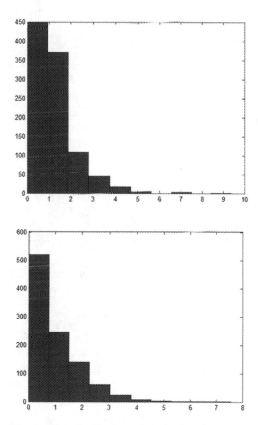

Fig. 1. The distribution of circle chaotic operator

4 Experimental Setting and Results from Benchmark Testing

For showing the merits of our proposed algorithm, seven of the well-known benchmarks used in [14] are employed to evaluate. The range of population initialization, the search arrange of these function, and the global optima are shown in Table 1, and they are tested on 10, 20 and 30 dimension separately.

The traditional PSO and QPSO algorithms are used for comparing with our algorithm. Since empirical experiments show that PSO does not need a large population size, we set the population size as 20 for all the compared algorithm, and each

Table 1. Benchmark test functions

F.	Formula	Range	X_{max}	f_{min}	X^*
f_1	$\sum_{i=1}^{n} x_i^2$	$[-100,100]$	100	0	0
f_2	$\sum_{i=1}^{n} i * x_i^2$	$[-100,100]$	100	0	0
f_3	$\sum_{i=1}^{n} (\lfloor x_i + 0.5 \rfloor)^2$	$[-100, 100]$	100	0	0
f_4	$\sum_{i=1}^{n} |x_i| + \prod_{i=1}^{n} |x_i|$	$[-10, 10]$	100	0	0
f_5	$\sum_{i=1}^{n} (x_i)^2 + \prod_{i=1}^{n} (x_i)^2$	$[-10, 10]$	10	0	0
f_6	$\sum_{i=1}^{n} \max |x_i|$	$[-100, 100]$	100	0	0
f_7	$\sum_{i=1}^{n} \left(x_i^2 - 10\cos(2\pi x_i) + 10 \right)$	$[-5.12, 5.12]$	5.12	0	0
f_8	$-20\exp\left(-0.2\sqrt{\frac{1}{n}\sum_{i=1}^{n} x_i^2}\right) - \exp\left(\frac{1}{n}\sum_{i=1}^{n} \cos 2\pi x_i\right) + 20 + e$	$[-32, 32]$	100	0	0
f_9	$\pi/n\{10\sin^2(\pi y_1) + \sum_{i=1}^{n-1} (y_i - 1)^2 * [1 + 10\sin^2(\pi y_{i+1})] + (y_n - 1)^2\}$	$[-50,50]$	50	0	0
f_{10}	$0.1\{\sin^2(3\pi x_1) + \sum_{i=1}^{n-1} (x_i - 1)^2 * [1 + \sin^2(\pi x_{i+1})] + (x_n - 1)^2[1 + \sin^2(2\pi x_n)]\}$	$[-50,50]$	50	0	0

algorithm is tested by 50 times for eliminate the influence of random seed in MATLAB. The maximum iteration are set as 100*dimension.

The results for the 7 benchmark functions show the merits of the COQPSO. For the unimodal functions, it is easily to find our algorithm performs the best achievements among the compared algorithm. The convergence rate of comparison algorithms is shown on Fig. 2 also testifies this conclusion. The main reason is that our proposed circle chaotic operator enables particles to not only have the chances to search nearby the leading point but also generate some relative large values to search regions far from the point. Furthermore, the leading point defined by the pbest and gbest also helps the particles to exploit in a small valuable region, which should enable particle to get precise results.

As the results shown in Table 2, our proposed algorithm also gets superior or even equal achievements on multimodal functions. This is due to our proposed circle chaotic operator has more chances to generate relative large values for making particles to explore a un-explore solution space, which enhances their global search abilities. Very similar results to the previous ones are obtained despite the large difference in the dimensionality of functions. COQPSO still outperforms the compared algorithm even when the dimension is low.

Table 2. The comparison between different algorithms on the benchmark function (mean value/standard deviation)

Alg.	f_1		f_2		f_3		f_4	
	Dim = 20	30	20	30	20	30	20	30
	G = 2000	4000	2000	4000	2000	4000	2000	4000
PSO	2.5E−17	3.9E−14	2.6E−16	2.1E−13	0	0.1	3.9E−10	9.5E−5
	(4.6E−17)	(3.6E−14)	(2.9E−16)	(3.8E−13)	(0)	(0)	(6.8E−10)	(2.7E−4)
QPSO	8.2E−29	1.4E−21	9.5E−28	2.5E−19	0	0	4.5E−16	9.5E−14
	(1.6E−28)	(2E−21)	(2.7E−27)	(4.6E−19)	(0)	(0)	(1.3E−15)	(5.7E−13)
COQPSO	**1.6E−118**	1.8E−134	2.6E−117	**2.7E−134**	0	0	3.9E−70	1.4E−80
	(3E−118)	(2.6E−134)	(2.7E−117)	**(3.6E−134)**	(0)	(0)	(9.4E−69)	(1.7E−80)

Alg.	f_5		f_6		f_7		f_8	
	Dim = 20	30	20	30	20	30	20	30
	G = 2000	4000	2000	4000	2000	4000	2000	4000
PSO	1E−16	4.1E−10	0.67	6.78	23.79	46.134	2.1E−9	0.1969
	(1.7E−16)	(8.6E−10)	(0.544)	(2.58)	(7.79)	(9.74)	(1.46E−9)	(0.402)
QPSO	0.0052	3.5E−4	9.4E−4	0.103	16.53	26.41	0.02	2.77E−11
	(0.016)	(8.8E−4)	(8.1E−4)	(0.07)	(16.36)	(3.41)	(0.015)	(4.5E−11)
COQPSO	**4.9E−105**	5.5E−80	1E−36	**5.2E−35**	0	0	2.6E−15	2.7E−15
	(1.5E-104)	(1.6E−79)	(1.5E−36)	**(5E−35)**	(0)	(0)	(3.9E−31)	(3.9E−31)

Alg.	f_9		f_{10}	
	Dim = 20	30	20	30
	G = 2000	4000	2000	4000
PSO	0.0156	0.197	96.93	423.58
	(0.047)	(0.52)	(132.3)	(229.04)
QPSO	1.88E−24	0.586	4.24E−12	30.62
	(5.6E−24)	(1.07)	(1.27E−11)	(109.62)
COQPSO	1.9E−31	0.0014	3.45E−15	**17.331**
	(3.4E−30)	(0.087)	(5.9E−15)	**(1.899)**

5 Conclusion

In this paper, a novel quantum-behaved particle swarm optimization with a circle chaotic operator is presented for designing a promising PSO variant. Our main objective is to further enhance the achievements of PSO. In the proposed algorithm, the circle chaotic operator is used to not only explore the unreached search space but also exploit the potential solution. The application of COQPSO should be further expanded in our future work.

Acknowledgments. The authors acknowledge support from the National Nature Science Foundation of China (Nos. 61571236, 61533010, 61602255 and 61320106008), the Macau Science and Technology Fund (FDCT 093/2014/A2, 008/2013/A1), the Research Committee of University of Macau (MYRG2015-00011-FST, MYRG2015-00012-FST).

References

1. Deb, K.: Optimization for Engineering Design: Algorithms and Examples. Prentice-Hall, New Delhi (1995)
2. Mitchell, M.: An Introduction to Genetic Algorithms. MIT Press, Cambridge (1996)
3. Storn, R., Price, K.: Differential evolution-a simple and efficient heuristic for global optimization over continuous spaces. J. Glob. Optim. **11**(4), 341–359 (1997)
4. Kennedy, J., Eberhart, R.C.: Particle swarm optimization. In: Proceeding IEEE International Conference on Neural Network, pp. 1942–1948. IEEE Press, New York (1995)
5. Sun, J., Palade, V., Wu, X.J., Fang, W.: Solving the power economic dispatch problem with generator constraints by random drift particle swarm optimization. IEEE Trans. Ind. Inform. **10**, 222–232 (2014). IEEE Press, New York
6. Gao, H., Pun, C.M., Kwong, S.: An efficient image segmentation method based on a hybrid particle swarm algorithm with learning strategy. Inf. Sci. **369**, 500–521 (2016). Elsevier Press, Holland
7. Li, Y.Y., Jiao, L.C., Shang, R.H., Stolkin, R.: Dynamic-context cooperative quantum-behaved particle swarm optimization based on multilevel thresholding applied to medical image segmentation. Inf. Sci. **294**, 408–422 (2015). Elsevier Press, Holland
8. Ding, C., Choi, J., Tao, D., Davis, L.: Multi-directional multi-level dual-cross patterns for robust face recognition. IEEE Trans. Pattern Anal. Mach. Intell. **38**, 518–531 (2015). IEEE Press, New York
9. Pehlivanoglu, Y.V.: A new particle swarm optimization method enhanced with a periodic mutation strategy and neural networks. IEEE Trans. Evol. Comput. **17**, 436–452 (2013). IEEE Press, New York
10. Chan, K.Y., Dillon, T.S., Kwong, C.K.: Modeling of a liquid epoxy molding process using a particle swarm optimization-base fuzzy regression approach. IEEE Trans. Ind. Inform. **7**, 148–158 (2011). IEEE Press, New York
11. Shen, K., Zhao, D., Mei, J., Tolbert, L.M.: Elimination of harmonics in a modular multilevel convert using particle swarm optimization-based staircase modulation strategy. IEEE Trans. Ind. Electron. **61**, 5311–5322 (2014). IEEE Press, New York
12. Sun, J., Feng, B., Xu, W.B.: Particle swarm optimization with particle having quantum behavior. In: IEEE Congress on Evolutionary Computation, pp. 325–331. IEEE Press, New York (1995)
13. Kolmogorov, A.N.: A new metric invariant of transient dynamical systems. Dok. Akad. Nauk SSSR, vol. 119, p. 861. Russian Press (1958)
14. Yao, X., Liu, Y.: Evolutionary programming made faster. IEEE Trans. Evol. Comput. **3**, 82–102 (1999). IEEE Press, New York

A Method of Ridge-NNG-Based Multivariate Fault Isolation in Presentence of Collinearity

Yimin Guo[1], Jianguo Wang[1(✉)], Banghua Yang[1], Shiwei Ma[1],
Minrui Fei[1], Yao Yuan[2], and Chen Tao[3]

[1] Shanghai Key Lab of Power Station Automation Technology,
School of Mechatronical Engineering and Automation,
Shanghai University, Shanghai 200072, China
jgwang@shu.edu.cn, yyao@mx.nthu.edu.tw
[2] Department of Chemical Engineering, National Tsing-Hua University,
Hsin-Chu 30013, Taiwan
[3] Department of Chemical and Process Engineering,
University of Surrey, Guildford GU2 7XH, UK

Abstract. Multivariate fault isolation is a critical step for monitoring industrial chemical and biological processes. For some complex cases with strong correlation variables which commonly exist in the industry process, conventional methods may perform poorly. Therefore, to further improve the fault prediction accuracy, a fault isolation method based on the ridge nonnegative garrote variable selection algorithm (R-NNG) was proposed in this dissertation, it transformed the multivariate fault isolation problem into a variable selection problem in discriminant analysis, which is proven to be capable for handling strongly correlated variables by the application to the benchmark Tennessee Eastman (TE) process.

Keywords: Fault isolation · Variable selection · Ridge nonnegative garrote · Multicollinearity · TE process

1 Introduction

In the continuous production process of chemical industry, the production system in the long term operation will inevitably occur a variety of failures, affecting the quality of production, and even cause significant economic losses, so theoretical fault monitoring and isolation has attracted great deal of attention in academic realm. As discussed in [1], the goal of fault detection is to recognize process exception immediately when it occurred, and the aim of fault isolation is to find the procedure variable that contributes to the failure detection biggest.

In the industrial chemical and biological processes, contribution plots [2] have been widely used to isolate faulty variables, it can make judgment to the status of each process variable based on the contribution to the detection of indicators and the pre-set control constraints. However, this approach may suffers from faulty variables the influence of faulty variables on the contributions of normal variables, leading to mislead isolation results [3].

© Springer Nature Singapore Pte Ltd. 2017
D. Yue et al. (Eds.): LSMS/ICSEE 2017, Part II, CCIS 762, pp. 171–180, 2017.
DOI: 10.1007/978-981-10-6373-2_18

Reconstruction-based method [4] was proposed by Dunia is also widely used in MSPM [5], which isolates faulty variables by minimizing the rebuild detection of indicators along determinate fault directions, it is assumed that all the potential fault directions are known which is almost impossible in practice. A method was proposed in [6] for extracting the fault directions from historical fault data, which relaxes the requirement for reconstruction. However, historic failure data are often inadequate in real industry.

In order to eliminate the shortcoming of contribution plots and the conventional reconstruction-based methods, the fault isolation method based on the nonnegative garrote (NNG) [7] and LASSO [8] are proposed, which transform multivariate fault isolation problem into a variable selection problem. The proposed method which sorts the multivariate according to its importance on the detected fault rather than give a group of suggested faulty variables according to the improper control limits, which can contributes to the next root-cause diagnosis step after fault isolation, but also to avoid the smearing effect [3].

However, the NNG-based isolation method may perform poorly when predictive variables are highly correlated. To further improve the fault prediction accuracy, R-NNG [9–11] is adopted for multivariate fault isolation, which can further revise the NNG-based isolation method by use the ridge regression instead of the OLS estimator as the initial estimate. So the Ridge-based-on the NNG model can be used to describe the multivariate fault isolation problem

2   Multicollinearity

In the classical hypothesis of the multivariate linear regression model, one of the most important assumptions is the variables x_1, x_2, ..., x_k are irrelevant, that is to say, there is no linear relationship among them. If there are some constants c_0, c_1, ...,c_p (p > 2), such that the linear equation

$$c_1 x_1 + c_2 x_2 + \ldots\ldots + c_p x_p = c_0 \tag{1}$$

The data is approximately established, which means that at least one variable like x_k can be determined by other variables

$$x_k \cong \left(c_0 + \sum_{j \neq k} c_j x_j \right) / c_k \tag{2}$$

There is a linear relationship among the argument x_1, x_2, ...x_p, that is to say, there are multiple variables in the model that are collinear.

3   Definition of Ridge Regression Estimation

3.1   Ordinary Least Squares Method

The multiple regression equation is written in the form of a matrix:

$$Y = X\beta + \varepsilon \tag{3}$$

The regression coefficient vector β can be obtained by minimizing the residual sum of squares (RSS). The RSS of β is

$$RSS(\beta) = (y - X\beta)^{\mathrm{T}}(y - X\beta) \tag{4}$$

If $(X^T X)^{-1}$ is present, the least squares estimate of β is:

$$\hat{\beta} = (X'X)^{-1}(X'X) \tag{5}$$

When the jth argument is collinear with other independent variables

$$\mathrm{var}(\hat{\beta}_j) = \sigma^2 \left(\frac{1}{1 - R_j^2}\right)\left(\frac{1}{X_j X_j}\right) \tag{6}$$

where R_j^2 is the square of the complex correlation coefficient, $\mathrm{VIF}_j = 1/(1 - R_j^2)$ is the variance expansion factor or variance expansion factor of the independent variable x_j.

When the collinearity is generated, the variance of the coefficient estimation of the explanatory variables in the model is typically increased, so that the t statistic of each variable is reduced, so that some important explanatory variables become insignificant. When the model has multiple collinearity, the t-test and the F-test fail, the prediction will fail, so the result is meaningless.

3.2 Ridge Regression

When there is multiple collinearity among the independent variables, i.e. $|X^T X| \approx 0$, it is assumed that a positive matrix kI ($k > 0$, I is a unit matrix) is added to $X^T X$. The estimated amount of ridge regression is

$$\hat{\beta}_R = (X'X + kI)^{-1}X'Y \tag{7}$$

Obviously, when $k = 0$, the estimation of the ridge regression is the least squares estimate. When $k \to \infty$, the estimate of the ridge regression tends to 0, so k should not be too large.

4 Motivation

In this section, we transform the multivariate fault isolation problem into a variable selection problem in discriminant analysis. Therefore, the problem of fault isolation is equivalent to a classification problem, the whole data set can be divided to 2 parts: the normal data and the detected faulty data. FDA [12] is one of the most popular classification techniques. Assume that a set of d-dimensional samples $\Xi = \Xi_1 \cup \Xi_2 = \{X_1, \ldots X_n\}$ consists of 2 parts of samples $\Xi_1 = \left\{X_1^1, \ldots, X_{n_1}^1\right\}$ and $\Xi_2 =$

$\left\{X_1^1, \ldots, X_{n_2}^1\right\}$, n, n_1 and n_2 are the numbers of observations in Ξ, Ξ_1 and Ξ_2 respectively, and $n = n_1 + n_2$. The aim of FDA is to acquire a projection vector that maximizes group means and minimizes the variance between two groups. In general, it can be realize by solving optimizing problem. To connect least squares regression with FDA, Define a predictor matrix x as

$$x = \begin{bmatrix} 1_1 & X_1 \\ -1_2 & -X_2 \end{bmatrix} \qquad (8)$$

where 1_i is a column vector containing n_i ones, and X_i is a $n_i - by - d$ matrix whose rows are the samples belonging to Ξ_i. A predictor matrix is defined as

$$y = \begin{bmatrix} \frac{n}{n_1} l_1 \\ \frac{n}{n_2} l_2 \end{bmatrix} \qquad (9)$$

where the constants n/n_i compensate the influence of the unbalanced sample sizes. For a least squares regression problem $X\beta = y$, the regression coefficient vector β can be gotten by minimizing the residual sum of squares (RSS). The objective function is formulated as

$$\min_{\beta}(y - X\beta)^T(y - X\beta) \qquad (10)$$

Denote $\beta = \begin{bmatrix} W_0 \\ \omega \end{bmatrix}$, where W_0 is the coefficient corresponding to the leading column in X and the vector ω is the residual coefficients. In [13], it is be proved that is the direction vector of FDA searches. That is to say, the solution of FDA is the same as that of the least squares regression problem.

5 R-NNG-Based Multivariate Fault Isolation

In recent years, the method of nonnegative garrote (NNG) is regarded as a highly successful technique which is used to simultaneously address estimation and variable selection. It can shrinks the OLS estimators directly through multiplying it by some constriction factors, and the constriction factors can be gotten by the penalized least-squares method. It gives a natural penalty based on the expression of degree of freedom.

The R-NNG-based multivariate fault isolation can be considered as a two-step fault isolation method. In the first step, ordinary least squares procedure is used to acquire a group of regression coefficients for each variable. Assumed that a set of observation $\{X, y\}$ is given and $X \in R^{n \times p_x}$ is the input matrix, the column of which signifies each measured candidate variable. $y \in R^{n \times 1}$ is the corresponding variable of response value. If desired, X and y may be normalized. $\hat{\beta} \in \mathcal{R}^{p_x \times 1}$ is a set of the ordinary least square estimates which is the coefficients of the following linear model

$$Y = X\beta + \varepsilon \tag{11}$$

The second step is the process of the corresponding coefficients shrunken with s decreasing from the amount of variables to zero:

$$J = \min_c \left\| y - X\hat{\beta}. * c \right\|^2 \text{ subject.to } c_j \geq 0, \sum_{j=1}^{p_x} c_j \leq s \tag{12}$$

In (12), s is a tuning parameter, the non-negative garrote is tightened with s decreasing. Therefore a smaller s usually lead to the fewer non-zero regression coefficients, while a larger s results in the more non-zero regression coefficients. And s is limited as: $s_0 = 0 < s_1 < \ldots\ldots < s_k = p_k$.

We use the ridge regression instead of the ordinary least squares as the initial estimate in defining the NG estimate. Accordingly, we define the ridge estimate of the regression coefficient:

$$\hat{\beta}_R = (X'X + sI_p)^{-1}X'Y \tag{13}$$

To make this method more simplified, using u_1 which get after one-step iteration as the final shrinking factor vector.

Based on R-NNG variable selection algorithm, the procedure to isolate faults can be developed as follows:

1. When a fault is detected, the operating process data related to the fault are stored in Ξ_2, while the historical normal process data are saved in Ξ_1.and then the data should be normalized.
2. Bulid the predictor matrix X and the response vector y according to the formula (8) and (9) mentioned above.
3. Start with $k = 0$.
4. Solve the penalized optimal problem described in (12) to get the active set.
5. Update $k = k + 1$ and return to step 4, until $s_k = p_x$.

When the regression coefficient of a variable turns into nonzero value, the variable enter the active set. The relationship between the process variable and the detected fault can be obtained from the order in which enter the valid set. The sooner a variable enters the active set, the greater the contribution to the fault. Operators can find out the root cause of the detected fault based on the information.

6 Case Study

In this section, The TE process [13] was used as the research object to illustrate the effectiveness of the proposed method, it was created by Eastman Chemicals, which aims to provide an actual industrial process for assessing process control and monitoring methods. The process is based on a real industrial project, it has been widely used to test process control strategies and MSPM methods [14]. A schematic view of the TE process is shown in Fig. 1. It consists of 5 main units: reactor, condenser, separator, tripper, and compressor, respectively. The gaseous components A, C, D and E and the inert component B are the reactants, which are fed to the reactor to product the liquid products G and H. The product of the reactor is cooled by a condenser and then fed to a vapor/liquid separator. The steam from the separator is recirculated into the reactor through a compressor. To prevent the accumulation of inert components and reaction by-products during the process, a portion of the recycle stream must be discharged. The condensing component (stream 10) from the separator is pumped to the stripper. Stream 4 is used for the residual reactants in stripping stream 10, which are bound to the recycle stream through stream 5. The products G and H from the bottom of the stripper are sent to the downstream process, which is mainly drained from the system in the form of a gas in a vapor-liquid separator.

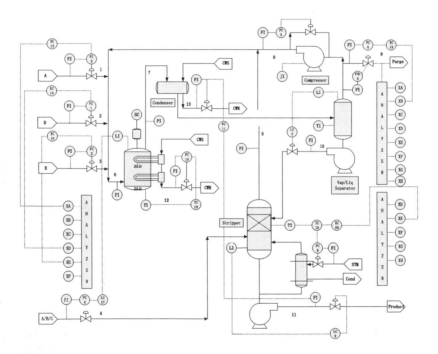

Fig. 1. The diagram of TE process

There are 41 measurement variables and 12 control variables are recorded in the data set, which are measured from historical normal program operation and different kinds of faulty operations. In each fault data set, the exceptional event is sparked after the 160th sampling interval. To illustrate the effectiveness of the proposed method, the isolation results of the fault by different method are compared in below.

In this dissertation, Fault 1 is used to illustrate the Superiority of the method of the R-NGG-based on fault isolation. Fault 1 is caused by a step change in the A/C feed ratio in Stream4, after the occurrence of such fault, the amount of A in the recycle stream was directly influenced and increased significantly. i.e. Stream5. And the ingredients of A in Stream6 was also reduced. Thus, the feedback control system reacted by adding an operating variable of the feed stream X_{44} to keep the ingredients of A in the flow 6 constant. The A feed in Stream 1, X_1, which is strongly related to X_{44} was also increased. The level of the reactor was increased due to the increase of the A

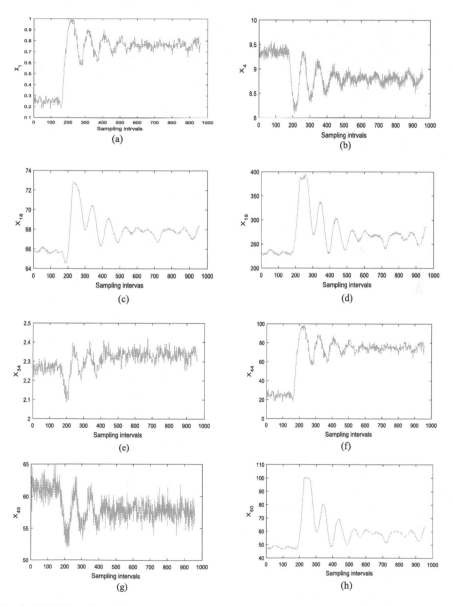

Fig. 2. Variable trajectories for Fault 2: (a) X_1, (b) X_4, (c) X_{18}, (d) X_{19}, (e) X_{34}, (f) X_{44}, (g) X_{45}, (h) X_{50}.

feed. As a result, the valve switch for controlling the total feed stream of flow 4, X_{45} is then reduced by the controller, which further affects the feed rate of stream 4, i.e. X_4. Since the C and E equal-molar reaction, the ingredients of E in the product streams (flow 11) was changed by the variations of C composition in the reactor feed streams. In order to adjust the ingredients of E, regulating steam valve X_{50} to make the extra ingredients E evaporation, leading to more steam flow (X_{19}) and higher stripper temperature (X_{18}). As a side effect, a by-product of F (X_{34}) also increased in the steam 9. Figure 2 shows the related variables trajectory.

To illustrate the validity of the selected method, compare it to the method of LASSO and NNG based on the fault isolation. The fault isolation results are shown in Figs. 3, 4 and 5, respectively, which is achieved based on 25 observations collected between the 936th and the 960th sampling points.

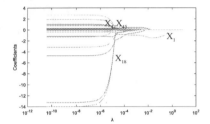

Fig. 3. LASSO-based isolation result

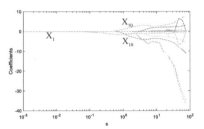

Fig. 4. NNG-based isolation result

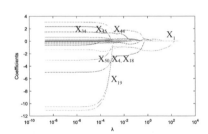

Fig. 5. Ridge-NNG-based isolation result

For LASSO, the sequence of the variables into the active set is $\Gamma(\lambda)$ {X_1, X_{18}, X_4, X_{45}......}. For NNG, the order is {X_1, X_{18}, X_{50}, ...}. Obviously, not all the faulty variables were revealed, although their behavior is abnormal. The reason is the strong correlations among process variables. E.g. X_{50} and X_{19} have strong correlation with X_{18}, while X_{44} is highly correlated to X_1.

The method of R-NNG based on the multivariate fault isolation is more suited to such situation. The variable sequence of entering the active set is{X_1, X_{44}, X_{19}, (X_{50}, X_{18}, X_4), X_{45}, X_{34}......}, which is more consistent with the above discussions on the mechanism of the fault. Such result as the superiority of R-NGG in dealing with highly relevant variables.

7 Conclusion

Multivariable fault isolation is a key step to find out the cause of the malfunction. In the dissertation, the task of fault isolation is converted to a variable selection problem In discriminant analysis, and solved by penalized regression techniques. The commonly used methods in such problem are NNG, LASSO, However, both of which may perform poorly when predictive variables are highly correlated. To solve the problem, this dissertation proposes R-NNG-based method for fault isolation, it use the ridge regression instead of the ordinary least squares as the initial estimate in defining the NG estimate. Which is proven to be capable for handling strongly correlated variables.

References

1. Zhao, C., Wang, W.: Efficient faulty variable selection and parsimonious reconstruction modelling for fault isolation. J. Process Control **38**, 31–41 (2016)
2. Westerhuis, J., Gurden, S., Smilde, A.: Generalized contribution plots in multivariate statistical process monitoring. Chemom. Intell. Lab. Syst. **51**, 95–114 (2000)
3. Liu, J., Wong, D.S.H., Chen, D.-S.: Bayesian filtering of the smearing effect: fault isolation in chemical process monitoring. J. Process Control **24**, 1–21 (2014)
4. Dunia, R., Qin, S.: Subspace approach to multidimensional fault identification and reconstruction. AIChE J. **44**, 1813–1831 (1998)
5. Qin, S.J.: Statistical process monitoring: basics and beyond. J. Chemom. **17**, 480–502 (2003)
6. Yue, H.H., Qin, S.J.: Reconstruction-based fault identification using a combined index. Ind. Eng. Chem. Res. **40**, 4403–4414 (2001)
7. Breiman, L.: Better subset regression using the nonnegative garrote. Technometrics **37**(4), 373–384 (1995)
8. Efron, B., Hastie, T., Johnstone, I., Tibshirani, R.: Least angle regression. Ann. Statist. **32**(2), 407–499 (2004)
9. Oh, Y.S., Mo, K.J., Yoon, E.S., Yoon, J.H.: Fault diagnosis based on weighted symptom tree and pattern matching. Ind. Eng. Chem. Res. **36**, 2672–2678 (1997)
10. Chu, Y., Qin, S., Han, C.: Fault detection and operation mode identification based on pattern classification with variable selection. Ind. Eng. Chem. Res. **43**, 1701–1710 (2004)
11. Musulin, E., Yélamos, I., Puigjaner, L.: Integration of principal component analysis and fuzzy logic systems for comprehensive process fault detection and diagnosis. Ind. Eng. Chem. Res. **45**, 1739–1750 (2006)
12. Fisher, R.A.: The use of multiple measurements in taxonomic problems. Ann. Eugenics **7**, 179–188 (1936)
13. Downs, J.J., Vogel, E.F.: A plant-wide industrial process control problem. Comput. Chem. Eng. **17**, 245–255 (1993)
14. Kuang, T.H., Yan, Z., Yao, Y.: Multivariate fault isolation via variable selection in discriminant analysis. J. Process Control **35**, 30–40 (2015)
15. Kariwala, V., Odiowei, P.E., Cao, Y., Chen, T.: A branch and bound method for isolation of faulty variables through missing variable analysis. J. Process Control **20**, 1198–1206 (2010)
16. He, B., Yang, X., Chen, T., Zhang, J.: Reconstruction-based multivariate contribution analysis for fault isolation: a branch and bound approach. J. Process Control **22**, 1228–1236 (2012)

17. Zou, H., Hastie, T.: Regularization and variable selection via the elastic net. J. R. Stat. Soc. Ser. B (Stat. Methodol.) **67**, 301–320 (2005)
18. Duda, R.O., Hart, P.E., Stork, D.G.: Pattern Classification, 2nd edn. Wiley, New York (2012)
19. Downs, J., Vogel, E.: A plant-wide industrial process control problem. Comput. Chem. Eng. **17**, 245–255 (1993)
20. Chiang, L.H., Kotanchek, M.E., Kordon, A.K.: Fault diagnosis based on Fisher discriminant analysis and support vector machines. Comput. Chem. Eng. **28**, 1389–1401 (2004)
21. Tibshirani, R.: Regression shrinkage and selection via the lasso. J. R. Stat. Soc. Ser. B (Methodol.), 267–288(1996)
22. Zou, H., Hastie, T.: Regularization and variable selection via the elastic net. J. R. Stat. Soc. Ser. B (Stat. Methodol.) **67**, 301–320 (2005)
23. Ricker, L.: Decentralized control of the Tennessee Eastman challenge process. J. Process Control **6**, 205–221 (1996)
24. Yoon, S., MacGregor, J.F.: Fault diagnosis with multivariate statistical models. Part I: using steady state fault signatures. J. Process Control **11**, 387–400 (2001)

Improved Artificial Weed Colonization Based Multi-objective Optimization Algorithm

Ruochen Liu[1(✉)], Ruinan Wang[1], Manman He[2], and Xiao Wang[1]

[1] Key Laboratory of Intelligent Perception and Image Understanding of Ministry of Education, Xidian University, Xi'an 710071, China
ruochenliu@xidian.edu.cn
[2] School of Computer, Xi'an Shi You University, Xi'an 710065, China

Abstract. Nondominated Neighbor Immune Algorithm (NNIA) is a Representative algorithm for multi-objective problems (MOPs). However, for some test problems, the diversity or convergence of NNIA cannot always keep very well. In order to avoid this phenomenon as well as not to increase the number of function evaluations as far as possible, a modified Invasive Weed Optimization (IWO) operator is introduced into NNIA and we proposed an improved NNIA for MOPs, denoted as NNIAIWO. There are three modifications for basic IWO. Firstly, each parent weed generates two weeds called associated parent weeds which do not join in the evaluation but produce new seeds; Secondly, these new seeds generated by the associated parent weeds distribute obey Cauchy distribution near them; Thirdly an oscillator factor is adopted in the calculation of the standard deviation during the iteration process. Fifteen benchmark problems are used to validate the performance of the proposed algorithm. Experimental results shows that NNIAIWO can obtain improved performance on some test problems, meanwhile the numbers of function evaluation do not increase. And for five complex unconstrained MOPs, namely UF, NNIAIWO also presents a better performance than NNIA.

Keywords: Multi-objective optimization · NNIA · IWO operator · MOEA/D · UF

1 Introduction

Optimization is an important problem in scientific research and engineering practice, which can be divided into single objective optimization and multi-objective optimization in the view of the number of objectives to be optimized. It is well-known that many real-world search and optimization problems are naturally posed as multi-objective optimization. Multi-objective optimization aims to optimize two or more conflicting objectives simultaneously, that means it cannot find one single best solution. Tremendous multi-objective optimization evolutionary algorithms (EMOAs) have been introduced [1–5].

NNIA is a typical multi-objective algorithm based on artificial immune system (AIS). The techniques of NNIA mainly include: the selection of nondominated neighbor technique, proportional cloning based on the crowding distance and the operation of

© Springer Nature Singapore Pte Ltd. 2017
D. Yue et al. (Eds.): LSMS/ICSEE 2017, Part II, CCIS 762, pp. 181–190, 2017.
DOI: 10.1007/978-981-10-6373-2_19

recombination and hypermutation. Although NNIA is an efficient algorithm for MOPs, the diversity of the solutions for some test problems is not stable or it tend to converge to local optimal Pareto solutions when the nondominated solutions selected as the active antibodies for cloning are very few. For the above, we introduced a new operator to improve NNIA so as to keep the diversity and avoid premature phenomenon as far as possible at the same time. The new operator is based on invasive weed optimization (IWO) algorithm [6]. And one aspect of IWO is its searching scope gradually changed during the iteration of the algorithm. With the increase of the iteration, the searching scope is transformed from the global search to local search, since the capability of the original IWO operator is limited. In this paper, we make some modifications in order to expand its search capability and keep the local search ability.

The remainder of this paper is organized as follows: Sect. 2 gives the background knowledge; Sect. 3 describes the modified IWO operator and the proposed algorithm; Sect. 4 presents the experimental results and analysis; Sect. 5 makes a conclusion and gives the future work for the next step.

2 Background Knowledge

2.1 NNIA

In NNIA [7], individuals adopt real-coded scheme, and the initial memory population is an empty set and the memory population is the external population to store the nondomianted individuals. The nondominated population individuals are selected firstly from the initial population, a few individuals called active antibodies are selected from the nondominated individuals according to the crowding distance value [3], the active antibodies are proportionally cloned to form the clone population, here, the clone proportion of each individual in the active population also depends on its crowding distance value, an active antibody with greater crowding distance value has a larger clonal size. Then a recombination operator is performed on the clone population and an active antibody is selected randomly from active population to generate two offspring. After recombination, a static hypermutation [8] operator is adopted and whether an offspring can join in the new population consist of a temporary population depends on the nondominated sorting and crowding distance [3] and then this temporary population is truncated to form a new population and go into the next generation.

2.2 Invasive Weed Optimization Algorithm

Mehrabian and Lucas abstracted a mathematic model to describe the process of weed colonization. There are four steps in this algorithm: (1) initialization, a finite number of seeds are dispread over the search area; (2) reproduction, every seed grows to a flowering plant (in this paper the plant means the weed) and produces seeds depending on its fitness; (3) spatial dispersal, the produced seeds are being randomly dispread over the search area and grow to new plants; (4) competitive exclusion, when the number of plants reach the maximum number which we give first, only the plants with lower fitness can survive and produce seeds, others are being eliminated [6].

3   The Proposed Algorithm

In order to increase the diversity of the individuals and without increasing the number of function evaluations as far as possible, a modified IWO operator is introduced to NNIA when the number of nondominated solutions is less than a certain number *NI*. In NNIA, after genetic operation, we get the new population, and the new individuals with the parent individuals together form the temporary population, we select the nondominated individuals form it. In the modified NNIA, if the size of the current memory population is less than *NI*, we selected $3 \times Na$ individuals from the new population which are generated after genetic operation randomly and remove them, then the active antibodies will be the prime weeds to reproduce seeds i.e. generate new individuals to join in the new population. We denoted the improved algorithm as NNIAIWO. The details of NNIAIW are shown in Algorithm 1.

Algorithm 1: NNIAIWO

NI: The limitation(number) of performing modified IWO operator

Step 1: Initialize the population P_0 with the size Nm, find nondominated population NP_0 , **if the size of NP_0 is less than Na, each individual in NP_0 generate one single seed with mean zero and variance** σ^2_{final} , **the new weeds and NP_0 form the memory population MP_0, otherwise, $MP_0=NP_0$,** $it=0$;

Step 2: Identify the dominant antibodies in MP_{it} called active population (AP_{it}) by computing the crowding distance, the size of AP_{it} is not more than Na;

Step 3: Proportional clone AP_{it} to form clone population (CP_{it});

Step 4: Perform recombination and hypermutation on CP_{it} to generate $CP_{it}^{'}$;

Step 5: **If the size of MP_{it} is less than NI, perform the modified IWO operator on the active population AP_{it} to generate the new population NW_{it+1}, and the associate parent weeds are not joined in the evaluation then go to Step 5,otherwise, go to Step 6;**

Step 6: **Randomly select $3 \times Na$ individuals from $CP_{it}^{'}$ and these individuals are replaced by the NW_{it+1} to form a new population $CP_{it}^{''}$;**

Step 7: Evaluate $CP_{it}^{'}$(without operating Step 5)or $CP_{it}^{''}$(operate Step 5) , $CP_{it}^{'}$ or $CP_{it}^{''}$ and MP_{it} form the population P_{it+1},

Step 8: Find the nondominated population (NP_{it+1}) in P_{it+1}, if the size of NP_{it+1} is no more than Nm, $MP_{it+1}=NP_{it+1}$, otherwise, truncation NP_{it} depending on the crowding distance form $NP_{it+1}^{'}$ and $MP_{it+1}=NP_{it+1}^{'}$, $it=it+1$;

Step 9: If $it=gmax$, output MP_{it}, otherwise, go to Step 2.

3.1   Modification I: Associated Parent Weed

With the increase of the number of iteration, the distribution area is shrinking. Since the searching range focus mainly on the neighborhood of the parent individual, the other space will be ignored, which may lead to premature convergence. In order to avoid this as far as possible, we introduce two parent individuals based on the parent weed and searching space to increase the diversity and extend the searching space. In order to more easily and more clearly expound, here we consider one-dimension situation, in each generation, the parent individual in the search space divide the searching space into two parts as shown in Fig. 1, the intermediate position of each part generate a new weed called as associated parent weed and Fig. 1 illustrates the distribution of the associate parent weed. That is, each parent weed have two associated parent weeds, and both of the associated parent weeds do not join in the function evaluations only response to generate two new seeds that is why we call it associated parent weed. The associated parent weeds are computed as follows:

$$associated\_weed_{i/parent} = \begin{cases} a\_weed_{ui/parent} = \frac{1}{2} \times (weed_i + UL) \\ a\_weed_{li/parent} = \frac{1}{2} \times (weed_i + LL) \end{cases} \quad (1)$$

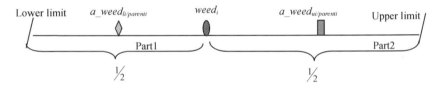

Fig. 1. The distribution of associated parent weeds in one-dimensional space

3.2   Modification II: Cauchy Distribution

In this paper, we adopt Cauchy distribution as the distribution area of the new weeds which are reproduced by the associated parents. The Cauchy density function is defined in Eq. (2):

$$f(x, \mu, \lambda) = \frac{1}{\pi} \left[\frac{\lambda}{(x - \mu)^2 + \lambda^2} \right] \quad (2)$$

where μ is the location parameter which is used to specify the peak of the distribution, and λ is the scale parameter which equals to the half width at the half peak value. The corresponding cumulative distribution function can be given as:

$$F(x, \mu, \lambda) = \frac{1}{2} + \frac{1}{\pi} \arctan(\frac{x - \mu}{\lambda}) \quad (3)$$

3.3 Modification III: Oscillating Factor

We introduced an oscillating factor when calculating the standard deviation, which has been proposed by Basak et al. [9]. Basak et al. introduced an oscillating factor *abs (cos (it))*, here '*it*' is the number of the current generation. In this way, and the searching space is no longer monotone decreasing with iterations.

The equation of standard deviation can be rewritten as follow:

$$\sigma_{it} = abs(\cos(it))(\frac{it_{max} - it}{it_{max}})^n(\sigma_{initial} - \sigma_{final}) + \sigma_{initial} \qquad (4)$$

4 Experimental Studies

In this section, we first introduce the test problems with two objectives and five problems with three objectives, and one metric used to evaluate the performance of algorithms. First, we compared our algorithm NNIAIWO with three MOEAs namely, NNIA, NSGAII and SPEAII in 30 independent runs in Experiment I; In Experiment II, we target the first two modifications of IWO operator specifically, in order to illustrate the improvement of our modifications; In Experiment III, we present the parameter analysis of NNIAIWO; and in Experiment IV, the proposed algorithm shows its potential of solving more complex MOPs.

4.1 Test Problems

5 test problems with two objectives [10, 11], i.e. ZDT1, ZDT2, ZDT3, ZDT4, ZDT6 and 5 three-objective problems [12], i.e. DTLZ1, DTLZ 2, DTLZ 3, DTLZ 4, DTLZ 6 are used to test the performance of the proposed algorithm.

4.2 Evaluation Criteria

In this work, we adopt inverted generational distance (IGD) [3] to evaluate the convergence and diversity of the algorithms, the equation is:

$$IGD(P_t, Q) = \frac{\sum\limits_{v \in P_t} d(v, Q)}{|P_t|} \qquad (5)$$

where P_t is the true Pareto set, Q is the approximate Pareto set find by the algorithm and $d(v, Q)$ is the minimum distance between v which is belonged to P_t to the points in Q.

4.3 Experiments Results and Analysis

Experiment I: Comparison of NNIAIWO with NNIA, NSGAII and SPEAII. In Experiment I, we compare the performance of the proposed algorithm with those of

Table 1. The parameter settings in Experiment I

Parameter	Parameter value
Nm (the size of the initial population/output population)	100
Na (the maximum size of active antibody)	20
c (the size of clone population)	100
$Gmax$ (the maximum number of iteration)	500(NNIAIWO, NNIA)/550(NSGAII, SPEAII)
$\sigma_{ini}/\lambda_{ini}$ (the initial standard deviation/scale parameter)	$0.6 \times$ (BU-BL)
$\sigma_{final}/\lambda_{final}$ (the final standard deviation/scale parameter)	0.0001
n (the nonlinear modulation index)	3
NI (The limitation(number) of performing modified IWO operator)	50

NNIA, NSGAII, SPEAII and MOEA/D [12]. The parameter settings of our algorithm (NNIAIWO) are given in Table 1. For ZDT4, $NI = 30$, for DTLZ1, $NI = 70$, and for DTLZ1 and DTLZ3, $\lambda_{it} = 0.5 \times \sigma_{it}$.

The results in Table 2 indicate that NNIAIWO indeed have best performance on ZDT3, DTLZ3, DTLZ4 and DTLZ6. And according to the statistic of IGD value, ZDT2, ZDT4, DTLZ1, DTLZ3 and DTLZ4, the performance of NNIA is not stable.

Table 2. The mean value and standard deviation of IGD of 30 independent runs

Test problems	IGD				
	NNIAIWO	NNIA	NSGAII	SPEAII	MOEA/D
ZDT1	0.004423	0.004456	0.00504	0.00387	0.003829
	0.000207	0.000201	0.00029	4.70E−05	1.32E−18
ZDT2	0.004578	0.186227	0.045548	0.064442	0.003756
	0.000168	0.281948	0.153346	0.18485	2.65E−18
ZDT3	0.005043	0.005159	0.006689	0.006786	0.010359
	0.000264	0.000289	0.005513	0.007638	0
ZDT4	0.004409	0.337718	0.004654	0.031826	0.003717
	0.000215	0.415145	0.000255	0.152175	2.65E−18
ZDT6	0.0028	0.002947	0.003433	0.002545	0.00185
	0.000252	0.00039	0.000393	0.000135	1.54E−18
DTLZ1	0.025576	0.268079	0.025348	0.236731	0.027055
	0.001495	1.325641	0.002008	0.140071	1.76E−17
DTLZ2	0.069928	0.070642	0.068097	0.054709	0.070669
	0.003798	0.004517	0.00336	0.000948	4.23E−17
DTLZ3	0.076979	4.020093	0.443545	0.207948	0.082802
	0.005296	9.018077	0.540973	0.331583	2.82E−17
DTLZ4	0.069435	0.155093	0.321178	0.352841	0.931184
	0.003287	0.263124	0.289868	0.271555	0
DTLZ6	0.079608	0.088849	0.149582	0.161862	0.84191
	0.004614	0.049751	0.121817	0.204965	5.65E−16

We give the mean numbers of function evaluations in these ten test problems in Fig. 2. Through the Experiment I, we found that NNIAIWO have a better performance than NNIA in most of the test problems, especially for ZDT2, ZDT4, DTLZ1, DTLZ3 and DTLZ4, and at the same time the mean numbers of the function evaluations of these test problems are not increase except ZDT2, DTLZ2 and DTLZ3. That means NNIAIWO make an improvement on most of these ten test problems without increasing the number of function evaluations basically.

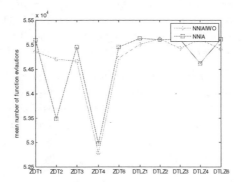

Fig. 2. The mean numbers of function evaluations in these ten test problems

Experiment II: Comparison of the IWO Operator with the Modified IWO Operators. In this section, in order to evaluate the usefulness of the proposed modified IWO operator (the first two modifications). Here, we make a comparison among three different cases. Case 1 is the original IWO operator, Case 2 just adopt modification I in NNIA. In Case 3, modifications I and II are both introduced to NNIA.

From Fig. 3, we can see that mean IGD value obtained by case 3 is lower than other two cases for all of the five two-objective problems and statistical results of 30 independent runs is more stable except ZDT4.

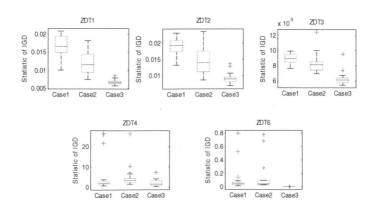

Fig. 3. The Boxplots of statistic of IGD in three different cases

Experiment III: Parameter Analysis. In this section, we analyze the affection of the initial standard deviation $\sigma_{initial}$ on the performance of NNIAIWO. We set $\sigma_{initial}$ as $0.2 \times$ (BU-BL), $0.4 \times$ (BU-BL), $0.6 \times$ (BU-BL), $0.8 \times$ (BU-BL) respectively, and make a survey of the impact of $\sigma_{initial}$ on IGD. 30 independent runs on ZDT and DTLZ problems are performed in the following experiments.

Figure 4 shows the box plots of NNIAIWO on IGD with four different $\sigma_{initial}$. From the results of five bi-objective test problems, we find that these four different setting of $\sigma_{initial}$ do not show significant difference. For ZDT3 and ZDT4, when σ_{inital} is $0.6 \times$ (BU-BL), the results of IGD are a little better than the other three cases. For five three-objective test problems, when $\sigma_{inital} = 0.6 \times$ (BU-BL), IGD are more stable than the other three cases. From the results of IGD, we can see that the IGD values are relatively more stable when $\sigma_{inital} = 0.6 \times$ (BU-BL) for most of the test problems.

Experiment IV: The Comparison of Performance Between NNIAIWO and NNIA on UF. In order to evaluate the performance of NNIAIWO for solving more difficult multi-objective optimization problem, we applied NNIAIWO to other five problems including UF1, UF2, UF3, UF4 and UF7. These test problems are proposed by Zhang et al. [13].

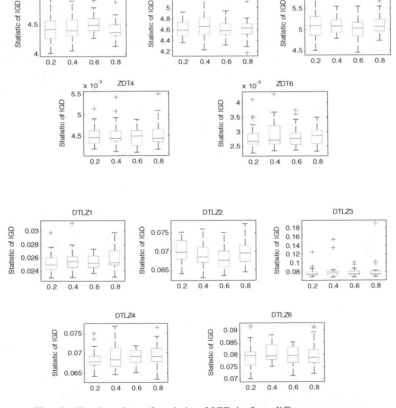

Fig. 4. The Boxplots of statistic of IGD in four different parameters

In Table 3, we give the mean and standard deviation of IGD of 30 independent runs. We find that the IGD values of NNIAIWO are better than NNIA and MOEA/D on UF1, UF2, UF3 and UF4. For these five test problems, the stable performance of MOEA/D is the best.

Table 3. The mean value and standard deviation of IGD of 30 independent runs

Test problems	IGD		
	NNIAIWO	NNIA	MOEA/D
UF1	0.037234	0.065741	0.139264
	±0.00632	±0.027502	±5.65E−17
UF2	0.019676	0.02302	0.06172
	±0.004466	±0.00408	±2.82E−17
UF3	0.076797	0.136719	0.706064
	±0.01345	±0.036669	±1.13E−16
UF4	0.041287	0.043209	0.061641
	±0.000414	±0.001182	±4.23E−17
UF7	0.043098	0.073211	0.032566
	±0.083556	±0.11107	±1.41E−17

5 Conclusion

By executing an extensive experiments, we conclude that the new operator introduced in NNIA can improve the convergence of some test problems and at the same time this operator docs not destroy the original advantages of NNIA, and it can also improve the stability of the diversity of the solutions of ZDT2, ZDT4, DTLZ3 and DTLZ4. The numbers of function evaluations does not increase on most of the test problems but decrease. Our algorithm also have a better performance than NNIA in UF1, UF2, UF3, UF4 and UF7, this further illustrates that our operator played a certain role in improving the original NNIA, but there are still many things to improve our algorithm: the convergence and diversity are not well in these five UF test problems.

Acknowledgments. This work was supported in part by the National Natural Science Foundation of China under Grant 61373111, Grant 61272279, Grant 61672405 and Grant 61203303; in part by the Fundamental Research Funds for the Central University under Grant K50511020014, Grant K5051302084, Grant JBG160229, Grant JB150227 and JBJ160229, and in part by the Provincial National Natural Science Foundation of Shanxi of China under Grant 2014JM8321.

References

1. Fonseca, C.M., Fleming, P.J.: Genetic algorithm for multi-objective optimization: Formulation, discussion and generation. In: Proceedings of the 5th International Conference on Genetic Algorithms, pp. 416–423. Morgan Kaufmann Publishers Inc. (1993)

2. Srinivas, N., Deb, K.: Multi-objective optimization using nondominated sorting in genetic algorithms. Evol. Comput. **2**(3), 221–248 (1994)
3. Deb, K., Pratap, A., Agarwal, S., Meyarivan, T.: A fast and elitist multi-objective genetic algorithm: NSGAII. IEEE Trans. Evol. Comput. **6**(2), 182–197 (2002)
4. Zitzler, E., Thiele, L.: Multi-objective evolutionary algorithms: a comparative case study and the strength Pareto approach. IEEE Trans. Evol. Comput. **3**(4), 257–271 (1999)
5. Zitzler, E., Laumanns, M., Thiele, L.: SPEA2: improving the strength Pareto evolutionary algorithm. In: Evolutionary Methods for Design, Optimization and Control with Applications to Industrial Problems, pp. 95–100. Springer, Berlin (2002)
6. Mehrabian, A.R., Lucas, C.: A novel numerical optimization algorithm inspired from weed colonization. Ecol. Inf. **1**, 355–366 (2006)
7. Gong, M., Jiao, L., Du, H., Bo, L.: Multi-objective immune algorithm with nondominated neighbor-based selection. Evol. Comput. **16**(2), 225–255 (2008)
8. Cutello, V., Nicosia, G., Pavone, M.: Exploring the capability of immune algorithms: a characterization of hypermutation operators. In: Nicosia, G., Cutello, V., Bentley, P.J., Timmis, J. (eds.) ICARIS 2004. LNCS, vol. 3239, pp. 263–276. Springer, Heidelberg (2004). doi:10.1007/978-3-540-30220-9_22
9. Basak, A., Pal, S., Das, S., Snasel, V.: A modified invasive weed optimization algorithm for time-modulated linear antenna array synthesis. In: IEEE Congress on Evolutionary Computation (CEC 2010), pp. 1–8 (2010)
10. Zitzler, E., Deb, K., Thiele, L.: Comparison of multi-objective evolutionary algorithm: empirical results. Evol. Comput. **8**(2), 173–195 (2000)
11. Zhang, Q., Li, H.: MOEA/D: a multi-objective evolutionary algorithm based on decomposition. IEEE Trans. Evol. Comput. **11**(6), 712–731 (2007)
12. Deb, K., Thiele, L., Laumanns, M., Zitzler, E.: Scalable multi-objective optimization test problems. In: Proceedings of the IEEE Congress on Evolutionary Computation (CEC 2002), pp. 825–830 (2002)
13. Zhang, Q., Zhou, A., Zhao, S.Z., Suganthan, P.N. Liu, W., Tiwari, S.: Multi-objective optimization test instances for the CEC 2009 special session and competition. Technical report CES-887, University of Essex and Nanyang Technological University (2009)

Noise-Removal Method for Manifold Learning

Zhonghua Hao[1], Jingjing Liu[2], ShiWei Ma[2(✉)], Xin Jin[1,4],
and Xin Lian[3]

[1] College of Automation and Electrical Engineering,
Qingdao University, Qingdao, China
[2] School of Mechatronical Engineering and Automation,
Shanghai University, Shanghai, China
masw@shu.edu.cn
[3] University of Western Australia, Perth, Australia
[4] Stage Grid Shandong Electric Power Company, Jinan, China

Abstract. Manifold learning algorithms are nonlinear dimensionality reduction methods which could find the intrinsic geometry structure of the data points and recover the latent main factors that influence object changes. However, noise is unavoidable for datasets in the process of sampling. The noisy data easily get wrong results when using manifold learning algorithms. This paper proposes a noisy-data pre-processing method for manifold learning algorithms. Firstly, we utilize shrink strategy and adopt the eigenvalue linear criterion to find the tangent hyperplane of each data point. Then, we construct the local coordinate system for each tangent hyperplane and get the projection coordinates of each data point. Finally, we reconstruct the high-dimensional coordinates of each data point by affine transformation. The experiments show that the proposed method is effective and useful.

Keywords: Noisy data · Manifold learning · Tangent space

1 Introduction

Since the objects in the world change gradually and regularly, the data points that describe the statues of objects lie on a low-dimensional nonlinear manifold in high-dimensional observation space [1, 2]. Discovering the structure of the manifold is a challenging unsupervised learning problem, which is called dimensionality reduction in pattern recognition [4–11]. The discovered low-dimensional structures can be further used in classification, motion analysis, clustering and data visualization [13, 14]. The key point is that the dimensions of the input spaces can be very high, however, the intrinsic dimensionality for dataset is limited by few factors. The purpose of manifold learning algorithms is to discover a low-dimensional embedding that preserves properties (e.g. geodesic distance or local relationships) of the high-dimensional input datasets.

Manifold learning algorithms [1, 2, 4–11] had attracted attention of researchers due to their geometric intuition, nonlinear nature and computational feasibility. However, noise is unavoidable in data collection process. Noisy data could make the proper neighbor set hard to obtain and lead the manifold learning algorithms failure. For this

D. Yue et al. (Eds.): LSMS/ICSEE 2017, Part II, CCIS 762, pp. 191–200, 2017.
DOI: 10.1007/978-981-10-6373-2_20

topic, Vellido and Velazco [3] discussed the effect of noise on an unsupervised feature selection method for manifold learning by Generative Topographic Mapping, however, they do not discuss how to remove the noise. Dadkhahi [12] utilized temporal information in out-of-sample points to make the embedding robust to noise. However, this method just suits for ISOMAP algorithm. Zhang et al. [9] promoted the robust of manifold learning from the aspect of algorithm. But it did not discuss the noise problem separately.

In this paper, we propose a noise-removal method for manifold learning. Since the scatter cloud points without noise lie on a manifold precisely, whereas the distribution of noise points is irregular. From the other point of view, points without noise lie on the tangent spaces of the manifold nearby and the noise data go out of them. Therefore, the noise point could be eliminated by tangent space projection.

Firstly, we construct tangent spaces for each point. If the neighbor set of a data point is 'flat' enough, it can be regard as the tangent space of this point. We utilize the ratio of summation of eigenvalues to measure the similarity between neighborhood and tangent space and adopt shrink strategy to obtain the eligible neighbor sets. Then, we construct the local coordinate system for each tangent space by principle component analysis (PCA) method and get the coordinates of each data point by projection. Finally, we recover the high-dimensional coordinates of each data point by affine transformation. Since the local tangent space alignment (LTSA) [8] method is regarded as the optimal manifold learning algorithm, this paper utilize this method to evaluate our noise removal method.

The rest of the paper is organized as follows. Section 2 presents the algorithm of LTSA and dimension reduction results influenced by different levels of noise. Section 3 details how to select tangent hyperplane of each point by shrink strategy and how to remove noise data points by projection. Experiments over several data discrete cloud point data sets are discussed in Sects. 4, and 5 draws some conclusions.

2 A Brief Review of LTSA and the Drawbacks of Noisy Data

2.1 LTSA Algorithm

The basic idea of LTSA is to construct local linear approximations of the manifold in the form of a collection of overlapping approximate tangent spaces at each sample point, and then align those tangent spaces to obtain a global parametrization of the manifold. This idea comes from the mathematical definition of a manifold. The algorithm steps are shown in Table 1.

2.2 Noisy Data for Nonlinear Dimensionality Reduction

The data points distribute on a low-dimensional manifold and the location of noise data points go out of the manifold. Generally, LTSA works well if the neighbor sets are well determined. However, when selecting neighbor set for noise data points by *KNN* or $\epsilon - ball$ method. It is easy to select a wrong neighbor set, which called 'short circuit' phenomenon.

Table 1. LTSA algorithm

Input:	data in high-dimensional observation space $X = \{x_i, \cdots, x_k\}$; neighborhood parameter k or ϵ
Output:	data in low-dimensional embedding space $Y = \{y_i, \cdots, y_k\}$
1. Set neighborhoods.	Obtain neighborhood N_i of each point x_i by *KNN*
or	
$\epsilon - ball$ method	
2. Extract local coordinates.	Decompose $X_i - \bar{x_i}\overline{1_k}^T$ by SVD. The local coordinates correspond to the first d singular vectors.
3. Align local coordinates.	Construct the arranging matrix $\emptyset = \sum_{i=1}^{N} S_i W_i W_i^T S_i^T$. Calculate the last $d + 1$ singular vectors, and $Y = [u_2, \cdots, u_{d+1}]^T$.

In Fig. 1, the data points distribute on curve that embeds in two-dimensional plane. In which, the solid dots stand for data points, the circles stand for noise data points and the points mark by triangle are the center points of the neighborhood which shows by dot line. The neighbor sets are determined by *KNN* method, and the parameter $k = 4$. It is obviously that the neighbor set of the noise data point p_{noise} at the bottom left contains three data points outside of data set and one point inside the data set which marked by "□". In this neighbor set, the geodesic distance between the inside point and other three outside points is extremely large. It leads to the low-dimensional coordinates of points could not reflect the geometrical structure rightly and makes the manifold algorithm failure.

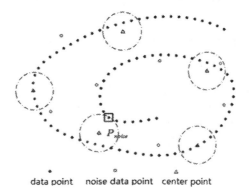

data point   noise data point   center point

Fig. 1. 'Short circuit' phenomenon

To illustrate the noise data set influence for manifold learning visually, we generate Swiss Roll Data Sets with different noise intensities and use LTSA algorithm to handle them (Table 2).

Table 2. MATLAB code for generating Noise Swiss Roll Data

Input:	the number of data set: n, noise parameter: $noise$
Output:	Swiss Roll Data set with Noise

```
t = (3 * pi / 2) * (1 + 2 * rand(n, 1));
height = 30 * rand(n, 1);
data = [t .* cos(t) height t .* sin(t)] + noise * randn(n, 3);
```

The Fig. 2(a) shows the Noise Swiss Roll Data Sets which the noise parameter increases from 0 to 0.8, in which n = 1000. The Fig. 2(b) is the nonlinear dimensionality reduction result by LTSA for each data set in (a) respectively, in which the KNN parameter k = 7. It is obvious that the low-dimensionality coordinate could reflect the real geometry structure of data points when $noise \leq 0.4$. As noise intensity increases, the location of low-dimensional points cat not reflect the right geometry structure of the data point. It shows that the true structure of data points could not be recovered in low-dimensional space when the noise is strength enough.

The Fig. 2(a) shows the Noise Swiss Roll Data Sets which the noise parameter increases from 0 to 0.8, in which n = 1000. The Fig. 2(b) is the nonlinear dimensionality reduction result by LTSA for each data set in (a) respectively, in which the KNN parameter k = 7. It is obvious that the low-dimensionality coordinate could reflect the real geometry structure of data points when $noise \leq 0.4$. As noise intensity increases, the location of low-dimensional points cat not reflect the right geometry structure of the data point. It shows that the true structure of data points could not be recovered in low-dimensional space when the noise is strength enough.

3   Noise Data Remove Method

The data points without noise lie on a manifold precisely, whereas, the location data points with noise is irregular out of manifold. If we focus on a local space on a manifold, a data point could regard as lie on its tangent space. Therefore, we could get the tangent space of each point firstly and then project data points on tangent spaces which contain them. That is the main idea of our noise data processing method.

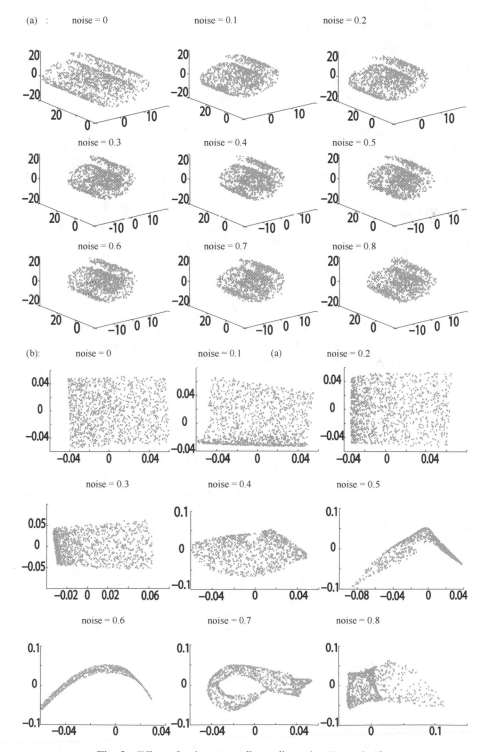

Fig. 2. Effect of noise on nonlinear dimensionality reduction

3.1   Tangent Space Construction

Since the dataset constructs by scattered points, which distribute on a low-dimensional manifold embedded in high-dimensional observation space, the neighborhood of a data point could regard as the tangent space of this point if it is plat enough as a plane or hyperplane. However, the neighborhood might be not 'plat' enough when the curvature of the manifold is large at this area.

Suppose cloud data points distribute on d-dimensional manifold embedded in D-dimensional observation space. A neighborhood N_i could be regarded as a tangent space if it similarity to Euclidean Space R^d. In other words, the data points in the neighbor set N_i of point P_i distribute on a d-dimensional hyperplane. It means that the variance of complementary $(D - d)$-dimensional subspace is zero. Therefore, we could adopt the ratio of variance of hyperplane and the variance of complementary subspace to measure the similarity of N_i and R^d. Suppose the data matrix of N_i is $X_i = [x_1, \cdots, x_k]$, the d biggest variance could obtain by PCA:

$$\left(X_i - \bar{x}e^T\right)\left(X_i - \bar{x}e^T\right)^T = V \wedge V^T \tag{1}$$

where $\quad \bar{x} = X_i e/k, e = \overbrace{[1, \cdots, 1]}^{k}{}^T, V = [v_1, \cdots, v_D], \wedge = diag(\lambda_1, \cdots, \lambda_D), (X_i - xe^T)$ is centralized symmetric matrix. In which, $\lambda_1, \cdots, \lambda_D$ are eigenvalues arranged from big to small and $v_1, \cdots, v_D$ are the corresponding eigenvectors.

Since the λ_i corresponds to value of variance on the v_i direction, the N_i could approximate to R^d satisfy:

$$\lambda_1 + \cdots + \lambda_d \approx \lambda_1 + \cdots + \lambda_D = > \frac{\sum_{i \leq d} \lambda_i}{\sum_{i \leq D} \lambda_i} = \delta \approx 1 \tag{2}$$

If ratio δ close to 1, the N_i close to R^d. Therefore, we utilize shrink strategy to guarantee that each neighbor set could regard as the tangent hyperplane. Firstly, we obtain initial neighbor sets by *KNN* or $\epsilon - ball$ method. Then, we sent a threshold δ_T and calculate the variance ratio δ. If $\delta < \delta_T$, we remove the largest distance point from the neighbor set utile $\delta > \delta_T$. The steps of tangent space construction are shown in Table 3.

3.2   Noise Removal Method

Suppose the data matrix of tangent space N_i is $X_i = [x_{i1}, \cdots, x_{ik_i}]$, $P = [u_1, \cdots, u_d]$ is the vector basis of tangent space, which obtain by decompose by SVD:

$$X_i = U \wedge V^T = \left[\underbrace{u_1 \cdots, u_d}_{P}, \cdots, u_D\right] \begin{bmatrix} \sigma_1 & \cdots & 0 \\ \vdots & \ddots & \vdots \\ 0 & \cdots & \sigma_D \end{bmatrix} \begin{bmatrix} v_1^T \\ \vdots \\ v_D^T \end{bmatrix} \tag{3}$$

where, the singular value $\sigma_1 \geq \cdots \geq \sigma_D$. If $\bar{x}_1$ is the date point x_j project on u_1, so:

Table 3. Tangent space construction

Input: data set: X, threshold ratio δ_T, initial neighbor parameter k

Output: tangent space set N_i of each point

---

1. Utilize KNN method to obtain the constant number neighbor N_i set for each point;

set $\delta_i = 0$

2. for i = 1: n:

while $\delta_i < \delta_T$:

calculate variance ratio δ_i by equ. (X)

if $\delta_i < \delta_T$:

      remove the point $P_j = \{j | \max ||P_j - P_i||\}$ from N_i

   end

      end

  end

$$u_1^T e = 0 \Rightarrow u_1^T \left(x_j - \hat{x}_1 u_1 \right) = 0 \Rightarrow \hat{x}_1 = \frac{u_1^T x_j}{u_1^T u_1} \tag{4}$$

Then, the project point $\bar{x}_{ij}$ of x_j on the tangent hyperplane x_i is:

$$\begin{bmatrix} u_1^T \\ \vdots \\ u_d^T \end{bmatrix} \left(x_j - P_i \hat{x}_{ij} \right) = 0 \Rightarrow P_i^T \left(x_j - P_i \hat{x}_{ij} \right) = 0 \tag{5}$$

$$\Rightarrow \hat{x}_{ij} = \left(P_i^T P_i \right)^{-1} P_i^T x_j$$

The coordinates of x_j on high-dimensional space is:

$$\tilde{x}_{ij} = P \hat{x}_{ij} + x_i e \tag{6}$$

where, $e = \overbrace{[1, \cdots, 1]}^{D}{}^{T}$. It should be noted that the point x_j has different coordinates on different tangent space, we adopt the mean value as the projection coordinate.

$$x_j' = \frac{1}{n} \sum_{i=1}^{N} \tilde{x}_{ij} S_i, \quad S_i = \begin{cases} 1 & if : x_j \in N_i \\ 0 & if : x_j \notin N_i \end{cases} \tag{7}$$

where, n is the point number of data set.

In this way, the noise data points are projected on the tangent hyperplane and the data points without noise stay same. The steps of noise data remove are shown in Table 4.

Table 4. Noisy data remove processing

Input: data set with noise $X = \{x_1, \cdots, x_n\}$; tangent hyperplane of each point $N =$

$\{N_1, \cdots, N_n\}$

Output: data set without noise $X' = \{x_1', \cdots, x_n'\}$

---

1. Calculate the basis vectors of tangent hyperplane for each point by Equation (3)

2. Calculate the coordinates of data points $\hat{x}_{ij}$ by Equation (5)

3. Calculate the coordinates of data point x_j', by Equation (7)

---

4   Experiments

To evaluate the performance of proposed method, we test it on Classical Swiss Roll Data sets with noise and compare the nonlinear dimensionality reduction results of noise data set and noise-removal data set.

In Fig. 3(a), we generate Swiss Roll Data set with $noise = 0.4$ by MATLAB, which contains 1000 points. (b) shows the noise-removal data set of (a) by proposed method. It is obviously that the data points lie on a manifold more regularly after noise elimination. (c) and (d) is the dimensionality reduction results of LTSA for (a), in which the KNN parameter is $k = 8$ and $k = 9$ respectivly. When $k \leq 5$, the LTSA is failure because of the number of intersection points is not enough. When $5 < k < 8$, the results are likely to (c); when $9 < k < 15$, the results are likely to (d). when $k \geq 15$, the result could not show the true geometry structure because of 'short circuit' phenomenon. For the noise data set, the reasonable results whatever the parameter k take. (e) and (f) are the nonlinear dimensionality reduction results for noise-removal data set (b) by LTSA. It could reflect the geometry structure of data points and it is robust to different parameter k.

Moreover, we do experiment on noise data set and the removed-noise data by LTSA with different parameter k 100 times and list the results in Table 5. In which, we use Embedded error, Fuzzy location error and Exact location error to evaluate the results. Embedded error refers to the error between the result and ground-truth data. Fuzzy location error refers to error of neighbor set location relationship between the result and ground-truth data. Exact location error refers to error of point location relationship between the result and ground-truth data. The mean value keeps three valid number and standard deviation keeps two valid number. It is obvious that the numerical indices are improved large after using the proposed noise-remove method.

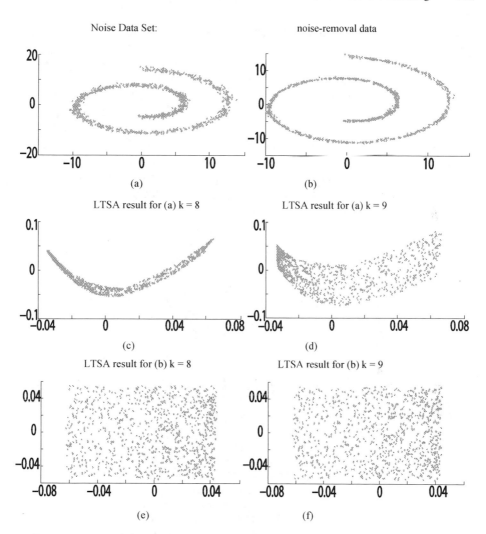

Fig. 3. Nonlinear dimensionality reduction for noise and noise-removed data set by LTSA

Table 5. Numerical indices comparison

	Noise swiss roll data set			Noise-removal swiss roll data set		
	Embedded error	Fuzzy location error	Exact location error	Embedded error	Fuzzy location error	Exact location error
k = 6	773 ± 5.1	55.4 ± 0.23	83.4 ± 0.10	5.40 ± 0.075	14.4 ± 0.062	67.2 ± 0.11
k = 7	608 ± 4.2	53.0 ± 0.21	81.0 ± 0.11	3.62 ± 0.051	17.3 ± 0.060	51.6 ± 0.13
k = 8	401 ± 3.8	49.8 ± 0.19	90.0 ± 0.13	3.31 ± 0.049	16.0 ± 0.067	36.9 ± 0.091
k = 9	65.0 ± 0.87	48.2 ± 0.23	89.9 ± 0.10	3.49 ± 0.048	16.2 ± 0.065	29.7 ± 0.083
k = 10	84.1 ± 0.56	60.6 ± 0.19	86.2 ± 0.10	3.77 ± 0.070	18.4 ± 0.71	31.7 ± 0.095
k = 11	93 ± 0.82	48.9 ± 0.18	91.4 ± 0.10	4.44 ± 0.083	23.2 ± 0.75	42.4 ± 0.10
k = 12	266 ± 2.8	51.9 ± 0.21	89.6 ± 0.21	4.64 ± 0.031	32.0 ± 0.61	45.1 ± 0.11

5 Discussions and Future Work

This paper proposed a noisy data pre-processing method for manifold learning algorithms. Firstly, we utilized shrink strategy and adopted the ratio of summation of eigenvalues as linear criterion to obtain the tangent space of each data point. Then, we constructed the local coordinate system for each tangent hyperplane by principle component analysis method and got the projection coordinates of each data point. Finally, we reconstructed the high-dimensional coordinates of each data point by affine transformation. The experiment showed the proposed method is effective and useful. This paper just considered the data sets that mixed with Gaussian noise. However, the type of noise has diversity under different situation. How to deal with different types of noise is the direction of our future work.

References

1. Tenenbaum, J., De Silva, V., Langford, J.: A global geometric framework for nonlinear dimensionality reduction. Science **290**, 2319–2323 (2000)
2. Roweis, S., Saul, L.: Nonlinear dimensionality reduction by locally linear embedding. Science **290**, 2323–2326 (2000)
3. Dadkhahi, H., Duarte, M.F., Marlin, B.: 2015 IEEE 25th International Workshop on Machine Learning for Signal Processing (MLSP) (2015)
4. Belkin, M., Niyogi, P.: Laplacian eigenmaps and spectral techniques for embedding and clustering. Adv. Neural. Inf. Process. Syst. **14**, 585–591 (2002)
5. Brand, M.: Charting a manifold. In: Advances in Neural Information Processing Systems, vol. 15, pp. 961–968 (2003)
6. Donoho, D.L., Grimes, C.: Hessian eigenmaps: new locally linear embedding techniques for high-dimensional data. Nat. Acad. Sci. **100**(10), 5591–5596 (2003)
7. Teh, Y., Roweis, S.: Automatic Alignment of Hidden Representations. Advances in Neural Information Processing Systems. MIT Press, Cambridge (2003)
8. Zhang, Z., Zha, H.: Principle manifolds and nonlinear dimensionality reduction via tangent space alignment. SIAM J. Sci. Comput. **26**(1), 313–338 (2004)
9. Zhang, Z., Wang, J., Zha, H.: Adaptive manifold learning. Pattern Anal. Mach. Intell. **34**(2), 253–365 (2012)
10. Lin, T., Zha, H.: Riemannian manifold learning. Pattern Anal. Mach. Intell. **30**(5), 796–809 (2008)
11. Wang, R., Shan, S., Chen, X., Chen, J., Gao, W.: Maximal linear embedding for dimensionality reduction. Pattern Anal. Mach. Intell. **33**(9), 1776–1792 (2011)
12. Vellido, A., Velazco, J.: The effect of noise and sample size on an unsupervised feature selection method for manifold learning. In: 2008 IEEE International Joint Conference on Neural Networks (IEEE World Congress on Computational Intelligence), pp. 522–527 (2008)
13. Tuzel, O., Porikli, F., Meer, P.: Pedestrian detection via classification on riemannian manifolds. Pattern Anal. Mach. Intell. **30**(10), 1713–1727 (2008)
14. Elgammal, A., Lee, C.: Tracking people on a torus. Pattern Anal. Mach. Intell. **31**(3), 520–538 (2009)

Dynamic Process Fault Isolation and Diagnosis Using Improved Fisher Discriminant Analysis and Relative Error of Variance

Huifeng Tian[1,2] and Li Jia[1(✉)]

[1] Shanghai Key Laboratory of Power Station Automation Technology, Department of Automation, College of Mechatronics Engineering and Automation, Shanghai University, Shanghai 200072, China
thf830@163.com, jiali@staff.shu.edu.cn
[2] College of Electric and Information Engineering, Jiangsu University of Science and Technology, Zhangjiagang, Jiangsu 215600, China

Abstract. The traditional fault detection methods have certain detection delay for dynamic processes with strong nonlinearity. In order to increase fault detection rate and decrease the fault detection delay, this paper proposed a new fault isolation and diagnosis method. The faulty and normal samples are separated using moving window Fisher discriminant analysis combining with mean and variance of projection error, then obtain the fault point position by hypothesis testing theory. Furthermore, the projection vector is revised by adding the auxiliary deviation. To identify the fault variables, relative error of variance is presented and compared with traditional complete deposition construction plots method. The simulation results of Tennessee Eastman benchmark process fault data sets show the advantages of this proposed method in fault isolation and diagnosis.

Keywords: Improved Ffisher discriminant analysis · Relative error of variance · Hypothesis testing · Canonical correlation analysis

1 Introduction

The fault diagnosis and isolation are key technology to ensure production safety and improve product quality and production efficiency in industrial processes. Many methods have been proposed over the past decade [1]. Multivariate statistical analysis method as a data-driven technique has been widely concerned by academic and industry, which does not need accurate mathematical model and prior knowledge, only using the historical data in the feature extraction, feature space construction statistics for fault detection, and according to the contribution of pattern recognition fault variables.

There are many multivariate statistical process monitoring (MSPM) methods, such as principal component analysis (PCA) and partial least squares (PLS), where the statistical model is built and the normal operating region is established using a series of normal operating data. However, the PCA and PLS are not suitable enough for fault

© Springer Nature Singapore Pte Ltd. 2017
D. Yue et al. (Eds.): LSMS/ICSEE 2017, Part II, CCIS 762, pp. 201–211, 2017.
DOI: 10.1007/978-981-10-6373-2_21

diagnosis due to the ignorance of the information between the classes during the period of deciding the lower dimensional representation.

Furthermore, the traditional fault detection in the industrial process usually adopts T^2 and squared prediction error (SPE) statistical indices, T^2 is Markov norm of the principal component vector of the sample and SPE is the prediction error square of the principal component model based on Euclidean distance, due to the inconsistency between the two statistics, leading to different fault detection results.

Nowadays, because of contribution plots can be obtained without prior process knowledge, they are widely used for fault diagnosis, which display the contribution of each process variable by observing the statistics T^2 and SPE [2]. However, the root cause of an abnormal condition may not be distinguished well by the contribution plots [3].

For industrial process fault diagnosis, the history data of the industrial process is divided into different classes, and each class denotes a specific fault. Fisher discriminant analysis (FDA) is a data classification technique in terms of maximizing the separability of these classes, which can isolate process fault from normal operation [4].

This paper proposed an improved Fisher discriminant analysis, which combines the moving window with FDA to solve single fault point problem. The fault interval can be quickly detected by mean and variance of time series data, then using hypothesis testing to determine the fault position. Differing from the contribution plots, relative error of variance of fault variables is performed to find out the fault variables.

The arrangement of the rest of this paper is following: Sect. 2 describes the fault isolation and identification method in detail. Then the improved FDA and relative error of variance are applied to data collected from the Tennessee Eastman process simulator in Sect. 3. Finally, conclusions are drawn in the Sect. 4.

2   Fault Isolation and Identification

2.1   Improved Fisher Discriminant Analysis

FDA is proved to be a very effective dimensionality reduction method, and its linear model is robust to noise. The main idea of this method is to find the vectors p separating different classes, for which the Fisher criterion has a maximum value.

$$\max \frac{p^T S_b p}{p^T S_w p} \tag{1}$$

where S_b denotes the between-class scatter matrix, and S_w is the within-class scatter matrix.

For the purpose of achieving the classification of information extraction and compression feature space dimension effect, the model of high dimension sample projection to optimal discriminant vector space, and projection ensures the minimum sample within-class distance and maximum between-class distance in the new subspace. In other words, the separability of data samples is the best in the space.

Hence, as an effective feature extraction method, it can create the largest projection of the inter class scatter matrix of the sample, and in the meantime the scatter matrix is the smallest in the class.

Assuming $\mathbf{X} \in R^{n \times m}$ is data set, which including n samples and c classes. And each sample has m variables.

The between-class scatter matrix S_b is defined as

$$S_b = \sum_{j=1}^{c} n_i(\bar{\mathbf{x}}_i - \bar{\mathbf{x}})(\bar{\mathbf{x}}_i - \bar{\mathbf{x}})^T \tag{2}$$

where $\bar{\mathbf{x}}_i, \bar{\mathbf{x}}$ are the average vector class i and the all samples of the matrix $\mathbf{X}$, respectively. Besides, n_i is the number of samples of class i.

Then, the between-class scatter matrix is given by

$$S_w = \sum_{i=1}^{c} S_i \tag{3}$$

where c is the number of classes, S_i is the within-class scattering matrix of class i, which is defined as

$$S_i = \sum_{\mathbf{x}_i \in \mathbf{X}_i} (\mathbf{x}_i - \bar{\mathbf{x}}_i)(\mathbf{x}_i - \bar{\mathbf{x}}_i)^T \tag{4}$$

where $\mathbf{x}_i$ is ith row of the matrix $\mathbf{X}$.

According to Fisher criterion (1), the solution of the optimal projection vector p is to solve the generalized eigenvalue problem as

$$J(p) = \frac{p^T S_b p}{p^T S_w p} \tag{5}$$

In order to compute the vector p, ensure the denominator normalization, otherwise whatever p to expand any times, the above function is right, it is not possible to determine p.

Assuming $\|p^T S_w p\| = 1$, and introducing Lagrange multiplier λ, then we can get function $f(p)$.

$$f(p) = p^T S_b p - \lambda(p^T S_w p - 1) \tag{6}$$

Then derivation of p, and assuming S_w is invertible.

$$S_b p = \lambda S_w p \tag{7}$$

Furthermore, Eq. (7) is multiplied by S_w^{-1}, we can obtain optimal projection vector p.

$$S_w^{-1} S_b p = \lambda p \tag{8}$$

where λ is a diagonal matrix, which is composed of eigenvalues of the matrix.

The optimal project vector p can be obtained by performing the eigenvalue decomposition on the scaled matrix $S_w^{-1} S_b$. By sorting the eigenvalues in descending order and recording the columns of the associated eigenvectors. And the optimal projection vector is the maximum eigenvalue corresponding eigenvector.

$$V_i = \mathbf{X}_i p \tag{9}$$

where $V_i \in R^{n \times 1}$ is the vector after projection, $\mathbf{X}_i \in R^{n \times m}$ and $p \in R^{m \times 1}$ are the samples and optimal projection vector, respectively.

According to error of the normal sample projection vector and the fault sample projection vector. The Eq. (9) can be revised as

$$V_i = \mathbf{X}_i p + w_k \tag{10}$$

where w_k is the auxiliary deviation, and k is the separation point.

2.2 Fault Identification

In industry dynamic process, assuming time serial data matrix $\mathbf{X} \in R^{n \times m}$ as

$$\mathbf{X}(k) = \begin{bmatrix} \mathbf{x}_t^T & \mathbf{x}_{t-1}^T & \cdots & \mathbf{x}_{t-k}^T \\ \mathbf{x}_{t-1}^T & \mathbf{x}_{t-2}^T & \cdots & \mathbf{x}_{t-k-1}^T \\ \vdots & \vdots & \ddots & \vdots \\ \mathbf{x}_{t+k-n}^T & \mathbf{x}_{t+k-n-1}^T & \cdots & \mathbf{x}_{t-n}^T \end{bmatrix} \tag{11}$$

where $\mathbf{x}_t^T$ is the m dimensional process variable at the time instance t.

Because of the different data types of variables in the industry process. The matrix $\mathbf{X}$ must be standardized, which is scaled to zero mean and unit variance as

$$s = \left(\frac{1}{n-1} \sum_{i=1}^{n} (\mathbf{x}_i - \mathbf{x})^2 \right)^{\frac{1}{2}} \tag{12}$$

Then covariance matrix is calculated as

$$\mathbf{C} = \frac{1}{n-1} \mathbf{X}^T \mathbf{X} \tag{13}$$

Further, perform the eigen-decomposed to the covariance matrix $\mathbf{C}$ and to obtain the principal and residual loading of $\mathbf{X}$ as follows

$$PS = \mathbf{P}\mathbf{P}^T \mathbf{x} \tag{14}$$

$$RS = (\mathbf{I} - \mathbf{P}\mathbf{P}^T)\mathbf{x} \tag{15}$$

where $\mathbf{P} \in R^{m \times l}$ is the principal loading. PS and RS denote principal space and residual space, respectively.

The contribution of the original *jth* measurement variable to the monitoring statistics T^2 and *SPE* are calculated as

$$CONT\_T^2i = \sum_{j=1}^{p} \left| t_i^T x_j / \lambda_i \right| \tag{16}$$

where t_i and x_j denote the *i*th nonlinear principal components and *j*th original measurement variable, respectively. And p denotes the number of the principal component, λ is eigenvalue.

$$CONT\_SPE = (x_i * (I - P * P^T))^2 \tag{17}$$

where x_i and P denote testing sample and loading matrix, respectively.

3 Case Study

3.1 Tennessee Eastman Benchmark Process

The Tennessee Eastman (TE) benchmark process is a simulation of an actual nonlinear dynamic industrial plant, which has been widely used as a benchmark simulation for comparing various process monitoring and fault detection [5].

The TE process is a complicated chemical process, which has one normal data set and 21 different fault data sets, which are divided into five types: step, random variation, sticking, unknown and constant position. The fault type is given in literature [6].

3.2 Fault Point Position Detection

Before analyzing the data, it need the standardized processing, which is mainly to eliminate dimension relationship between the variables, to make the data comparable. The attribute data which is in accordance with the proportion of the zoom, fell on a small specific interval, to further analyze the data attributes.

In order to determine the separation point of fault data from normal sample theoretically. The hypothesis testing method is applied. Assuming that the samples are consistent with normal distribution. According to the results of separation position of normal and fault samples of seven step type. Therefore, we proposed two contrary hypothesis: $H_0 : \mu = \mu_0 = 161$ and $H_1 : \mu \neq \mu_0$. Then on the basis of a reasonable rule Eq. (18), using known samples to make a decision whether to accept the assumption H_0 or accept the hypothesis H_1. If accept H_0, that is to say, the value 161 is deemed as the separation point position.

$$P\{H_0\} = P_{\mu_0} \left\{ \left| \frac{\bar{X} - \mu_0}{\sigma / \sqrt{n}} \right| \geq k \right\} = \alpha \tag{18}$$

where $H_0 : \mu = \mu_0$, $\bar{\mathbf{X}}$ is the mean of the separation point vector. The parameter σ and α denote the standard deviation and the significance level $(0 < \alpha < 1)$, respectively. Besides, k is the quantile.

We define testing statistic as

$$z = \left| \frac{\bar{\mathbf{X}} - \mu_0}{\sigma/\sqrt{n}} \right| \qquad (19)$$

According to the hypothesis testing theory, if z greater than or equal to k, denote that reject the hypothesis H_0, otherwise represent accept the hypothesis H_0.

In this experiment, the significance level α is set 0.05, then $k = z_{\alpha/2} = 1.96$ is computed. And $n = 7$, $\sigma = 3.9581$. Further, calculate the testing statistic $z = 1.3369$. Obviously, the value of testing statistic z less than the quantile k. Therefore, the result shows that hypothesis H_0 is accepted, thus the separation point position is 161.

3.3   Fault Isolation

In the industrial process, such as the chemical industry, the production process data is time serials data. Once the fault occurs, the obtained data after the fault point are fault data, because the fault cannot recover by itself. Therefore, the IFDA is used to separate fault from normal samples, and the position when separated is the fault detection delay. The detection results for fault 1 and 4 is shown in Fig. 1.

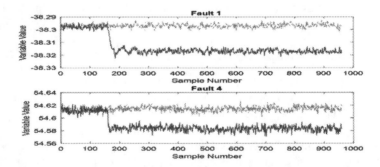

Fig. 1. Detection results of Fault 1 and 4 (red dashed lines denote normal samples and blue dotted lines represent fault samples) (Color figure online)

In the fault detection research field, fault detection rate (FDR) [7] is commonly used criteria, which is the percentage of fault samples identified correctly. It can be calculated as

$$FDR = \frac{N_{cf}}{N_{tf}} \times 100 \qquad (20)$$

where N_{cf} and N_{tf} are the number of fault identified correctly and the total fault samples.

For most of fault detection using fault detection rates and fault alarm rates, but not taking the fault detection delay into account. Fault detection delay is that when the fault occurs, failed to detected timely. The canonical correlation analysis (CCA) is used to dynamic process fault detection, which separates the fault from the normal time serial data [8]. Table 1 is the result that fault detection rates and detection delay with IFDA,

Table 1. FDRs (%) and detection delay (min)

Fault id	IFDA method		FDA method		CCA method	
	FDR	DD	FDR	DD	FDR	DD
1	100	0	99.375	15	99.375	15
2	100	0	98.75	30	100	0
3	100	0	97.375	63	92.625	177
4	100	0	100	0	95.625	105
5	100	0	99.875	3	100	0
6	100	0	100	0	100	0
7	100	0	99.875	3	98.75	30

FDA and CCA three different method, the improved Fisher discriminant analysis is the best of the three methods. Moreover, the FDA is better than the CCA method.

3.4 Fault Variable Diagnosis

After the fault occurs, we need to further determine which variables have significantly changed. The conventional fault diagnosis method is the construction plots method. And the most commonly used construction plots is complete decomposition construction (CDC) [9], which decomposes the fault detection index as the summation of the variable contributions.

This paper presented a method which can quickly detect significant variation of variables. Firstly, we compute the error of normal and fault samples, and obtain the variance of the error. Then the relative error of the variance is calculated as

$$REV = \frac{\text{var}_{fault} - \text{var}_{normal}}{\text{var}_{normal}} \tag{21}$$

where var_{fault} and var_{normal} denote variance of the normal and fault samples, respectively.

The Fault 1 and Fault 4 are selected to analyze. Many variables with interacting and counteracting effects are affected in Fault 1, and these effects consequently confuses fault identification methods. In Fault 4, a step change of cooling water flow rate in the reactor originates from the step change of the cooling water inlet temperature [10].

The relative error of the variables x_1 and x_{44} are 45.1308 and 45.0934, respectively. Obviously, the variables x_1 and x_{44} are the two most significant fault variables in Fig. 2. Then the actual plots of variable x_1 and x_{44} are shown in Fig. 3. The result illustrates that the relative error of variance method is feasible.

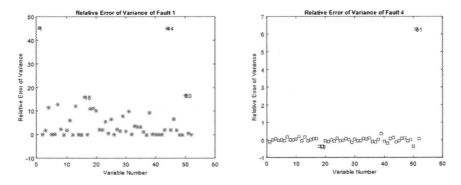

Fig. 2. Relative error of variance of Fault 1 and 4

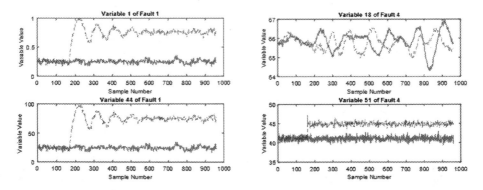

Fig. 3. Variable value of Fault 1 and Fault 4 (red dashed lines denote normal samples and blue dotted lines represent fault samples) (Color figure online)

The relative error of the variables x_{18} and x_{51} are -0.3575 and 6.2882, respectively. From the Fig. 2, we can easy find that the value of x_{51} is the largest, which just is the reactor cooling water flow rate. Through analysis of the Fault 4 above, this result conform to the actual situation.

In addition, comparing with the relative error of variances, the contribution plots are performed based on the PCA.

Usually, when CPV is greater than 85%, the former k principal component can contain most of the original data set information.

Figure 4 is the construction plots of the Fault 6. For example, the variable x_{49} is not diagnosed by CDC construction plots. However, variable x_{49} is a significant change

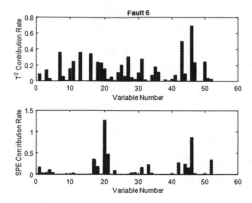

Fig. 4. Variables construction plots of Fault 6

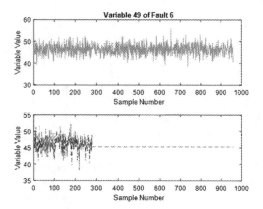

Fig. 5. Variable x_{49} value of Fault 6 (red dashed lines denote normal variables and blue dotted lines represent fault variables) (Color figure online)

Table 2. Fault error diagnosis rates (%)

Fault no.	Relative error of variances	Construction plots based on PCA
1	11.54	17.31
2	9.62	21.15
3	11.54	15.38
4	9.62	13.46
5	9.62	19.23
6	3.85	26.92
7	13.46	17.30

from the Fig. 5. But when using the relative error of the variance to diagnosis, the variable x_{49} can be diagnosed.

In order to compare the superiority of the two algorithms, the fault error diagnosis rate is defined, which is calculated the percentage of fault identified as normal samples.

$$FEDR = \frac{N_{nf}}{N_{tf}} \times 100 \qquad (22)$$

where N_{nf} denotes the number of fault samples which considered as normal samples, and N_{tf} is the number of total fault samples.

The results in Table 2. show that the fault error diagnosis rates of relative error of variance is less than that of construction plots based on PCA.

4   Conclusions

In the dynamic industry process, the data generated from production process is time serials data. Once the fault occurs, since the fault cannot be automatically repaired, all data obtained after the fault point is fault data. For this situation, a new method of fault isolation and diagnosis for a class of nonlinear multivariate process is proposed. Improved Fisher discriminant analysis can effectively detect the faults from the normal samples. By comparing IFDA with conventional FDA and CCA algorithm, the result shows that fault detection rates and fault detection delay of IFDA are better than the others.

Additionally, fault variables diagnosis is also a significant problem needed to be settled after the faults are isolated. This paper uses the relative error of variance of the normal and fault samples to determine which variables are fault variables. The fault error diagnosis rates are lower than CDC method. The simulation results of TE process fault detection data sets show the advantages of the proposed method in fault isolation and diagnosis.

References

1. Zhao, C., Wang, W.: Efficient faulty variable selection and parsimonious reconstruction modeling for fault isolation. J. Process Control **38**, 31–41 (2016)
2. Qin, S.J.: Statistical process monitoring: basics and beyond. J. Chemometr. **17**, 480–502 (2003)
3. He, Q.P., Qin, S.J., Wang, J.: A new fault diagnosis method using fault directions in Fisher discriminant analysis. AIChE J. **51**(2), 555–571 (2005)
4. Chiang, L.H., Russell, E.L., Braatz, R.D.: Fault diagnosis in chemical processes using Fisher discriminant analysis, discriminant partial least squares, and principal component analysis. Chemometr. Intell. Lab. Syst. **50**(2), 243–252 (2000)
5. Downs, J., Vogel, E.: A plant-wide industrial process control problem. Comput. Chem. Eng. **17**(3), 245–255 (1993)

6. Shen, Y., Ding, S.X., Haghani, A., et al.: A comparison study of basic data-driven fault diagnosis and process monitoring methods on the benchmark Tennessee Eastman process. J. Process Control **22**(9), 1567–1581 (2012)
7. Samuel, R.T., Cao, Y.: Nonlinear process fault detection and identification using kernel PCA and kernel density estimation. Syst. Sci. Control Eng. **4**, 165–174 (2016)
8. Chen, Z., Zhang, K., Ding, S.X., et al.: Improved canonical correlation analysis-based fault detection methods for industrial processes. J. Process Control **41**, 26–34 (2016)
9. Alcala, C.F., Qin, S.J.: Reconstruction-based contribution for process monitoring with kernel principal component analysis. Automatica **45**(7), 1593–1600 (2009)
10. Jiang, B., Huang, D., Zhu, X., et al.: Canonical variate analysis-based contributions for fault identification. J. Process Control **26**, 17–25 (2015)

An LMI Approach to Iterative Learning Control Based on JITL for Batch Processes

Liuming Zhou and Li Jia[(✉)]

Shanghai Key Laboratory of Power Station Automation Technology,
Department of Automation, College of Mechatronics Engineering
and Automation, Shanghai University, Shanghai 200072, China
jiali@staff.shu.edu.cn

Abstract. In this paper, in order to linearize the nonlinear model of batch processes, a batch process is modeled by just in time learning (JITL) method and dynamic updating locally linear model parameters along batch cycle is also proposed. Considering that the error between the actual model and the prediction model, iterative learning control strategy based on a quadratic performance criterion is proposed and the system controller is solved by linear matrix inequality (LMI) method. Moreover the convergence of tracking error based on ILC is also analyzed and the conditions of convergence is proposed. In order to satisfy the condition, a novel ILC method based on JITL is proposed. To improve the convergence speed, this paper further uses of ILC based on nominal trajectory. As a result, the simulation results show that the system has better accuracy of output. It provides a new way for the control of batch processes.

Keywords: Batch processes · Iterative learning control (ILC) · Linear matrix inequality (LMI) · Just in time learning (JITL)

1 Introduction

Modern process industry is gradually developing from the production of large quantities and basic materials to the production of small quantities, many varieties and serialization. Batch processes have the characteristics of small batch and multi production, which meets the requirements of modern process industries. It plays more and more important roles in many manufacturing fields [1, 2]. Although batch processes have been widely used in industry, there are no steady working points in batch processes, which has characteristic of highly nonlinearity. These characteristics determine that the control of batch processes is more complicated than that of continuous process control, so it needs new non-traditional technologies. The idea of iterative learning control is very suitable for the optimal control of batch processes [3, 4]. It uses the previous control experience and the output error to correct the current output of control. The actual output trajectory of the controlled system converges to the desired output trajectory in a finite time interval.

Because of batch processes have the characteristic of repetitive motion, iterative learning control is widely used in batch processes. It realizes improved tracking and control optimization [5, 6].The LMI technique has become a useful tool for solve

© Springer Nature Singapore Pte Ltd. 2017
D. Yue et al. (Eds.): LSMS/ICSEE 2017, Part II, CCIS 762, pp. 212–222, 2017.
DOI: 10.1007/978-981-10-6373-2_22

control problem. With the wide application of LMI, more and more scholars apply the LMI method to the batch processes. Ghaffari proposed a robust predictive control approach for additive discrete time uncertain nonlinear systems. A sufficient state feedback synthesis condition is provided in the form of a LMI optimization and is solved online at each time step [7]. Wang proposed a closed-loop robust iterative learning fault-tolerant guaranteed cost control scheme for batch processes with actuator failures [8]. However, most papers just consider model is linear or not consider the error between actual model and predict model. How to address these problems is worth studying.

To solve this problem, inspired by JITL technology, we first translate the nonlinear model into the locally linear model. Considering the model error, we present a design method of control system and propose a quadratic performance criterion for locally linear model. Since model error is uncertain, we introduce LMI techniques to design ILC algorithms. Control law is solved by LMI method.

The paper is structured as follows. Batch processes are modeled based on JITL technology in Sect. 2. Section 3 presents the proposed ILC control system, and the controller is obtained by solving the optimal problem. In Sect. 4, the convergence of the system is analyzed and Sect. 5 gives a simulation example. In the end, the concluding remarks is given in Sect. 6.

2 Locally Linear Model for Batch Processes

2.1 Batch Processes System Description

The batch length of batch processes is t_f, which can be divided into T equal intervals, and define that $U_k = [u_k(1), \cdots, u_k(T)]^T$ and $Y_k = [y_k(1), \cdots, y_k(T)]^T$ respectively are a vector of control input and product quality variables during k-th batch, where k denotes the batch. $y \in R^n$ and $u \in R^m$ represent the product quality and control action variables, respectively. In this paper, the nonlinear model can be represented as follow

$$\hat{y}_k(t+1) = f[y_k(t), y_k(t-1), \cdots, y_k(t-n_y+1), u_k(t), u_k(t-1) \cdots, u_k(t-n_u+1)] \quad (1)$$

where n_y and n_u are related to the order of the model.

2.2 Just-in-Time Learning

As shown in the Fig. 1, system predictive output can be obtained by JITL technology. Firstly, relevant data are obtained by similarity calculation between current query data and sample data in database. Secondly, we can get locally linear model based on relevant data. Lastly, system model output can be obtained based on the current input data and the locally model.

In this paper, the distance and angle information between samples are considered simultaneously. The Euclidean distance and the angle are weighted as a measurement of similarity between samples, so that we can obtain the neighborhood data of the model.

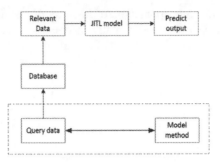

Fig. 1. Just-in-time learning model

Sample sets in database are consist of N process data $[y, X_i] = [y_i, X_{i1}, X_{i2}, X_{i3}\dots]$ $(i = 1, 2,\dots, n)$ and input sample point $X_q = [X_{q1}, X_{q2}, X_{q3}\dots]$. The formulas of similarity calculation are as follows

$$d(X_q, X_i) = \sqrt{\sum_{j=1}^{N} (X_{qi} - X_{ij})^2} \tag{2}$$

$$\cos \theta_i = \frac{\Delta X_q^T \Delta X_i}{\|\Delta X_q\|_2 \|\Delta X_i\|_2} \tag{3}$$

$$s_i = \lambda \sqrt{e^{-d(X_q \bullet X_i)}} + (1 - \lambda) \cos \theta_i, \cos \theta_i \geq 0 \tag{4}$$

where $\Delta X_q = X_q - X_{q-1}$, $\Delta X_i = X_i - X_{i-1}$, θ is angle between ΔX_q and ΔX_i, λ is weight coefficient, which influence the model precision. S_i is similarity between ΔX_q and ΔX_i. The larger the value of s_i, the greater similarity of samples.

A weight w_i is assigned to each data X_i and it is calculated by the kernel function, $w_i = \sqrt{K(d(x_q, x_i))/h}$, where h is the bandwidth of the kernel function K that normally uses a Gaussian function, $K(d) = e^{-d^2}$, the predict value is

$$\hat{y}_q = X_q^T (P^T P)^{-1} P^T v \tag{5}$$

where $P = W\Phi$, $v = Wy$, $W \in R^{NXN}$ is a weight matrix with diagonal elements w_i, $\Phi = R^{NXN}$ is the matrix with every row corresponding to X_i^T and $y = [y_1, y_2, \dots, y_N]^T$.

We can obtain the database by collect input and output data and select the appropriate modeling neighborhood by similarity between samples. The locally model for JITL can be represented by the ARX model and it can be described as follow

$$\hat{y}(t) = [y(t - 1), y(t - 2), \dots, y(t - n_y), u(t - 1), u(t - 2), \dots, u(t - n_u)]Z \tag{6}$$

where $Z = [\xi_1, \xi_2, \dots, \xi_{n_y + n_u}]^T$

So we obtain the model of batch processes by the JITL technology. In order to simplify the model, we select a two-order model with $n_y = n_u = 2$. It can be written as follow

$$\hat{y}(t) = \alpha_1 y(t-1) + \alpha_2 y(t-2) + \beta_1 u(t-1) + \beta_2 u(t-2) \tag{7}$$

3   Design of Control Strategy Based on LMI

As show in Fig. 2, due to the influence of external disturbance, uncertainty and linearization error. The locally linear model is impossible to approach the real system completely. There is a certain deviation between the predicted value and the actual output value. It can be written as follows

$$\tilde{e}_k(t) = y_d(t) - \tilde{y}_k(t) = y_d(t) - (\hat{y}_k(t) + \alpha(\hat{e}_k(t) + \theta\hat{e}_k(t))) \tag{8}$$

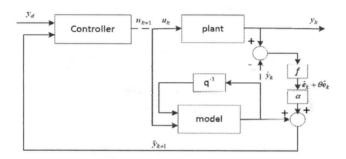

Fig. 2. Structure of optimal control system

where θ is uncertain parameters and satisfy $\|\theta - \bar{\theta}\|_W \le \rho$. $\hat{e}$ is model prediction errors of the previous batch as follow

$$\hat{e}_{k+1}(t) = y_k(t) - \hat{y}_k(t) \tag{9}$$

Quadratic object function is as follow

$$\min_{\Delta u_{k+1}} \max_{\theta \in \Phi} J = \|\tilde{e}_{k+1}(t+2)\|_Q^2 + \|\Delta u_{k+1}(t+1)\|_R^2 \quad 0 \le t \le N \tag{10}$$

where $\Delta u_{k+1}(t) = u_{k+1}(t) - u_k(t)$.

The constraint of control input in industry application is as follow

$$u^{low} \le u_{k+1}(t) \le u^{up} \tag{11}$$

Equation (11) can be written as follow

$$\prod \Delta u_{k+1} \geq P_{k+1} \tag{12}$$

where

$$\prod = [I \quad -I]^T \tag{13}$$

$$P_k = \begin{bmatrix} u^{low} - u_k \\ -(u^{up} - u_k) \end{bmatrix} \tag{14}$$

Lemma 1 [9]: If there exist $\tilde{y} \in R^m$, such that $\sigma_1(\tilde{y}) > 0$ for $\sigma_1(y) = y^T Q_1 y + 2s_1^T y + r_1 \geq 0$, the following two conditions are equivalent

S1: if for every y such that $\sigma_1(y) > 0$,

$$\sigma_1(y) = y^T Q_1 y + 2s_1^T y + r_1 \geq 0 \tag{15}$$

S2: there exist $\tau \geq 0$, such that the following linear matrix inequality is feasible

$$\begin{bmatrix} Q_0 & s_0 \\ s_0^T & r_0 \end{bmatrix} + \tau \begin{bmatrix} Q_1 & s_1 \\ s_1^T & r_1 \end{bmatrix} \geq 0 \tag{16}$$

Theorem 1: For a given system (7), the quadratic object function (10) is equivalent to

$$\min \lambda$$
$$\text{subject to}$$
$$\begin{bmatrix} \lambda - \tau(\rho - \bar{\theta}^T W \bar{\theta}) & -\tau \bar{\theta}^T W & Y(\Delta u_{k+1}) & Z(\Delta u_{k+1}) \\ * & \tau W & X & 0 \\ * & * & I & 0 \\ * & * & * & I \end{bmatrix} \geq 0 \tag{17}$$
$$\prod \Delta u_k \geq P_k$$

where X, Y, Z is as follows

$$X = Q^{\frac{1}{2}} \alpha \bar{\theta} \hat{e}_{k+1}(t+2) \tag{18}$$

$$Y(\Delta u_{k+1}) = Q^{\frac{1}{2}}(\alpha \hat{e}(t+2) - (\alpha_1 y_{k+1}(t) + \alpha_2 y_{k+1}(t+2) \\ + \beta_1(u_k(t)) + \beta_2(u_k(t+1) + \Delta u_{k+1}(t+1))) \tag{19}$$

$$Z(\Delta u_{k+1}) = \Delta u_{k+1}^T(t+1) R \Delta u_{k+1}(t+1) \tag{20}$$
$$(0 \leq t \leq N)$$

Proof. The quadratic objective performance function can be written as

$$\tilde{e}_{k+1}^T(t+2)Q\tilde{e}_{k+1}(t+2) + \Delta u_{k+1}^T(t+1)R\Delta u_{k+1}(t+1)$$
$$= (e_{k+1}(t+2) - \alpha\hat{e}_{k+1}(t+2) - \alpha\theta\hat{e}_{k+1}(t+2))^T Q(e_{k+1}(t+2) -$$
$$\alpha\bar{\hat{e}}_{k+1}(t+2) - \alpha\theta\hat{e}_{k+1}(t+2)) + \Delta u_{k+1}^T(t+1)R\Delta u_{k+1}(t+1)$$
$$= \left\|\alpha Q^{\frac{1}{2}}\theta\hat{e}_{k+1}(t+2) + Q^{\frac{1}{2}}(\alpha\hat{e}_{k+1}(t+2) - e_{k+1}(t+2))\right\|_2^2 + \left\|R^{\frac{1}{2}}\Delta u_{k+1}(t+1)\right\|_2^2$$

(21)

define X, Y, Z as show in Eqs. (18)–(20).

The min-max problem is equivalent to

$$\min \lambda$$

$$\|X\theta + Y(\Delta u_{k+1})\|_2^2 + \|Z(\Delta u_{k+1})\|_2^2 \leq \lambda$$

(22)

$$\forall\theta\left\{\theta\big|\|\theta - \bar{\theta}\|_W \leq \rho\right\}$$

(23)

Equation (23) can be rewritten as

$$\begin{bmatrix} 1 \\ \theta \end{bmatrix}^T \begin{bmatrix} \rho - \bar{\theta}^T W\bar{\theta} & \bar{\theta}^T W \\ W\bar{\theta} & -W \end{bmatrix} \begin{bmatrix} 1 \\ \theta \end{bmatrix} \geq 0$$

(24)

So according to Eq. (21), we get

$$\begin{bmatrix} 1 \\ \theta \end{bmatrix}^T \begin{bmatrix} \lambda - \|Y(\Delta u_{k+1})\|_2^2 - \|Z(\Delta u_{k+1})\|_2^2 & -Y(\Delta u_{k+1})^T X \\ -X^T Y(\Delta u_{k+1}) & -X^T X \end{bmatrix} \begin{bmatrix} 1 \\ \theta \end{bmatrix} \geq 0$$

(25)

Using the Lemma 1, we have if there exist a scalar t > 0 such that

$$\begin{bmatrix} 1 \\ \theta \end{bmatrix}^T \begin{bmatrix} \lambda - \|Y(\Delta u_{k+1})\|_2^2 - \|Z(\Delta u_{k+1})\|_2^2 - \tau(\rho - \bar{\theta}^T W\bar{\theta}) & -Y(\Delta u_{k+1})^T X - \tau(\bar{\theta}^T W) \\ -X^T Y(\Delta u_{k+1}) - \tau W\bar{\theta} & -X^T X + \tau W \end{bmatrix} \begin{bmatrix} 1 \\ \theta \end{bmatrix} \geq 0$$

(26)

Thus

$$\begin{bmatrix} \lambda - \|Y(\Delta u_{k+1})\|_2^2 - \|Z(\Delta u_{k+1})\|_2^2 - \tau(\rho - \bar{\theta}^T W\bar{\theta}) & -Y(\Delta u_{k+1})^T X - \tau(\bar{\theta}^T W) \\ -X^T Y(\Delta u_{k+1}) - \tau W\bar{\theta} & -X^T X + \tau W \end{bmatrix} \geq 0$$

(27)

Using the schur complements theorem, we have

$$\begin{bmatrix} \lambda - \tau(\rho - \bar{\theta}^T W \theta) & -\tau \bar{\theta}^T W & Y(\Delta u_{k+1}) & Z(\Delta u_{k+1}) \\ * & \tau W & X & 0 \\ * & * & I & 0 \\ * & * & * & I \end{bmatrix} \geq 0 \qquad (28)$$

This is a LMI in regard to Δu_{k+1}, so the input increment Δu_{k+1} can be obtained by solving LMIs, and the input of iterative learning control system can be written as follow

$$u_{k+1}(t+1) = \Delta u_{k+1}(t+1) + u_k(t+1) \qquad (29)$$

4 Convergence Analysis

Theorem 2: Consider a batch process described by Eq. (7). The optimal iterative control policy will converge to a constant along batch cycle under the condition (30), namely $\Delta u_k = u_{k+1} - u_k \to 0$ as $k \to \infty$.

$$G_k u_k + \hat{e}_k(\theta) \geq G_{k+1} u_k + \hat{e}_{k+1}(\theta) \qquad (30)$$

where $e_{k+1}(\theta) = \hat{e}_k + \theta \hat{e}_k$ and the locally linear model can be written as $y_k = G_k u_k$

Proof. The error update model is described as follow

$$e_{k+1} = y_d - \hat{y}_{k+1} = e_k + \hat{y}_k - \hat{y}_{k+1} = e_k - (G_{k+1} u_{k+1} - G_k u_k) \qquad (31)$$

According to Eq. (30), we get

$$e_{k+1} - \hat{e}_{k+1}(\theta) \geq e_k - (G_{k+1} u_{k+1} - G_{k+1} u_k) - \hat{e}_k(\theta) = e_k - G_{k+1} \Delta u_{k+1} - \hat{e}_k(\theta) \qquad (32)$$

Then the objective function in Eq. (10).

$$\begin{aligned} J &= (e_{k+1} - e_{k+1}(\theta))^T Q(e_{k+1} - e_{k+1}(\theta)) + \Delta u_{k+1}^T R \Delta u_{k+1} \\ &\geq (e_k - G_{k+1} \Delta u_{k+1} - \hat{e}_k(\theta))^T Q(e_k - G_{k+1} \Delta u_{k+1} - \hat{e}_k(\theta)) + \Delta u_{k+1}^T R \Delta u_{k+1} \\ &= \Delta u_{k+1}^T (G_{k+1}^T Q G_{k+1} + R) \Delta u_{k+1} - 2(e_k - \hat{e}_k(\theta))^T Q G_{k+1} \Delta u_{k+1} + (e_k - \hat{e}_k(\theta))^T Q(e_k - \hat{e}_k(\theta)) \end{aligned} \qquad (33)$$

define as

$$F(e_k) = \min_{\Delta u_{k+1}} \max_{\theta \in \Phi} J \qquad (34)$$

Assume θ^* is the optimizer of min-max problem for the previous batch, since $e_{k+1} = e_k$ with $\Delta u_{k+1} = 0$, we have

$$F(e_k) \leq (e_k - \hat{e}_k(\theta))^T Q(e_k - \hat{e}_k(\theta)) \leq (e_k - \hat{e}_k(\theta^*))^T Q(e_k - \hat{e}_k(\theta^*))$$
$$\leq F(e_{k-1}) - \Delta u_k^T R \Delta u_k \tag{35}$$

According to Eq. (35), we get

$$F(e_k) + \sum_{j=1}^{k} \Delta u_j^T R \Delta u_j \leq F(e_0) \tag{36}$$

We have the conclusion that $\Delta u_k \to 0$ as $k \to \infty$, and thus $\{u_k\}$ converges.

The dynamic model update based on JITL technology is proposed in the paper. But the optimal iterative control policy converges under constraint condition (30). In order to satisfy condition, we proposed novel ILC Algorithm as follows

Step 1: Initialization. Let $k = 1$ and initialize $U_1, \hat{e}_1$ and parameters Q and R.
Step 2: We can get model G_k by using JITL technology and update the model based on previous input and output.
Step 3: Calculate fist time input $u_k(1)$ by the theorem 1, then we can get input $u_{k_0}(1)$ such that $y_d(2) - y_{k_0}(2) < \delta$, where δ is small scalar.
Step 4: We can get second time model G_k by using previous k_0-th batch input and output, thus we can get second time input $u_{k_0}(2)$ by the method which step 2 and step 3 shows.
Step 5: Increase time by 1 and until end time.

Remark1. The above-mentioned method can ensure the condition (30) by getting the first time input to end time input. The paper gets system model by JITL technology based on similarity between input data and sample sets, so we can reduce the number of input data change, and thus we can get controller by above ILC algorithm.

Although above-mentioned method can ensure the condition (30), but since initial value of U_1 is set to 0, the algorithm convergence speed is slowly. In order to solve this problem, we can first get nominal trajectory by using Theorem 1 where $\Delta u_{k+1} \in R^n$ and $X = Q^{\frac{1}{2}} \alpha \bar{\theta} \hat{e}_{k+1}(tf)$ and set it as initial value. Then we can perform the algorithm step 2 to step 5 based on nominal trajectory.

5 Example

The algorithm presented in this paper is applied to a typical batch reactor, in which a first-order irreversible exothermic reaction $A \xrightarrow{k_1} B \xrightarrow{k_2} C$ takes place. This reaction process are described by the dynamic equations as follows

$$\dot{x}_1 = -k_1 \exp(-E_1/T)x_1^2$$
$$\dot{x}_2 = -k_1 \exp(-E_1/T)x_1^2 - k_2 \exp(-E_2/T)x_2 \tag{37}$$

where x_1 and x_2 respectively represent the reactant concentration of A and B, and T denote the reaction temperature. The values of parameter k_1, k_2, E_1 and E_2 are given in Table 1.

Table 1. Parameter values for the batch reactor

Parameter	Value
k_1	4.0×10^3
k_2	6.2×10^5
E_1	2.5×10^3
E_2	5.0×10^3

In this simulation, the reactor temperature is normalized by using $u = (T - T_{min})/(T_{max} - T_{min})$, where T_{min} and T_{max} are 298(K) and 398(K), respectively. u is the control variable confined by $0 \leq u \leq 1$, and $x_2(t)$ is the output signal. The control objective is control concentration of B at the end-time by adjusting input u of system.

The initial batch input $U = 0$ and system output approximate to $yd(tf) = 0.61$. In order to verify the convergence, we first set different run number according to different time and we can get each moment input increment as batch increase. The figures are as follows (Fig. 3).

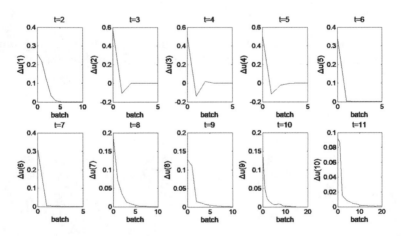

Fig. 3. The curves of each time input increment

From the above diagram, we can see input increment convergence to zero.

According to step 1 to step 5, we can get control output and error of the terminal point by calculating. The figure of control output trajectories based on zero initial value at 5th, 10th, 30th and 50th batches and error of the terminal point as batch increase are as follows (Fig. 4).

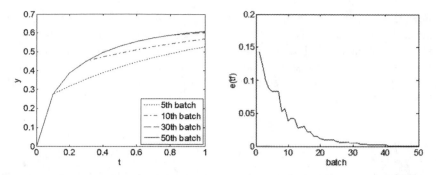

Fig. 4. The control output trajectories at 5th, 10th, 30th and 50th batches based on zero initial value and the curve of error based on zero initial value

The figure of control output trajectories based on nominal trajectory at 1st, 5th, 15th and 30th batches and error of the terminal point as batch increase are as follows (Fig. 5).

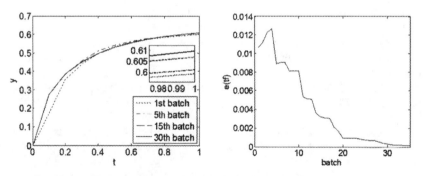

Fig. 5. The control output trajectories at 1st, 5th, 15th and 30th batches based on nominal trajectory and the curve of error based on nominal trajectory

Seen from the chart of the simulation, the algorithm based on nominal trajectory has faster convergence speed.

The proposed control strategy based on LMI and JITL was compared with tradition iterative learning control(ILC) strategy [10],which is the representative method in batch processes control. The final output error values can be seen from Table 2. It is clear that the proposed control strategy has faster convergence rate and yields a more accurate final output than that obtained by traditional ILC.

Table 2. Final output error value based on two controller systems

Methods	1st batch	20th batch	35th batch	50th batch
The proposed control strategy	1.0×10^{-2}	9.0×10^{-4}	1.4×10^{-4}	5.2×10^{-5}
Tradition iterative learning control	1.1×10^{-1}	1.6×10^{-3}	1.5×10^{-3}	1.5×10^{-3}

Remark2. The convergence of control algorithm is strictly proved and tracking performance is analyzed in this paper. The proposed control system verify that perfect tracking can be attained. The simulation has indicated that this method has greatly improved the accuracy of system output. The proposed control strategy was applied to a simulation example and the results demonstrate that the control system has good tracking performance.

6 Conclusion

This paper first gives locally linear model based on JITL method, thus it realizes that nonconvex optimization problem of nonlinear system is translated into convex optimization problem of linear system. Then we proposed a novel ILC algorithm which ensure convergence of control input. In addition, this paper gives design method of the controller based on LMI method and studies performance of convergence. The simulation studies show the proposed algorithm have better tracking performance.

References

1. Yu, X.D., Xiong, Z.H., Huang, D.X., et al.: Model-based iterative learning control for batch processes using generalized hinging hyperplanes. Ind. Eng. Chem. Res. **52**(4), 1627–1634 (2014)
2. Zhang, R., Jin, Q., Gao, F.: Design of state space linear quadratic tracking control using GA optimization for batch processes with partial actuator failure. J. Process Control **26**, 102–114 (2015)
3. Xiong, Z.H., Zhang, J., Wang, X., Xu, Y.M.: Integrated tracking control strategy for batch processes using a batch-wise linear time-varying perturbation model. IET Control Theory Appl. **1**(1), 178–188 (2007)
4. Lee, J.H., Lee, K.S.: Iterative learning control applied to batch processes: an overview. Control Eng. Pract. **15**(10), 1306–1318 (2007)
5. Liu, T., Wang, X.Z., Chen, J.: Robust PID based indirect-type iterative learning control for batch processes with time-varying uncertainties. J. Process Control **24**(12), 95–106 (2014)
6. Chen, C., Xiong, Z.H., Zhong, Y.: Design and analysis of integrated predictive iterative learning control for batch process based on two-dimensional system theory. Chin. J. Chem. Eng. **22**(7), 762–768 (2014)
7. Ghaffari, V., Naghavi, S.V., Safavi, A.A.: Robust model predictive control of a class of uncertain nonlinear systems with application to typical CSTR problems. J. Process Control **23**(4), 493–499 (2013)
8. Wang, L., Chen, X., Gao, F.: An LMI method to robust iterative learning fault-tolerant guaranteed cost control for batch processes. Chin. J. Chem. Eng. **21**(4), 401–411 (2013)
9. Boyd, S., Ghaoui, L.E., Feron, E., Balakrishnan, V.: Linear Matrix Inequalities in System and Control Theory. SIAM, Philadelphia (1994)
10. Jia, L., Shi, J.P., Chiu, M.S.: Integrated neuro-fuzzy model and dynamic R-parameter based quadratic criterion-iterative learning control for batch process control technique. Neurocomputing **98**(18), 24–33 (2012)

Theme-Based Spider for Academic Paper

Peifeng Yin[1], Qiyu Shao[2], Xingfu Wang[1], Weihua Wang[1],
Fuyou Miao[1], and Chenxi Shao[1,3(✉)]

[1] College of Computer Science and Technology,
Unviersity of Science and Technology of China, Hefei 230027, China
ypftxbb@mail.ustc.eud.cn,
{Wangfu,whwang,mfy,cxshao}@ustc.edu.cn
[2] Department of Computer Science, Dayananda Sagar Institutions,
Bangalore University, Bangalore, India
shaofromchina@gmail.com
[3] Anhui Province Key Laboratory of Software in Computing and
Communication, Hefei 230027, China

Abstract. Nowadays contents of the web multiply everyday. However, for particular company or individual, some kind of information has higher priority. For example, among so much information on the internet, web pages containing academic papers are definitely more attractive to a researcher. And the problem lies in how to find that kind of data. Therefore we design a spider that targets only on online academic papers. Besides reserving three major parts of a traditional spider, we make some modifications on Filter and Parser so that our spider is competent enough to accomplish the mission. And the essential mechanism of recognizing and extracting expected pages primarily lies on keyword-matching and Finite State Machine Theory. After roaming on two web sites, the spider successfully collects desirable information. We can safely see from the result that in future by optimization and modification this theme-based spider may work more efficiently or even expands to other fields of interest.

Keywords: Theme-based · Spider · Paper

1 Introduction

Information on the internet has been growing faster and faster everyday since the build of the World Wide Web. The information bomb makes it extremely difficult for user to find useful data, and to solve the problem, spider and search engine were born. Spider has been defined as "software programs that traverse the World Wide Web information space by following hypertext links and retrieving Web documents by standard HTTP protocol" [1].

This work are supported by Natural Science Foundation of China (Nos. 61472381, 61472382, 61572454 and 61174144), NOE-Micrsoft Key Laboratory of Multimedia Computing and Communication Foundation, Anhui Province Key Laboratory of Software in Computing and Communication.

© Springer Nature Singapore Pte Ltd. 2017
D. Yue et al. (Eds.): LSMS/ICSEE 2017, Part II, CCIS 762, pp. 223–230, 2017.
DOI: 10.1007/978-981-10-6373-2_23

Today internet users are familiar with such search engines as Google [A.1] and Baidu [A.2], which are supported by general-purpose spiders browsing web pages on a breath-first strategy. If the task is to find pages of "a particular kind or on a particular topic" [2], a more advanced spider, theme-based spider or "focused-crawler" [3] is needed.

This paper describes the structure and kernel mechanism of the theme-based spider which targets only on academic papers. Compared with other themes, paper has characteristics that are easier to extract and generalize, which will be discussed later. And this is the reason we choose paper as our initial focus of research. In the following chapters, "Intelligent Spider" will be used as a nickname of the theme-based spider for academic papers.

2   Structure of Intelligent Spider

Usually, a general-purpose spider consists of three major parts: Crawler or "Page-Collector" [4], Filter and Parser or "Page-Indexer" [4]. Crawler aims at fetching web pages, according to the URL (Uniform Resource Locators) provided by Filter. Filter takes charge in extracting new URL and texts of the web pages. New URL will be sent back to Crawler and texts back to Parser, which parses the contents and creates index for later retrieving.

More advanced than spider, Intelligent Spider is supposed to fetch pages discriminatively. It has to recognize pages containing information about the paper (called Key-Info below) and extract such information (Fig. 1).

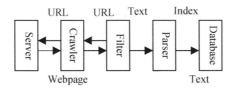

Fig. 1.   Classic three parts of a spider

To complete such task, we make some modifications on the second part, the Filter. As the Fig. 2 shows, a module in charge of Key Information recognition and extraction is integrated into filter, whose output now becomes Key-Info as a result.

Also, another module, Format is added into parser in order to get a better representation of Key-Info.

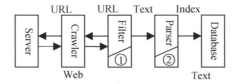

Fig. 2.   Structure of Intelligent Spider. ①: Key-Info recognition, ②: Key-Info format.

"As for the implement, there are generally two ways: recursive and non-recursive" [5]. And our spider adopts the latter one since recursive spider does not agree with multi-thread running. Also, as experiment [6] shows, non-recursive spider works more efficiently than recursive one.

3   Kernel Mechanism and its Evolution

Key-Info recognition and extraction, which seems naturally easy for people, is quite difficult for web spider, since it can not understand human languages. Before going further, we need to consider how human brain accomplishes this task. Actually, not all people can recognize Key Information. A baby certainly can not, a junior student may be unlikely to tell, and even an adult, if he or she knows little about academic paper, may fail. Therefore, it is the knowledge about academic paper that leads us to recognize the Key-Info. Keywords such as "title", "author", and "abstract" may be an obvious hint. To put it straight, the appearance of "title" in some page suggests that reader will read the title later in the same page. And so does that of "author" and "abstract". This mechanism is common in daily life. For example, if a person receives a pretty packed box on his birthday, he will expect it to be his birthday gift, though he does not know what exactly is in the box until it is opened. Therefore, after matching some keyword, Intelligent Spider may "expect" to meet the relative content, even if it does not understand the meaning and neither does it need to.

Besides keywords, there is another obvious hint for Key-Info. Since all contents are viewed through a web browser, web page designer adds many ornamental elements to get a tidy appearance for Key-Info. And HTML tags such as <table>, <td> and <tr> may be of great help in Key-Info recognition (Fig. 3).

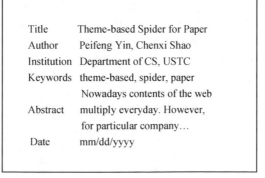

Fig. 3. Classic appearance of Key-Info in web page

So we get the kernel mechanism of Key-Info recognition, a combination of keywords-match and HTML-tag- assistance. The process of recognition is something like a FSM (Finite State Machine), as Fig. 4 indicates.

1:Keywords-match 2: Content-obtain

Fig. 4. Original state switching

However, it is not the whole story. Sometimes the web page only contains a list of papers, which may be misjudged as Key-Info. And it's necessary to introduce a new state, Keywords-Recorder, to eliminate such unpleasant circumstances. Keywords-Recorder records keywords in one page and recognize the repeatedly appearing keywords. When Filter meets the same keyword more than once, it can be sure that the information is just a list of papers and desert the page immediately (Fig. 5).

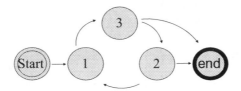

1: Keywords-match 2: Content-obtain
3: Keywords-recorder

Fig. 5. Revised state switching

There is another situation worth considering. Sometimes a web page contains the Key-Info of some paper. However, this Key-Info is a brief version and a detailed one can be obtained by visiting the hypertext link provided by the page (called Bait-page). In this case, Filter is supposed to discard the Bait-page wisely and wait for the detailed one. Therefore, we add another state to count the frequency of keywords since a Bait-page usually displays low frequency of keywords (Fig. 6).

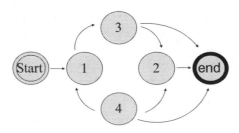

1: Keywords-match 2: Content-obtain
3: Keywords-recorder 4: Counter

Fig. 6. Re-modified state switching

Sometimes, Key-Info is split into several parts, each put in a different page. This situation is due to the tag "<iframe>", which allows designer to store the data in different pages and leave to internet browser the integrating task. That means, a page bonded with a specific URL may serve as a frame, and contents actually come from other URLs. To get a complete picture of Key-Info, Filter has to use a stack to reserve different data streams. So we have the final FSM as Fig. 7.

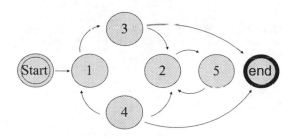

1: Keywords-match   2: Content-obtain
3: Keywords-recorder 4: Counter
5: Push & Pop data stream

Fig. 7. Final state switching

4 Algorithm

Now we provide an algorithm to describe the mechanism introduced above. It goes as:

a. Match keywords? If yes, go to b; else return to a;
b. Keywords appeared before? If yes, go to f; else record the keyword and go to the next step;
c. Read the following content until tag </td> is met; counter++ and go on;
d. Has tag </table> occurred? If yes, go to e; else return to a;
e. Is counter greater than x? If yes, submit the information; else, discard it;
f. Quit.

In the algorithm, the x is the value that judges whether the page being parsed is a Bait-page and its value is manually determined, usually ranging from 3 to 5. By our experience, a proper value is 4.

5 Results

After programming work is done, we make the spider run on two web sites, Science Paper Online[A.3] and CNKI[A.4], for experiment. One thing worth mentioning is that the spider usually works from night to dawn of next day, about 23:00–7:00, when network suffers less burden. Moreover, Crawler will sleep for a random time, between 5 to 10 s, whenever it fetches a web page, so that the server is free of frequent queries.

All of these are to be "a responsible spider designer" [7]. So far, it has successfully recognized 9753 web pages which contain Key-Info out of 38208 pages in total. Figures 8, 9 and 10 clearly shows the input and output of the spider, or exactly, the Filter. And Table 1 displays some of the working records.

Fig. 8. Classic view of a page through web browser

Fig. 9. Web page in the spider's eye

With these data at hand, a search engine, PaperSo[A.5] is built, providing service of online search for academic papers.

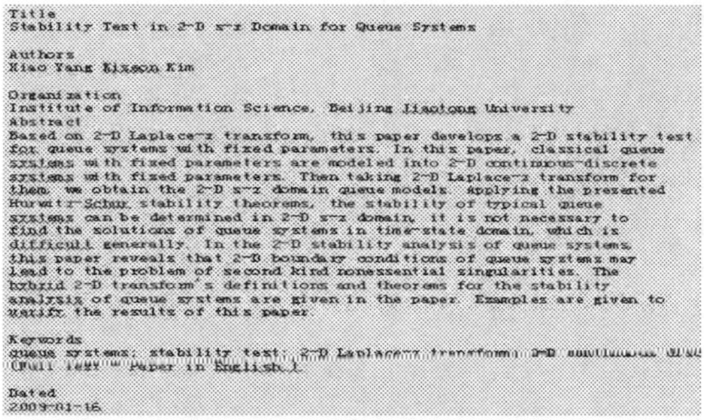

Title
Stability Test in 2-D x-z Domain for Queue Systems

Authors
Xiao Yang Kixson Kim

Organization
Institute of Information Science, Beijing Jiaotong University
Abstract
Based on 2-D Laplace's transform, this paper develops a 2-D stability test
for queue systems with fixed parameters. In this paper, classical queue
systems with fixed parameters are modeled into 2-D continuous-discrete
systems with fixed parameters. Then taking 2-D Laplace's transform for
them, we obtain the 2-D x-z domain queue models. Applying the presented
Hurwitz-Schur stability theorems, the stability of typical queue
systems can be determined in 2-D x-z domain. it is not necessary to
find the solutions of queue systems in time-state domain, which is
difficult generally. In the 2-D stability analysis of queue systems,
this paper reveals that 2-D boundary conditions of queue systems may
lead to the problem of second kind nonessential singularities. The
hybrid 2-D transform's definitions and theorems for the stability
analysis of queue systems are given in the paper. Examples are given to
justify the results of this paper.

Keywords
queue systems; stability test; 2-D Laplace's transform; 2-D continuous-di...
(Full text : Paper in English)

Dated
2009-01-16

Fig. 10. Output of filter

Table 1. Work records of Intelligent Spider.

Date (mm/dd/yyyy)	Running time (min)	Number of pages fetched	Number of pages recognized
07/15/2008	40	961	114
07/31/2008	40	958	237
08/03/2008	40	982	258
08/11/2008	40	778	248
10/10/2008	40	310	114

6   Conclusion and Future Work

Over the past decade, Web spiders have evolved from "simple breadth-first search spiders to intelligent, adaptive spiders" [8]. By adding new mechanism and making modifications, spiders can focus on specific kind of information and therefore work better on information recognition and classification. However, more work has to be done on spider to catch up with the web whose content is growing, both in quantity and scope, day after day. For a theme-based spider, we think there are two aspects in which it may be improved.

6.1   Optimization in Crawler

URLs of pages coming from the same web site may have something in common, which allows the Crawler to evaluate URLs extracted by Filter. That is to say, instead of fetching pages mechanically, Crawler may give higher priority to some kind of URL, based on its working experience. As a result, web spider can access pages of interest in shorter time. Specific knowledge of Artificial Intelligence, such as SVM (Support Vector Machine), Neutral Network and so on may be useful in this part.

6.2   Human-Spider Interaction

A perfect theme-based spider can always keep its focus accordant with master's interest. Through human-spider interaction, user may conveniently control the working of spider. The problem lies in how to make spider understand its user's interest. One possible solution is to use Characteristic Vector, a common term in Text Clustering. However, more research has to be done before any conclusion comes out.

Appendix: URLs of Search Engines

1. Google: http://www.google.cn
2. Baidu: http://www.baidu.com
3. Science Paper Online: http://www.paper.edu.cn
4. CNKI: http://dlib.cnki.net/kns50
5. PaperSo: http://202.38.79.80:8080/ps/search.jsp

References

1. Cheong, F.C.: Internet Agents: Spiders, Wanderers, Brokers, and Bots. New Riders Publishing, Indianapolis (1996)
2. Rennie, J., McCallum, A.K.: Using reinforcement learning to spider the web efficiently. In: ICML 1999 Workshop, Machine Learning in Text Data Analysis (1999)
3. Jin-hong, L., Yu-liang, L.: Survey on topic-focused web crawler. Appl. Res. Comput. **24**(10), 26–29 (2007)
4. Yuanchao, X., Jianghua, L., Lizhen, L., Yong, G.: Design and implementation of spider on web-based full-text search engine. Control Autom. **23**(7–3), 119–121 (2007)
5. Wang, J., Peng, J.: Design and research of web spider's structure. Sci. Technol. Inf. **27**, 96–99 (2007)
6. Jia, N., Huang., W.: Non-recursive crawling schema of mobile web spider. J. Xihua Univ.-Nat. Sci. **26**(3), 51–53 (2007)
7. Heaton, J.: Programming Spiders, Bots, and Aggregators in Java. Sybex, San Francisco (2002)
8. Chau, M., Chen, H.: Personalized and focused web spiders. In: Zhong, N., Liu, J., Yao, Y. (eds.) Web Intelligence, pp. 197–217. Springer, Heidelberg (2003). doi:10.1007/978-3-662-05320-1_10

Iterative Learning Identification with Bias Compensation for Stochastic Linear Time-Varying Systems

Fazhi Song[1], Yang Liu[1]($\boxtimes$), Zhile Yang[2], Xiaofeng Yang[2], and Ping He[1]

[1] Department of Control Science and Engineering,
Harbin Institute of Technology, Harbin, China
hitlg@hit.edu.cn
[2] School of Microelectronics, Fudan University, Shanghai, China

Abstract. A novel iterative learning algorithm is proposed for the identification of linear time-varying (LTV) output-error (OE) systems that perform tasks repetitively over a finite-time interval. Conventional LTV system identification normally relies on recursion algorithms in time domain, which are unable to follow fast changing parameters because of an inevitable estimation lag. To overcome this problem, an extra iteration axis is introduced besides the time axis in the parameter estimation process, and identification algorithm performed in iteration domain is proposed. Firstly, a norm-optimal identification approach is presented to balance the tradeoff between convergence speed and noise robustness. Then a bias compensation algorithm is further proposed to improve the estimation accuracy. Finally, numerical examples are provided to validate the algorithm and confirm its effectiveness. The algorithm is effective to estimate both slow and abrupt parameter changes with high accuracy without estimation lags.

Keywords: System identification · Linear time-varying systems · Output error systems · Bias compensation

1 Introduction

Time-varying systems exist extensively in manufacturing processes, aerospace industry and biomedical systems [1]. Most practical industrial processes are inherently time-varying, and they cannot be effectively characterized by time invariant models. Time-varying behavior can come from the actuation system or the process itself. In [2], a pick-and-place robot working in an assembly line is investigated. A significant dynamic variation occurs when a mass is picked up or released. Identification of such linear time-varying systems is often a challenging problem, and thus is of wide interest in the community of control engineers [3,4].

Recursive least squares (RLS) algorithm is one of the most popular methods for linear time-invariant (LTI) system identification [5]. However, RLS algorithm fails to track time-varying parameters due to asymptotically vanishing gains.

© Springer Nature Singapore Pte Ltd. 2017
D. Yue et al. (Eds.): LSMS/ICSEE 2017, Part II, CCIS 762, pp. 231–239, 2017.
DOI: 10.1007/978-981-10-6373-2_24

To estimate varying parameters, many identification algorithms have been proposed. One of the most commonly used approaches is the recursive least squares method with a forgetting factor (FFRLS). The tracking performance of FFRLS has been discussed in [6]. And various scalar forgetting factor RLS algorithms have been developed to attain the minimal misadjustment as well as to estimate the optimal forgetting factor [7,8]. Adaptive filter based methods work reasonably well to track time-varying parameters if their variations are slow. However, if the parameters change quickly with time, these adaptive approaches fail to track the drastic changes due to their slow converging speed.

Since many systems execute the same task repetitively such as robot arms, hard-disk drivers and the wafer stage in a lithographic tool [9], iterative learning methods have draw lots of attentions [10–14]. A novel learning identification based on least squares (ILLS) was proposed by Sun and Bi [15] to identify repetitive ARX systems with time-varying parametric uncertainties. This method performs recursive identification in iteration domain instead of time domain for every time index. Compared with the time-varying system identification algorithms mentioned above which aimed for a fast tracking speed, it achieves tracking parameter variation satisfactorily. However, this method results in biased estimates when identifying OE systems. That is because OE systems could be considered as equation-error type (EET) systems with colored noise, while ARX systems are white noise EET systems.

The purpose of the paper is two-fold. One is to propose a new identification algorithm, which is norm-optimal iterative learning identification (NOILI) algorithm to estimate the time-varying parameters with no time lag. The other is to propose a bias compensation method in iteration domain to improve the estimation accuracy in the presence of measurement noise.

The rest of this paper is organized as follows. Section 2 describes the LTV system considered in this paper. Section 3 derives the norm-optimal iterative learning identification algorithm for LTV OE systems. Section 4 proposes a bias compensation scheme to improve the estimation accuracy. Section 5 provides examples to show effectiveness of the proposed method. Concluding remarks are given in Sect. 6.

2   Preliminaries and System Description

Since most system identification algorithms are performed based on sampled data and described in discrete time, here the system identification for the following time-varying OE system is considered

$$y(k) = \frac{B(k,z)}{A(k,z)}u(k) + v(k), k = 0, 1, 2, \ldots, N \tag{1}$$

where $\{u(k)\}$ and $\{v(k)\}$ are the input and output sequences respectively; $\{v(k)\}$ is a white-noise sequence with zero mean and unknown variance σ^2; N is the pre-specified time interval. $A(k,z)$ and $B(k,z)$ are time-varying polynomials of the backward shift operator z^{-1} with the following forms

$$A(k, z) = 1 + a_1(k)z^{-1} + a_2(k)z^{-2} + \ldots + +a_n(k)z^{-n}$$
$$B(k, z) = b_1(k)z^{-1} + b_2(k)z^{-2} + \ldots + +b_m(k)z^{-m}$$

The system described in (1) can be rewritten in a regressive form as

$$y(k) = \boldsymbol{\varphi}(k)\boldsymbol{\theta}(k) + \boldsymbol{\psi}(k)\boldsymbol{\theta}(k) + v(k) \tag{2}$$

where the information vector $\boldsymbol{\varphi}(k)$ and the noise vector $\boldsymbol{\psi}(k)$ are defined respectively as

$$\boldsymbol{\varphi}(k) \triangleq [-y(k-1) \ -y(k-2) \ \ldots \ -y(k-n) \ u(k-1) \ u(k-2) \ \ldots \ u(k-m)]$$
$$\boldsymbol{\psi}(k) \triangleq [v(k-1) \ v(k-2) \ \ldots \ v(k-n) \ 0 \ \ldots \ 0]$$

The unknown but true time-varying parameter set is defined as

$$\boldsymbol{\theta}(k) \triangleq [a_1(k) \ a_2(k) \ \ldots \ a_n(k) b_1(k) \ b_2(k) \ \ldots \ b_m(k)]^T$$

Assumption 1. It is assumed that the system described in (1) satisfies the following conditions

(1) The plant can be operated multiple times over a pre-specified finite-time interval — $t \in [0 \ N]$. Although the system is time-varying, for each operation, the parameters at the same time are invariant, i.e., $\boldsymbol{\theta}(k) = \boldsymbol{\theta}_1(k) = \ldots = \boldsymbol{\theta}_j(k) = \ldots$, for $k = 0, 1, \ldots, N$. The subscripts $1, 2, \ldots, j, \ldots$ represent iteration times.
(2) For each iteration, $v(k)$ is white noise with zero mean. $u(k)$ and $v(k)$ are statistically independent.
(3) All the time-varying parameters at each time index are bounded and the orders n and m are fixed and known.

The system output at the jth iteration can be written as

$$y_j(k) = \boldsymbol{\varphi}_j(k)\boldsymbol{\theta}(k) + \boldsymbol{\psi}_j(k)\boldsymbol{\theta}(k) + v_j(k) \tag{3}$$

For all iteration (j times), the stacked output vector $\boldsymbol{Y}_j(k)$, the stacked noise vector $\boldsymbol{V}_j(k)$, the stacked information matrix $\boldsymbol{\Phi}_j(k)$ and the stacked noise matrix $\boldsymbol{\Psi}_j(k)$ at time k, are defined respectively as

$$\boldsymbol{Y}_j(k) \triangleq [y_1(k) \ y_2(k) \ \ldots \ y_j(k)]^T \in \mathbb{R}^{j \times 1}$$
$$\boldsymbol{V}_j(k) \triangleq [v_1(k) \ v_2(k) \ \ldots \ v_j(k)]^T \in \mathbb{R}^{j \times 1}$$
$$\boldsymbol{\Phi}_j(k) \triangleq [\boldsymbol{\varphi}_1(k) \ \boldsymbol{\varphi}_2(k) \ \ldots \ \boldsymbol{\varphi}_j(k))]^T \in \mathbb{R}^{j \times (n+m)}$$
$$\boldsymbol{\Psi}_j(k) \triangleq [\boldsymbol{\psi}_1(k) \ \boldsymbol{\psi}_2(k) \ \ldots \ \boldsymbol{\psi}_j(k))]^T \in \mathbb{R}^{j \times (n+m)}$$

Then the following equation can be obtained

$$\boldsymbol{Y}_j(k) = \boldsymbol{\Phi}_j(k)\boldsymbol{\theta}(k) + \boldsymbol{\Psi}_j(k)\boldsymbol{\theta}(k) + \boldsymbol{V}_j(k) \tag{4}$$

3   Norm-Optimal Iterative Learning Identification

Different from the recursive identification, which is performed in the time axis in the form of $\widehat{\boldsymbol{\theta}}(k) = \widehat{\boldsymbol{\theta}}(k-1) + \boldsymbol{L}(k)e(k)$, iterative identification estimates parameters along the iteration axis as follows

$$\widehat{\boldsymbol{\theta}}_j(k) = \widehat{\boldsymbol{\theta}}_{j-1}(k) + \boldsymbol{L}_j(k)\boldsymbol{E}_j(k) \tag{5}$$

where $\widehat{\boldsymbol{\theta}}_j(k)$ is the estimate at time k at the jth iteration, $\boldsymbol{L}_j(k)$ is the learning gain and $\boldsymbol{L}_j(k)$ is the estimation error defined as

$$\boldsymbol{E}_j(k) \triangleq \boldsymbol{Y}_j(k) - \boldsymbol{\Phi}_j(k)\widehat{\boldsymbol{\theta}}_j(k) \tag{6}$$

Here a norm-optimal approach is proposed to design the learning law in Eq. (5). The quadratic cost function is chosen for the balance between convergence speed and noise robustness, given as

$$J_j(k, \widehat{\boldsymbol{\theta}}_j(k)) = \boldsymbol{E}_j^T(k)\boldsymbol{W}_1\boldsymbol{E}_j(k) + \left[\widehat{\boldsymbol{\theta}}_j(k) - \widehat{\boldsymbol{\theta}}_{j-1}(k)\right]^T \boldsymbol{W}_2\left[\widehat{\boldsymbol{\theta}}_j(k) - \widehat{\boldsymbol{\theta}}_{j-1}(k)\right] \tag{7}$$

where $\boldsymbol{W}_1 = w_1\boldsymbol{I}^{j \times j}, \boldsymbol{W}_2 = w_2\boldsymbol{I}^{(n+m) \times (n+m)}$ are the positive definite weighting matrices.

For the optimization problem in (7), minimizing $J_j(k, \widehat{\boldsymbol{\theta}}_j(k))$ by taking the partial derivative with respect to $\widehat{\boldsymbol{\theta}}_j(k)$ and setting it to zero leads to

$$\widehat{\boldsymbol{\theta}}_j(k) = \widehat{\boldsymbol{\theta}}_{j-1}(k) + \boldsymbol{W}_2^{-1}\boldsymbol{\Phi}_j^T(k)\boldsymbol{W}_1\boldsymbol{E}_j(k) \tag{8}$$

When the iteration index j is large enough, at least $n + m$, $\boldsymbol{W}_2 + \boldsymbol{\Phi}_j^T(k)\boldsymbol{W}_1\boldsymbol{\Phi}_j(k)$ will be full-rank. Substituting Eq. (6) into (8) yields

$$\begin{aligned}\widehat{\boldsymbol{\theta}}_j(k) &= \left[\boldsymbol{W}_2 + \boldsymbol{\Phi}_j^T(k)\boldsymbol{W}_1\boldsymbol{\Phi}_j(k)\right]^{-1}\boldsymbol{W}_2\widehat{\boldsymbol{\theta}}_{j-1}(k) \\ &+ \left[\boldsymbol{W}_2 + \boldsymbol{\Phi}_j^T(k)\boldsymbol{W}_1\boldsymbol{\Phi}_j(k)\right]^{-1}\boldsymbol{\Phi}_j^T(k)\boldsymbol{W}_1\boldsymbol{Y}_j(k)\end{aligned} \tag{9}$$

which provides an implementable parameter update law.

Lets define

$$\boldsymbol{P}_j(k) \triangleq \left[\boldsymbol{W}_2 + \boldsymbol{\Phi}_j^T(k)\boldsymbol{W}_1\boldsymbol{\Phi}_j(k)\right]^{-1} \tag{10}$$

Obviously,

$$\boldsymbol{P}_j^{-1}(k) = \boldsymbol{P}_{j-1}^{-1}(k) + w_1\boldsymbol{\varphi}_j^T(k)\boldsymbol{\varphi}_j(k) \tag{11}$$

$$\boldsymbol{P}_j(k) = \boldsymbol{P}_{j-1}(k) - \frac{w_1\boldsymbol{P}_{j-1}(k)\boldsymbol{\varphi}_j^T(k)\boldsymbol{\varphi}_j(k)\boldsymbol{P}_{j-1}(k)}{1 + w_1\boldsymbol{\varphi}_j(k)\boldsymbol{P}_{j-1}(k)\boldsymbol{\varphi}_j^T(k)} \tag{12}$$

Denote $\Delta\widehat{\boldsymbol{\theta}}_j(k) \triangleq \widehat{\boldsymbol{\theta}}_j(k) - \widehat{\boldsymbol{\theta}}_{j-1}(k)$ as the increment of estimates. Then substituting Eq. (10) into (9) gives the iterative update law for $\Delta\widehat{\boldsymbol{\theta}}_j(k)$ as follows

$$\Delta\widehat{\boldsymbol{\theta}}_j(k) = w_2\boldsymbol{P}_j(k)\Delta\widehat{\boldsymbol{\theta}}_{j-1}(k) + \boldsymbol{L}_j(k)\left[y_j(k) - \boldsymbol{\varphi}_j(k)\widehat{\boldsymbol{\theta}}_{j-1}(k)\right] \tag{13}$$

$$L_j(k) = w_1 P_j(k)\varphi_j^T(k) = \frac{w_1 P_{j-1}(k)\varphi_j^T(k)}{1 + w_1\varphi_j(k)P_{j-1}(k)\varphi_j^T(k)} \tag{14}$$

4   Bias Compensation Algorithm

Considering the above knowledge, we are now in a position to state the converged estimates in the following theorem.

Theorem 1. *Consider the LTV system (1) satisfying Assumption 1. Provided that the inputs are persistent-excitation along the iteration axis, and that they are stationary and ergodic, then the converged estimates can be represented as*

$$\lim_{j\to\infty} \widehat{\boldsymbol{\theta}}_j(k) = \boldsymbol{\theta}(k) - w_1\sigma^2 \left[\lim_{j\to\infty} jP_j(k)\right]\boldsymbol{\Omega\theta}(k) \tag{15}$$

where $\boldsymbol{\Omega} \triangleq \begin{bmatrix} I_n & 0 \\ 0 & 0_m \end{bmatrix}.$

Theorem 1 shows that a bias exists between the estimate $\widehat{\boldsymbol{\theta}}_j(k)$ and the true parameter $\boldsymbol{\theta}(k)$. It results primarily from the measurement noise. Next, a bias-compensation term will be introduced into $\widehat{\boldsymbol{\theta}}_j(k)$ to improve the estimation accuracy.

Equation (15) can be rewritten as

$$\boldsymbol{\theta}(k) = \lim_{j\to\infty} \left[\widehat{\boldsymbol{\theta}}_j(k) + jw_1\sigma^2 P_j(k)\boldsymbol{\Omega\theta}(k)\right]$$

Obviously, $\widetilde{\boldsymbol{\theta}}_j(k) \triangleq \widehat{\boldsymbol{\theta}}_j(k) + jw_1\sigma^2 P_j(k)\boldsymbol{\Omega\theta}(k)$ is unbiased estimate of the true parameter $\boldsymbol{\theta}(k)$. Thus, a compensation term $jw_1\sigma^2 P_j(k)\boldsymbol{\Omega\theta}(k)$ can be introduced into estimate $\widehat{\boldsymbol{\theta}}_j(k)$ to improve the estimation accuracy. Since noise variance σ^2 and the true parameter $\boldsymbol{\theta}(k)$ are unknown, here the compensation term is designed as $jw_1\widehat{\sigma}^2 P_j(k)\boldsymbol{\Omega}\widetilde{\boldsymbol{\theta}}_{j-1}(k)$, where $\widehat{\sigma}^2$ is the estimate of σ^2. Thus, the bias compensation algorithm can be represented in an iterative form as

$$\widetilde{\boldsymbol{\theta}}_j(k) = \widehat{\boldsymbol{\theta}}_j(k) + jw_1\widehat{\sigma}^2 P_j(k)\boldsymbol{\Omega}\widetilde{\boldsymbol{\theta}}_{j-1}(k) \tag{16}$$

The estimate of noise variance and the iterative equation about the cost function can be obtained as follows

$$\widehat{\sigma}^2 = \frac{J_j(k)}{jw_1\left[1 + \widetilde{\boldsymbol{\theta}}_{j-1}^T(k)\boldsymbol{\Omega}\widehat{\boldsymbol{\theta}}_j(k)\right]} \tag{17}$$

$$J_j(k) = J_{j-1}(k) - w_2\left[\Delta\widehat{\boldsymbol{\theta}}_{j-1}(k)\right]^T\left[\Delta\widehat{\boldsymbol{\theta}}_j(k) + \Delta\widehat{\boldsymbol{\theta}}_{j-1}(k)\right] + w_1$$

$$\frac{\left[y_j(k) - \varphi_j(k)\widehat{\boldsymbol{\theta}}_{j-1}(k)\right]^2 - w_2\varphi_j(k)P_{j-1}(k)\Delta\widehat{\boldsymbol{\theta}}_{j-1}(k)\left[y_j(k) - \varphi_j(k)\widehat{\boldsymbol{\theta}}_{j-1}(k)\right]}{1 + w_1\varphi_j(k)P_{j-1}(k)\varphi_j^T(k)}$$

$$\tag{18}$$

5   Simulation Results

The following second-order LTV OE system is considered

$$y(k) = \frac{B(k, z)}{A(k, z)} u(k) + v(k)$$

where

$$A(k, z) = 1 + a_1(k)z^{-1} + a_1(k)z^{-2} \quad B(k, z) = b_1(k)z^{-1} + b_2(k)z^{-2}$$

with $k = 0, 1, \ldots, 40$ and

$$a_1(k) = -1.5 + \sin\left(\frac{120}{k+1}\right) \quad a_2(k) = 0.7 + 0.01k \sin\left(\frac{k\pi}{5}\right)$$
$$b_1(k) = 1 + \frac{\sin(2k\pi/61)}{k+1} \quad b_2(k) = \begin{cases} 0.8 & k \in [0\ 10] \cup [20\ 30] \\ 0.2 & k \in (10\ 20) \cup (30\ 40) \end{cases}$$

The time-varying system chosen above involves not only soft variations, but also abrupt changes in the parameters. The input $u_j(k)$ is taken as i.i.d. persistent-excitation sequence distributed uniformly in $[-0.5\ 0.5]$. $v_j(k)$ is i.i.d white noise sequence $v_j(k) \in \mathbb{N}(0, \sigma^2)$, where $\sigma^2 = 0.04^2$. To describe the estimation accuracy, the parameter estimation error versus iteration index j is defined as

$$\delta \triangleq \frac{1}{N} \sum_{k=1}^{N} \frac{\| \overline{\boldsymbol{\theta}}_j(k) - \boldsymbol{\theta}(k) \|}{\| \boldsymbol{\theta}(k) \|}$$

where $\overline{\boldsymbol{\theta}}_j(k)$ represents the estimate $\widehat{\boldsymbol{\theta}}_j(k)$ before bias compensation (BC) or the estimate $\widetilde{\boldsymbol{\theta}}_j(k)$ after BC.

The time-varying parameters are identified by the NOILI algorithm where the weight value w_1 and w_2 are both set to be 1. Figure 1 shows the estimation error versus the iteration index j. We can see that after bias compensation, the estimation error is reduced remarkably, which validates the effectiveness of bias compensation algorithm.

To illustrate visually the NOILI algorithm's tracking performance for parameter variation, after 200 iterations, the plots of estimates are shown in Fig. 2(a)–(d) respectively. Clearly, although bias exists between estimates and true parameters before BC, NOILI algorithm can track perfectly not only soft but also abrupt parameter variations with high accuracy after BC.

To indicate the role of weights w_1 and w_2 in the balance between convergence speed and noise robustness, the parameters are identified by the NOILI algorithm under different weights. The solid and dotted bule lines in Fig. 3 represent the estimation error δ before and after BC respectively under $w_1 = 1$ and $w_2 = 10^{-6}$, while the red lines represent the estimation error under $w_1 = 1$ and $w_2 = 1$.

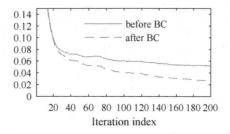

Fig. 1. Estimation error before and after bias compensation respectively

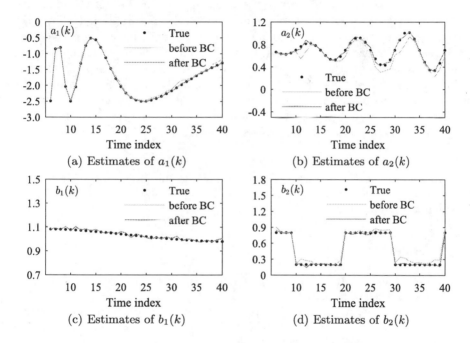

(a) Estimates of $a_1(k)$

(b) Estimates of $a_2(k)$

(c) Estimates of $b_1(k)$

(d) Estimates of $b_2(k)$

Fig. 2. Estimates by the NOILI algorithm under $\sigma^2 = 0.04^2$ when $j = 200$

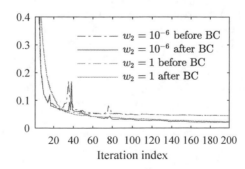

Fig. 3. Estimation error under different weights (Color figure online)

We can see that the blue lines has a faster convergence speed than the red lines in the initial several iterations before and after BC. However, severe fluctuation exists between some iterations in the blue lines. With a larger wight w_2, which means a heavier penalty on the changing rate of the estimates, the red lines before and after BC both become more smooth than the blue ones, which indicates that the weight w_2 in Eq. (7) improves the robustness against noise.

6   Concluding Remarks

This paper proposes a novel norm-optimal learning algorithm for the identification of time-varying output-error systems under the Assumption 1. This algorithm performs recursion in iteration domain instead of time domain, making it effective to estimate both slow and abrupt parameter changes without estimation lag. To eliminate the estimation bias resulting from the measurement noise, a bias compensation method is proposed to improve the estimation accuracy. The effectiveness of this algorithm is validated by simulations. Future directions include estimation for time-varying parameters under colored or just bounded noise and the application of the proposed method to a real-world identification problem.

Acknowledgments. This work was supported by the State Key Program of National Natural Science of China under Grant 51537002, and Chinese National Science Foundation under Grant 51405097.

References

1. Zou, R., Chon, K.: Robust algorithm for estimation of time-varying transfer functions. IEEE Trans. Biomed. Eng. **51**(2), 219–228 (2004)
2. Liu, N., Alleyne, A.: Time-varying norm optimal iterative learning identification. In: 2013 American Control Conference (ACC), pp. 6715–6720. IEEE (2013)
3. Shan, X., Burl, J.B.: Continuous wavelet based linear time-varying system identification. Sig. Process. **91**(6), 1476–1488 (2011)
4. Majji, M., Juang, J.N., Junkins, J.L.: Observer/kalman-filter time-varying system identification. J. Guid. Control Dyn. **33**(3), 887–900 (2010)
5. Ding, F., Shi, Y., Chen, T.: Performance analysis of estimation algorithms of nonstationary ARMA processes. IEEE Trans. Signal Process. **54**(3), 1041–1053 (2006)
6. Ljung, L., Gunnarsson, S.: Adaptation and tracking in system identification - a survey. Automatica **26**(1), 7–21 (1990)
7. Peters, S., Antoniou, A.: A parallel adaptation algorithm for recursive-least-squares adaptive filters in nonstationary environments. IEEE Trans. Signal Process. **43**(11), 2484–2495 (1995)
8. Leung, S., So, C.: Gradient-based variable forgetting factor RLS algorithm in time-varying environments. IEEE Trans. Signal Process. **53**(8), 3141–3150 (2005)
9. Heertjes, M.F., Van der Velden, B., Oomen, T.: Constrained iterative feedback tuning for robust control of a wafer stage system. IEEE Trans. Control Syst. Technol. **24**(1), 56–66 (2016)

10. Bolder, J., Oomen, T.: Rational basis functions in iterative learning controlwith experimental verification on a motion system. Int. J. Robust Nonlinear Control **23**(2), 722–729 (2015)
11. Sugie, T., Sakai, F.: Noise tolerant iterative learning control for identification of continuous-time systems. In: 44th IEEE Conference on Decision and Control, 2005 and 2005 European Control Conference, CDC-ECC 2005, pp. 4251–4256. IEEE (2005)
12. Campi, M., Sugie, T., Sakai, F.: An iterative identification method for linear continuous-time systems. IEEE Trans. Autom. Control **53**(7), 1661–1669 (2008)
13. Kim, T.H., Sugie, T.: An iterative learning control based identification for a class of mimo continuous-time systems in the presence of fixed input disturbances and measurement noises. Int. J. Syst. Sci. **38**(9), 737–748 (2007)
14. Liu, N., Alleyne, A.G.: Iterative learning identification for an automated off-highway vehicle. In: 2011 American Control Conference (ACC), pp. 4299–4304. IEEE (2011)
15. Sun, M., Bi, H.: Learning identification: least squares algorithms and their repetitive consistency. Acta Autom. Sin. **38**(5), 698–706 (2012)

A Skylight Opening Prediction Method Based on Parallel Dirichlet Process Mixture Model Clustering

Yue Yu[1,2], Li Deng[1,2(✉)], Lili Wang[1,2], and Honglin Pang[1,2]

[1] School of Mechatronics Engineering and Automation, Shanghai University,
Shanghai 200072, China
dengli@shu.edu.cn
[2] Shanghai Key Laboratory of Power Station Automation Technology,
Shanghai 200072, China

Abstract. In order to process the massive distributed data, control the agricultural facilities intelligently and improve the production efficiency, a parallel Dirichlet Process Mixture Model (DPMM) clustering method is proposed in this paper based on Spark, which is a memory computing framework. Firstly, the prediction model of skylight opening degree in greenhouse is obtained by training the agricultural environmental and facilities data. Secondly, the model is used to predict the greenhouse skylight opening degree. Thirdly, by compared experiments, both the feasibility and the efficiency of the proposed parallel clustering are verified, the prediction accuracy is also calculated. The experimental results show that the proposed approach has higher efficiency and accuracy.

Keywords: Dirichlet Process Mixture Model · Agriculture environmental data · Skylight opening value prediction · Spark

1 Introduction

In recent years, with the rapid development of automatic control and cloud computing, many new technologies have increasingly applied to traditional agricultural production, for example, intelligent greenhouse monitoring system and agricultural expert knowledge database.

The accurate environmental control strategy of greenhouse agriculture is the key to crop breeding; therefore, it is significant to predicting and controlling the action of agricultural environment facilities. The Priva intelligent greenhouse agriculture system has accumulated a great deal of agricultural production data for a long time, Data mining methods are introduced into agricultural data mining, which can better guide agricultural production1.

As an important method of machine learning, cluster analysis has been successfully applied to the establishment of crop yield prediction model, environmental anomaly detection and the division of plant species. Ananthara et al. [2] built a prediction model of crop yield based on the method of bee hive clustering. Shi [3] has utilized clustering

© Springer Nature Singapore Pte Ltd. 2017
D. Yue et al. (Eds.): LSMS/ICSEE 2017, Part II, CCIS 762, pp. 240–251, 2017.
DOI: 10.1007/978-981-10-6373-2_25

ensemble algorithm based on Clustering with Obstructed Distance(COD) and STORM to detect environment data anomalies during wheat growth. Ruß et al. [4] proposed a management zone delineation strategy based on clustering approach. By using fuzzy clustering algorithm, Cao et al. [5] produced fertilizer prescription figure which can provide reasonable suggestions for fertilizer decision. Wu et al. [6] proposed a clustering algorithm to realize the quality evaluation in the whole life cycle of farm products.

However, traditional clustering methods need to specify the number of initial clusters, which is sensitive to the model. Meanwhile, with the scale expansion of agricultural production and the increase of data type and data amount, the performance defects using traditional single machine for data storage and operation have gradually shown. Aiming at these problems, a clustering method base on parallel Dirichlet process mixture model is proposed to predict the greenhouse skylight opening degree.

Dirichlet process mixed model clustering can deal with complex data sets, without specifying initial values of clusters, and has the characteristics of fuzzy clustering and hierarchical clustering. This method has been widely used in sample clustering, topic modeling, tag extraction and other fields. Yu et al. [7] carried out text clustering by using Dirichlet process mixed model, solving the problem of estimating the clusters number for text. Crook et al. [8] lclustered dialogue act using Dirichlet process mixed model, which can be used to analyze the possible dialogue acts people might represent. Hu et al. [9] proposed an incremental DPMM-based method, and applied to trajectory analysis.

Apache Spark is an open source distributed computing framework based on memory computing, it outperforms MapReduce [10] when dealing with the iteration task in machine learning.

Combining with the characteristics of agricultural data, we propose a parallel Dirichlet process mixed model clustering method based on Spark API (Application Program Interface) and train this model with the data in Priva. In order to improve the generalization ability of the model for agricultural environmental data processing, cross validation is adopted to choose the parameters of prediction model. The prediction task of skylight opening degree is carried out then, which support the control decision for intelligent greenhouse environment. Finally, to evaluate the prediction effect, the test dataset in Priva is used to predict the execution accuracy of the model.

2 Preprocessing of Agricultural Environmental Data Based on MapReduce

The principle of data cleaning is to analyze the causes and existing forms of "dirty data", transform the data that does not meet the quality requirements or application requirements. Data cleaning involves consistency checking, invalid and missing processing. The data consistency check is based on specification requirements and check if the data conform to definitions, such as scope checking and logical checks. For invalid values and missing values, the most commonly used method is to delete data, correct data or estimate data according to certain rules.

2.1 Data Source

About 45,000 data are used in this paper, which were collected from tomato green-house in ChongMing between 2014.11 and 2015.3. The time intervals between samples are 5 min. Six features of the dataset are time, temperature (°C), relative humidity (%), concentration of carbon dioxide (ppm), photosynthetically active radiation (umol/s/m^2), skylight opening degree (%), as shown in Table 1.

Table 1. Structure of Data.

Time	TEMP	RH	CO$_2$	PAR	Skylight opening degree
......	......	......	......	......	......
2014–11–16 08:00:00	20.1	89	403.84	2.00	47.62
2014–11–16 08:05:00	20	89.98	424.58	2.00	47.60
......	......	......	......	......	......

2.2 Data Preprocessing

Missing data should be detected and treated firstly. In the actual acquisition process, the dataset is very easy to be affected by noise, missing values, etc. For instance, there are 127 missing data between 3:40 and 14:10 on 2014.11.30 including environment fields and actuator fields.

The linear interpolation method is used to fill the missing value in the period. In this paper, it is implemented by using MapReduce framework. In order to fill a missing value, the first step is to find the interpolated increment $\Delta d = (x_n - x_1)/n$, where x_1 and x_n are the data points at both ends of the missing data. Interpolation of dataset is achieved by two iterations. During the first iteration, the Δd can be calculated and written to HashMap until read to x_n. When the Mapper function reads the input data, the default data row offset in the data file is the input "Key" value to Mapper interface and the "Value" value is data in each row. The output value is still in original format. The time that is in the first field of missing value and the increments of other field are saved in the key value pairs in the variable "map". During the second iteration, the original dataset containing the missing value will still be read and filled by the field of the variable "map" in first iteration that matches acquisition time of x_1.

3 Preprocessing of Agricultural Environmental Data Based on MapReduce

3.1 Process of Dirichlet Clustering

The most important application of the Dirichlet process is the prior distribution of the parameters for the probabilistic model. Suppose there are observation variables: $y_1, y_2, \ldots$ are variables subject to the following independent and identically distribution:

$$G \sim DP(\alpha, H)$$
$$x_i | G \sim G \tag{1}$$
$$y_i | x_i \sim F(x_i)$$

The variable y_i obeys distribution $F(x_i)$ parameterized by x_i, G is a priori distribution with parameter x_i, if G obeys the Dirichlet process with base distribution H and lumped parameter α, then this model is called Dirichlet Process mixture model. For calculation convenience, $F(x_i)$ usually belongs to exponential family distribution and H is the corresponding conjugate prior distribution.

The Priva dataset to be analyzed is generated from different multi-dimensional Gaussian distribution, the parameters of the Gaussian distribution $\theta_{z_i}, (\mu_{z_i}, \sum_{z_i})$ are independent of each other, θ_{z_i} is generated from Gaussian-inverse-Wishart distribution. The mean vector is μ_{z_i}, where the subscript denotes the class of vectors corresponding to label $z_i (z_i = j$ indicates that the ith data is assigned to the jth cluster). The correlation matrix is $\sum_{z_i}$. The hierarchical representation of the DPMM distribution for the data set description is as follows:

$$x_i = (c_{i1}, \ldots, c_{id}) | \mu_i, z_i \Sigma_i^{-1} \sim N(\mu_{z_i}, \Sigma_{z_i}), i = 1, \ldots, n \tag{2}$$

$$\mu_{z_i} = (\mu_{z_i}1, \ldots, \mu_{z_id}) | \Sigma_{z_i}^{-1} \sim N(\varepsilon_0, (\gamma_0 \Sigma_{z_i}^{-1})^{-1}), 1 \leq z_i \leq K \tag{3}$$

$$\Sigma_{z_i}^{-1} \sim W(\lambda_0, \beta_0), 1 \leq \sim z_i \leq K \tag{4}$$

$$z_i \sim Multi(\Pi), i = 1, \ldots, n \tag{5}$$

$$\Pi = (\pi_1, \ldots, \pi_{K+1}) \sim DP(G_0, \alpha_0) \tag{6}$$

The parameters $\varepsilon_0, \lambda_0, \gamma_0, \beta_0, \alpha_0$ in (2) to (6) are hyper parameters. DP stands for the Dirichlet process, N and W represent Gaussian distribution and Wishart distribution respectively. The multi-dimensional Gaussian distribution in (2) is used to produce each class cluster in the mixed model, the mean and covariance in formula (2) are generated by formulas (3) and (4), as a prior distribution in Bayesian statistics, the number of clusters K depends on the sampling data. In order to reduce the computational complexity of Gibbs sampling, the distributions in (3) and (4) are chosen as conjugate prior distributions of the parameters of Gauss distribution in (2).

The distribution in (5) is used to describe the allocation process of each sample point to a class cluster. This is equivalent to sampling an element from the multinomial distribution with parameter Π. These elements π are corresponding to the weights of the mixed model, and obey the distribution described in (6). The sampling of DP is implemented according to the Stick-Breaking construct. The probability that a sample is assigned to an existing cluster is shown in formula (6.1a), where n_k represents the number of all current sample points belonging to cluster k. The probability of assigning a sample is shown in the formula (6.1b).

$$\frac{n_k}{\alpha_0 + n - 1}, 1 \le k \le K \tag{6.1a}$$

$$\frac{\alpha_0}{\alpha_0 + n - 1} \tag{6.1b}$$

The mean μ_{z_i} and precision\roman$\Sigma_{z_i}^{-1}$ of conditional posterior distributions are generated by formulas (7) and (8).The parameters $\varepsilon_{z_i}^*, \gamma_{z_i}^* \Sigma_{z_i}^{-1}$ in (7) are generated by (8), (9) and (10), respectively. Where n_{z_i} represents the sample number in the cluster z_i.The parameter $\beta_{z_i}^*$ in (8) is generated by an Eq. (12).

$$\mu_{z_i} | x_i, z_i, \Sigma_{z_i}^{-1} \sim N(\varepsilon_{z_i}^*, (\gamma_{z_i}^* \Sigma_{z_i}^{-1})^{-1}), 1 \le z_i \le K \tag{7}$$

$$\varepsilon_{z_i}^* = \frac{\gamma_0 \varepsilon_0 + n_{z_i} \bar{x}_{z_i}}{\gamma_0 + n_{z_i}} \tag{8}$$

$$\gamma_{z_i}^* = \gamma_0 + n_{z_i} \tag{9}$$

$$\Sigma_{z_i}^{-1} | x_i, z_i \sim W(\lambda_0 + n_{z_i}, \beta_{z_i}^*), 1 \le z_i \le K \tag{10}$$

$$\bar{x}_{z_i} = \frac{\sum_{i=1}^{n} x_{z_i}}{n_{z_i}} \tag{11}$$

$$\beta_{z_i}^* = \beta_0 + (\sum_{i=1}^{n} (x_{z_i} - \bar{x}_{z_i})(x_{z_i} - \bar{x}_{z_i})^T) + \frac{\gamma_0 n_{z_i}}{\gamma_0 + n_{z_i}} (\varepsilon_{z_i} - \bar{x}_{z_i})(\varepsilon_{z_i} - \bar{x}_{z_i})^T \tag{12}$$

3.2   Clustering Process Based on Gibbs Sampling

Using Gibbs sampling, the probability of redistribution for agricultural environmental data x_i to a new class of cluster z_i' is iteratively obtained.

The redistribution of posterior distribution $(\pi_1, \ldots, \pi_{K+1})$ in formula (6) will be recalculated at each iteration, the allocation probability of the sample points after the ith iteration is calculated as follows:

$$\pi_k = P(z_i = k | Z_{-i}, X) = \frac{1}{c} \frac{n_k}{\alpha_0 + n - 1} P(x_i | z_i = k), 1 \le k \le K \tag{13}$$

$$\pi_{K+1} = P(z_i = K + 1 | Z_{-i} X) = \frac{1}{c} \frac{\alpha_0}{\alpha_0 + n - 1} P(x_i | z_i = K + 1) \tag{14}$$

where k is the index of a cluster, the sample point x_i is assigned to the cluster k, the zi = K+1 indicates that the sample is assigned a whole new cluster. As a normalization variable, C guarantees the sum of probability convergent to 1. Z-i indicates that all hidden variables Z except the tags are Zi. The conditional probability $P(x_i | z_i = k)$ is the likelihood of the sample point x_i, which is used to assign the label K of the cluster to x_i. The conditional probability cannot be obtained by direct calculation, the integral of the parameters $\theta_{z_i}(\mu_{z_i}, \sum_{z_i})$ of the normal distribution is calculated as follows:

$$P(x_i|z_i = k) = \int_{\theta_k} F(x_i|\theta_k)G(\theta_k)d\theta_k$$

$$P(x_i|z_i = K+1) = \int_{\theta_{K+1}} F(x_i|\theta_{K+1})G_0(\theta_{K+1})d\theta_{K+1}$$

The $F(x_i|\theta_k)$ in Eq. (15) is the probability mass function of the Gaussian-Wishart distribution, which considers the parameter x_i and parameterized by $\theta_{z_i}(\mu_{z_i}, \sum_{z_i})$. $G(\theta_k)$ represents all observations according to the base distribution H except x_i, the posterior Gaussian-Wishart distribution is given by formulas (7) and (10).

Formula (15) represents the probability that data points are assigned to an existing cluster in the mixed model, formula (16) represents the probability that a data point is assigned to a new cluster not included in the mixed model. $F(x_i|\theta_{K+1})$ in formula (16) stands for the posterior distribution in formula (2). $G_0(\theta_{K+1})$ in formula (16) is the representation of a priori Gaussian-Wishart distribution, whose parameters are given by formulas (3) and (4), respectively.

DP is used to determine the ratio of the hybrid model. Gibbs sampling for estimating DPMM parameters can be seen as a simulation of data allocation implemented by DP. The Spark framework is applied to encapsulate the DPMM algorithm, the Gibbs sampling process of the DPMM algorithm based on Spark is as follows:

1. Initialize parameter $\varepsilon_0, \lambda_0, \gamma_0, \beta_0, \alpha_0$;

2. Initialize sample point allocation, according to the formulas (6.1a) and (6.1b), allocate the sample point X = (x1,... xn) to cluster $Z^{(0)} - (z_1^{(0)}, \ldots, z_n^{(0)})$;

3. When no stopping condition is satisfied, perform the ith iteration: when Z does not satisfy the condition, the probability distributions described in formulas (13) and (14) are adopted, each sample point is redistributed to a cluster $z_i^{(I)}$ according to $z_i^{(I-1)}$. Update $k^{(I)}$ on the basis of the clusters number in $Z^{(I)}$ and recalculate α_0 with $k^{(0)}, \ldots, k^{(I)}$ according to formula (17).

Firstly, initialize hyper parameter $\varepsilon_0, \lambda_0, \gamma_0, \beta_0$ with a priori arguments, and the precision is initialized by a nonparametric prior constant. Secondly, the sample redistribution process is implemented in the Spark framework, the redistribution process for Gibbs sampling can be described as follows: Firstly, in the ith iteration, the current model is calculated based on the previous parameter $\theta_{z_i}^{(I-1)}(\mu_{z_i}^{(I-1)}, \sum_{z_i}^{(I-1)})$ and the cluster label $z_i^{(I-1)}$, this process is implemented via the Spark mapToPair interface. Then, the mapToPair function is used to scan the whole key value pairs for two times to calculate $\theta_{z_i}^{(I-1)}(\mu_{z_i}^{(I-1)}, \sum_{z_i}^{(I-1)})$ in the current iteration stage. Secondly, scan all data rows in the mapToPair function, the number of samples and model parameters $\varepsilon_{z_i}^{(I)}, \gamma_{z_i}^{(I)}, \beta_{z_i}^{(I)}, \overline{x}_{z_i}^{(I)}$ of each cluster are updated and prepared for calculating the parameters $\theta_{z_i}^{(I)}(\mu_{z_i}^{(I)}, \sum_{z_i}^{(I)})$ of $k^{(I)}$ Gauss models in next iteration. Finally, model parameters are derived according to formulas (13) and (14), then, the sample points are assigned to the model whose parameters are updated. The redistribution process is implemented by using two Spark interfaces: updateStateByKey and mapToPair, MapToPair split data rows, updateStateByKey updates class variables $z_i^{(l)}$ based on the sampling results of formula (5), the parameters in formula (5) are solved according to formulas (13) and (14).

3.3 Prediction of Skylight Opening Degree Based on Clustering Model

The Priva dataset are distinguished when the prediction model is trained to effectively predict the skylight opening degree. In the prediction section, the Priva test data set is selected. The fields are the same as those used for the training data set.

According to latitude and longitude information [11] in Shanghai, the time of sunrise and sunset in different periods is calculated, so as to distinguish between day and night. In this paper, only daytime model is under consideration.

The results of the prediction model is shown in Tables 2, where μ stands for mean and σ stands for standard deviation. The daytime data are clustered and finally generate 10 Gauss models. The 10 models consists of the whole Gauss mixture model, which is used to perform the predicting task. The first column is the ID number of the Gauss model and the last column of the table represents the proportion of samples in each model to the total samples.

Table 2. Model of daytime.

ID	TEMP		RH		CO_2		PAR		Opening degree		Proportion of model
	μ	σ	μ	σ	μ	σ	μ	σ	μ	σ	
0	16.3	1.6	89.0	4.7	425.2	25.2	1138.5	267.4	95.3	4.7	0.365
1	24.3	3.6	64.4	16.1	358.8	20.5	475.8	35.6	73.7	1.1	0.055
2	20.6	1.5	86.7	5.1	331.1	32.4	229.9	23.	64.8	5.1	0.204
3	17.1	0.7	82.8	3.5	442.7	21.5	157.6	12.5	47.6	1.4	0.148
4	17.6	0.7	87.8	3.0	495.7	29.7	46.9	4.8	15.6	1.0	0.026
5	19.0	0.6	93.1	4.0	378.3	35.6	170.4	15.8	50.4	1.9	0.033
7	18.2	2.2	85.9	6.1	380.1	38.8	14.4	1.8	2.2	0.4	0.097
8	18.8	0.6	90.0	5.4	416.1	32.2	70.1	6.4	20.1	0.7	0.022
9	23.2	1.4	89.1	2.9	283.9	18.0	637.7	64.6	89.4	0.01	0.044
10	19.3	0.2	86.2	1.8	410.0	10.6	846.9	81.4	93.3	0.9	0.006

The main task of the analysis system described in this paper is to predict the skylight opening degree value. The Gauss mixture model trained on the Priva data is used as a predictive model. The prediction process is as follows. First, load the resulting model files into memory. Then, read the Priva test data set, the model is called for daytime or nighttime according to the timestamp to execute the prediction. The prediction process is similar to the allocation process of sample points.

Firstly, calculate the probability of each model which generate the sample. Then, refer to Table 3, to find the according model, calculate the probability P0temp, P0HD, P0CO2. To predict the skylight opening degree, suppose the degree probability is P0sky, the probability of the input data generated by the No. 0 model is P0temp * P0HD * P0CO2 * P0sky. After calculating the probability for all sub-models, the corresponding model with the highest probability is selected.

Table 3. Kmeans results of the daytime clustering model.

ID	TEMP(°C)	RH	CO_2	PAR	Skylight opening degree
0	16.402	89.161	425.431	58.672	56.462
1	24.310	63.829	359.207	463.896	37.923
2	20.859	87.404	328.592	219.457	22.952
3	17.182	83.271	443.519	157.492	14.635
4	17.727	88.097	497.579	46.954	3.923
5	19.020	93.057	376.914	7.452	0.694
6	19.155	87.116	368.907	1024.450	91.550
7	18.528	90.981	421.054	0.103	0.004
8	23.487	90.253	288.336	637.748	61.462
9	19.111	87.507	423.534	846.980	82.923

Secondly, compare to the skylight opening degree of the test dataset and then calculate the accuracy of predicting task according to the clustering model. The indicator of successful prediction are shown below as formula (23), where Xpred is the predictive value, and Xreal is the actual value.

$$\left|1 - \frac{X_{pred}}{X_{real}}\right| \leq 0.1 \tag{23}$$

4   Experimental Results and Analysis

4.1   Experimental Environment

The experiments were carried out under the cluster environment built by two computers. One work as both the master node and the work node (Intel Core i3-6100 CPU @3.70 GHz, RAM: 8 GB), the other one work as the work node only (Intel Core 2 Duo CPU E8200 @2.66 GHz, RAM: 4 GB).

Ubuntu 14.04, jdk1.8, Scala-2.11.8 and SSH (Secure Shell) were installed and configured on the two machines. Then, Hadoop 1.2.1 and Spark 1.6.1 were installed.

4.2   Comparison of Clustering Methods

Firstly, the influence of different clustering methods on the accuracy of skylight opening is compared.

Using the same training dataset with DPMM, the data is divided into daytime part and night part. We use Kmeans and FCM method to training and get two sets of clustering results, as shown in following tables. Tables 3 and 4 are clustering results of Kmeans and FCM during daytime, respectively.

Table 4. FCM results of the daytime clustering model.

ID	TEMP	RH	CO_2	PAR	Skylight opening degree
0	21.630	87.960	305.615	1058.672	95.342
1	18.447	87.217	490.690	475.896	73.753
2	18.658	87.568	453.343	229.947	64.876
3	19.478	87.955	398.774	157.692	47.647
4	18.776	87.960	433.814	46.954	39.693
5	20.954	84.417	352.875	7.452	10.464
6	21.151	85.451	331.162	14.450	28.244
7	19.098	87.544	417.590	0.103	0.120
8	20.222	85.733	375.306	637.748	89.476
9	22.303	89.096	275.556	846.980	93.385

Then, each model is used to predict the skylight opening degree on the test set, and the accuracy is calculated respectively. In order to maintain consistency with the DPMM clustering condition, the initial cluster number of Kmeans and FCM is set to 10 at daytime. The convergence threshold of FCM membership is set to 1, and the fuzzy coefficient of FCM is set to 3. As shown in Table 5, the prediction results for the three clustering models are presented.

Table 5. Prediction results of three clustering models.

Model	DPMM	Kmeans	FCM
Correct number	42474	36537	39735
Error number	3198	9135	5937
accuracy	93%	80%	87%

Among them, Kmeans was the basis of the hard cluster control group. Since the cluster of Kmeans is described by the center, it is hard to constraint the cluster scope and boundary in detail by simply dividing the center point, so there is little data in line with the forecast index (23) and it shows poor predictive ability on the opening degree. FCM is the Kmean method in combination with fuzzy sets, the data clusters are classified in the form of membership, so the intersection between data clusters is the same point between FCM and DPMM.The different dimension data of the mixed model controls the distribution range through different variance values, for irregularly distributed data clusters, it is found that DPMM has better adaptability than FCM, therefore, DPMM has the highest accuracy in predicting the skylight opening degree.

4.3 Comparison of Clustering Methods

To test the efficiency of the Spark based skylight opening prediction program when performing clustering, the operation process of different volume data are specifically recorded. The data set is shown in Table 6.

Table 6. Test data set.

	Data100	Data200	Data400	Data800
Size	4.2G	8.4G	16.8G	33.6G
Sample number	100000000	200000000	400000000	800000000
Number of fields	5	5	5	5

In this section, we compare the execution time and speedup ratio by comparing parallel DPMM with DPMM on single machine (Fig. 1 and Table 7).

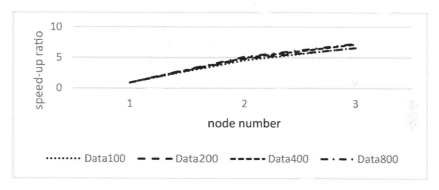

Fig. 1. Speed-up radio.

Table 7. Result of execution and speed-up ratio.

Execution time (speed-up ratio)	Stand-alone	One machine	Two machines	Three machines
Data100	4m33s320	4m52s134(0.93)	1m0s299(4.55)	41s246(6.66)
Data200	11m8s169	12m31s908(0.89)	2m19s716(4.80)	1m41s163(6.61)
Data400	22m15s906	24m24s628(0.91)	4m29s334(4.96)	3m5s919(7.21)
Data800	44m24s847	48m30s7(0.92)	8m38s897(5.14)	6m3s658(7.33)

As can be seen from the chart above, the parallel DPMM algorithm based on Spark takes less executing time than the single version DPMM algorithm on the 5 data sets. When a cluster contains only one node, the speed-up radio is usually less than 1, this is because the Hadoop cluster has a lot of expense on the framework in addition to executing the Spark task. With the increasing number of nodes in the Hadoop cluster, the speed-up radio is also increasing, which is in line with expectations. The more nodes are, the finer the distribution granularity of data blocks is, and the higher concurrent operation level. The speed-up ratio decreases as the number of nodes increases. This is because data blocks need to occupy a lot of time to transfer between nodes, affecting the efficiency of the entire cluster.

5   Conclusions

In view of the characteristics and development trend of agricultural intelligent greenhouse, a prediction method for greenhouse skylight opening degree based on parallel Dirichlet process mixed model clustering is presented in this paper. The accuracy of different clustering models for predicting the opening of skylights are compared in the experiment. The experimental results in Spark distributed platform show that the method can predict the skylight opening degree in crop growth process with high efficiency and accuracy.

Acknowledgments. This work is supported by the Key Project of Science and Technology Commission of Shanghai Municipality under Grant No. 14DZ1206302. The authors would like to thank editors and anonymous reviewers for their valuable comments and suggestions to improve this paper.

References

1. Zhan, J., Song, Z., Li, F., Wang, X.: Enlightenment of the development of agricultural facilities in Japan, the Netherlands and Israel to China. Tianjing Agric. Sci. **17**(6), 97–101 (2011)
2. Ananthara, M.G., Arunkumar, T., Hemavathy, R.: CRY – An improved crop yield prediction model using bee hive clustering approach for agricultural data sets. In: 2013 International Conference on Pattern Recognition, Informatics and Mobile Engineering (PRIME)
3. Shi, L.: Research on Data Collection and Data Mining of Wheat Growth Environment based on the Internet of Things. Henan Agricultural University, (2013)
4. Ruß, G., Kruse, R., Schneider, M.: A clustering approach for management zone delineation in precision agriculture. In: Khosla, R. (ed.) 2010 Proceedings of the International Conference on Precision Agriculture, July 2010
5. Cao, L., Zhang, X., San, X., et al.: Application of fuzzy clustering algorithm in precision agriculture. In: 2012 World Automation Congress (WAC), pp. 1–4. IEEE (2012)
6. Wu, M., Wang, Y., Liao, Z.A.: New clustering algorithm for sensor data streams in an agricultural IoT. In: IEEE International Conference on High Performance Computing and Communications, pp. 2373–2378 (2013)
7. Yu, G., Huang, R., Wang, Z.: Document clustering via dirichlet process mixture model with feature selection. In: ACM SIGKDD International Conference on Knowledge Discovery and Data Mining, Washington, DC, USA, pp. 763–772. DBLP, July 2010

8. Crook, N., Granell, R., Pulman, S.: Unsupervised classification of dialogue acts using a dirichlet process mixture model. In: SIGDIAL 2009 Conference: The Meeting of the Special Interest Group on Discourse and Dialogue. Association for Computational Linguistics, pp. 341–348 (2009)
9. Hu, W., Li, X., Tian, G., et al.: An incremental DPMM-based method for trajectory clustering, modeling, and retrieval. IEEE Trans. Pattern Anal. Mach. Intell. **35**(5), 1051 (2013)
10. Zaharia, M., Chowdhury, M., Franklin, M.J., et al.: Spark: cluster computing with working sets. In: Usenix Conference on Hot Topics in Cloud Computing. USENIX Association, pp. 1765–1773 (2010)
11. Yang, Q., Wei, L., Liu, W., Cheng, R., Zhang, Y., Tong, Y.: The research situation and development strategy of controlled environmental agriculture in China. China Agric. Inf. 22–27, (2012)

Two-Layer Harmony Search Algorithm for a Robust Flow Shop Scheduling Problem

Bo Wu, Bing Wang$^{(\boxtimes)}$, and Xingbao Han

School of Mechatronic Engineering and Automation, Shanghai University,
Shanghai 200072, China
susanbwang@shu.edu.cn

Abstract. This paper discusses a two machines permutation flow-shop scheduling problem with uncertain job processing times, where the criterion is the weighted earliness and tardiness. Uncertain processing times are described by interval scenarios, and a robust scheduling model is established to minimize the maximum penalties for earliness and tardiness. The property for the worst-case scenario of processing times is discussed for this scheduling model. Based on the obtained conclusion, a two-layer harmony search algorithm is proposed to address the characteristic of two-layer searching space. The inner-layer harmony search algorithm is used for searching the scenario space for a given schedule, while the outer-layer harmony search algorithm is used for searching the min-max schedule space. Finally, an extensive experiment is conducted to testify the effectiveness of the proposed algorithm and the characteristics of the min-max robust solution obtained.

Keywords: Flow-shop scheduling · Min-max model · Uncertain processing time · Harmony search algorithm

1 Introduction

Since there are a lot of uncertainties in the actual manufacturing environment, the manufacturing system is more complex under the uncertain environment, and therefore, the study for uncertain production scheduling problem is more challenging compared to certain production scheduling problem [1]. Processing time uncertainty is one of the uncertain factors mostly encountered in production scheduling. These have certain advantages that using the interval number to describe the uncertain operation processing time and using the method of scenario planning to model the uncertain operation processing time [2].

There are two kinds of scenarios to describe the uncertain processing time: interval scenario and discrete scenario [3]. Liu et al. [4] propose the uncertainty Just-in-time scheduling system whose processing time is expressed by interval scenario, and establish absolute robust scheduling model, meanwhile conclude that the worst-case scenario is obtained in the interval bound point, and design a two-layer co-evolutionary algorithm to solve problems based on the conclusion. To job shop scheduling problem, Yang et al. [5] establish absolute robust scheduling model under the uncertain

© Springer Nature Singapore Pte Ltd. 2017
D. Yue et al. (Eds.): LSMS/ICSEE 2017, Part II, CCIS 762, pp. 252–261, 2017.
DOI: 10.1007/978-981-10-6373-2_26

processing time described by interval scenarios, and propose a two-layer co-evolutionary genetic algorithm.

With the development of JIT (Just-In-Time) production, earliness/tardiness scheduling problems have become a hot research topic. When earliness/tardiness are viewed as the objective, the certainty two machines flow shop scheduling problem is NP - hard problem [6]. Baker and Scudder [7] do a good study about the initial work of earliness/tardiness scheduling problem. Moslehi et al. [8] present an optimal scheduling in a two-machine flow shop, in which the objective function is to minimize the sum of maximum earliness and tardiness. Zegordi et al. [9] apply a simulated annealing algorithm to solve the permutation flow-shop scheduling problem with earliness/tardiness costs. Schaller and Valente [10] consider the problem of scheduling jobs in a permutation flow shop with the objective of minimizing total earliness and tardiness. A genetic algorithm is proposed for the problem, and comparisons are executed between the proposed algorithm and a variety of algorithms.

This paper discusses a two machines permutation flow-shop scheduling problem with uncertain job processing times described by intervals, where the objective is to minimize the worst-case earliness and tardiness penalty cost. Then a two-layer harmony search algorithm is proposed. The outer-layer harmony search algorithm is used for searching the scheduling space while the inner-layer harmony search algorithm is used for searching the worst-case scenario of each scheduling.

The remainder of this paper is organized as follows. In Sect. 2, we present the problem statement and property of the permutation flow shop problem. The two-layer harmony search algorithm is introduced in Sect. 3. In Sect. 4, the computational experiment was conducted and the computational results and analysis are given. In Sect. 5, conclusions are given.

2   Problem Statement and Property

Suppose there are n jobs from the set $J = \{J_1, J_2, \cdots, J_n\}$ to be processed in a flow shop with $M = \{M_1, M_2\}$ two machines. Each job need to be performed first on machine M_1 and then on M_2 for p_{i1} and p_{i2} time units, respectively. At any time, each machine can process at most one job, and each job can be processed on at most one machine. Let o_{ij} denote the operation of job J_i on machine M_j, where the processing time p_{ij} of operation o_{ij} follows the uniform distribution on the interval $[\underline{p_{ij}}, \overline{p_{ij}}]$, where $\underline{p_{ij}}$ and $\overline{p_{ij}}$ denote the processing time lower and upper bounds of operation o_{ij}, respectively. Let s denote a feasible scheduling, and S denote all feasible scheduling set. Let $\lambda = \{p_{ij} | i = 1, 2, \cdots, n; j = 1, 2\}$ represent a scenario that contains the processing time of each operation, where the processing time of each operation in the scenario λ satisfies $\underline{p_{ij}} \leq p_{ij} \leq \overline{p_{ij}} (i = 1, 2, \cdots, n, j = 1, 2)$. Each scenario represents an implementation of the processing time of each operation, and Λ is a set of all possible scenarios, namely $\Lambda = \left\{ p_{ij} \middle| p_{ij} \in \left[\underline{p_{ij}}, \overline{p_{ij}} \right], i = 1, 2, \cdots, n; j = 1, 2 \right\}$. d_i is the due date of job J_i, which is known in advance. $c_{ij}(s, \lambda)$ represent the completion time of job J_i on machine M_j in the scenario λ under the scheduling s. Under the scheduling s and the scenario λ, the earliness and tardiness of each job can be expressed as

$$E_i(s, \lambda) = \max\{0, d_i - c_{i2}(s, \lambda)\}, i = 1, 2, \cdots, n$$
$$T_i(s, \lambda) = \max\{0, c_{i2}(s, \lambda) - d_i\}, i = 1, 2, \cdots, n$$

The objective function can be expressed as follows:

$$\min_{s \in S} \max_{\lambda \in \Lambda} \sum_{i=1}^{n} \alpha_i E_i(s, \lambda) + \beta_i T_i(s, \lambda) \tag{1}$$

Where α_i and β_i are the earliness and tardiness penalties of job, respectively. Since $\alpha_i E_i(s, \lambda) + \beta_i T_i(s, \lambda) = \max\{\alpha_i(d_i - c_{i2}(s, \lambda)), \beta_i(c_{i2}(s, \lambda) - d_i)\}$, note:

$$f_i(c_{i2}(s, \lambda)) = \max\{\alpha_i(d_i - c_{i2}(s, \lambda)), \beta_i(c_{i2}(s, \lambda) - d_i)\} \tag{2}$$

Then the formula (1) can be expressed as:

$$\min_{s \in S} \max_{\lambda \in \Lambda} \sum_{i=1}^{n} f_i(c_{i2}(s, \lambda)) \tag{3}$$

The problem is a min-max optimization problem, which is composed of inner Max optimization and outer Min optimization. The min-max model is also called the Absolute Robust Model (ARM).

For the uncertain single machine scheduling problem described by scenario, literature [3] proves that the worst-case scenario of every scheduling belongs to the scenario set composed by each operation processing time taking the upper or lower bounds. Therefore, authors only need to search the scenario space constituted by each operation processing time taking the upper or lower bounds, which greatly decreases the search space of solving the worst-case scenario of each scheduling. For the flow-shop scheduling min-max model proposed in this paper, we can get a property of the inner Max optimization problem when the processing time of the operation is satisfied with certain conditions.

Property 1: For a given scheduling s, job total weighted earliness and tardiness penalties function $f_i(c_{i2}(\lambda))$ is a convex function with regard to the operation processing time vector $\lambda = [p_{11}, p_{21}, \cdots p_{n1}, p_{12}, p_{22}, \cdots, p_{n2}]^T$ when the operation processing time satisfies $\overline{p_{i1}} \leq \underline{p_{k2}}(k = 1, 2, \cdots, n)$ or $\underline{p_{i1}} \geq \overline{p_{k2}}(k = 1, 2, \cdots, n)$.

According to the property of convex function: the linear combination of a finite number of convex functions is still a convex function. We can draw the following corollary by Property 1.

Corollary 1: $\sum_{i=1}^{n} f_i(c_{i2}(s))$ is a linear convex function about the processing time vector $\lambda = [p_{11}, p_{21}, \cdots p_{n1}, p_{12}, p_{22}, \cdots, p_{n2}]^T$.

Theorem 1: When the operation processing time satisfy $\overline{p_{i1}} \leq \underline{p_{k2}}(k = 1, 2, \cdots, n)$ or $\underline{p_{i1}} \geq \overline{p_{k2}}(k = 1, 2, \cdots, n)$, for a given job processing sequence s, the worst-case scenario under the sequence belongs to the scenario set constituted by the extremum of processing time. In this paper, the Theorem 1 is also called the inner-layer max optimization convex function theorem.

According to Theorem 1, given a job-sequence, the worst-case scenario of the scheduling belongs to the scenario set composed by each operation processing time taking the upper or lower bounds. Based on this feature, it can only search the scenario which is composed of the processing time boundary value of each operation instead of searching the whole space of each interval variables when we solve the worst-case scenario of a scheduling. Thus, this can greatly reduce the processing time space, which is beneficial to improve the searching efficiency of the algorithm.

3 Two-Layer Harmony Search Algorithm

In view of the function (3) min-max model, especially, a Two-Layer Harmony Search Algorithm (TLHS) is designed, which consists of Outer Harmony Search (OHS) and Inner Harmony Search (IHS). The OHS is used to optimize the job processing sequence, whose harmony memory is called Outer Harmony Memory (OHM); the IHS is used to search each operation processing time (the worst-case scenario) with worst performance for a given scheduling sequence, whose harmony memory is called Inner Harmony Memory (IHM). OHM contains only the individual on behalf of job processing sequence while IHM contains only the individual on behalf of the scenario λ. OHS and IHS cooperate to solve the min-max problem described by function (3). The overall algorithm block diagram is shown in Fig. 1.

3.1 Inner Harmony Search Algorithm

For a given job-sequence, IHS mainly searches the processing time of each operation with the worst performance under the sequence. Based on Theorem 1, for a sequence, the worst-case scenario of the sequence belongs to the scenario set composed by the processing time of each operation P_{ij} taking the upper $P_{ij} = \overline{P_{ij}}$ or lower $P_{ij} = \underline{P_{ij}}$. So, we just need to search the scenario space constituted by the processing time of each operation taking the upper or lower bounds.

(1) Initializing IHM

$x(iner) = [x_{11}, x_{21}, \cdots x_{n1}, x_{12}, x_{22}, \cdots x_{n2}]$, where $x_{ij} \in \{0, 1\}$. And $p_{ij} = \underline{p_{ij}}$ if $x_{ij} = 0$; $p_{ij} = \overline{p_{ij}}$ if $x_{ij} = 1$.

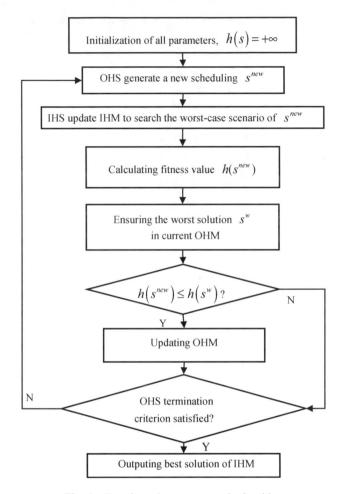

Fig. 1. Two-layer harmony search algorithm

$$IHM = \begin{bmatrix} X^1(iner) \\ X^2(iner) \\ \vdots \\ X^{IHMS}(iner) \end{bmatrix} = \begin{bmatrix} x_{11}^1 & \cdots & x_{n1}^1 & x_{12}^1 & \cdots & x_{n2}^1 \\ x_{11}^2 & \cdots & x_{n1}^2 & x_{12}^2 & \cdots & x_{n2}^2 \\ \vdots & \cdots & \vdots & \vdots & \cdots & \vdots \\ x_{11}^2 & \cdots & x_{n1}^2 & x_{12}^2 & \cdots & x_{n2}^1 \end{bmatrix}$$

Where $X^k(iner)$ $k = 1, 2 \cdots, IHMS$ means the first k individual of IHM, and IHMS represents the size of IHM, and each individual in the IHM is a vector made up of variable values by 0 or 1. The initialization IHM in this paper, variables in $X^1(iner)$ are all 0, variables in $X^2(iner)$ are all 1, variables in other individuals $X^k(iner)$ ($k = 3, \cdots, IHMS$) are randomly generated. Individual $X(iner)$ in IHM and scenario is one-to-one correspondence.

(2) Generating a new solution

Each variable value in the new solution is generated as follow:

$$x_{ij}^{new} = \begin{cases} x_{ij}^{r_1} + (-1)^{\Lambda} x_{ij}^{r_1} * \left| x_{ij}^{best} - x_{ij}^{r_2} \right| & if\,(rand < IHMCR) \\ rand\{0,1\} & else \end{cases} \tag{4}$$

Where, IHMCR is the harmony memory considering probability of IHS, X_{ij}^{best} is x_{ij} value of the optimal solution of the current harmony memory in the corresponding position, best is the location of the best individual in the current harmony memory, r_1 and r_2 are randomly chosen two different integers from $\{1, 2, \cdots, IHMS\}$ and they are different from best, $rand\{0,1\}$ randomly generates 0 or 1 with equal probability.

(3) Updating IHM

After a new solution is obtained, the IHM will be updated by the survival of the fitter competition between the new solution and the worst solution in the current IHM. That is, the new will replace the worst and become a new member of the IHM if the new is better than the worst.

(4) Stopping criterion

In this paper, the maximum number of evolution generations $Imaxiter$ is predefined to determine when to stop the IHS.

3.2   Outer Harmony Search Algorithm

The purpose of OHS algorithm is to search the processing sequence of jobs. This subsection mainly introduces the outer harmony search algorithm designed for this problem.

(1) Initializing OHM

A heuristic method based on NEH is designed to generate the initial harmony memory of OHS. EDD rule is applied to generate initial solution in deterministic flow shop scheduling, and NEH rule is often very effective. An EDD rule based on NEH is adopted to generate an initial solution for the uncertain PFSP with total weighted E/T.

(2) Generating a new solution

$$X^{new} = [x_1^{new}\ x_2^{new}\ \cdots\ x_n^{new}]$$

Where,

$$x_j^{new} = \begin{cases} x_j^{rand[i]} & if\,(rand1 < OHMCR) \\ rand(0,4) & else \end{cases}$$

$$while(x_j^{new} = x_j^{rand[i]})$$
$$x_j^{new} = \begin{cases} x_j^{new} \pm OBW * rand & if(rand2 < OPAR) \\ x_j^{new} & else \end{cases}$$

Where, $rand[i]$ is a random integer selected from $\{1, 2, \cdots, HMS\}$, $rand1, rand2$ are random real number generated from 0 to 1 with uniform distribution, OHMCR is outer harmony memory consideration rate, OPAR is outer pitch adjustment rate, OBW is outer distance bandwidth.

(3) Updating Outer Harmony Memory

The LOV rule [11] is applied in this paper to translate the real vector stored in the outer harmony memory into scheduling. After obtaining the new scheduling, IHS is adopted to search the worst-case scenario of the scheduling, and the performance of the scheduling in the worst-case scenario is evaluated as the objective value of the solution. The new solution will replace the worst of the HM if the objective value of the new solution is less than the worst solution in the current HM. Otherwise, the OHM will not charge.

(4) Stopping criterion

If the maximum number of iteration $Omaxiter$ is reached, the OHS is terminated. Otherwise, Step 3 and Step 4 are repeated.

4   Computational Results and Comparisons

An extensive experiment is conducted in this section. The parameters are set as follows: n = 20, 30, 40, 50, 60. p_{ij} is in uniform distribution $p_{ij} \in \left[\underline{p_{ij}}, \overline{p_{ij}}\right]$, where $\underline{p_{ij}} \in U[10, 50\theta_1], \overline{p_{ij}} \in U\left[\underline{p_{i2}}, \underline{p_{i2}}(1 + \theta_2)\right]$ (taking $\theta_1 = \{0.2, 0.4\}$ and $\theta_2 = \{0.2, 0.4, 0.6, 0.8, 1.0\}$ respectively). For the processing time of the operation is uncertain in this paper, the expected processing time of each operation $\widetilde{p_{ij}} = (\underline{p_{ij}} + \overline{p_{ij}})/2$ is adopted as the processing time of each operation, and the Johnson rule is adopted to obtain the completion time M. The due date of each job is integer discrete uniformly distributed in interval [0, 1.1M], and the weight coefficient α_i/β_i are discrete uniformly distributed in interval [1, 3]. (Outer Harmony Memory Size) OHMS = 10, OHMCR = 0.9, OPAR = 0.3, OBW = 0.05, $Omaxiter = n \times 10^2$, IHMCR = 0.9, $Imaxiter = 500$, IHMS = 20. All the procedures were coded in C++ and all tests are conducted on a Pentium G630 at 2.7 GHz with 2.0 GB of RAM.

4.1   Comparison of TLHS and OHS-BRS

In this section, the method that OHS searches the outer scheduling and BRS (Border Random Search) searches the worst-case scenario of each scheduling is defined as the OHS-BRS algorithm. Table 1 shows comparison results of TLHS with OHS-BRS

Table 1. Results of TLHS with OHS-BRS under different examples

θ_1	θ_2	WIR(%)				
		n = 20	n = 30	n = 40	n = 50	n = 60
0.2	0.2	3.253	7.331	6.403	8.308	6.453
	0.4	9.252	7.376	9.302	4.838	0.749
	0.6	7.262	9.323	4.138	3.586	3.851
	0.8	13.72	8.466	11.46	1.288	11.79
	1.0	20.22	10.43	10.63	5.464	9.391
0.4	0.2	−0.574	2.657	5.613	−1.316	7.453
	0.4	2.657	2.681	13.579	8.152	7.213
	0.6	6.177	8.478	7.683	1.797	9.180
	0.8	13.13	10.39	11.89	1.895	10.18
	1.0	9.031	9.941	9.957	6.439	5.627

under different examples. For each example, the two algorithms search for a pre-scheduling respectively, then generating randomly 5000 scenarios (the processing time of operation taking the upper or lower bounds), then calculating the objective value of the two pre-scheduling in each scenario. The worst performance of the two pre-scheduling in the 5000 simulations is done as the objective function value of the simulation. For each example simulation 10 times, the average value of the TLHS and OHS-BRS respectively in the 10 simulation results are recorded as f_{TLHS} and $f_{OHS-BRS}$. The worst-case scenario Improvement Rate (WIR) of TLHS algorithm relative to the OHS-BRS algorithm is calculated as follows:

$$WIR = (f_{OHS-BRS} - f_{TLHS})/f_{TLHS} \times 100\% \qquad (5)$$

As can be seen from the Table 1, WIR is positive in most examples, which shows that the worst performance of pre-scheduling in random simulation scenarios obtained by TLHS algorithm is better than that obtained by OHS-BRS algorithm, in other words, the robust pre-scheduling of TLHS is able to maintain a good performance in the face of the disturbance of uncertain processing time. This may be because that the ability of IHS searching for the worst-case scenario is better than that of BRS method in the process of max optimization for each scheduling. The worst-case scenario searched by BRS has a certain deceptive for each schedule, which is easy to guide the outer search in the wrong direction, and then lead to the searched robust pre-scheduling has a larger deceptive, then the larger total weighted E/T is generated in the simulation. This also shows that the proposed TLHS algorithm is effective for solving this problem and has certain advantages compared with OHS-BRS.

4.2   Comparison of Min-Max Model and Mean Scenario Model

Based on the TLHS algorithm, we compare the min-max model, namely the absolute robust model (ARM), with the expected scenario model (ESM) [12]. Since the researched deterministic problem is still the NP-hard problem in this section, the OHS algorithm is adopted to search the optimal scheduling under the expected scenario, whose parameters are generated the same as that in TLHS algorithm.

The ARM is compared with the ESM with various types of processing time for all the generated examples, where the two-layer harmony search algorithm proposed in this paper is denoted as TLHS and the harmony search algorithm for solving the expected scenario problem is denoted as EHS. For ARM and ESM of each example simulating 10 times respectively, the average value of the 10 objective function values of the solution ARM (denoted as f_{ARM}) is recorded as the performance of the pre-scheduling of ARM while the average value of the 10 objective function values of the solution ESM (denoted as f_{ESM}) is recorded as the performance of the ESM under the pre-scheduling. For each example, the worst performance index (WPI) of the pre-scheduling obtained by ARM relative to EMS is calculated as follow:

$$WPI = (f_{ESM} - f_{ARM})/f_{ARM} \qquad (6)$$

Table 2 shows the worst performance index of the pre-scheduling obtained by ARM relative to ESM under different parameters and scales of the problem. WPI value is positive, which indicates that the robustness of the pre-scheduling obtained by ARM is better than that obtained by ESM, and the greater the WPI value is, the greater the advantage of ARM is. This is because that, in the ESM, the main consideration of the EHS algorithm in the process of searching is the mean performance rather than the searching for the worst-case scenario. But in ARM, the IHS algorithm ensures that the scheduling with high robustness obtained by the OHS algorithm is more likely to be survived when the TLHS is in the process of searching, so the scheduling has stronger robustness. This also indicates that ARM is able to optimize the scheduling robustness in uncertain environments.

Table 2. Improvement rate of TLHS relative to EHS under different examples

θ_1	θ_2	WPI(%)				
		n = 20	n = 40	n = 60	n = 80	n = 100
0.2	0.2	0.717	2.033	0.805	2.313	7.747
	0.4	16.02	0.711	1.116	7.913	3.832
	0.6	20.07	3.762	5.211	3.206	5.527
	0.8	21.09	14.50	4.604	13.82	6.388
	1.0	17.27	3.326	2.524	1.255	4.597
0.4	0.2	6.686	0.631	4.517	2.198	15.39
	0.4	12.21	6.151	1.326	10.47	8.731
	0.6	2.044	6.556	1.032	7.895	9.067
	0.8	5.580	1.951	6.974	4.320	0.341
	1.0	11.37	3.623	4.707	3.185	3.057

5   Conclusions

This paper discusses a two machines permutation flow shop scheduling problem with uncertain job processing times described by interval scenarios, where the target is to obtain robust scheduling with minimal E/T weighted sum under the worst-case scenario. In view of the problem with the property of two spaces optimization, a two-layer harmony search algorithm is designed to solve the problem. Through a lot of simulation experiments, this paper verifies the validity of the proposed Min-max model and the designed two-layer harmony search algorithm.

References

1. Wang, B., Yang, X.F., Li, Q.Y.: Bad-scenario set based risk-resisting robust scheduling model. Acta Autom. Sin. **38**(2), 270–278 (2012)
2. Allahverdi, A., Aydilek, H.: Heuristics for the two-machine flow-shop scheduling problem to minimize makespan with bounded processing times. Int. J. Prod. Res. **48**(21), 6367–6385 (2010)
3. Kouvelis, P., Yu, G.: Robust Discrete Optimization and its Applications, vol. 14. Springer Science & Business Media, Heidelberg (2013)
4. Liu, L., Gu, H.Y., Xi, Y.G.: Robust scheduling in a Just-in-time single machine system with processing time uncertainty. Control Decis. **22**(10), 1151–1154 (2007)
5. Yang, H.A., Xi, Z.C., Xia, C.K., et al.: Minimax model and two space co-evolutionary genetic algorithm for job shop scheduling problem. China Mech. Eng. **26**(3), 330–338 (2015)
6. Lenstra, J.K., Kan, A.R., Brucker, P.: Complexity of machine scheduling problems. Ann. Discret. Math. **1**(4), 343–362 (1977)
7. Baker, K.R., Scudder, G.D.: Sequencing with earliness and tardiness penalties: a review. Oper. Res. **38**(1), 22–36 (1990)
8. Moslehi, G., Mirzaee, M., Vasei, M., et al.: Two-machine flow shop scheduling to minimize the sum of maximum earliness and tardiness. Int. J. Prod. Econ. **122**(2), 763–773 (2009)
9. Zegordi, S.H., Itoh, K., Enkawa, T.: A knowledgeable simulated annealing scheme for the early/tardy flow shop scheduling problem. Int. J. Prod. Res. **33**(5), 1449–1466 (1995)
10. Schaller, J., Valente, J.S.: A comparison of metaheuristic operations to schedule jobs in a permutation flow shop to minimise total earliness and tardiness. Int. J. Prod. Res. **51**(3), 772–779 (2013)
11. Bean, J.C.: Genetic algorithms and random keys for sequencing and optimization. Informs J. Comput. **6**(2), 154–160 (1994)
12. Daniels, R.L., Kouvelis, P.: Robust scheduling to hedge against processing time uncertainty in single-stage production. Manag. Sci. **41**(2), 363–376 (1995)

Heuristic Based Terminal Iterative Learning Control of ISBM Reheating Processes

Ziqi Yang, Zhile Yang$^{(\boxtimes)}$, Kang Li, Wasif Naeem, and Kailong Liu

School of Electronics, Electrical Engineering and Computer Science,
Queen's University Belfast, Belfast BT9 5AH, UK
{zyang06,zyang07,k.li,w.naeem,kliu02}@qub.ac.uk

Abstract. The injection stretch blow moulding (ISBM) process is widely used to manufacture plastic bottles for the beverage and consumer goods industry. The majority of the production processes are open-loop systems, often suffering from high raw material and energy waste. In this paper, a heuristic based norm-optimal terminal iterative learning control (ILC) method is proposed to control the preform temperature profiles in the reheating process. The reheating process is a batch process, and ILC can achieve improved tracking performance in a fixed time interval. The terminal ILC (TILC) is a useful strategy when only the terminal temperature profile can be measured in a batch process like the preform reheating in ISBM. To balance the control performance and energy cost, a norm-optimal method is applied, leading to a proposal of the new norm-optimal TILC method in this paper. Heuristic methods including the swarm optimisation (PSO), differential evolution (DE) and teaching-learning based optimization (TLBO) are used to calculate the sequence of norm-optimal control inputs for this non-linear batch process. Simulation results confirm the efficacy of the proposed control strategy.

Keywords: Iterative learning control · Reheating process · Temperature control · Heuristic optimisation method

1 Introduction

Over the last few decades, the use of plastics has experienced continuous growth due to many advantages including lightweight with high tensile/impact/tear strengths, high temperature/chemical resistance, high clarity/modulus/plasticity and low cost [1]. The injection stretch blow moulding (ISBM) is a typical processing method in the plastic industry. The numerical simulation, as an efficient tool, has been applied in the polymer industry [2–4], endorsing improved process design for this conventional energy intensive industry. However, the majority of plastic production process control systems are still open-loop, leading to significant energy and material waste.

The batch process is widely used in the manufacturing industry. Among various batch process control methods, iterative learning control (ILC) is a popular

© Springer Nature Singapore Pte Ltd. 2017
D. Yue et al. (Eds.): LSMS/ICSEE 2017, Part II, CCIS 762, pp. 262–271, 2017.
DOI: 10.1007/978-981-10-6373-2_27

one first proposed in 1971 [5]. It has been widely applied in a numbers of areas such as robot manipulators [6], injection moulding [7], and rapid thermal processing (RTP) [8], etc. To control the RTP, a terminal ILC (TILC) was proposed in [9]. In TILC, only the terminal states and outputs are measured, and the control objective involves the terminal output trajectory. TILC has also been applied in polymer reheating [10] and robot manipulators [11].

This paper proposes a new ILC control method which is then used to control the infrared lamp settings to achieve the desired preform terminal temperature profiles in the reheating process in ISBM. Since the reheating process is a batch process, the traditional control methods are not suitable to achieve the desired control objective, namely desired temperature profile of the preform. On the contrary, this repeatability can be utilized to improve the system control performance by using the ILC method. In the reheating process, only the terminal system states and outputs of each iteration can be measured. Hence, the terminal ILC strategy is used in this paper. Unlike the traditional terminal ILC methods where only the control performance is considered, a new cost function which considers both the control performance and the energy consumption that are directly related to the control input is proposed, leading to the proposal of a new norm-optimal terminal ILC. In order to obtain a sequence of nom-optimal TILC control inputs, several popular heuristic methods including PSO, TLBO and DE are used. Simulation studies are carried out to verify the effectiveness and performance of the proposed algorithm.

2 Norm-Optimal TILC Controller Design

Consider a discrete MIMO nonlinear dynamic batch process formulated as

$$x_k(t+1) = f(x_k(t), u_k) + \omega_k(t)$$
$$y_k(t) = h(x_k(t)) + \nu_k(t) \tag{1}$$

where $t = 0, 1, 2, ..., N$ is the sampling time index, N is the final sample time point of each batch process; $f(\cdot, \cdot)$ and $h(\cdot)$ are some consistent non-linear vector-value functions respectively; k is the system iteration number; $x_k(t) \in \Re^n$ is system state; $u_k \in \Re^m$ is system control input, $y_k(t) \in \Re^l$ is system output where only $y(N)$ is measurable at the end of each trial; $\omega_k(t) \in \Re^n$, $\nu_k(t) \in \Re^l$ are state disturbance and output noise respectively. The control objective is to obtain the appropriate control input u_k to make the associated output $y_k(N)$ approach the desired output y_d as the iteration number k increases. In this case, the system terminal dynamic model can be represented as [12]

$$y_k(N) = g(u_k) + V_k(N) + W_k(N) \tag{2}$$

where $g(\cdot)$ is the consistent non-linear vector-value function depending on $f(\cdot, \cdot)$ and $h(\cdot)$; $V_k(N) = \nu_k(N)$ and $W_k(N) = \sum_{j=0}^{N-1} h^{N-j}(\omega_k(j))$.

In this case, the system error can be written as

$$e_k(N) = y_d - y_k(N) = (y_d - y_{k-1}(N)) - (y_k(N) - y_{k-1}(N)) \tag{3}$$

where y_d is the system desired output signal and assumed to be a constant vector.

In this work, an improved norm-optimal ILC learning algorithm is employed given by (4).

$$u_k = L_u u_{k-1} + L_e e_{k-1}(N) - L_d(\Delta) \tag{4}$$

where L_u, L_e and L_d are the solutions of a new quadratic optimization problem presented below, and Δ is the system noise and disturbance.

Unlike existing ILC learning algorithms [13,14] where the cost function only considers the control performance, a new norm-optimal TILC is proposed in this paper by introducing a new cost function for TILC method. Here, the cost function consists of three terms introduced below,

$$J(u_k) = e_k(N)^T Q e_k(N) + (u_k - u_{k-1})^T R(u_k - u_{k-1}) + u_k^T S u_k \tag{5}$$

where the weighting Q, R and S are symmetric positive definite matrices with a general form as $(Q, R, S) = (qI, rI, sI)$, and $0 \leq (q, r, s) \leq 1$. In this new cost function, the first item concerns about system output tracking error during each iteration, the second item guarantees that the control inputs do not vary too much between two iterations, and the last item estimates the control input energy in each iteration. This new cost function balances the control performance (tracking error of the desired temperature profile of performs) and the control energy.

Due to the limitation of space, controller convergence analysis is not detailed in this paper.

3   Heuristic Based Norm-Optimal TILC

In many real industrial applications, it is difficult or even impossible to work out the optimal control input due to the non-linearity of the batch processes under investigation. Heuristic methods are useful computational tools to solve the optimal control input for each iteration. In this work, three heuristic methods including particle swarm optimization (PSO) [15], teaching-learning based optimization (TLBO) [16] and differential evolution (DE) [17] are applied to solve the norm-optimal TILC control problem.

Here the heuristic methods are used to find proper control inputs u to minimise the cost function $J(u)$ at the terminal point of each iteration. In a given iteration, the control inputs which minimize the cost function are considered as the best solutions, thus as the optimal inputs. For the $(k + 1)^{th}$ iteration (where $k \geq 1$), as an example, based on the control inputs u_k from the kth iteration, a number of candidate solutions u_{k+1}^* are generated randomly in an appropriate range. Then the control inputs u_{k+1}^* are applied to system model to obtain corresponding system output y_{k+1}^* and error $e_{k+1}^*(N)$. Substituting the $(k + 1)^{th}$ iteration information u_{k+1}^*, $e_{k+1}^*(N)$ along with the previous kth iteration information u_k and e_k to the cost function, then the value of $J_{k+1}(u_{k+1}^*)$ is found. Heuristic methods test all candidate control inputs u_{k+1}^* and comparing the value of $J_{k+1}(u^*_{k+1})$. Finally, the best control inputs u_{k+1} with the minimum value of cost function $J_{k+1}(u_{k+1})$ for the $(k+1)^{th}$ iteration are obtained and recorded with corresponding system error $e_{k+1}(N)$. The structure of heuristic based norm-optimal TILC is illustrated in Fig. 1.

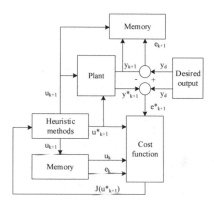

Fig. 1. The structure of heuristic based norm-optimal TILC

4   Application to the Preform Reheating Process

A practical reheating process for the perform is conducted in this section. The infrared heating oven used here was manufactured by VITALII & SON and was made available by the Polymer Processing Research Center (PPRC) at Queens University Belfast. A side view of the infrared heating oven is shown in Fig. 2.

It can be noted that there are eight infrared lamp tubes (No. 1–No. 8 from bottom to top) vertically arranged on the right-hand side. Behind each lamp

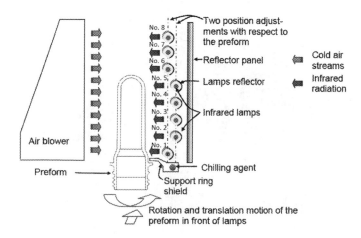

Fig. 2. Side view of the infrared heating oven [18]

tube, a reflector is fixed to increase the radiation efficiency. The infrared lamp tube positions can be adjusted with respect to the preform. In addition, each lamp tube can be turned on individually depending on the preform type. In this research, the preform used has a height of 90 mm, due to which five lamp tubes (No. 1–No. 5) were deemed sufficient for the reheating process.

Utilising the heating oven, terminal temperature of five different positions (from top to bottom) in a preform during the reheating processes illustrated in Fig. 3 will be controlled by adjusting the infrared lamp settings, where the system control input matrix u_k is given by the matrix below:

$$u_k = \begin{bmatrix} u_1 \ u_2 \ u_3 \ u_4 \ u_5 \ p_1 \\ u_1 \ u_2 \ u_3 \ u_4 \ u_5 \ p_2 \\ u_1 \ u_2 \ u_3 \ u_4 \ u_5 \ p_3 \\ u_1 \ u_2 \ u_3 \ u_4 \ u_5 \ p_4 \\ u_1 \ u_2 \ u_3 \ u_4 \ u_5 \ p_5 \end{bmatrix}_k$$

The matrix u_k represents five infrared lamp settings $(u_1, u_2, u_3, u_4, u_5)$ and position information $(p_1, p_2, p_3, p_4, p_5)$ as shown in Fig. 3. Five thermocouples are placed in the corresponding positions p_1–p_5 where the preform is heated by five infrared lamps. The control objective is to automatically regulate the lamp settings to achieve a desired temperature profile of the preform. In the following simulation, uniform temperature profile are taken as the example, of which the temperature is set at $100\,°C$. However, since the system is highly coupled, it is extremely difficult to guarantee the control objective. Fortunately, a small error is acceptable in the practical reheating process. Therefore, the control objective is adjusted to make the terminal temperature of each position approach the desired temperature as closely as possible. Moreover, because infrared lamp power is directly proportional to the electric energy consumed, the level of lamp setting can be treated as the energy consumption during the reheating process.

The heuristic based norm-optimal TILC proposed above is applied to the reheating process to control the preform external terminal temperature profiles.

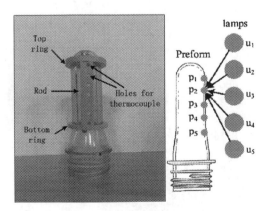

Fig. 3. The physical interpretation of reheating process control input

Three popular heuristic methods, including PSO, TLBO, and DE are applied
to the cost function (5) to find out the sequence of optimal control input for
this norm-optimal TILC. For each heuristic method, the settings of the algorithm parameters are given in Table 1, and the convergence of the algorithm is
illustrated in Fig. 4. The statistical analysis results are presented in Fig. 5.

Consider the preform terminal temperature model in a RBF neural network
structure as given below:

$$y_k(N) = \sum_{j=1}^{n} \theta_j \varphi_j(u_k; \mathbf{c}_j; \boldsymbol{\Sigma}_j) + \varepsilon(N) \tag{6}$$

where $y_k(N) \in \Re^l$ denotes the system output vector (e.g. the terminal temperature of corresponding positions) at the terminal sample time $t = N$; $u_k \in \Re^{p \times m}$
represents the control input matrix; $\varphi_j(u_k; \mathbf{c}_j; \boldsymbol{\Sigma}_j)$ is the RBF activation function, θ_j denotes the output layer weight for each RBF node; $\varepsilon_k(N) \in (0, 1)$

Table 1. Parameter settings of applied heuristic methods

Method	Parameter	Value	Description
PSO	S	10	Number of particles
	G	20	Number of generations
	C_1	$(1-3)*G/G_{max}+3$	Acceleration coefficient of the cognitive part, G_{max} is the maximum number of generation
	C_2	$(3-1)*G/G_{max}+1$	Acceleration coefficient of the social part, G_{max} is the maximum number of generation
	r_1, r_2	$\in (0,1)$	Coefficients randomly generated from the specified range
	w_0	1	Inertia weight in velocity updating
	$\mathbf{v}_{min}$	0	Minimum value of speed
	$\mathbf{v}_{max}$	3	Maximum value of speed
TLBO	S	10	Population size
	G	10	Maximum number of generations
	T_F	1 or 2	Teaching factor
	r_1, r_2, r_3	$\in (0,1)$	Coefficients randomly generated from the specified range
DE	S	10	Population size
	G	20	Maximum number of generations
	F	0.8	Weight of vector difference
	C_r	0.6	Crossover constant
	r	$\in (0,1)$	Coefficient randomly generated from the specified range

represents the networks error at terminal sample time $t = N$, and k is the iteration number. Model (6) is obtained from fitting to the model to a number of experimental data collected according to the experiment set up shown in Fig. 3. More details in terms of RBF neural network model could be found in [19].

The heuristic based norm-optimal TILC is then applied to the developed model to find the optimal control input. For heuristic optimization methods, their parameter settings are detailed in Table 1.

Low and upper boundaries of the search space are set as [25.5, 22.5, 22.3, 22.6, 23.3] and [38.9, 38.4, 39.7, 33.6, 34.5] respectively. The first iteration lamp settings are randomly generated as [30, 28.6, 37, 31.7, 25.8]. The results are evaluated based on the root mean square error (RMSE) of the terminal temperature at each iteration. Figures 4 and 5 represent the performance of different heuristic (including PSO, TLBO, DE) based norm-optimal TILC controllers.

Figure 4 shows the RMSE of the terminal temperature behaviour when the desired temperatures are uniform at 100 °C. It is clear that the three heuristic methods are able to guarantee that the terminal temperature errors are in the same range. Comparing the three heuristic methods, PSO works better than the other two in terms of the convergence rate while DE has a better performance in final state error. Conversely, TLBO has the worst performance for these two indexes.

However, due to the stochastic nature of heuristic optimal methods, it is not suitable to compare the performance of different heuristic methods using a single simulation result. Therefore, Monte Carlo method is applied to evaluate the performance of the three heuristic methods. Here, 100 repetitive simulations are carried out for each heuristic method in each of the conditions. In addition, different values of weighting parameter S are tested to investigate its effect on

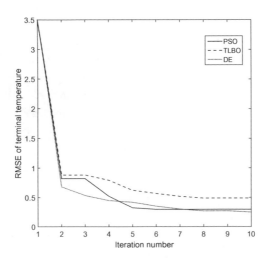

Fig. 4. The terminal tracking RMSE profiles when desired temperature is uniform at 100 °C with respect to iteration

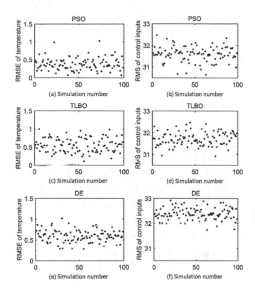

Fig. 5. Statistical results based on 100 simulations for heuristic based norm-optimal TILC with respect to simulation number (desired temperature is uniform at 100 °C and system disturbance is considered)

the system output error and control inputs. RMSE of temperature and RMS of control inputs at final iteration are represented to indicate algorithm performance and energy consumption respectively. The statistical results are presented in Table 2.

Table 2. Statistical analysis based on 100 simulations for heuristic based norm-optimal TILC (desired output temperature is uniform as 100 °C)

Method	Parameters	Average error	Average lamp setting
PSO	Q = 1 R = 0.1 S = 0	0.2909	**32.1450**
	Q = 1 R = 0.1 S = 0.001	0.3094	**32.1050**
TLBO	Q = 1 R = 0.1 S = 0	0.5125	32.2000
	Q = 1 R = 0.1 S = 0.001	0.5245	32.1470
DE	Q = 1 R = 0.1 S = 0	**0.2583**	32.3970
	Q = 1 R = 0.1 S = 0.001	**0.2632**	32.1206

It could be observed in Table 2 that if parameter S is kept the same, DE produces the best performance with the smallest RMSE and PSO has the least energy consumption with the smallest control input. For the same method, the average error increases while the average lamp setting decreases if parameter S changes form 0 to 0.001.

5   Conclusion

In this paper, a heuristic based norm-optimal terminal iterative learning control method is proposed to control the preform terminal temperature profiles in a ISBM reheating process. It balances both the control performance and the control energy sonsumption. In the real ISBM process, it is difficult or even impossible to determine the optimal control input due to the non-linearity of the process. In this case, heuristic methods were used as computational tools to solve this problem. In order to verify the effectiveness of the proposed method, three different heuristic methods including PSO, TLBO and DE were applied to find the optimal control inputs. Simulation results confirmed that the proposed heuristic based norm-optimal TILC method can achieve the control objective, and three popular heuristic methods were used in the control method, and their performances are compared and analysed. The control results are sufficiently precise for the real reheating process [18]. Future work will be addressing the control of practical reheating system in ISBM process subject to significant disturbances.

Acknowledgement. This paper was partially funded by the EPSRC under grant EP/P004636/1. Dr. Ziqi Yang would like to thank the UK-CHINA Science Bridge for financially support his research.

References

1. Abeykoon, C., Li, K., McAfee, M., Martin, P.J., Irwin, G.W.: Extruder melt temperature control with fuzzy logic. In: Preprints of the 18th IFAC World Congress Milano, Italy, pp. 8577–8582 (2011)
2. Liu, X., Li, K., McAfee, M., Deng, J.: Soft-sensor for real-time monitoring of melt viscosity in polymer extrusion process. In: 2010 49th IEEE Conference on Decision and Control (CDC), pp. 3469–3474. IEEE (2010)
3. Yan, J., Li, K., Deng, J., Yang, Z.: Efficient Gaussian process modelling of section weights in polymer stretch blow moulding. In: 2014 UKACC International Conference on Control (CONTROL), pp. 192–197. IEEE (2014)
4. Deng, J., Yang, Z., Li, K., Menary, G., Harkin-Jones, E.: Heuristically optimized RBF neural model for the control of section weights in stretch blow moulding. In: 2012 UKACC International Conference on Control (CONTROL), pp. 24–29. IEEE (2012)
5. Murray, G.: Learning control of actuators in control systems. US Patent 3,555,252, 12 Jan 1971
6. Arimoto, S., Kawamura, S., Miyazaki, F.: Bettering operation of robots by learning. J. Robot. Syst. 1(2), 123–140 (1984)
7. Shi, J., Gao, F., Wu, T.: Robust iterative learning control design for batch processes with uncertain perturbations and initialization. AIChE J. 52(6), 2171–2187 (2006)
8. Yang, D.R., Lee, K.S., Ahn, H.J., Lee, J.: Experimental application of a quadratic optimal iterative learning control method for control of wafer temperature uniformity in rapid thermal processing. IEEE Trans. Semicond. Manuf. 16(1), 36–44 (2003)

9. Xu, J., Chen, Y., Lee, T., Yamamoto, S.: Terminal iterative learning control with an application to rtpcvd thickness control. Automatica **35**(9), 1535–1542 (1999)
10. Gauthier, G., Boulet, B.: Terminal iterative learning control applied to thermoforming machine reheat phase. In: 2006 IEEE International Symposium on Industrial Electronics, vol. 1, pp. 353–357. IEEE (2006)
11. Mondal, S., Yun, Y., Chung, W.K.: Terminal iterative learning control for calibrating systematic odometry errors in mobile robots. In: 2010 IEEE/ASME International Conference on Advanced Intelligent Mechatronics (AIM), pp. 311–316. IEEE (2010)
12. Lin, T., Owens, D., Hatonen, J.: Newton method based iterative learning control for discrete non-linear systems. Int. J. Control **79**(10), 1263–1276 (2006)
13. van de Wijdeven, J., Bosgra, O.: Residual vibration suppression using hankel iterative learning control. Int. J. Robust Nonlinear Control **18**(10), 1034–1051 (2008)
14. Bristow, D., Hencey, B.: A Q, L factorization of norm-optimal iterative learning control. In: 2008 47th IEEE Conference on Decision and Control, CDC 2008, pp. 2380–2384. IEEE (2008)
15. Eberhart, R.C., Shi, Y.: Comparing inertia weights and constriction factors in particle swarm optimization. In: Proceedings of the 2000 Congress on Evolutionary Computation, vol. 1, pp. 84–88. IEEE (2000)
16. Rao, R., Savsani, V., Vakharia, D.: Teaching-learning-based optimization: a novel method for constrained mechanical design optimization problems. Comput. Aided Des. **43**(3), 303–315 (2011)
17. Das, S., Suganthan, P.N.: Differential evolution: a survey of the state-of-the-art. IEEE Trans. Evol. Comput. **15**(1), 4–31 (2011)
18. Salomeia, Y.M.: Improved understanding of injection stretch blow moulding through instrumentation, process monitoring and modelling. Ph.D. thesis, Queen's University Belfast (2009)
19. Yang, Z.: Advanced batch process modelling, control and optimization for injection stretch blow moulding. Ph.D. thesis, Queen's University Belfast (2016)

Advanced Machine Learning Methods and Applications

Application of LSSVM in Performance Test of Pneumatic Valves

Jiayuan Li and Wei Sun[✉]

School of Mechatronic Engineering and Automation, Shanghai University,
Shanghai, China
2478509517@qq.com

Abstract. Pneumatic valve is an important component of the car and also widely used in the automation industry. The performance of the pneumatic valves can be measured by a number of testing parameters which mainly depend on manual testing in China until now. In order to lessen the labor intensity and improve the test efficiency, we propose a pneumatic valve performance test method based on LSSVM algorithm. This method has tested the parameters of the leakage and pressure of the pneumatic valve so that multi-class data can be divided into multiple regions according to different characteristics. The experimental result shows that the proposed method is more accurate than the manual testing in improving the efficiency.

Keywords: Pneumatic valve · LSSVM · Performance testing

1 Introduction

Pneumatic valve has been widely used in automobile industry (one example as shown in Fig. 1). It is a guarantee of the safe driving which can be installed in the fuel pump flanges of the vehicle's fuel supply system and keep the pressure of the fuel tank constant by adjusting the gas in and out [1, 2]. When the vehicle tilts, the rollover valve can automatically cut off the oil to prevent fuel leakage. Undoubtedly the application of pneumatic valve is an appropriate way to ensure driving safety. The pressure and the leakage are the decisive parameters of the valve's performance. Accurately forecasting the malfunction of the pneumatic valve should have great significance [3, 4].

With the rapid growth of the automobile production, the demand for pneumatic valves is also rising. But the pneumatic valves fault detection nowadays still mainly depend on manual testing in China [5, 6]. In this paper a method to predict the malfunction of the valve based on least square support vector machines (LSSVM) is proposed. The LSSVM develop from Support Vector Machine (SVM) [7, 8]. The LSSVM guided by statistical theory, it has theoretical and mathematical foundation which is suitable for small samples and high nonlinearity. It has transformed the problems of quadratic programming in SVM into linear equations, which can greatly reduce the computational complexity and at the same time guarantee the accuracy with quick disposition [9–11]. Test data input into the LSSVM model and classify according to the pressure and leakage. The simulation results show that the high classification accuracy of LSSVM can improve the efficiency of data analysis and find out the

© Springer Nature Singapore Pte Ltd. 2017
D. Yue et al. (Eds.): LSMS/ICSEE 2017, Part II, CCIS 762, pp. 275–281, 2017.
DOI: 10.1007/978-981-10-6373-2_28

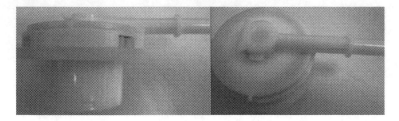

Fig. 1. Pneumatic valve

difference of the performance between the different batches, so as to avoid the influence on the performance during the production and further ensure traffic safety.

2 Least Square Support Vector Machines

For a classification problem with M classes, we have N known observation samples, xi as the input sample, and y_i as the category which the i-th sample belongs. First, all the samples are mapped to the decision space, in which the optimal partition hyperplane is defined:

$$f_j(x) = w_j \varphi(x) + b_j \quad j = 1,\ldots, M \tag{1}$$

where w_j is the weight and b_j is the threshold value.

For the solution of LSSVM, it should consider the following optimization problem:

$$\min \frac{1}{2} \sum_{j=1}^{M} w_j w_j + \frac{1}{2} \gamma \sum_{i=1}^{N} \sum_{j=1}^{M} (\sum p_{ij} \xi_{ij})^2 \tag{2}$$

$$\text{s.t} \quad y_i - \sum_{j=1}^{M} p_{ij}(w_j \varphi(x_i) + b_j) = \sum_{j=1}^{M} p_{ij} \xi_{ij} \tag{3}$$

where γ is the regularization parameter, ξ_{ij} is the error which generate when the data xi input to the j-th class, and pij is the membership degree of the i-th data for the j-th class.

When LSSVM comes to multi-class classification, there would have an indivisible region due to the problem of mixed and missing sub-samples. Based on the LSSVM, we introduce the fussy membership value, so that different samples could separately contribute to the decision-making function learning and reduce the noise interference to eliminate the non-sub-regional ultimately.

3 Experiment

In order to realize the automatic detection of equipment, we designed a four-station pneumatic valve detection device based on LSSVM. Due to this article limitations, Fig. 2 shows only one station of the test schematic. The pneumatic valve which needs to be detected is placed at the test chamber. The left side are the airway channels. In order to obtain the test data, we installed pressure sensor and flow sensor in channels to get feedback measurements of pressure and leakage. At the beginning of the test, the gas in the external gas source flow into the test chamber through some of the electromagnetic reversing valves on the left airway channels. Cut off the left gas path when the chamber's pressure reaches the test value and begin to test the pneumatic valve in the chamber, access the relevant data. After the end of the test open the valves on the airway, so that the pressure inside the test chamber back to atmospheric pressure.

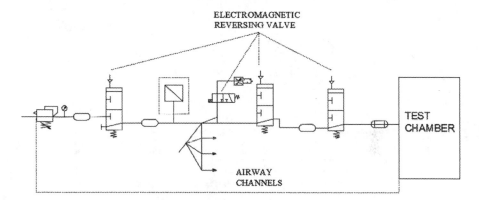

Fig. 2. Test schematic of station 1

We conducted a performance test on a batch of fuel pneumatic valves using a four-station inspection system, which simultaneously measures four valves at a time. The electromagnetic reversing valves control the opening and closing of the airway. The operating frequency is 4 Hz. Six months later after the test, some valve began to malfunction and then began to collect and record the operating status of the valve. A total of 172 effective records were obtained. Each set of data included air pressure, leakage characteristics. There were 103 sets of normal operating state records and 69 sets of fault status records, as shown in Fig. 3. In Fig. 3, class 1 is the normal operating state, and class 2 is the fault state. Table 1 shows the range of the air pressure and leakage value corresponding to each state when the valve is closed.

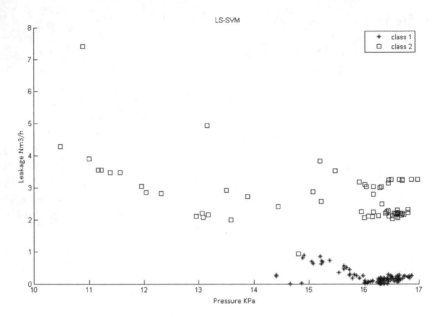

Fig. 3. The running state of the pneumatic valves

Table 1. Each status of the valve corresponds to the data range

	Pressure(KPa)	Leakage (Nm3/h)
Class 1	14.4–17	0–0.9
Class 2	10–17	0.9–8.6

4 Fault Prediction Method Based on LSSVM

All the data records were randomly divided into training set and prediction set. The training set which is used to train the fault classification model takes up two-thirds of the data records; the prediction set which is used to test the model's performance takes up one-third of the data records. The training performance and predictive performance of the model are evaluated by the correct classification rate of the sample (Eq. (4)). The letter N means the number of the correctly classified samples, the letter T means the total number of test samples and the letter P means performance of the model.

$$P = \frac{N}{T} \times 100\% \qquad (4)$$

Located in the decision space, the distance between the sample and its nearest neighbor is used to judge whether the neighbor belongs to the isolated point and thereby determine the adjacent point's membership. Let xi as the primary test sample and there are k samples which need to be distinguished nearest to xi. The average distance of the k samples to xi is di. The sample which deviation is large in the decision space can be regarded as an isolated point. In order to reduce its influence on the accuracy classification, a smaller membership degree is given. To this end, the membership functions are defined as follow:

$$u_i = 1 - (1 - \delta)(\frac{d_i - d\min}{d\max - d\min})^f \tag{5}$$

δ is a small positive number given in advance. The letter f is the parameter that controls the mapping function and the value of f should be chosen according to the actual situation. The symbol dmax is the maximum value of di and dmin is the minimum value of di.

5   Experimental Results and Discussion

The fault prediction method of medical valve based on LSSVM proposed in Sect. 4 is implemented, and training performance and prediction performance are evaluated by formula (4) in the MATLAB.

Figure 4 shows the results of the LSSVM on the valve running state data training and prediction results. Table 2 shows the training performance and prediction performance of LSSVM.

According to Table 2, LSSVM has 100% training and prediction performance for state 1. For state 2, LSSVM has 100% training performance and 98.55% prediction performance, but it remains at a high accuracy despite of certain errors. The device can simultaneously measure four pneumatic valves and each measurement takes only 3 min. We will be able to measure 640 rollovers per day which will greatly improve the measurement efficiency as well as ensure high measurement accuracy.

Table 2. LSSVM training performance and predictive performance

	LSSVM	
	Training performance	Predictive performance
Status 1	100%	100%
Status 2	100%	98.55%
Average	100%	99.28%

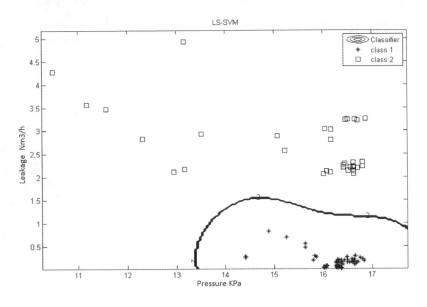

(a) Training results

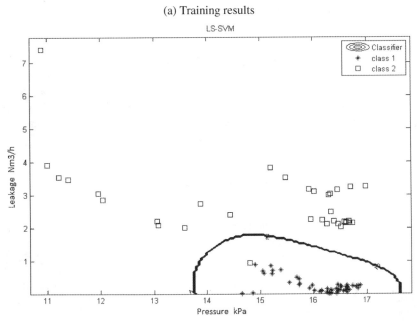

(b) Forecast results

Fig. 4. LSSVM training and prediction results

6 Conclusion

Pneumatic valve can protect the car and guarantee safety driving. It has practical significance to diagnose and forecast the pneumatic valve.

In this paper, we present a fault diagnosis and prediction method based on least squares support vector machines. Experimental results demonstrate that the training performance and test performance of the least squares support vector machine are kept at a good level, which is more accurate and more efficient than the artificial measurement and explicitly shows the superiority of the least squares support vector machine.

The four-station pneumatic valve detection system based on least squares support vector machine (LSSVM) designed in this paper can improve the efficiency by three times compared with manual measurement. This system not only saves labor but also improves measurement accuracy.

References

1. Agashe, S., Rege, P., Agashe, S.: Control valve fault detection. In: Proceedings of the International Instrumentation Symposium, vol. 474, pp. 297–305 (2008)
2. Chen, P., Yu, X., Liu, L.: Simulation and experimental study of electro-pneumatic valve used in air-powered engine. J. Zhejiang Univ.-Sci. A (Appl. Phys. Eng.) **10**(3), 377–383 (2009)
3. Jia, M., Gouming, Z., Harold, S., Jim, W.: Adaptive control of a pneumatic valve actuator for an internal combustion engine. In: Proceedings of the 2007 American Control Conference, pp. 3678–3685 (2007)
4. Chuanhu, Z., Kun, L.: New calibration technology for safety valves of utility boiler. Electricity **4**, 44–49 (2001)
5. Lin, C., Wang, S.: Training algorithm for fuzzy support vector machines with noisy data. Pattern Recogn. Lett. **25**(14), 1647–1656 (2004)
6. You, M., Zhang, J., Sun, D., Gou, J.: Characteristics analysis and control study of a pneumatic proportional valve. In: Proceedings of 2015 IEEE Advanced Information Technology, Electronic and Automation Control Conference, pp. 242–247 (2015)
7. Chapelle, O., Vapnik, V., Bousquet, O., Mukherjee, S.: Choosing multiple parameters for support vector machines. Mach. Learn. **46**(1–3), 131–159 (2002)
8. Xue, X., Yang, X., Chen, X.: Application of a support vector machine for prediction of slope stability. Sci. China Technol. Sci. **57**(12), 2379–2386 (2014)
9. Wang, Y.Q., Wang, S.Y., Laik, K.: A new fuzzy support vector machine to evaluate credit risk. IEEE Trans. Fuzzy Syst. **13**(6), 820–831 (2005)
10. Zhang, Y., Chi, Z., Liu, X.-D., Wang, X.: A novel fuzzy compensation multi-class support vector machine. Appl. Intell. **27**, 21–28 (2007)
11. Suykens, J.A.K., Vandewalle, J.: Least squares support vector machines classifiers. Neural Process. Lett. **9**(3), 293–300 (1999)

A Two-Stage Optimal Detection Algorithm Research for Pedestrians in Front of the Vehicles

Yunlian Shao[1,2], Mei-hua Xu[1(✉)], Feng Ran[3], and Dong-yang Shen[1]

[1] Department of Automation, College of Mechatronics Engineering and
Automation, Shanghai University,
No. 149, Yanchang Road, Shanghai 200072, China
mhxu@shu.edu.cn
[2] School of Physics and Electronic Electrical Engineering,
Huaiyin Normal University, Huai'an, China
[3] Microelectronic R&D Center,
Shanghai University, No. 149, Yanchang Road, Shanghai 200072, China

Abstract. In this paper, a two-stage optimal detection algorithm is presented for pedestrians in front of the vehicles. It uses the idea of combing the coarse-grain and fine-grain to effectively classify and filter. First, it uses the combination of Color Self-Similarity features based on rectangular block summing and AdaBoost classifier based on greedy strategy to coarse-grained screen the pedestrian detection window, then it uses the combination of HOG feature and libsvm classifier to fine-grained confirm the previous screened pedestrian detection window, Finally, the target windows is integrated by the greedy strategy. The AdaBoost classifier's training time is theoretically shorten to the 1/T time of original algorithm. With the training process, The Color Self-Similarity features shorten to 250 dimensions by the feature selection. Then, the method makes full use of the image information and ensures the detection accuracy.

Keywords: Color Self-Similarity features based on rectangular block summing · AdaBoost classifier based on greedy strategy · Feature dimensionality reduction · Grain filter screening · Libsvm

1 Introduction

The study of pedestrian detection systems began in the mid-1990s, and it has become one of the core research fields in assistant driving. People generally obtain the road images by using cheap and ordinary optical cameras and improve the comprehensive performance of pedestrian detection system by the optimized algorithm.

In 2010, Wojek et al. added the CSS (Color Self-Similarity) feature and motion features to extend the Wojek and Schieles' feature framework and the measures improve the detection effect [1]. However, the original CCS feature contains a lot of redundant information and its' high vector dimension which lead to the feature extraction and feature classification more time-consuming. In 2005, Dalal and Triggs

© Springer Nature Singapore Pte Ltd. 2017
D. Yue et al. (Eds.): LSMS/ICSEE 2017, Part II, CCIS 762, pp. 282–292, 2017.
DOI: 10.1007/978-981-10-6373-2_29

proposed HOG (Histograms of Oriented Gradients) pedestrian feature descriptor [2], which has become a milestone in the pedestrian detection research. Since then a lot of HOG variants are proposed by the researchers. From the present point of view, HOG feature expression is the best in the single feature extraction. But the redundant cal-culation and the large amount of computational in the HOG feature extraction lead to slow the detection speed.

Therefore, this paper presents a two-stage pedestrian detection algorithm for road image provided by the monocular camera. It is my contribution. It uses the idea of combing the coarse-grain and the fine-grain to effectively classify and filter. In the first stage, the CSS feature based on the sum of rectangular blocks and the AdaBoost classifier based on greedy strategy are used to carry out the coarse-grain screening of pedestrian window; In the second stage, The combination of HOG feature and libsvm classifier is used to fine-grained the previous screening of the pedestrian detection window. Compared with the single pedestrian feature and classifier, the method makes full use of the image information and shortens the pedestrian detection time and ensures the detection accuracy.

2   CCS Feature Based on Rectangular Block Summing

According to the CSS feature of Walk et al., the local color feature of the pedestrian image is analyzed such as the following images. Figure 1(a) is the original pedestrian image; The face and arm skin color in the Fig. 1(b) is similar; The color of pedestrians' clothing is also self-similar in Fig. 1(c) and (d).

(a)   (b)   (c)   (d)

Fig. 1. Local structural similarity of pedestrians

According to the CSS theory feature, the 128 × 64 images are divided into 8 × 8 blocks and the histogram information of every block in HSV color space is calculated. Then there is a total of 128 (16 × 8) blocks. The histogram intersection distance is respectively calculated between the first block and the other 127 blocks, and the histogram intersection distances of the second block and subsequent 126 blocks are calculated as well. Finally the feature with 8128 dimensions is got. In the concrete calculation, the tricolor interpolation is used to reduce the regional aliasing effect. However, according to the image sensor structure, the interaction between the pixel colors in the image is not significant [3], and the three-linear interpolation is time-consuming. At the same time when the color similarity of the blocks is calculated, the more complicated histogram intersection is applied. In this paper, the rectangular block summing is used to replace the mentioned method, which greatly reduces the computational complexity of CSS feature [4, 5]. These measures improve the calculation speeds:

(1) Converting an RGB image to HSV color space;
(2) Rectangular Block Feature Extraction and Similarity Calculation: R is defined as the 8 × 8 rectangular block, and the sum of the matrix blocks are calculated in H, S and V channels respectively:

$$Sum_{RH} = \sum_{x,y \in R} sum(x_H, y_H) \tag{1}$$

$$Sum_{RS} = \sum_{x,y \in R} sum(x_S, y_S) \tag{2}$$

$$Sum_{RV} = \sum_{x,y \in R} sum(x_V, y_V) \tag{3}$$

(3) Calculating the similarity of rectangular blocks: The ratio of two rectangular blocks is calculated in three channels, the ration is decided the similarity of two rectangular.

$$F(R_1, R_2) = \frac{Sum_{R_1 H}}{Sum_{R_2 H}} + \frac{Sum_{R_1 S}}{Sum_{R_2 S}} + \frac{Sum_{R_1 V}}{Sum_{R_2 V}} \tag{4}$$

The modified feature extraction algorithm is still calculated according to the method proposed by Walk et al., Finally the 8128 dimension features is got. The dimensions of the CSS feature are still high, so the dimensionality reduction of the features must be taken for the real-time scenarios, which is an effective measure to reduce the feature dimension and improve the efficiency of a given task. It can be divided into feature extraction and feature selection. The feature extraction regenerates a feature space with a smaller dimension and a more independent dimension by transforming the original feature [6].

The feature selection is to select proper subset from the original set. The feature extraction involves semantic analysis. The natural language semantic processing technology is not yet developed, so the feature extraction method is not significant. In contrast, the feature selection is the proper subsets of the origin features, so it is easier to implement. The feature selection method is used to reduce the CSS feature in the paper as shown in Fig. 2. In the AdaBoost training process, the each weak classifier corresponds to a feature. So AdaBoost training process is the feature selection process. The CSS feature is selected by the AdaBoost training which is directly related to the classification results. The feature selection result is fed back to the character extraction stage, the specified feature is only extracted which effectively reduce the time in the character extraction.

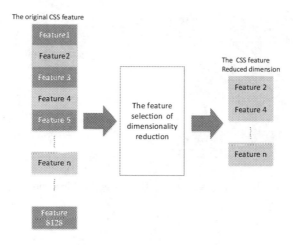

Fig. 2. Feature selection diagram

3   The AdaBoost Classifier Based on Greedy Strategy

In 1995, Freund and Schapire jointly proposed the AdaBoost algorithm which is an iterative algorithm. The core idea is to train different weak classifiers for the same training set, and then the weak classifier is combined to form a strong classifier.

The most time-consuming part of the original AdaBoost algorithm is to compute the weight error rate of the weak classifier. At the end of a round training, all the training sample weight is updated, and all weak classifiers must be retrained again in the next round training. The original AdaBoost algorithm training process is shown in Fig. 3(a). In the training process, the number of training samples and weak classifiers is very large; the AdaBoost algorithm training time is mostly spent on the weak classifier training. Although the updated weight samples can focus on the error detection samples, but it is the very time consuming. If the weak classifier training process is separated from the cycle, the training time will be significantly reduced as shown in Fig. 3(b) [7].

The method of serialized tables is implemented to shorten the weak classifier training time. A training set is given as $T = \{(x_1, y_1), (x_2, y_2) \cdots (x_N, y_N)\}$, $x \in X$, $X \subset R^n$. $y_i \in (0, 1)$, the $y_i = 1$ represents the positive samples; the $y_i = 0$ represents the negative samples; l represents the number of positive samples; m represents the number of negative samples; n represents the total number of training samples. The algorithm flow is as follows:

(1) Initialize the weight $w_{1,i} = D(i)$; the negative samples: $D(i) = \frac{1}{2m}$; the positive samples: $D(i) = \frac{1}{2l}$

(2) Each feature of the sample trains a weak classifier. The sample classifier of the jth feature is $h_j(x)$.

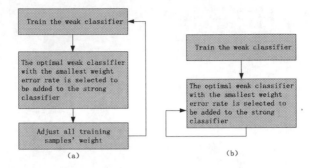

Fig. 3. Analysis of AdaBoost training algorithm

$$h_j(x) = \begin{cases} 1 & if\ p_j ft_j(x) < p_j \theta_j \\ 0 & otherwise \end{cases} \tag{5}$$

The classifier is determined by the threshold θ_j and the offset $p_j, p_j = \pm 1$; $ft_j(x)$ represents the jth feature value

(3) Build the following serialized tables.

In the *Tables*, the $error_i$ represents the weighted error rate of a trained weak classifier. The $error_1\ error_2\ \cdots\ error_N$ is an incremental sequence. The $f_{ij}(x_k, y_k) = 0$ or $f_{ij}(x_k, y_k) = 1$ indicates the test result of the $h_{ij}(x)$ weak classifier detection on the training sample k. (Where 1 represents positive samples; where 0 represents negative samples) [8] (Table 1).

Table 1. The serialized tables

$error_1$	$h_{i1}(x)$	$f_{i1}(x_1, y_1)$	$f_{i1}(x_2, y_2)$	$\cdots$	$f_{i1}(x_n, y_n)$
$error_2$	$h_{i2}(x)$	$f_{i2}(x_1, y_1)$	$f_{i2}(x_2, y_2)$	$\cdots$	$f_{i2}(x_n, y_n)$
$\vdots$	$\vdots$	$\vdots$	$\vdots$	$\cdots$	
$error_N$	$h_{iN}(x)$	$f_{iN}(x_1, y_1)$	$f_{iN}(x_2, y_2)$	$\cdots$	$f_{iN}(x_n, y_n)$

In the improved algorithm, the updated weight of the original algorithm and the process of the weak classifier cycle training are omitted. The algorithm doesn't find the optimal solution but treatment each sample equally by the greedy strategy. After the end of a round of training, the sample weight is not updated. Then the next best weak classifier is selected by the serializing table and the histogram. It can shorten the training time to the $1/T$ time of the original AdaBoost algorithm [9].

4 Simulation of Algorithm and Comparison of Experimental Results

Based on the road image of the monocular camera, this paper designs the two-stage detection system of the pedestrian in front of the vehicle. The experiments are carried out on the INRIA pedestrian database [10], and Computer configuration: Intel Corei5 2.8 GHz, 12 GB RAM, 64-bit Windows7; Simulation environment: Matlab R2013a. The DET curve is shown as Fig. 4. It can achieve the precision of 92.6% in our own detection database with false rate of 7.0%.

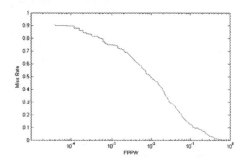

Fig. 4. The DET curve of detection pedestrian

The algorithm is divided into several modules: image preprocessing module, coarse-grained screening module, fine-grained confirmation module, target fusion module. It is shown in Fig. 5.

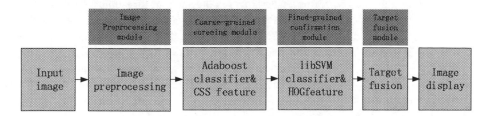

Fig. 5. The two-stage detection system of the pedestrian in front of the vehicle

4.1 Image Preprocessing Module

A First, the input image is cropped and the cropped image is converted to HSV color space. Second, the cropped image is scaled according to the design desire, the two scaled levels are selected as grade 1 and grade 1.25 in this paper. Finally, the pixels in 8×8 rectangular block units of H channel, S channel and V channel is summed respectively in each scaled image. The sums prepare for extracting CSS features. The image preprocessing process is shown in Fig. 6.

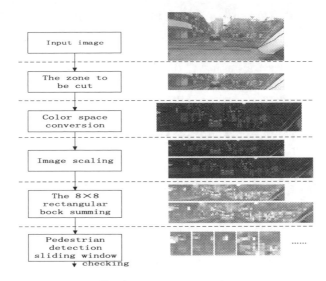

Fig. 6. Image preprocessing

4.2 Coarse-Grained Screening Module

The image preprocessing module has complete the color space conversion and 8×8 rectangular sum, so the rectangular block similarity can be directly calculated when the CSS feature is extracted in the 64×128 pedestrian detection window, According to the proposed CCS feature dimension reduction processing at the same time, it is not necessary to extract the full CCS feature of the 8128 dimension as long as some of the dimensions are sufficient to fulfill the detection requirements. During the AdaBoost training process, the number of weak classifiers is the same as the number of iterations, that is to say, the number of selected features is equal to the number of iterations. By analyzing the number of iterations and false positives in the AdaBoost classifier, it can be found that the error rate of the classifier is less than 7.5% when the number of iterations is more than 250 times. Considered the accuracy and feature extraction speed, the most important 250 features of the CSS feature only are extracted. The whole process is shown in Fig. 7.

4.3 Coarse-Grained Screening Module

The image preprocessing module has complete the color space conversion and 8×8 rectangular sum, so the rectangular block similarity can be directly calculated when the CSS feature is extracted in the 64×128 pedestrian detection window, According to the proposed CCS feature dimension reduction processing at the same time, it is not necessary to extract the full CCS feature of the 8128 dimension as long as some of the dimensions are sufficient to fulfill the detection requirements. During the AdaBoost training process, the number of weak classifiers is the same as the number of iterations, that is to say, the number of selected features is equal to the number of iterations.

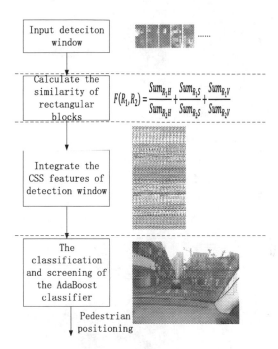

Fig. 7. Coarse-grained pedestrian screening process

By analyzing the number of iterations and false positives in the AdaBoost classifier, it can be found that the error rate of the classifier is less than 7.5% when the number of iterations is more than 250 times. Considered the accuracy and feature extraction speed, the most important 250 features of the CSS feature only are extracted. The whole process is shown in Fig. 7.

4.4 Fine-Grained Confirmation Module

The suspected pedestrian detection window is passed to the fine-grained confirmation module of the HOG feature. The sliding window consists of a 3780 dimension HOG vector. The trained the libsvm of HOG feature is loaded into the memory; then the y value of the sliding window is calculated according to $y = w^T x + b$. If the y value is greater than a certain threshold (the threshold is 0), then the sliding window is considered as the pedestrian zone; if the y value is less than a certain threshold, the sliding window is considered as the non-pedestrian zone [11, 12]. The fine-grained confirmation process is shown in Fig. 8.

4.5 Target Fusion Module

After the fine-grained confirmation module is processed, the pedestrians are distributed in the different layers. The overlapping pedestrian zones need to be integrated. In this

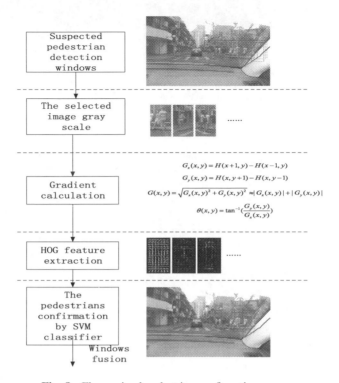

$$G_x(x,y) = H(x+1,y) - H(x-1,y)$$

$$G_y(x,y) = H(x,y+1) - H(x,y-1)$$

$$G(x,y) = \sqrt{G_x(x,y)^2 + G_y(x,y)^2} \approx |G_x(x,y)| + |G_y(x,y)|$$

$$\theta(x,y) = \tan^{-1}\left(\frac{G_y(x,y)}{G_x(x,y)}\right)$$

Fig. 8. Fine-grained pedestrian confirmation process

Fig. 9. Windows fusion process

paper, we improve the non-maximal suppression by introducing the fractional ratio and neighborhood window. The different strategies are taken for individual windows in the same layer and peripheral windows in different layers. For the individual window, the window detection score decides whether it is a false window; for the peripheral windows, the neighborhood windows score gap decides whether the peripheral windows is retained or the neighborhood window is weighted. The actual results are shown in Fig. 9.

5   Conclusion

In this paper, we have presented a two-stage pedestrian detection algorithm for road image. Compared with the single pedestrian feature and classifier, the method can make full use of the image features' information and shorten the pedestrian detection time; ensure the detection accuracy. And in the future, we plan to transplant the proposed method to embedded platforms for the vehicle-borne mobile systems for practical application.

Acknowledgements. This work was financially supported by the national natural science foundation of China under Grant (No. 61376028) and (No. 61674100).

References

1. Wojek, C., Walk, S., Schiele, B.: Multi-cue onboard pedestrian detection. In: IEEE Conference on Computer Vision and Pattern Recognition, pp. 794–801 (2009)
2. Dalal, N., Triggs, B.: Histograms of oriented gradients for human detection. In: Computer Vision and Pattern Recognition, pp. 886–892 (2005)
3. Heidari, H., Gatti, U., Maloberti, F.: CMOS vertical hall magnetic sensors on flexible substrate. IEEE Sens. J. **16**, 1 (2016)
4. Zeng, B., Wang, G., Lin, X.: Color self-similarity feature based real-time pedestrian detection. J. Tsinghua Univ. **4**, 030 (2012)
5. Shen, D.-y., Xu, M.-h., Guo, A.-y.: A novel method of pedestrian detection aided by color self-similarity feature. In: Zhang, L., Song, X., Wu, Y. (eds.) AsiaSim/SCS AutumnSim - 2016. CCIS, vol. 646, pp. 21–29. Springer, Singapore (2016). doi:10.1007/978-981-10-2672-0_3
6. Schutzeh, H., Hull, D.A., Pedersen, J.O.: A comparison of classifiers and document representations for the routing problem. In: Proceedings of 18th ACM International Conference on Research and Development in Information Retrieval, pp. 229–237. ACM, New York (1995)
7. Kong, K.K., Hong, K.S.: Design of coupled strong classifiers in AdaBoost framework and its application to pedestrian detection. Pattern Recogn. Lett. **68**, 63–69 (2015)
8. Qian, Z.-M., Xu, D.F.: Fast AdaBoost training algorithm. Comput. Eng. **35**, 187–189 (2009)
9. Zhang, P.B., Yang, Z.X.: A novel AdaBoost framework with robust threshold and structural optimization. IEEE Trans. Cybern. **99**, 1–13 (2016)
10. INRIA'S Person Dataset. http://pascal.inrialpes.fr/data/human/

11. Guo, A., Xu, M., Ran, F.: A novel real-time pedestrian detection system on monocular vision. In: Zhang, L., Song, X., Wu, Y. (eds.) AsiaSim/SCS AutumnSim - 2016. CCIS, vol. 646, pp. 293–303. Springer, Singapore (2016). doi:10.1007/978-981-10-2672-0_30
12. Kachouane, M., Sahki, S., Lakrouf, M., et al.: HOG based fast human detection. eprint arXiv **12**(24), 1–4 (2015)

Collision Free Path Planning for Welding Robot Based on CG-MOPSO

Xuewu Wang$^{(\boxtimes)}$, Yixin Yan, and Xingsheng Gu

Key Laboratory of Advanced Control and Optimization for Chemical Processes
of Ministry of Education, East China University of Science and Technology,
Shanghai 200237, China
{wangxuew,xsgu}@ecust.edu.cn, 578135034@qq.com

Abstract. For spot welding task, reasonable welding path is useful for welding efficiency improvement. Obstacle avoidance is essential for safe welding, and energy consumption is another factor needed to be considered in the process of welding robot path planning. The shortest path length and energy consumption are considered as optimization objectives, and obstacle avoidance is set as the constraint condition in this article. After analysis of geometric obstacle avoidance strategy, energy consumption, and robot path length, the multi-objective welding path optimization model is given first. Then, the clustering guidance multi-objective particle swarm algorithm (CG-MOPSO) is presented. At last, the improved algorithm is applied to realize the welding robot path optimization, and the algorithm effectiveness is verified through the Pareto optimal solution.

Keywords: Welding robot · Obstacle avoidance strategy · Energy consumption · Path planning · CG-MOPSO

1 Introduction

Manual planning is still widely used for industrial welding robot task planning, which is time-consuming when there are large-scale weld joints. Hence, it is necessary to apply intelligent algorithms for path planning and realize efficient path optimization. Welding robot path optimization was simplified as the travelling salesman problem (TSP) and the path length was minimized based on double-global optimal particle swarm optimization algorithm [1]. In Ref [2], task sequencing and path planning in remote laser welding was studied based on TSP and meta-heuristic algorithm. The energy consumption and cycle time were optimized based on restarted simulated annealing algorithm [3]. In Ref [4], the robot performance was optimized and energy consumption was reduced. Besides optimization of time and energy consumption, obstacle avoidance strategy is also necessary to be studied. Hence, obstacle avoidance and cycle time were considered to optimize the robot path.

In this article, the welding robot path optimization is studied as a multi-objective problem. Where the shortest path length and energy consumption are considered as optimization objectives, and obstacle avoidance is set as the constraint condition. The multi-objective welding path optimization model is analyzed in Sect. 2. The clustering multi-objective particle swarm algorithm (CG-MOPSO) is presented in Sect. 3. Then,

© Springer Nature Singapore Pte Ltd. 2017
D. Yue et al. (Eds.): LSMS/ICSEE 2017, Part II, CCIS 762, pp. 293–303, 2017.
DOI: 10.1007/978-981-10-6373-2_30

the improved algorithm is used to realize the welding robot path optimization in Sect. 4. And the conclusion is given in Sect. 5.

2 Analysis of Welding Robot Path Planning

2.1 Optimization Problem Description

In this article, the weld joints sequence for the automobile front baffle is used for optimization. Path planning for single robot is considered, the path length and energy consumption are taken as optimization goal, and obstacle avoidance of welding torch is also taken into account. The welding robot used here is ABB IRB2400-10. For this multi-objective optimization problem, the shortest path length and least energy consumption are desired. The optimization problem is described as follows

$$\begin{cases} \min J_1(X) \\ \min J_2(X) \\ \text{s.t. path is collision free} \end{cases} \tag{1}$$

where X denotes welding path sequence, $J_1(X)$ denotes path length, $J_2(X)$ denotes energy consumption.

In this article, an improved multi-objective particle swarm and algorithm is proposed for path length and energy consumption planning. The path between two weld joints is obtained after trajectory planning of two welding positions. Straight line is adopted to avoid obstacles. The linear path of the manipulator is realized by linear interpolation of position and pose of two weld joints in Cartesian space. Then, corresponding joint parameters are obtained according to the inverse kinematics of the robot. Calculation of energy consumption is obtained after inverse kinetic solution for joint kinematic parameters based on the robot D-H parameter model.

The spot welding robot path can be regarded as the point-to-point motion of the robot end, and the robot path planning is simplified as TSP. If the optimization goal is set as the path length, it could be presented as follows:

$$s = \sum_{I=1}^{N-1} d\left(c_{\varphi(i)}, c_{\varphi(i+1)}\right) + d\left(c_{\varphi(N)}, c_{\varphi(1)}\right) \tag{2}$$

where $d\left(c_{\varphi(i)}, c_{\varphi(i+1)}\right)$ denotes the distance between point $c_{\varphi(i)}$ and point $c_{\varphi(i+1)}$.

Energy saving is also needed to be considered for welding robot path optimization. Hence, energy consumption analysis is studied based on industrial robot dynamics. There are various methods for studying robot dynamics, for example, Lagrange, Newton-Euler, Gauss, and Kane. For Lagrangian dynamics, very complex system dynamics equation can be obtained in a simple form based on the system energy concept. Besides, it has an explicit structure, and the physical meaning is explicit.

2.2   Obstacle Avoidance Analysis

In the actual welding process, the movement between weld joints is not a simple point-to-point movement, the collision between the robot and work-piece should be avoided. In this article, the geometrical obstacle avoidance strategy with the transition point is introduced due to the complex obstacle avoidance of welding process. According to the weld joints distribution in different regions, the transition points with the shortest path length are obtained based on the geometrical method. Because the work-piece is much smaller than the robot, only the gun is considered to avoid obstacle.

For obstacle avoidance, the model of the work-piece should be established first. The welding work-piece model and weld joints distribution for the car component is shown in Fig. 1. The work-piece model is established according to three points determining a plane. As transition points are used to realize welding obstacle avoidance, some details of the work-piece is ignored when the work-piece model is established, and the tangency surface is used for approximation of the work-piece surface.

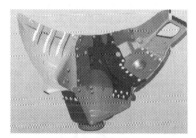

Fig. 1. 3D figure of welding work-piece

Obstacle avoidance for welding robot is different from obstacle avoidance for mobile robot, it does not need to be close to or move around obstacle. Hence, geometric obstacle avoidance strategy is used in this article, and the obstacle avoidance intermediate point is obtained using geometric reasoning. The geometric obstacle avoidance strategy is described as follows:

(1)   Two weld joints are in adjacent planes as shown in Fig. 2. The starting point is in the plane 1, and terminal point is in the plane 2. The shortest path length is demanded for the path from the starting point, after the middle point belong to intersection line of two planes, and to the terminal point. Solving method for the transition point is that Connection starting point and terminal point, which is called line 1, the intersection of two planes is called line 2, Line 1 and line 2 locate in different surface. A transition point on line 2 is obtained to make the path shortest, which moves through the starting point, the transition point, and reach the terminal point. This transition point is the intersection of the line 2 and the middle vertical line of the two lines.

(2)   Two weld joints are not in adjacent planes as shown in Fig. 3. In this case, the middle point outside the work-piece is found, the torch moves from the starting point of the work-piece through the middle point and then reaches the terminal

point. For transition point selection, the safety distance should be set according to the width of the torch. Then, a transition line can be obtained, the distance between the line and work-piece is bigger than the width of the torch. Furthermore, the transition point with the shortest path is found through iteration after the transient line discretization. Obtained transient points are shown by the blue dots in Fig. 3. Besides, the in-point and out-point can be got using the same method mentioned in above paragraph. The final path can be seen in the Fig. 3. The path starts from the start point to the out-point, through the transition point to the in-point, and finally to the terminal point.

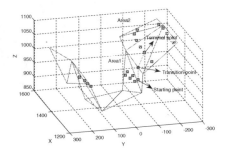

Fig. 2. Weld joints on adjacent surfaces (Color figure online)

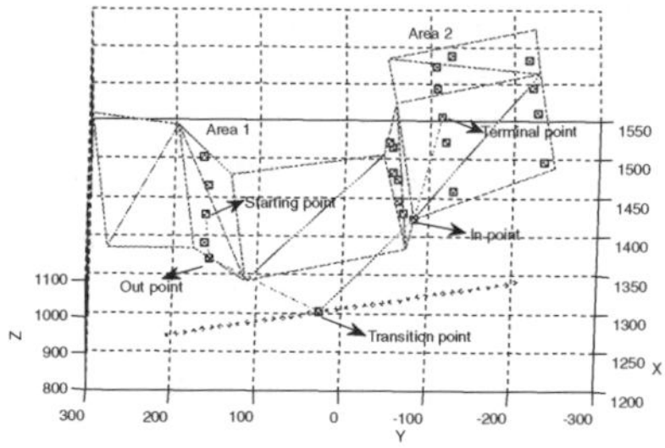

Fig. 3. Weld point on nonadjacent surfaces (Color figure online)

3   Multi-objective Particle Swarm Optimization Algorithm

In 1995, Kennedy and Eberhart [5] presented the particle swarm optimization (PSO) algorithm based on the regularity of hunting birds. The best position of a particle is called p_i^k, the best position of the whole swarm is called p_g^k. The state of the particle is described by the D-dimensional velocity $v_i = (v_{i1}, v_{i2}, \ldots, v_{iD})$ and the position $X_i = (x_{i1}, x_{i2}, \ldots, x_{iD})$. Then, every particle updates its state according to the Eqs. (3) and (4), and the next generation are generated.

$$v_i^{k+1} = \omega v_i^k + c_1 r_1 \left(p_i^k - x_i^k \right) + c_2 r_2 \left(p_g^k - x_i^k \right) \tag{3}$$

$$x_i^{k+1} = x_i^k + v_i^{k+1} \tag{4}$$

where w denotes inertia weight, k is the current iterations. c_1, c_2, which are learning factor, are usually positive and adjust the traction force of personal optimal position and global optimal position. r_1, r_2 are random numbers between 0 and 1.

For multi-objective problem, following two aspects is necessary to be considered [6]. (1) Reasonable fitness function and selection strategy are applied to make the searching results approach to the Pareto front step by step. (2) Keep the diversity of evolutionary population, and make sure the solution set has better distribution in the target space.

The global and local search capabilities of algorithm have to be coordinated to solving these two problems. When multi-objective particle swarm optimization is used to solve the multi-objective optimization problem, different guidance particle selection strategies will greatly affect the local and global search ability of the algorithm. In this article, the guide particle selection strategy is improved, and it is selected according to the state of particles. The new particle selection strategy can increase the local searching efficiency and coordinate global searching ability through considering particles information communication. In addition, the external archives update mechanism of non-dominated solution generated by the multi-objective algorithm is also important to the algorithm. The uniform distribution of the non-dominated solution at the Pareto front is enhanced through iterative elimination of superfluous solutions in this article.

3.1 Optimization Problem Description

In order to balance the local and global search ability, the clustering partitioning strategy [7] is adopted to guide the particles, increase the population diversity and optimize the searching effect. In this article, clustering analysis is conducted for two optimization objectives (path length and energy). Hence, the simple Q-type hierarchical clustering method is used to realize cluster analysis for the sample indexes (path length and energy), and it makes the algorithm structure simple.

The process is presented as follows:

Step 1: One particle is clustered as a group, and the clustering process will be terminated when the number of groups is in the range (a, b). Then, current clustering result of particles is accepted. Experiments show that suitable particle clustering results can be obtained when a = 5, b = 15.

Step 2: Assuming that the number of samples is m, and the number of sample index is n, the particle data can be expressed as m * n order matrices:

$$Data = \begin{bmatrix} x_{11} & \cdots & x_{1n} \\ \vdots & \ddots & \vdots \\ x_{m1} & \cdots & x_{mn} \end{bmatrix} \tag{5}$$

where x_{mn} denotes the n-th index value of the m-th particle.

Step 3: Determine the similarity measuring method. The similarity measurement commonly used in Q-type clustering is "distance". Common distance calculation methods include Euclidean distance, Manhattan distance, Chebyshev distance, Power distance, and Mahalanobis distance. Un-weighted Euclidean distance method is used in this article:

$$d_{ij} = \left(\sum_{z=1}^{n} \left(x_{iz} - x_{jz} \right)^2 \right)^{0.5} \tag{6}$$

where d_{ij} is the "distance" between particle i and particle j, which is the sum of unweighted Euclidean distance of n sample indices, the distance matrix of samples can be got:

$$Distance = \begin{bmatrix} d_{11} & \cdots & d_{1m} \\ \vdots & \ddots & \vdots \\ d_{m1} & \cdots & d_{mm} \end{bmatrix} \quad (7)$$

The distance matrix is a symmetric matrix, where $d_{11}, d_{22}, \ldots, d_{mm} = 0$.

Step 4: The two samples with shortest distance are further clustered into one group, and the group number is updated to m−1. Then, Return to step 2, continue the above steps until the number of group is in the range (a, b).

3.2   Guidance Particle Selection Strategy

In this article, all particles are divided into three states: unconstrained state, constrained excited state, constrained non-excited states. Before particle classification, the decision space is divided using unweighted average distance method and is numbered $Region_i(i = 1, 2, \ldots, n)$. The center of each region is obtained based on the average coordinate value of all non-inferior solutions in the region

$$center_{i,j} = \frac{1}{nn_i} \sum_{s=1}^{nn_i} x_{s,j} \quad (8)$$

where, $center_{i,j}$ is the $jth(j = 1, 2)$ dimension coordinate of the $Region_i$, $x_{s,j}$ is the jth dimensional coordinate of the $s-th$ non-inferior solution in the $Region_i$. In this article, there are two dimensions for every solution, and they are path length and energy consumption.

Then, the Euclidean distance between the centers of the regions is obtained:

$$d_{m,n} - \left(\sum_{j=1}^{2} \left(center_{m,j} - center_{n,j} \right)^2 \right)^{0.5} \quad (9)$$

where $d_{m,n}$ is the distance between the $Region_m$ and the $Region_n$.

At the same time, the Euclidean distance between each particle and region center is calculated:

$$d_{k,i} = \left(\sum_{j=1}^{2} \left(x_{k,j} - center_{i,j} \right)^2 \right)^{0.5} \quad (10)$$

where k denotes number of particle in $Region_i$. Find the region closest to the particle, if the distance between a particle and the region is less than the average distance between all particles and the region, the particle is constrained particle, otherwise non-constrained particles.

Then, the excitation strategy for constrained particles is conducted. When there are too many constrained particles in a certain region, some particles in the region are excited. For constrained particles, it is set as non-excited particle when rand $<ratio_i$. Otherwise, it is excited particle. Here, rand is a random number in (0, 1), and $ratio_i$ is obtained based on Eq. 11. Where nn_i represents the number of non-inferior solution in

the $Region_i$, np_i is the number of constrained particles in $Region_i$, N is the population size, and R is the upper limit of external files.

$$ratio_i = \begin{cases} 4 \times \frac{nn_i}{np_i} \times \frac{N}{R}, nn_i < 3; \\ \frac{nn_i}{np_i} \times \frac{N}{R}, otherwise; \end{cases} \tag{11}$$

From Eq. 11, it can be known that the particles have more chance to become excited particles when more constrained particles exist in the region. The guidance particle selection strategy of the excited particles adopts global selection strategy in this article. This excitation mechanism can make the particle jump out the region, and balance the search probability of each region.

In Fig. 4, the clustering result is described in nine regions. From down to up, these nine regions are denoted by green star, blue circle, blue block, green block, green circle, blue hexagon, blue star, green hexagon, and red block. In every region, the solid shape represents constrained particles, the hollow shape represents non-constrained particles and the diamond represents the centre of region, and the red asterisk represents Pareto solution.

The selection strategy is presented in Fig. 5. Circles denote particles in a region, solid circles represent constrained particles, and the rest represent non-constrained particles. Then, the non-inferior solution nearest to the region centre in the region is selected as region guidance particle, which is shown as red circle. Besides, the global guidance particle is selected in global non inferior solution randomly, which is shown in the Fig. 5. In Fig. 4, for the region denoted by red block at the upper right corner, the region is too far from the non-constrained particles, and $nn_i = 0$. Hence, region selection strategy is not applied, and only global selection strategy is used here to obtain guidance particle.

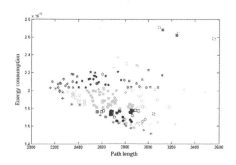

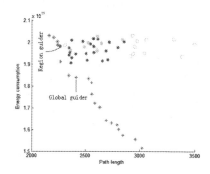

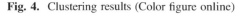

Fig. 4. Clustering results (Color figure online)

Fig. 5. Guidance particle selection (Color figure online)

In conclusion, all particles are divided into constrained particles and unconstrained particles. The particles that are far from all regions are unconstrained particles, and the particles near to a certain region are constrained particles. Then, the particles are divided into excited and non-excited states using the particle excitation mechanism. Global selection strategy is used for guidance particle selection of excited state and the unconstrained particle, and region selection strategy is used for guidance particle selection of the non-excited particle.

3.3   External Archive Save Mechanism

For traditional external archiving mechanism, the distance between non-inferior solutions is calculated first. Then, all non-inferior solutions with too large density are removed according to the distance of non-inferior solution when the scale of the external files exceeds the maximum size. However, this kind elimination method for non-inferior solution will lead to bad distribution uniformity of the non-inferior solutions.

According to the shortcomings of the traditional external archiving mechanism, the distance between adjacent non-inferior solutions is calculated first based on the target space [8]. The average distance between the non-inferior solution and its adjacent two solutions is taken as its density value. The smaller the average distance is, the greater the density is. When the size of the external file exceeds the maximum size, the non-inferior solutions with biggest density are eliminated based on the density value. And the density of the non-inferior solution is calculated after each removal. When the non-inferior density is calculated, only the density of the non-inferior solution which are adjacent to the eliminated non-inferior solution need to be recalculated because the non-inferior solution density adjacent to the non-inferior solution is changed. As a result, computation complexity can be reduced to a great extent, and make sure the reserved non-inferior solution can be uniformly distributed in the target space as much as possible.

3.4   Discretization of Improved Multi-objective Particle Swarm Algorithm

PSO is mostly used to solve continuous optimization problems, but the welding robot path planning in this article is a discrete optimization problems. Hence, appropriate discrete transformation of PSO need to be conducted to realize welding robot path planning. Improved exchange strategy for discrete sequences, individual optimal and global optimal in the iterative process is presented as follows

$$v_i^{t+1} = \omega * v_i^t + c_1 * \left(p_i - x_i^t\right) + c_2 * \left(p_{gbest} - x_i^t\right) \tag{12}$$

$$x_i^{t+1} = x_i^t \oplus v_i^{t+1} \tag{13}$$

The operators $+, -, \oplus$ have new definitions, which contains the rules of crossover and union among particle, individual optimal solution and global optimal solution.

(I)   Subtraction operator (e.g. $p_i - x_i^t$): It represents the difference between the optimal position of the individual and the current particle position. The purpose of the difference is to calculate the conversion formula between current particle position (sequence) and individual historical optimal position (sequence). A TSP problem for 5 cities is taken as example:

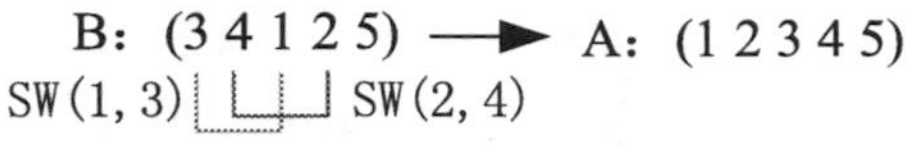

$$\text{B:} \ (3\ 4\ 1\ 2\ 5) \longrightarrow \text{A:} \ (1\ 2\ 3\ 4\ 5)$$
$$\text{SW}\,(1,\ 3) \underline{\sqcup\sqcup} \ \text{SW}\,(2,\ 4)$$

Fig. 6. Subtraction calculation

For position A (1 2 3 4 5) and position B (3 4 1 2 5), an exchange operation $SW(i,j)$ is defined to exchange the elements of the sequence i and j position. Here, $A(1) = B(3)$, $A(2) = B(4)$. Hence, difference set of position A, B is: $A - B = SW(1,\ 3) + SW(2,\ 4)$.

(II) Multiplication operator (e.g. $x_i^t \oplus v_i^{t+1}$): Here, v_i^{t+1} means the particle exchange order, $\oplus$ operator means executing exchange operation of order v_i^{t+1} for x_i^t.

(III) Additive operators (e.g. speed + speed): It means union of several exchange operation.

3.5 Realization Steps of CG-MOPSO

Based on above algorithm description, the detailed steps of the discrete clustering guiding multi-objective particle swarm optimization (CG-MOPSO) are given as follows:

Step 1: Initializing position and velocity for individual particles.

Step 2: The non-inferior solution is obtained and stored in the external file based on the Pareto dominance method, and the distance of non-inferior solution is calculated based on the target space.

Step 3: Guidance particle selection: If the number of non-inferior solutions was no more than 20, a non-inferior solution is selected randomly in the non-inferior solution set as the guidance particle. If the number of non-inferior solutions was more than 20, the clustering strategy is used to obtain guidance particle.

Step 4: Update the position and velocity of each particle, evaluate the fitness of particles, and update the individual history of the particle according to the fitness.

Step 5: Put the non-inferior solution of the external file and the particles based on current iteration into a temporary file. Find the non-inferior solution set in the temporary file based on the Pareto dominance method, and store it in the external file. Then, calculate the density of non-inferior solution. If the external file size exceeds the upper limit, preserve thirty non-inferior solutions using the external file preservation mechanism proposed in this article.

Step 6: Conduct mutation in the current iteration particle using mutation factors based on probability.

Step 7:   Increase the number of iterations t, if t is less than Tmax, skip to step 4. Otherwise, terminate the iteration, output the solutions in external file as the final solution.

4   Multi-objective Particle Swarm Optimization Path Planning

The overall optimization process is given as follows: (1) D-H parameters model establishment for robot; (2) Import the work-piece model; (3) Teaching the position and pose of welding joint; (4) Obtain transition points based on geometrical obstacle avoidance; (5) Calculate the straight path length between two points; (6) Conduct trajectory planning for straight path between two points; (7) Calculate the energy consumption between two points; (8) Realize multi-objective path planning for path length and energy consumption; (9) Output optimization result.

Where, the robot inverse kinematics and inverse dynamics are used to obtain energy consumption. After the energy consumption computation between any two weld joints, the total energy consumption is solved according to the order of weld joints. Then, above calculated path length and energy consumption are applied to realize multi-objective optimization. The number of segments between two weld joints in this article is proportional to the distance, and the length for a segment is set as 10 mm.

When target weights for path length and energy consumption are set as (1, 0), the optimal welding path is shown in Fig. 7(a), Starting point → 1 → 2 → 3 → 4 → 7 → 10 → 6 → 9 → 8 → 5 → 12 → 13 → 14 → 15 → 16 → 17 → 18 → 19 → 20 → 11 → terminal point. Where the path length and energy consumption are 1874.42 mm and 3352.17 J respectively. When the two target weights are (0.5, 05), the optimal welding path is shown in Fig. 7(b), Starting point →1 → 2 → 3 → 4 → 7 → 10 → 6 → 9 → 8 → 5 → 14 → 15 → 16 → 17 → 18 → 19 → 20 → 13 → 12 → 11 → Terminal point. Where the path length and energy consumption are 2106.51 mm and 1695.76 J respectively.

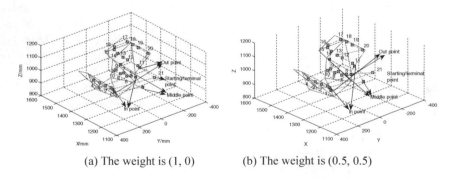

(a) The weight is (1, 0)   (b) The weight is (0.5, 0.5)

Fig. 7. Optimization results for different weights

5   Conclusion

Reasonable robot welding path is useful for welding efficiency improvement, and intelligent welding robot path optimization was studies in this article. Clustering guidance multi-objective particle swarm optimization (CG-MOPSO) algorithm was presented first. Then, the guidance particle selection strategies and external archives update mechanism were used to improve the optimization performance for CG-MOPSO. Simulation results show the advantage of CG-MOPSO algorithm to MOPSO and NSGA-II in both optimization results and stability. And it can be applied to the multi-objective path planning problem of spot welding robot. The improved optimization algorithm can provide an optimized welding sequence reference for spot welding operation, which will save the teaching time for engineers and improve production efficiency.

References

1. Wang, X.W., Shi, Y.P., Ding, D.Y., et al.: Double global optimum genetic algorithm–particle swarm optimization-based welding robot path planning. Eng. Optim. **48**(2), 299–316 (2016)
2. Kovács, A.: Integrated task sequencing and path planning for robotic remote laser welding. Int. J. Prod. Res. **54**(4), 1210–1224 (2016)
3. Li, Z., Tang, Q., Zhang, L.P.: Minimizing energy consumption and cycle time in two-sided robotic assembly line systems using restarted simulated annealing algorithm. J. Clean. Prod. **135**, 508–522 (2016)
4. Chen, C.Y., Liao, H.L., Montavon, G., et al.: Nozzle mounting method optimization based on robot kinematic analysis. J. Therm. Spray Technol. **25**(6), 1138–1148 (2016)
5. Kennedy, J., Eberhart, R.: Particle swarm optimization. IV. In: Proceedings of IEEE International Conference on Neural Networks, pp 1942–1948. IEEE Press, New Jersey (1995)
6. Akbari, M., Rashidi, H.: A multi-objectives scheduling algorithm based on cuckoo optimization for task allocation problem at compile time in heterogeneous systems. Expert Syst. Appl. **60**, 234–248 (2016)
7. Emmons, S., Kobourov, S., Gallant, M., et al.: Analysis of network clustering algorithms and cluster quality metrics at scale. PloS ONE **11**(7), e0159161 (2016)
8. Wang, X.W., Xue, L.K., Gu, X.S.: Multi-objective particle swarm optimization algorithm based on three status coordinating searching. Control Decis. **30**(11), 1945–1952 (2015)

Taxi Driving Anomalous Route Detection Using GPS Sampling Data

Zhiguo Ding$^{(\boxtimes)}$

College of Mathematics, Physics and Information Engineering,
Zhejiang Normal University, Jinhua 321004, Zhejiang, China
dingzhiguo@zjnu.cn

Abstract. This paper proposed a method of detecting taxi driving anomalous route using the GPS sampling data. After analyzing the characteristics of sampling data, such as discrete and uneven, and taking into account that the traditional anomaly detection methods are hard to be applied directly in this field as well as high computation complexity, the mapping trajectory is defined and the new anomaly detection method is proposed based on the grid concept, which doesn't require measure the distance or density during anomaly detection procedure and thus alleviates the computing resource requirements. To validate the proposed method, the real-life GPS sampling dataset is used and the experimental results confirm that our proposed method is effective.

Keywords: Anomaly detection · Taxi driving route · Mapping trajectory · Grid · GPS sampling

1 Introduction

With the fast development of urbanization, the harmonious urban public transport play an important role to reflect the degree of civilization, city taxi, as an important way of short distance travel, gives greatly convenience and enjoyment for the people. However, there are some taxi drivers who maliciously select a longer route than the normal route for earning much more money. To prevent the occurrence of such uncivilized event and improve the city civilization, some measures should be taken. Consequently, monitoring the taxi driving event and detecting timely the current driving route normal or not is critical.

Nowadays, GPS devices are installed on most of the modern city taxies, which makes the monitoring and detecting possible based on the IT development. These devices usually record some important information when the taxi is driving, such as the vehicle position, instantaneous speed, the time, average speed and so on. Collecting and analyzing these data can find some value information, for example, from start point to end point, a normal or popular route usually is known and is selected by most of the taxi driver. If the specified taxi driving route significantly deviated from the expected normal ones based on some historical dataset, it maybe mean some anomalous driving process and some further measure should be taken, such as monitoring closely, warning and so on [6, 12, 13].

© Springer Nature Singapore Pte Ltd. 2017
D. Yue et al. (Eds.): LSMS/ICSEE 2017, Part II, CCIS 762, pp. 304–312, 2017.
DOI: 10.1007/978-981-10-6373-2_31

To detect the current taxi driving route anomalous or not, a straightforward strategy is to employ some used widely anomaly detection methods in the data mining and machine learning community, such as distance-based methods [1, 10], density-based methods [2, 7], model-based method [8] and so on [4, 11, 14]. Although there are many anomaly detection methods available up to now, most of them do not take some concrete constraint into account, such as the discrete and non-uniform characteristics of GPS sampling data and are not designed specifically for taxi driving anomaly detection application. For example, the driving route in the modern urban is numerous and complicated, every position in the normal route would be a start point or a destination; besides, there are different traffic flow in different route; further, some density-based or distance-based method would be judge a shortcut as an anomalous driving because it is not met some predefined threshold.

The main contributions of this paper are as follows:

(1) Analyzing the characteristics of sampling data, such as discrete and uneven, the mapping trajectory is defined.
(2) To alleviate the computing resource requirements, a new anomaly detection method is proposed based on the grid concept, which doesn't require measure the distance or density during anomaly detection procedure.
(3) To validate the proposed method, the real-life GPS sampling dataset is used and the acceptable result has been obtained, which can be assisted to build the civilized urban taxi driving system.

The rest of this paper is organized as follows. The problem description about the anomaly detection of taxi driving route and proposed grid-based anomaly detection method are present in Sect. 2. Section 3 shows our dataset, experiment and result analysis. At last, a conclusion and future work are given in Sect. 4.

2　Anomaly Route Detection of Taxi Trajectory

2.1　The Problem Description

Detecting the taxi anomalous driving trajectory has important value of research and application for the construction of modern civilized metropolis [3, 9]. For example, when a person arrives in a strange city and wants to go somewhere by taxi, he/she would suffer from the deception by the bad taxi driver. Most of such uncivilized events are hard to find and solve effectively. Usually, such deception event is solved by the experienced staff based on the passenger's complaints. The common method is that the GPS monitoring data of the complained taxi is extracted and analyzed, whether it is anomalous or fraudulent is decided by the staff's experience, which is low efficiency. In fact, the passenger usually is hard to know whether he/she has suffered from the taxi deception because the concrete route is unknown. Consequently, most of such bad events were not be detected timely, which damages the image of the city significantly. As an important part of the modern civilized urban building, monitoring the taxi driving and finding the anomalous driving trajectory timely are critical to construct harmonious taxi marketing.

Usually, some historic taxi driving trajectory data should be trained to build a detection model for finding the anomaly route automatically, which can be collected by the mobile localization technology. The positioning and communication component are installed on the vehicle and the routing trajectory data can be recorded when the vehicle is driving. There are many available techniques, such as mobile wireless positioning, satellite positioning combined with the geographic information system(GIS), global position system (GPS) and so on.

In this paper, the routes between the start points (S) and the destination (D) can be depicted by Fig. 1. There are three normal routes between S and D, where the black line denotes the normal route, and the width of the line means the quantity of normal routes, the more the historical routes are, the wider the line is. There are other three routes depicted in Fig. 1, i.e., t_1 (the red line), t_2 (the green line) and t_3 (the blue line), obviously, the three line is slim and different to the three bold black line. Conclusion maybe obtained preliminary that all three routes are anomalous. That is to say, $t1$, $t2$ and $t3$ are all anomalous, but an obvious fact is that from the Fig. 1, $t1$ and $t3$ are anomalous surely and t2 is a shortcut. Hence, the problem of anomalous taxi driving route can be described as follows.

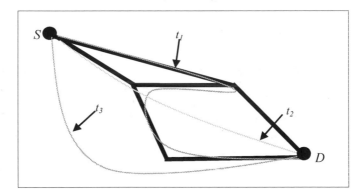

Fig. 1. An illustration of taxi driving trajectory between start point and destination (Color figure online)

Problem Description: Given a taxi driving route between the start points(S) and the destination (D), detection of this specified route is anomalous or normal based on the historic cumulated driving trajectory dataset of this route.

Usually, data sampled by the GPS device has two characteristics described as follows:

(1) Discrete, because the low sampling frequency of GPS devices, the time interval of most current used widely GPS devices is about 50 s or 1 min. Consequently, the GPS sampling points are discrete in most of time.
(2) Uneven, because the speed of the vehicle usually is not same in the whole driving process. When the traffic is smooth and the speed of the vehicle is high, the distance between any two adjacent sampling points would be big; On the contrary,

when the traffic jam is met or the vehicle speed is low, the sampling points is dense and the distance between any two adjacent sampling points would be small.

In the real taxi driving process, the dataset obtained by GPS devices is a time series data and each sampling points consists of many data item, such as timestamp of data sampled, the current vehicle position (denoted by geographical latitude and longitude), the vehicle instant velocity, the status of vehicle and so on. Usually, the dataset has the format described as Table 1.

Table 1. GPS dataset

	Attribute	Description
1	TimeStamp	The time of data sampled
2	Latitude	Geographical position
3	Longitude	Geographical position
4	Speed	Vehicle instantaneous velocity
5	Status	The status of taxi, i.e., loaded or unloaded

Consequently, the route of taxi driving can be depicted simply by some discrete GPS sample points in a specific time interval on a two dimensional plane. To clearly describe this problem, we name the real route of taxi driving as taxi driving route and the discrete GPS sampling points linked orderly as the taxi driving trajectory, which defined as follows.

Definition 1: Taxi Driving Trajectory (T)

T is a simulative route and is built by n discrete GPS sampling points linked orderly. Represented as $T : p_1 \rightarrow p_2 \rightarrow, \cdots, \rightarrow p_n, p_i \in R^2$ is a sampled geographical position and denotes a two-tuples consisted of latitude and longitude, which can be depicted by the yellow circle points in Fig. 2. $(p_1, p_2, \ldots, p_n)$ denotes the taxi driving trajectory from start point to destination. $(p_i, p_{i+1}, \ldots p_j)(1 \leq i \leq j \leq n)$ denotes the driving trajectory between the interval $[t_i, t_j]$. p_1 and p_n denotes the start point and destination point, respectively. The tax driving route (depicted by the blue line in Fig. 2) can be represented by the taxi driving trajectory (depicted by the red arrow line in Fig. 2).

In fact, detecting the taxi anomalous driving trajectory just is a similarity measure between the current driving route and the expected driving route. Apparently, only the distance between the target driving route and the expected driving route is calculated to accomplish this task, i.e., if the distance exceeds the predefined threshold, it is an anomalous driving route, otherwise it is normal. But there are some problems existed, such as the real route is continuous and the sampling is discrete, it is difficult to calculate the distance between of them, further, because the GPS sampling points are not regular, finding the exact matching points for the different sampling points is hard to accomplished.

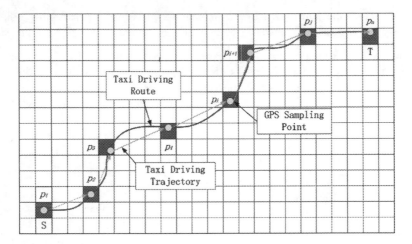

Fig. 2. Taxi driving trajectory from start point to destination (Color figure online)

2.2   The Grid-Based Anomaly Detection of Driving Trajectory

The driving trajectories are some discrete GPS sampling points linked orderly, while the real driving route is continuous. When two taxies are driving on the same road and from the same start point to the same destination, the GPS sampling points maybe different greatly and hard to match each other because of the different driving instantaneous speed, sampling time stamp and so on. Generally to speak, the GPS sampling rate are usually low then the driving trajectory is discrete, such as the yellow dots in Fig. 2, to obtain the continuous driving trajectory, some pre-processing are needed. Here, only one driving route, i.e., from the fixed start point to the fixed destination, is selected to description proposed method.

Firstly, the target region is divided evenly into same square g_i based on the latitude and longitude data (Fig. 2). Let $G = \{g_i | i = 1 \ldots n\}$, further, mapping function $f : R^2 \rightarrow G$, $p_i \in R^2$ is defined. Thus, if the GPS sampling points (yellow dots) are located in the same region, such as small grey square depicted in Fig. 2, they are regarded as same and do not need any distance computation, which only need simple position calculation and save the computation resource to some extent.

Secondly, because the GPS sampling rate usually is low, the driving trajectory is discrete, some artificial position are generated and inserted into the initial GPS sampling series. Here, to clearly present proposed method, the driving mapping trajectory is defined.

Definition 2: Driving Mapping Trajectory $\left(\widehat{T}\right)$

$$\widehat{T} : \hat{p}_1 \rightarrow \hat{p}_2 \rightarrow, \cdots, p_i \rightarrow \hat{p}_{i+1}, \cdots, \rightarrow \hat{p}_n$$

where $\hat{p}_i \in G$, $(\hat{p}_1, \hat{p}_2, \ldots, \hat{p}_n)$ is mapping trajectory of $(p_1, p_2, \ldots, p_n)$, which is inserted some artificial generated points based on the driving direction and is continuous. That is to say, the adjacent two square are linked each other and forms the continuous driving mapping trajectory.

(1) Building the grid based detector
     The size of grid, i.e., the side length of square, is a key parameter, which usually is specified by the domain experts based on some prior knowledge, such as the city road information, the average taxi driving speed and so on, or learned based on the data mining or machine learning method using the historical driving dataset. The detail content about the grid can be find in [5]. The steps of building the detector are described as follows:

> Step 1: Extracting the available taxi driving trajectory from the raw GPS sampling dataset.
> Step 2: Dividing the target area into the same square/grid and mapping the historical taxi driving trajectories onto it.
> Step 3: Forming some hot spot region based on the clustering method, which would be some start points or destination.
> Step 4: Building the mapped driving trajectory.
> Step 5: Counting the number of GPS mapping points along the driving mapping trajectory.

     Based on the building detector, the route, across the sparse square or the mapped GPS sampling points is less than a predefined threshold k, is detected as the anomalous route; on the contrary, it is a normal route. This strategy does not need the distance computation between the current driving route and the expected driving route, thus it is a light weight algorithm. Besides, with the time pass by, more and more taxi GPS sampling data of the normal driving trajectory are cumulated and the detector can become more accurate.

(2) Detection of Anomalous Driving Route
     When the target taxi is monitored, its current driving data is sampled based on the GPS device. Whether it shows some unusual characteristics, the aforementioned method is triggered. That is to say, if the square where the GPS sampling points located is sparse, then the current driving route regard as anomalous, otherwise as normal.

3   Experiment and Result Analysis

3.1   Dataset

In order to evaluate the effectiveness of proposed method, a real dataset of taxi driving trajectories derived from the GPS logs of smart car networking was employed. For the sake of describing our method simply and concisely, only the sub-dataset between a relative fixed start point and destination was extracted from the original raw dataset, besides, some data pre-processing was firstly done, such as discarding the unload driving route and the information of car speed. Finally, a dataset composed of 2672 route trajectories was used to validate proposed method. Further, the rectangle area was selected which covered the whole driving route from start point to destination and it was split into 50 * 70 grids with the same area. For the obtained dataset, the interpolation method was used to generate the relative regular driving trajectory to solve the few GPS sampling points for some driving routes.

Besides, because the obtained 2672 driving routes are all normal, the anomalous 80 driving routes were generated by modifying the existed 80 normal driving routes to validate proposed algorithm. The anomaly rate is about 3% (80/2672 * 100% $\approx$ 3%) and the final summary of dataset can be seen in Table 2.

Table 2. Dataset information of taxi driving route

Training dataset		Testing dataset	
Normal	Anomaly	Normal	Anomaly
1800	0	792	80

3.2 Experimental Results and Analysis

To evaluate our proposed algorithm, three performance metrics are selected. The first is the *ACC*, which can be calculated by formula (1).

$$ACC = (TP + TN)/(TP + FP + FN + TN) \tag{1}$$

where *TP*, *FP*, *TN* and *FN* denotes the number of true positive samples, the number of false positive samples, the number of true negative samples and the number of false negative samples, respectively. *ACC* is commonly used to evaluate the performance of classification problem in data mining and machine learning community, which denotes the classification accuracy. But some researchers regard that *ACC* would not appropriately evaluate the algorithm performance of unbalanced learning problem. Further, another two performance metrics, *TPR* and *FAR*, are employed, which are the acronyms of true positive rate and false alarm rate, respectively. The former represents the percentage of anomalies that are correctly detected, i.e., the ratio between the number of correctly detected anomalies and the total number of anomalies. Usually, the higher this value is, the better the algorithm performance can be obtained; the latter is renamed as false positive rate (*FPR*), which represents the percentage of normal data that are incorrectly considered as anomalies, i.e., the ratio between the number of normal data which was detected as anomalies and the total number of normal data. Usually, the lower this value is, the better the algorithm performance can be obtained. *TPR* and *FAR* can be calculated by formula (2)

$$TPR = TP/(TP + FN)$$
$$FAR = FP/(FP + TN) \tag{2}$$

1800 normal driving route trajectories, about 69.4% of the whole dataset, were used to build the grid based detector. The remainder 792 data item, including of 80 artificial generated anomalous driving routes, were used as the test dataset. Our experiment was conducted 10 times independently and the average result is represented in Table 3.

Table 3. Algorithm performance of grid-based anomaly detection method of taxi driving route

TP	FP	FN	TN	TPR	FAR	ACC
58.8	1.6	21.2	790.4	0.7350	0.0020	0.9739

From the experimental results presented in Table 3, an obvious fact is that a relative high detection performance, i.e., *ACC* is 97.36%, has obtained, but the relative low *TPR* and relative high *FAR* demonstrates that proposed method is not effective very much. After analyzing the experimental results and finding that the main reason is that there were some circle detour driving routes which were not detected successfully, which results in the poor detection performance. How to detect the circle detour driving routes successfully is our next work to do.

4   Conclusion and Future Work

In this paper, a grid-based anomaly detection method for taxi driving route is proposed based on the grid concept, which does not calculate the distance or density between the target driving route and expected driving route. The experimental results conducted on the real taxi GPS dataset shows that proposed method has relative good detection performance.

Based on the proposed method in this paper, some anomalous driving route can be detected timely when it driving route deviates the expected driving route. But the taxi driving trajectory is a dynamic and changed time series in the real situation, the proposed method does not take the circle detour into account and it does not deal with this complex situation. In the next work, we will further optimize our proposed method for taking the circle detour into account and apply it to a real software platform for building the smart car networking monitoring system.

Acknowledgments. This work is supported by the Open Project of Top Key Discipline of Computer Software and Theory in Zhejiang Provincial (ZC323014100, ZC323016038), the Doctoral Research Start-up Fund of Zhejiang Normal University(ZC304016020), Project of Science and Technology Department of Zhejiang Province (2015C33085), besides, we also thank the anonymous reviewers for their constructive suggestions to improve the quality of the paper.

References

1. Angiulli, F., Fassetti, F.: Dolphin: an efficient algorithm for mining distance-based outliers in very large datasets. ACM Trans. Knowl. Discov. Data (TKDD) **3**, 1–57 (2009)
2. Breunig, M.M., Kriegel, H.-P., Ng, R.T., Sander, J.: LOF: identifying density-based local outliers. In: ACM SIGMOD Record, pp. 93–104. ACM (2000)
3. Chen, C., Zhang, D., Samuel Castro, P., Li, N., Sun, L., Li, S.: Real-time detection of anomalous taxi trajectories from GPS traces. In: Puiatti, A., Gu, T. (eds.) MobiQuitous 2011. LNICSSITE, vol. 104, pp. 63–74. Springer, Heidelberg (2012). doi:10.1007/978-3-642-30973-1_6

4. Daneshpazhouh, A., Sami, A.: Entropy-based outlier detection using semi-supervised approach with few positive examples. Pattern Recogn. Lett. **49**, 77–84 (2014)
5. Ding, Z., Fei, M., Du, D., Yang, F.: Streaming data anomaly detection method based on hyper-grid structure and online ensemble learning. Soft Comput. 1–13 (2016)
6. Ge, Y., Xiong, H., Liu, C., Zhou, Z.-H.: A taxi driving fraud detection system. In: 2011 IEEE 11th International Conference on Data Mining (ICDM), pp. 181–190. IEEE, Vancouver (2011)
7. Huang, H., Yoo, S., Qin, H., Yu, D.T.: Physics-based anomaly detection defined on manifold space. ACM Trans. Knowl. Discov. Data **9**, 1–39 (2014)
8. Liu, F.T., Ting, K.M., Zhou, Z.H.: Isolation-based anomaly detection. ACM Trans. Knowl. Discov. Data **6**, 1–39 (2012)
9. Liu, S.Y., Ni, L.M., Krishnan, R.: Fraud detection from taxis' driving behaviors. IEEE Trans. Veh. Technol. **63**, 464–472 (2014)
10. Moshtaghi, M., Havens, T.C., Bezdek, J.C., Park, L., Leckie, C., Rajasegarar, S., Keller, J. M., Palaniswami, M.: Clustering ellipses for anomaly detection. Pattern Recogn. **44**, 55–69 (2011)
11. Noto, K., Brodley, C., Slonim, D.: FRaC: a feature-modeling approach for semi-supervised and unsupervised anomaly detection. Data Min. Knowl. Discov. **25**, 109–133 (2012)
12. Zhang, D., Li, N., Zhou, Z.-H., Chen, C., Sun, L., Li, S.: iBAT: detecting anomalous taxi trajectories from GPS traces. In: Proceedings of 13th International Conference on Ubiquitous Computing, pp. 99–108. ACM (2011)
13. Zhang, L., Hu, Z.M., Yang, G.: Trajectory outlier detection based on multi-factors. IEICE Trans. Inf. Syst. **E97D**, 2170–2173 (2014)
14. Zhang, Y., Meratnia, N., Havinga, P.: Outlier detection techniques for wireless sensor networks: a survey. IEEE Commun. Surv. Tutor. **12**, 159–170 (2010)

Study on Flame Combustion Stability Based on Particle Swarm Optimization Feature-Weighted SVM

Rongbao Chen[✉], Honghui Jiang, and Yang Liu

Hefei University of Technology, Hefei 230009, China
crhwish@126.com, hhui92@aliyun.com, 294960097@qq.com

Abstract. In order to achieve the automatic monitoring of the combustion stability of the boiler, and to quantitatively determine the stability of the combustion, the combustion stability evaluation model of the particle swarm optimization feature weighted support vector machine is proposed. The eigenvalues of the combustion state in the flame image is extracted, and the feature weight of each eigenvalue is obtained. Then, the kernel function of the support vector machine is modified by feature weighting vector. Particle swarm is used to optimize penalty factors and kernel parameters, and the same set of samples are used to test the classification ability of support vector machine and feature weighted support vector machine. The results show that the support vector machine model with feature weighting has higher recognition rate and can judge the combustion state accurately and effectively, which can meet the real-time requirement of stability judgment.

Keywords: Feature weighting · Support vector machine · Particle swarm optimization · Combustion stability judgment · Flame image processing

1 Introduction

At present, the thermal power is still china's most important form of electric production, and thermal power consumes a lot of coal. The consumption of the boiler burned coal accounts for more than half of the total produced coal. So improving the efficiency of coal combustion in the boiler to reduce pollution caused by coal combustion is an important part of achieving sustainable energy development. The basic requirement for the combustion of a power plant boiler is to establish and maintain a stable, uniform combustion flame. Burning instability will reduce boiler thermal efficiency, generate noise, increase pollutant emissions, and in extreme cases may cause furnace fire, and even lead to furnace explosion. Therefore, in order to make the boiler run safely and economically, it is necessary to real-time effectively detect the combustion condition inside the furnace cavity [1].

The key problem of flame detection with digital image is feature extraction and state recognition based on flame image segmentation. At present, the flame image's feature extraction and state recognition methods are divided into four categories: ① Neural Network Classification. In order to solve the problem of judging the stability of

© Springer Nature Singapore Pte Ltd. 2017
D. Yue et al. (Eds.): LSMS/ICSEE 2017, Part II, CCIS 762, pp. 313–323, 2017.
DOI: 10.1007/978-981-10-6373-2_32

the boiler combustion, a rough - fuzzy neural network method is proposed in reference [2]. The combustion stability decision database is established by extracting the flame burning parameters, and use the roughness theory to extract the rules, and then sent it into the neural network to identify the combustion state. And the combustion state is judged as four states: very stable, generally stable, slightly unstable and very unstable. ② The Rough Set Theory Classification Method. In the reference [3], a method of detecting the combustion state based on rough set is proposed. Through the region detection and feature extraction of the flame image, the combustion state of the flame is recognized by the knowledge of the rough set. ③ Support Vector Machine(SVM) classification. In the reference [4], seven feature quantities such as flame brightness, flame high temperature brightness, flame area, flame high temperature area, flame high temperature area ratio, center of mass shift distance and circularity were extracted. And then, use support vector machine algorithm for classification. ④ Other methods.

Compared with the neural network which is easy to fall into local minimum characteristics and can't get the global optimum, support vector machine's final decision function is only determined by a few support vectors, so the method can grasp the key samples when "removing" the redundant samples, and the complexity of the calculation depends on the number of support vectors, rather than the dimension of the sample space, therefore the algorithm is not only simple but also has good robustness. On the one hand, the SVM classification overcomes the inherent problems of neural network method which are the over learning and the less learning problems, on the other hand, it has a strong ability of nonlinear classification.

2 Pretreatment of Flame Image and Selection of Combustion Parameters

Pretreatment of Flame Image
The analysis of flame combustion characteristics is essential to determine the flame detection algorithm. Figure 1a is the image of flame in the chamber, which may be affected by various noise sources [5]. In order to obtain more accurate and realistic flame characteristics, and to obtain the flame combustion parameters more clearly, the flame image need to be pretreated. The method described in literature [6] is applied in this paper for pretreatment, including grayscale and median filtering. The process is shown in Fig. 1b and c.

Grayscale is the process of converting a color image into a grayscale image. According to the corresponding transformation relation between RGB color space and

a. Original flame image

b. Gray flame image

c. image edge processing

Fig. 1. Flame image and its treatment

YUV color space, The luminance value Y of each pixel is calculated by the formula: Y = 0.3R + 0.59G + 0.11B, and the luminance value information is used as the gradation value of the gradation image. The random noise in the flame image can be filtered out by median filter, and because of its non-linear characteristic, it does not affect the step signal so will not cause image blur. The numerical expression of the median filter is shown in formula (1).

$$g(x, y) = med\{f(x - i, y - j)\}, i, j \in S \tag{1}$$

where g(x, y), f(x, y) is the pixel gray level of the image data matrix, and S is the sliding window.

Selection of Combustion Sample Parameters

Some combustion parameters are mentioned in the reference [3, 4, 6, 7], which including the average gray level of the flame, the average gray level of the effective area, the area of the high temperature area, roundness, the deviation of the flame center and the abundance of the flame et al. The sample used in this study is from the tangentially round coal-fired boiler, so that the roundness is not ideal. When too much combustion parameters are chosen, the complexity of the model will be increased. So five combustion parameters are selected in this paper, including the average gray level of the flame, the average gray scale of the effective area, the abundance of the flame, the area ratio of the high temperature area and the deviation of the flame center. All of the five parameters are extracted from the pretreatment of flame image

Because the pulsation frequency of pulverized coal is 10–30 Hz and the flame center frequency is 5–10 Hz [7], the flame parameters of the flame image are averaged for each 5 frames of the flame video in order to eliminate the influence of flame pulsation on the determination of combustion stability, so that each sample data contains at least one flame pulse. The normalization of the sample data, which can reduce the impact of the difference in the sample data on the test results, allows the model to be better trained and identified. The normalized formula is represented by (2):

$$u_i = \frac{x_i - x_{min}}{x_{max} - x_{min}} \tag{2}$$

where x_i is the original value of the sample, u_i is the normalized value, and x_{max}, x_{min} are respectively the maximum and minimum values of the sample data, then the combustion parameter database can be get.

3 Particle Swarm Optimization Algorithm and Feature Weighted Support Vector Machine

Relief-F Feature Weighting

Relief-F algorithm is improved on the basis of Relief algorithm. It can deal with multi-class classification problem. The Relief-F method can effectively implement feature weighting, which is described as follows:

There are several different classes of samples for each class called X_n.

① From all samples, a sample R was randomly taken out.
② In the sample group of which classification is the same as the sample R, k nearest neighbor samples are taken out.
③ In all other sample groups of which classification are different from the sample R, k nearest neighbor samples are also taken out separately.
④ Calculate the weight of each feature.

For each feature weight:

$$w(A) = w(A) - \sum_{i=1}^{k} \frac{diff(A, R, H_i)}{mk} + \sum_{c \notin class(R)} \frac{\frac{p(C)}{1-p(class(R))} \sum_{i=1}^{k} diff(A, R, M_i(C))}{mk} \tag{3}$$

In the above formula $diff(A, R_1, R_2)$ represents the difference between the sample R_1 and the sample R_2 on the eigenvalue A.

$$diff(A, R_1, R_2) = \begin{cases} 0 & R_1[A] = R_2[A] \\ 1 & R_1[A] \neq R_2[A] \end{cases} \tag{4}$$

where p(C) represents the distribution probability of the class, class(R) represents the category to which R belongs. H_i represents the i-th nearest neighbor of R in class(R), $M_i(C)$ represents the i-th nearest neighbor in class C. $R_1[A]$ and $R_2[A]$ refer to the values of the A-th feature of the samples R_1 and R_2, respectively, $diff(A, R_1, R_2)$ represents the difference between the samples R_1 and R_2, on the F-th feature [8].

Particle Swarm Optimization Algorithm
The essence of Particle Swarm Optimization (PSO) [9, 10] is simulating the principle that birds can maintain a complete flight formation in the process of flight, PSO is an optimization algorithm based on group intelligence theory, corresponding to the problem of finding optimal solution, and the parameters to be optimized are taken as a particle of the entire space. Initialize a group of random particles, and each particle represents a candidate solution of the solution space, and the superiority of solution is determined by the fitness function. Suppose that in a certain space, a total of n particles fly at a certain speed, the position vector of the i-th particle in the N-dimensional space is expressed as $X_i = (x_{i1}, x_{i2}, \cdots, x_{iN})$ and the flight speed is expressed as $v_i = (v_{i1}, v_{i2}, \ldots, v_{iN})$, each particle memory and following the current optimal particle, search in the solution space. Particles track the best individual extremes $pbest = (p_{i1}, p_{i2}, \cdots, p_{iN})$ which found by the particle itself and record all the best global extreme points $gbest = (p_{g1}, p_{g2}, \cdots, p_{gN})$ experienced by all particles in the whole group. Where i = 1, 2, ···, n, represents its position. In each algorithm iteration, the particles update their position and speed according to formulas (5) and (6).

$$v_{iN}(t+1) = wv_{iN}(t) + c_1 r_1 (p_{iN} - x_{iN}(t)) + c_2 r_2 (p_{gN} - x_{iN}(t)) \tag{5}$$

$$x_{iN}(t+1) = x_{iN}(t) + v_{iN}(t+1) \tag{6}$$

where 't' is the evolutionary algebra; 'w' is the inertia weight, which maintains the balance of global and local search capabilities; c_1 and c_2 are the learning factors, also known as the acceleration constants, which respectively regulate the maximum step size in the direction of global best particle and individual best particle. According to experience, usually $c_1 = c_2 = 2$; r_1 and r_2 are the uniform random number within [0, 1], $v_{iN} \in [-v_{max}, v_{max}]$, v_{max} is constant, which is set by the user to limit the speed of particles.

Support Vector Machine and Feature Weighted Support Vector Machine

The support vector machine (SVM) is based on the principle of VC dimension theory and structural risk minimization principle, and search for the best compromise between model complexity and learning ability based on the limited sample information, largely overcome dimension disaster and local minimum problems of traditional machine learning, so as to obtain good generalization ability [10, 11, 13, 14].

For a set of training sample sets with category markers (x_i, y_i), $x_i \in R^n$, $y_i \in (+1, -1)$, $i = 1, 2, \cdots, l$. if the hyperplane $w^\circ x + b = 0$ can correctly classify the samples into two categories, the optimal hyperplane should maximize the sum of the minimum distance between the two classes of samples and hyperplane. For linear indivisible cases, a non-linear mapping $\emptyset : R^n \to H$ is used to map the data to a high-dimensional feature space H, which is for achieving linearly classification. After defining the function $k(x_i, x_j) = \emptyset(x_i) \cdot \emptyset(x_j)$, by using the Lagrange multiplier, the problem of the optimal hyperplane can be transformed into a dual problem.

$$\left. \begin{array}{c} \max \sum_{i=1}^{l} a_i - \frac{1}{2} \sum_{i,j=1}^{l} a_i a_j y_i y_j k(x_i, x_j) \\ s.t. \sum_{i=1}^{l} a_i y_i = 0 \\ 0 \leq a_i \leq C, \quad i = 1, 2, \ldots, l \end{array} \right\} \tag{7}$$

where a_i is the Lagrange multiplier of the sample point x_i, and there exists a unique solution. It can be proved that only a part of solution a_i is not zero, and the corresponding sample is the support vector. The decision function is thus obtained.

$$f(x) = sign \left(\sum_{i=1}^{l} a_i y_i k(x_i \cdot x) + b \right) \tag{8}$$

where $k(x_i, x_j) = \emptyset(x_i) \cdot \emptyset(x_j)$ is called a kernel function. The kernel function should be chosen as an inner product of the feature space. Here choose to use a wide range of good performance of the Gauss kernel function.

$$k(x_i, x_j) = \exp(-\gamma \parallel x_i - x_j \parallel^2) \tag{9}$$

According to a certain criterion, assigning a certain weight to each feature in a data set which is called a feature weighting. The study on the application of feature weighting to improve the performance of machine learning algorithms can be found in the reference [12, 13], which is the extension of the standard Euclidean distance with the feature weight vector. Reference [13] proposed a method of support vector machine based on feature weighting, which is called Feature Weighted Support Vector Machine (FWSVM). The definition of feature weighted kernel function is as follows:

Let 'k' be a kernel function defined on $X \times X, X \in R^n$, P is n-order linear transformation matrix for a given input space, where 'n' is the dimension of the input space. The feature weighting kernel function is defined as formula (10):

$$k_p(x_i, x_j) = k\left(x_i^T p, x_j^T p\right) \tag{10}$$

The matrix P is called the feature weighting matrix. Here select P for n-order diagonal matrix, the literature [14] gives detailed proof process.

By the formula (10), the feature weighted Gaussian radial basis kernel function can be obtained:

$$k_p(x_i, x_j) = \exp\left(-\gamma \parallel x_i^T p - x_j^T p \parallel^2\right) = \exp\left(-\gamma\left(\left(x_i - x_j^T\right)pp^T\left(x_i - x_j\right)\right)\right) \tag{11}$$

The FWSVM first evaluates the importance of the various features corresponding to the classification task, and sets the corresponding weights for each feature according to the importance. The weights obtained are then applied to the calculation of the kernel function, thereby avoiding the problem that the calculation of the kernel function is dominated by some weakly related or irrelevant features. The examples in the reference [13] prove that FWSVM has better generalization ability and robustness than the traditional SVM. The construction steps of the FWSVM based on Relief-F are as follows:

(I)　Collect data set S, the sample in S is described by feature set $\langle (f_s, d) \rangle$, in which d is class label (classification feature), $f_s = (f_1, f_2, \ldots, f_n)$ is a non-class label feature set;

(II)　Calculate the weight of each eigenvalues according to the Relief-F algorithm, and structure feature weight vector 'w' and linear transformation matrix 'P' (diagonal matrix);

$$w = \sqrt{G} = \left(\sqrt{Gain(f_1)}, \cdots, \sqrt{Gain(f_n)}\right), P = diag(w), (P)_{kk'} = w_k \delta_{kk'} \tag{12}$$

(III)　Replace the kernel function in the libsvm toolbox with the feature weighting kernel function, and the appropriate model and training algorithm are used to construct the classification decision function (classifier) for the data set S.

4 Simulation of Combustion Stability Model Based on Particle Swarm Optimization FWSVM

Select 200 training samples in the processed sample library, and choose a set of samples with a sample number of 150 as the test samples, the training samples and test samples contain combustion label value (1,2,3,4) in this characteristic state, and each contains four states of flame combustion.

Firstly, the feature weights of the eigenvalues of the training samples under the Relief F algorithm are obtained, and the feature weights $w_1 = [0.34135, 0.20871, 0.432031, 0.00841, 0.009497]$ are obtained by the experimental calculation. 1, 2, 3, 4, 5, respectively, the average gray level of the flame, the average gray scale of the effective area, the abundance of the flame, the area ratio of the high temperature area, the deviation of the flame center. The characteristic weight distribution of the selected sample set is shown in Fig. 2. It can be seen that the weights occupied by features 1, 2 and 3 play a dominant role in the classification of new samples, and features 4 and 5 account for less impact on the classification of new samples.

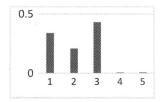

Fig. 2. Sample feature weight coefficient

The penalty coefficient 'c' is the tolerance of the error, the higher the 'c' can't tolerate the error, the more easily over fitting. The smaller 'c' the easier it is to underfitting, too large or too small will reduce its generalization ability. The parameter of the RBF function implicitly determine the distribution of the data after mapping to the new feature space. The larger the γ, the smaller the support vector, the smaller the γ, the more the support vector, the number of support vectors affects the speed of training and prediction. In this paper, the particle swarm optimization algorithm is used to obtain the optimal solution of 'c' and γ. The penalty parameter 'c' and the kernel parameter γ are optimized as follows:

Step 1: Read the existing sample data, randomly initialize a set of penalty parameters c and the kernel parameter γ as the initial position of the particle.

Step 2: The whole sample data is divided into a uniform set of m subsets that are not mutually exclusive.

Step 3: According to the current penalty parameter c and the kernel parameter γ training model, the cross validation error can be calculated: Assuming i = 1, the subset is used as the test set, and the rest of the subsets are used as training sets for the training model; Calculate the generalization error of the subset according to;

Then i = i + 1, repeat Step2 until i = k + 1; Finally, the K generalization error is taken as the cross validation error.

Step 4: The cross validation error in Step 3 is taken as the fitness value, and the best adaptive position of the individual and the best adaptive position of the group are recorded. When these two optimal values are found, the particle swarm is updated according to the formulas (5) and (6) to find the better penalty parameter c and the kernel parameter γ.

Step 5: If the maximum number of iterations is reached, go to Step 6, otherwise go to Step 2.

Step 6: Stop the operation.

The initialization termination algebra is 200 and the population number is 20. The fitness curve of the parameter selection is shown in Fig. 3: The optimization result of the parameter is: c = 3.952, γ = 1.528. If the sample data is changed, the SVM model parameters need to be re-optimized, and different training samples will be different optimization results.

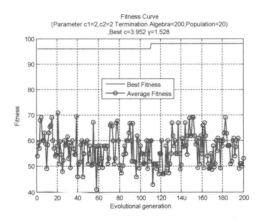

Fig. 3. PSO algorithm adaptability curve

In order to conveniently test of the performance of the model, "1–4" is respectively used to represent four combustion states [8], such as: "1: very stable", "2: generally stable", "3: slightly unstable", "4: Unstable". Due to the impact of flame pulsation and flame image noise, there will be an imprecise situation, so when the output state of the model is adjacent to the sample state, there is little effect on the determination of the combustion stability. For example, "1" and "2" are both represent steady state, only the degree is different. However, when the stability is differ by two degrees, such as "1" and "3", the difference between these two combustion state will be larger. Therefore, if the recognition result does not appear the case of two degrees difference, it will be considered acceptable.

SVM was originally used for two classification problems. but it need to deal with multi-classes problem in practical applications, so it is necessary to break the multi-classes problem into multiple two-classes problems, and train each of the two-classes classifiers to solve the classification problems. For multi-classification problems, SVM has three classification methods: one to one, one to many and decision-oriented acyclic graphs. In this paper, one to one method is used, each classifier can only separate a class from another class, regardless of other classes. Because the flame combustion state is divided into 4 categories, there are 6 classifiers for SVM to solve classification problems. In classification, the test samples are input into the SVM model and the FWSVM model respectively. Finally, the voting strategy is used to vote on the results. When all the decision-making functions have judged, the class with the highest number of votes is considered to be the class to which the result belongs.

Firstly, the training samples are used to train the SVM model and the FWSVM model respectively, and then the test samples are input into the trained two models respectively. The results are shown in Figs. 4, 5, 6 and 7. The blue circle represents the combustion state of the output of the model. The red plus sign indicates the real combustion state of the given flame combustion parameter. If the blue circle coincides with the red plus, it means that the output of the model is correct, otherwise the output of the model is error.

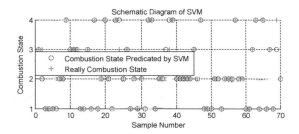

Fig. 4. The SVM recognition results of the first 70 data of the test samples

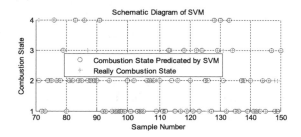

Fig. 5. The SVM recognition results of the last 80 data of the test samples

As can be seen from the results, the output value of 14 samples in the SVM model is not matched successfully, where the 71th sample's output value is 4, but the real value of the original sample is 2, and there is a difference of two degrees between them, the rest of the differences are all one degree. In practical applications, the model should try to avoid the situation of two degrees difference, so as to get a more accurate classification. In the model of FWSVM, only 7 samples did not match successfully, and

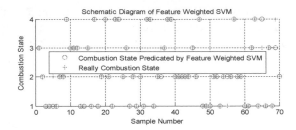

Fig. 6. The FWSVM recognition results of the first 70 data of the test samples

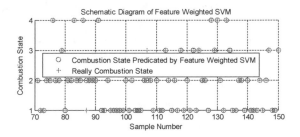

Fig. 7. The FWSVM recognition results of the last 80 data of the test samples

did not appear a difference of two degrees. Particle Swarm Optimization Support Vector Machine (PSO-SVM) model and Particle Swarm Optimization Feature Weighted Support Vector Machine (PSO-FWSVM) model for the correct judgment rate of the flame state stability were 90.67% and 95.33% respectively. The FWSVM model has only one degree difference for the unknown flame state, and when the judgment of the single picture in the video sequence appear error, it does not affect the judgment of the flame stability state at that time. Only when the judgment of the successive multiple pictures appear error, it can result in a failure in judging stability. In practical applications, it is not concerned about whether the single frame image is unstable, but whether there is a continuous picture value of 3 and 4, especially in the state of 4, and ultimately determine the combustion state. Therefore, the FWSVM model based on PSO is feasible for judging the stability of flame combustion.

5   Conclusion

In this paper, a judgment model of flame-combustion stability based on PSO-FWSVM is proposed. The model has a great advantage in solving small sample, nonlinear and high-dimensional problems in pattern recognition. The global optimal solution can be obtained. According that the importance of different eigenvalues is different for final judgment, the weight of different eigenvalues will be obtained, so as to avoid the situation that the calculation of the kernel function is dominated by some weak or irrelevant features. PSO algorithm is used to solve the influence of key parameters on the performance of the algorithm, so it improves the accuracy of the algorithm. At the same time, it is compared with the PSO-SVM model, and the experimental results show that, the influence of the weak correlation feature on the classification result is reduced by feature weighting, by which the robustness and recognition rate of the learning algorithm is effectively improved. Therefore, the particle swarm optimization feature-weighted support vector machine model can accurately and effectively determine the combustion state, and it is an effective method to judge the combustion stability.

References

1. Kamarthi, S.V., Pittner, S.: Accelerating neural network training using weight extrapolations. Neural Netw.rks **12**(9), 1285–1299 (1999)
2. Rongbao, C., Fanghui, M., Benxian, X., et al.: Research on combustion stability based on interval number and multiple attribute decision making. Chin. J. Sci. Instrum. **36**(3), 552–559 (2015)
3. Rongbao, C., Wuyong, M., Benxian, X., et al.: Research on the rough set attribute reduction algorithm based on significance of attributes. In: International Conference on Control, pp. 1–9 (2016)
4. Weidong, B., Jianhua, Y., Zengyi, M., et al.: Method of flame identification based on support vector machine. Power Eng. **4**, 548–551 (2004)
5. Junfei, Q., Honggui, H.: Optimal structure design for RBFNN structure. Acta Automatica Sinica **36**(6), 865–872 (2010)
6. Rongbao, C., Wuting, F., et al.: Research on stability criterion of furnace flame combustion based on image processing. In: International Conference on Control Engineering and Communication Technology (ICCECT 2012), vol. 2012, pp. 568–572 (2012)
7. Rongbao, C., Jingci, B.: Research on closed-loop control system based on image-signal processing of furnace flame. In: International Conference on Energy, Environment and Sustainable Development (ICEESD 2013), vol. 2013, pp. 1095–1100 (2013)
8. Feihu, Y.: Research on Feature selection approach and its application in network traffic identification. In: Nanjing University of Posts and Telecommunications (2012)
9. Fengning, Z., Minglong, F.: Chaos particle swarm optimization algorithm for optimizing the parameter of SVM. Comput. Simul. **27**(11), 183–186 (2010)
10. Yiquan, W., Song, Y., Huaichun, Z.: State identification of boiler combustion flame images based on gray entropy multiple thresholding and support vector machine. Proc. CSEE **33**(20), 66–73 (2013)
11. Yan, Z., Hao, C., Guochun, H.: An optimization algorithm of K-NN classifier. In: Proceedings of 5th International Conference on Machine Learning and Cybernetics, Dalian, China, pp. 2246–2251 (2006)
12. Xizhao, W., Yadong, W., Lijuan, W.: Improving fuzzy c-means clustering based on feature weight learning. Pattern Recogn. Lett. **25**(10), 1123–1132 (2004)
13. Tinghua, W., Shengfeng, T., Houkuan, H.: Feature weighted support vector machine. J. Electron. Technol. **31**(3), 514–518 (2009)
14. Yanhao, L.: Research on measurement of temperature field of furnace flame based on SVM. Hefei University of Technology (2012)

Study on Lamb Wave Dispersion Curves
for the Testing of Metal Plates

Jinggang Xu[1,2(✉)] and Jingshan Deng[1,3]

[1] Shanghai University, Shanghai 200444, China
xjgczie@163.com
[2] Changzhou Vocational Institute of Engineering, Changzhou 213164, China
[3] State Nuclear Power Plant Service Company, Shanghai 200233, China

Abstract. For using Lamb wave to test metal plates extensively, Lamb wave dispersion curves [1–5] for the testing of metal plates are studied. A suit of software for drawing Lamb wave dispersion curves specially has been designed though the arithmetic analyzing of symmetrical and asymmetrical modes of Lamb wave frequency characteristic equation, and achieves it by the software of VC++. And the problem of drawing and application for Lamb wave dispersion curves has been resolved. It is fit for metal plates of different materials and types.

Keywords: Metal plates · Lamb wave · Non-destructive testing · Dispersion curves

1 Introduction

It's essential to know Lamb wave principle and characteristic, and confirm detection scheme according to Lamb wave dispersion characteristic [6] for applying effectively in non-destructive field. The problem of drawing Lamb wave dispersion curves [1] must be resolved before popularization and application. It's difficult to meet the demand of practical detection objects although some Lamb wave dispersion curves of special parameters can be searched in document literatures. Therefore the study on Lamb wave dispersion curves has very important significance, and it's the effective way of resolving the application of Lamb wave.

Lamb wave dispersion curves include phase velocity curve (C_p—f d), group velocity curve (C_g—f d), stimulant angle curve (α—f d), and displacement amplitude distribution curve (U, V—x). Phase velocity curve is solved from Lamb wave frequency characteristic equation. Other three curves are solved from the different equations which constitute by the relationship of group velocity, stimulant angle and particles displacement amplitude with phase velocity [7]. Group velocity curve shows energy propagation speed of Lamb wave in different modes and homologous frequency and plate thickness. Stimulant angle curve shows incident angles in different modes and homologous frequency and plate thickness. Particles displacement amplitude curve shows particle vibration displacement in the direction of parallel and perpendicular to the plate surface. It has some Corresponding relations between particle displacement amplitude curve and the energy distribution of Lamb wave in plate. Longitudinal wave

© Springer Nature Singapore Pte Ltd. 2017
D. Yue et al. (Eds.): LSMS/ICSEE 2017, Part II, CCIS 762, pp. 324–332, 2017.
DOI: 10.1007/978-981-10-6373-2_33

velocity, shear wave velocity, plate thickness and detection frequency are four separated variables of Lamb wave frequency characteristic equation. Plate thickness and detection frequency are determined by actual detection conditions, so longitudinal and shear wave velocity are the key factors of solving Lamb wave frequency characteristic equation and drawing Lamb wave dispersion curves.

In this paper, Lamb wave dispersion curves for the testing of metal plates are studied. A suit of software for drawing Lamb wave dispersion curves specially has been designed though the arithmetic analyzing of symmetrical and asymmetrical modes of Lamb wave frequency characteristic equation [8, 9], and achieves it. And the problem of drawing and application for Lamb wave dispersion curves has been resolved. It is fit for metal plates of different materials and types. So the application of Lamb wave is further promoted effectively in engineering. So the application of Lamb wave is further promoted effectively in engineering.

2 Numerical Solution of Lamb Wave Frequency Characteristic Equation

Lamb wave divides into symmetric mode and asymmetric mode according to vibration characteristics of particles. Every mode has different order. It usually shows by $S_0, S_1, S_2 \ldots$; $A_0, A_1, A_2 \ldots$. On the condition of free boundary, Lamb wave frequency characteristic equations are shown as follows.

Symmetric mode:

$$4pq\tan\frac{\pi fd}{C_p}q + \left(p^2 - 1\right)^2\tan\frac{\pi fd}{C_p}p = 0 \tag{1}$$

Asymmetric mode:

$$\left(p^2 - 1\right)^2\tan\frac{\pi fd}{C_p}q + 4pq\tan\frac{\pi fd}{C_p}p = 0 \tag{2}$$

The meanings of parameters's in formulas are as shown below.

$$p = \left[\left(\frac{C_p}{C_s}\right)^2 - 1\right]^{\frac{1}{2}}, \quad q = \left[\left(\frac{C_p}{C_l}\right)^2 - 1\right]^{\frac{1}{2}},$$

C_p: Phase Velocity,
C_s: Shear Wave Velocity,
C_l: Longitudinal Wave Velocity,
f: Frequency,
d: Plate Thickness.

The phase velocity $\left(C_p\right)$ is not a constant. It changes along with the change of frequency and thickness. The frequency dispersion curve gives expression to the characteristic.

2.1   Analysis and Solution of Symmetric Mode Equation

2.1.1   Equation Analysis

x is defined as f·d. From formula (1), it is very complex to solve C_p if x is independent variable. But it will be relatively simple to solve x with C_p as independent variable. So C_p is chosen as independent variable. In view of engineering application, C_p and x are real numbers which are greater than zero.

Formula (1) could be modified as formula (3) when C_p is a given value except special values.

$$A\tan(Bx) + C\tan(Dx) = 0 \tag{3}$$

The values of the coefficient of A, B, C and D are changes over C_p. For genera materials, C_s is less than C_l. And the coefficient values are shown as Table 1.

Table 1. Coefficient values

Coefficient	$0 < C_p < C_s$	$C_s < C_p < C_l$	$C_l < C_p$
A	$-a$	ai	a
B	bi	bi	b
C	c	c	c
D	di	d	d

Note:

$$a = 4|p\,q| > 0, \quad b = \left|\frac{\pi \cdot q}{C_p}\right| > 0, \qquad c = (p^2 - 1)^2 > 0;$$

$$d = \left|\frac{\pi \cdot p}{C_p}\right| > 0, \quad i : \text{imaginary unit.}$$

2.1.2   Numerical Solution [8, 9]

q is equal to zero when C_p is equal to C_l. At this time, formula (1) will turn into simple trigonometric equation, just as formula (4).

$$(p^2 - 1)^2 \tan\frac{\pi \cdot p}{C_p} x = 0 \tag{4}$$

The solution of the above equation is $x = k\frac{C_p}{p}(k = 1, 2, 3, \ldots)$.

In the same way, p is equal to one when C_p is equal to $\sqrt{2}\,C_s$. And the solution of equation is $x = \frac{(2k-1)C_p}{2q}$ $(k = 1, 2, 3\ldots)$.

The above two cases in k = 1, 2, 3..., correspond to 1, 2, 3, ... order modes solution.

p is equal to zero when C_p is equal to C_s. At this time, formula (1) is identical equation. It makes no sense.

(1) $0 < C_p < C_s$

Formula (3) could be written as Formula (5).

$$F(x) = ath(bx) - cth(dx) = 0 \tag{5}$$

Analysis shows that if there is real solution for formula (5), it must satisfy the conditions for c > a, and a b > c d. When the above condition meets, formula (5) only has one solution in the interval $\left[0, \frac{1}{2d} \ln \frac{c+a}{c-a}\right]$. And at the two endpoints of the interval, function F (x) has opposite sign. Now it's easy to solve the equation by the dichotomy, and it corresponds to zero order modes solution.

(2) $C_s < C_p < C_l$

Formula (3) could be written as Formula (6).

$$F(x) = ath(bx) - ctan(dx) = 0 \tag{6}$$

Analysis shows that formula (6) only has one solution in the interval $\left[\frac{k\pi}{d}, \frac{(2k+1)\pi}{2d}\right]$ (k = 1, 2, 3, ...) by two adjacent discontinuous points. And at the two endpoints of the interval, function F(x) has opposite sign. And it corresponds to 1, 2, 3, ... order modes solution when k = 1, 2, 3, ...

Specially, the Formula (6) also only has one solution in the interval $\left[0, \frac{1}{d} \arctan \frac{a}{c}\right]$ when it satisfies the condition for a b > c d. At the two endpoints of the interval, function F(x) has opposite sign. And it corresponds to zero order modes solution.

Similarly, it could be also to get the solutions of the equation in every interval by the dichotomy [5].

(3) $C_l < C_p$

Formula (3) could be written as Formula (7).

$$F(x) = atan(bx) + ctan(dx) = 0 \tag{7}$$

bx and dx are defined as $\frac{(2k-1)\pi}{2}$ (k = 1, 2, 3, ...). Lots of discontinuous points are solved by function F(x), and these points are in the order since the childhood stand in line, as $\{J_1, J_2, J_3, ...\}$. Formula (8) could be found as below when the derivative of function F (x) is calculated in the interval (J_k, J_{k+1}) by two adjacent discontinuous points.

$$F'(x) = absec^2(bx) + cdsec^2(dx) > 0 \tag{8}$$

And $F(J_k^+) < 0, F(J_{k+1}) > 0$, so formula (7) only has one solution in the interval (J_k, J_{k+1}). The solutions of the equation in every interval could be to get by the dichotomy. And it corresponds to 1, 2, 3, ... order modes solution when k = 1, 2, 3, ...

2.2 Analysis and Solution of Asymmetric Mode Equation

The analysis and numerical solution of asymmetric mode equation are similar to symmetric mode equation. So it's no longer go into details here.

3 Program Flow Chart of Algorithm

The analysis of algorithm for Lamb wave frequency characteristic with Symmetric and asymmetric mode has been done, and makes it come true with VC++ software. The program flow chart is shown as Fig. 1.

Calculating module 1 is the solving program of simple trigonometric equation, and Calculating module 2, 3 and 4 are the process of solving program by the dichotomy.

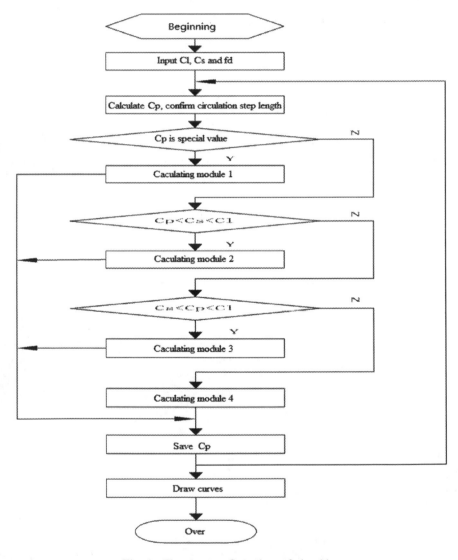

Fig. 1. The program flow chart of algorithm

4 Application of the Drawing Software for Lamb Wave Dispersion Curves

The Lamb wave dispersion curves are drawn by VC++ software, and the interface is beautiful and easy to understand. The drawing software for applying includes six interfaces. Such as parameters settings, data output, phase velocity curve (C_p—f d), group velocity curve (C_g—f d), stimulant angle curve (α—f d), and particles displacement amplitude curve (U, V—x). The stainless steel plate (1Cr18Ni9Ti) with three millimeters will be detailed introduction as an example in following content.

4.1 Phase Velocity Curve

Phase velocity curve is drawn on the basis of the Lamb wave frequency characteristic equation. When parameters' have been set, phase velocity curve will be shown after running program. Known from the analysis of algorithm, it makes no sense while C_p is equal to C_s. There is some reflex for this characteristic in Fig. 2. As f d increases, C_p tends to be C_s in addition to zero order modes. That's an example in Fig. 2.

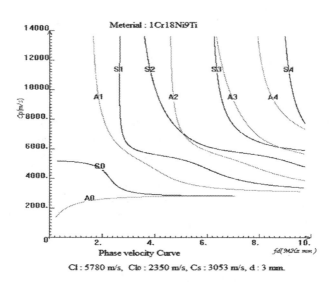

Fig. 2. Phase velocity curve

4.2 Group Velocity Curve

Lamb wave are made up of wave with different frequency and different velocity [2]. Group velocity is the most greatly velocity of synthesis vibration. Actually, Lamb wave in the plate are transmitted in the form of group velocity. The drawing of group velocity curve is similar to phase velocity. Firstly, the value of C_p is calculated though calculation subroutine, then estimate it symmetric or asymmetric mode, and calculate group velocity (C_g) by C_p and corresponding expression. Finally, group velocity curve will be drew though program designed. It's an example in Fig. 3.

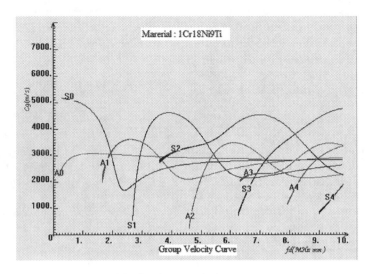

Fig. 3. Group velocity curve

4.3   Displacement Distribution Curve

Particles will vibrate when Lamb wave spreads in the plate. The displacement amplitude distribution of vibration reflects energy flow distribution at different depth. It is related directly to the detection sensitivity at different depth of the plate. U, V and x are defined respectively as vertical displacement amplitude, horizontal displacement amplitude and the distance between particle and waveguide axis (z axis in Fig. 4).

Symmetric and asymmetric Lamb wave U and V expression in different range could be reduced by the relationship between hyperbolic function and trigonometric function. The value of U and V can be calculated according to the U, V expression after C_p is calculated, and displacement amplitude curve (U, V—x) can also be drew. That's a case in Fig. 4.

4.4   Stimulant Angle Curve

The stimulant angle curve is the basis of choosing probe angle. The stimulant angle is chose by formula (17) when Lamb wave are stimulated. It's an example in Fig. 5.

$$\sin \alpha = \frac{C_1}{C_p} \tag{9}$$

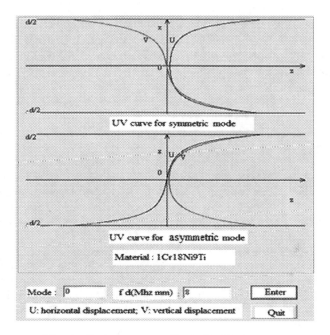

Fig. 4. displacement amplitude distribution curve

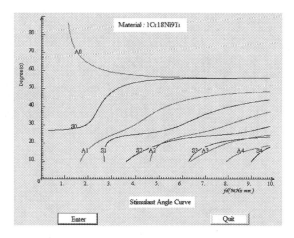

Fig. 5. Stimulant angle curve

5   Conclusion

Defined phase velocity as independent variable, Lamb wave frequency characteristic equation is analyzed and solved with the method that dividing interval by function discontinuities. Dichotomy is chosen in the numerical solution method, because it will make programming relatively simple to use this method. The running result of program shows that this solution method achieved good effect, and is quite feasible. Under the condition that Lamb wave dispersion curves are scanty in the current, the problem of drawing Lamb wave dispersion curves for different material and different thickness metal plates testing is solved, and the practical application of Lamb wave is further promoted in engineering.

References

1. Sorazu, B., Culshaw, B., Thursby, G.: Obtaining complementary Lamb wave dispersion information by two signal processing methods on an all-optical non-contact configuration. Sens. Actuators, A **217**, 95–104 (2014)
2. Hayashi, T., Song, W.J., Rose, J.L.: Guided wave dispersion curves for a bar with an arbitrary cross-section, a rod and rail example. Ultrasonics **41**, 175–183 (2003)
3. Raghavan, A., Cesnik, C.E.S.: Guided-wave signal processing using chirplet matching pursuits and mode correlation for structural health monitoring. Smart Mater. Struct. **16**(2), 61741B (2007)
4. Draudvilienė, L., Raišutis, R., Žukauskas, E., Jankauskas, A.: Validation of dispersion curve reconstruction techniques for the A0 and S0 modes of Lamb waves. Int. J. Struct. Stab. Dyn. **14**, 14–24 (2014)
5. Hedayatrasa, S., Bui, T.Q., Zhang, C., Lim, C.W.: Numerical modeling of wave propagation in functionally graded materials using time-domain spectral Chebyshev elements. J. Comput. Phys. **258**, 381–404 (2014)
6. Harley, J.B., Moura, J.M.F.: Sparse recovery of the multimodal and dispersive characteristics of Lamb waves. J. Acoust. Soc. Am. **133**, 2732–2745 (2013)
7. Gao, W., Christ, G., Jan, T.: Laser ultrasonic study of Lamb waves: determination of the thickness and velocities of a thin plate. Int. J. Eng. Sci. **41**(2), 219–228 (2003)
8. Singh, R.K., Ramadas, C., Misal, R.D., Thakur, D.G.: Numerical analysis of Lamb wave propagation in delaminated composite laminate. Int. Conf. Modell. Opt. Comput. **38**, 2510–2519 (2012)
9. Packo, P., Uhl, T., Staszewski, W.J.: Generalized semi-analytical finite difference method for dispersion curves calculation and numerical dispersion analysis for Lamb waves. J. Acoust. Soc. Am. **136**, 993–1002 (2014)

Automatic Character Detection System for IC Test Handler Based on Active Learning SVM

Tianshan Wang, Fan Jiang, Xiaojin Zhu, Hesheng Zhang,
and Zhiyuan Gao$^{(\boxtimes)}$

School of Mechatronic Engineering and Automation, Shanghai University,
Shanghai 200072, People's Republic of China
gaozhiyuan86@shu.edu.cn

Abstract. An automatic character detection system for IC test handler is designed to recognize the characters on the surface of IC chip based on active learning SVM. Firstly, industrial camera is employed to collect a large number of chips' surface image. Secondly, image preprocessing is carried out, including image grayscale, binarization and filter processing. Thirdly, the features of the preprocessed image are extracted. To reduce the annotation cost for training data and improve recognition rate, active learning algorithm is used to label the training data, while support vector machine algorithm is used to classify those data. Comparison with SVM algorithm, template matching and BP neural network shows the effectiveness of the proposed algorithm.

Keywords: Active learning · SVM · IC chips · Character recognition

1 Introduction

Semiconductor manufacturing, testing and packaging have a high requirement for automation [1, 2]. For example, the character on the surface of IC chips is used to indicate the manufacturer, the chip type, serial number information. Before the test of Chip, the workers need to identify the chip whether it is correct or not [3]. This is a time-consuming job which leads to production efficiency reduction. Therefore, it is necessary to develop a set of system which can automatically recognize the characters on the chip's surface [4, 5].

Optical character recognition technology is widely used in the field of production, such as automatic recognition of mail and automatic license plate recognition [6]. Support vector machine (SVM) is one of the most commonly used algorithm in pattern recognition and it has excellent classification function [7]. However, SVM algorithm takes a lot of time to label the sample, to solve this problem, active learning algorithm is used to alleviate the training data annotation burden [8].

Z. Gao—This work is supported by National Natural Science Foundation (NNSF) of China under Grant 31570998. Mechatronics Engineering Innovation Group project from Shanghai Education Commission and Shanghai Key Laboratory of Power Station Automation Technology.

© Springer Nature Singapore Pte Ltd. 2017
D. Yue et al. (Eds.): LSMS/ICSEE 2017, Part II, CCIS 762, pp. 333–342, 2017.
DOI: 10.1007/978-981-10-6373-2_34

This paper mainly introduces the following contents. Section 2 introduces the process of image preprocessing and feature extraction. Section 3 analyzes the principle of active learning and support vector machine algorithm. Section 4 is the design of IC character detection system. Section 5 is the experiment result of active learning SVM used in IC character detection, comparison with SVM, template matching and BP neural network algorithm.

2   Image Preprocessing and Feature Extraction

Optical character recognition is mainly composed of two parts: sample training and recognition. Both need to preprocess the images and extract the image feature value. These two steps can directly influence the recognition rate of the image [9].

2.1   Image Preprocessing

Image preprocessing is illustrated in Fig. 1, including binarization, filtering and denoising, skew correction and character segmentation [10, 11].

Fig. 1. Image preprocessing process

Image Graying and Morphological Transformations. Image gray processing can reduce a number of unimportant information and good for subsequent processing.

Two basic morphological operations are erosion and dilation. The basic idea of erosion is just like soil erosion. It erodes away the boundaries of foreground object. Dilation is just opposite of erosion. It escalates the white region in the image or the size of foreground object. Normally, in cases like noise elimination, erosion is followed by dilation. Opening is erosion followed by dilation. It is useful in removing noise. Top hat is the difference between input image and opening of the image. Here we use the function of top hat before image binarization.

Image Binarization. The image binarization can highlight the outline of the target. And threshold selection is very important for image binarization. Threshold selection method is mainly divided into the following three categories: the global threshold method, local threshold method and dynamic threshold method. Global threshold method is chosen to set the threshold. Using Otsu algorithm can successfully divide the image into target and background.

Image Filtering. The image acquired by a camera have some noise caused by illumination or electromagnetic interference. Including salt and pepper noise, Gaussian noise, and impulse noise. And there are three kinds of popular filtering methods: Linear smoothing filtering, median filtering, Wiener filtering and Gaussian filtering. Figure 2

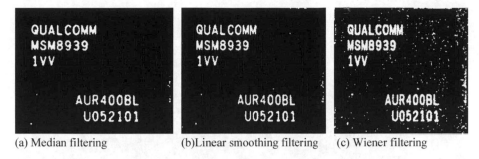

| (a) Median filtering | (b)Linear smoothing filtering | (c) Wiener filtering |

Fig. 2. Comparison of different filtering methods

show the images filtered by median filtering, linear smoothing filtering and wiener filtering respectively. A comprehensive comparison of the three filtering methods, the median filtering has the best effect of filtering noise.

Skew Correction. The original chip image usually exists a certain of tilt degree, which will affect the next step's character segmentation and decrease the character recognition accuracy. The tilt angle of the chip image can be detected by Hough transform algorithm. The classical Hough transform can detect the straight lines in the chip image [12]. Figure 3 shows the skew correction result. First, to dilate the binary image and get the dilate image, then, use the Canny algorithm to detect the edge of the characters. Thirdly, use Hough transform to detect straight lines in the Canny image. Finally, rotate the image according to the slope of straight lines.

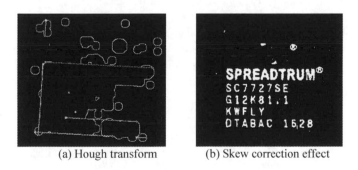

| (a) Hough transform | (b) Skew correction effect |

Fig. 3. Skew correction process

Image Segmentation. Image segmentation including two steps. Firstly, separate a single chip image from the whole picture, and then separate out each character from the single chip image. There are numbers of chips displayed neatly on one plate, and the chip's color is close to the plate's background color. Here, opening function is used to remove some noise in the binary image and makes each chip separate out clearly. Then, dilate the image, so that the whole outline of the characters can be linked together. Using projection method to add each column and each row's pixel value. And the chip image is separated out according the crest and trough of the total pixel value.

After separating out each single chip image, select one of the chip image and also use the projection method explained above to spilt each character (Fig. 4).

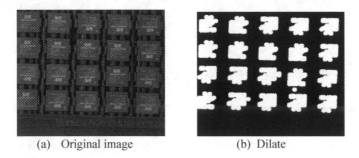

(a)   Original image   (b) Dilate

Fig. 4. Image segmentation

Image Feature Extraction

The purpose of feature extraction is to extract the information from the image which reflect the characteristics of the character itself. Feature extraction based on structure and feature extraction based on statistic features are used in this paper [13].

Firstly, Grid the character image into 8 areas equally, shown in Fig. 5(a). Add up each area's pixel value as one feature. Secondly, select two rows and two columns in the middle of character image and calculate their pixel values respectively as the feature. Thirdly, the total pixel value will be the thirteenth feature. The other method to extract features is based on the character contour information. Scanning each row of the image from left and right side until meet the first black pixel. This pair of black pixel marks the edge information of the Character and use their position as a feature. For a 32*32 pixel image, we can get 32 features, similarly, we can get another 32 features by scanning each column from top to the bottom.

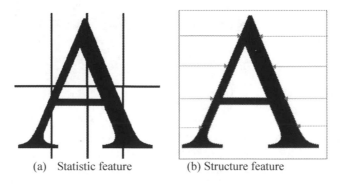

(a)   Statistic feature   (b) Structure feature

Fig. 5. Image feature extraction

3   Active Learning Support Vector Machine

Active Learning

Active learning, also called query learning, is an effective machine learning method that generated to solve the problem of unlabeled binary classification. It was first presented by Simon in 1974 [14]. The main idea is to select the most valuable samples in a large pool of unlabeled data and ask the expert to label them, and then add these labeled samples to the training set. Initially, there is only a small part of labeled data and a large pool of unlabeled data, we called it initial training data set, and then select the lowest confidence of unlabeled data and request their labels. End of the loop after a series of iteration.

Active learning can be characterized into three categories based on different ways to select the unlabeled samples [15]:

(1)   Active learning based on membership queries ask active learners to construct the examples for which annotations will be requested.
(2)   Stream-based active learning is used in situations where samples are incoming in a stream one by one, classifier decides whether to ask the learner to label it or not.
(3)   Pool-based active learning value all the unlabeled samples and sort them according to their value, this is the most widely used method among these three categories.

In this paper, the pool-based active learning method is used to select the unlabeled character images which have the lowest confidence to classify. The following is the definition of confidence [16]:

$$x^* = \arg\left\{ \max\left[1 - p_\theta\left(\frac{\hat{y}}{x}\right)\right]\right\} \tag{1}$$

x is the character sample and y is its label. x^* is this character sample's confidence. $\hat{y}$ is the value of y when this character sample has the biggest Posterior Probability.

$$\hat{y} = \arg\left\{ \max\left[p_\theta\left(\frac{y}{x}\right)\right]\right\} \tag{2}$$

Support Vector Machines

In the field of machine learning, support vector machine (SVM) is a supervised learning model. A support vector machine constructs a hyperplane or set of hyperplanes in a high or infinite dimensional space, which can be used for classification and regression. A good separation is achieved by the hyperplane that has the largest distance to the nearest training-data point of any class. SVM can solve the problem of data can't linearly separate by using a kernel function.

Given training samples in two classes [17]:

$$(x_1, y_1)\ldots(x_l, y_l), x \in R^n, y \in \{-1, +1\} \tag{3}$$

Here, l is the number of character samples and n is the input dimension. The optimal hyper-plane divide those samples into two classes:

$$w \cdot x + b = 0 \tag{4}$$

The classification formula is:

$$\begin{aligned} w \cdot x_i + b \geq 0, y_i = +1 \\ w \cdot x_i + b \leq 0, y_i = -1 \end{aligned} \tag{5}$$

The distance from sample to optimal hyper-plane is as follows:

$$d = \frac{w \cdot x + b}{\|w\|} \tag{6}$$

x is a positive sample when $d \geq 1$, similarly, x is a negative sample when $d \leq -1$. Only those characters between $-1 < d < 1$ need to ask expert for their labels.

In our experiments, the initial sample set is 615 character images that contains all the character types in the chip, some characters look like similar, such as "0" and "o", "1" and "I", those character images have low confidence which makes SVM algorithm difficult to classify them. Active learning algorithm selects these low confidence character images to ask expert for their labels.

4 Design of IC Character Recognition System

The recognition system mainly includes two parts: hardware and software design.

Hardware Design

Hardware design is mainly composed of industrial camera, auxiliary light and communication controller. The image collected by the ordinary camera is not clear enough. It is important to select an industrial camera which can capture high-definition images. In this system, the industrial camera's model is GS3-U3-51S5 M, which produced by Point Gray company. Its maximum resolution is 2448 × 2048 and data transfer rate up to 5 Gbit/s.

The auxiliary light source is installed to improve the recognition rate of the system. Auxiliary light can overcome some of the ambient light interference, to ensure that the image on the chip has good brightness. At present, the common types of light source in industry are surface array light source, ring light source and strip light source. In this system, the size of IC tray is 335 mm × 145 mm and the entire chip tray needs uniform illumination, only strip light source is the most suitable for the needs above. Figure 6(a) shows the IC tray and Fig. 6(b) shows the camera mounting position and light effect under the strip light source.

Communication controller is an important bridge between hardware and software. Its main function includes: (1) Check whether the IC tray reaches the image acquisition area; (2) Send commands to the camera to capture the image; (3) Receive and parse the message send by software; (4) Send different control instructions according to the recognition results. For example, send alarm signals when recognition result is wrong.

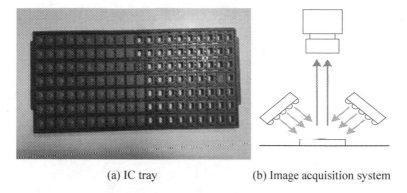

(a) IC tray   (b) Image acquisition system

Fig. 6. (a) IC tray, (b) image acquisition system

Software Design

The main function of the software are as follows: sample training and character recognition. Sample training is to collect a number of IC images as the sample data, using active learning SVM algorithm to train the classifier. The main process of sample training: first, the initialization of the system, such as open the camera and serial port, and then the communication controller module for serial port monitoring, monitoring image acquisition commands. When the communication control module received the image acquisition instruction, the image acquisition is notified to collect a plurality of IC images, and do preprocess and feature extraction for those images. Then, to initialize label those character images, and the initial classifier is trained and judge whether the classifier meets the criteria. If the classifier does not meet the standard, the active learning method is used to select some of the samples to be labeled, and then the classifier is trained again after the completion of the label. Finally, save the classification information when the classification performance of the classifier meets the standard. Figure 7 shows the sample training process.

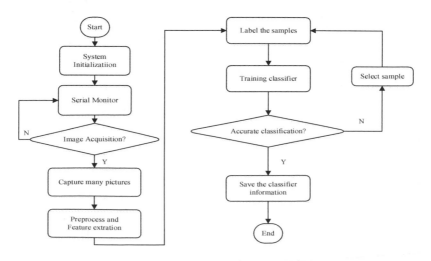

Fig. 7. Sample training process

The process of character recognition is as follows: first, the system initialization, including the opening of the camera, serial port, load the chip information and classifier information. Then the communication control module monitoring serial port. Capture one IC image when communication control module received the acquisition instruction, to preprocess and feature extraction for this image. Then, the classifier is used to recognize the character image and judge whether the IC character is matched with the standard IC character. Alarm and notify the relevant personnel to deal with the problem when the character recognition is wrong. Figure 8 shows the software interface and recognition result.

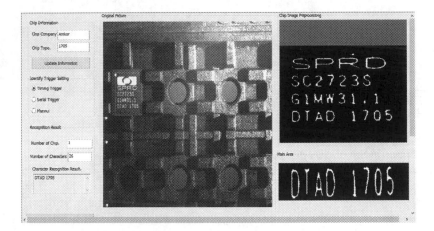

Fig. 8. Software interface

5   Experiment and Analysis

In this experiment, we took 15 pieces of Spreadtrum company's SC7727SE chip as the experiment sample, preprocess and segment those images, each chip has 41 characters and can get 615 characters in total. 12 statistical features and 6 structural features in each character image are selected for training.

Firstly, 50 samples were randomly selected to form the initial sample set and label those them. Then use the active learning SVM and SVM algorithm for training respectively. Both methods need to use the initial sample set to train an initial classifier. The active learning SVM algorithm select 10 unlabeled samples whose distance are shortest to the optimal classification surface, to label those 10 samples and add them to the training set, retrain the classifier and repeat the process above. However, SVM algorithm select 10 unlabeled samples randomly form the unlabeled samples set, other steps are the same as active learning SVM.

Figure 10 is the active learning SVM and SVM sample training comparison chart, showing the relationship between training times and recognition rate. The abscissa of the curve is the number of training times and the ordinate is the recognition rate. It can be seen that with the increase of training samples, the recognition rate is higher. The

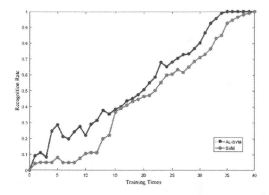

Fig. 9. Comparison of active learning SVM and SVM in sample training

recognition rate of the classifier can reach 100% after training by active learning SVM 35 times, and the number of samples need to be labeled is 390, and the number of support vectors is 285. While the SVM requires training 40 times to make the training classifier recognition rate reached 100%. The numbers of sample to be labeled is 440 and the number of support vector is 327. Comparing two kinds of methods, active learning SVM can reduce the number of labeled samples and support vectors in training, Active learning SVM can greatly reduce the time when the classifier is used for classification and recognition.

We also compare the active learning algorithm with template matching and BP neural network algorithm. 25 chip images were selected in this experiment and get 1025 character images after image preprocess and segment. Template matching method needs to prepare the template library in advance, there are 150 character images in the template library and each kind of character contains at least three template images. BP neural network and Active Learning SVM used the same sample library when training character samples, a total of 680 images in this experiment were used for training. The experiment results are shown in the Table 1.

Table 1. Recognition rate comparison of different character recognition algorithms

Recognition algorithm	Total number of characters	Correct	Wrong	Recognition rate
AL-SVM	1025	1001	24	97.67%
Template matching	1025	985	40	96.10%
BP neural network	1025	963	62	93.95%

As shown in Table 1, active learning SVM has the highest character recognition rate in these three algorithms, and its recognition rate is up to 97.67%.

6   Conclusion

An automatic IC character recognition system is designed and implemented based on active learning SVM algorithm in this paper. The experimental results show that the active learning SVM algorithm has faster training speed and higher recognition rate than SVM algorithm.

References

1. Tummala, R., Rymaszewski, E.J., Klopfenstein, A.G.: Microelectronics Packaging Handbook: Technology Drivers. Springer Science & Business Media, Heidelberg (2012)
2. Chen, Y.M., Chiang, J.-H.: Recognition of the making on integrated circuit chips based on the hybrid Fourier-AFMT. Glob. J. Comput. Sci. Technol. **10**(2), 64–70 (2010)
3. Blaes, P., Young, C.: Mobile IC package recognition. Technical report, EE368 Project, Stanford University (2008)
4. Chen, S.-H., Liao, T.-T.: An automated IC chip marking inspection system for surface mounted devices on taping machines. J. Sci. Ind. Res. **68**(5), 361–366 (2009)
5. Nagarajan, R., Yaacob, S., Pandian, P., et al.: A real time marking inspection scheme for sem-iconductor industries. Int. J. Adv. Manuf. Technol. **34**(9), 926–932 (2007)
6. Aghaie, M., Shokri, F., Tabari, M.Y.Z.: Automatic iranian vehicle license plate recognition system based on Support Vector Machine (SVM) algorithms. Comput. Appl. Eng. Educ. **2** (1), 161–174 (2013)
7. Schölkopf, B., Smola, A.J., Williamson, R.C., et al.: New support vector algorithms. Neural Comput. **12**(5), 1207–1245 (2000)
8. Schohn, G., Cohn, D.: Less is more: active learning with support vector machines. In: ICML, pp. 839–846 (2000)
9. Jain, A.K.: Fundamentals of Digital Image Processing. Prentice Hall, Upper Saddle River (2011)
10. Zhou, H., Li, X., Schaefer, G.: Mean shift based gradient vector flow for image segmentation. Comput. Vis. Image Underst. **117**(9), 1004–1016 (2013)
11. Zhang, K., Croookes, D., Fei, M.: Multi-scale colorectal tumour segmentation using a novel coarse to fine strategy. In: BMVC (2016)
12. Aggarwal, N., Karl, W.C.: Line detection in images through regularized Hough transform. IEEE Trans. Image Process. **15**(3), 582–591 (2006)
13. Zitova, B., Flusser, J.: Image registration methods: a survey. Image Vis. Comput. **21**(11), 977–1000 (2003)
14. Guo, H., Wang, W.: An active learning-based SVM multi-class classifica-tion model. Pattern Recogn. **48**(5), 1577–1597 (2015)
15. Vladimir, N.V.: An overview of statistical learning theory. IEEE Trans. Neural Netw. **10**(5), 988–999 (1999)
16. Tong, S., Koller, D.: Support vector machine active learning with applications to text classification. J. Mach. Learn. Res. **2**(11), 45–66 (2001)
17. Amari, S., Si, W.: Improving support vector machine classifiers by modifying kernel functions. Neural Netw. **12**(6), 783–789 (1999)

Active RFID Tags for Smart Shelf Based on LF Assistant Devices

Bing Bai, Xiaojin Zhu$^{(\boxtimes)}$, Hesheng Zhang, and Zhaoxun Zhang

School of Mechatronic Engineering and Automation, Shanghai University,
Shanghai 200072, People's Republic of China
mgzhuxj@shu.edu.cn

Abstract. An active RFID tag with 2.4 GHz radio communication function and LF wake-up module is designed in this paper. On the basis of this, a smart shelf system is proposed to reduce the time of searching for specified goods and improve operation efficiency of warehousing management. The location of the tags attached to the items on the shelf is estimated by the weighted centroid localization algorithm. With the deployments of the assistant LF label nodes, the shelf doesn't have to be divided into several fixed electromagnetic shielding space. These advantages help the shelf to achieve greater flexibility of cargo storage management.

Keywords: RSSI · Active RFID tag · Smart shelf · LF wake-up

1 Introduction

The rapid development of electronic and information industry calls for higher efficiency and automation level in logistics and warehousing department. Semiconductor industry is a representative example of technology and knowledge intensive industries among all the electronic and information industry. It requires the production line to be able to track the market changes and make adjustments in a short time; this also requests the supporting warehousing department to have the ability to transport and update the contents in cargo shelf with a highly efficient management system. In addition, the definite functions and divisions of work between the upstream and downstream enterprises results in a variety of package of the products, and this is often true even for the IC comes from one same order, which usually costs troubles in the management of the items on the shelf.

Radio Frequency Identification (RFID) is an advanced form of contactless identification and communication [1, 2]. The system of RFID is simple and low cost, and could run in reliability and flexibility; it can work without manual intervention and read information from multiple tags simultaneously. It's has obviously advantages over bar code and 2-dimensional bar code in the transmitting cryptograph and storage size, and

X. Zhu—This work is supported by Mechatronics Engineering Innovation Group project from Shanghai Education Commission and Shanghai Key Laboratory of Power Station Automation Technology.

© Springer Nature Singapore Pte Ltd. 2017
D. Yue et al. (Eds.): LSMS/ICSEE 2017, Part II, CCIS 762, pp. 343–352, 2017.
DOI: 10.1007/978-981-10-6373-2_35

the application of RFID has been considered to be the future tendency into the automation of warehousing.

In recent years the research on the applications of RFID into the logistics and warehousing has attracted great attention from the experts all over the world. Dr. Yunhao Liu present an RFID-based system, Tagoram, for real time object localization and tracking using COTS RFID tags and readers. The system had been tested and deployed for automatic baggage sortation in two airports. It was announced in his paper that the location accuracy has been improved to millimeter level, which is a remarkable progress [3]. ZHANG Tian-cheng developed a wireless positioning system based on low-frequency (LF) wake-up and ELM classification algorithm, the real-time positioning computation is realized on MCU systems. His test result shows that the positioning precision in effective range can reach 15 cm, correctness rate of positioning is positioning is over 95% [4]. Other researchers tried to apply the RFID system to the smart shelf, WANG Jian-wei worked to solve the problems existing in data information acquisition and automation level of traditional warehouse management and tried to combine RFID with ID barcode technology to realizing the automated warehousing management and real-time inventory control [5] .

So far, the RF communication technology and received signal strength (RSS) detection has become the main technical means of indoor positioning technology [6–8]. In this paper, a method of setting fixed low-frequency assistant card on the shelf to help locating the active RFID tags is introduced. By acquired the RSSI value of the neighboring LF assistant cards and their pre-coded number, the correlation level to the neighboring LF assistant tags could be calculated, and therefore estimation coordinates of the active RFID tags would be acquired to show their locations on the shelf. This method doesn't need to separate the shelf to certain space and the electromagnetic shielding is not needed between each tag on the shelf.

2 RFID Smart Shelf System

The main objective of this paper is to overcome the issues and challenges of the warehousing management system in semiconductor industry. In many situations the raw materials with different sizes and shapes need to be stored together during the producing procedure and separated after production, making it extremely difficult to keep track of the position of specified IC product on the shelf.

2.1 Basic RFID System

RFID system works with radio-frequency signal for wireless transmit and receive of the data. The information of the goods is stored in the tag it attached with. As shown in Fig. 1, the typical RFID system is usually consist of tags, reader, and background processing software system, which mostly running on the PC. The reader is responsible to transmit the radio signals at certain frequency through the antenna it matched to. When the RFID tags enter the working zone of the reader, the antenna of the tags will

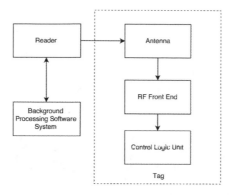

Fig. 1. Typical radio frequency identification system block diagram

have the inductive current from the signal from the reader. Thus the tags will be active and then try to transmit their own information back to the reader; the information is usually modulated in the carrier of the same frequency to the reader. Then the reader could receiver and demodulate RF signal, finished the decoding and verification work, after that the information is sent to the background processing software system to process. The software system will judge the legitimacy of the tag by processing the verification code and UUID, and then interact differently to the different items and situations. If the legitimacy is valid, the reader will sent back corresponding command signal, and the RF front end of the tag will demodulate and recover the information from the radio frequency. Then those information data are transported to the control logic unit, which will take operation according to the command signal it receives.

2.2 Proposed System

In this paper, a RFID smart shelf system is proposed based on the LF trigger signal. The low frequency band is chosen because it has relatively even field strength, which is ideal for the situation of the items detection on the shelf. The hardware is mainly based on the 125 kHz LF wake-up communication technique, and location algorithm is based on weighted centroid localization algorithm.

As shown in Fig. 2, the proposed system structure of smart shelf using active RFID tags is consist of LF assistant label nodes, active tags, reader and software system running on PC.

The LF assistant label nodes are preset on the shelf according to an established Cartesian coordinate grid. Knowing the actual location of each label node, we give the label nodes a three dimensional vector to demonstrate their positions. The LF assistant label nodes will then actively transmit wake-up signal through 125 kHz at a certain interval. When the active RFID tag carrying with the cargo enters the working field of the LF assistant label nodes, the LF detection circuit will activate the tag. The RSSI and the position vectors of neighboring label nodes will be acquired simultaneously from the wake-up signal.

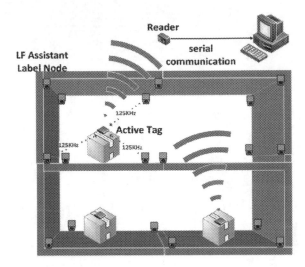

Fig. 2. Structure of smart shelf system

The tag will compared the receiving vectors with the previous transaction vectors. If there are some new faces appeared, the tag will then activate its 2.4 GHz band to transmit each RSSI value with the corresponding vector to the reader along with the information of the tag itself. The work of reader is comparatively simple, it handles to pick up the data frames on the 2.4 GHz band and try not be fuzzed by the noisy air interface jammed by Tag collision and other ISM band users. As to the task of calculating the location of the tags on the shelf, we decided to let the MCU in the reader to do the work instead of the logic control unit on the tags, to reduce the energy consuming of the tags. The location algorithm is detailed in the Sect. 4. After figuring out the real-time location of the tag, the reader will send the information of the tag and the location to the background processing software system via RS485 serial bus.

The tags on the shelf will enter the low power mode ever since a successful communication to the reader and a sleep-timer will be started. If the tag reaches sleep time limit, the circuit will be activated again to receive LF signal. But the tag won't start a new communication to the reader via 2.4 GHz band until it detect a new location vector of the LF label node, to help the tag reduce the power consumption, and to increase the battery life.

3   Circuit Design

3.1   Circuit of LF Assistant Label Node

The function of the circuit of LF assistant label node is to transmit 125 kHz wake-up signal. While the format of the signal and the radio frequency is correct and accurate, the tags in the range could be effectively triggered and the data correctly demodulated. The signal amplitude should be as stable as possible, to ensure a trustworthy precision for the detected RSSI value. Based on these considerations, we adopt the integrated advanced base station IC PCF7991AT. This device is operating at 125 kHz and employing Amplitude Shift Keying (ASK) for write and AM/PM for the read operation. The PCF7991AT IC has a high degree of integration and very low external component dependency. The device integrates a powerful antenna driver and modulator, a low-noise adaptive sampling time demodulator, and provides three wire SPI microcontroller interface for programming. The power supply of the LF assistant label node is supported from the 9 V battery and the voltage stabilizing circuit.

The schematic diagram of the antenna of the LF assistant label node is designed based on the model of RLC series resonant circuit, as shown in Fig. 3.

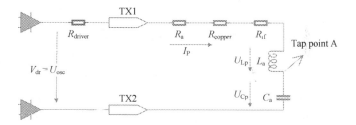

Fig. 3. Antenna resonance loop equivalent circuit diagram

R_{driver} is the internal resistance of the driving component (i.e. the equivalent resistance of the antenna driving IC PCF7991). R_{copper} is the resistance of the wire of the antenna coil, which includes the contact resistance between the coil and the circuit and the equivalent resistance of electric current concentrating effect at 125 kHz. R_a is used to adjust the current of the lope. R_{rf} stands for the equivalent resistance caused by eddy current loss from the metal near the coil. L_a is the inductance of the coil. C_a is the tuning capacitance. U_{Cp} is the peak voltage on the C_a. U_{Lp} is the peak voltage on the L_a. Q_{op} is the energy factor at resonant state. U_{osc} is the driving signal of the antenna. I_p is the peak current when the circuit works at resonant state of 125 kHz and the Q_{op} is 10. The tap point A is the test point of the circuit.

As shown in the data sheet of PCF7991AT, if the digital square wave signal is converted into an equivalent sine wave signal, the equivalent voltage $U_{osc} = 6.37$ V. As we known, when the energy factor $Q_{op} = 10$, the energy factor Q_a at tap point A should be much larger than 10. So that we can figure out the inductance of the coil is:

$$L_a = \frac{6.37 \times 10}{I_P \times 0.785} \qquad (1)$$

Generally we can choose the needed value of I_p from 150 mA to 250 mA to determine the inductance of the 125 kHz emission coil.

The application circuit of the LF assistant label node is shown in Fig. 4, TX1 pin and TX2 pin of the IC PCF7991 are connected to the frequency selective network.

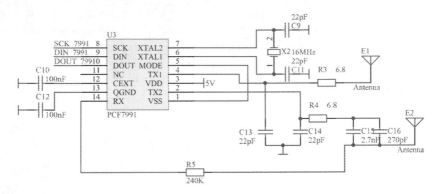

Fig. 4. PFC7991 and LF selective network circuit diagram

3.2 Circuit of Active Tags

Active tags are used for receiving the incoming LF wake up signals and communicating with the readers at 2.4 GHz ISM band. When the tag detecting the LF signal in the field, it will verify the legitimacy of the wake up frames, measure the received signal strength indication (RSSI) and finish an effective dialogue with the reader.

The circuit of active tag can be divided into three main function parts: the LF signal module, the digital process module and the 2.4 GHz communication module. To ensure that at least one set of coils can obtain sufficient signal strength to demodulate the data, the 3-D orthogonal antenna ZSUCORE 3D15-722 is applied to the LF signal module to acquire better signal uniformity and sensitivity. In generally, the 3-D receiving antenna is a combination of 3 single coils oriented in the 3 space axis, so that the LF signal can be detected and measured on three dimensions at the same time. The antenna is connected to the AS3933 which is a 3-channel low power ASK receiver IC. This IC is able to generate a wake-up signal to MCU upon detection of a LF carrier frequency data signal. Each dimension of the antenna is attached to one of the channels of AS3933. The digital process module is handled by IC MSP430F149, it communicates with AS3933 on board via 3 wires SPI interface to receive the LF data and RSSI value. The 2.4 GHz communication module is handled by nRF24L01; it can transfer and receive RF data on worldwide 2.4 GHz ISM band with 2Mbps air data. Considering the carrying convenience of active tags, the button battery is used since both nRF24L01 and MSP430F149 have very low power consumption. The application circuit of AS3933 is shown in Fig. 5.

The LF frequency selection network employs parallel resonance. The inductance of three dimensions coil is 7.2 mH, the parallel capacitance can be calculated by the parallel resonant formula shown in formula 2.

$$f = \frac{1}{2\pi\sqrt{LC}} \tag{2}$$

So when resonance point frequency is designed to be 125 kHz, the resonant capacitance is 225 pF. Considering the practice of the circuit board, a pair of two

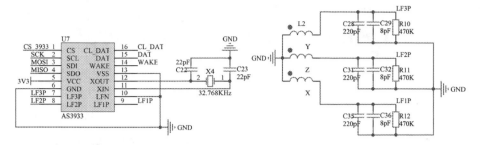

Fig. 5. AS3933 application circuit diagram

capacitors is applied in the circuit. The internal tuning resonant capacitor can also be programmed to a maximum of 31 pF at the step size of 1 pF.

4 Algorithm Analysis

Weighted centroid localization algorithm featuring low communication overhead and low complexity, is our basis of localization on the energy constrained RFID tags. In this smart shelf system, we introduce the concept of calibrated reference tags. The basic idea is to use the stationary LF assistant label nodes to measure RSSI of the calibrated reference tags, and thus we can compare those RSSI with the testing tag, find the several most related calibrated reference tags of the testing tag. Because we have set the stationary LF assistant label nodes by given precise 3-D coordinates, we can calculate the relational grades of target tag and all the calibrated reference tags to indicate the real-time location of the target tag.

5 Software and Hardware Implementation

5.1 Embedded Software

The LF communication process can be break down in two parts: one of the LF trigger transmission with the circuit of PCF7991AT and the other is the LF detection with the circuit of AS3933. Both of them communicate via the 125 kHz air channel with the ASK modulation.

The wake-up protocol of AS3933 is shown in Fig. 6. When the radio frequency is 125 kHz, the minimum time duration of Carrier Burst is $16T_{clk} +16T_{carr}$. T_{clk} is the period of the clock generator of AS3933. Here the clock is 32.765 kHz. T_{carr} is the period of the carrier. So the minimum time duration is 616 μs, and the maximum time is $155T_{clk}$, i.e. 4727.5 μs.

The embedded software of the active tags consists of four parts: initialization module, sleep mode module, low-frequency wake-up receive module and the high-frequency transceiver module. The initialization module includes MCU and external device initialization. The sleep mode is mainly to reduce power consumption, including turn off some peripherals and MCU into the suspended state, and turn off the

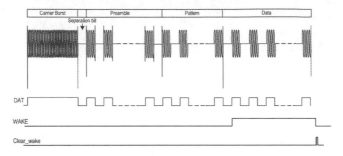

Fig. 6. Wake-up protocol overview with the pattern detection

nRF24L01. The low-frequency wake-up receive section used to verify the pairing data is mainly consisted of the wake-up pin configuration of the MCU and the reception of low frequency data. High-frequency transceiver module is responsible to send high-frequency information to the reader and complete the high-frequency response after a successful transmission.

5.2   Communication Protocol

The communication between the reader and the active RFID tags is based on the 2.4G ISM band. nRF24L01 is a single chip 2.4 GHz transceiver with an embedded baseband protocol engine, suitable for ultra-low power wireless applications. Using high data rate gives lower average current consumption and reduces probability of collisions. The communication rate is set to 2Mbps in this system.

We define the communication protocol of nRF24L01 with the chart shown in Fig. 7. In every frame nRF24L01 actually send 32 bytes data. The first byte is the length of this sending frame, so that the reader can count the right bytes of the data in one frame during a continuous transmission stream.

Buff[0]	Buff[1]	Buff[2]	Buff[3]	Buff[..]	Buff[..]	Buff[31]
Length	Byte1	Byte2	Byte3	..	..	Byte31

Fig. 7. RF communication protocol of the active tag

5.3   System Implementation

The development platform of PCB and schematic design is finished on Altium Designer 16. The circuit is manufactured on the FR-4 with thickness of 1.6 mm. The circuit boards of LF assistant node and the active tag is shown as below in Fig. 8.

According to the structure of smart shelf system, there is background software running on the computer to help release the real-time visualized inventory management and automatic cargo localization in warehouse. We designed a software system running on the computer, it communicates with the readers via RS485 serial bus to acquire the

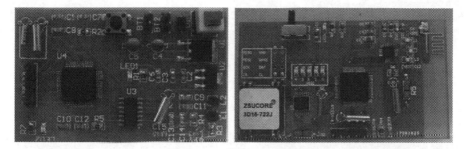

Fig. 8. Circuit board of LF assistant label node (*left*) and active tag (*right*)

information of the tags and the shelves and land a basic implementation of automation warehousing system. The software interface is shown in Fig. 9. There are three function windows which show the items on the shelf, leaving the shelf and entering the shelf. All the items are attached with an active tag with a unique UUID, and the software will display the UUID of the tags and their real time position estimations.

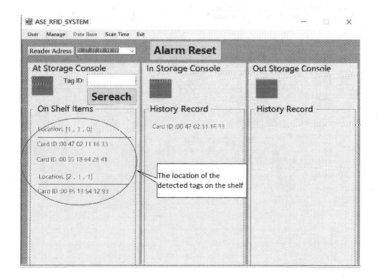

Fig. 9. An example of automatic storage detection

6 Conclusion

Based on the LF detection, communication method and RFID technology, we put forwards an approach to solve the problem of how to improve the inventory management and operations in warehousing. In order to achieve that, the LF assistant location device was proposed in this paper, which achieves the real-time visualized locating of the active tags on the shelf. With the help of RFID technology, the digital pallet and smart shelf are implemented. They ensure that the products and their stored places can be bound together and identified uniquely.

References

1. Lim, M.K., Bahr, W., Leung, S.C.H.: RFID in the warehouse: a literature analysis (1995–2010) of its applications, benefits, challenges and future trends. Int. J. Prod. Econ. **145**, 409–430 (2013)
2. Prakash, G., Renold, A.P., Venkatalakshmi, B.: RFID based mobile cold chain management system for warehousing. Procedia Eng. **38**, 964–969 (2012)
3. Yang, L., Chen, Y., Li, X.Y., Xiao, C., Li, M., Liu, Y.: Tagoram: real-time tracking of mobile RFID tags to high precision using COTS devices. In: 20th International Conference on Mobile Computing and Networking, pp. 237–248. ACM Press, Hawaii (2014)
4. Zhang, T.C.: Wireless positioning system based on LF wake-up and ELM. Transducer Microsyst. Technol. **146**, 102–104 (2016)
5. Wang, J.W., Xie, Y., Ji-Sheng, W.U.: Design & implementation of digital warehouse management system based on RFID. Logistics Technol. **28**, 130–132 (2009)
6. Ni, L.M., Liu, Y., Lau, Y.C., et al.: LANDMARC: indoor location sensing using active RFID. Wirel. Netw. **10**, 701–710 (2004)
7. Wang, P.: The Design And Application of Combinational RFID Positioning System Based on Multi-frequency. Xidian University (2014)
8. Wu, Y.P.: Design of the Antenna for the Dual-frequency Positioning System Based on RFID. Xidian University (2014)

Mean Squared Error vs. Frame Potential for Unsupervised Variable Selection

Federico Zocco and Seán McLoone[(✉)]

School of Electronics, Electrical Engineering and Computer Science,
Queen's University Belfast, Belfast, Northern Ireland
{fzocco01,s.mcloone}@qub.ac.uk

Abstract. Forward Selection Component Analysis (FSCA) provides a pragmatic solution to the NP-hard unsupervised variable selection problem, but is not guaranteed to be optimal due to the multi-modal nature of the mean squared error (MSE) selection metric used. Frame potential (FP) is a metric that has recently been shown to yield near-optimal greedy sensor selection performance for linear inverse problems. This paper explores if FP offers similar benefits in the unsupervised variable selection context. In addition, the backward elimination counterpart of FSCA is introduced for the first time (BECA) and compared with forward and backward FP based variable selection on a number of simulated and real world datasets. It is concluded that FP does not improve on FSCA and that while BECA yields comparable results to FSCA it is not a competitive alternative due to its much higher computational complexity.

Keywords: Unsupervised dimensionality reduction · Variable selection · Frame potential · Greedy algorithm

1 Introduction

Principal Component Analysis (PCA) is a powerful technique for unsupervised dimensionality reduction, but as the resulting reduced representation is a linear combination of all variables, it is not, in general, straightforward to use it to identify a subset of key variables [2]. This is especially true if there is a high level of correlation among candidate variables. Various enhancements to PCA have been developed, such as SCoTLASS [4], DSPCA [5], sparse PCA [6]. These attempt to constrain PCA to produce sparse solutions, but are generally computationally intensive and do not necessarily yield good variable selection.

Directly solving the unsupervised variable selection problem is an NP-hard combinatorial optimization problem, and quickly becomes intractable as the number of candidate variables increases. Therefore, sub-optimal approaches which approximately solve the problem are generally employed. These fall into three categories: convex optimization relaxations of the cardinality constraint

© Springer Nature Singapore Pte Ltd. 2017
D. Yue et al. (Eds.): LSMS/ICSEE 2017, Part II, CCIS 762, pp. 353–362, 2017.
DOI: 10.1007/978-981-10-6373-2_36

such as [7], heuristic approaches such as the aforementioned PCA enhancements, and greedy search methods such as Forward Selection Component Analysis (FSCA) [3].

Mathematically the unsupervised variable selection problem can be stated as follows. Given a dataset $\boldsymbol{X} \in \mathbb{R}^{m \times v}$ with m measurements of v variables, and an index set $\mathcal{N} = \{1, 2, ..., v\}$ of the columns of $\boldsymbol{X}$ we wish to find the subset $\mathcal{S}$ of length k of the columns of $\boldsymbol{X}$ that best approximates $\boldsymbol{X}$ according to some metric, $G(\mathcal{S})$, that is:

$$S^* = \underset{\mathcal{S} \subset \mathcal{N}, |\mathcal{S}|=k}{\arg \min} \ G(\mathcal{S}) \tag{1}$$

In algorithms such as FSCA and sparse PCA $G(\mathcal{S})$ is the reconstruction error of the optimum linear reconstruction of $\boldsymbol{X}(= \boldsymbol{X}([\mathcal{N}])$ by $\boldsymbol{X}([\mathcal{S}])$, that is

$$G(\mathcal{S}) = \frac{1}{mv} ||\boldsymbol{X} - \hat{\boldsymbol{X}}([\mathcal{S}])||_F^2 \tag{2}$$

where $\hat{\boldsymbol{X}}([\mathcal{S}]) = \boldsymbol{X}([\mathcal{S}])\boldsymbol{X}([\mathcal{S}])^\dagger \boldsymbol{X}$. Here, for a generic matrix $\boldsymbol{M}$, the notation $\boldsymbol{M}^\dagger$ signifies the Moore-Penrose pseudoinverse of $\boldsymbol{M}$, $\boldsymbol{M}([\mathcal{R}])$ is a matrix containing only the columns of $\boldsymbol{M}$ specified by index set $\mathcal{R}$, and $||\boldsymbol{M}||_F$ is the Frobenius norm of $\boldsymbol{M}$. Essentially (2) is the mean squared error (MSE) of the approximation, or equivalently a proxy for the variance explained metric $V_{\boldsymbol{X}}(\mathcal{S})$ if the columns of $\boldsymbol{X}$ are mean-centred, that is:

$$V_{\boldsymbol{X}}(\mathcal{S}) = 100 \cdot \left(1 - mv\frac{G(\mathcal{S})}{||\boldsymbol{X}||_F^2}\right) \tag{3}$$

Hence, minimizing $G(\mathcal{S})$ is equivalent to maximizing the variance explained.

Recently a metric referred to as the frame potential (FP) has been shown to guarantee near-optimal sensor selection solutions in terms of MSE for linear inverse problems when using a greedy selection algorithm [8]. The frame potential of a matrix $\boldsymbol{X}$ is defined as

$$FP(\boldsymbol{X}) = \sum_{i,j=1}^{v} |\langle \boldsymbol{x}_i, \boldsymbol{x}_j \rangle|^2 = \sum_{i,j=1}^{m} |\langle \overrightarrow{\boldsymbol{x}_i}, \overrightarrow{\boldsymbol{x}_j} \rangle|^2 \tag{4}$$

where $\boldsymbol{x}_i$ and $\overrightarrow{\boldsymbol{x}_i}$ are the i-th column and i-th row of $\boldsymbol{X}$, respectively [12], and minimizing it encourages orthogonality among the selected variables. Its attractiveness with regard to greedy selection algorithms arises from the *submodularity* property [8–10], which is defined as follows.

Definition 1. *(Submodular function [8]) Given three sets $\mathcal{X}$, $\mathcal{Y}$ and $\mathcal{N}$ such that $\mathcal{X} \subset \mathcal{Y} \subset \mathcal{N}$ and given an element $i \in \mathcal{N} \backslash \mathcal{Y}$, a function G is submodular if it satisfies $G(\mathcal{X} \cup i) - G(\mathcal{X}) \geq G(\mathcal{Y} \cup i) - G(\mathcal{Y})$.*

The significance of this property is that in the field of combinatorial optimization it has been proven that greedy maximization of normalised, monotone, submodular functions is near-optimal in the sense of being bounded to be within a factor $(1 - e^{-1})$ of the global maximum [11], that is:

$$G(\mathcal{S}_{\text{greedy}}) \geq (1 - e^{-1})G(\mathcal{S}_{\text{opt}}) \tag{5}$$

where $\mathcal{S}_{\text{opt}} = \underset{\mathcal{S} \subset \mathcal{N}, |\mathcal{S}| = k}{\arg \max} G(\mathcal{S})$. Ranieri et al. [8] showed that the FP based cost function

$$F(\mathcal{Q}) = FP(\boldsymbol{X}) - FP(\boldsymbol{X}([\mathcal{N} \backslash \mathcal{Q}])) \tag{6}$$

is a normalized, monotone and submodular function with respect to $\mathcal{Q}$, and hence satisfies the optimality bound requirements. Maximizing $F(\mathcal{Q})$ is equivalent to minimizing $FP(\mathcal{S})$, where $\mathcal{S} = \mathcal{N} \backslash \mathcal{Q}$.

The sensor selection problem considered by Ranieri et al. [8] can be expressed as $\boldsymbol{f} = \boldsymbol{X}\boldsymbol{\alpha}$, where $\boldsymbol{f} \in \mathbb{R}^{m \times 1}$ is the measured physical field, $\boldsymbol{\alpha} \in \mathbb{R}^{v \times 1}$ are the parameters to be estimated and $\boldsymbol{X} \in \mathbb{R}^{m \times v}$ is a known linear model. Then, given a limited number of sensor locations $r < m$ corresponding to the rows specified in the index set $\overrightarrow{\mathcal{S}}$, and denoting $\boldsymbol{X}([(\overrightarrow{\mathcal{S}})])$ as the matrix containing the rows of $\boldsymbol{X}$ indexed by $\overrightarrow{\mathcal{S}}$, solving the sensor placement problem equates to minimizing

$$G(\overrightarrow{\mathcal{S}}) = MSE(\hat{\boldsymbol{\alpha}}(\overrightarrow{\mathcal{S}})) = \|\hat{\boldsymbol{\alpha}}(\overrightarrow{\mathcal{S}}) - \boldsymbol{\alpha}\|_2^2 \tag{7}$$

with respect to $\overrightarrow{\mathcal{S}}$, subject to $|\overrightarrow{\mathcal{S}}| = r$, where $\hat{\boldsymbol{\alpha}}(\overrightarrow{\mathcal{S}}) = \boldsymbol{X}([(\overrightarrow{\mathcal{S}})])^{\dagger} \boldsymbol{f}([\overrightarrow{\mathcal{S}}])$.

Ranieri et al. [8] showed that by employing a backward elimination greedy search algorithm to maximize (6) near optimal MSE performance can be obtained. It should be noted that a near-optimal solution in terms of FP does not guarantee near-optimality with regards to the MSE. In the case of the sensor selection inverse problem considered in [8], the authors show that a strong link exists between the MSE of the model parameters being estimates ($\boldsymbol{\alpha}$) and FP, with the result that a near-optimal solution is guaranteed for that specific problem formulation. However, for the general unsupervised variable selection problem, where the focus is on the MSE of the reconstruction of $\boldsymbol{X}$, and not the MSE of the model parameters, such links are not readily established and hence MSE performance is not guaranteed. Nevertheless, it is interesting to explore if optimizing with respect to FP with its *orthogonality encouraging* property provides performance benefits over FSCA, which is a greedy forward selection algorithm that directly optimizes with respect to the reconstruction MSE. As such, this paper presents an empirical investigation of the performance of FP versus reconstruction MSE as a variable selection metric for unsupervised variable selection problems. The standard FSCA algorithm performs variable selection using forward selection, while the FP algorithm in [8] uses backward elimination. Therefore, to enable a fair comparison, forward and backward versions of each algorithm are considered. These are denoted FSCA, BECA, FSFP and BEFP.

The remainder of the paper is organized as follows: Sect. 2 introduces the greedy selection algorithms under investigation. Section 3 presents the results of two simulated experiments, while Sect. 4 presents the results for two real world cases. Finally, conclusions are provided in Sect. 5 The nomenclature used is as follows: matrices are denoted by bold capital letters, vectors are denoted by bold lowercase letters, $\boldsymbol{X}_0$ and $\boldsymbol{X}_u$ are the data matrix variants of $\boldsymbol{X}$ with zero mean columns and one norm columns, respectively.

2   Algorithms

The four greedy unsupervised variable selection algorithms investigated are:

1. Forward Selection Component Analysis (**FSCA**): The implementation used here is equivalent to, but less computationally efficient than the algorithms presented in [3], and is used to allow direct comparison with the FP selection criteria.
2. Backward Elimination Component Analysis (**BECA**): This implements the classic backward elimination algorithm, where all variables are initially selected and then the least important variables are successively eliminated using the change in reconstruction MSE as the selection metric.
3. Forward Selection Frame Potential (**FSFP**): This implements the forward selection approach using $F(\mathcal{Q})$ in (6) as the selection metric.
4. Backward Elimination Frame Potential (**BEFP**): This uses the backward elimination approach of BECA but with MSE replaced by $F(\mathcal{Q})$ as the selection metric.

The pseudo-code for the forward selection and backward elimination algorithms is presented in General Algorithm 1 and General Algorithm 2, respectively, where the *Selector* flag allows selection of the specific algorithm of interest. Note that the FP algorithms use X_u instead of X, as recommended in [8], as this has been found to improve selection performance.

General algorithm 1. Forward greedy variable selection

Input: $X, k, Selector$
Output: s
  Initialisation: $s = [\,], a = [1, 2, 3, ..., v]$
  for $j = 1$ to k **do**
    switch *Selector* **do**
      case FSCA
        (a) $\hat{\Theta}(a_i) = X_0([s, a_i])^\dagger X_0$
        (b) $\hat{X}_0(a_i) = X_0([s, a_i])\hat{\Theta}(a_i)$
        (c) $a_{i*} = \arg\min_{a_i} ||X_0 - \hat{X}_0(a_i)||_F^2$

      case FSFP
        (a) $a_{i*} = \arg\max_{a_i}\{FP(X_u) - FP(X_u([s, a_i]))\}$

    end switch
    $s = [s, a_{i*}], a = a\backslash a_{i*}$
  end for

In all experiments conducted, algorithm performance is evaluated using the percentage of dataset variance explained by reconstruction using the selected variables, as defined in (3) (with $X = X_0$).

General algorithm 2. Backward greedy variable elimination

Input: $X, k, Selector$

Output: s

Initialisation: $s = [\,], a = [1, 2, 3, ..., v]$

for $j = 1$ to $(v - k)$ do

    switch *Selector* do

        case BECA

            (a) $\hat{\Theta}(a_i) = X_0([a \backslash a_i])^\dagger X_0$

            (b) $\hat{X}_0(a_i) = X_0([a \backslash a_i]) \hat{\Theta}(a_i)$

            (c) $a_{i*} = \arg \min\limits_{a_i} ||X_0 - \hat{X}_0(a_i)||_F^2$

        case BEFP

            (a) $a_{i*} = \arg \max\limits_{a_i} \{FP(X_u) - FP(X_u([a \backslash a_i]))\}$

    end switch

    $a = a \backslash a_{i*}$

end for

$s = a$

---

3 Simulated Case Studies

This section presents results comparing FSCA, BECA, FSFP and BEFP on two simulated case studies introduced in [3]. Since PCA provides an upper bound on the achievable variance explained by variable selection algorithms for a fixed number of components [3], the algorithms are also benchmarked against PCA. Following [1], the performance comparison focuses on variable selection to achieve 99% variance explained. The number of variables/components needed to achieve 99% variance explained is denoted as $k_{99\%}$.

3.1 Simulated Dataset 1: Four Distinct Variables

The generation of this dataset begins by defining four base variables w_0, x_0, y_0, $z_0 \sim N(0, 1)$, 20 noise variables $\epsilon_1, \ldots, \epsilon_{20} \sim N(0, 0.1)$ and two larger noise variables $\epsilon_{21}, \epsilon_{22} \sim N(0, 0.4)$. These are then used to define the dataset $X = [w_0, \ldots, w_5, x_0, \ldots, x_5, y_0, \ldots, y_5, z_0, \ldots, z_5, h_1, h_2] \in \mathbb{R}^{n \times 26}$, where the columns of X are n realizations of the variables $\{w_i = w_0 + \epsilon_i\}_{i=1,\ldots,5}$, $\{x_i = x_0 + \epsilon_{i+5}\}_{i=1,\ldots,5}$, $\{y_i = y_0 + \epsilon_{i+10}\}_{i=1,\ldots,5}$, $\{z_i = z_0 + \epsilon_{i+15}\}_{i=1,\ldots,5}$, $h_1 = w_0 + x_0 + \epsilon_{21}$ and $h_2 = y_0 + z_0 + \epsilon_{22}$. Hence, the dataset is highly redundant with just 4 independent variables. The algorithms have been evaluated over 200 realizations of X with $n = 1000$. The results reported are the average performance over the 200 realizations.

Figure 1(a) shows the percentage variance explained (V_X) with respect to the variance explained by PCA (V_{PCA}) as a function of k. Among the four algorithms, only FSCA shows a significantly different trend, rapidly achieving 95%, but then showing no improvement until $k = 5$. With reference to the $k_{99\%}$ results in Table 1, FSCA performs best, followed by BECA and FSFP. BEFP is inferior to the other algorithms requiring 21 variables to achieve the 99% target.

3.2   Simulated Dataset 2: Block Redundancy

This dataset is defined as follows: $\boldsymbol{X} = [\boldsymbol{X}^0, \boldsymbol{X}^1] \in \mathbb{R}^{m \times v}$, where $\boldsymbol{X}^0 \in \mathbb{R}^{m \times u}$ with $\boldsymbol{X}_{i,j}^0 \sim N(0,1)$, $\boldsymbol{X}^1 = \boldsymbol{X}^0 \cdot \boldsymbol{\Phi} + \boldsymbol{E}$, $\boldsymbol{\Phi} \in \mathbb{R}^{u \times (v-u)}$ with $\boldsymbol{\Phi}_{i,j} \sim N(0,1)$ and $\boldsymbol{E} \in \mathbb{R}^{m \times (v-u)}$ with $\boldsymbol{E}_{i,j} \sim N(0, 0.1)$. Hence, this dataset contains $u \leq v$ independent variables. Three different (u, v) combinations are considered: (10, 30), (15, 50) and (20, 75). Results are presented in each case for the average of 200 realizations of $\boldsymbol{X}$ with $m = 1000$.

Figure 1(b) shows the performance of each algorithm relative to PCA for different values of k when $u = 10$. As can be seen, FSCA yields the best results followed closely by BECA. Both FP algorithms perform poorly for this problem when $k < 10$, with the forward implementation superior to the backward implementation. As k increases the differences between the algorithms decrease, and they all converge at $k = 10$. Table 2 shows the $k_{99\%}$ results and the corresponding V_X in parentheses for the different (u, v) combinations. All algorithms need u variables to achieve the 99% threshold. The difference between the worst and the best is less than 0.2%. To demonstrate the robustness of the results, box plots showing the distribution of the variance explained by each algorithm over the 200 realizations are presented in Fig. 2 for the case $u = 10$, for $k = 5$ and $k = 10$.

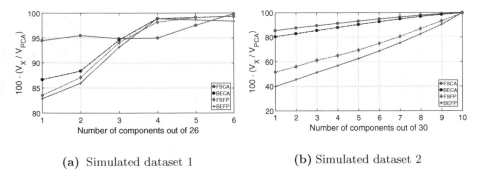

(a) Simulated dataset 1   (b) Simulated dataset 2

Fig. 1. Percentage explained variance with respect to V_{PCA} for different values of k for: (a) Simulated dataset 1 and; (b) Simulated dataset 2 for $u = 10$.

Table 1. (Simulated dataset 1) values of $k_{99\%}$ achieved and the corresponding V_X. In bold the winner algorithm after PCA.

	PCA	**FSCA**	BECA	FSFP	BEFP
$k_{99\%}$	5	**6**	8	8	21
V_X	99.01	**99.30**	99.07	99.06	99.14

Table 2. (Simulated dataset 2) values of $k_{99\%}$ achieved and, between brackets, the corresponding V_X.

u	v	PCA	FSCA	BECA	FSFP	BEFP
10	30	10(99.95)	10(99.72)	10(99.86)	10(99.75)	10(99.89)
15	50	15(99.96)	15(99.76)	15(99.89)	15(99.69)	15(99.93)
20	75	20(99.97)	20(99.77)	20(99.90)	20(99.68)	20(99.95)

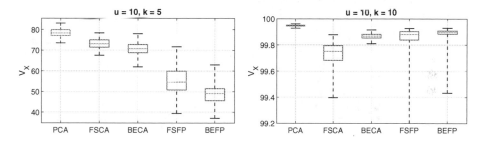

Fig. 2. (Simulated dataset 2) Boxplot of V_X by each algorithm for the case $u = 10$ with $k = 5$ (left) and $k = 10$ (right).

4   Real World Case Studies

In this section the algorithms are compared on two different real world datasets: wafer metrology data from a semiconductor manufacturing process and gas sensor array data collected from a gas delivery system.

4.1   Real Dataset 1: Wafer Site Optimization

This dataset, which is described in detail in [1], consists of wafer metrology data from a semiconductor manufacturing process for a set of 316 wafers. The goal is to improve the efficiency of wafer profile monitoring by reducing the number of measured sites from a candidate set of 50 sites, without discarding valuable information. This can be cast as a variable selection problem, with the columns of the data matrix representing the candidate sites and the rows representing the measurements from individual wafers, hence $X \in \mathbb{R}^{316 \times 50}$. The goal is to select the number of sites needed to achieve 99% variance explained. The results of the analysis of this dataset are presented in Fig. 3(a) and in Tables 3 and 4.

Figure 3(a) and Table 3 show that the MSE-based algorithms (FSCA and BECA) substantially outperform the FP-based algorithms for this problem achieving consistently higher explained variance for a given number of selected variables. FSCA yields the best performance for low values of k while BECA is marginally superior at higher values. Both algorithms identify 7 sites as necessary to achieve 99% variance explained. In contrast, the best FP-based result is 10 sites.

Table 3. (Real dataset 1) Values of $k_{99\%}$ achieved and the corresponding V_X.

	PCA	FSCA	**BECA**	FSFP	BEFP
$k_{99\%}$	5	7	**7**	10	11
V_X	99.07	99.02	**99.17**	99.24	99.17

Table 4. (Real dataset 1) Mean, minimum and standard deviation of V_X for the unmeasured sites using the sites selected by FSCA and BECA as regressors.

	Best 7 sites	Mean V_X	Min V_X	σ
FSCA	45, 27, 1, 24, 9, 49, 14	98.74	93.74	1.34
BECA	4, 15, 16, 31, 42, 44, 48	99.06	96.70	0.86

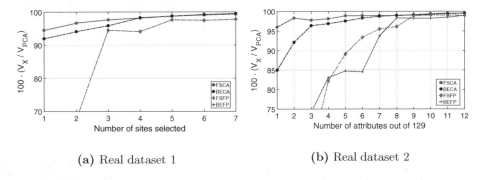

(a) Real dataset 1   (b) Real dataset 2

Fig. 3. Percentage explained variance with respect to V_{PCA} for different values of k for: (a) Real dataset 1 (left) and; (b) Real dataset 2 (right).

As described in [1], the unmeasured sites can be estimated from the measured sites using a linear model with the selected sites as regressors. Table 4 provides a comparison of the performance of the seven sites selected by FSCA and BECA with regard to their ability to predict the 43 unmeasured sites on each wafer. Performance is expressed in terms of the mean, standard deviation and minimum variance explained over the 43 unmeasured sites. As can be seen, BECA selects completely different sites to FSCA, and in this instance produces significantly better results.

4.2   Real Dataset 2: Gas Sensor Array Analysis

This dataset was selected from the UCI Machine Learning Repository [13,14] and consists of measurements from 16 chemical sensors exposed to 6 gases at different concentration levels gathered in a gas delivery platform facility at the BioCircuits Institute, University of California, San Diego. From each sensor, 8 features have been extracted giving a total of 128 variables plus the concentration of the analyte gas. Here, only the data from batch 3 is considered giving a dataset

$X \in \mathbb{R}^{1586 \times 129}$ for analysis. Due to the large variation in the magnitude of the variables in the dataset, all variables were standardized prior to analysis. Results are presented in Fig. 3(b) and Table 5 for the standardized dataset.

Table 5. (Real dataset 2) Values of $k_{99\%}$ achieved and the corresponding V_X.

	PCA	FSCA	**BECA**	FSFP	BEFP
$k_{99\%}$	8	12	**12**	17	17
V_X	99.00	99.05	**99.07**	99.02	99.01

Here again, the MSE-based algorithms outperform FP, particularly for lower numbers of selected variables. In addition, to achieve 99% variance explained FSFP and BEFP need 17 variables while FSCA and BECA achieve the same performance with only 12 variables.

5   Conclusions

Motivated by its effectiveness in a recently reported optimum sensor placement application, this paper has explored the value of FP as an alternative to MSE as a selection metric in unsupervised variable selection problems. Both forward selection and backward elimination greedy selection algorithms have been considered. The results of two simulated and two real case studies show that, in general, for a fixed number of selected variables, selection based on MSE significantly outperforms FP, and therefore FP is not a good choice for this type of problem. An explanation for this is that while greedy FP-based algorithms enjoy guarantees on near-optimal solutions in terms of FP this does not automatically extend to guarantees on MSE performance. In general FSCA outperforms BECA when the number of variables selected is low, but BECA has comparable and sometimes marginally better performance when approaching 99% variance explained. However, FSCA has the advantage of being computationally much more efficient, and therefore is the preferred algorithm.

Acknowledgments. The first author gratefully acknowledges Irish Manufacturing Research (IMR) for its financial support of his PhD.

References

1. Prakash, P., et al.: Optimal wafer site selection using forward selection component analysis. In: 2012 23rd Annual SEMI Advanced Semiconductor Manufacturing Conference (ASMC), pp. 91–96. IEEE (2012)
2. McCabe, G.P.: Principal variables. Technometrics **26**(2), 137–144 (1984)
3. Puggini, L., McLoone, S.: Forward selection component analysis: algorithms and applications. IEEE Transactions on Pattern Analysis and Machine Intelligence (2017). doi:10.1109/TPAMI.2017.2648792

4. Jolliffe, I.T., et al.: A modified principal component technique based on the lasso. J. Comput. Graph. Stat. **12**(3), 531–547 (2003)
5. d'Aspremont, A., et al.: A direct formulation for sparse PCA using semidefinite programming. SIAM Rev. **49**(3), 434–448 (2007)
6. Zou, H., et al.: Sparse principal component analysis. J. Comput. Graph. Stat. **15**(2), 265–286 (2006)
7. Masaeli, M., et al.: Convex principal feature selection. In: SDM. SIAM, pp. 619–628 (2010)
8. Ranieri, J., et al.: Near-optimal sensor placement for linear inverse problems. IEEE Trans. Sig. Process. **62**(5), 1135–1146 (2014)
9. Das, A., Kempe, D.: Algorithms for subset selection in linear regression. In: Proceedings of ACM Symposium on Theory of Computing (STOC) (2009)
10. Das, A., Kempe, D.: Submodular meets spectral: greedy algorithms for subset selection, sparse approximation and dictionary selection. In: Proceedings of International Conference on Machine Learning (ICML) (2011)
11. Nemhauser, G., et al.: An analysis of approximations for maximizing submodular set functions-I. Math. Prog. **14**, 265–294 (1978)
12. Waldron, S.: Generalised welch bound equality sequences are tight frames. Department of Mathematics, University of Auckland, Auckland, New Zealand, Technical report (2003)
13. Vergara, A., et al.: Chemical gas sensor drift compensation using classifier ensembles. Sens. Actuators B: Chem. **166**, 320–329 (2012)
14. Rodriguez-Lujan, I., et al.: On the calibration of sensor arrays for pattern recognition using the minimal number of experiments. Chemometr. Intell. Lab. Syst. **130**, 123–134 (2014)

Zero-Shot Image Classification via Coupled Discriminative Dictionary Learning

Lehui Liu, Songsong Wu[(⊠)], Runqing Chen, and Mengquan Zhou

Nanjing University of Post and Telecommunication, Nanjing, China
raleighliu@163.com, sswu@njupt.edu.cn,
crq13843838438@163.com, 18251957682@126.com

Abstract. In this paper, we propose a Coupled Discriminative Dictionary Learning framework to tackle the zero-shot image classification problem. Instead of the original attribute vectors and sample feature vectors, we use their corresponding sparse coefficients attained from sparse coding to do the classification. The purpose of our framework is that, when an unseen-class sample shows during test time, we first attain its corresponding sparse coefficient through learned feature dictionary. Then we use a mapping method to map it to the attribute sparse coefficients category histogram domain where we can accomplish the classification. We evaluate our method performance on two benchmark datasets for zero-shot image classification. The results are compelling to other state-of-the-art, especially on fine-grained dataset.

Keywords: Coupled Discriminative Dictionary Learning · Zero-shot image classification · Sparse representation · Category histogram

1 Introduction

Traditional supervised model is faced with an overwhelming problem. According to Bishop and Bishop [1], recognition of target class samples always requires sufficient manually labeled data. However, it seems impossible to collect well-labeled data for every classes. Thus, zero-shot image classification [2–6] has been proposed to cope with this problem.

Zero-shot image classification often gives the following situation: during training time, we are given side information of all the classes. However, we are given training samples only for some of the classes called seen classes. The biggest difference between traditional supervised learning and zero-shot image classification is that we lack the training sample images of the rest of the classes called unseen classes.

Most of the exist methods mainly focus on using side information such as attributes [7–12], Words or phrases [13–15], Learned classifiers [5, 16]. When the sample of the novel class shows up during test, it will generate the corresponding side information vectors. Since the side information is shared among all classes, the result will be reached. Some further works learn an embedding space and the mapping function between side information space and embedding space as well as the one between sample space and embedding space [14, 15, 17–19].

D. Yue et al. (Eds.): LSMS/ICSEE 2017, Part II, CCIS 762, pp. 363–372, 2017.
DOI: 10.1007/978-981-10-6373-2_37

Inspired by the SSE [20], our method does not include the prediction of side information. However, the method used in the SSE works less accurately in the fine-grained databases such as CUB-200-2011. One of the reason is that the embedded histogram space used in the SSE has a limited number of bars. The number of bars is restricted by the class number in the database. As a result, we introduce a coupled dictionary [21] framework into zero-shot image classification, which can also learn the relationships between class but an unlimited number of bars in the histogram.

Shown in Fig. 1, inspired by semi-coupled dictionary learning, we manage to learn coupled dictionaries over the attribute domain (D_1) and feature domain (D_2) and the mapping method W simultaneously.

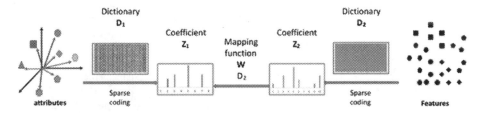

Fig. 1. Our method uses sparse coding method to embed attributes and features into coefficient domain respectively. Blue shapes in attribute space represent the attribute vectors of unseen classes. In zero-shot image classification problem, we lack the corresponding unseen class instances in the feature space. (Color figure online)

Our method mainly contributes in two aspects. First, we introduce the coupled dictionary framework into zero-shot image classification, which is suitable for cross-domain problem. Second, we improve the accuracy of the zero-shot image classification compared to the traditional methods, especially we improve the accuracy on the fine-grained databases.

The rest of the paper is organized as follows. Section 2 provides a review of the related work; Sect. 3 illustrates the details of our coupled dictionary learning method; Sect. 4 presents our experimental evaluation; Sect. 5 presents the discussion and our conclusions.

2 Related Work

2.1 Zero-Shot Image Classification

Since side information shared among seen classes and unseen classes, most of the existed methods rely on side information learning to solve zero-shot image classification. Side information can be categorized into different sources. Attributes are widely used side information in zero-shot image classification. Besides attribute, methods using word vector from textual databases [13–15] are also trending. Moreover, [16] proposed that we can use learned classifiers to reconstruct the classifier for zero-shot image classification. Most of the above-mentioned literature rely on predicting the side information vector for the novel unseen class sample, which is suboptimal according to [19].

Then further studies introduce the label embedding methods [14, 15, 17–19]. These methods manage to find an embedding space and corresponding mapping functions where we can classify the samples in a direct way. However, these methods may suffer from missing or incorrectly annotated side information according to [20].

2.2 Coupled Dictionary Learning

Coupled dictionary learning has shown great performance in different areas [21, 22, 23]. [21] proposed a semi-coupled dictionary learning framework that can be applied to super-resolution. And [21, 24] shows that the frame work can also be used to the field of photo-synthesis.

According to Coupled Dictionary and Feature Space Learning with Applications to Cross-Domain Image Synthesis and Recognition [24], they learn the dictionaries to describe the relationship between cross-domain images. Because of the outstanding performance coupled dictionary shows on transfer knowledge from different domains. We think it's reasonable to introduce the framework to zero-shot image classification.

3 Coupled Discriminative Dictionary Learning

3.1 Model

Terminology and Notation. In this section, we summarize all the terminology and notations we used in our framework. In the zero-shot image classification setting, we are given the attribute matrix $C = \{(c_i, y_i) | c_i \in \mathbb{R}^{d_s}, y \in S \cup U, i = 1, \ldots, N\}$, where S denotes the label set for the seen classes, y_i denotes the corresponding label for c_i; U denotes the label set for the unseen classes; N denotes the number of N' seen classes and N'' unseen classes put together. Therefore, $N = N' + N''$; d_s denotes the dimension of attributes. Besides, we are given the training set which only contains the samples for seen classes $T = \{(x_i, y_i) | x_i \in \mathbb{R}^{d_t \times M}, y_i \in S, i = 1, \ldots, M\}$, where M denotes the number of training samples, y_i denotes the corresponding label for x_i, d_t denotes the dimension of features.

In this paper, we use sparse coding method to get the learned attribute dictionary and the corresponding sparse coefficients in the attribute domain. Meanwhile, we in the feature domain. We use the sparse coefficients instead of the original vectors because we want to explore the similarity among the attributes and features of different classes. Then we learn a mapping function between the two coefficients domain since they have different dimensions.

To model this rule function, we can minimize the following object function:

$$\min_{D_1,Z_1,D_2,Z_2,W} E_c(D_1,C) + E_x(D_2,X) + J_{map}(Z_1,Z_2,W) + E_{reg}(D_1,Z_1,D_2,Z_2,W) \quad (1)$$

Our objective function in Eq. (1) includes 4 parts, where $E_c(\cdot,\cdot), E_x(\cdot,\cdot)$ represent data description error [21] via sparse coding in attribute domain and feature domain respectively; $J_{map}(\cdot,\cdot,\cdot)$ represents the target object term of regulating coefficients to separate the sample from each other in the attribute coefficient embedded space; E_{reg} is the regulation term to regulate the dictionaries, their corresponding coefficients and the mapping function.

For the first and second part, our main model is to use coupled dictionary learning to get the coefficients which can replace the original attribute vectors and sample feature vectors. Based on the SCDL [21], $E_c(D_1,C)$ and $E_x(D_2,X)$ can be depicted as $\|C - D_1Z_1\|_F^2 + \lambda_1\|Z_1\|_1$ and $\|X - D_2Z_2\|_F^2 + \lambda_2\|Z_2\|_1$, where $\|Z_1\|_1$ and $\|Z_2\|_1$ represents the sparsity constraint term of the coefficients.

For the third part, we use fisher discrimination criterion [25] to demonstrate our learning theory, which can be achieved by maximizing the between-class scatter, denoted by $S_B(Z_1)$, and minimizing the gap between mapped term WZ_2^j and its belonging class attribute coefficient Z_1^j, denoted by $S_{map}(Z_1,Z_2)$.

$$S_B(Z_1) = tr(\frac{1}{N}\sum_{i=1}^{N}(Z_1^i - P_1)(Z_1^i - P_1)^T) \quad (2)$$

$$S_{map}(Z_1,Z_2) = tr(\frac{1}{N'}\sum_{j\in S}\frac{1}{M}\sum_{l(i)=l(j)}(WZ_2^i - Z_1^j)(WZ_2^i - Z_1^j)^T) \quad (3)$$

where P_1 stands for the mean vector of Z_1, thus $P_1 = \frac{1}{N}\sum_{i=1}^{N}Z_1^i, l(i) = l(j)$ represents that the seen class feature and attribute coefficients Z_2^i and Z_1^i should belong to the same label. M_j denotes the different numbers of class j provided in the database.

However, since we lack the samples for unseen class, in the mapping gap $S_{map}(Z_1,Z_2)$ only seen class feature coefficients are mapped to the Z_1 space.

To sum up, our framework can be turned into the following coupled dictionary learning problem:

$$\min_{D_1,Z_1,D_2,Z_2,W} \|C - D_1Z_1\|_F^2 + \lambda_1\|Z_1\|_1 + \eta_1(\|X - D_2Z_2\|_F^2 + \lambda_2\|Z_2\|_1)$$
$$+ \eta_2(tr[\frac{1}{N'}\sum_{j\in S}\frac{1}{M}\sum_{l(i)=l(j)}(WZ_2^i - Z_1^j)(WZ_2^i - Z_1^j)^T])$$
$$+ \eta_3(tr[\frac{1}{N}(Z_1^i - P_1)(Z_1^i - P_1)^T]) \quad (4)$$
$$+ \lambda_w\|W\|_F^2$$

where $\lambda_1, \lambda_2, \lambda_w, \eta_1, \eta_2, \eta_3$ are the regulation parameters to balance the corresponding terms in the framework function.

3.2 Optimization Algorithm

To tackle the minimization of the objective function, basically we divide it into three main parts. Overall, we use an iteration method to solve the optimization problem.

We use FDDL [28] to cope with the initialization for its good representation power. We then have the initialized mapping function W.

With D_1, D_2, Z_2, W are fixed, the objective function can be reduced to a convex problem. And we compute $Z_1 = \left[Z_1^1, Z_1^2, \ldots, Z_1^c\right]$ class by class. When we compute Z_1^i, the rest $Z_1^j, j \neq i$ are fixed. Thus the objective function can be turned into:

$$\min_{Z_1^i} Q(Z_1^i) + \lambda_1 \left\|Z_1^i\right\|_1 \tag{5}$$

where:

$$
\begin{aligned}
Q(Z_1^i) = &\left\|C - D_1 Z_1^i\right\|_F^2 \\
&+ \eta_2 tr[\frac{1}{N' \cdot M_i} \sum_{l(i)=l(j)} (WZ_2^j - Z_1^i)(WZ_2^j - Z_1^i)^T] \\
&+ \eta_3 tr[\frac{1}{N}(Z_1^i - P_1)(Z_1^i \quad P_1)^T]
\end{aligned}
\tag{6}
$$

M_i represents the number of samples in the ith class. We employ the Iterative Projection Method(IPM) [27] to solve the above-mentioned equation. All the terms in the equation are differentiable except $\left\|Z_1^i\right\|$.

Algorithm.1. Coding Algorithm for coefficient
1. **Input**: σ, τ >0.
2. **Initialization**: $Z_1^i = 0, h = 1$
3. **While** convergence and the maximum iteration number are not reached **do:** $h = h + 1$ $Z_1^{i(h)} = S_{\tau/\sigma}(Z_1^{i(h-1)} - \frac{1}{2\sigma} \nabla Q(Z_1^{i(h-1)}))$ where $\nabla Q(Z_1^{i(h-1)})$ is the derivative of the $Q(Z_1^{i(h-1)})$ and $S_{\tau/\sigma}$ is a soft thresholding function defined in [29].   **end**
4. **Output:** $Z_1^i = Z_1^{i(h)}$

With Z_1, D_2, Z_2, W are fixed, D_1 can be refined as follows:

$$\min_{D_1} \|C - D_1 Z_1\|_F^2 \ s.t \ \forall i, \|d_{1,i}\|_{l_2} \le 1 \tag{7}$$

The above equation is a quadratically constrained quadratic program problem (QCQP) and can be solved by applying the atom-by-atom updating algorithm in [26].

With D_1, D_2, Z_1, Z_2 are fixed, we can update the mapping function W by using the following equation:

$$W = B(\lambda_w I + A)^{-1} \tag{8}$$

where: I is an identity matrix, $A = \sum_{j \in S} \frac{Z_2^j Z_2^{jT}}{M_j}$, $B = \sum_{j \in S} \widetilde{Z_1^j} Z_2^{jT}$. $\widetilde{Z_1^j}$ is the matrix that take M_j Z_1^j s as its column vector.

The refinement algorithm of Z_2 and D_2 is similar to the way we do to refine Z_1 and D_1 by using IPM [27] and atom-by-atom updating algorithm in [26].

To sum up our algorithm, we list our whole optimization process in Algorithm 2.

Algorithm.2. Zero-Shot Image Classification via CDDL
1.   **Input:** The attribute matrix C , The feature matrix X ,   Parameters $\lambda_1, \lambda_2, \lambda_w, \eta_1, \eta_2, \eta_3$

2.   **Update:**
     2.1 **Initialize** D_1, Z_1, D_2, Z_2, W
     2.2 **While** convergence and the maximum iteration number are not reached **do:**
             fix D_1, D_2, Z_2, W , refine Z_1 ;
             fix Z_1, D_2, Z_2, W , refine D_1 ;
             fix D_1, D_2, Z_1, W , refine Z_2 ;
             fix Z_1, D_1, Z_2, W , refine D_2 ;
             fix Z_1, D_1, Z_2, D_2 , refine W ;
     end

3.   **Output:**   Learned dictionary of attributes D_1 ; Learned dictionary of features D_2 ; Learned coefficient of attributes Z_1 ; Learned coefficient of features Z_2 ; The mapping method W between Z_1 and Z_2

3.3   Test

When the test sample x^* of an unseen class shows during test time, we first can derive the corresponding feature coefficient z_2^* by using the learned dictionary D_2.

Then we use our learned mapping function W to map z_2^* to the Z_1 space. Finally, we compare $W z_2^*$ with $Z_1^i, i \in U$ to determine the label for the test sample.

Thus, our zero-shot image classification test rule is defined as followed:

$$i^* = \arg\max_{i\in U} f(x, c) = \arg\max_{i\in U} <WZ_2^*, Z_1^i> \qquad (9)$$

4 Experiment

4.1 Datasets

To evaluate our method's performance on zero-shot image classification problem, we test our method on three benchmark datasets, i.e. aPascal & aYahoo (aP&Y) [7] and Animals With Attributes (AWA) [8]. Both aP&Y and AWA are benchmark databases often used to evaluate the performance of zero-shot image classification methods. Table 1 gives the settings of our evaluation.

Table 1. The statics of the two benchmark datasets we used in our experiment.

	Total		Train set		Test set	
	Images	Classes	Images	Classes	Images	Classes
aP&Y	15339	32	12695	20	2644	12
AwA	30475	50	24295	40	6180	10

We follow other state-of-art settings to maintain the same input for the purpose of comparison. For all the datasets, we use a 4096-dim CNN feature vector [20] for image samples. For side information, we use the continuous attribute vectors provided in the datasets as input. We conclude the recognition accuracy averaged over 3 trials.

Implementation Details. Our framework use FDDL [28] to initialize the dictionaries D_1, D_2 and their corresponding coefficients Z_1 and Z_2. Then we gain the initialization of mapping function W. We then follow the algorithm listed in Sect. 3 to solve the objective function optimization. As for the parameters, we set $\lambda_1, \lambda_2, \lambda_w, \eta_1, \eta_2, \eta_3 \in \{0, 10^{-3}, 10^{-2}, 10^{-1}, 1, 10, 10^2\}$ in Eq. (4) for parameters selection.

4.2 Comparison with State-of-the-Art

We use the same split of datasets as other methods. The statics of the database are summarized in Table 1. In AwA there are 50 different classes. we choose 40 classes randomly as training set and use the left 10 classes as test set. In aP&Y, we utilize the 32 classes as seen classes for training and 10 classes as unseen classes for testing.

We report absolute classification accuracy on AwA and aP&Y for direct comparison to published results. The zero-shot image classification accuracy comparison is listed in % on aP&Y and AwA. Except our results, the rest numbers are cited from their original papers. The results of the performance on the aforementioned benchmark datasets of our framework are summarized in Table 2.

Table 2. The classification accuracy (%) of the two benchmark datasets

Method	aP&Y
Farhadi *et al.*	32.5
Lampert *et al.*	19.1
Jayaraman and Grauman [29]	26.02±0.05
Romera-Paredes and Torr [30]	24.22±2.89
CDDL	**35.83**

Method	AwA
Wang and Ji	42.78
Rohrbach et al.	42.7
Yu et al.	48.3
Akata et al.	43.5
Fu et al.	47.1
Lampert et al.	57.23
Jayaraman and Grauman	43.01±0.07
Romera-Paredes and Torr	49.30±0.21
CDDL	**61.5**

First of all, we reduce our feature vectors to 100 dimensions using PCA to improve the speed of our experiments.

We can observe that our framework achieves better performance on than the baseline methods, such as DAP [7] and IAP [8]. The performance of our CDDL framework achieve the classification accuracies are 35.83% and 61.5% respectively, improves 10.25% on aP&Y dataset compared with DAP [7]. Besides, our framework improves 24.75% on the AwA dataset compared with IAP [8]. One may argue that the result improvement is related to the strong visual feature we used in the experiments, such as 4096-dim CNN feature vector. We admit that CNN-feature indeed enhance the recognition framework. Yet the gap between our work and the state-of-the-art shows that our framework do have an impact on improving the classification accuracy.

Firstly, we can observe from Fig. 2 that the value of objective function defined in Eq. (4) can decrease via more iterations and can finally converge within 10 iterations, which validates the algorithm we proposed in Sect. 3.2.

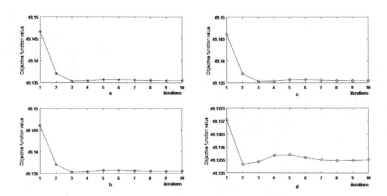

Fig. 2. (a) Objective function value decreases w.r.t. the number of iterations when Z_1 is fixed; (b) Objective function value decreases w.r.t. the number of iterations when D_1 is fixed; (c) Objective function value decreases w.r.t. the number of iterations when Z_2 is fixed; (d) Objective function value decreases w.r.t. the number of iterations when D_2 is fixed.

Since we use sparse coding to represent each sample with sparse coefficients, we suppose that our framework will work well on fine-grained datasets rather than those methods using simple feature vectors and attribute vectors.

5 Conclusion

We introduce a Coupled Discriminative Dictionary Learning (CDDL) framework to solve the zero-shot image classification. We jointly learn two dictionaries and corresponding sparse coefficients space in the attribute domain and the feature domain and learn the mapping function between the coefficient space for classification at the same time. In our experiment, we conduct our method on several benchmark databases. The result is competitive to the existed method. We will discuss about how the proposed method will perform the fine-grained databases and introduce kernel dictionary learning method to address the classification problem in our future work.

References

1. Bishop, C., Bishop, C.M.: Pattern recognition and machine learning. J. Electron. Imaging **16** (4), 140–155 (2006). Springer
2. Palatucci, M., Pomerleau, D., Hinton, G., et al.: Zero-shot learning with semantic output codes. In: International Conference on Neural Information Processing Systems, pp. 1410–1418. Curran Associates Inc. (2009)
3. Lampert, C.H., Nickisch, H., Harmeling, S.: Learning to detect unseen object classes by between-class attribute transfer. IEEE (2009)
4. Akata, Z., Perronnin, F., Harchaoui, Z., et al.: Label-embedding for attribute-based classification. In: Computer Vision and Pattern Recognition, pp. 819–826. IEEE (2013)
5. Yu, F.X., Cao, L., Feris, R.S., et al.: Designing category-level attributes for discriminative visual recognition. In: IEEE Conference on Computer Vision and Pattern Recognition, pp. 771–778. IEEE Computer Society (2013)
6. Fu, Y., Hospedales, T.M., Xiang, T., Fu, Z., Gong, S.: Transductive multi-view embedding for zero-shot recognition and annotation. In: Fleet, D., Pajdla, T., Schiele, B., Tuytelaars, T. (eds.) ECCV 2014. LNCS, vol. 8690, pp. 584–599. Springer, Cham (2014). doi:10.1007/978-3-319-10605-2_38
7. Farhadi, A., Endres, I., Hoiem, D., et al.: Describing objects by their attributes. In: IEEE Conference on Computer Vision and Pattern Recognition, CVPR 2009, pp. 1778–1785. IEEE (2009)
8. Lampert, C.H., Nickisch, H., Harmeling, S.: Attribute-based classification for zero-shot visual object categorization. IEEE Trans. Pattern Anal. Mach. Intell. **36**(3), 453–465 (2014)
9. Mensink, T., Verbeek, J., Perronnin, F., Csurka, G.: Metric learning for large scale image classification: generalizing to new classes at near-zero cost. In: Fitzgibbon, A., Lazebnik, S., Perona, P., Sato, Y., Schmid, C. (eds.) ECCV 2012. LNCS, pp. 488–501. Springer, Heidelberg (2012). doi:10.1007/978-3-642-33709-3_35
10. Parikh, D., Grauman, K.: Interactively building a discriminative vocabulary of nameable attributes. In: The IEEE Conference on Computer Vision and Pattern Recognition, CVPR 2011, DBLP, 20–25 June, Colorado Springs, Co, USA, pp. 1681–1688 (2011)

11. Duan, K., Parikh, D., Crandall, D., et al.: Discovering localized attributes for fine-grained recognition. In: Computer Vision and Pattern Recognition, pp. 3474–3481. IEEE (2012)
12. Rohrbach, M., Stark, M., Schiele, B.: Evaluating knowledge transfer and zero-shot learning in a large-scale setting. In: Computer Vision and Pattern Recognition, pp. 1641–1648. IEEE (2011)
13. Berg, T.L., Berg, A.C., Shih, J.: Automatic attribute discovery and characterization from noisy web data. In: Daniilidis, K., Maragos, P., Paragios, N. (eds.) ECCV 2010. LNCS, vol. 6311, pp. 663–676. Springer, Heidelberg (2010). doi:10.1007/978-3-642-15549-9_48
14. Frome, A., Corrado, G.S., Shlens, J., et al.: DeViSE: a deep visual-semantic embedding model. In: International Conference on Neural Information Processing Systems, pp. 2121–2129. Curran Associates Inc. (2013)
15. Socher, R., Ganjoo, M., Sridhar, H., et al.: Zero-shot learning through cross-modal transfer. In: Advances in Neural Information Processing Systems, pp. 935–943 (2013)
16. Mensink, T., Gavves, E., Snoek, C.G.M.: COSTA: co-occurrence statistics for zero-shot classification. In: Computer Vision and Pattern Recognition, pp. 2441–2448. IEEE (2014)
17. Akata, Z., Reed, S., Walter, D., et al.: Evaluation of output embeddings for fine-grained image classification. 2927–2936 (2015)
18. Norouzi, M., et al.: Zero-shot learning by convex combination of semantic embeddings. arXiv preprint arXiv:1312.5650 (2013)
19. Akata, Z., Perronnin, F., Harchaoui, Z., et al.: Label-embedding for image classification. IEEE Trans. Pattern Anal. Mach. Intell. **38**(7), 1425–1438 (2015)
20. Zhang, Z., Saligrama, V.: Zero-shot learning via semantic similarity embedding. In: IEEE International Conference on Computer Vision, pp. 4166–4174. IEEE (2015)
21. Liang, Y.: Semi-coupled dictionary learning with applications to image super-resolution and photo-sketch synthesis. In: IEEE Conference on Computer Vision and Pattern Recognition, pp. 2216–2223. IEEE Computer Society (2012)
22. Li, F., Zhang, S.: Double sparse dictionary learning for image super resolution. In: Chinese Control and Decision Conference, pp. 4344–4348. IEEE (2016)
23. Skau, E., Wohlberg, B., Krim, H., et al.: Pansharpening via coupled triple factorization dictionary learning. In: IEEE International Conference on Acoustics, Speech and Signal Processing, pp. 1234–1237. IEEE (2016)
24. Huang, D.A., Wang, Y.C.F.: Coupled dictionary and feature space learning with applications to cross-domain image synthesis and recognition. In: IEEE International Conference on Computer Vision, pp. 2496–2503. IEEE (2013)
25. Duda, R., Hart, P., Stork, D.: Pattern Classification, 2nd edn. En Broeck the Statistical Mechanics of Learning (2001)
26. Yang, M., Zhang, L., Yang, J., et al.: Metaface learning for sparse representation based face recognition. In: IEEE International Conference on Image Processing, 1601–1604. IEEE (2010)
27. Rosasco, L., Verri, A., Santoro, M., et al.: Iterative projection methods for structured sparsity regularization. Computation (2009)
28. Yang, M., Zhang, L., Feng, X., et al.: Fisher discrimination dictionary learning for sparse representation. In: International Conference on Computer Vision, pp. 543–550. IEEE (2011)
29. Jayaraman, D., Grauman, K.: Zero-shot recognition with unreliable attributes. In: NIPS, pp. 3464–3472 (2014)
30. Romera-Paredes, B., Torr, P.H.S.: An embarrassingly simple approach to zero-shot learning. In: ICML (2015)

Multivariate Fault Isolation in Presence of Outliers Based on Robust Nonnegative Garrote

Jianguo Wang[1], Zhifu Deng[1(✉)], Banghua Yang[1], Shiwei Ma[1],
Minrui Fei[1], Yuan Yao[2], and Tao Chen[3]

[1] Shanghai Key Lab of Power Station Automation Technology,
School of Mechatronical Engineering and Automation,
Shanghai University, Shanghai 200072, China
jgwang@shu.edu.cn, dzf625096527@outlook.com
[2] Department of Chemical Engineering, National Tsing-Hua University,
Hsin-Chu 30013, Taiwan
yyao@mx.nthu.edu.tw
[3] Department of Chemical and Process Engineering, University of Surrey,
Guildford GU2 7XH, UK
t.chen@surrey.ac.uk

Abstract. Fault isolation is essential to fault monitoring, which can be used to detect the cause of the fault. Commonly used methods include contribution plots, LASSO, Nonnegative garrote, construction-based methods, branch and bound algorithm (B & B), etc. However, these existing methods have shortcomings limiting their implementation when there exist vertical outliers and leverage points, Therefore, to further improve the fault prediction accuracy, this paper present a strategy based on robust nonnegative garrote (R-NNG) variable selection algorithm, which is proved to be robust to outliers in the TE process.

Keywords: Fault isolation · Variable selection · Outliers · Robust nonnegative garrote · TE process

1 Introduction

With the industrial processes expanding in scale and increasing in complexity, effective process monitoring and fault diagnosis is the key to ensure plane safety, enhance product quality and economic benefit. For complex industrial processes, accurate and mathematical models are often difficult to obtain. Even if it can be obtained, these predigested equations can only describe partial relationship of the system energy and material balance. As discussed in [1], it is proposed that the multivariate statistical process monitoring process (MSPM) mainly includes fault detection fault isolation, fault diagnosis and fault recovery. Fault detection aims to identify process abnormality

This work is supported by National Natural Science Foundation (NNSF) of China under Grant 61171145 and 61374044.

D. Yue et al. (Eds.): LSMS/ICSEE 2017, Part II, CCIS 762, pp. 373–382, 2017.
DOI: 10.1007/978-981-10-6373-2_38

after it occurs, while the target of fault isolation is to recognize the most responsible variable of the detected fault [2].

Variable selection has become a key issue in applied data analysis, since often many variables are measured. However, models including all the covariates are difficult to interpret and irrelevant variables increase the variance [3]. One method of variable selection is the least angle regression (LARS) [3], which sorts the multivariate according to its importance. The other approach is to impose a penalty term $n\lambda \sum_{j=1}^{p} g(\beta_j)$ to the objective function of the least squares regression to enforce the sparsity of the model. An example is LASSO [4] and Bridg [5], which add Lq-type of penalty function to the regression coefficients, i.e., $g(\theta) = \|\theta\|^q$, with $q = 1$ and $\theta > 0$ respectively. Another penalty function $g_\lambda(|\bullet|) = \lambda g(|\bullet|)$ called the Smoothly Clipped Absolute Deviation (SCAD) [6] is proposed. which satisfies $g_\lambda(0) = 0$ and has a first-order derivative

$$g'_\lambda(\theta) = \lambda \left\{ I(\theta \le \lambda) + \frac{(a\lambda - \theta)+}{(a-1)} I(\theta > \lambda) \right\}, \tag{1}$$

when $\alpha > 2$ and $\theta > 0$. NNG [7] use a penalty function on shrinkage factors of the regression coefficients. The method is derived from the ordinary least squares estimator (OLS), and then it shrinks some coefficients of OLS to zero by the NNG shrinkage factors. Let $\hat{\beta}_j^{OLS}$ denote the OLS estimator of the coefficient β_j, then the NNG shrinkage factors $\hat{c} = (\hat{c}_1, \cdots, \hat{c}_p)^T$ are found by solving

$$\begin{cases} \hat{c} = \arg\min_{c} \{ \frac{1}{2n} \sum_{i=1}^{n} (Y_i - \sum_{j=1}^{p} c_j \hat{\beta}_j^{OLS})^2 + \lambda \sum_{j=1}^{p} c_j \} \\ s.t.\, 0 \le c_j\, (j = 1, \cdots, p), \end{cases} \tag{2}$$

For given $\lambda > 0$, Breiman [7] recommends to choose regularization parameter λ with five folds cross-validation. The NNG estimator of the coefficient $\beta_j, j = 1, \cdots p$, is then given by $\hat{\beta}_j^{NNG} = \hat{c}_j \cdot \hat{\beta}_j^{OLS}$.

Although many variable selection methods are available, few of them are designed to avoid sensitivity to outliers which commonly exist in the industry process. Therefore, R-NNG [8–10] is adopted for multivariate fault isolation. To investigate the performance of LASSO, NNG and R-NNG, three methods are respectively applied to the simulation of the Tennessee Eastman (TE) [11] process and the simulation results are compared. The results indicate that a carefully designed robust NNG method performs quite well and outperforms other two methods.

The rest of this paper is organized as follows. In Sect. 2, Multivariate fault isolation is transformed into variable problem. Then the target of fault isolation can be regarded as a variable selection problem in discriminant analysis. In Sect. 3, R-NNG method is interpreted and applied to the variable selection problem. In Sect. 4, we give two simulation cases to compare the performance of R-NNG, NNG and LASSO. Section 5 provides some further discussions and conclusions.

2 Problem Transformation

In this section, we transform the multivariate fault isolation problem into a variable selection problem in discriminant analysis. Therefore, to recognize the most responsible variable form all the fault variables is the task of fault isolation in the process monitoring. In other words, this task is equivalent to identifying the discriminating variables in a two-class problem, where the whole data set can be divided to 2 classes which are the historical normal operating data and the detected faulty process data.

One of the most popular techniques in discriminant analysis is FDA [12]. Suppose that a set of d-dimensional samples $\Xi = \Xi_1 \cup \Xi_2 = \{X_1, \ldots, X_n\}$ consists of 2 classes of samples $\Xi_1 = \left\{X_1^1, \ldots, X_{n_1}^1\right\}$ and $\Xi_2 = \left\{X_1^1, \ldots, X_{n_2}^1\right\}$, where $\Xi = \Xi_1 \cup \Xi_2$, n, n_1 and n_2 are the numbers of observations in Ξ Ξ_1, and Ξ_2, respectively, $n = n_1 + n_2$. The purpose of FDA is to acquire a projection direction with maximal class means and minimal the within-class variance, which is identical to an optimization problem. In order to link least squares regression to FDA, a predictor matrix is defined as (3)

$$x = \begin{bmatrix} 1_1 & X_1 \\ -1_2 & -X_2 \end{bmatrix}, \tag{3}$$

where 1_i is a column vector containing n_i ones, and X_i is a $n_i - by - d$ matrix whose rows are the samples belonging to Ξ_i. A response vector y is defined as (4)

$$y = \begin{bmatrix} \frac{n}{n_1} 1_1 \\ \frac{n}{n_2} 1_2 \end{bmatrix}, \tag{4}$$

where the constant n/n_i compensate the effect of the unbalanced sample sizes. $X\beta = y$ is a least squares regression problem, where β can be obtained by minimizing the residual sum of squares. Formulate the objective function as (5)

$$\min_{\beta}(y - X\beta)^T(y - X\beta). \tag{5}$$

Denote $\beta = \begin{bmatrix} W_0 \\ \omega \end{bmatrix}$, where W_0 is the coefficient corresponding to the first column in X and the vector ω contains the remaining coefficients. It is proved in [13] that ω is the direction vector for FDA.

Accordingly, the multivariate fault isolation problem can be further transformed to a variable selection problem in regression analysis. Motivated by above findings, this paper proposes to apply the NNG method in variable selection problem, which is useful with its high efficiency in variable selection for regression models for its robustness to outliers.

3   R-NNG-Based Multivariate Fault Isolation

In this paper, a linear regression model with unspecified error distribution is considered to solve the issue of simultaneous estimation and variable selection in regression models. The standard NNG is widely used [14–16], however, it is not directly applicable in high-dimension case. Fortunately, this problem is also resolved in [17]. The theoretical properties of the NNG algorithm are well studied in [10] and are extended for variable selection in additive regression models and varying coefficient models in [18, 19]. Since NNG algorithm has not been studied in presentence of the outliers which are commonly existed in the industry process, to eliminate its influence for fault isolation, a strategy based on robust nonnegative garrote (R-NNG) variable selection algorithm is presented in [20].

Thus, the algorithms of the S- and M-NNG can be utilized to compute the shrinkage factors. Possible loss function for ρ_0 and ρ_1 are loss function of the Tukey's bi-square family with d equal to $1.547(b = 0.5)$ and 5.182 respectively. How to compute the shrinkage factors and selection of regularization parameter λ is interpreted in [21].

4   Industry Case Study

A schematic view of the TE process is shown in [11]. There are five main units in this plant, which are reactor, condenser, separator, stripper, and compressor, respectively. The TE process [11] is used to compare the effectiveness of the presented methods in this section. As a challenging problem for a wide variety of process control technology studies, TE process, in short, consisting of five main units, which, are reactor, condenser, separator, stripper, and compressor, respectively, is widely used to test MSPM methods [21]. In this process, 2 products (G, H) are produced from 4 reactants (A, C, D, E), 1 byproduct (F) being produced at the same time. Besides, trace amounts of an inert component (B) is contained in the feed streams of A, C and D. The reactions are:

$$
\begin{array}{ll}
A + C + D \rightarrow G & \text{Product 1} \\
A + C + E \rightarrow H & \text{Product 2} \\
A + E \rightarrow F & \text{Byproduct 1} \\
3D \rightarrow 2F & \text{Byproduct 2.}
\end{array}
$$

There are 41 measured variables and 11 manipulated variables contained in the data collection, which are measured from historical normal operation and different types of faulty operations. The list of variables [21] is shown in Table 1. In each fault dataset, the fault appears after the 160th sampling interval. Simulation results of two types of fault by different method are compared.

Table 1. Isolation results of Fault 4

Sampling interval	NNG	LASSO	R-NNG
161	51, 9	51, 9	51,9
162	51	51	51
163	51	51	51
...	...	...	...
201	51	51	51
...	...	...	...
960	51	51	51

4.1   Case 1: Without Outliers

When outliers are not contained in the data set, simulation results about Fault 4 and Fault 5 are as follows.

- Scenario 1: Fault 4

Fault 4, firstly investigated in [11], is caused by a step change in the reactor cooling water inlet temperature. Figure 1 shows, the reactor temperature X_9 rose suddenly as the Fault 4 occurs. At the same time, to bring X_9 back to its normal state in a short time, the reactor cooling water flow rate X_{51} is adjusted by the feedback controller. Although the adjustment of X_{51} is very efficient, X_{51} itself cannot return to its original state any longer and reached a new steady state later. No other variables were influenced in this case. Figure 1 shows the trajectories X_9 and X_{51}. Other process variables were not affected by the fault.

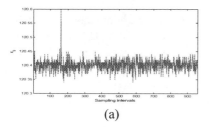
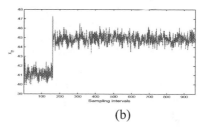

(a)   (b)

Fig. 1. Variable trajectories for Fault 4: (a) X9, (b) X51

Since the steady-state fault signature is informative for root-cause diagnosis, the fault isolation was conducted based on 25 observations collected between the 936th and the 960th sampling intervals. To get the root-cause of steady-state fault information, NNG, LASSO and R-NNG are utilized to trace the fault propagation path. After the fault occurred, by using the historical normal data and the fault data collected at the corresponding sampling interval, an NNG model was built for each fault observation. The isolation results for each time point based on NNG, LASSO and R-NNG are shown in Table 1. Both of them consistently show that, at the 161th sampling interval, i.e. the first sampling interval after Fault 4 occurred, X_{51} and X_9 were most responsible. After the 161th sampling interval, since the efficient closed-loop control restored X_9 to its normal state quickly, X_{51} was the only variable to blame, which is consist with what we discuss at the beginning. These results of Fig. 2 are in accord with the process analysis above.

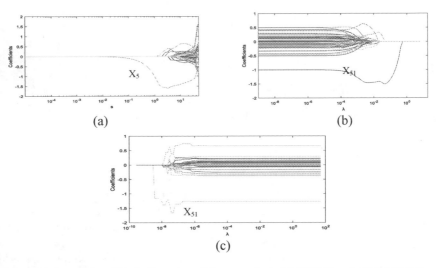

(a)   (b)

(c)

Fig. 2. Isolation results of Fault 4 based on different method: (a) NNG-Based, (b) LASSO-Based, (c) R-NNG-Based

- Scenario 2: Fault 5

The values of the selected measurements are adjusted in a random manner and within a certain range. Another fault to be isolated in this paper is Fault 5 [11], which is caused by a step change in the condenser cooling water. The downstream process characteristics were influenced directly. Since the condenser was connected to the separator, this fault affected the process variables related to the separator (e.g. X_{22} and X_{11}) firstly. After that, the abnormality gradually propagated to other separator variables (e.g. X_{13}, X_{11} and X_{22}) and other operation units, such as the reactor (e.g. X_7), the stripper (e.g. X_{16}, X_{19} and X_{50}) and the compressor (e.g. X_{20} and X_{46}). Thus, the concentrations of the inert component, products and byproducts changed (e.g. X_{31}, X_{33}, X_{35}, X_{30}, X_{38}, X_{44}, X_{25} and X_{34}). Because of the feedback concentration control, the flow rates and the amounts of the feed stocks (e.g. X_1, X_3, X_{43} and X_{44}) were adjusted as well. In general, a large amount of variables were affected in this case. To compensate the effect of such fault, the feedback controller had to adjust the condenser cooling water flow rate X_{52}. After the process reached a new steady-state, X_{52} did not return to its original state, while all other variables became normal again. Figure 3 displays the trajectory of X_{52}, X_{18} for reference.

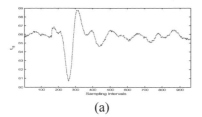
(a)

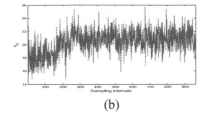
(b)

Fig. 3. Variable trajectories for Fault 4: (a) X18, (b) X52

The isolation results for each time point based on NNG, LASSO and R-NNG are shown in Table 2. Again, such results were obtained by investigating 25 observations collected between the 936th and the 960th sampling intervals. After the process reached a new steady state, X_{52} is considered as the most indicative faulty variable. According to Fig. 4, the isolation results of Fault 5 based on NNG, LASSO, R-NNG respectively are almost the same. The second potential faulty variable is X_{18}. However, no abnormality is found in the behavior of this variable in the corresponding time intervals, indicating that X_{18} is actually normal while the process reached the new steady state. Therefore, the conclusion is that X_{52} is the only abnormal variable identified, which is consistent with the above discussions. The root cause of such fault can then be diagnosed easily based on the isolation result.

Table 2. Isolation results of Fault 5

Sampling interval	NNG	LASSO	R-NNG
161	52, 18	52, 18	52,18
162	52	52	52
163	52	52	52
...	...	...	...
201	52	52	52
...	...	...	...
960	52	52	52

4.2 Case 2: With Outliers

For further comparison, outliers are added into the training data before process modeling for further comparison. Five process variables out of the total 52 are randomly chosen to be faulty with the probability of 0.05. The values are adjusted in a random manner and within a certain range.

The following simulation result show that only the R-NNG based method is robust to the outliers while the simulation results based on NNG and LASSO is inconsistent with the former. From which we can see that R-NNG outperforms the existing other two methods.

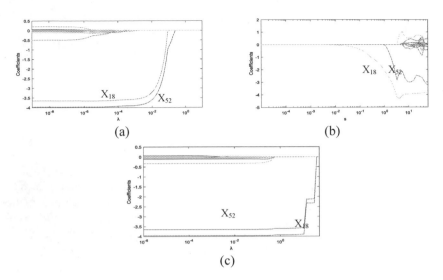

Fig. 4. Isolation results of Fault 5 based on different method: (a) NNG-Based, (b) LASSO-Based, (c) R-NNG-Based

- Scenario 1: Fault 4

The steady-state fault isolation results based on different methods are shown in Fig. 5, which is achieved based on 25 observations collected between the 936th and the 960th sampling points. It shows the changes in the active set along with the tuning factor λ and c. Based on NNG, X16 is the most responsible variable and the counterpart is X1 while using LASSO, in spite of their normal behaviors. Obviously, as shown in Fig. 5 (c), the first variable entering the active set is X51, the result is the same as it is in

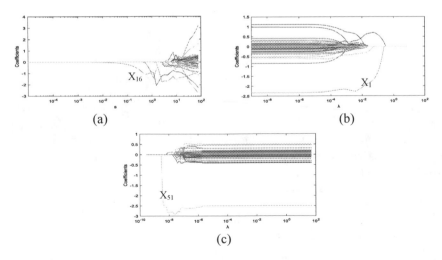

Fig. 5. Isolation results of Fault 4 based on different method: (a) NNG-Based, (b) LASSO-Based, (c) R-NNG-Based

scenario 1 when outliers do not exist in the data set of fault 4. Such result demonstrates the superiority of R-NNG in fault isolation in presence of outliers.

- Scenario 2: Fault 5

For further comparison, outliers are added in the data set of fault 5. Isolation result based on different methods are shown in Fig. 6. Comparing the results of NNG, LASSO and R-NNG, it is noted that X_{52} is only identified by R-NNG and not revealed by LASSO and NNG. In contrast R-NNG is better suited to such situation where outliers exist.

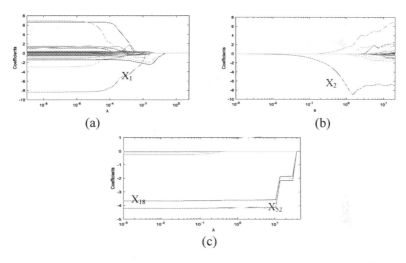

Fig. 6. Isolation results of Fault 4 based on different method: (a) NNG-Based, (b) LASSO-Based, (c) R-NNG-Based

5 Conclusion

Fault isolation is critical to fault monitoring, which can help engineers to diagnose the root cause of the fault. In this paper fault isolation problem is transformed into a variable selection problem in discriminant analysis, therefore, it can be solved by penalized regression techniques. The commonly used methods in such problem are NNG, LASSO, unfortunately, both of which are not robust to outliers. This paper proposes R-NNG-based method for fault isolation. The isolation results based on NNG, LASSO and R-NNG are almost the same when the data set does not contain outliers. In comparison, in presentence of outliers, wrong variables are selected when adopting NNG and LASSO methods, while the proposed R-NNG algorithm selects the correct variables and outperforms other two methods for its strong robustness.

References

1. Zhao, C., Wang, W.: Efficient faulty variable selection and parsimonious reconstruction modelling for fault isolation. J. Process Control **38**, 31–41 (2016)
2. Chiang, L.H., Russell, E.L., Braatz, R.D.: Fault Detection and Diagnosis in Industrial Systems. Springer, London (2001)
3. Efron, B., Hastie, T., Johnstone, I., Tibshirani, R.: Least angle regression. Ann. Statist. **32**(2), 407–499. (2004). With discussion, and a rejoinder by the authors
4. Frank, I.E., Friedman, J.H.: A statistical view of some chemometrics regression tools. Technometrics **35**(2), 109–135 (1993)
5. Fu, W.J.: Penalized regressions: the bridge versus the lasso. J. Comput. Graph. Statist. **7**(3), 397–416 (1998)
6. Fan, J., Li, R.: Variable selection via nonconcave penalized likelihood and its oracle properties. J. Am. Statist. Assoc. **96**(456), 1348–1360 (2001)
7. Breiman, L.: Better subset regression using the nonnegative garrote. Technometrics **37**(4), 373–384 (1995)
8. Yohai, V.J.: High breakdown-point and high efficiency robust estimates for regression. Ann. Statist. **15**(2), 642–656 (1987)
9. Yohai, V.J., Zamar, R.H.: High breakdown-point estimates of regression by means of the minimization of an efficient scale. J. Am. Statist. Assoc. **83**(402), 406–413 (1988)
10. Yuan, M., Lin, Y.: On the non-negative garrote estimator. J. R. Stat. Soc. Ser. B Stat. Methodol. **69**(2), 143–161 (2007)
11. Downs, J.J., Vogel, E.F.: A plant-wide industrial process control problem. Comput. Chem. Eng. **17**, 245–255 (1993)
12. Duda, R.O., Hart, P.E., Stork, D.G.: Pattern Classification, 2nd edn. Wiley New York (2012)
13. Fisher, R.A.: The use of multiple measurements in taxonomic problems. Ann. Eugenics, 7, 179–188 (1936)
14. Wang, J.G., Shieh, S.S., Jang, S.S., Wong, D.S.H., Wu, C.W.: A two-tier approach to the data-driven modeling on thermal efficiency of a BFG/coal co-firing boiler. Fuel **111**, 528–534 (2013)
15. Wang, J.G., Jang, S.S., Wong, D.S.H., Shieh, S.S., Wu, C.W.: Soft-sensor development with adaptive variable selection using nonnegative garrote. Control Eng. Practice **21**, 1157–1164 (2013)
16. Breiman, L.: Better subset regression using the nonnegative garrote. Technometrics **37**(4), 373 (1995)
17. Medina, M.A., Ronchetti, E.: Robust and consistent variable selection for generalized linear and additive models. Technical report. University of Geneva, Switzerland. http://archive-ouverte.unige.ch/unige:36961 (2014)
18. Antoniadis, A., Gijbels, I., Verhasselt, A.: Variable selection in additive models using P-splines. Technometrics **54**(4), 425–438 (2012)
19. Antoniadis, A., Gijbels, I., Verhasselt, A.: Variable selection in varying-coefficient models using P-splines. J. Comput. Graph. Stat. **21**(3), 638–661 (2012)
20. Gijbels, I., Vrinssen, I.: Robust nonnegative garrote variable selection in linear regression. Comput. Stat. Data Anal. **85**, 1–22 (2015)
21. Kuang, T.H., Yan, Z., Yao, Y.: Multivariate fault isolation via variable selection in discriminant analysis. J. Process Control **35**, 30–40 (2015)

Intelligent Modeling, Monitoring, and Control of Complex Nonlinear Systems

Secant Method Based U-Model Identification and Generalized Predictive Controller for Nonlinear Dynamic Systems

Ting Zhou, Jie Ding$^{(\boxtimes)}$, and Hui Deng

School of Automation, Nanjing University of Posts and Telecommunications,
Nanjing 210023, China
dingjie@njupt.edu.cn

Abstract. Generalized predictive controller of nonlinear systems are analyzed, to improve the efficiency, a secant method is employed to estimate the parameters of U-model that considered as an easy and effective modelling method for nonlinear dynamic plants. In this way, the final controller output of the nonlinear systems is transformed into solving a polynomial equation based on the available controller output, which greatly decreases the difficulties in the design of nonlinear control systems. The controller output can be derived from the secant method, which does not need to calculate the derivative, reduces the computational complexity and have faster convergence rate. In order to illustrate the design process and its effectiveness of the algorithm, a simulation is conducted to verify the method.

Keywords: U-model · Generalized predictive control · Secant method · Nonlinear systems

1 Introduction

In practical world, nonlinearity is ubiquitous, such as the petrochemical sector, heating furnace and reactor process. The linearization method is a commonly used method to deal with nonlinear problems in the most common cases, for example, Taylor linearization, piecewise linearization. Generalized predictive control (GPC) is very effective model predictive control methods theoretically and practically [1, 2]. Most research on generalized predictive control concentrate on the linear discrete systems, the main difficulty is to construct the predictive model of the nonlinear control systems, which leads to the difficulty of solving the GPC law. Therefore, it is very important to construct a suitable or general mathematical model, U-model is such an effective model first proposed by Professor Zhu et al. [3]. They constructed a U-model for control purpose, and the designed controller was used to realize a pole placement. From then on, a lot of work have been done in the analysis of nonlinear systems based on the U-model [4–11]. In most of them, the output of the controller is derived by using

This work was supported by Hatching Foundation of NJUPT (No. NY217063).

D. Yue et al. (Eds.): LSMS/ICSEE 2017, Part II, CCIS 762, pp. 385–394, 2017.
DOI: 10.1007/978-981-10-6373-2_39

Newton-Raphson iteratively. But there may occur some problems, e.g., the derivative in the algorithm may be approximately equal to zero. This is due to plant changes, calculation errors, and/or an inappropriate initial value, thus the results may be incorrect. In addition, the polynomial equation may not have a real root condition leading to a wrong algorithm. Du et al. [12] proposed the least-squares support vector machine to solve the controller output, but the method is relatively poor in real time.

In control of U-model, by using secant method recursively for the controller output, the problems above can be improved in some degree. The main advantage of the secant method is that the derivative can be avoided, the computational complexity and computing time can be reduced, at the same time, it has faster convergence rate.

The rest of the paper is organized as follows: Sect. 2 specifically introduces the basic idea of GPC. Section 3 describes a control-oriented U-model. In Sect. 4, the parameters of the U-model is estimated based on a secant method and the controller output is obtained. In Sect. 5, a simulation example is demonstrated for the proposed design process, and the feasibility and effectiveness of the method are verified.

2 GPC of Linear Systems

The linear GPC design [13, 14] starts from a discrete-time dynamic model as follows:

$$A(z^{-1})y(k) = B(z^{-1})u(k-1) + \frac{C(z^{-1})\xi(k)}{\Delta} \tag{1}$$

where $y(k)$, $u(k)$ and $\xi(k)$ are the output, the input (or controller output) and the white noise disturbance with zero mean and finite variance, respectively, $\Delta = 1 - z^{-1}$ as the differencing operator.

The conventional performance function is as follows:

$$J = E\{\sum_{j=N_1}^{P} q_j[y(k+j) - y_r(k+j)]^2 + \sum_{j=1}^{M} \lambda_j[\Delta u(k+j-1)]^2\} \tag{2}$$

where N_1 and P are the minimum and maximum prediction horizon, respectively, M denotes the maximum control horizon, q_j and λ_j are the weighting coefficients of prediction error and control increment, respectively, $y(k+j)$ and $y_r(k+j)$ is the actual output and the expected output at time $k+j$.

The reference trajectory is

$$\begin{cases} y_r(k+j) = \beta_r^j y_r(k) + (1 - \beta_r^j)\omega(k) \\ y_r(k) = y(k) \end{cases} \tag{3}$$

where $0 < \beta_r < 1$ is the softening coefficient; $\omega(k)$ is the predefined reference, $j = 1, 2, \ldots, P$.

Then rewriting the performance function in vectors as:

$$J = E[Y(k+1) - Y_r(k+1)]^{\mathrm{T}} Q[Y(k+1) - Y_r(k+1)] + \Delta U_P^{\mathrm{T}} \lambda \Delta U_P \qquad (4)$$

with

$Y(k+1) = [y(k+1), \ldots, y(k+j), \ldots, y(k+P)]^{\mathrm{T}}$,
$Y_r(k+1) = [y_r(k+1), \ldots, y_r(k+j), \ldots, y_r(k+P)]^{\mathrm{T}}$,
$\Delta U_P(k) = [\Delta u(k), \ldots, \Delta u(k+j-1), \ldots, \Delta u(k+M-1)]^{\mathrm{T}}$, $\Delta u(k+j\ \ 1)$ are the future control increment, $Q = diag(q_1, q_2, \ldots, q_j, \ldots, q_P)$, $\lambda = diag(\lambda_1, \lambda_2, \ldots, \lambda_j, \ldots, \lambda_M)$.

The minimized solution of performance index J is to determine the controller output by setting its derivative to zero,

$$\frac{\partial J}{\partial \Delta U_P(k)} = 0 \qquad (5)$$

The linear generalized predictive control theory has been more mature, however, for nonlinear systems, it is not easy to obtain the predictive model needed for generalized predictive control, the U-model is a very important part in getting the model as introduced in following.

3 U-Model

Consider a class of nonlinear systems in terms of

$$y(k) = f(y(k-1), y(k-2), \cdots, y(k-n), u(k-1), u(k-2), \cdots, u(k-n)) \qquad (6)$$

where $f(\cdot)$ is a nonlinear function, $y(k)$ and $u(k)$ are the output and input of the system, respectively, at discrete time instant k, n is the plant order.

The control-oriented model can be obtained by rescheduling $f(\cdot)$ into a polynomial of $u(k-1)$ as follows

$$y(k) = \sum_{i=0}^{N} \alpha_i(k) u^i(k-1) \qquad (7)$$

where N is the new degree of model (7) with respect to $u(k-1)$, $\alpha_i(k)$ is a function only containing the inputs $u(k-2), \ldots, u(k-n)$ and outputs $y(k-1), \ldots, y(k-n)$. Noticing that the coefficient function $\alpha_i(k)$ is time varying, the control model in (7) can be considered as a power series of $u(k-1)$ associated with $\alpha_i(k)$.

By defining

$$y(k) = U(k-1) = \Phi(u(k-1)) = \sum_{i=0}^{N} \alpha_i(k) u^i(k-1) \qquad (8)$$

Equation (8) is a U-model of (6). Namely, the nonlinear models in (6) are transformed by the U-model into nonlinear polynomials of control input with time-varying parameters, as shown in Fig. 1.

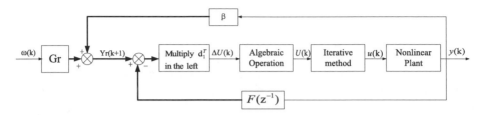

Fig. 1. Structure of U-model GPC

Note that, the U-model can convert the nonlinear autoregressive moving average model into a simple one which is convenient for control analysis. $U(k-1)$ can be considered as a polynomial of the actual input $u(k-1)$ with some unknown parameters. By designing $U(k-1)$ in some way, the control input $u(k-1)$ can be obtained by some iterative methods, e.g., Newton-Raphson method or least-squares support vector machine method. But Newton-Raphson method requires gradient derivative, giving rise to a large amount of calculation, the secant method [15, 16] can avoid derivative and reduce the calculation time greatly, the details are in the next section.

4   Derivation of GPC Algorithm Based on U-Model

4.1   Secant Method

First, we give the Newton-Raphson iteration formula

$$x_{s+1} = x_s - \frac{f(x_s)}{f'(x_s)}$$

Then, substituting the $\frac{f(x_s)-f(x_{s-1})}{x_s-x_{s-1}}$ with derivative $f'(x_s)$, yields the iteration formula of secant method

$$x_{s+1} = x_s - \frac{f(x_s)}{f(x_s)-f(x_{s-1})}(x_s - x_{s-1}) \quad s = 1, 2, \cdots$$

Through this iterative equation, the next iteration is determined by the value of the previous iteration, two initial values x_0 and x_1 are given.

The following gives a stop criterion

$$|x_s - x_{s+1}| < \varepsilon$$

Secant method is based on root solving process which utilizes succession of roots of secant lines to approach the true root of functions with the assumption that the local region of the function is approximately linear, and takes the cross point of secant line connecting the previous two points on a curve and the X-axis as the new reference point. The following iteration starts at the new reference point and then gets another secant line. It is characteristic of super linear convergence.

The main advantage is that the derivative can be avoided, the computational complexity and computing time can be reduced, at the same time, it has faster convergence rate.

4.2 Stochastic U-Model

Fitting the U-model into GPC, the entries of $\Delta U_P(k)$ is reformed by $\Delta U(k+j-1)$, $j = 1, 2 \cdots$. Taking the effects of external noise or disturbance into the deterministic model of Eqs. (9)–(10), then the stochastic U-model is written as

$$y(k) = U(k-1) + \xi(k)/\Delta \tag{9}$$

Multiplying Δ on both sides of Eq. (9) gives

$$(1 - z^{-1})y(k) = \Delta U(k-1) + \xi(k) \tag{10}$$

In the following, a new Diophantine equation is presented

$$1 = (1 - z^{-1})E_j(z^{-1}) + z^{-j}F_j(z^{-1}) \tag{11}$$

where

$$E_j(z^{-1}) = 1 + \sum_{i=1}^{j-1} e_{j,i} z^{-i}, \deg E_j(z^{-1}) = j - 1$$

$$F_j(z^{-1}) = f_{j,0}, \deg F_j(z^{-1}) = 0, j = 1, 2, \ldots, P$$

Multiplying (10) by $E_j(z^{-1})$ gives

$$(1 - z^{-1})E_j(z^{-1})y(k) = E_j(z^{-1})\Delta U(k-1) + E_j(z^{-1})\xi(k) \tag{12}$$

Substituting (11) into (12), and multiplying the z^j on both sides of (12) give

$$y(k+j) = E_j(z^{-1})\Delta U(k+j-1) + F_j(z^{-1})y(k) + E_j(z^{-1})\xi(k+j) \tag{13}$$

Given the following definition

$$y_P(k+j|k) = E_j(z^{-1})\Delta U(k+j-1) + F_j(z^{-1})y(k) \tag{14}$$

Thus

$$y(k+j) = y_P(k+j|k) + E_j(z^{-1})\xi(k+j) \tag{15}$$

where $y_P(k+j|k)$ is the optimal prediction output and $E_j(z^{-1})\xi(k+j)$ is the prediction error.

4.3   U-Model Based Diophantine Equation

Since the direct solution of the Diophantine equation is computationally large, recursive algorithm is used to solve $E_j(z^{-1})$, $F_j(z^{-1})$

$$1 = (1 - z^{-1})E_{j+1}(z^{-1}) + z^{-(j+1)}F_{j+1}(z^{-1}) \tag{16}$$

Subtracting (11) from (16) yields

$$(1 - z^{-1})[E_{j+1}(z^{-1}) - E_j(z^{-1})] + z^{-j}[z^{-1}F_{j+1}(z^{-1}) - F_j(z^{-1})] = 0 \tag{17}$$

Then

$$E_{j+1}(z^{-1}) - E_j(z^{-1}) = -\frac{z^{-j}[z^{-1}F_{j+1}(z^{-1}) - F_j(z^{-1})]}{1 - z^{-1}}$$

Since all $(j-1)$ time of the low power terms of the right side in the above equation are zero. So the coefficients of the first $(j-1)$ terms of E_{j+1} and E_j are equal and therefore

$$\begin{cases} E_{j+1}(z^{-1}) = E_j(z^{-1}) + e_{j+1,j}z \\ e_{j+1,i} = e_{j,i} \end{cases} \quad (i = 0, 1, \ldots, j-1) \tag{18}$$

Subtracting (18) into (11)

$$F_{j+1}(z^{-1}) = z[F_j(z^{-1}) - e_{j+1,j}(1 - z^{-1})] \tag{19}$$

By expanding (19), we can obtain

$$\begin{cases} f_{j+1,0} = e_{j+1,j} \\ e_{j+1,j} = f_{j,0} \end{cases}$$

Then we can get the following recursive formula

$$\begin{cases} f_{j+1,0} = f_{j,0} \\ E_{j+1}(z^{-1}) = E_j(z^{-1}) + f_{j,0}z^{-j} \end{cases} \tag{20}$$

where $j = 1$, set $E_1(z^{-1}) = 1$, from Eq. (13), $F_1(z^{-1}) = 1$.

4.4   Multi-step Output Prediction

As j varies from 1 to P, the corresponding multi-step optimal predictive output $y_P(k+j|k)$ can be obtained by using Eqs. (14) and (20)

$$y_P(k+1|k) = E_1(z^{-1})\Delta U(k) + F_1(z^{-1})y(k) = \Delta U(k) + F_1(z^{-1})y(k)$$
$$y_P(k+2|k) = E_2(z^{-1})\Delta U(k) + F_2(z^{-1})y(k) = \Delta U(k+1) + e_{2,1}\Delta U(k) + F_2(z^{-1})y(k)$$

$$\vdots$$

$$y_P(k+M|k) - E_M(z^{-1})\Delta U(k) + F_M(z^{-1})y(k)$$
$$= \Delta U(k+M-1) + e_{M,1}\Delta U(k+M-2) + \ldots + e_{M,M-1}\Delta U(k) + F_M(z^{-1})y(k)$$

$$\vdots$$

$$y_P(k+P|k) = E_P(z^{-1})\Delta U(k) + F_P(z^{-1})y(k)$$
$$= \Delta U(k+P-1) + e_{P,1}\Delta U(k+P-2)$$
$$+ \ldots + e_{P,P-M}\Delta U(k+M-1) + \ldots + e_{P,P-1}\Delta U(k) + F_P(z^{-1})y(k)$$

According to the recurrence formula of Diophantine equation, we can get the multi-step prediction output value

$$Y_P(k+1) = G\Delta U_P + F(z^{-1})y(k) \tag{21}$$

Where

$$Y_P(k+1) = [y_P(k+1|k), y_P(k+2|k), \cdots, y_P(k+P|k)]^T$$
$$\Delta U_P = [\Delta U(k), \Delta U(k+1), \cdots, \Delta U(k+M-1)]^T$$

$$G = \begin{bmatrix} 1 & 0 & \cdots & 0 \\ e_{2,1} & 1 & \cdots & 0 \\ \vdots & \vdots & \vdots & \vdots \\ e_{M,M-1} & e_{M,M-2} & \cdots & 1 \\ \vdots & \vdots & \vdots & \vdots \\ e_{P,P-1} & e_{P,P-2} & \cdots & e_{P,P-M} \end{bmatrix}_{P\times M} \tag{22}$$

$$F(z^{-1}) = [F_1(z^{-1}), F_2(z^{-1}), \cdots, F_P(z^{-1})]$$
$$E(z^{-1}) = [E_1(z^{-1}), E_2(z^{-1}), \cdots, E_P(z^{-1})]^T$$

4.5   Calculate the Optimal Control Law

Referring to Eqs. (13), (14) and (21), the future output vector $Y(k+1)$ can be expressed as

$$Y(k+1) = Y_p(k+1) + E(z^{-1})\xi(k+1) = G\Delta U_p + F(z^{-1})y(k) + E(z^{-1})\xi(k+1) \tag{23}$$

Substitute (23) into (4) to obtain

$$\begin{aligned}J_P =& E[G\Delta U_P + F(z^{-1})y(k) + E(z^{-1})\xi(k+1) - Y_r(k+1)]^T \\ & Q[G\Delta U_P + F(z^{-1})y(k) + E(z^{-1})\xi(k+1) - Y_r(k+1)] + \Delta U_P^T(k)\lambda\Delta U_P(k)\end{aligned}$$

Resolving the following equation

$$\frac{\partial J_P}{\partial \Delta U_P} = G^T Q[G\Delta U_P + F(z^{-1})y(k) + E(z^{-1})\xi(k+1) - Y_r(k+1)] + \lambda\Delta U_P(k) = 0$$

Gives the optimal law

$$\Delta U_P(k) = (G^T QG + \lambda)^{-1} G^T Q[Y_r(k+1) - F(z^{-1})y(k)]$$

$$\Delta U(k) = d_1^T[Y_r(k+1) - F(z^{-1})y(k)] \tag{24}$$

d_1^T represents the first row of matrix $(G^T QG + \lambda)^{-1} G^T Q$, The controller output $U(k)$ can be derived by some algebraic operations

$$U(k) = \Delta U(k) + U(k-1)$$

Thus, the generalized predictive controller design based on the Eq. (9) is completed. But, $U(k)$ is only pseudo-input of the system, we need to calculate the control input $u(k)$ by the secant method. The recursive computation is listed below

$$u_{s+1}(k) = u_s(k) - \frac{\sum\limits_{i=0}^{N}\alpha_i(k)u_s^i(k) - U(k)}{\sum\limits_{i=0}^{N}\alpha_i(k)u_s^i(k) - \sum\limits_{i=0}^{N}\alpha_i(k)u_{s-1}^i(k)}(u_s(k) - u_{s-1}(k)) \tag{25}$$

where $s \geq 0$ is the iteration index.

5   Case Study

Consider a nominator polynomial [17, 18],

$$y(k) = \frac{y(k-1)}{1+y^2(k-1)} + u^3(k-1) \tag{26}$$

The corresponding U-model can be described as follows

$$U(k-1) = \alpha_0(k) + \alpha_1(k)u(k-1) + \alpha_2(k)u^2(k-1) + \alpha_3(k)u^3(k-1)$$

where

$$\alpha_0(k) = \frac{y(k)}{1+y^2(k)}, \alpha_1(k) = 0, \alpha_2(k) = 0, \alpha_3(k) = 1$$

The parameters are initialized as follows: $N_1 = 1, P = 8, M = 3, \lambda_j = 0.02, q_j = 1,$ $\beta_r = 0.05$. Reference input $\omega(k)$ is normally a periodic function, thus the square wave is taken into account. The result indicates that the predictive output can track the reference input as shown in Fig. 2.

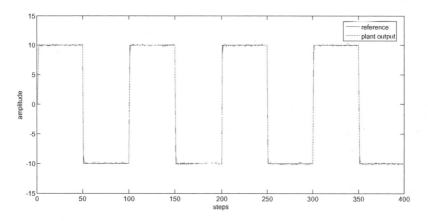

Fig. 2. System output under U-model GPC based on secant method

6   Conclusions

This paper designs a generalized predictive controller by using the U-model frame-work, employs the secant method to derive the controller output, since the secant method does not need to solve the derivative, so some problems with the use of Newton-Raphson algorithm are avoided, greatly reducing the computational complexity and computational time, simultaneously, have faster convergence rate. In order to verify the effectiveness of the proposed method, a nonlinear system is taken as the simulation model.

Acknowledgments. Great thank Professor Quanming Zhu for explanation of U-model estimation with Newton-Raphson iteration.

References

1. Abdeldjebar, B., Khier, B.: Generalized predictive control: application of the induction motor. In: Proceedings of the International Conference on Smart Manufacturing Application, 9–11 April, Gyeonggi-do, Korea, pp. 526–529 (2008)
2. Min, X., Shaoyuan, L.: A fast generalized predictive control algorithm for the typical industrial processes. In: Proceedings of the 4th World Congress on Intelligent Control and Automation (Cat. No. 02EX527), pp. 2416–2421 (2002)
3. Zhu, Q.M., Guo, L.Z.: A pole placement controller for nonlinear dynamic plant. Proc. IMechE, Part I: J. Syst. Control Eng. **216**(16), 467–476 (2002)
4. Zhu, Q.M., Warwocl, K., Douce, J.L.: Adaptive general predictive controller for nonlinear systems. IEEE Proc. Control Theory Appl. **138**(1), 33–40 (1991)
5. Chang, W.C.H., Wang, W.J., Jia, H.R.: Radial basis functions neural network of vary learning rate based stochastic U-model. In: International Conference on Electrical and Control Engineering (ICECE), Yichang, pp. 278–281 (2011)
6. Muhammad, S., Butt, N.R.: Real-time adaptive tracking of DC motor speed using U-model based IMC. Autom. Control Comput. Sci. **41**(1), 31–38 (2007)
7. Tahir, K., Muhammad, S.: A novel internal model control scheme for adaptive tracking of nonlinear dynamic plants. In: 2006 1st IEEE Conference on Industrial Electronics and Applications, Wuhan, pp. 123–130. IEEE (2006)
8. Shafiq, M., Haseebuddin, M.: U-model-based internal model control for non-linear dynamic plants. Proc. IMechE, Part 1: J. Syst. Control Eng. **219**(6), 449–458 (2005)
9. Shafiq, M., Butt, N.R.: U-model based adaptive IMC for nonlinear dynamic plants. In: 10th IEEE International Conference on Emerging Technologies and Factory Automation, pp. 955–959 (2005)
10. Du, W.X., Wu, X.L., Zhu, Q.M.: Direct design of a U-model-based generalized predictive controller for a class of non-linear (polynomial) dynamic plants. Proc. Inst. Mech. Eng. Part I: J. Syst. Control Eng. **226**(1), 27–42 (2012)
11. Zhu, F., Yu, Z.J., Hu, Y.Z.: Proportional-integral generalized predictive control for nonlinear systems based on U-model. In: Proceedings of the 25th Chinese Process Control Conference, Dalian, pp. 958–965 (2014)
12. Du, W.X., Zhu, Q.M., Wu, X.L.: Support vector machine based U-model generalized predictive controller for nonlinear dynamic plants. In: Proceedings of the 33rd Chinese Control Conference, Nanjing, pp. 2178–2182 (2014)
13. Pang, Z.H., Cui, H.: System Identification and Adaptive Control MATLAB Simulation. Beijing University of Aeronautics and Astronautics Press, Beijing, vol. 8 (2013)
14. Ding, B.C.: Theory and Methods of Prediction control. Machinery Industry Press, Beijing, vol. X, p. 3 (2013)
15. Luo, W.C., Yi, X.B.: Calculate the common normal line's distance of single arc gear based on secant method. In: The 1st International Conference on Information Science and Engineering (ICISE2009), pp. 158–161 (2009)
16. Hu, J.: A comparative study on the application of Newton method and Secant method. J. Yangtze Univ. **3**(2), 479–480 (2006)
17. Narendra, K.S., Parthasarathy, K.: Identification and control of dynamical systems using neural networks. IEEE Trans. Neural Netw. **1**(1), 4–27 (1990)
18. Ford, I., Kitsos, C.P., Titterington, D.M.: Recent advances in nonlinear experimental design. Technometrics **31**(1), 49–60 (1989)

Research on Nonlinear Lamb Wave Based Structural Damage Monitoring

Qiang Wang$^{(\boxtimes)}$, Dongchen Ji, and Chen Zhou

College of Automation, Nanjing University of Posts and Telecommunications,
Nanjing 210023, China
wangqiang@njupt.edu.cn

Abstract. Due to limitation of traditional Lamb wave based structural damage monitoring methods, early micro damages which are smaller than the wavelength of the waves usually can hardly be detected and evaluated. In this paper, major efforts were focused on nonlinear Lamb wave, including its propagation characteristic and sensitivity to micro damages. The relationship between the nonlinear characteristic parameters of Lamb wave and the degree of damage is revealed by experimental study. The cumulative (S1, S2) symmetric mode Lamb wave were adopted in the research so that nonlinear second harmonic signals could be obtained to measure metallic structural material's nonlinear changes quantitatively. In view of dispersion and multiple models characteristic that affect signal analysis, the time-frequency analysis method, STFT, was adopted to extract the fundamental Lamb wave mode and second harmonic mode respectively. Experimental results on T6061 aluminum plates shown that the nonlinear characteristic parameters were sensitive to the artificial fatigue damages. It can be also found that the nonlinear characteristic parameters were grown with the degree of the damages.

Keywords: Nonlinear lamb wave · Nonlinear characteristic parameters · STFT

1 Introduction

Metal materials are widely used in industrial fields, such as large tanks, aircraft fuselage, wing, door and car making. Due to the metal material itself apparent weakness, metal material in the internal factors (such as moving parts transfer alternating load) and environmental factors (such as corrosion, temperature, external loads, etc.), will gradually aging, different degrees of damage in service process. In a wide range of damage, more than 80% of the failure of mechanical components is caused by fatigue damage. The study found that fatigue damage is a defect of the instability, under the operation conditions of the structure, even a small crack, under the effect of alternating load, corrosion, temperature and other factors may also accelerate the expansion, suddenly fracture, lead to the occurrence of catastrophic accidents. If these local structural damage can be detected in a timely manner, the location and degree of damage can be determined, and the necessary remedial measures can be taken to reduce the risk and the risk to the lowest.

Traditional based on linear Lamb wave monitoring technology use Lamb wave defects in the process of wave propagation encountered reflection, scattering and the

© Springer Nature Singapore Pte Ltd. 2017
D. Yue et al. (Eds.): LSMS/ICSEE 2017, Part II, CCIS 762, pp. 395–405, 2017.
DOI: 10.1007/978-981-10-6373-2_40

propagation of energy absorption of linear feature were defect detection and evaluation. However, use linear Lamb wave method to detect the signal wavelength is much smaller than that of the early micro damage and micro cracks, is not very sensitivity. Nonlinear Lamb wave monitoring technique is based on the nonlinear effects of fatigue induced changes in the structural damage. The study shows that the micro damage in the plate is very sensitive.

The existing theory on the basis of the results in today. Experimental study on the cumulative effect of the nonlinear Lamb wave second harmonic of fatigue damage sensitivity and injury changes caused by the nonlinear characteristic parameters change trends, provide basic for micro damage monitoring and assessment.

2 Fundamental Theory

In a solid medium, stress perturbations caused by the propagation of ultrasonic waves cause longitudinal strain:

$$\varepsilon = \varepsilon_e + \varepsilon_{p1} \tag{1}$$

ε_e is an elastic strain component, ε_{p1} is a plastic strain component related to the dislocation motion of dislocations in the dipole configuration. The stress perturbation $\bar{\sigma}$ and the elastic strain component ε_e are related to the nonlinear Hooke's law using the quadratic nonlinear approach:

$$\bar{\sigma} = A_2^e \varepsilon_e + \frac{1}{2} A_3^e \varepsilon_e^2 + \cdots \tag{2}$$

According to relevant literature introduction:

$$u = \frac{1}{8} \beta k^2 u_0^2 X + u_0 \cos(kX - \omega t) - \frac{1}{8} \beta k^2 u_0^2 X \cos[2(kX - \omega t)] + h.o.t. \tag{3}$$

Neglect of the higher order terms can produce the fundamental and the second harmonic frequency in the output wave signal. Assigning the amplitudes $A_1 = u_0$ and $A_2 = \frac{1}{8} \beta k^2 u_0^2 X$ for fundamental and two harmonics, nonlinear parameters can be represented by these amplitudes:

$$\beta = \frac{8}{k^2 X} \left(\frac{A_2}{A_1^2} \right). \tag{4}$$

By using the definition of wavenumber, another equation can be derived (4):

$$\beta = 8 \frac{c^2}{\omega^2 X} \left(\frac{A_2}{A_1^2} \right). \tag{5}$$

As mentioned earlier, these expressions for calculating absolute nonlinear parameter β are valid only for longitudinal and fundamental and two harmonic amplitudes measured by longitudinal waves. Introducing relative nonlinear parameters:

$$\beta' = \frac{A_2}{A_1^2} \propto \beta \tag{6}$$

It provides a method for quantifying the degree of nonlinearity in lamb waves. The β' is the relative parameter, considering only the amplitudes A_1 and A_2, so it is impossible to use absolute β statements as benchmarks. Also note that in this study, amplitudes A_1 and A_2 are surface normal velocities.

3   Experimental Research

3.1   Nonlinear Lamb Wave Signal Analysis and Separation Method

Due to the dispersion and multimode nature of Lamb wave, the amplitude of the fundamental frequency and the two harmonic wave is difficult to be extracted directly from the signal, and each wave packet is mixed together, so it is difficult to directly separate the signal in time domain. The two harmonic excitation point is defined as the point at which the first phase is divided into two symmetrical modes, and the same phase velocity is controlled by the fundamental frequency and the second harmonic frequency, respectively. Excitation frequency signal in different propagation position two order nonlinear Lamb wave mode signal is often not superimposed and bad lost, difficult to capture. In this paper, the short time Fourier transform is used to analyze the time and frequency domain, and then to extract the corresponding frequency signal to realize the mode separation:

$$F(\omega, t) = \frac{1}{2\pi} \int_{-\infty}^{\infty} e^{-i\omega t} f(\tau) h(\tau - t) d\tau \tag{7}$$

F(T) is the sensing signal, H(T) is the window function, and the length of the window function is selected according to the time domain pulse width of the excitation signal. According to the time frequency analysis results, the frequency and the two harmonic Lamb wave response signals are extracted respectively, and the amplitude of the fundamental frequency amplitude A_1 and the two harmonic amplitude A_2 are obtained. The relative nonlinear parameters are obtained by the formula (6).

3.2   Experimental Process

Based on the cumulative effect of the nonlinear Lamb wave theory analysis and the second order harmonic, the key steps of the nonlinear Lamb wave method to realize the structure fatigue and micro crack damage monitoring are nonlinear Lamb wave signal capture and separation, nonlinear characteristic parameters and damage characterization.

Nonlinear Lamb Wave Two Harmonic Excitation with Additive Effect. Due to the presence of the properties of dispersion and multi-mode Lamb wave structure response signal in the part of the fundamental and second harmonic generation part will with different speed, different models, and different frequency propagation, so the communication signal is very complex, the analysis is more difficult. Therefore, when the fundamental frequency and the two harmonic phase velocity, group velocity equal or approximate equal, the formation of cumulative effect, in order to better extraction and analysis of the two frequency. According to Figs. 1 and 2 of the phase velocity and group velocity frequency dispersion curve, it can be seen that the frequency thickness product is 3.6 mw can be seen when the baseband signal signal S1 is Stimulated to have (S0, S1, S2, S3) the several modes of signal can be as the second harmonic signal of candidate signals. Combined with frequency dispersion curve to select the better separation signal S1 mode baseband signal and second harmonic signal S2 mode to meet with additive effects on the nonlinear Lamb wave conditions, and S1 mode speed is fast and easy to with the other modes separately, so the final choice of the S1 mode signal as the excitation signal.

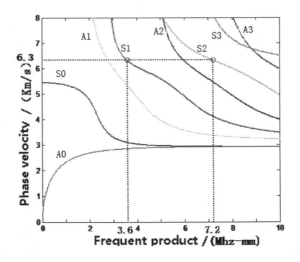

Fig. 1. Phase velocity dispersion curve of aluminum plate

Experimental Scheme and Experimental System. Experiment is divided into two parts: the first is the nonlinear Lamb wave characteristic parameters to simulate fatigue damage sensitivity test, in experiment through the same path on the nonlinear characteristic parameters changes before and after comparing the damage to validate the parameter sensitivity; the second is nonlinear characteristic parameters change with different degree of injury of experimental analysis. In the experiment, the local heating method is used to simulate the occurrence of fatigue, the damage is defined as the health state, the structural state of the heating 60 s, 120 s and 180 s is defined as the damage state 1, the damage state 2 and the damage state 3. The experimental research object is (400 mm * 600 mm * 4 mm^3) T6061 aluminum plate, the layout of the

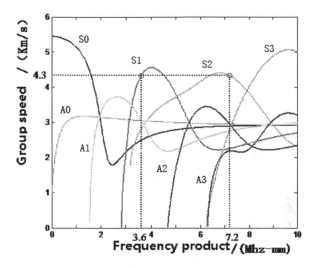

Fig. 2. Group velocity dispersion curves of aluminum plate

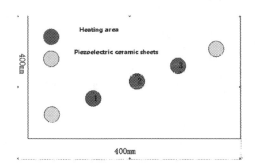

Fig. 3. T6061 aluminum plate

piezoelectric chip is shown in Fig. 3. According to the previous incentive signal selection conditions, the choice of frequency signal frequency is 900 Hz. The experimental system and the schematic as shown in Fig. 4 of the sample, in which a piezoelectric excitation signal. By Ni PXI-1071 chassis with NI5781 acquisition card issued 15 cycles of narrowband sine wave modulation signal excitation signal and the signal after peak to the amplification of the power amplifier Krohn-Hite company peak 100 V loaded into the actuator, signal in structure propagation from the other end of the piezoelectric ceramic piece received signal, after the charge amplifier also by NI5781 acquisition card to 50 MHz sampling rate (Fig. 5).

Typical sensor signals such as shown in Fig. 6, the short-time Fourier transform of sensor signal acquisition to the frequency domain analysis, processing spectrum results as shown in Fig. 7, from sheet we can see S1 and S2 mode is arriving at the same time. This energy spectrum were extracted from the fundamental frequency and the second frequency doubling of energy values as shown in Sheet 8, can clearly see

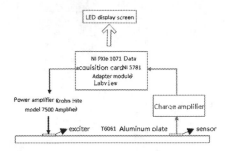

Fig. 4. Schematic of experimental system

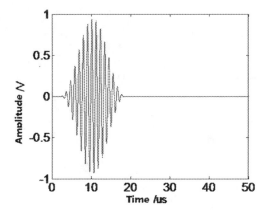

Fig. 5. Excitation signal

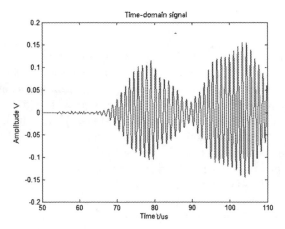

Fig. 6. Typical sensing signal

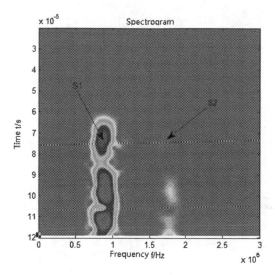

Fig. 7. Spectrum of STFT

the fundamental and second harmonic generation arrival time is consistent, meanwhile it can quantitatively express the amplitude of A_1 and A_2, using formula (6) can calculate the material nonlinear value (Fig. 8).

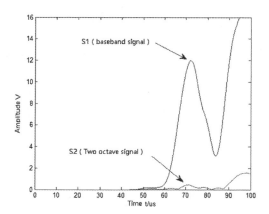

Fig. 8. Extracted fundamental and second harmonic signal

Experimental Result Analysis. Simulation of 1 point damage before and after the fundamental frequency and the two harmonic energy values compared to Fig. 9 and Fig. 10 shows that Fig. 9 for the healthy state of the basic frequency and the two frequency response signal, Fig. 10 for the damage state of the basic frequency and the two frequency response signal. According to Eq. (6) clearly see the damage simulation appear, value increases, in Fig. 3 the No. 2 and No. 3 points to do the same experiment,

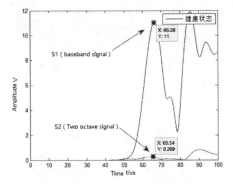

Fig. 9. Typical fundamental frequency and second harmonic response signal of health state

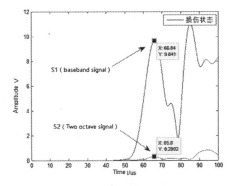

Fig. 10. Typical fundamental frequency and second harmonic response signal of damage state

experimental results such as Table 1 shows, from Table 1, it can be seen, when damage occurs, values are significantly increased, indicating that the nonlinear lamb Potter syndrome reference number on fatigue damage has better sensitivity.

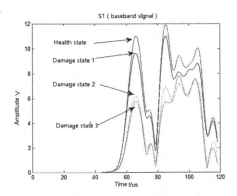

Fig. 11. Fundamental frequency response signal

Figure 11 is fundamental frequency response signal. Figure 12 is second harmonic response signal, according to formula (6) can be calculated the value of nonlinear characteristic parameters, are compared.

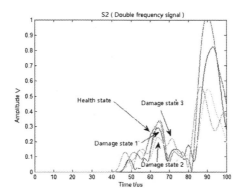

Fig. 12. Second harmonic response signal

Figure 13 shows the growth rate of the characteristic parameters of the 1 point damage state, it can be found that with the deepening of the degree of damage, the higher the value of the growth rate. In order to prevent the data from accidental, in Fig. 3 (T6061 aluminum plate) on the 2 points and 3 points to do the same experiment, the results of the experiment as shown in Sheet 14, with the degree of damage to deepen, the value of the growth rate is also getting higher and higher (Fig. 14).

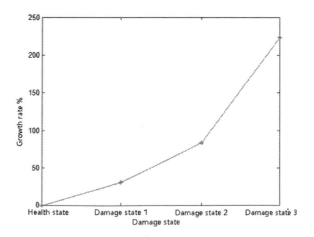

Fig. 13. Growth rate of characteristic parameter after damage

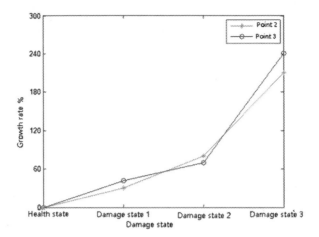

Fig. 14. Growth rate of characteristic parameters after 2 and 3 point damage

4 Conclusion

In this paper, we mainly study the sensitivity of nonlinear Lamb wave to the early micro damage of structures. Experimental results show that the change of material nonlinearity of structure of the nonlinear Lamb wave is more sensitive when the damage occurs, the nonlinear characteristic parameters will increase, and with the deepening of the degree of injury, the value of the growth rate is also more and more high. The study results for structural fatigue, crack, and other early micro damage of on-line monitoring provides the basic research.

References

1. Deng, M.X., Pei, J.F.: Nondestructive evaluation of fatigue damage nonlinear ultrasonic Lamb wave method. Acoust. Sinica **33**(4), 360–369 (2008)
2. Matsuda, N., Biwa, S.: Phase and group velocity matching for cumulative harmonic generation in Lamb waves. J. Appl. Phys. **109**, 094903 (2011)
3. Matlack, K.H., Kim, J.Y., Jacobs, L.J., et al.: Experimental characterization of efficient second harmonic generation of Lamb wave modes in a nonlinear elastic isotropic plate. J. Appl. Phys. **109**, 014905 (2011)
4. Deng, M., Xiang, Y., Liu, L.: Time-domain analysis and experimental examination of cumulative second-harmonic generation by primary Lamb wave propagation. J. Appl. Phys. **109**, 113525 (2011)
5. Qiang, W., Shenfang, Y., Xiaohui, C., et al.: Active Lamb wave synthesis wavefront and damage imaging monitoring method. Chin. J. Sci. Instrum. **32**(11), 2468–2474 (2011)
6. Boon, M.J.G.N., Zarouchas, D., Martinez, M., et al.: Temperature and load effects on acoustic emission signals for structural health monitoring applications. In: 7th European Workshop on Structural Health Monitoring, 8–11 July, La Cité, Nantes, France (2014)

7. Xiang, Y., Deng, M., Xuan, F.-Z.: Creep damage characterization using nonlinear ultrasonic guided wave method: a mesoscale model. J. Appl. Phys. **115**, 044914 (2014)

8. Shui, G., Wang, Y.-S., Huang, P., Jianmin, Q.: Nonlinear ultrasonic evaluation of the fatigue damage of adhesive joints. NDT E Int. **70**, 9–15 (2015)

9. Zhou, Z.G., Liu, S.M.: Non-linear non-destructive research, application and development of detection technology. J. Mech. Eng. **47** (8), 002-011 (2011)

10. Xiang, Y., Xuan, F., Deng, M.: Evaluation of thermal degradation induced material damage using nonlinear Lamb waves. Chin. Phys. Lett. **27**(1), 016202 (2010)

11. Müller, M.F., Kim, J.Y., Qu, J.M., et al.: Characteristics of second harmonic generation of Lamb waves in nonlinear elastic plates. J. Acoust. Soc. Am. **127**(4), 2141–2152 (2010)

12. Matlack, K.H., Kim, J.Y., Jacobs, L.J., et al.: Experimental characterization of efficient second harmonic generation of Lamb wave modes in a nonlinear elastic isotropic plate. J. Appl. Phys. **109**, 014905 (2011)

Second-Order Average Consensus with Buffer Design in Multi-agent System with Time-Varying Delay

Junxian Yang[1,2], Li Hui[1,2], Peidong Wang[3], and Yang Li[4,5(✉)]

[1] Shandong Provincial Key Laboratory of Ocean Environment Monitoring Technology, Qingdao, China
yjxwork@126.com, qd_hl@qingdaonews.com
[2] Shandong Academy of Sciences Institute of Oceanographic Instrumentation, Qingdao, China
[3] Qingdao Institute of Product Quality Supervision and Inspection, Qingdao, China
qdrnocking@yahoo.com.cn
[4] College of Mechanical and Electronic Engineering, Shandong Agricultural University, Tai'an, China
mtlyab@sdau.edu.cn
[5] Shandong Provincial Key Laboratory of Horticultural Machinery and Equipment, Tai'an, China

Abstract. In this paper, we focus on the average consensus problem with varying time-delays for second-order dynamic agents within a network of fixed topologies. Some typical network effects are elaborated, such as network conditions that induced delays, packet dropouts, error-sequence, etc. Based on Gersgorin Disks theorem, we discuss in-depth the necessary condition and the time delays' upper bound for system stability. Then the stability theory is used in consensus strategy design, avoiding the communication error caused by network time-delays. A group agents consensus algorithm with transmission-receive buffer and buffer length a selection method are proposed. Using this buffer design method, agent can transmit and receive data with original order. The proposed algorithm is test in MATLAB simulation environment with 2 typical examples. The simulation results show the effectiveness of the algorithm. With the proposed consensus algorithm, all agents are matched with the average speed, and network time-delay effects are reduced.

Keywords: Buffer design · Multi-agent system · Average consensus · Time-varying delay

1 Introduction

Due to its wide application in sensor networks, UAV formation and robot team, the consensus problem in recent years has attracted great interest [1–4]. A variety of distributed control and estimation strategies are designed based on the consensus algorithm. The research of distributed consensus is closely related to the nature of

© Springer Nature Singapore Pte Ltd. 2017
D. Yue et al. (Eds.): LSMS/ICSEE 2017, Part II, CCIS 762, pp. 406–417, 2017.
DOI: 10.1007/978-981-10-6373-2_41

complexity science, that is, how the local communication and collaboration between individuals lead to some ideal global behavior. More research aims at understanding cooperation group's collective behavior become distributed local mutually beneficial results in mobile personal, only share information with their neighbors, trying to reach some common concern global standards at the same time [5, 6].

The average-consensus is a basic consensus strategy, originated from distributed computation and decision-making. It generally means to design a network protocol, with which the states of all agents asymptotically reach the average of the original states with time [7–9]. The mathematical problems are considered as the simplest coordinated task examples. In reality, it can be used to model the control of multiple autonomous, and these home-made quantities have to be driven to the initial position of the centroid or from the distributed sensors with multiple measures of the decentralized estimator. It can be used for modeling processors to balance the load too. Because of the work in [5], now we can solve the mean consensus problem with mild conditions on graphs and evolutionary matrices. Here we study network topology, 2-way communication protocols, additional performance requirements and control assumptions. In these works, many considered the average-consensus when communication is affected by communication time-delays [10–19]. More specifically, assume the proxy behavior is similar to an integrator, and the communication latency is constant and consistent over time.

As well known, the induced time delays in a network is unavoidable. In the networked multi-agent system, the time delay is definitely inevitable, called network induced delay, in particular. It tends to change a lot of uncertainty, and cause the system instability. The existence of induced information lag plays an important role in the stability, and seriously affects the consensus and convergence of the system. Considering the time delay cannot be eliminated, it is important to design an efficient algorithm for communication average consensus in time delay environment. Before we start discussing the follow-up content, another point to note is that the actual latency in the multi-agent system is usually divided into 2 types. One is the statement information detection delay in the system itself, and the contract is the induced network induced delay among agents network. According 2 type time-delays has different properties; the consensus algorithms in the network with time-delays are mainly defined as symmetric ones and asymmetric ones. The main difference between them is that the former takes both the statement delay and the network induced delay into account, the other of which only considers the network delay among the agents.

In this paper, we propose a distributed average consistency problem based on buffer design. Assuming that each agent interacts with its partners in a desired bounded workspace, our goal is to make each agent finally match the average state. This paper's main contribution is to avoid the sequence of mis-sequences effectively using the proposed algorithm to exchange data among agents. Finally, we give some simulation examples, which show that the algorithm is effective.

2 Preliminaries

Consider a n-agent system under the fixed topology. The agents reach consensus if and only if $x_i = x_j$ ($i \neq j$) for all $i, j \in N$. Suppose the agents operate in the same Euclidean space $W \subset R^3$. Let $q_i = [z_{xi}, z_{yi}, z_{zi}]^T \in R^3$ denote the agent's (x, y, z)-position on a 3-dimension coordinates, and let $p_i = [v_{xi}, v_{yi}, v_{zi}]^T \in R^3$ denote an agent's velocities on axes x, y and z. Then denote $[q_i^T, p_i^T]^T$ as the position and velocity of agent $i = 1, 2, 3, \ldots, n$, respectively.

Furthermore, let $u_i = [u_{xi}, u_{yi}, u_{zi}]^T \in R^3$ denote the agent i's control input, in other words, u_i can also be considered as the agent i's input command. Furthermore, the each second order agent's kinematic model is defined using the following formula.

$$\begin{cases} \dot{q}_i = p_i \\ \dot{p}_i = u_i \end{cases} i = 1, 2, 3, \ldots, n \tag{1}$$

where, the location and speed of all agents are defined as

$$q = [q_1^T \; q_2^T \; q_3^T \cdots q_n^T]^T$$
$$p = [p_1^T \; p_2^T \; p_3^T \cdots p_n^T]^T$$

Assume the representation of all agents in internal behavior. We can use vector graphics to describe the relations conveniently, so as to establish an interactive topological model, which is consisted of a vertex set $v(G) = \{v_i : i \in l_n\}$, $l_n = \{1, 2, \ldots, n\}$ and an edge set

$$e(G) \subset \{\langle v_i, v_j \rangle : v_i, v_j \in v(G)\}$$

The adjacency matrix $A = [a_{ij}(q)] \in R^{n \times n}$ of the directed graph is a matrix with elements according to the properties that if $\langle v_i, v_j \rangle \subset e(G)$, $a_{ij}(q) > 0$; otherwise $a_{ij} = 0$. The matrix G degree is a diagonal matrix $\Delta(A)$ with diagonal elements $\sum_{i=1}^{n} a_{ij} \sum_{i=1}^{n} a_y$. The graph Laplacian matrix $L = [l_{ij}] \in R^{n \times n}$ is defined as $L = \Delta(A) - A$.

We believe that the movement of followers depends on the movement of other neighbours. So, we define the neighbor let of agent i as follows

$$N_i(t) = \{j \in v : \|q_j - q_i\| < r_d\}, \tag{2}$$

where r_d is the maximum range of activity between the two agents, and $\|\cdot\|$ is Euclidean distance. So we make the following assumptions for this dynamic system.

(a) Although the relative distance between them may change during the agent movement, the topology of the system is fixed.
(b) Each agent i can get other agents' locations and speeds information only located in the circular neighborhood of the agent location and speed. This means that every agent has the longest communication distance.
(c) Speed of the reagent must not exceed the maximum value given.

One classical second-order consensus proposed algorithm without constraint condition such as time delay is proposed in [5], as

$$u_i^a(t) = -\sum_{j\in N_i(t)} a_{ij}\{\gamma[q_i(t) - q_j(t)] + [p_i(t) - p_j(t)]\} \tag{3}$$

where N_i represents the neighbor set of agent i. Here the communication is not necessarily symmetric, i.e. $a_{ij} \neq a_{ji}$.

Vector closed loop multi-agent systems with integral agents are

$$\dot{x} = -Lx \tag{4}$$

where $x = [q(t)^T p(t)^T]^T$.

The research [5] shows that abide by the distributed consensus protocol (3), all initial state values tend to the average state as $t \to +\infty$.

3   Preliminaries

As what has mentioned, the time delays in multi-agent systems are sorted into two categories [12, 20]. One type is caused by the specific conditions of the network induced delay. Here we give a delay restriction of $0 < \tau_{ij} \leq \tau_d$ $(\tau_d > 0)$, where τ_d is a constant. It is easy to know the specific value τ_{ij} mainly relies on the distance between agent i and agent j. That means, the further the distance is, the larger the τ_{ij} will be. Another thing to mention is the network induced delay is varied following the time changing. The unstable network is the major reason causes this phenomenon. Another type is caused by the system controller, which equals to the elapsed time from getting the sensor values to process them. Define it as τ_s, considering the process procedure is rapid, it can be reasonably estimated that τ_s is obviously smaller than τ_{ij}. Therefore, we can assume $\tau_s \ll \tau_{ij}$ in the system, and the time delays in self-processing are ignored.

The networked induced delay can cause the unstable information transmissions, such as accident consequence, packet-loss, etc. In Fig. 1, it is shown how these transmission errors occur. Indicates that during the sampling period T_s, then we get $\tau_{ij} = i \times T_s$, $i = 1, 2, 3, \ldots, n$. Furthermore, denote as x_{ji} the statement agent j to i, and $t_{k,\tau}^{ji}$ is kth the agent j to i through time delay τ. There is the statements of agent j at

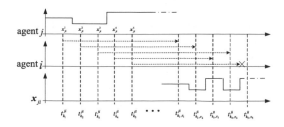

Fig. 1. Error sequence and packet loss in network communications

$t_{k_1}^{ji}, t_{k_2}^{ji}, t_{k_3}^{ji}, t_{k_4}^{ji}, t_{k_5}^{ji}$ will arrive to agent i at $t_{k_1,\tau_1}^{ji}, t_{k_2,\tau_2}^{ji}, t_{k_3,\tau_3}^{ji}, t_{k_4,\tau_4}^{ji}, t_{k_5,\tau_5}^{ji}$. In consideration of the delays' variation, only statement x_{ji}^1 and x_{ji}^2 are transferred to the receiver as expected. Statement x_{ji}^3 and x_{ji}^4 are mis-sequence packets, noticing that x_{ji}^4 reaches agent j earlier, even though it is sent later. Otherwise, x_{ji}^5 is lost because of $\tau_5 > \tau_d$, where τ_d is upper bound of delays [23].

Assume that there is a communication delay τ_{ji} between i-th agent and j-th, and $|\tau_{ji}| \leq \tau_d$. In a distributed protocol, all agent states eventually converge to the average state

$$u_i^d(t) = -\sum_{i \in N_i} a_{ij}\left[\gamma\big(q_i(t) - q_j(t - \tau_{ji})\big) + \big(p_i(t) - p_j(t - \tau_{ji})\big)\right] \tag{5}$$

where, $\gamma > 0$ is control gain, and τ_{ji} is data transfer time lag from j-th agent to the i-th. Furthermore, we discuss the range of network induced delays which ensure the multi-agent system salable.

Lemma 1 [21]: For system (1), if and only if 0 is a simple eigenvalue L, the graph has a global reachable node..

Take (5) into (1), and take the Laplace transform of both sides of (5) and get

$$sq_i(s) = -\sum_{j \in N_i} a_{ij}\left[\gamma\big(q_i(s) - e^{-s\tau_{ji}}q_j(s)\big) + \big(sq_i(s) - e^{-s\tau_{ji}}sq_j(s)\big)\right]$$

$$= -\sum_{j \in N_i} a_{ij}(\gamma + s)\left[q_i(s) - e^{-s\tau_{ji}}q_j(s)\right]$$

where $q_j(s)$ is the Laplace transform of $q_i(t)$ $(i \in N)$.

Denote $L(s) = \{l_{ij}(s)\}$ as a $n \times n$ matrix, which $l_{ij}(s)$ can be defined as

$$l_{ij}(s) = \begin{cases} -e^{-s\tau_{ij}}a_{ij}, & j \in N_i \\ \sum_{j \in N_i} a_{ij}, & j = i \\ 0, & others \end{cases}$$

When $s = 0$, $L(0) = L$ is the Laplacian matrix. Thus we get the characteristic polynomial of multi-agent system in the vector form. Then we consider the following

$$\det(sI + (\gamma + s)L(s)) = 0 \tag{6}$$

If the system (1) is to be stable, the root of (6) should on the closed left half complex plane. Here we check the characteristic of the Nyquist curve to discuss the system stability. Now we consider in two cases, namely $s = 0$ and $s \neq 0$.

Let $N(s) = \det(sI + (\gamma + s)L(s))$, if $s = 0$, then we get

$$N(0) = \det(0I + (\gamma + 0)L(0)) = \gamma \det(L(0)), \quad \gamma \neq 0$$

from Lemma 1, since the topology G has a globally reachable node, we can get $rank(L) = n - 1$, and 0 is the single eigenvalue of L. Thus $N(0) = 0$ and $N(0)$ has a single root with $s = 0$.

Now we discuss the situation when $s \neq 0$. Denote the Nyquist curve as

$$G(j\omega) = (\gamma + j\omega)L(j\omega)/j\omega \tag{7}$$

Based on the Nyquist stability criterion, the roots of $G(j\omega)$ lie on the open left half complex plane if and only if the Nyquist curve $G(j\omega)$ does not enclose the point $(-1, j0)$ for any $\omega \in R$.

Lemma 2 (Gersgorin disks theorem) [22]: For $A = [a_{ij}]_{n \times n}$, let $d_i = \sum_{i \neq j} |a_{ij}|$, then the set $D_i = \{z \in C : |z - a_{ii}| \leq d_i\}$ is called the ith Gershgorin disc of the matrix A. The circle has a radius d_i and is centered at a_{ii}.

Lemma 2 means each eigenvalue of matrix A satisfies $|\lambda - a_{ii}| \leq \sum_{i \neq j} |a_{ij}|$, $i \in \{1, 2, 3 \ldots, n\}$. Note that when ω changes from $(-\infty, +\infty)$, the disks of the eigenvalue change. Let $M_{\max} = \max_{i \in N} \sum_{i \neq j} a_{ij}$, then we can get

$$|\lambda - G(j\omega)| = |\lambda - (\gamma + j\omega)L(j\omega)/j\omega| \leq |\lambda - M_{\max}(\gamma + j\omega)/j\omega| \leq |M_{\max}(\gamma + j\omega)/j\omega|$$

Furthermore, for $\omega \in R$, given any constant $c \geq 1$, consider

$$|-c + 0j - M_{\max}(\gamma + j\omega)/j\omega| > |M_{\max}(\gamma + j\omega)/j\omega|$$

It can be proved the point $(-c, j0)$ satisfies $|-c + j0 - G(j\omega)| > |G(j\omega)|$, where $c \geq 1$ is not in a disk, and the system can maintain stable. Consider the system satisfies the given assumptions, the upper bounder τ_d should have

$$2(\tau_d + \gamma)M_{\max} < 1$$

Therefore, all roots of (6) are located on the closed left-hand complex plane. The conclusions above give the time-delays' boundary.

4 Consensus Algorithm Design

In the Sect. 2, we discussed the upper bound of the networked induced delays, which can maintain the system stable. However, these conclusions doesn't give an applied method to avoid the undesirable situations such as mis-sequence, packet dropout, etc. Next, we propose an effective way to compensate the network induced delays for deterministic predictor. We preset an auto-order data buffer in controller. The information in the buffer is re-ordered by the time stamp. Using this buffer, the received state data from its neighbors is resorted, and all the transferred information are guaranteed to be used in the right sequence. Thus, the adverse impact of the varied delays is reduced. The buffer enhances the error-tolerance of the system. In this section, we discuss the method of buffer design and how it works based on the conclusions in the last section.

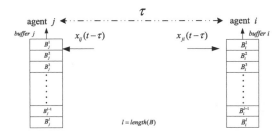

Fig. 2. Communication buffer in a multi agent system

Take the buffers in agent i and its neighbor j into account, the statements from j to i are stored in buffer B_i, and the statements from i to j are stored in buffer B_j. For a necessary condition of the system stability, the maximum delay time from one to another should be less than τ_d. Define the buffer level as $l(B)$, to determine its value, that means

$$T_s l(B) + \tau_{\min} \leq \tau_d$$

where T_s presents the sampling period, $\tau_{\min}$ presents the minimum delay under the networked environment. So we can get

$$l(B) \leq \frac{\tau_d - \tau_{\min}}{T_s} \qquad (8)$$

When the agent receives the report, all the data is based on a time stamp. When sending information to a neighbor, the time of the statement is marked. These time stamps can not be changed for any reason. Therefore, we can determine which information is sent first according to the time mark, and then sort them in the correct order. Fault tolerance of the system is improved.

The buffers resort all the information are not sent, and the resorted statements in a buffer of agent i are described as

$$\begin{cases} B^k = s(t)x_{ji}^\tau + (1 - s(t))B^{k-1} \\ k = \frac{\tau_{ji}}{T} \end{cases}$$

where

$$s(t) = \begin{cases} 0 & \tau_{ij} > \tau_d \\ 1 & \tau_{ij} \leq \tau_d \end{cases}$$

x_{ji}^{τ} and τ_{ji} are the statement under time delay τ and the time delay from j to i respectively, B^k is the kth statement in the buffer, and the output of buffer is always the first data of the buffer. Then denote it as $O(\cdot)$, thus, $O(B) = B^k|_{k=1} = B^1$. Then, consensus algorithm with buffer is described as

$$u_i^B(t) = -\sum_{i \in N_i} a_{ij}[\gamma(q_i(t) - O(B_i^q)) + (p_i(t) - O(B_i^p))] \tag{10}$$

where, B^q and B^p represent the buffer of positions and velocities respectively.

Note 1: Different buffer level is designed for each agent. Under the ideal network, buffers' level can use the following restriction

$$l(B)_{\max} \leq \frac{\tau_d}{T} \tag{11}$$

The multi-agent system is the unified negotiation under protocol (10). In that case, $\tau_{\max}$ is the network maximum delay, and $\tau_{\max} < \tau_d$. Because the fault tolerance of the system is limited, although the buffer layer design can be different, but the long buffer design with a limit inevitable increases the delay of the system, it is recommend to design a short buffer can reduce the difficulty and cost of system, and for the system limited fault tolerance. The implementation should be carried out according to the actual needs of the system.

5 Simulation

In this part, we use the algorithm in Sect. 3 to simulate the consistency of two multi-agent systems.

Example 1. Consider a 7 agents multi-agent system, whose communication network topology is shown in Fig. 3.

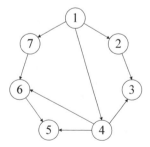

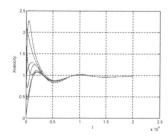

Fig. 3. Communication topology of agents   **Fig. 4.** The x-axis velocity consensus curves

Suppose every agent is a second-order agent with the kinetic Eq. (1). Set parameter γ an reasonable value to let $\tau_d = 0.16$. Assuming that $\tau_{min} = 0.06$ is the ideal network induce time delay. And set the simulation step to $\Delta T = 0.01$, the simulation time is $T = 20$. Then according to Sect. 3, the agent communication buffer length is designed as $length(B) = 10$.

The instantaneous communication delays in the system are defined as $\tau_{12} = 0.10$, $\tau_{14} = 0.07$, $\tau_{23} = 0.08$, $\tau_{43} = 0.11$, $\tau_{45} = 0.09$, $\tau_{46} = 0.09$, $\tau_{65} = 0.06$, $\tau_{76} = 0.16$, $\tau_{17} = 0.10$. Furthermore, let $(P_x^i(t_0), P_y^i(t_0), P_z^i(t_0))$ and $Q^i(t_0)$ defines the initial position and velocity of agent i, and

$$P_x^i(t_0) = 1 + 7 \cdot \text{rand}(1, 1), \ P_y^i(t_0) = 1 + 7 \cdot \text{rand}(1, 1), \ P_z^i(t_0) = 1 + 7 \cdot \text{rand}(1, 1)$$
$$Q_x^i(t_0) = 2.5 \cdot \text{rand}(1, 1), \ Q_y^i(t_0) = 2.5 \cdot \text{rand}(1, 1), \ Q_z^i(t_0) = 2.5 \cdot \text{rand}(1, 1)$$

In these figures, showing the cooperative operation of the agent under the algorithm. It is shown that the agents get velocity consensus on each axis finally.

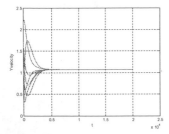

Fig. 5. The y-axis velocity consensus curves   **Fig. 6.** The z-axis velocity consensus curves

Example 2. Now we verify the time delay value to validate the results of multi-agent consensus. We consider using a multi-agent system with eight agents, with the communication topology shown as Fig. 7.

Let every agent is a second-order agent with the kinetic Eq. (1). Also set parameter γ a reasonable value to let $\tau_d = 0.20$ this time. We also assume that $\tau_{min} = 0.02$ is the ideal network induce time delay. In this example we also set the simulation step $\Delta T = 0.01$, simulation time $T = 15$. The agent communication buffer length is designed as $length(B) = 18$.

We change the instantaneous communication in the system delays are defined as $\tau_{12} = 0.20$, $\tau_{23} = 0.17$, $\tau_{24} = 0.06$, $\tau_{53} = 0.07$, $\tau_{45} = 0.19$, $\tau_{76} = 0.09$, $\tau_{46} = 0.09$, $\tau_{87} = 0.05$, $\tau_{17} = 0.16$, $\tau_{18} = 0.12$. Furthermore, we set the initial position and velocity as

$$P_x^i(t_0) = 2\mathrm{rand}(1,1), \ P_y^i(t_0) = 2\mathrm{rand}(1,1), \ P_z^i(t_0) = 2\mathrm{rand}(1,1)$$
$$Q_x^i(t_0) = 2.5 \cdot \mathrm{rand}(1,1), \ Q_y^i(t_0) = 2.5 \cdot \mathrm{rand}(1,1), \ Q_z^i(t_0) = 2.5 \cdot \mathrm{rand}(1,1)$$

In Figs. 8, 9 and 10 shows that agents get cooperative operation on the basis of algorithm. It is shown that the agents get velocity consensus on each axis finally.

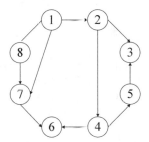

Fig. 7. Communication topology of agents

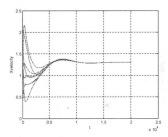

Fig. 8. The x-axis velocity consensus curves

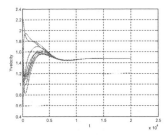

Fig. 9. The y-axis velocity consensus

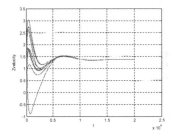

Fig. 10. The z-axis velocity consensus

6 Conclusion

The consistency problem of multi-agent systems with time-varying delay is studied in this paper. The distributed consistency control of the second order multi-agent with time-varying delay is considered. An improved consensus state derivative control is proposed. We define a specific buffer design function to avoid the networked time delays impacts. The theoretical results are verified by two simulation examples. Under this function, we propose a practical control protocol, which leads the agent in the system to the system and allows the agent to obtain the consensus state. In this paper, some sufficient and necessary conditions of special case are obtained, and the theory is applied to some simulation problems and the results are given. The proposed algorithm is test in MATLAB simulation environment with 2 typical examples. The simulation results show the effectiveness of the algorithm. With the proposed consensus algorithm, all agents are matched with the average speed, and network time-delay effects are reduced.

Acknowledgement. This work supported by the National Key Research and Development Program (2016YFC1400403), and the Youth Science and Technology Innovation Fund Of Shandong Agricultural University.

References

1. Li, S.B., Wang, J., Luo, X.Y., Guan, X.P.: A new framework of consensus protocol design for complex multi-agent systems. Syst. Control Lett. **60**, 19–26 (2011)
2. Cortés, J., Martínez, S., Bullo, F.: Robust rendezvous for mobile autonomous agents via proximity graphs in arbitrary dimensions. IEEE Trans. Autom. Control **51**, 1289–1298 (2006)
3. Xiao, L., Boyd, S.: Fast linear iterations for distributed averaging. Syst. Control Lett. **53**, 65–78 (2004)
4. Li, S.H., Du, H.B., Lin, X.Z.: Finite-time consensus algorithm for multi-agent systems with double-integrator dynamics. Automatica **47**, 1706–1712 (2011)
5. Ren, W.: Consensus strategies for cooperative control of vehicle formations. IET Control Theory Appl. **1**, 502–512 (2007)
6. Angeli, D.: Bliman PA: Convergence speed of unsteady distributed consensus: decay estimate along the setting spanning-trees. SIAM J. Control Optim. **48**, 1–32 (2009)
7. Jadbabaie, A., Lin, J., Morse, A.S.: Coordination of groups of mobile autonomous agents using nearest neighbor rules. IEEE Trans. Autom. Control **48**, 985–1001 (2003)
8. Yu, W., Chen, G., Cao, M.: Some necessary and sufficient conditions for second-order consensus in multi-agent dynamical systems. Automatica **46**, 1089–1095 (2010)
9. Moreau, L.: Stability of continuous-time distributed consensus algorithms. In: Proceedings of 43rd IEEE Conference on Decision Control, Atlantis, Paradise Island, Bahamas, pp. 3998–4003 (2004)
10. Nedic, A., Ozdaglar, A.: On the rate of convergence of distributed asynchronous sub-gradient methods for multi-agent optimization. In: Proceedings of 46th IEEE Conference Decision Control, New Orleans, LA, pp. 4197–4202, December 2007
11. Ren, W., Atkins, E.: Second-order consensus protocols in multiple vehicle systems with local interactions. Presented at the AIAA Guidance Navigation, Control Conference and Exhibit (2005)
12. Saber, O.R., Murray, R.M.: Consensus problems in networks of agents with switching topology and time-delays. IEEE Trans. Autom. Control **49**, 1520–1534 (2004)
13. Ren, W.: Multi-vehicle consensus with a time-varying reference state. Syst. Control Lett. **56**, 474–483 (2007)
14. Li, Z.G., Jia, Y.M., Du, J.P., Yuan, S.Y.: Flocking for multi-agent systems with switching topology in a noisy environment. In: American Control Conference, pp. 111–116 (2008)
15. Yang, Y., Souissi, S., Défago, X., Takizawa, M.: Fault-tolerant flocking for a group of autonomous mobile robots. J. Syst. Softw. **84**, 29–36 (2011)
16. Yang, W., Bertozzi, A.L., Wang, X.F.: Stability of a second order consensus algorithm with time delay. In: The 47th IEEE Conference on Decision and Control, Cancun, Mexico, pp. 2926–2931 (2008)

17. Gazi, V.: Stability of an asynchronous swarm with time-dependent communication links. IEEE Trans. Syst. Man Cybern. B **38**, 267–274 (2008)
18. Bliman, P.A., Iwasaki, T.: Application of semi-definite programming to robust stability of delay systems. Appl. Math. Comput. **200**, 517–528 (2008)
19. Lu, W., Chen, T.: Synchronization of coupled connected neural networks with delays. IEEE Trans. Circ. Syst. I **51**, 2491–2503 (2004)
20. Liu, C.L., Liu, F.: Consensus problem of second-order multi-agent systems with time-varying communication delay and switching topology. J. Syst. Eng. Electron. **22**, 672–678 (2011)
21. Lin, Z.Y., Francis, B., Maggiore, M.: Necessary and sufficient graphical conditions for formation control of unicycles. IEEE Trans. Autom. Control **50**, 121–127 (2005)
22. Desoer, A.C., Wang, T.Y.: On the generalized Nyquist stability criterion. IEEE Trans. Autom. Control **25**, 187–196 (1980)
23. Yang, L., Yuan, J.: A consensus algorithm with buffer in second-order multi-agent with time-varying delayed communication. Adv. Mater. Res. **1039**, 305–312 (2014)

Adaptive Consensus-Based Distributed Target Tracking in Sensor Networks

Xue Zhou[1], Hao Zhang[1(✉)], and Huaicheng Yan[2]

[1] The Department of Control Science and Engineering, Tongji University,
Shanghai 200092, People's Republic of China
zhang.hao@tongji.edu.cn

[2] The Key Laboratory of Advanced Control and Optimization for Chemical Processes
of Ministry of Education, School of Information Science and Engineering, East China
University of Science and Technology, Shanghai 200237, People's Republic of China

Abstract. This paper is concerned with the distributed Kalman state estimation with an adaptive consensus factor for a discrete-time target linear system over a sensor network. Both optimal filter gain and average disagreement of the estimates are considered in the filter design. In order to estimate the state of the target more accurately, an optimal Kalman gain is obtained by minimizing the mean-squared estimation error. The considered disagreement is employed to adjust the optimal gain as well as to acquire a better filtering performance. An illustrative example has been presented to prove the correctness of the conclusion and show the tracking performance of the filters.

1 Introduction

During the past decades, wireless sensor network (WSN) has been widely used in supervisory systems, rescue operation, intelligent transportation [1–4], etc. Especially the consensus-based distributed estimation has caused widespread interest due to its less use of communication resource and higher robustness in data fusion compared with centralized state estimation.

Although traditional centralized filtering is relatively easy to design, it requires powerful communication, and once there exist sensor failures, the whole system won't work [5,6]. Besides, in dynamic target tracking, only local information from neighboring sensors are available at each sensor, so the centralized estimation is not applicable [7–9]. As a result, some decentralized works have developed. In [10], authors propose a fully decentralized Kalman filter to reduce the coupling between sensor nodes. However, since each sensor needs to know all other sensor's information to compute its local estimates, this method is not extensible with the network size. Then the more general distributed algorithms

H. Yan—This work is supported by National Natural Science Foundation of China (61673178), Shanghai Natural Science Foundation (17ZR1445800) and Shanghai Shuguang Project (16SG28).

© Springer Nature Singapore Pte Ltd. 2017
D. Yue et al. (Eds.): LSMS/ICSEE 2017, Part II, CCIS 762, pp. 418–425, 2017.
DOI: 10.1007/978-981-10-6373-2_42

are proposed. It does not need a central processing facility nor a global information about the topology. Every sensor in the network, observe the state of the target, and form their own estimates only with the information from their neighbor's [11, 12].

In the aforementioned distributed filtering, the disagreement of estimates between sensors are overlooked. But, in many real networks, the coordinated estimation in the whole network is very important. In [13], authors developed a consensus-based distributed mixture Kalman filter, combining the particle filter with the traditional Kalman filter, which can estimate the state of conditional dynamic linear systems with a satisfactory disagreement of estimates. Besides, optimization approach and adaptive method are also used to solve distributed estimation problems. Authors in [14] studied an optimal adaptive filter. It introduces an adaptive factor for the filter gain to control its outlying disturbance influences. However, so far, almost no one in the design of filter, consider to automatically adjust the consensus parameter with an adaptive factor according to the disagreement. This motivate us to design such a filter.

The main contribution of this paper is to deal with the relationship between adjustable disagreement and filtering performance. We have designed a novel consensus-based distributed filter with an adaptive factor. With this factor, it is feasible to adjust the filter gain according to the disagreement of estimates. Different from existing literature, the adaptive factor under consideration is to adapt the consensus gain. From the illustrative example, it is shown that with this consensus adaptive factor, the estimation performance is improved and the disagreement between sensors also arrives to a satisfactory level.

2 Problem Statement

Consider a sensor network described as a directed graph $\mathcal{G} = \{\mathcal{V}, \mathcal{E}, \mathcal{A}\}$ consisting of a set of sensors $\mathcal{V} = \{1, 2, 3, \ldots, n\}$ and a set of edges $\mathcal{E} \subseteq \mathcal{V} \times \mathcal{V}$. The existence of edge (i, j) means that the ith sensor can communicate with the jth sensor. The set of neighbors of sensor i is denoted by $\mathcal{N}_i = \{j; (i, j) \in \mathcal{V}\}$. Let $d_i = |\mathcal{N}_i|$ be the number of neighboring sensors of the ith sensor. The adjacent matrix $\mathcal{A}(k) = [a_{ij}(k)]$ with nonnegative adjacency elements is defined by $a_{ij}(k) = 1$ if $(i, j) \in \mathcal{E}$, otherwise $a_{ij}(k) = 0$. The degree matrix is described by $\mathcal{D}(k) = diag\{D_1(k), D_2(k), \ldots, D_n(k)\}$, where the diagonal element is represented as $D(k) = \sum_{j \in \mathcal{N}_i} a_{ij}(k)$. The Laplacian matrix of the directed graph $\mathcal{G}$ is defined as $\mathcal{L}(k) = \mathcal{D}(k) - \mathcal{A}(k)$ and $\mathcal{L}(k) = [l_{ij}(k)]$. The discrete-time target plant is described as follows:

$$x(k + 1) = Ax(k) + \omega(k), \tag{1}$$

where $x \in \mathbb{R}^m$ is the state vector, the initial state $x(0)$ is zero-mean Gaussian with covariance $\Pi_0 \geq 0$. $\omega(k) \in \mathbb{R}^m$ is the process noise, which is also assumed to be zero-mean white Gaussian with covariance matrix $Q \geq 0$. $x(0)$ is independent of $\omega(k)$ for all $k \geq 0$. Suppose that the state of Eq. (1) is observed by n sensors distributed in a directed graph $\mathcal{G} = \{\mathcal{V}, \mathcal{E}, \mathcal{A}\}$, then the measurement equation of the ith sensor is given by

$$y_i(k) = H_i x(k) + v_i(k), \tag{2}$$

where $v_i(k) \in \mathbb{R}^m$ is the zero-mean Gaussian measurement noise with covariance $R_i > 0$. $v_i(k)$ is independent of $x(0)$ and $\omega(k), \forall k, i$, and is independent of $v_j(s)$ when $i \neq j$ or $k \neq s$. Besides, A and H_i have the suitable dimensions.

The state estimator of the ith node is

$$\hat{x}_i(k+1) = A\hat{x}_i(k) + K_i(k)[y_i(k) - H_i\hat{x}_i(k)] - \alpha_i(k)\varepsilon A \sum_{j \in \mathcal{N}_i} a_{ij}(k)[\hat{x}_i(k) - \hat{x}_j(k)], \tag{3}$$

where $K_i(k)$ is the gain matrix, ε is the consensus gain with the range of $(0, 1/\Delta)$, $\Delta = \max(di)$, $\hat{x}_i$ is the estimated target state. Define the estimated error of the ith sensor as $e_i(k) = \hat{x}_i(k) - x(k)$, and the cross error covariance $P_{ij}(k) = \mathbb{E}\{e_i(k)e_j(k)^T\}$. Let $F_i(k) = A - K_i(k)H_i$, the iterative equation of P_i can be obtained as

$$
\begin{aligned}
P_i(k+1) = {} & A\{P_i(k) - 2\alpha_i(k)\varepsilon \sum_{r \in \mathcal{N}_i} a_{ir}(k)P_i(k) + (\alpha_i(k)\varepsilon)^2 \sum_{r \in \mathcal{N}_i} a_{ir}^2(k)P_i(k) \\
& + (\alpha_i(k)\varepsilon)^2 \sum_{r,s \in \mathcal{N}_i, r \neq s} a_{ir}(k)a_{is}(k)P_i(k)\}A^T \\
& + A\{\sum_{r \in \mathcal{N}_i} a_{ir}(k)(\alpha_i(k)\varepsilon - (\alpha_i(k)\varepsilon)^2 a_{ir}(k) \\
& - (\alpha_i(k)\varepsilon)^2 \sum_{s \in \mathcal{N}_i, r \neq s} a_{is}(k))[P_{ri}(k) + P_{ir}(k)]\}A^T + (\alpha_i(k)\varepsilon)^2 A \\
& \times \sum_{r,s \in \mathcal{N}_i, r \neq s} a_{ir}(k)a_{is}(k)P_{rs}(k)A^T + (\alpha_i(k)\varepsilon)^2 A \sum_{r \in \mathcal{N}_i} a_{ir}^2(k)P_r(k)A^T \\
& - A\{P_i(k) + \alpha_i(k)\varepsilon \sum_{r \in \mathcal{N}_i} a_{ir}(k)[P_{ri}(k) - P_i(k)]\}H_i M_i(k)^{-1} H_i^T \\
& \times \{P_i(k) + \alpha_i(k)\varepsilon \sum_{r \in \mathcal{N}_i} a_{ir}(k)[P_{ir}(k) - P_i(k)]\}A^T \\
& + [K_i(k) - K_i^*(k)]M_i(k)[K_i(k) - K_i^*(k)]^T, \tag{4}
\end{aligned}
$$

where $M_i(k) = H_i P_i(k)H_i^T + R_i$, following from Eq. (4), the optimal gain is

$$K_i^*(k) = A\{P_i(k) + \alpha_i(k)\varepsilon \sum_{r \in \mathcal{N}_i} a_{ir}(k)[P_{ri}(k) - P_i(k)]\}H_i M_i(k)^{-1}. \tag{5}$$

Remark 1. It is noted that the optimal gain contains the adaptive term, if the disagreement meets the requirement, then $\alpha_i(k)$ won't be changed. Moreover, if the initial value of $\alpha_i(k)$ is given as 1, and it always meets the demand, then $\alpha_i(k) \equiv 1$, [15] becomes a special case of this adaptive estimator.

3   Convergence Analysis

In this section, the stability of the proposed estimator (3) with the optimal estimator gain (5) is analysed. Due to the coupling of the estimation errors among neighboring sensors, it is difficult to prove that the estimation error covariance converges to a unique positive definite matrix such as in the centralized Kalman filter, so only an upper and a lower bound of the estimation error covariance is derived.

Before moving on, the following assumptions are introduced.

Assumption 1. There exist nonzero real constants $\underline{f}$, $\bar{f}$, $\underline{h}_i$, $\bar{h}_i$, $\underline{q}$, $\bar{q}$, $\underline{r}_i$ and $\bar{r}_i$, for all $k \geq 0$, $i \in N$, such that the following bounds on the matrices are satisfied

$$\underline{f}^2 I_m \leq AA^T \leq \bar{f}^2 I_m, \tag{6}$$

$$\underline{h}_i^2 I_m \leq H_i H_i^T \leq \bar{h}_i^2 I_m, \tag{7}$$

$$\underline{q}^2 I_m \leq Q \leq \bar{q}^2 I_m, \tag{8}$$

$$\underline{r}_i^2 I_m \leq R_i \leq \bar{r}_i^2 I_m. \tag{9}$$

Assumption 2. The initial error covariance $P_i(0)$ is positive semidefinite.

Now, we are ready to present the main results of this paper.

Theorem 1. When k approaches to infinite, under assumptions 1 and 2, there exist a constant φ and ϱ, making the error covariance of each sensor bounded, $P_i(k+1) < \varphi I_m$, $P_i(k+1) \geq \varrho I_m$, where $\varrho = \underline{q} + \kappa$, $\varphi = \bar{P}_k(\bar{f}^2 + \bar{h}_i^2 K^2)(1 + \xi)$.

Proof. According to Eq. (4), $P_i(k+1)$ can be written as

$$P_i(k+1) = F_i(k)P_i(k)F_i(k) + Q + K_i(k)R_iK_i(k)^T + \Delta P_i(k), \tag{10}$$

where $\Delta P_i(k) = (\alpha_i(k)\varepsilon)^2 A \times \sum_{r,s \in N_i, r \neq s} a_{is}(k)a_{ir}(k)[P_i(k) - P_{ir}(k) - P_{si}(k) + P_{rs}(k)]A^T + (\alpha_i(k)\varepsilon)^2 A \sum_{r \in N_i} a_{ij}(k)[P_i(k) + P_r(k) - P_{ir}(k) - P_{ri}(k)]A^T - \alpha_i(k)\varepsilon F_i(k) \sum_{r \in N_i} a_{ij}(k)[P_i(k) - P_{ir}(k)]A^T - \alpha_i(k)\varepsilon A \sum_{r \in N_i} a_{ij}(k)[P_i(k) - P_{ri}(k)]F_i(k)^T$.
Similar to [15], there exist a small enough ε making $\|\Delta P_i(k)\| < \kappa$, $K_i(k)K_i(k)^T \leq \bar{K}^2 I_m$. As a result, $P_i(k+1)$ can be written approximatively as

$$P_i(k+1) = F_i(k)P_i(k)F_i(k)^T + K_i(k)R_iK_i(k)^T + Q + \kappa I_m. \tag{11}$$

Denote $K_i(k)R_iK_i(k)^T + Q + \kappa I_m$ as $\Phi(k)$, by continuously using the matrix inverse lemma, it can be obtained that

$$P_i(k+1) \geq (\underline{q} + \kappa)I_m. \tag{12}$$

Besides, $P_i(k+1)$ can be written in another form

$$
\begin{aligned}
(P_i(k+1))^{-1} &= (F_i(k)P_i(k)F_i(k)^T + F_i(k)F_i(k)^{-1}\Phi(k)F_i(k)^{-T}F_i(k)^T)^{-1} \\
&= F_i(k)^{-T}(P_i(k) + F_i(k)^{-1}\Phi(k)F_i(k)^{-T})^{-1}F_i(k)^{-1}.
\end{aligned}
\tag{13}
$$

So,

$$
P_i(k+1) \le F_i(k)P_i(k)F_i(k)^T(1 + \frac{\bar{r}_i\bar{K}^2 + \bar{q} + \kappa}{\bar{f}^2(\underline{q} + \kappa)}).
\tag{14}
$$

Next, by using mathematical induction and assumption(2), the upper bound of $P_i(k+1)$ can be acquired.

For $l=0$, since $P_i(0)$ is positive semidefinite, $P_i(0) \le \lambda_{\max}(P_i(0))I_m$, a $\bar{P}_0 = \max\{\lambda_{\max}(P_i(0))\}$ can be got to make $P_i(0) \le \bar{P}_0 I_m$.

For $l=1$, based on Eq. (12), it is obtained that

$$
P_i(1) \le \{(\bar{f}^2 + \bar{h}_i^2\bar{K}^2)\bar{P}_0 + \bar{r}_i\bar{K}^2 + \bar{q}\}I_m,
\tag{15}
$$

where $(\bar{f}^2 + \bar{h}_i^2\bar{K}^2)\bar{P}_0 + \bar{r}_i\bar{K}^2 + \bar{q}$ is denoted as $\bar{P}_1$. Then use inductive step, the upper bound of $P_i(k+1)$ is given

$$
P_i(k+1) \le \bar{P}_k(\bar{f}^2 + \bar{h}_i^2\bar{K}^2)(1 + \xi)I_m,
\tag{16}
$$

where $\bar{P}_k = (\bar{f}^2 + \bar{h}_i^2\bar{K}^2)\bar{P}_{k-1} + \bar{r}_i\bar{K}^2 + \bar{q}$, $\xi = \frac{\bar{r}_i\bar{K}^2 + \bar{q} + \kappa}{\bar{f}^2(\underline{q} + \kappa)}$.

Now, the form of adaptive factor will be considered. As [8] defined, the average disagreement of the estimates (DoE) among all sensors is $DoE = \frac{1}{N}\sum_{i=1}^{N}\|\hat{x}_i - \frac{1}{N}\sum_{i=1}^{N}\hat{x}_i\|^2$. Given the form of $\alpha_i(k)$ as follows

$$
\alpha_i(k) = \begin{cases} \alpha_i(k), & \text{if } DoE \le \beta, \\ \alpha_i(k) - a\alpha_i(k)(l - \dfrac{1}{l - DoE})^b, & \text{if } DoE > \beta, \end{cases}
\tag{17}
$$

where a is used to decide the rangeability, b coordinate the decrease proportion, l represents the past l steps. They all need to be chosen appropriately. β is the needed threshold value, it's decided by your demand. In the past l steps, computing the consensus degree, if it's beyond the requirement, then it's necessary to decrease DoE to achieve the demand. Moreover, from Eq. (5), we know when $\alpha_i(k)$ decreases, $\bar{K}$ decreases. According to Eq. (14), the upper bound of $P_i(k+1)$ is also decreased, then the estimation performance is improved.

4   Simulation Results

In this section, simulations of a maneuvering target tracking system [16] are presented to demonstrate the effectiveness of the proposed estimator design method, where the parameters of state space model in 1 and 2 are

$$
A = \begin{bmatrix} 1 & 0.5 \\ 0 & 1 \end{bmatrix}, \quad Q = \begin{bmatrix} 0.1 & 0 \\ 0 & 0.1 \end{bmatrix}.
$$

Here, 25 sensors are considered in the networks. $H_i = [2\delta_i \quad 0; 0 \quad 2\delta_i]$. $v_i(k)$ has covariance matrix $R_i = 0.01I_2$. Besides, the topology of sensor network is depicted in Fig. 1. The initial position of the target is chosen as $x = 1.553\,\mathrm{m}$, $y = 1.877\,\mathrm{m}$. According to Eq. (1), we can plot the target's location at every moment k. Through the given initial condition and the sensors' estimate Eq. (3), the estimated trajectory of each sensor can be plotted. Figure 2 displays the true value of target position (the black curve) and the estimated trajectory (the blue curve) of sensor i ($i = 1, 2, \ldots, 25$), from which, we can observe that the 25 sensors all can well track the target location and maintain a satisfactory disagreement between them. It is shown that as time goes on, the tracking performance is getting better and better. By omitting the adaptive factor in the estimation Eq. (3), a specified estimation equation is got. And its error covariance is depicted in Fig. 3 (the black one). Besides, the adaptive estimation error covariance is also presented in Fig. 3 (the red one). For clarity, only sensor 1's error covariance is plotted. According to Fig. 2, it is noted that the estimator with an adaptive factor has lower error covariance, this implies that an adaptive factor can improve the estimation results. Besides, it is demonstrated that $P_i(k)$ indeed converges.

Fig. 1. The topology of sensor networks.

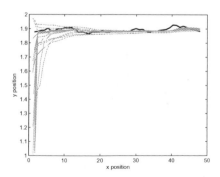

Fig. 2. The tracking performance of the distributed system. (Color figure online)

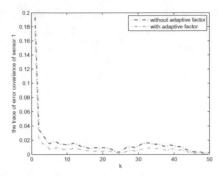

Fig. 3. The adaptive factor's influence to estimation performance. (Color figure online)

To show the performance of the method in this paper is over existing methods, we make a comparison among this method (ACDF) and the consensus-based distributed Kalman filtering method (CDF) as well as the average distributed Kalman filtering method (DF). Similarly to [2], we define an improvement factor (IF) of the ACDF algorithm, as compared with DCF and DF, which is

$$IF = \frac{\text{RMSE of the compared one - RMSE of ACDF}}{\text{RMSE of the compared one}},$$

where RMSE represents for the average of the root-mean-square error.

$$RMSE = \frac{1}{N} \sum_{i=1}^{N} \sqrt{\frac{1}{K - [k/2] + 1} \sum_{k=[K/2]}^{K} \|e_i(k)\|^2},$$

where K is the total number of time steps of simulations, and $[K/2]$ is the nearest integer around $K/2$. Table 1 summarizes the RMSE of the three distributed algorithms. Compared with the DCF algorithm, the ACDF algorithm improve the filtering performance by 17.7% and 13.3%, compared with the DF, improved by 37.7% and 35.7%.

Table 1. RMSE and IF of the proposed ACDF algorithm compared with some other algorithms

	RMSE	IF
ACDF	x:0.6603	
	y:0.6302	
CDF	x:0.7770	17.7 %
	y:0.7268	13.3 %
DF	x:1.0600	37.7 %
	y:0.9802	35.7 %

5 Conclusion

In this paper, a distributed estimator with an adaptive factor is designed. Through the adaptive factor, the disagreement is associated with the estimation performance. By calculating the average disagreement of the estimates, the form of adaptive factor is proposed and it can improve the tracking performance. Compared with existing works, the filtering method proposed in this paper, has higher precision, but there is still some problem for improvement. In future works, some analysis on the selection of adaptive parameters should be started to get the best results. In addition, it is important to consider how to get the best filtering performance under the packet loss, attack and other situations.

References

1. Yu, W., Chen, G., Wang, Z., Yang, W.: Distributed consensus filtering in sensor networks. IEEE Trans. Syst., Man, Cybern. B, Cybern. **39**, 1568–1577 (2009)
2. Zhu, S., Chen, C., Guan, X., Long, C.: An estimator model for distributed estimation in heterogenous wireless sensor networks. In: Proceedings of Workshop Wireless Sensor, Actuator and Robot Networks, pp. 1–6 (2010)
3. Olfati-Saber, R.: Kalman-consensus filter: optimality, stability, and performance. In: Proceedings of IEEE Conference Decision Control, pp. 7036–7042 (2009)
4. Olfati-Saber, R.: Distributed Kalman filter with embedded consensus filters. In: Proceedings of 44th IEEE Conference Decision Control, pp. 8179–8184 (2005)
5. Speyer, J.: Computation and transmission requirements for a decentralized linear-quadratic-Gaussian control problem. IEEE Trans. Autom. Contr. **24**, 266–269 (1979)
6. Foderaro, G., Zhu, P.: Distributed optimal control of sensor networks for dynamic target tracking. In: IEEE Trans. Control Netw. Syst. (2016)
7. Carli, R., Chiuso, A., Schenato, L., Zampieri, S.: Distributed Kalman filtering based on consensus strategies. IEEE J. Sel. Areas Commun. **26**, 622–633 (2008)
8. Zhu, S., Chen, C.: Distributed optimal consensus filter for target tracking in heterogeneous sensor network. IEEE Trans. Cybern. **43**, 1963–1975 (2013)
9. Olfati-Saber, R.: Distributed Kalman filtering for sensor networks. In: Proceedings of 46th IEEE Conference Decision Control, pp. 5492–5498 (2007)
10. Rao, B., Durrant-Whyte, H., Sheen, J.: A fully decentralized multi-sensor system for tracking and surveillance. Int. J. Robot. Res. **12**, 20–44 (1993)
11. Federico, S., Ali, H.: Diffusion strategies for distributed Kalman filtering and smoothing. IEEE Trans. Autom. Control **55**, 2069–2084 (2010)
12. Ribeiro, A., Schizas, I., Roumeliotis, S., Giannakis, G.: Kalman filtering in wireless sensor networks. IEEE Control Syst. Mag. **30**, 66–86 (2010)
13. Yu, Y.: Consensus-based distributed mixture Kalman filter for maneuvering target tracking in wireless sensor networks. IEEE Trans. Veh. Technol. **65**, 8669–8681 (2016)
14. Yang, Y., Gao, W.: An optimal adaptive Kalman filter. Orig. Art. **80**, 177–183 (2006)
15. Yang, W., Chen, G.: Stochastic sensor activation for distributed state estimation over a sensor network. Automatica **50**, 2070–2076 (2014)
16. Zhang, W.A., Feng, G., Yu, L.: Multi-rate distributed fusion estimation for sensor networks with packet losses. Automatica **48**, 2016–2028 (2012)

Event-Triggered Consensus Tracking Control of Multi-agent Systems with Lipschitz-Type Dynamics

Yang Yang[1,2(✉)] and Dong Yue[1,2]

[1] College of Automation, Nanjing University of Posts and Telecommunications,
Nanjing 210023, China
yyang@njupt.edu.cn

[2] The Jiangsu Engineering Laboratory of Big Data Analysis and Control for Active
Distribution Network, Nanjing University of Posts and Telecommunications,
Nanjing 210023, China

Abstract. In this paper, we consider the leader-following tracking control problem for a class of nonlinear multi-agent systems (MASs) with Lipschitz-type dynamics via event-triggered approaches. For a directed communication topology, a distributed consensus control scheme is developed on the basis of event-triggered mechanism. In addition, to avoid continuous monitor of measurement information, a technical approach is presented for generation of the combinational information from their own neighboring agents only at event instants. The stability of the closed-loop system is given, and it is proven that the Zeno behavior is ruled out.

Keywords: Multi-agent systems · Event-triggered control · Consensus · Nonlinear systems

1 Introduction

Fruitful results about cooperative control methods for MASs have recently been reported and provided a mature theoretical background as well as numerous practical examples, e.g. [1–6] and the references therein. The aperiodic control has emerged for the networked systems with limited communication as an alternative to periodic triggered one [7,8]. In [9], event-scheduling consensus control mechanisms for a class of single-integrator MASs were introduced. Average consensus event-triggered control approaches were developed in [10] for single-integrators and double-integrators. Zhang *et al.* discussed consensus control schemes for linear dynamics connected through an undirected topology in [11]. In [12,13], Hu and Zhu *et al.* discussed the event-based broadcasting algorithms to achieve consensus for linear from MASs and the linear ones with time-delay inputs, respectively. Self-triggered control strategies [9,14,15] were employed to avoid continuous measurement using current measurement information. The leader-following issues are also taken into account in the past years.

© Springer Nature Singapore Pte Ltd. 2017
D. Yue et al. (Eds.): LSMS/ICSEE 2017, Part II, CCIS 762, pp. 426–434, 2017.
DOI: 10.1007/978-981-10-6373-2_43

Hu *et al.* discussed a dynamic tracking problem for a first-order directed linear MASs by an event-triggered strategy in [16]. The event-based leader-following consensus control protocols strategy for second-order MASs were investigated in [17,18]. Authors in [17–20] paid less attention to the nonlinear ones. In this paper, we devote to consider the leader-following tracking issue for a class of nonlinear MASs regulated by an event-triggered mechanism. In details, a distributed leader-following control strategy is developed on the basis of event-triggered mechanism. Furthermore, to avoid continuous measurement information monitor, we present a technical approach for generation of the combinational information from their own neighboring agents only at event-triggered instants. The main contributions of this paper consist of the following aspects. (1) First, compared with the associated research work [19], it is nontrivial to be concentrated on the extension of the recent leading-following control results to a class of nonlinear systems with a directed diagraph in an event-triggered manner. Moreover, the dynamics of the leader agent can be marginally stable or even unstable. (2) Second, unlike [21], a computing algorithm for combinational state information is presented and it avoids additional sampling and removes requirement of continuous monitor measurement information to check whether triggered conditions are satisfied.

2 Problem Formulation

We consider a class of nonlinear MASs including one leader and N follower agents connected through a directed digraph, and the dynamics of the ith follower are

$$\dot{x}_i = Ax_i + Bu_i + Cf(x_i(t), t), \tag{1}$$

where $i = 1, \cdots, N$, $x_i \in \mathbb{R}^n$ is the state variable vector of the ith agent, $u_i \in \mathbb{R}^p$ represents the control input signal, and $A \in \mathbb{R}^{n \times n}$, $B \in \mathbb{R}^{n \times p}$, $C \in \mathbb{R}^{n \times n}$. $f(x_i(t), t) = (f_1(x_i(t), t), \ldots, f_n(x_i(t), t))^{\mathrm{T}}$ is a continuous vector function standing for the nonlinear dynamics of the ith agent. It is assumed that the inner states are of availableness for measurement. The dynamics of the leader are expressed as

$$\dot{x}_l = Ax_l + Cf(x_l(t), t), \tag{2}$$

where $x_l \in \mathbb{R}^n$ is the measurable and trajectory vector of the leader.

Assumption 1. There exists a positive constant ρ such that

$$||f(y, t) - f(z, t)|| \leq \rho ||y - z||, \tag{3}$$

where $\forall y, z \in \mathbb{R}^n$, $t \geq 0$.

Remark 1. This assumption is the so-called Lipschitz condition, and it is mild and normal, which can be referred in [3].

The preliminaries about communication topology is omitted, and the more details can be found in [19]. A diagonal matrix $S = \text{diag}(s_1, \cdots, s_N)$ is the accessibility of the leader for the ith follower node with $s_i = 1$ if possible and $s_i = 0$ otherwise. It is also assumed that the graph G contains a spanning tree and $-(L + S)$ is a nonsingular M-matrix, where L is the Laplacian matrix. This implies that there exists a positive diagonal matrix $\Theta = \text{diag}(\theta_1, \cdots, \theta_N)$ satisfying that $Y = \Theta^{-1}(L+S) + (L+S)^{\text{T}}\Theta^{-1} > 0$. Define that $\beta = \frac{1}{2}\lambda_{\min}(Y)$, $\theta_{\max} = \max\limits_{i=1,\ldots,N}\{\theta_i\}$, $\theta_{\min} = \min\limits_{i=1,\ldots,N}\{\theta_i\}$, $\underline{\theta} = \min\limits_{i=1,\ldots,N}\{\theta_i^{-1}\}$, and $F = (L+S)^{\text{T}}(L+S)$.

For the ith follower agent, a state denoted as $\eta_i(t)$ is introduced

$$\eta_i(t) = \sum_{j \in \mathcal{N}_i} \Big(x_j(t) - x_i(t)\Big) + s_i\Big(x_l(t) - x_i(t)\Big). \tag{4}$$

Denote t_k^i as the event time sequence of the ith follower agent, $k = 0, 1, 2, \cdots$, and $\eta_i(t_k^i)$ represents its latest broadcast value of Agent i. The measurement signal is $\breve{\eta}_i(t) = \eta_i(t_k^i)$, where $t \in [t_k^i, t_{k+1}^i)$. The controller is based on sampling data and we consider the following controller

$$u_i(t) = -K\breve{\eta}_i(t), \tag{5}$$

where $t \in [t_k^i, t_{k+1}^i)$, $K \in \mathbb{R}^{p \times n}$ is a gain matrix.

In the above data transmission framework, the event-triggered consensus tracking is said to be achieved, as $t \to \infty$,

$$\sum_{i=1}^{N} ||x_l(t) - x_i(t)||^2 \leq \varpi, \tag{6}$$

and Zeno behavior is also excluded, where ϖ is a positive constant. The overall goal of this paper is to develop such a control strategy for the system (1) satisfying (6).

3   Distributed Event-Triggered Control Approach

In this part, we are going to derive a leader-following tracking control scheme for the system (1) in an event-triggered manner. Define the measurement error

$$e_i(t) = \breve{\eta}_i(t) - \eta_i(t), \tag{7}$$

and tracking error

$$\zeta_i(t) = x_l(t) - x_i(t), \tag{8}$$

for the ith agent.

As for $t \in [t_k^i, t_{k+1}^i)$, the triggered function is designed as

$$h_i = \frac{||e_i||^2}{\beta\varsigma_1} - \vartheta_i\theta_i^{-1}\eta_i^{\text{T}}P\eta_i - \mu_i e^{-\sigma_i t} - \delta, \tag{9}$$

where $\vartheta_i > 0$, $\mu_i > 0$, $\sigma_i \in (0, \varepsilon_{\min})$, $\varepsilon_i = \beta_1 - \vartheta_i - \frac{\varsigma_1}{\beta}\beta_2 - \varsigma_2\beta_3 > 0$, $\beta_1 = \frac{\lambda_{\min}(Q)}{\lambda_{\max}(P)}$, $\beta_2 = \frac{\lambda_{\max}(Y)\lambda_{\max}^2(PBR^{-1}B^{\mathrm{T}}P)}{\underline{\theta}\lambda_{\min}(P)}$, $\beta_3 = \frac{\lambda_{\max}(Y)\lambda_{\max}(P^{\mathrm{T}}P)}{\underline{\theta}\lambda_{\min}(P)}$, $\varepsilon_{\min} = \min\limits_{i=1,\ldots,N}\{\varepsilon_i\}$, $\sigma_i \in (0, \varepsilon_{\min})$, and $\varsigma_1 > 0$, $\varsigma_2 > 0$, $\delta > 0$. And there exists a positive and symmetrical matrix P satisfying the following inequality

$$PA + A^{\mathrm{T}}P - 2\theta_{\min}PBR^{-1}B^{\mathrm{T}}P + \frac{\rho^2}{\varsigma_2}\lambda_{\max}(C^{\mathrm{T}}C)\lambda_{\max}(D)\theta_{\max}I_n + Q \le 0, \tag{10}$$

where $\varsigma_2 > 0$, D will be given later, and I_n is a nth identify matrix.

The definition of event triggered time instant is given by

$$t_{k+1}^i - \inf\{t > t_k^i : h_i \ge 0\}. \tag{11}$$

Now, we are going to present the main result of this paper.

Theorem 1. *Given the MASs* (1) *in a directed graph satisfying Assumption 1, then the control scheme* (5) *with* $K = -\frac{1}{\beta}R^{-1}B^{\mathrm{T}}P$ *is able to steer the inner states of the system* (1) *to achieve leader-following tracking target* (6) *if the triggered time sequence for each follower agent is defined by* (11). *Also, the Zeno behavior is excluded.*

Proof. From (1), (7) and (8), we have

$$\dot{\zeta}_i - A\zeta_i + C\Big(f(x_l, t) - f(x_i, t)\Big) + BKe_i + BK\eta_i. \tag{12}$$

Then, by denoting $\zeta = [\zeta_1^{\mathrm{T}}, \cdots, \zeta_N^{\mathrm{T}}]^{\mathrm{T}}$, $e = [e_1^{\mathrm{T}}, \cdots, e_N^{\mathrm{T}}]^{\mathrm{T}}$, $\eta = [\eta_1^{\mathrm{T}}, \cdots, \eta_N^{\mathrm{T}}]^{\mathrm{T}}$, the aforementioned equation can be written in vector

$$\dot{\zeta} = (I_N \otimes A)\zeta + \widetilde{f} + (I_N \otimes BK)e + (I_N \otimes BK)\eta, \tag{13}$$

where $\widetilde{f} = \Big[C\Big(f(x_l, t) - f(x_1, t)\Big); \cdots ; C\Big(f(x_l, t) - f(x_N, t)\Big)\Big]$, and I_N is the Nth identify matrix.

Consider the Lyapunov function candidate

$$V = \eta^{\mathrm{T}}(\Theta^{-1} \otimes P)\eta, \tag{14}$$

where $\eta = ((L + S) \otimes I_n)\zeta$.

Noting (18), the time derivative of V yields

$$\begin{aligned}
\dot{V} &= \dot{\eta}^{\mathrm{T}}(\Theta^{-1} \otimes P)\eta + \eta^{\mathrm{T}}(\Theta^{-1} \otimes P)\dot{\eta} \\
&= \zeta^{\mathrm{T}}((L+S)^{\mathrm{T}}\Theta^{-1} \otimes A^{\mathrm{T}}P)\eta + \eta^{\mathrm{T}}(\Theta^{-1}(L+S) \otimes PA)\zeta \\
&\quad + \eta^{\mathrm{T}}(\Theta^{-1}(L+S) \otimes P(BK))\eta + e^{\mathrm{T}}((L+S)^{\mathrm{T}}\Theta^{-1} \otimes (BK)^{\mathrm{T}}P)\eta \\
&\quad + \eta^{\mathrm{T}}((L+S)^{\mathrm{T}}\Theta^{-1} \otimes (BK)^{\mathrm{T}}P)\eta + \eta^{\mathrm{T}}(\Theta^{-1}(L+S) \otimes P(BK))e \\
&\quad + \widetilde{f}^{\mathrm{T}}((L+S)^{\mathrm{T}}\Theta^{-1} \otimes P)\eta + \eta^{\mathrm{T}}(\Theta^{-1}(L+S) \otimes P)\widetilde{f}. \tag{15}
\end{aligned}$$

Taking the relationship between ζ and η, the definition of ζ, $K = -\frac{1}{\beta}R^{-1}B^{\mathrm{T}}P$, (3) and completely square inequalities into account, one has

$$e^{\mathrm{T}}((L+S)^{\mathrm{T}}\Theta^{-1} \otimes (BK)^{\mathrm{T}}P)\eta + \eta^{\mathrm{T}}(\Theta^{-1}(L+S) \otimes P(BK))e$$
$$\leq \frac{e^{\mathrm{T}}e}{\beta\varsigma_1} + \frac{\varsigma_1}{\beta}\eta^{\mathrm{T}}(Y \otimes (2\theta_{\min}PBR^{-1}B^{\mathrm{T}}P)^2)\eta, \tag{16}$$

$$\tilde{f}^{\mathrm{T}}((L+S)^{\mathrm{T}}\Theta^{-1} \otimes P)\eta + \eta^{\mathrm{T}}(\Theta^{-1}(L+S) \otimes P)\tilde{f}$$
$$\leq \frac{1}{\varsigma_2}\eta^{\mathrm{T}}(\Theta^{-1} \otimes (\lambda_{\max}(C^{\mathrm{T}}C)\rho^2\eta^{\mathrm{T}}\lambda_{\max}(D)\theta_{\max})I_m)\eta + \varsigma_2\eta^{\mathrm{T}}(Y \otimes (P^{\mathrm{T}}P))\eta, \tag{17}$$

$$\eta^{\mathrm{T}}((L+S)^{\mathrm{T}}\Theta^{-1} \otimes (BK)^{\mathrm{T}}P)\eta + \eta^{\mathrm{T}}(\Theta^{-1}(L+S) \otimes P(BK))\eta$$
$$\leq -\eta^{\mathrm{T}}(\Theta^{-1} \otimes (2\theta_{\min}PBR^{-1}B^{\mathrm{T}}P)I_m)\eta, \tag{18}$$

where $D = (L+S)^{-\mathrm{T}}(L+S)^{-1}$. Then, it follows that

$$\dot{V} \leq -\eta^{\mathrm{T}}(\Theta^{-1} \otimes Q)\eta + \frac{e^{\mathrm{T}}e}{\beta\varsigma_1} + \varsigma_2\eta^{\mathrm{T}}(Y \otimes (P^{\mathrm{T}}P))\eta$$
$$+ \frac{\varsigma_1}{\beta}\eta^{\mathrm{T}}(Y \otimes (2\theta_{\min}PBR^{-1}B^{\mathrm{T}}P)^2)\eta. \tag{19}$$

Since the triggered condition (11) enforces the property

$$\frac{\|e_i\|^2}{\beta\varsigma_1} \leq \vartheta_i\theta_i^{-1}\eta_i^{\mathrm{T}}P\eta_i + \mu_ie^{-\sigma_it} + \delta, \tag{20}$$

during the time interval $[t_k^i, t_{k+1}^i)$, it leads to

$$\dot{V} \leq -\sum_{i=1}^{N}\varepsilon_i\theta_i^{-1}\eta_i^{\mathrm{T}}P\eta_i + \sum_{i=1}^{N}\mu_ie^{-\sigma_it} + N\delta$$
$$\leq -\chi V + \sum_{i=1}^{N}\mu_ie^{-\sigma_it} + N\delta, \tag{21}$$

where $\chi = \varepsilon_{\min}$.

Then, we can obtain that

$$V \leq e^{-\chi t}\left[V(0) - \sum_{i=1}^{N}\frac{\mu_i}{\chi - \sigma_i} - \frac{N\delta}{\chi}\right] + \sum_{i=1}^{N}e^{-\sigma_it}\frac{\mu_i}{\chi - \sigma_i} + \frac{N\delta}{\chi} \leq \xi, \tag{22}$$

where $\xi \triangleq V(0) + \sum_{i=1}^{N}\frac{\mu_i}{\chi - \sigma_i} + \frac{N\delta}{\chi}$ is a constant.

By virtual of the Lyapunov function candidate (14), it follows that

$$\underline{\theta}\lambda_{\min}(P)\sum_{i=1}^{N}||\eta_i||^2 \le \eta^{\mathrm{T}}(\Theta^{-1}\otimes P)\eta \le \xi, \tag{23}$$

which means that $||\eta_i||$ is bounded satisfying that

$$||\eta_i|| \le \sqrt{\frac{\xi}{\underline{\theta}\lambda_{\min}(P)}} \triangleq \bar{\xi}, \tag{24}$$

where $\bar{\xi}$ is a positive constant.

In the following part, the Zeno-free behaviour of the designed system are analyzed. During the internal $t \in [t_k^i, t_{k+1}^i)$, $||e_i|| > 0$ and one can derive

$$\frac{\mathrm{d}||e_i||}{\mathrm{d}t} = \frac{\mathrm{d}}{\mathrm{d}t}(e_i^{\mathrm{T}}e_i)^{\frac{1}{2}} = \frac{e_i^{\mathrm{T}}\dot{e}_i}{||e_i||} < ||\dot{e}_i||. \tag{25}$$

By the definition of e_i, the following result comes

$$\dot{e}_i = -\dot{\eta}_i, \tag{26}$$

then invoking (4), we can see that

$$
\begin{aligned}
||\dot{e}_i|| &= \left|\left| \sum_{j\in\mathcal{N}_i}\Big(\dot{x}_j(t) - \dot{x}_i(t)\Big) + s_i\Big(\dot{x}_l(t) - \dot{x}_i(t)\Big) \right|\right| \\
&= \left|\left| A\eta_i(t) + BK\Big[\sum_{j\in\mathcal{N}_i}\Big(\eta_i(t_k^i) - \check{\eta}_j(t)\Big) + s_i\eta_i(t_k^i)\Big] \right.\right. \\
&\quad \left.\left. + C\Big[\sum_{j\in\mathcal{N}_i}\Big(f(x_j,t) - f(x_i,t)\Big) + s_i\Big(f(x_l,t) - f(x_i,t)\Big)\Big] \right|\right|.
\end{aligned}\tag{27}
$$

It follows, from (7) and Assumption 1, that

$$||\dot{e}_i|| \le ||A||\,||e_i(t)|| + \gamma_k^i + ||C||\rho\sqrt{N}\bar{\xi}(2|\mathcal{N}_i| + s_i), \tag{28}$$

where $\gamma_k^i = \max\limits_{t\in[t_k^i, t_{k+1}^i)}\left(\left|\left| A\eta_i(t_k^i) + BK\Big(\sum_{j\in\mathcal{N}_i}\Big(\eta_i(t_k^i) - \check{\eta}_j(t)\Big) + s_i\eta_i(t_k^i)\Big) \right|\right|\right).$

Combining (11) with (28), it yields

$$\sqrt{\beta_{\varsigma_1}\delta} \le ||e(t_{k+1}^{i-})|| \le \frac{\gamma_k^i + ||C||\rho\sqrt{N}\bar{\xi}(2|\mathcal{N}_i| + s_i)}{||A||}\left(\mathrm{e}^{||A||(t_{k+1}^i - t_k^i)} - 1\right), \tag{29}$$

and for any k, the property holds $\gamma_k^i \le (||A|| + (2|\mathcal{N}|_i + s_i)||BK||)\bar{\xi} = \bar{\gamma}$. Hence, we have

$$t_{k+1}^i - t_k^i \ge \frac{1}{||A||}\ln\left(1 + \frac{||A||\sqrt{\beta_{\varsigma_1}\delta}}{\bar{\gamma} + ||C||\rho\sqrt{N}\bar{\xi}(2|\mathcal{N}_i| + s_i)}\right) > 0. \tag{30}$$

Therefore, the Zeno behavior is excluded.

For all agent, this can be shown as follows

$$\lim_{t \to \infty} \sum_{i=1}^{N} ||\eta_i||^2 \leq \frac{N\delta}{\chi \underline{\theta} \lambda_{\min}(P)}, \tag{31}$$

and from the relationship between η and ζ, we further obtain that

$$\lim_{t \to \infty} \sum_{i=1}^{N} ||\zeta_i||^2 \leq \frac{N\delta}{\chi \underline{\theta} \lambda_{\min}(P)\lambda_{\min}(F)}. \tag{32}$$

This completes the proof of Theorem 1.

From the event-triggered conditions (11), it is apparent that the control scheme should monitor the state information continuously to check whether triggered conditions are satisfied. Such information transformation mechanisms might result in the phenomenon of heavy burdens in communication networks. We are going to generate combinational state $\eta_i(t)$ from its neighbors at event-triggered instants. The dynamics of $x_i(t)$ and $x_j(t)$, during the time interval $t \in [t_k^i, t_{k+1}^i)$, are

$$x_i(t) = e^{A(t-t_k^i)}x_i(t_k^i) - \int_{t_k^i}^{t} e^{A(t-\tau)}BK\eta_i(t_k^i)d\tau + C\int_{t_k^i}^{t} e^{A(t-\tau)}f(x_i(\tau),\tau)d\tau \tag{33}$$

and

$$x_j(t) = e^{A(t-t_k^i)}x_j(t_k^i) - \int_{t_k^i}^{\check{t}_j} e^{A(\check{t}_j-\tau)}BK\eta_j(t_g^j)d\tau$$

$$- \sum_{h:t_k^i < t_h^j < t} \int_{t_h^j}^{\min(t_{h+1}^j,t)} e^{A(\min(t_{h+1}^j,t)-\tau)}BK\eta_j(t_h^j)d\tau$$

$$+ C\int_{t_k^i}^{\check{t}_j} e^{A(\check{t}_j-\tau)}f(x_j(\tau),\tau)d\tau$$

$$+ \sum_{h:t_k^i < t_h^j < t^h} \int_{t_h^j}^{\min(t_{h+1}^j,t)} e^{A(\min(t_{h+1}^j,t)-\tau)}f(x_j(\tau),\tau)d\tau, \tag{34}$$

where

$$j \in \mathcal{N}_i, \ \check{t}_j = \begin{cases} t_{g+1}^j, \text{if the } j\text{th agent occurs at least one event during } [t_k^i, t), \\ t, \text{otherwise}, \end{cases}$$

and $t_{g+1}^j = \min(t_h^j : t_h^j \in [t_k^i, t))$. Triggered-events of the jth agent may happen several times according to the instant sequence t_h^j, $h = g+1, \cdots$, during $t \in [t_k^i, t_{k+1}^i)$.

We denote that $\Psi(t,t^*) = \int_t^{t^*} e^{(A-K_{ob}C)(t^*-\tau)}BKd\tau$, and $\Phi_m(t,t^*) = \int_t^{t^*} e^{A(t^*-\tau)}f(x_m(\tau),\tau)d\tau$. Then, from (33) and (34), the following result comes

$$
\begin{aligned}
\eta_i(t) &= e^{A(t-t_k^i)}\eta_i(t_k^i) + s_i\Psi(t_k^i,t)\eta_i(t_k^i) + s_iC\Big(\Phi_l(t_k^i,t)-\Phi_i(t_k^i,t)\Big) \\
&+ \sum_{j\in\mathcal{N}_i}\sum_{h:t_k^i<t_h^j<t}\Big(\Psi(t_h^j,\min(t_{h+1}^j,t))\big(\eta_i(t_k^i)-\eta_j(t_h^j)\big)\Big) \\
&+ \sum_{j\in\mathcal{N}_i}\sum_{h:t_k^i<t_h^j<t}C\Big(\Phi_j(t_h^j,\min(t_{h+1}^j,t)) - \Phi_i(t_h^j,\min(t_{h+1}^j,t))\Big) \\
&+ \sum_{j\in\mathcal{N}_i}\Big(\Phi_j(t_k^i,\check{t}_j) - \Phi_i(t_k^i,\check{t}_j)\Big) + \sum_{j\in\mathcal{N}_i}\Psi(t_k^i,\check{t}_j)\big(\eta_i(t_k^i) - \eta_j(t_g^j)\big). \quad (35)
\end{aligned}
$$

From (35), the ith agent must obtain the following knowledge $\eta_i(t_k^i)$ and $\eta_j(t_h^j)$ to predict the combinational state $\eta_i(t)$, where $t_h^j \in (t_k^i,t)$. As one can see, the former three ones are available from themselves whereas the other information are taken from the jth nodes when their triggered-events come about during the time interval $[t_k^i,t_{k+1}^i)$, $j\in\mathcal{N}_i$.

4   Conclusion

In this paper, an event-driven leader-following tracking control has been designed for a class of nonlinear MASs under a directed communication topology. Within the event-triggered framework, the consensus control mechanism is presented for such MASs, and then the stability of the closed-loop system has been analyzed.

Acknowledgments. This work is supported in part by National Natural Science Foundation of China under Grant 61533010 and 61503194, in part by the Research and Development Program of Jiangsu Province under Grant BE2016184, in part by Natural Science Foundation of Jiangsu Province under Grant BK20140877, in part by Scientific Foundation of Nanjing University of Posts and Telecommunications (NUPTSF) under Grant NY214076.

References

1. Olfati-Saber, R., Murray, R.M.: Consensus problems in networks of agents with switching topology and time-delays. IEEE Trans. Autom. Control **49**(9), 1520–1533 (2004)
2. Chen, C.L.P., Wen, G.X., Liu, Y.J., et al.: Adaptive consensus control for a class of nonlinear multiagent time-delay systems using neural networks. IEEE Trans. Neural Netw. Learn. Syst. **25**(6), 1217–1226 (2014)
3. Wen, G., Duan, Z., Chen, G., et al.: Consensus tracking of multi-agent systems with Lipschitz-type node dynamics and switching topologies. IEEE Trans. Circuits Syst. I, Reg. Papers. **61**(2), 499–511 (2014)

4. Yuan, D., Ho, D.W.C., Xu, S.: Regularized primal-dual subgradient method for distributed constrained optimization. IEEE Trans. Cybern. **46**(9), 2109–2118 (2016)
5. Yoo, S.J.: A low-complexity design for distributed containment control of networked pure-feedback systems and its application to fault-tolerant control. Int. J. Robot. Res. **27**(3), 363–379 (2017)
6. Yang, Y., Yue, D., Dou, C.: Distributed adaptive output consensus control of a class of heterogeneous multi-agent systems under switching directed topologies. Inform. Syst. **345**, 294–312 (2016)
7. Tallapragada, P., Chopra, N.: On event triggered tracking for nonlinear systems. IEEE Trans. Autom. Control **58**(9), 2343–2348 (2013)
8. Yue, D., Tian, E., Han, Q.L.: A delay system method for designing event-triggered controllers of networked control systems. IEEE Trans. Autom. Control **58**(2), 475–481 (2013)
9. Dimarogonas, D.V., Frazzoli, E., Johansson, K.H.: Distributed event-triggered control for multi-agent systems. IEEE Trans. Autom. Control **57**(5), 1291–1297 (2012)
10. Seyboth, G.S., Dimarogonas, D.V., Johansson, K.H.: Event-based broadcasting for multi-agent average consensus. Automatica **49**(1), 245–252 (2013)
11. Zhang, H., Feng, G., Yan, H., et al.: Consensus of multi-agent systems with linear dynamics using event-triggered control. IET Control Theory Appl. **8**(18), 2275–2281 (2014)
12. Hu, W., Liu, L., Feng, G.: Consensus of linear multi-agent systems by distributed event-triggered strategy. IEEE Trans. Cybern. **46**(1), 148–157 (2016)
13. Zhu, W., Jiang, Z.P.: Event-based leader-following consensus of multi-agent systems with input time delay. IEEE Trans. Autom. Control **60**(5), 1362–1367 (2015)
14. Fan, Y., Feng, G., Wang, Y., et al.: Distributed event-triggered control of multi-agent systems with combinational measurements. Automatica **49**(2), 671–675 (2013)
15. Fan, Y., Liu, L., Feng, G., et al.: Self-triggered consensus for multi-agent systems with Zeno-free triggers. IEEE Trans. Autom. Control **60**(10), 2779–2784 (2015)
16. Hu, J., Chen, G., Li, H.X.: Distributed event-triggered tracking control of leader-follower multi-agent systems with communication delays. Kybernetika **47**(4), 630–643 (2011)
17. Li, H., Liao, X., Huang, T., et al.: Event-triggering sampling based leader-following consensus in second-order multi-agent systems. IEEE Trans. Autom. Control **60**(7), 1998–2003 (2015)
18. Mu, N., Liao, X., Huang, T.: Leader-following consensus in second-order multiagent systems via event-triggered control with nonperiodic sampled data. IEEE Trans. Circ. Syst. II: Express Br. **62**(10), 1007–1011 (2015)
19. Cheng, Y., Ugrinovskii, V.: Event-triggered leader-following tracking control for multivariable multi-agent systems. Automatica **70**, 204–210 (2016)
20. Yang, D., Ren, W., Liu, X., et al.: Decentralized event-triggered consensus for linear multi-agent systems under general directed graphs. Automatica **69**, 242–249 (2016)
21. Xie, D., Xu, S., Li, Z., et al.: Event-triggered consensus control for second-order multi-agent systems. IET Control Theory Appl. **9**(5), 667–680 (2015)

Formation Problem of Second-Order Multi-agent Systems with Input Delay and Communication Delay

Yun Chai[1](✉) and Ke-cai Cao[1,2]

[1] Nanjing University of Posts and Telecommunications, Nanjing 210023, China
chaiyun_nupt@163.com
[2] Nanjing University of Aeronautics and Astronautics, Nanjing 210016, China

Abstract. Distributed formation control of Second-order Multi-agent Systems has been discussed in this paper. A consensus-based cooperative formation control strategy with both input delay and communication delay has been proposed. The control strategy not only consider the deviation between the actual speed and the standard speed, but also, on the basis of this, consider the deviation between the actual displacement and the standard displacement. In order to achieve a faster consensus seeking, the tow-hop relay protocol has been introduced into the strategy. The control strategy makes agents can build up stable and desired formation and move at expected speed. Based on the frequency-domain analysis and matrix theory, the distributed conditions are proved for the formation control of system. A six-vehicle formation control example is shown in simulation as an illustrative example.

Keywords: Multi-agent system · Formation control · Two-hop relay protocol · Heterogencous delays

1 Introduction

Formation control problem of multi-agent system has attracted growing attention in recent years [1–3], due to its widely practical applications in the spacecraft exploration, disaster investigation, sensor networks and so on. Compared with the single agent, multi-agent system can be more efficiently.

In the formation structure of the multi-agent system, each agent's delayed or current states are used to compare with neighboring agents. Formation of the multi-agent system with time delays have been studied by many methods including frequency domain analysis [4, 5], Lyapunov functions [6, 7], the concept of delayed and hierarchical graphs [8, 9], etc.

For consensus-based formation control, the consensus convergence speed is very important. Note that some literature focuses on how to find a suitable connection topology to increase the convergence speed of the known algorithm [10, 11], However, physically changing the topology may be difficult in some applications. It is very necessary to consider how to improve the convergence speed in the case of a given communication topology. In the Social network, you can find an interesting

© Springer Nature Singapore Pte Ltd. 2017
D. Yue et al. (Eds.): LSMS/ICSEE 2017, Part II, CCIS 762, pp. 435–444, 2017.
DOI: 10.1007/978-981-10-6373-2_44

phenomenon, the friend of your friends are usually very easy to become your friends, and you two can maintain contact and cooperation [12–14], which means the second-order neighbors are also important in the network. Jin and Murray proposed a first-order consensus protocol based on multi-hop relay protocols which can make the convergence speed faster compared with the normal first-order consensus protocol [15]. Yuan et al. proposed a distributed average consensus in the discrete-time case by using the information of second-order neighbors [16]. Kim and Mesbahi concentrate on how to maximize the second smallest eigenvalue of a graph Laplacian in a first-order integrator system [17].

In this paper, formation problem is studied for the second-order multiple dynamic agents with communication delay and input delay under the new consensus algorithm which introduces absolute position and relative velocity deviation into the control strategy and combines with the two-hop relay protocol. A six-vehicle formation control example is shown in simulation as an illustrative example.

2 Problem Formulation

Consider m agents indexed with $1, 2 \cdots, m$ which are moving on a plane. For simplicity, we assume that each member of the group has the same mechanical structure and each agent can be described by the following equation in global coordinates:

$$\begin{cases} \dot{r}_i = v_i \\ \dot{v}_i = u_i \end{cases} \tag{1}$$

where $i = 1, 2 \cdots, m$.

The Laplacian matrix of the weighted graph is defined as $L = [\ell_{ij}]$, where $\ell_{ii} = \sum_{j \neq i} a_{ij}$ and $\ell_{ij} = -a_{ij}, \forall i \neq j$. For an undirected graph, the Laplacian matrix is symmetric positive semi-definite. Let $\mathbf{1}$ and $\mathbf{0}$ denote the $n \times 1$ column vector of all ones and all zeros respectively. Let I_n denote the $n \times n$ identity matrix and $0_{m \times n}$ denote the $m \times n$ matrix with all zero entries. Let $M_n(IR)$ represent the set of all $n \times n$ real matrices. Given a matrix $A = [a_{ij}] \in M_n(IR)$, the digraph of A, denoted by $\Gamma(A)$, is the digraph on nodes $v_i, i \in \{1, 2, \cdots, n\}$, such that there is a directed edge in $\Gamma(A)$ from v_j to v_i if and only if $a_{ij} \neq 0$.

Formation Control Problem:
Design formation protocol for each vehicle based on its states and its neighbors' states such that the group of vehicles moves expected velocity and form a fixed formation, design consensus protocols for systems (1) such that

$$r_i - r_j \rightarrow \delta_i - \delta_j,$$
$$v_i \rightarrow v_j \rightarrow v^d(t).$$

In order to solve the formation control problem, some lemmas are recalled that will be used in next Section.

Lemma 1 [18]: Given a matrix $A = [a_{ij}] \in M_n(R)$, where $a_{ij} \geq 0, \forall i \neq j$, and $\sum_{j=1}^{n} a_{ij} = 0$ for each j, then A has at least one zero eigenvalue and all of the nonzero eigenvalues are in the open left half plane. Furthermore, A has exactly one zero eigenvalue if and only if the directed graph associated with A has a spanning tree.

Lemma 2 [19]: Let O be the origin of coordinate axes, the prolongation of the line OG_{io} that links the origin and the center of the disc, crosses the circle of the disc G_i at point W_i that is furthest from the origin. The point W_i plots a trajectory-tracking $W_i(j\omega)$ when the disc G_l changes with ω varying from $-\infty$ to $+\infty$. $\cup_{i \in I} G_i$ is contained in the convex hull $C_o(0 \cup \{W_i(j\omega), i \in I\})$.

Lemma 3 [20]: For any given natural number $m \geq 2$, let

$$F_i(j\omega) = k_i \frac{e^{-j\omega T_i}}{j\omega} \tag{2}$$

$i = 1, \cdots, m, k_i = \pi/2T_i$. Where $0 < T_i \in R$ is divers nonnegative delay constant. Then $kCo(0 \cup \{E_i(j\omega), i = 1, \cdots, m\})$ does not contain the point $(-1, j0)$ for any given real number $0 \leq k < 1$ and for all $\omega \in (-\infty, +\infty)$, where $Co\{\bullet\}$ denotes the convex hull of $set\{\bullet\}$.

3 Main Results

3.1 Second-Order Formation Without Time-Delays

In view of the importance of formation speed for formation protocol, this paper proposes an improved formation protocol:

$$u_i = \dot{v}^d - \alpha(v_i - v^d) - \beta(r_i - r^d - e_{id}) - \sum_{j=1}^{n} g_{ij} k_{ij}[(r_i - r_j - \delta_{ij})$$
$$+ \sum_{j=1}^{n} g_{jk}(r_i - r_k - \delta_{ik}) + \gamma(v_i - v_j) + \gamma \sum_{j=1}^{n} g_{jk}(v_i - v_k)] \tag{3}$$

where $v^d \in R$ represents the velocity tracking value, $r^d \in R$ represents position tracking value. $e_{id} \in R$ represents expected displacement deviation between r^d and r_i. In this formation protocol, what each vertex sends to its child vertices is not only its own state, but also a collection of its instantaneous neighbors' states. It is equal to adding virtual "two-hop" paths as additional edges to original graph. For a directed graph G, a two-hop directed graph $\tilde{G} = (\mathcal{N}, \tilde{\mathcal{E}})$ is a graph that has the same vertex set and all the edges are "two-hop" paths of G. This means vehicle v_i can not only get the state of itself and neighbor nodes, but also can obtain a collection of its instantaneous neighbors' states. Moreover, between any pair of vertices in G, multiple two-hop paths may exist. They are considered as one edge in $\tilde{G}$ and the weight associated with it is equal to the sum of two-hop paths' weights. Thus, the adjacency matrix $\tilde{A} = \{\tilde{g}_{ik}\}$ of $\tilde{G}$ are:

$$\tilde{g}_{ik} = \begin{cases} \sum_{j \in V} g_{ij} g_{jk}, (v_i, v_k) \in \tilde{\mathcal{E}} \\ 0, otherwise \end{cases}$$

The corresponding out-degree diagonal and Laplacian matrices are denoted by $\tilde{D}$ and $\tilde{L}$ respectively. For a directed graph G with two-hop relay protocol (3), the whole system can also be described as:

$$
\begin{aligned}
u_i = \dot{v}^d - \alpha(v_i - v^d) - \beta(r_i - r^d - e_{id}) - \sum_{j=1}^{n} g_{ij} k_{ij}[(r_i - r_j - \delta_{ij}) \\
+ \gamma(v_i - v_j)] - \sum_{j=1}^{n} g_{ij} g_{jk} k_{ik}[(r_i - r_k - \delta_{ik}) + \gamma(v_i - v_k)]
\end{aligned}
\tag{4}
$$

3.2   Second-Order Formation with Time-Delays

Now, the formula (3) is split into four parts:

$$
\begin{aligned}
u_i &= u_{i1} + u_{i2} + u_{i3} + u_{i4}, \\
u_{i1} &= \dot{v}^d, \\
u_{i2} &= -\alpha(v_i - v^d), \\
u_{i3} &= -\beta(r_i - r^d - e_{id}), \\
u_{i4} &= -\sum_{j=1}^{n} g_{ij} k_{ij}[(r_i - r_j - \delta_{ij}) + \sum_{j=1}^{n} g_{jk}(r_i - r_k - \delta_{ik}) \\
&\quad + \gamma(v_i - v_j) + \gamma \sum_{j=1}^{n} g_{jk}(v_i - v_k)]
\end{aligned}
\tag{5}
$$

The formula (5) can be divided into two control parts: u_{i2} and u_{i3} are tracking control, u_{i4} is the coordination control between agents. Input delay exists for each agent processing information, and communication delay exists between agents. Here, considering the input delay and communication delay in u_{i3} and u_{i4}:

$$
\begin{aligned}
u_{i3}(t) &= -\beta(r_i(t - T_i) - r^d - e_{id}), \\
u_{i4}(t) &= -\sum_{j=1}^{n} g_{ij} k_{ij}[(r_i(t - T_i) - r_j(t - T_j - T_{ij}) - \delta_{ij}) \\
&\quad + \sum_{j=1}^{n} g_{jk}(r_i(t - T_i) - r_k(t - T_k - T_{ik}) - \delta_{ik}) \\
&\quad + \gamma(v_i(t - T_i) - v_j(t - T_j - T_{ij})) \\
&\quad + \gamma \sum_{j=1}^{n} g_{jk}(v_i(t - T_i) - v_k(t - T_k - T_{ik}))]
\end{aligned}
$$

where T_i is the input delay of agent i and T_{ij} is the communication delay between agent i and agent j.

Here, the formation control protocol with both input delay and communication delay is shown as follows:

$$u_i = \dot{v}^d - \alpha(v_i - v^d) - \beta(r_i(t - T_i) - r^d - e_{id})$$
$$- \sum_{j=1}^{n} g_{ij}k_{ij}[(r_i(t - T_i) - r_j(t - T_j - T_{ij}) - \delta_{ij})$$
$$+ \sum_{j=1}^{n} g_{jk}(r_i(t - T_i) - r_k(t - T_k - T_{ik}) - \delta_{ik}) \quad (6)$$
$$+ \gamma(v_i(t - T_i) - v_j(t - T_j - T_{ij}))$$
$$+ \gamma \sum_{j=1}^{n} g_{jk}(v_i(t - T_i) - v_k(t - T_k - T_{ik}))]$$

3.3   Main Theorem

Theorem 1: Formation algorithm (6) guarantees that $r_i - r_j \to \delta_i - \delta_j, r_i - r_k \to$ $\delta_i - \delta_k, v_i \dashrightarrow v_j \to v_k \to v^d(t)$ asymptotically if the information exchange topology has a (directed) spanning tree and

$$(\alpha + 2\gamma q_i + h_i)T_i < \pi, \forall i \in V \quad (7)$$

where $q_i = \sum\limits_{j \in V} g_{ij}k_{ij}$ and $h_i = \sqrt{4\gamma^2 q_i^2 + 4(\alpha\gamma - 2)q_i + \alpha^2 - 4\beta}$.

Proof: Let $\tilde{r}_i(t) = r_i(t) - 1 \int_0^t v^d(\tau)d\tau - e_{id}$ and $\tilde{v}_i(t) = v_i(t) - 1v^d$, Eq. (6) can be written as:

$$\begin{cases} \dot{\tilde{r}}_i(t) = \tilde{v}_i(t) \\ \dot{\tilde{v}}_i(t) = -\alpha\tilde{v}_i(t) - \beta\tilde{r}_i(t - T_i) - \sum_{j=1}^{n} g_{ij}k_{ij}[(\tilde{r}_i(t - T_i) - \tilde{r}_j(t - T_j - T_{ij})) \\ \quad + \sum_{j=1}^{n} g_{jk}(\tilde{r}_i(t - T_i) - \tilde{r}_k(t - T_k - T_{ik})) \\ \quad + \gamma(\tilde{v}_i(t - T_i) - \tilde{v}_j(t - T_j - T_{ij})) \\ \quad + \gamma \sum_{j=1}^{n} g_{jk}(\tilde{v}_i(t - T_i) - \tilde{v}_k(t - T_k - T_{ik}))] \end{cases} \quad (8)$$

Applying the Laplace transform to (8), we get

$$\begin{cases} s\tilde{r}_i(s) = \tilde{v}_i(s) \\ s\tilde{v}_i(s) = -\alpha\tilde{v}_i(s) - \beta\tilde{r}_i(s)e^{-sT_i} - \sum_{j=1}^{n} g_{ij}k_{ij}[(\tilde{r}_i(s)e^{-sT_i} - \tilde{r}_j(s)e^{-s(T_j + T_{ij})}) \\ \quad + \sum_{j=1}^{n} g_{jk}(\tilde{r}_i(s)e^{-sT_i} - \tilde{r}_k(s)e^{-s(T_k + T_{ik})}) \\ \quad + \gamma(\tilde{v}_i(s)e^{-sT_i} - \tilde{v}_j(s)e^{-s(T_j + T_{ij})}) \\ \quad + \gamma \sum_{j=1}^{n} g_{jk}(\tilde{v}_i(s)e^{-sT_i} - \tilde{v}_k(s)e^{-s(T_k + T_{ik})})] \end{cases} \quad (9)$$

where $\tilde{r}_i(s)$ and $\tilde{v}_i(s)$ are the Laplace transform of $\tilde{r}_i(t)$ and $\tilde{v}_i(t)$ respectively.

Let $\bar{L}(s) = L(s) + \tilde{L}(s)$, and $\bar{L}(s) = [l_{ij}(s)]$, we get

$$l_{ij}(s) = \begin{cases} -g_{ij}k_{ij}e^{-s(T_i+T_{ij})} - \tilde{g}_{ik}k_{ik}e^{-s(T_k+T_{ik})}, j \neq i \\ (\sum_{j\neq i} g_{ij}k_{ij})e^{-sT_i} + (\sum_{j\neq i} \tilde{g}_{ik}k_{ik})e^{-sT_k}, j = i \\ 0, 其他 \end{cases} \tag{10}$$

Then, we let $A = diag\{\alpha\}$, $B(s) = \{\beta e^{-sT_i}, i \in V\}$, $R = diag\{\gamma\}$, and we also let $\tilde{r}(s) = [\tilde{r}_1(s), \tilde{r}_2(s), \cdots, \tilde{r}_n(s)]^T$, $\tilde{v}(s) = [\tilde{v}_1(s), \tilde{v}_2(s), \cdots, \tilde{v}_n(s)]$, Eq. (9) can be written in matrix form as:

$$s \begin{bmatrix} \tilde{r}(s) \\ \tilde{v}(s) \end{bmatrix} = \begin{bmatrix} 0 & 1 \\ -B(s) \otimes I_2 - \bar{L}(s) \otimes I_2 & -A \otimes I_2 - (R\bar{L}(s)) \otimes I_2 \end{bmatrix} \begin{bmatrix} \tilde{r}(s) \\ \tilde{v}(s) \end{bmatrix} \tag{11}$$

Therefore, the eigenvalues of (11) are given by

$$s_{1,2}I_n = -\frac{1}{2}(A + R\bar{L}(s)) \pm \sqrt{R^2\bar{L}^2(s) + 2(AR - 2I_n)\bar{L}(s) + A^2 - 4B(s)}$$

Let $H(s) = \sqrt{R^2\bar{L}^2(s) + 2(AR - 2I_n)\bar{L}(s) + A^2 - 4B(s)}$, then we get

$$s_1 I_n = -\frac{1}{2}(A + R\bar{L}(s) + H(s)),$$

$$s_1 I_n = -\frac{1}{2}(A + R\bar{L}(s) - H(s))$$

Thus, the above equivalent to the next:

$$\det\left(sI_n + \frac{1}{2}(A + R\bar{L}(s) + H(s))\right) = 0, \det\left(sI_n + \frac{1}{2}(A + R\bar{L}(s) - H(s))\right) = 0.$$

Let $N(s) = \det(sI_n + \frac{1}{2}(A + R\bar{L}(s) + H(s)))$, and when $s = 0$, we can get $N(0) = \det(sI_n + \frac{1}{2}(A + R\bar{L}(0) + H(0)))$, from Lemma 1, we can have the result $rank(\bar{L}) = n - 1$, so we can get that $N(0) = \det(\frac{1}{2}(A + \sqrt{A^2 - 4B(0)}))$, thus $N(0) \neq 0$. Here, Let $M(s) = \det(I_n + \frac{1}{2s}(A + R\bar{L}(s) + H(s)))$, Based on the general Nyquist stability, the zeros of $M(s)$ lie on the open left half complex plane, if the trajectory-tracking of $\lambda(D(j\omega))$ does not enclose the point $(-1, j0)$, where we let $D(s) = \frac{1}{2s}(A + R\bar{L}(s) + H(s))$, and $D(j\omega) = \frac{1}{2s}(A + R\bar{L}(j\omega) + H(j\omega))$.

We use the Gershgorin disc theorem to estimate the matrix eigenvalue, i.e.

$$\lambda(D(j\omega)) \in \cup_{i\in v} D_i \tag{14}$$

where $D_i = \left\{\eta : \eta \in C \middle| \eta - \frac{1}{2}(\alpha + \gamma q_i + h_i)\frac{e^{-j\omega T_i}}{j\omega}\middle| \leq \middle|\frac{1}{2}(\alpha + \gamma q_i + h_i)\frac{e^{-j\omega T_i}}{j\omega}\middle|\right\}$, and $h_i = \sqrt{\gamma^2 q_i^2 + 2(\alpha\gamma - 2)q_i + \alpha^2 - 4\beta}$.

The disc D_i changes with ω from $-\infty$ to $+\infty$, Let O be the origin of coordinate axes, the prolongation of the line OD_{io} that links the origin and the center of the disc, crosses the circle of the disc D_i at point W_i that is furthest from the origin. The point W_i plots a trajectory-tracking $W_i(j\omega)$:

$$W_i(j\omega) = \frac{1}{2}(\alpha + 2\gamma q_i + h_{i0})\frac{e^{-j\omega T_i}}{j\omega} \tag{15}$$

where $h_i = \sqrt{\gamma^2 q_i^2 + 2(\alpha\gamma - 2)q_i + \alpha^2 - 4\beta}$. Then, Let $Z_i(j\omega) = k_i\frac{e^{-j\omega T_i}}{j\omega}$, and we transform Eq. (15) to $W_i(j\omega) = \xi Z_i(j\omega)$ with $\xi_i = \frac{T_i}{\pi}(\alpha + 2\gamma q_i + h_{i0})$. we can konw that $\xi_i < 1$, Let $\xi = \max\{\xi_i, i \in V\}$, and it is obviously that $\xi < 1$. Then, we get $Co(0 \cup \{W_i(j\omega), i \in V\}) \subseteq \xi(0 \cup \{Z_i(j\omega), i \in V\})$, it can be verified that $\cup_{i \in V} D_i \subseteq Co(0 \cup \{W_i(j\omega), i \in V\})$ from Lemma 2, so we can get that:

$$\cup_{i \in V} D_i \subseteq \xi Co(0 \cup \{Z_i(j\omega), i \in V\})$$

Then, From Lemma 3, we also can get $(-1, j0) \notin \xi Co(0 \cup \{Z_i(j\omega), i \in V\})$, so that $(-1, j0) \notin \cup_{i \in V} D_i$.

Now, we obtain that the track of $\lambda(D(j\omega))$ does not contain the point $(-1, j0)$ by Greshgorin disc theorem. Based on the general Nyquist stability criterion, the zeros of $M(s)$ lie on the open left half complex plane. Thus, the formation of multi-agent delayed systems is obtained. Theorem 1 is proved.

4 Simulation

Let us illustrate the performance of the proposed formation scheme by conducting a simulation using a network of six two-DOF (degree-of-freedom) vehicles.

By employing two-hop paths in the network, more information is passed around and each vehicle enlarges its "available" neighborhood. The interaction graph among the vehicles can also be shown as below (Fig. 1):

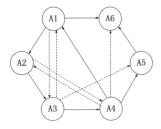

Fig. 1. Interaction with second-order information

For simplicity, all the weights of the edges are assumed to be 1. For the system (6) with both communication delay and input delay, we take the input delay $T_i = 0.2s$, and the communication delay $T_{ij} = 0.25s$. We also design the given control parameters α, β, γ as 2, 1, 0.5.

In order to highlight the advantages of the formation control strategies in this paper, a formation control strategy with one-hop relay protocol will be introduced firstly and the control strategy with one-hop relay protocol is given as below:

$$
\begin{aligned}
u_i = \dot{v}^d &- \alpha(v_i - v^d) \\
&- \sum_{j=1}^{n} g_{ij} k_{ij}[(r_i(t - \tau) - r_j(t - \tau) - \delta_{ij}) + \gamma(v_i(t - \tau) - v_j(t - \tau))]
\end{aligned}
\tag{16}
$$

Compared with the strategy (16), the formation control strategy (6) not only consider the relative velocity deviation and the absolute position deviation, but also introduce the tow-hop relay protocol into it. Then, this strategy (16) and the formation control strategy with the tow-hop relay protocol (6) in this paper are applied respectively to coordinate the movement of six vehicles.

Firstly, it is needed to verify whether the speed of the multiple vehicles system can be consistent. At the same time, the simulation results of the formation control strategy with the tow-hop relay protocol (6) and the control strategy (16) are compared to show the high efficiency of the formation control strategy (6) in this paper. The simulation results of the formation control strategy (16) are shown as below (Figs. 2 and 3):

The simulation results of the formation control strategy with the tow-hop relay protocol (6) are shown as below (Figs. 4 and 5):

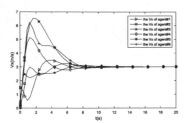

Fig. 2. Velocity variation in X direction.

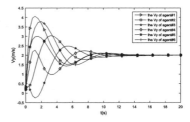

Fig. 3. Velocity variation in Y direction.

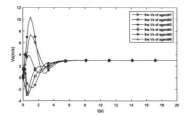

Fig. 4. Velocity variation in X direction.

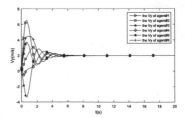

Fig. 5. Velocity variation in Y direction.

It is very obviously that when using the control strategy (16) and (6), it takes about 14 s and 6 s respectively for the agents to approach the desired speed $v^d = (3, 2)^T$. Secondly, it is needed to verify whether the system can form a desired formation. The simulation result is shown as below (Figs. 6 and 7):

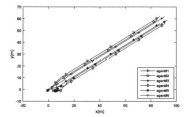

Fig. 6. Trajectories when $v^d = (3, 2)^T$

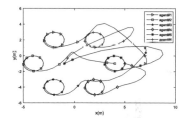

Fig. 7. Trajectories when $v^d = (\sin(t), \cos(t))^T$

From the simulation result above, it is easily to draw the conclusion: the formation control strategy with both input delay and communication delay in this paper is very efficient compared with other control strategy.

5 Conclusion

In this paper, the distributed formation problem for multiple agent system in two-dimensional space is studied. A new formation protocol with both input delay and communication delay was proposed, which consisted of the absolute deviation and relative deviation of velocity and position and also employs two-hop paths in the network. The simulation results has showed that the proposed algorithm is validated and effective for the formation control of agent system.

References

1. Murray, R.M.: Recent research in cooperative control of multi-vehicle systems. J. Dyn. Syst. Meas. Control **129**, 571–598 (2007)
2. Chang, B.L., Ng, Q.S.: A flexible virtual structure formation keeping control for fixed-wing UAVs. In: 9th IEEE International Conference on Control and Automation, pp. 621–626. IEEE Press, Santiago (2011)
3. Kuriki, Y., Namerikawa, T.: Formation control of UAVs with a fourth-order flight dynamics. In: 52th IEEE Conference on Decision and Control, pp. 6706–6711. IEEE Press, Florence (2013)
4. Liu, C.: Consensus of multi-agent system with diverse communication delays. J. Southeast Univ. **38**, 726–730 (2008)
5. Wang, J., Elia, N.: Consensus over network with dynamic channels. In: 27th American Control Conference, pp. 2637–2642, Seattle (2008)

6. Moreau, L.: Stability of continuous-time distributed consensus algorithms. In: 44th IEEE Conference on Decision and Control, pp. 3998–4003. IEEE Press, Seville (2005)
7. Wang, W., Slotine, J.J.E.: Contraction analysis of time-delayed communication delays. IEEE Trans. Autom. Control **51**, 712–717 (2006)
8. Cao, M., Morse, A.S., Anderson, B.D.O.: Reaching an agreement using delayed information. In: 45th IEEE Conference on Decision and Control, pp. 3375–3380. IEEE Press, San Diego (2006)
9. Wang, L., Xiao, F.: A new approach to consensus problems for discrete-time multiagent systems with time-delays. In: 25th American Control Conference, p. 6, Minneapolis (2006)
10. Xiao, L., Boyd, S.: Fast linear iterations for distributed averaging. Syst. Control Lett. **53**, 65–78 (2004)
11. Xiao, L., Boyd, S., Lall, S.: A scheme for robust distributed sensor fusion based on average consensus. In: 4th International Conference on Information Processing in Sensor Networks, pp. 63–70, Los Angeles (2005)
12. Zhou, S., Cox, I.J., Hansen, L.K.: Second-order assortative mixing in social networks. Physics (2009)
13. Cao, Y.J., Wang, G.Z., Jiang, Q.Y., et al.: A neighbourhood evolving network model. Phys. Lett. A **349**, 462–466 (2006)
14. Li, C., Chen, G.: A comprehensive weighted evolving network model. Phys. A Stat. Mech. Appl. **343**, 288–294 (2004)
15. Jin, Z., Murray, R.M.: Multi-hop relay protocols for fast consensus seeking. In: 45th IEEE Conference on Decision and Control, pp. 1001–1006. IEEE Press, San Diego (2006)
16. Yuan, D.M., Xu, S.Y., Zhao, H.Y., et al.: Accelerating distributed average consensus by exploring the information of second-order neighbors. Phys. Lett. A **374**, 2438–2445 (2010)
17. Kim, Y., Mesbahi, M.: On maximizing the second smallest eigenvalue of a state-dependent graph Laplacian. IEEE Trans. Autom. Control **51**, 116–120 (2006)
18. Ren, W., Beard, R.W.: Consensus seeking in multiagent systems under dynamically changing interaction topologies. IEEE Trans. Autom. Control **50**, 655–661 (2005)
19. Yang, H.Y., Zhu, X.L., Zhang, S.Y.: Consensus of second-order delayed multi-agent systems with leader-following. Eur. J. Control **15**, 1–12 (2010)
20. Tian, Y.P., Yang, H.Y.: Stability of distributed congestion control with diverse communication delays. In: 5th Intelligent Control and Automation, pp. 1438–1442. IEEE Press, Hangzhou (2004)

Fault Estimation Observer Design of Nonlinear Systems with Actuator Faults

Xiangpeng Xie[1,3] and Yanan Liu[2(✉)]

[1] Institute of Advanced Technology,
Nanjing University of Posts and Telecommunications,
Nanjing 210023, People's Republic of China
xiexp@njupt.edu.cn
[2] School of Automation, Nanjing University of Posts and Telecommunications,
Nanjing 210023, People's Republic of China
827507039@qq.com
[3] Hubei Province Collaborative Innovation Center for New Energy Microgrid,
China Three Gorges University, Yichang 443002, People's Republic of China

Abstract. This paper introduces a relaxation design of fault estimation observer for some nonlinear dynamical plants by means of the Takagi–Sugeno method. A featured fuzzy fault estimation observer is produced by utilizing the named maximum-priority-based switching law, which is different from these existing ones. For each enabled switching signal, the appropriate piece of enabled matrices can be produced to explore certain serviceable properties of the considered plants by introducing a piece of matrix-valued variables. Owing to the more useful information of the considered nonlinear plant could be properly updated and effectively employed at each time instant, the conservatism of the given result can be significantly released, at the same time, the result is less restraint than that previous ones. At last, there are some simulation results of the considered nonlinear truck-trailer plant are given to prove the profit of our theoretic approach.

Keywords: Fuzzy systems · Relaxation method · Fault estimation · Slack matrix

1 Introduction

In the past twenty years, it has taken much interest in nonlinear control fields based on fuzzy logic, because the reason that fuzzy models can be used to as general approximators in reported references [2,3]. In these results, Takagi-Sugeno (T-S) fuzzy models that given by [1] are composed of a pile of IF-THEN-based fuzzy rules, so most nonlinear dynamical models can be described. Hence, many

This work was sponsored by "Six Talent Peaks Project" in Jiangsu Province of China under Grant XNY-040, in part sponsored by "Qing Lan Project" in Jiangsu Province of China.

© Springer Nature Singapore Pte Ltd. 2017
D. Yue et al. (Eds.): LSMS/ICSEE 2017, Part II, CCIS 762, pp. 445–454, 2017.
DOI: 10.1007/978-981-10-6373-2_45

of the results of fuzzy state/output feedback control designs with the aid of T-S fuzzy models have been reported in previous literature [4,5]. Similarly, T-S fuzzy models is also used to handle the problem with fuzzy filters [6,7], fuzzy tracking controls [8], adaptive sliding mode controls [9], etc. Nevertheless, a large number of previous references depend on the common Lyapunov function but too conservative results are produced [10]. Much effort has been given to produce other effective ways to reduce the conservatism of results obtained [11,12]. Recently, by applying appropriate homogenous polynomially parameter-dependent(HPPD) Lyapunov functions, we have been benefited from the powerful analysis tool of homogenous polynomial solutions [13], that less conservative results have been developed for stabilization of discrete-time T-S fuzzy control systems [14,15]. However, although the distribution of real-time normalized fuzzy weighting functions usually varies between any two adjacent time instants, no information is used, and all the previous results must reach any possible distribution. As a trade-off, that will add a lot of conservatism. All in all, if the distribution of real-time normalized fuzzy weighting functions could be considered in some way, there may be a lot of room for improvement that is quite significant.

On another angle of this field, fault detection/isolation/tolerant control were taken into account because component malfunctions may lead to serious practical problems that may result in performance degradation or even instability of the original system [16]. Through a major branch, the issue of nonlinear fault detection/estimation was mightily investigated and some featured methods were given in [17], respectively. Particularly, with regard to the special case that external noises/disturbances belong to finite-frequency range [18], authors study some finite-frequency range of fault estimation in [19]. Taking into account an important fact that correlation results of the entire-frequency domain are still valid once the finite-frequency range of external noises or disturbances is not determinate, it becomes an interesting term of the so-called entire-frequency domain for the study of the issue of less conservative fuzzy fault estimation conditions. For example, with a valid piecewise Lyapunov functions [20], a relaxed result is investigated in [21]. However, there are few studies on fuzzy fault estimation based on the HPPD method, not to mention the improved HPPD methods that are given. In other words, some embedded research is worth proceeding, which promoted the authors to carry out this presented result.

The main contribution of the study is through some improved HPPD methods to develop a relaxed fuzzy fault estimation(FE) observer. With the help of the alleged maximum-priority-based switching law, we have discussed an improved fuzzy fault estimation observer. For each enabled switching state, it is possible to produce its appropriate group of enabled matrices to explore some of key attributes of the considered plants by introducing a piece of matrix-valued variables. Because the useful information of the considered plants can be properly updated and effectively used at each time instant, the conservatism of the given result could be significantly released, and at the same time, it is less restraint than previous ones. At last, there are some simulation results on one nonlinear truck-trailer plant are given to prove the profit of theoretic methods are discussed in our paper.

2   Preliminaries

As presented in [21], the alleged holistic T–S fuzzy system which represents a piece of discrete-time nonlinear plants with process/actuator faults can be written as follows:

$$x(t+1) = \sum_{i=1}^{r} h_i(z(t))\left(A_i x(t) + B_i u(t) + E_i f(t) + D_{1i} w(t)\right)$$

$$y(t) = \sum_{i=1}^{r} h_i(z(t))\left(C_i x(t) + D_{2i} w(t)\right), \tag{1}$$

where $x(t) \in C^{n_1}$ represents system state vector, $u(t) \in R^{n_2}$ is control input vector, $y(t) \in R^{n_3}$ represents measurable output vector, $f(t) \in R^{n_4}$ represents process/actuator fault vector, $w(t) \in R^{n_3}$ represents disturbance and model uncertainties which could be supposed to be part of $l_2[0, \infty)$. $z(t)$ represents the fuzzy premise variable, $h_i(z(t))$ stands for the i-th current-time normalized fuzzy weighting function. $A_i \in R^{n_1 \times n_1}, B_i \in R^{n_1 \times n_2}, E_i \in R^{n_1 \times n_4}, D_{1i} \in R^{n_1 \times n_5}, C_i \in R^{n_3 \times n_1}, D_{2i} \in R^{n_3 \times n_5}$ are constant real matrices. It is supposed that as follows: both E_i and C_i are of full rank, rank$(E_i)=n_4$, rank$(C_i)=n_3$, the pair of (A_i, C_i) must be observable.

3   Main Result

3.1   An Improved Fuzzy FE Observer by Means of a Maximum-Priority-Based Switching Law

In the interest of our presented switching law, we can achieve an improved fuzzy FE observer as follows:

$$\hat{x}(t+1) = A_{z(t)}\hat{x}(t) + B_{z(t)}u(t) + E_{z(t)}\hat{f}(t)$$
$$+ L(i, z(t))(y(t) - \hat{y}(t)),$$
$$\hat{y}(t) = C_{z(t)}\hat{x}(t),$$
$$\hat{f}(t+1) = \hat{f}(t) + F(i, z(t))(y(t) - \hat{y}(t)), \tag{2}$$

where $i \in \{1, 2, \cdots, r\}$; $\begin{bmatrix} L(i, z(t)) \\ F(i, z(t)) \end{bmatrix} = \{S_{z(t)}^i\}^{-1} \begin{bmatrix} L_{z(t)}^i \\ F_{z(t)}^i \end{bmatrix}$. $L_{z(t)}^i$, and we have some special structures for $F_{z(t)}^i$, $S_{z(t)}^i$:

$$L_{z(t)}^i = \sum_{j \in \{1, \cdots, r\}} \{h_j L_j^i\}, \quad F_{z(t)}^i = \sum_{j \in \{1, \cdots, r\}} \{h_j F_j^i\},$$

$$S_{z(t)}^i = \sum_{j \in \{1, \cdots, r\}} \{h_j S_j^i\}. \tag{3}$$

$L_j^i \in R^{n_1 \times n_3}$, $F_j^i \in R^{n_4 \times n_3}$, $S_j^i \in R^{(n_1+n_4) \times (n_1+n_4)}$ are a piece of matrix variables which will be solved by LMIs.

According to $e_f(t) = \hat{f}(k) - f(k)$ with $e_x(t) = \hat{x}(t) - x(t)$, then the plant's error dynamics can be produced in terms of two formulas:

$$
\begin{aligned}
e_x(t+1) &= A_{z(t)} e_x(t) + E_{z(t)} e_f(t) - D_{1z(t)} w(t) \\
&\quad - L(i, z(t)) C_{z(t)} e_x(t) \\
&\quad + L(i, z(t)) D_{2z(t)} w(t) \\
&= \left(A_{z(t)} - L(i, z(t)) C_{z(t)} \right) e_x(t) + E_{z(t)} e_f(t) \\
&\quad + \left(L(i, z(t)) D_{2z(t)} - D_{1z(t)} \right) w(t),
\end{aligned}
\tag{4}
$$

$$
\begin{aligned}
e_f(t+1) &= \hat{f}(t) - F(i, z(t))(\hat{y}(t) - y(t)) - f(t+1) \\
&= \hat{f}(t) - F(i, z(t)) \left(C_{z(t)} e_x(t) - D_{2z(t)} w(t) \right) - f(t+1) \\
&= e_f(t) - F(i, z(t)) \left(C_{z(t)} e_x(t) - D_{2z(t)} w(t) \right) - \Delta f(t),
\end{aligned}
\tag{5}
$$

the notation $\Delta f(t) = f(t+1) - f(t)$ expresses fault increment for instant t.

3.2   Relaxed Conditions of Designing the Fuzzy FE Observer

Theorem 1. Preset a circular area $\mathcal{D}(\alpha, \tau)$ (one of which has center $\alpha + j0$ and radius τ) and one prescribed H_∞ performance level γ. If there are a piece of symmetric matrices $P_{1k''} \in R^{(n_1+n_4) \times (n_1+n_4)}$ and $P_{2k''} \in R^{(n_1+n_4) \times (n_1+n_4)}$, a piece of matrices $S_j^i \in R^{(n_1+n_4) \times (n_1+n_4)}$, $L_j^i \in R^{n_1 \times n_3}$, $F_j^i \in R^{n_4 \times n_3}$, for $k'' \in \mathcal{K}(g)$, $i, j \in \{1, \cdots, r\}$; a piece of symmetric positive-definite matrices $W_m^{1i} \in R^{2(n_1+n_4) \times 2(n_1+n_4)}$, and $W_m^{2i} \in R^{(2n_1+4n_4+n_5) \times (2n_1+4n_4+n_5)}$, for $i, m \in \{1, \cdots, r\}$, $i \neq m$, to meet that a piece of LMIs (6)–(7) should be determined as follows:

$$
\begin{bmatrix} \Lambda_{kk'}^{i11} & \Lambda_{kk'}^{i12} \\ * & \Lambda_{kk'}^{i22} \end{bmatrix} + \sum_{\substack{(l \in \{1, \cdots, r\}) \\ k - \chi_l \geq 0}} \phi_{kk'l} \Upsilon_{il} \leq 0,
\tag{6}
$$

$$
\begin{bmatrix} \Theta_{kk'}^{i11} & \Theta_{kk'}^{i12} & \Theta_{kk'}^{i13} & 0 \\ * & \Theta_{kk'}^{i22} & 0 & \Theta_{kk'}^{i24} \\ * & * & \Theta_{kk'}^{i33} & 0 \\ * & * & * & \Theta_{kk'}^{i44} \end{bmatrix} + \sum_{\substack{(l \in \{1, \cdots, r\}) \\ k - \chi_l \geq 0}} \varphi_{kk'l} \Sigma_{il} \leq 0,
\tag{7}
$$

where $\forall\ k' \in \mathcal{K}(g + d_2)$, $k \in \mathcal{K}(g + d_1)$, $g, d_1, d_2 \in Z_+, i \in \{1, \cdots, r\}$;, $\phi_{kk'l} = \varphi_{kk'l} = \dfrac{(g+d_1-1)!}{\pi(k-\chi_l)} \dfrac{(g+d_2)!}{\pi(k')}$, $\Upsilon_{il} = \left\{ \sum_{m \in \{1, \cdots, r\}, m \neq i} W_m^{1i}, \right.$ for $l = i, -W_l^{1i}$, for $l \neq i$,

$\Sigma_{il} = \left\{ \sum_{m \in \{1, \cdots, r\}, m \neq i} W_m^{2i}, \right.$ for $l = i, -W_l^{2i}$, for $l \neq i$, $\hat{L}_j^i = \begin{bmatrix} L_j^i \\ F_j^i \end{bmatrix}$,

$$\Lambda_{kk'}^{i11} = \sum_{j \in \{1,\cdots,r\}, k \geq \chi_j} \left\{ \frac{(g+d_1-1)!}{\pi(k-\chi_j)} \frac{(g+d_2)!}{\pi(k')} \left(-S_j^i - \{S_j^i\}^T \right) \right\}$$

$$+ \sum_{k'' \in \mathcal{K}(g), k \geq k''} \left\{ \frac{(d_1)!}{\pi(k-k'')} \frac{(g+d_2)!}{\pi(k')} \left(P_{1k''} \right) \right\},$$

$$\Lambda_{kk'}^{i12} = \sum_{\binom{j,l \in \{1,\cdots,r\},}{k-\chi_j-\chi_l \geq 0}} \left\{ \frac{(g+d_1-2)!}{\pi(k-\chi_j-\chi_l)} \frac{(g+d_2)!}{\pi(k')} \left(S_j^i \bar{A}_l - \hat{L}_j^i \bar{C}_l - \alpha S_j^i \right) \right\},$$

$$\Lambda_{kk'}^{i22} = \sum_{k'' \in \mathcal{K}(g), k'-k'' \geq 0} \left\{ \frac{(g+d_1)!}{\pi(k)} \frac{(d_2)!}{\pi(k'-k'')} \left(-\tau^2 P_{1k''} \right) \right\},$$

$$\Theta_{kk'}^{i11} = \sum_{j \in \{1,\cdots,r\}, k \geq \chi_j} \left\{ \frac{(g+d_1-1)!}{\pi(k-\chi_j)} \frac{(g+d_2)!}{\pi(k')} \left(-S_j^i - \{S_j^i\}^T \right) \right\}$$

$$+ \sum_{k'' \in \mathcal{K}(g), k \geq k''} \left\{ \frac{(d_1)!}{\pi(k-k'')} \frac{(g+d_2)!}{\pi(k')} \left(P_{2k''} \right) \right\},$$

$$\Theta_{kk'}^{i12} = \sum_{\binom{j,l \in \{1,2,\ldots,r\},}{k-\chi_j-\chi_l \geq 0}} \left\{ \frac{(g+d_1-2)!}{\pi(k-\chi_j-\chi_l)} \frac{(g+d_2)!}{\pi(k')} \left(S_j^i \bar{A}_l - \hat{L}_j^i \bar{C}_l \right) \right\},$$

$$\Theta_{kk'}^{i13} = \sum_{\binom{j,l \in \{1,2,\ldots,r\},}{k-\chi_j-\chi_l \geq 0}} \left\{ \frac{(g+d_1-2)!}{\pi(k-\chi_j-\chi_l)} \frac{(g+d_2)!}{\pi(k')} \left(\hat{L}_j^i \bar{D}_{2l} - G_j^i \bar{D}_{1l} \right) \right\},$$

$$\Theta_{kk'}^{i22} = \sum_{k'' \in \mathcal{K}(g), k'-k'' \geq 0} \left\{ \frac{(g+d_1)!}{\pi(k)} \frac{(d_2)!}{\pi(k'-k'')} \left(-P_{2k''} \right) \right\},$$

$$\Theta_{kk'}^{i24} = \left\{ \frac{(g+d_1)!}{\pi(k)} \frac{(g+d_2)!}{\pi(k')} \bar{I}_{n_4} \right\}, \quad \bar{I}_{n_4} = \begin{bmatrix} 0_{n_1 \times n_4} \\ I_{n_4 \times n_4} \end{bmatrix},$$

$$\Theta_{kk'}^{i33} = \left\{ \frac{(g+d_1)!}{\pi(k)} \frac{(g+d_2)!}{\pi(k')} \left(-\gamma I_{(n_4+n_5) \times (n_4+n_5)} \right) \right\},$$

$$\Theta_{kk'}^{i44} = \left\{ \frac{(g+d_1)!}{\pi(k)} \frac{(g+d_2)!}{\pi(k')} \left(-\gamma I_{n_4 \times n_4} \right) \right\},$$

Consequently, it could be thought that all eigenvalues of $\bar{A}_{z(t)} - \bar{L}_{z(t)}^i C_{z(t)}$ $(i \in \{1, \cdots, r\})$ are part of $\mathcal{D}(\alpha, \tau)$, and its H_∞ performance index $\|e_f(t)\|_2 \leq \gamma \|\nu(t)\|_2$ must be guaranteed.

Proof. By utilizing the considered fuzzy FE observer (2) and the conventional Lyapunov stability theory, the proof process can be proved to be straightforward, and for saving space, it is abbreviated here.

Remark 1: Unlike to existing references, by means of the alleged maximum-priority-based switching law which is given in this section, we have considered an improved version of fuzzy FE observer in terms of (2). Actual process of this proposed result could be described with three steps:

Step (1) representing fault nonlinear plant by using the T-S fuzzy method;
Step (2) determining one appropriate pair of (g, d_1, d_2), and then solving feasible solutions via off-line LMIs (7)–(8);
Step (3) actualizing our FE observer (2) online in order to accomplish the fault estimation.

4   An Illustrative Example

Example 1. Use that nonlinear truck-trailer plant employed at one time or another by the authors in [21]. As that described in [21], we can also set:

$$T = 2\,\mathrm{s}, \ v = -1.0\,\mathrm{m/s}, \ l = 2.8\,\mathrm{m}, \ L = 5.5\,\mathrm{m}, \ A_1 = \begin{bmatrix} 1 - \frac{vT}{L} & 0 & 0 \\ \frac{vT}{L} & 1 & 0 \\ \frac{(vT)^2}{2L} & vT & 1 \end{bmatrix},$$

$$A_2 = \begin{bmatrix} 1 - \frac{vT}{L} & 0 & 0 \\ \frac{vT}{L} & 1 & 0 \\ \frac{0.01(vT)^2}{2L\pi} & \frac{0.01vT}{\pi} & 1 \end{bmatrix}, \text{ and the other matrices are all the same as before.}$$

Those applied normalized weighting functions will be specified to the same form as those described in [21]. So as to express our benefit over other ones, we try to use Theorem 1 and firstly select $g = 1$, $d_1 = d_2 = 0$, then we can calculate a pair of feasible solutions according to the LMIs (6)–(7) and the results ate listed as below:

$$P_{110} = \begin{bmatrix} 6.5499 & 21.4431 & 0.0503 & 4.8008 \\ 21.4431 & 76.7624 & 0.1283 & 13.5566 \\ 0.0503 & 0.1283 & 0.0027 & 0.0586 \\ 4.8008 & 13.5566 & 0.0586 & 4.4066 \end{bmatrix},$$

$$P_{101} = \begin{bmatrix} 6.5499 & 21.4431 & 0.0504 & 4.8008 \\ 21.4431 & 76.7616 & 0.1278 & 13.5566 \\ 0.0504 & 0.1278 & 0.0028 & 0.0586 \\ 4.8008 & 13.5566 & 0.0586 & 4.4066 \end{bmatrix},$$

$$P_{210} = \begin{bmatrix} 3.9042 & 13.5984 & 0.0015 & 2.4614 \\ 13.5984 & 52.8033 & 0.0445 & 6.7942 \\ 0.0015 & 0.0445 & 0.0034 & -0.0053 \\ 2.4614 & 6.7942 & -0.0053 & 2.5124 \end{bmatrix},$$

$$P_{201} = \begin{bmatrix} 3.8425 & 13.3208 & -0.0015 & 2.4360 \\ 13.3208 & 51.5527 & 0.0296 & 6.6799 \\ -0.0015 & 0.0296 & 0.0030 & -0.0065 \\ 2.4360 & 6.6799 & -0.0065 & 2.5020 \end{bmatrix},$$

Setting 1 (when $i = 1$):

$$\begin{bmatrix} L_1^1 \\ F_1^1 \end{bmatrix} = \begin{bmatrix} 14.0890 & 0.0291 \\ 60.1778 & 0.1031 \\ 0.2292 & 0.0042 \\ 6.0151 & 0.0180 \end{bmatrix},$$

$$S_1^1 = \begin{bmatrix} 5.0575 & 17.2647 & -0.0000 & 3.5221 \\ 17.7052 & 66.3603 & 0.0047 & 10.2520 \\ 0.1057 & 0.3244 & 0.0067 & 0.1040 \\ 3.1128 & 8.7861 & -0.0002 & 3.1409 \end{bmatrix},$$

$$\begin{bmatrix} L_2^1 \\ F_2^1 \end{bmatrix} = \begin{bmatrix} 14.0716 & 0.0292 \\ 60.0709 & 0.1032 \\ 0.2340 & 0.0046 \\ 6.0142 & 0.0182 \end{bmatrix},$$

$$S_2^1 = \begin{bmatrix} 5.0553 & 17.2511 & -0.0000 & 3.5228 \\ 17.6867 & 66.2558 & 0.0048 & 10.2545 \\ 0.1053 & 0.3138 & 0.0067 & 0.1052 \\ 3.1137 & 8.7881 & -0.0002 & 3.1414 \end{bmatrix},$$

Setting 2 (when $i = 2$):

$$\begin{bmatrix} L_1^2 \\ F_1^2 \end{bmatrix} = \begin{bmatrix} 14.0813 & 0.0290 \\ 60.1293 & 0.1012 \\ 0.2223 & 0.0042 \\ 6.0134 & 0.0181 \end{bmatrix},$$

$$S_1^2 = \begin{bmatrix} 5.0554 & 17.2548 & -0.0003 & 3.5226 \\ 17.6943 & 66.3019 & 0.0010 & 10.2551 \\ 0.1064 & 0.3226 & 0.0064 & 0.1045 \\ 3.1121 & 8.7838 & -0.0001 & 3.1410 \end{bmatrix},$$

$$\begin{bmatrix} L_2^2 \\ F_2^2 \end{bmatrix} = \begin{bmatrix} 14.0574 & 0.0291 \\ 59.9954 & 0.1009 \\ 0.2448 & 0.0043 \\ 6.0111 & 0.0183 \end{bmatrix},$$

$$S_2^2 = \begin{bmatrix} 5.0509 & 17.2344 & -0.0003 & 3.5211 \\ 17.6658 & 66.1731 & 0.0010 & 10.2466 \\ 0.1060 & 0.3198 & 0.0063 & 0.1055 \\ 3.1123 & 8.7835 & -0.0001 & 3.1409 \end{bmatrix}.$$

Secondly, we use Theorem 1 with $g = 1$ and $d_1 = 1, d_2 = 0$, then we can calculate a pair of feasible solutions according to the LMIs (6)–(7) and the results ate listed as below:

$$P_{110} = \begin{bmatrix} 6.5503 & 21.4454 & 0.0524 & 4.8011 \\ 21.4454 & 76.7722 & 0.1336 & 13.5587 \\ 0.0524 & 0.1336 & 0.0030 & 0.0610 \\ 4.8011 & 13.5587 & 0.0610 & 4.4068 \end{bmatrix},$$

$$P_{101} = \begin{bmatrix} 6.5503 & 21.4454 & 0.0525 & 4.8010 \\ 21.4454 & 76.7714 & 0.1332 & 13.5587 \\ 0.0525 & 0.1332 & 0.0030 & 0.0610 \\ 4.8010 & 13.5587 & 0.0610 & 4.4068 \end{bmatrix},$$

$$P_{210} = \begin{bmatrix} 3.9065 & 13.6083 & 0.0009 & 2.4623 \\ 13.6083 & 52.8466 & 0.0430 & 6.7981 \\ 0.0009 & 0.0430 & 0.0036 & -0.0058 \\ 2.4623 & 6.7981 & -0.0058 & 2.5128 \end{bmatrix},$$

$$P_{201} = \begin{bmatrix} 3.8451 & 13.3325 & -0.0023 & 2.4370 \\ 13.3325 & 51.6067 & 0.0278 & 6.6844 \\ -0.0023 & 0.0278 & 0.0033 & -0.0070 \\ 2.4370 & 6.6844 & -0.0070 & 2.5024 \end{bmatrix},$$

Setting 1 (when $i = 1$):

$$\begin{bmatrix} L_1^1 \\ F_1^1 \end{bmatrix} = \begin{bmatrix} 14.0910 & 0.0303 \\ 60.1875 & 0.1075 \\ 0.2346 & 0.0046 \\ 6.0161 & 0.0187 \end{bmatrix},$$

$$S_1^1 = \begin{bmatrix} 5.0579 & 17.2663 & -0.0001 & 3.5223 \\ 17.7087 & 66.3716 & 0.0051 & 10.2548 \\ 0.1096 & 0.3355 & 0.0073 & 0.1082 \\ 3.1130 & 8.7868 & -0.0002 & 3.1410 \end{bmatrix},$$

$$\begin{bmatrix} L_2^1 \\ F_2^1 \end{bmatrix} = \begin{bmatrix} 14.0726 & 0.0304 \\ 60.0781 & 0.1076 \\ 0.2419 & 0.0051 \\ 6.0149 & 0.0190 \end{bmatrix},$$

$$S_2^1 = \begin{bmatrix} 5.0556 & 17.2518 & -0.0001 & 3.5232 \\ 17.6898 & 66.2640 & 0.0051 & 10.2582 \\ 0.1095 & 0.3255 & 0.0074 & 0.1095 \\ 3.1139 & 8.7888 & -0.0002 & 3.1417 \end{bmatrix},$$

Setting 2 (when $i = 2$):

$$\begin{bmatrix} L_1^2 \\ F_1^2 \end{bmatrix} = \begin{bmatrix} 14.0848 & 0.0302 \\ 60.1470 & 0.1056 \\ 0.2280 & 0.0046 \\ 6.0148 & 0.0188 \end{bmatrix},$$

$$S_1^2 = \begin{bmatrix} 5.0562 & 17.2579 & -0.0003 & 3.5231 \\ 17.6997 & 66.3207 & 0.0012 & 10.2591 \\ 0.1105 & 0.3343 & 0.0070 & 0.1087 \\ 3.1125 & 8.7849 & -0.0001 & 3.1412 \end{bmatrix},$$

$$\begin{bmatrix} L_2^2 \\ F_2^2 \end{bmatrix} = \begin{bmatrix} 14.0583 & 0.0303 \\ 60.0029 & 0.1051 \\ 0.2526 & 0.0048 \\ 6.0118 & 0.0191 \end{bmatrix},$$

$$S_2^2 = \begin{bmatrix} 5.0511 & 17.2350 & -0.0003 & 3.5213 \\ 17.6684 & 66.1806 & 0.0012 & 10.2493 \\ 0.1101 & 0.3313 & 0.0069 & 0.1098 \\ 3.1125 & 8.7840 & -0.0001 & 3.1411 \end{bmatrix}.$$

5   Conclusion

Our study has successfully given relaxed conditions of proposing effective FE conditions with the aid of producing a different fuzzy FE observer. Actually, by means of the alleged maximum-priority-based switching law, we have developed a more effective FE observer. For each enabled switching state, it is possible to produce its proper piece of designed matrices to explore some of key attributes of the underlying systems by constructing a piece of matrix-valued variables. Considering that the useful information of the considered nonlinear plants can be properly updated and effectively used at each time instant, previous conservatism can be obviously reduced to another level. At last, simulation results of the used nonlinear truck-trailer plant are given to prove the profit of theoretic approach.

References

1. Takagi, T., Sugeno, M.: Fuzzy identification of systems and its applications to modeling and control. IEEE Trans. Syst. Man Cybern. **15**(1), 116–132 (1985)
2. Su, X., Shi, P., Wu, L., Nguang, S.K.: Induced l2 filtering of fuzzy stochastic systems with time-varying delays. IEEE Trans. Cynern. **43**(4), 1251–1264 (2013)
3. Zhang, H., Xie, X.: Relaxed stability conditions for continuous-time T-S fuzzy control systems via augmented multi-indexed matrix approach. IEEE Trans. Fuzzy Syst. **19**(3), 478–492 (2011)
4. Liu, D., Wu, C., Zhou, Q., Lam, H.-K.: Fuzzy guaranteed cost output tracking control for fuzzy discrete-time systems with different premise variables. Complexity **21**(5), 265–276 (2016)

5. Li, H., Wang, J., Wu, L., Lam, H.K., Gao, Y.: Optimal guaranteed cost sliding mode control of interval type-2 fuzzy time-delay systems. IEEE Trans. Fuzzy Syst. (2017). doi:10.1109/TFUZZ.2017.2648855

6. Zhang, D., Cai, W., Xie, L., Wang, Q.: Nonfragile distributed filtering for T-S fuzzy systems in sensor networks. IEEE Trans. Fuzzy Syst. **23**(5), 1883–1890 (2015)

7. Wang, L., Lam, H.K.: Local stabilization for continuous-time Takagi-Sugeno fuzzy systems with time delay. IEEE Trans. Fuzzy Syst. (2016). doi:10.1109/TFUZZ.2016.2639564

8. Li, H., Wu, C., Jing, X., Wu, L.: Fuzzy tracking control for nonlinear networked systems. IEEE Trans. Cybern. **47**, 2020–2031 (2016). doi:10.1109/TCYB.2016.2594046

9. Li, H., Shi, P., Yao, D.: Adaptive sliding mode control of Markov jump nonlinear systems with actuator faults. IEEE Trans. Autom. Control **62**, 1933–1939 (2016). doi:10.1109/TAC.2016.2588885

10. Wang, H., Yang, G.-H.: Dynamic output feedback controller design for affine T-S fuzzy systems with quantized measurements. ISA Trans. **64**, 202–215 (2016)

11. Ding, B.C.: Stabilization of Takagi-Sugeno model via nonparallel distributed compsensation law. IEEE Trans. Fuzzy Syst. **18**(1), 188–194 (2010)

12. Hou, L., Cheng, J., Qi, H.: Event-triggered reliable control for fuzzy Markovian jump systems with mismatched membership functions. ISA Trans. **66**, 96–104 (2016). doi:10.1016/j.isatra.2016.09.006

13. Oliveira, R.C.L.F., Peres, P.L.D.: Parameter-dependent LMIs in robust analysis: characterization of homogeneous polynomially parameter-dependent solutions via LMI relaxations. IEEE Trans. Autom. Control **52**(7), 1334–1340 (2007)

14. Ding, B.C.: Homogeneous polynomially nonquadratic stabilization of discrete-time Takagi-Sugeno systems via nonparallel distributed compensation law. IEEE Trans. Fuzzy Syst. **18**(5), 994–1000 (2010)

15. Xie, X., Yue, D., Zhang, H., Xue, Y.: Control synthesis of discrete-time T-S fuzzy systems via a multi-instant homogenous polynomial approach. IEEE Trans. Cybern. **46**(3), 630–640 (2016)

16. Ding, S.X.: Model-Based Fault Diagnosis Techniques: Design Schemes, Algorithms, and Tools. Springer, Berlin (2008). doi:10.1007/978-1-4471-4799-2

17. Zhang, K., Jiang, B., Shi, P.: Integrated fault estimation and accommodation design for discrete-time Takagi-Sugeno fuzzy systems with actuator faults. IEEE Trans. Fuzzy Syst. **19**(2), 291–304 (2011)

18. Ding, D.-W., Yang, G.-H.: Fuzzy filter design for nonlinear systems in finite-frequency domain. IEEE Trans. Fuzzy Syet. **18**(5), 935–945 (2010)

19. Yang, H., Xia, Y., Liu, B.: Fault detection for T-S fuzzy discrete systems in finite-frequency domain. IEEE Trans. Syst. Man Cybern. B Cybern. **41**(4), 911–920 (2011)

20. Feng, G.: Controller synthesis of fuzzy dynamic systems based on piecewise Lyapunov functions. IEEE Trans. Fuzzy Syst. **11**(5), 605–612 (2003)

21. Zhang, K., Jiang, B., Shi, P.: Fault estimation observer design for discrete-time Takagi-Sugeno fuzzy systems based on piecewise Lyapunov functions. IEEE Trans. Fuzzy Syst. **20**(1), 192–200 (2012)

Advanced Methods for Networked Systems

Stability Analysis of Event-Triggered Networked Control Systems with Time-Varying Sampling

Huaibin Xie[1(⊠)] and Songlin Hu[2]

[1] College of Automation, Nanjing University of Posts and Telecommunications,
Nanjing 210000, China
1012579727@qq.com

[2] Hubei Provincial Collaborative Innovation Center for New Energy Microgrid,
CTGU, Institute of Advanced Technology,
Nanjing University of Posts and Telecommunications, Nanjing 210000, China

Abstract. In this paper, the stability analysis of event-triggered networked control systems is investigated. First, a more advanced event-triggered algorithm is introduced. Second, the nonperiodic sampled-data system is modeled as a state delay system. Third, a stability result is derived based on Lyapunov-Krasovskii functional approach. Finally, some simulation results are given to verify the effectiveness of the proposed method.

Keywords: Sampled-data systems · Event-triggering scheme · Linear matrix inequalities

1 Introduction

In recent years, sampled-data systems have attracted the attention of many researchers [1, 2] due to the high-speed development of the digital control systems and networked control systems. Most results about sampled-data systems use a periodic triggered control method [3], periodic sampling method is easy for system modeling and analysis [4], but considering the resource utilization, this way has its limitations. When the system is running smoothly, periodical transmission will result in a waste of resources and bandwidth. At the same time, we should have noticed another fact, with the growing of the systems scale [5, 6], the amount of data transmitted by the network is great, thus, it is necessary to save resources and bandwidth. From the two aspects, the event-triggering mechanism shows its unique advantages [7]. Recently, the research of networked control system based on event-driven mechanism gets an increasing attention, and so far, many research results have been achieved [8–10]. Therefore, it is necessary to analyze and design the networked control system based on the event-driven mechanism.

In the event-triggered mechanism, the transmission of data mainly depends on the predefined trigger algorithm [11]. Therefore, the advantage of an event-triggered mechanism depends on the choice of trigger algorithm and the corresponding parameters settings. At the same time, the stability analysis based on the event-triggered

© Springer Nature Singapore Pte Ltd. 2017
D. Yue et al. (Eds.): LSMS/ICSEE 2017, Part II, CCIS 762, pp. 457–466, 2017.
DOI: 10.1007/978-981-10-6373-2_46

mechanism is dependent on the selection of the Lyapunov-Krasovskii equation, an appropriate Lyapunov-Krasovskii equation and the treatment of the corresponding integral term will reduce the conservativeness of the system to a certain extent. A smaller degree of conservatism will make the proposed solution more valuable.

Inspired by literature [12, 13], compared to other aperiodic sampling methods, we take nonperiodic sampled-data system into account and model it as a state delay system, then we proposed a more advanced event-triggered algorithm based on non-periodic sampling, this algorithm has its own unique advantage. Simultaneously, after changing the corresponding parameters, the different set of the element in Θ can reduce the amount of transmitted sampled data. In the selection of the Lyapunov-Krasovskii equation, we choose a discrete Lyapunov-Krasovskii equation to reduce the conservative. At the same time, in the processing of some integral items, we choose the improved Jason inequality [14] and some results in literature [15] to further reduce the conservative.

2 Problem Formulation

Consider a class of linear systems:

$$\dot{x}(t) = Ax(t) + Bu(t) \tag{1}$$

where $x(t) \in R^n$ is the state vector, $u(t) \in R^m$ is the control input, $A \in R^{n \times n}$, $B \in R^{n \times m}$ are known constant matrices with appropriate dimensions.

Similar to [13], this paper considers an event-triggered mechanism, the last released instant $r_k, k = 1, 2, \ldots$ the next released instant $r_{k+1} = r_k + \sum_{s=0}^{l_k} \Delta t_s$ $1 \leq l_k < \infty$, $l_k \in N$, then we divide the time interval $[r_k, r_{k+1})$ into the following subintervals:

$$[r_k, r_{k+1}) = U_{d=-1}^{l_k - 1} I_d^k \tag{2}$$

where $I_d^k = [r_k + \sum_{s=0}^{d} \Delta t_s, r_k + \sum_{s=0}^{d+1} \Delta t_s), d \in [0, l_k - 1]$, and the trigger instants r_k satisfying $0 = r_0 < r_1 < \ldots < r_k < \ldots$ and $0 \leq \underline{r} \leq r_{k+1} - r_k \leq \bar{r}$, for $\forall k \in N$.

The triggered algorithm proposed in this paper is:

$$\varepsilon^2 e^T (r_k + \sum_{s=0}^{d} \Delta t_s) \Omega_1 e(r_k + \sum_{s=0}^{d} \Delta t_s) \leq x^T(r_k) \Theta \, \Omega_2 \Theta x(r_k)$$

where

$$e(r_k + \sum_{s=0}^{d} \Delta t_s) = x(r_k + \sum_{s=0}^{d} \Delta t_s) - x(r_k), \Theta = diag\{\sqrt{\sigma_1}, \sqrt{\sigma_2}, \ldots, \sqrt{\sigma_n}\} \text{ with } \sigma_i$$
$$> 0(i = 1, 2, \ldots, n), \Omega_1 > 0, \text{ and } \Omega_2 > 0 \text{ are two weighting matrices.}$$

Remark 1. Notice that, compared with traditional event-triggered algorithm, this algorithm introduces a diagonal matrix Θ, this matrix contains different weighting factor σ_i which corresponds to each component x_i of the latest transmitted sampled state x, the different set of the element in Θ can reduce the amount of transmitted sampled data, in this way, the communication and computation resources will be saved deeply. Another point, we can see: if taking $\Theta = diag\{\sqrt{\sigma}, \sqrt{\sigma}, \ldots, \sqrt{\sigma}\}$, $\varepsilon = 1$, this event-triggered algorithm turns into a traditional algorithm. Therefor, this event-triggered algorithm is more general than some existing ones.

Similar to [13], define a time-varying delay $\iota(t)$ as:

$$\tau(t) = \begin{cases} t - r_k, t \in [r_k, r_k + \Delta t_0) \\ t - r_k - \sum_{s=0}^{d} \Delta t_s, t \in [r_k + \sum_{s=0}^{d} \Delta t_s, r_k + \sum_{s=0}^{d+1} \Delta t_s) \end{cases}$$

where $d \in [0, l_k - 1]$.

Then we have

$$e\left(r_k + \sum_{s=0}^{d} \Delta t_s\right) = e(t - \tau(t)) = e_\tau(t),$$

$$x(r_k) = x(t - \tau(t)) - e\left(r_k + \sum_{s=0}^{d} \Delta t_s\right) = x_\tau(t) - e_\tau(t)$$

The event-triggered algorithm can be written as:

$$\varepsilon^2 e_\tau^T(t)\Omega_1 e_\tau(t) \leq [x_\tau(t) - e_\tau(t)]^T \Theta \Omega_2 \Theta[x_\tau(t) - e_\tau(t)]$$

Considering the event-triggered mechanism, we can design the controller as follow:

$$u(t) = Kx(r_k), t \in [r_k, r_{k+1}) \tag{3}$$

where $u(t) \in R^m$ is the control input satisfying $u(t) = u(r_k)$.

$$x(r_k) = x_\tau(t) - e_\tau(t) \tag{4}$$

Substituting (3) into (1) yields.

$$\dot{x}(t) = Ax(t) + BKx(r_k) \tag{5}$$

Then substituting (4) into (5) yields, the original model can be converted into:

$$\dot{x}(t) = Ax(t) + A_1(x_\tau(t) - e_\tau(t)), t \in [r_k, r_{k+1}) \tag{6}$$

where $A_1 = BK$.

Lemma 1 [14]. For a given matrix $R \in S_+^n$, any differentiable function x in $[a, b] \rightarrow R^n$, the inequality holds:

$$\int_a^b \dot{x}^T(u)R\dot{x}(u)du \geq \frac{1}{b-a}\Omega^T diag(R, 3R)\Omega$$

where

$$\Omega = \begin{bmatrix} x(b) - x(a) \\ x(b) + x(a) - \frac{2}{b-a}\int_a^b x(u)du \end{bmatrix}$$

3   Stability Analysis

Theorem 1. For given positive $\underline{r}$ and $\bar{r}$, $1 \times n$ matrix K, if there exist symmetric matrix $P > 0$, $Q > 0$, $\Omega > 0$, $Q_1 > 0$, $Q_2 \in R^{n \times n} M_1, M_2 \in R^{n \times n}$ and $N_{1j}, N_{2j}, N_{3j} \in R^{n \times n}(j = 1, 2, 3, 4)$, the following inequalities hold.

$$\begin{bmatrix} \Pi_{11} & * & * & * & * & * \\ \Pi_{21} & \Pi_{22} & * & * & * & * \\ \Pi_{31} & \Pi_{32} & \Pi_{33} & * & * & * \\ \Pi_{41} & \Pi_{42} & \Pi_{43} & \Pi_{44} & * & * \\ rN_{11}^T & rN_{12}^T & rN_{13}^T & rN_{14}^T & -rQ & * \\ 3rN_{21}^T & 3rN_{22}^T & 3rN_{23}^T & 3rN_{24}^T & 0 & -3rQ \end{bmatrix} < 0$$

$$\begin{bmatrix} X_{11} & * & * & * & * \\ X_{21} & X_{22} & * & * & * \\ X_{31} & X_{32} & X_{33} & * & * \\ X_{41} & X_{42} & X_{43} & X_{44} & * \\ rAQ & rA_1Q & -rA_1Q & 0 & -rQ \end{bmatrix} < 0$$

where

$$\Pi_{11} = A^T P + PA - N_{11} - N_{11}^T - N_{31} - N_{31}^T - 3N_{21} - 3N_{21}^T - 2M_1$$

$$\Pi_{21} = A_1^T P - N_{12} + N_{11}^T - N_{32} + N_{31}^T - 3N_{22} - 3N_{21}^T - M_2 + M_1 + rA_1^T N_{31}^T$$

$$\Pi_{22} = N_{12} + N_{12}^T + N_{32} + N_{32}^T - 3N_{22} - 3N_{22}^T + 2M_2 + rN_{32}A_1 + rA_1^T N_{32}^T$$
$$- rQ_2 + \Theta\Omega\Theta$$

$$\Pi_{31} = A_1^T P - N_{13} - N_{11}^T - N_{33} - N_{31}^T - 3N_{23} + 3N_{21}^T + M_2 - M_1 - rA_1^T N_{31}^T$$

$$\Pi_{32} = N_{13} - N_{12}^T + N_{33} - N_{32}^T - 3N_{23} + 3N_{22}^T - 2M_2 + rN_{33}A_1 - rA_1^T N_{32}^T$$
$$+ rQ_2 - \Theta\Omega\Theta$$

$$\Pi_{33} = -N_{13} - N_{13}^T - N_{33} - N_{33}^T + 3N_{23} + 3N_{23}^T + 2M_2 - rN_{33}A_1 - rA_1^T N_{33}^T$$
$$- rQ_2 - \varepsilon^2\Omega + \Theta\Omega\Theta$$

$$\Pi_{41} = -N_{14} - N_{34} - 3N_{24} + 6N_{21}^T + rA^T N_{31}^T$$
$$\Pi_{42} = N_{14} + N_{34} - 3N_{24} + 6N_{22}^T + rN_{34}A_1 + rA^T N_{32}^T$$
$$\Pi_{43} = -N_{14} - N_{34} + 3N_{24} + 6N_{23}^T - rN_{34}A_1 + rA^T N_{33}^T$$
$$\Pi_{44} = 6N_{24} + 6N_{24}^T + rN_{34}A + rA^T N_{34}^T - rQ_1$$

$$X_{11} = A^T P + PA - N_{11} - N_{11}^T - N_{31} - N_{31}^T - 3N_{21} - 3N_{21}^T - 2M_1 + rA^T M_1$$
$$\quad + 2rM_1A + rA^T M_1 + rQ_1$$
$$X_{21} = A_1^T P - N_{12} + N_{11}^T - N_{32} + N_{31}^T - 3N_{22} - 3N_{21}^T - M_2 + M_1 + rA_1^T M_1$$
$$\quad + rM_2A + rA_1^T M_1 - rM_1A$$
$$X_{22} = N_{12} + N_{12}^T + N_{32} + N_{32}^T - 3N_{22} - 3N_{22}^T + 2M_2 - rA_1^T M_1 + rM_2A_1$$
$$\quad - rM_1A_1 + rA_1^T M_2 + rQ_2$$
$$X_{31} = A_1^T P - N_{13} - N_{11}^T - N_{33} - N_{31}^T - 3N_{23} + 3N_{21}^T + M_2 - M_1 - rA_1^T M_1$$
$$\quad - rM_2A - rA_1^T M_1 + rM_1A$$
$$X_{32} = N_{13} - N_{12}^T + N_{33} - N_{32}^T - 3N_{23} + 3N_{22}^T - 2M_2 + rA_1^T M_1 - rM_2A_1$$
$$\quad + rM_1A_1 - rA_1^T M_2 - rQ_2$$
$$X_{33} = -N_{13} - N_{13}^T - N_{33} - N_{33}^T + 3N_{23} + 3N_{23}^T + 2M_2 - rA_1^T M_1 + rM_2A_1$$
$$\quad - rM_1A_1 + rA_1^T M_2 + rQ_2$$
$$X_{41} = -N_{14} - N_{34} - 3N_{24} + 6N_{21}^T$$
$$X_{42} = N_{14} + N_{34} - 3N_{24} + 6N_{22}^T$$
$$X_{43} = -N_{14} - N_{34} + 3N_{24} + 6N_{23}^T$$

Then the system (6) is asymptotically stable.

Proof. Similar to [12], select a Lyapunov-like functional:

$$V(x(t), t) = V_1(x(t)) + V_2(x(t), t) + V_3(x(t), t)$$

where

$$V_1(x(t)) = x^T(t)Px(t)$$

$$V_2(x(t), t) = 2(r_{k+1} - t)(x^T(t)M_1 + x^T(r_k)M_2)(x(t) - x(r_k)) + (r_{k+1} - t)\int_{r_k}^t \dot{x}(s)Q\dot{x}(s)ds$$

$$V_3(x(t), t) = (r_{k+1} - t)\int_{r_k}^t x^T(s)Q_1x(s)ds + (r_{k+1} - t)(t - r_k)x^T(r_k)Q_2x(r_k)$$

Then define $\xi(t) = \begin{bmatrix} x^T(t) & x_\tau^T(t) & e_\tau^T(t) & v^T(t) \end{bmatrix}^T$
where $v(t) = \frac{1}{t - r_k}\int_{r_k}^t x(s)ds$.

Taking the derivative of $V(x(t), t)$ along the trajectory of system (6).

$$\dot{V}(x(t),t) = \dot{V}_1(x(t)) + \dot{V}_2(x(t),t) + \dot{V}_3(x(t),t)$$

$$\dot{V}_1(x(t)) = x^T(t)(A^T P + PA)x(t) + 2x^T(t)PA_1 x_\tau(t) - 2x^T(t)PA_1 e_\tau(t)$$

$$\dot{V}_2(x(t),t) = 2\xi^T(t)Z_1\xi(t) + (r_{k+1} - t)\xi^T(t)(He(Z_2) + Z_3)\xi(t) - \int_{r_k}^t \dot{x}^T(s)Q\dot{x}(s)ds$$

$$\dot{V}_3(x(t),t) = (r_{k+1} - t)\xi^T(t)\Gamma_1\xi(t) + (r_{k+1} - t)\xi^T(t)\Gamma_2\xi(t) - (t - r_k)\xi^T(t)\Gamma_2\xi(t) - \int_{r_k}^t x^T(s)Q_1 x(s)ds$$

where

$$Z_1 = \begin{bmatrix} -M_1 & M_1 & -M_1 & 0 \\ -M_2 & M_2 & -M_2 & 0 \\ M_2 & -M_2 & M_2 & 0 \\ 0 & 0 & 0 & 0 \end{bmatrix}$$

$$Z_2 = \begin{bmatrix} A^T M_1 + M_1 A & M_1 A_1 - A^T M_1 & -M_1 A_1 + A^T M_1 & 0 \\ A_1^T M_1 + M_2 A & -A_1^T M_1 + M_2 A_1 & A_1^T M_1 - M_2 A_1 & 0 \\ -A_1^T M_1 - M_2 A & A_1^T M_1 - M_2 A_1 & -A_1^T M_1 + M_2 A_1 & 0 \\ 0 & 0 & 0 & 0 \end{bmatrix}$$

$$Z_3 = \begin{bmatrix} A^T QA & * & * & * \\ A_1^T QA & A_1^T QA_1 & * & * \\ -A_1^T QA & -A_1^T QA_1 & A_1^T QA_1 & * \\ 0 & 0 & 0 & 0 \end{bmatrix}$$

$$\Gamma_1 = \begin{bmatrix} Q_1 & * & * & * \\ 0 & 0 & * & * \\ 0 & 0 & 0 & * \\ 0 & 0 & 0 & 0 \end{bmatrix} \quad \Gamma_2 = \begin{bmatrix} 0 & * & * & * \\ 0 & Q_2 & * & * \\ 0 & -Q_2 & Q_2 & * \\ 0 & 0 & 0 & 0 \end{bmatrix}$$

Integrating both sides of system (5) On $[r_k, t)$, we have

$$x(t) - x(r_k) = A \int_{r_k}^t x(s)ds + (t - r_k)A_1 x(r_k) \tag{7}$$

According to (7), there exists $N_3 \in R^{4n \times n}$ such that

$$-2\xi^T(t)N_3(e_1 - e_2 + e_3)\xi(t) + 2(t - r_k)\xi^T(t)N_3 A e_4 \xi(t) \\ + 2(t - r_k)\xi^T(t)N_3 A_1(e_2 - e_3)\xi(t) = 0 \tag{8}$$

By Lemma 1, we have

$$-\int_{r_k}^{t} \dot{x}^T(s)Q\dot{x}(s)ds \le -\frac{1}{t-r_k}\xi^T(t)(e_1 - e_2 + e_3)^T Q(e_1 - e_2 + e_3)\xi(t)$$

$$-\frac{3}{t-r_k}\xi^T(t)(e_1 + e_2 - e_3 - 2e_4)^T Q(e_1 + e_2 - e_3 - 2e_4)\xi(t)$$

In addition, there exist $N_1, N_2 \in R^{4n \times n}$ satisfies the following inequalities.

$$-\int_{r_k}^{t} \dot{x}^T(s)Q\dot{x}(s)ds \le (t-r_k)N_1 Q^{-1}N_1^T \quad N_1(e_1 - e_2 + e_3) - N_1^T(e_1 - e_2 + e_3)^T$$
$$+3(t-r_k)N_2 Q^{-1}N_2^T - 3N_2(e_1 + e_2 - e_3 - 2e_4) - 3N_2^T(e_1 + e_2 - e_3 - 2e_4)^T \tag{9}$$

where
$$e_1 = [I \;\; 0 \;\; 0 \;\; 0], e_2 = [0 \;\; I \;\; 0 \;\; 0], e_3 = [0 \;\; 0 \;\; I \;\; 0], e_4 = [0 \;\; 0 \;\; 0 \;\; I]$$
According to Jensen inequality, we have the following inequality.

$$-\int_{r_k}^{t} x^T(s)Q_1 x(s)ds \le -(t-r_k)v^T(t)Q_1 v(t) \tag{10}$$

From (8)–(10), by Schur complement lemma, Theorem 1 can be derived for $r \in \{\underline{r}, \bar{r}\}$.

4 Numerical Examples

In this section, a numerical simulation is given to verify the results proposed in the previous section.

Example 1. Consider the system in [12] with the parameter matrices.

$$A = \begin{bmatrix} 0 & 1 \\ 0 & -0.1 \end{bmatrix}, \quad A_1 = \begin{bmatrix} 0 & 0 \\ -0.375 & -1.15 \end{bmatrix}$$

When $\underline{r} = 0$, the admissible upper bound $\bar{r}$ can be calculated by Matlab LMI toolbox according to Theorem 1.

(1) Case 1: Set event-trigger parameters

$$\varepsilon = 1, \Theta = diag\{0.59, 0.47\}$$

The admissible upper bound $\bar{r}$ and some results in [12, 16, 17] are shown in Table 1.
From Table 1, it can be seen clearly that Theorem 1 has a less conservatism than the results in [12, 16, 17].

Table 1. Admissible upper bound $\bar{r}$ under different schemes

Schemes	[12]	[16]	[17]	Theorem 1
$\bar{r}$	1.729	1.69	1.7216	2.44

So as to further verify the effectiveness of the event-triggered algorithm, we make the following experiments.

(2) Case 2: we set different ε to do several simulations.

$$\varepsilon_1 = 10, \varepsilon_2 = 15, \varepsilon_3 = 30$$

The admissible upper bounds corresponding to different ε are shown in Table 2.

From Table 2, we can see clearly that different ε can reduce the conservatism to different degrees.

Table 2. Admissible upper bound $\bar{r}$ with different ε

Different ε	ε_1	ε_2	ε_3
$\bar{r}$	2.51	2.54	2.59

Example 2. Consider the system in [12].

$$A = \begin{bmatrix} 0.05 & 0.6 & 0.1 \\ -3 & -2 & 0.1 \\ 0.1 & 0 & -2 \end{bmatrix}, \quad A_1 = \begin{bmatrix} 0.05 & 0.05 & 0.4 \\ -1 & 1 & 0.05 \\ 0.5 & 0.05 & -0.9 \end{bmatrix}$$

(1) Case 1: Set event-trigger parameters

$$\varepsilon = 15, \quad \Theta = diag\{0.59, 0.47, 0.51\}$$

The admissible upper bound and some results in [14, 17] are shown in Table 3.

For the different simulation model, the Table 3 shows that Theorem 1 has a less conservatism than the results in [14, 17].

Table 3. Admissible upper bound $\bar{r}$ under different schemes

Schemes	[14]	[17]	Theorem 1
$\bar{r}$	2.33	2.00	2.51

(1) Case 2: Now we set $\Theta = diag\{0.59, 0.47, 0.51\}$ and choose different ε to do several simulations.

$$\varepsilon_1 = 20, \varepsilon_2 = 25, \varepsilon_3 = 30$$

The admissible upper bounds $\bar{r}$ corresponding to different ε are shown in Table 4.

From Table 4, we can see clearly that different ε can reduce the conservatism to different degrees.

From Tables 1 and 3, it is seen clearly that Theorem 1 is less conservative than the results in literature [16, 17]. From Tables 2 and 4, we can see clearly that the event-triggering algorithm has a certain effect in reducing conservatism.

Table 4. Admissible upper bound $\bar{r}$ with different ε

Different ε	ε_1	ε_2	ε_3
$\bar{r}$	2.66	2.77	2.84

5 Conclusion

In this paper, based on the sampling-dependent stability for sampled-data systems, a more general event-triggering mechanism is taken into account. In terms of reducing conservatism, we utilize a Lyapunov-like functional including the integral of the state. Simultaneously, we use the improved Jensen inequality for the derivative of the Lyapunov-like functional. At last, a sampling-dependent stability theorem is derived. The validity of this theorem is verified by several simulation experiments.

References

1. Fujioka, H.: A discrete-time approach to stability analysis of systems with aperiodic sample-and-hold devices. IEEE Trans. Autom. Control 54(10), 2440–2445 (2009)
2. Ghantasala, S., El-Farra, N.H.: Active fault-tolerant control of sampled-data nonlinear distributed parameter systems. Int. J. Robust Nonlinear Control 22(1), 24–42 (2012)
3. Chen, T., Francis, B.A.: Optimal sampled-data control systems. Proc. IEEE 86(6), 1293–1294 (1998)
4. Zhang, W., Branicky, M.S., Phillips, S.M.: Stability of networked control systems. IEEE Control Syst. 21(1), 84–99 (2001)
5. Zhou, Y., Yang, X., Guo, X., et al.: A design of greenhouse monitoring and control system based on ZigBee wireless sensor network. In: 2007 International Conference on Wireless Communications, Networking and Mobile Computing, pp. 2563–2567. IEEE (2007)
6. Ulusoy, A., Gurbuz, O., Onat, A.: Wireless model-based predictive networked control system over cooperative wireless network. IEEE Trans. Industr. Inf. 7(1), 41–51 (2011)
7. Rabi, M., Johansson, K.H.: Event-triggered strategies for industrial control over wireless networks. In: Proceedings of the 4th Annual International Conference on Wireless Internet. ICST (Institute for Computer Sciences, Social-Informatics and Telecommunications Engineering), p. 34 (2008)
8. Lunze, J., Lehmann, D.: A state-feedback approach to event-based control. Automatica 46(1), 211–215 (2010)
9. Peng, C., Han, Q.L.: A novel event-triggered transmission scheme and control co-design for sampled-data control systems. IEEE Trans. Autom. Control 58(10), 2620–2626 (2013)

10. Aranda-Escolástico, E., Guinaldo, M., Dormido, S.: A novel approach for periodic event-triggering based on general quadratic functions. In: 2015 International Conference on Event-Based Control, Communication, and Signal Processing (EBCCSP), pp. 1–6. IEEE (2015)
11. Wang, X., Lemmon, M.D.: Event-triggering in distributed networked control systems. IEEE Trans. Autom. Control **56**(3), 586–601 (2011)
12. Zhao, J., Shao, H., Zhang, D.: A new approach to sampling-dependent stability for sampled-data systems under aperiodic samplings. In: 2016 Chinese Control and Decision Conference (CCDC), pp. 5732–5737. IEEE (2016)
13. Hu, S., Yue, D., Xie, X., et al.: Stabilization of neural-network-based control systems via event-triggered control with nonperiodic sampled data. In: IEEE Transactions on Neural Networks and Learning Systems (2016)
14. Seuret, A., Gouaisbaut, F.: Wirtinger-based integral inequality: application to time-delay systems. Automatica **49**(9), 2860–2866 (2013)
15. Gu, K.: An integral inequality in the stability problem of time-delay systems. In: Proceedings of the 39th IEEE Conference on Decision and Control, vol. 3, pp. 2805–2810. IEEE (2000)
16. Fridman, E.: A refined input delay approach to sampled-data control. Automatica **46**(2), 421–427 (2010)
17. Seuret, A.: A novel stability analysis of linear systems under asynchronous samplings. Automatica **48**(1), 177–182 (2012)

State Estimation-Based Security Control for Networked Systems Under Hybrid Attacks

Hao Zhang$^{(\boxtimes)}$, Chen Peng$^{(\boxtimes)}$, and Hongtao Sun

Shanghai Key Laboratory of Power Station Automation Technology,
School of Mechatronic Engineering and Automatic, Shanghai University,
Shanghai 200072, China
zhyk1117@163.com, c.peng@shu.edu.cn

Abstract. This paper is concerned with the security control of networked systems under denial of attacks and false data injection attacks. Firstly, an observer is designed to estimate the system state under hybrid attacks, and the system is modelled as a stochastic closed-loop system with an observer-based security controller. Then, by use of the Lyapunov theory, sufficient security stability and stabilization criteria are derived to ensure the asymptotically stable of the studied system in the mean-square sense under hybrid attacks. Finally, an example is given to illustrate the effectiveness of developed method.

Keywords: State estimation · DoS attacks · False data injection attacks · Security control

1 Introduction

Industry networks based-network are complex systems. It plays an crucial role in power networks, coal industry and other energy fields. It enriches our life, however, fatal consequences will be caused when the networked control systems (NCS) suffered from malicious attacks [1]. Currently, the question of energy security has been a focus for nations around the world. As is well known, in industry energy system, sensors, controllers and physical plants are connected via a common network medium. Owing to the openness and sharing of network, energy system suffer from the security problems, inevitably. For example, the data will be easily exploited by attacks when the exchanged data are transmitted to the next device without any security protection. Therefore a security defense system is necessary to defend network attacks.

Nowadays, two types of attack models, namely, denial of service (DoS) attacks [2] and false data injection (FDI) attacks [3], generally occurs. The two kinds of attack can cause date packets dropout and injection of vicious information, respectively. Besides, there are some other attacks appearing in NCS, such as deception attacks [4], replay attacks [5] and sparse attacks [6] etc. In order to reduce or eliminate the adverse effects caused by unsafe factors, some state estimation strategies are imperative for NCS under malicious attacks. Consequently,

© Springer Nature Singapore Pte Ltd. 2017
D. Yue et al. (Eds.): LSMS/ICSEE 2017, Part II, CCIS 762, pp. 467–476, 2017.
DOI: 10.1007/978-981-10-6373-2_47

state estimation has attacked extensive attention by researchers from a variety of disciplines, see, e.g. [1,7–13].

For the state estimation strategies, the existing approaches can be classified into two categories: (a) estimation based on special attacks [7–9]. In such case, the attacks destroy system through a special behaviour. [7] transforms Kalman filtering into χ^2 estimation problem, the method is effective against DoS attacks, however, it can't defend FDI attacks. Shoukry and Tabuada [9] limits the attack targets within a certain subset, then, a Lunberger observer is designed to estimate system state, and an event-triggered strategy is used to reduce unnecessary date transmission. Besides, Dai W [10] proposes a novel kind of FDI attacks in smart grids, then, a method based on extended distributed state estimation is provided. However, the above approaches are not applicable when attack behavior does not conform to the special hypothesis, not to mention the case that two kinds of attack exist simultaneously; (b) estimation based on optimization [1,11,12], L_0 and $L_1/L_r (r > 1)$ are the main optimization methods. Fawzi et al. [1] describes the process of L_0 decoder and illustrates that the algorithm is the best decoder for sparse attacks. Based on the above works, Tabuada proposes a convex optimization L_1/L_r and a novel gradient descent algorithm [11]. Moreover, [12] gives a new method, which can been seen as an extension of the normalized iterative hard threshold (NIHT) algorithm.

In this paper we consider the problem of state estimation with both randomly occurring DoS attacks and randomly occurring FDI attacks. Unlike most of the works we mentioned above, we do not need to restrict the behavior and type of attack. Inspired by the work [14,15], an observer-based security controller is designed to guarantee the stability of the system. The main contributions of this paper can be highlighted as:

1. A general model of observer-based security control is constructed when considering randomly occurring DoS attacks and randomly occurring FDI attacks together; and
2. An observer-based security controller are well designed to guarantee the asymptotically stable of the studied system in the mean-square sense under hybrid attacks.

The remainder of this paper is organized as follows. In Sect. 2, the attacks model and observer model are established. In Sect. 3, Analogously to [15], the main results are presented for system analysis and synthesis. In Sect. 4, a numerical example is given to demonstrate the usefulness of the proposed design method. Finally, Sect. 5 concludes our work.

2   Problem Formulation and Modeling

2.1   System Description

Considering the following discrete linear time-invariant system with sensor attacks

$$\begin{cases} x(k+1) = Ax(k) + Bu(k) \\ y(k) = Cx(k) + Du(k) \end{cases} \tag{1}$$

where $x(k) \in R^n$, $u(k) \in R^m$, and $y(k) \in R^p$ are the state vector, control inputs and detectable outputs, respectively. A, B, C, D are the corresponding constant matrices with appropriate dimensions. The $y_o(k)$ is used to denote the signal received from the Zero Order Hold (ZOH).

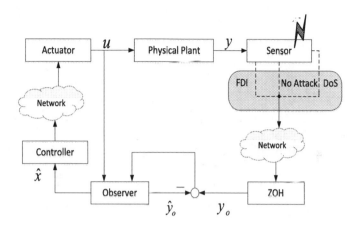

Fig. 1. The networked control system with sensor attacks

The schematic block diagram of a NCS with hybrid attacks is shown in Fig. 1, for convenience, some basic assumptions are stated for the system.

1. Sensors and controller are the time-driven and clock synchronization, the sampling period is T, simultaneously, the actuator is event-driven.
2. Network-induced delay and data dropout are neglected.
3. Only investigate the case that sensors are destroyed with both randomly occurring DoS attacks and randomly occurring FDI attacks.

The stochastic variable $\alpha(k)$ is Bernoulli-distributed white sequences, and takes values on either 0 or 1. Besides,

$$Prob\{\alpha(k) = 0\} = 1 - \bar{\alpha}, \quad Prob\{\alpha(k) = 1\} = \bar{\alpha} \tag{2}$$

where $\bar{\alpha} \in [0, 1)$ is a known constant.

Remark 1. In Fig. 1, the three cases can be interpreted as follows: (1) the data will be discarded when the sensors suffer from DoS attacks, and the recent received signal from sensors will be regarded as the input of observer at time $t = k$, $y_o(k) = y_o(k-1)$; (2) when the sensors suffer from FDI attacks, the received signal for observer can be regarded as $y_o(k) = y(k) + w(k)$, where $w(k)$ is the injection of error information; (3) for the last case, the sensors do not suffer from attacks, $y_o(k) = y(k)$. Apparently, the second case can be seen as the third case when $w(k) = 0$.

Summing up the above remark, the following formulas are hold.

$$y_o(k) = \begin{cases} y_o(k-1), & \text{if suffered DoS attacks;} \\ y(k) + w(k), & \text{if suffered FDI attacks;} \\ y(k), & \text{otherwise.} \end{cases} \tag{3}$$

where $w(k)$ is a random sequence. Consequently, the input signal of observer can be represented as

$$y_o(k) = (1 - \alpha(k))y_o(k-1) + \alpha(k)(y(k) + w(k)) \tag{4}$$

2.2 Modelling of Closed-Loop System with an Observer-Based Security Controller

Different from the prevalent method [16], the observer can not only tolerate DoS but also allow the existence of FDI attacks. In this subsection, an observer under malicious attacks will be first designed to estimate the unmeasured state, then an observer-based controller will be designed to guarantee the desired stability properties. Then the global dynamics of the observer can be represented as

$$observer: \begin{cases} \hat{x}(k+1) = A\hat{x}(k) + Bu(k) + L(y_o(k) - \hat{y}_o(k)) \\ \hat{y}_o(k) = (1 - \alpha(k))y_o(k-1) + \alpha(k)c\hat{x}(k) \end{cases} \tag{5}$$

where $\hat{x}(k+1) \in R^n$ is the estimated observer state, $\hat{y}_o(k) \in R^p$ is the measured output. L is observer gain to be designed.

Since we do not consider the effects of communication network and attacks between controller and actuator, it is reasonable to assume that the output signal of controller can be transmitted directly into the actuator. Then the following observer-based controller can be devised.

$$u(k) = K\hat{x}(k) \tag{6}$$

where K is the controller parameter to be determined.

Define the estimation error as $e(k) = x(k) - \hat{x}(k)$, then the dynamic error of the observer can be obtained as

$$\begin{aligned} e(k+1) &= x(k+1) - \hat{x}(k+1) \\ &= Ae(k) - \alpha(k)L[Ce(k) + w(k)] \end{aligned} \tag{7}$$

Moreover, considering (5) and (7) together, denote $\xi(k) = [\hat{x}(k), e(k)]$, then the augmented system can be obtained as

$$\begin{aligned} \xi(k+1) =& \bar{A}\xi(k) + (\alpha(k) - \bar{\alpha})\bar{L}\xi(k) + \bar{\alpha}\tilde{L}w(k) \\ &+ (\alpha(k) - \bar{\alpha})\tilde{L}w(k) \end{aligned} \tag{8}$$

where $\bar{\alpha}$ denotes the mathematical expectation of the random variable $\alpha(k)$, or equivalently, $\bar{\alpha} = E\{\alpha(k)\}$.

$$\bar{A} = \begin{bmatrix} A + BK & \bar{\alpha}LC \\ 0 & A - \bar{\alpha}LC \end{bmatrix},$$

$$\bar{L} = \begin{bmatrix} 0 & LC \\ 0 & -LC \end{bmatrix}, \tilde{L} = \begin{bmatrix} L \\ -L \end{bmatrix}$$

It can be known from (8) that the argument system is a time-variable para-meter system including random parameter. Consequently, a definition for (8) is given as follows.

Definition 1. *The system (8) is random mean-square stability for $w(k) = 0$ and any initial state $\eta(0)$ ($\eta(k) = [x^T(k), e^T(k)]^T$), if there exists a positive definite matrix W such that the following inequalities is hold.*

$$E\{\sum_{k=0}^{\infty} \|\eta(k)\|^2 |\eta(0)\} < \eta^T(0)W\eta(0) \tag{9}$$

The purpose of this paper is to design an observer to estimate state for system (1) with both randomly occurring DoS attacks and randomly occurring FDI attacks. In other words, we are going to devise an observer gain L and an observer-based controller gain K such that the system state can be estimated accurately and the system is random mean-square stability.

3   Main Results

In this section, the stability is analysed for the closed system (8) with randomly occurring attacks, simultaneously, the system state is estimated. A sufficient condition is provided to guarantee the security of the closed system (8). Then, in terms of the solution of certain matrix inequalities, the explicit expression of the desired observer gain and controller gain are obtained.

By introduction of the following Lemmas, the main results will be developed more clearly in this paper.

Lemma 1. *For given constant matrices S_1, S_2, S_3, where $S_1 = S_1^T$ and $S_2 = S_2^T$. Then $S_1 + S_3^T S_2^{-1} S_3$ if and only if*

$$\begin{bmatrix} S_1 & S_3^T \\ S_3 & S_2 \end{bmatrix} < 0 \quad or \quad \begin{bmatrix} -S_2 & S_3 \\ S_3^T & S_1 \end{bmatrix} < 0$$

Lemma 2. *[15] For full rank matrix $rank(C) = m, C \in R^{m\times n}$, the Singular Value Decomposition (SVD) for C can be described as $C = U[S \ 0]V^T$, where $U \cdot U^T = I$ and $V \cdot V^T = I$. Let matrices $X > 0, M \in R^{m\times m}, N \in R^{n\times n}$. Then, there exits $\bar{X}$ such that $CX = \bar{X}C$ if and only if the following condition holds:*

$$X = V \begin{bmatrix} M & 0 \\ 0 & N \end{bmatrix} V^T.$$

Then, the following results are established.

Theorem 1. *For given the controller gain K and observer gain L. The closed system (8) is security if there exist matrices $P > 0, Q > 0$ such that the following matrix inequality hold:*

$$\begin{bmatrix} -P & * & * & * \\ 0 & 0 & * & * \\ P\bar{A} & \bar{\alpha}P\tilde{L} & P & * \\ \theta' P\bar{L} & \theta' P\tilde{L} & 0 & \theta' P \end{bmatrix} < 0 \tag{10}$$

In which, $\theta = E\{(\alpha(k) - \bar{\alpha})^2\}$ and $\theta' = \theta + \varepsilon$, ε is a sufficiently small positive number.

Proof: Set $\xi(k) = (x(k), e(k))$, Construct the Lyapunov function

$$V(\xi(k)) = x^T(k)Px(k) + e^T(k)Pe(k) \tag{11}$$

It is worth noting that $E\{\alpha(k) - \bar{\alpha}\} = 0$, $E\{(\alpha(k) - \bar{\alpha})^2\} < \theta + \varepsilon$. By calculating the difference of $V(\xi(k))$ along the trajectory of system (8) and taking the mathematical expectation, one has

$$
\begin{aligned}
&E\{V(\xi(k+1))|\xi(k)\} - V(\xi(k)) \\
&= E\{\xi^T(k+1)P\xi(k+1) - \xi^T(k)P\xi(k)\} \\
&\leq \xi^T(k)[\bar{A}^T P\bar{A} + (\theta + \varepsilon)\bar{L}^T P\bar{L}]\xi(k) - 2\xi^T(k)[\bar{A}^T P\bar{\alpha}\tilde{L} \\
&\quad + (\theta + \varepsilon)\bar{L}^T P\tilde{L}]w(k) + w^T(k)[\bar{\alpha}^2\tilde{L}^T P\tilde{L} + (\theta + \varepsilon)\tilde{L}^T \\
&\quad \cdot P\tilde{L}]w(k) = \eta^T(k)\Omega\eta(k)
\end{aligned}
\tag{12}
$$

where $\eta(k) = [\xi^T(k), w^T(k)]^T$,

$$\Omega = \begin{bmatrix} \bar{A} & \bar{\alpha}\tilde{L} \\ \bar{L} & \tilde{L} \end{bmatrix}^T \cdot \begin{bmatrix} P & 0 \\ 0 & \theta'P \end{bmatrix} \cdot \begin{bmatrix} \bar{A} & \bar{\alpha}\tilde{L} \\ \bar{L} & \tilde{L} \end{bmatrix} - \begin{bmatrix} P & 0 \\ 0 & 0 \end{bmatrix}$$

First, in term of Lyapunov stability theorem, the following inequality is obtained.

$$E\{V(\xi(k+1))|\xi(k)\} - V(\xi(k)) \leq \eta^T(k)\Omega\eta(k) < 0 \tag{13}$$

That is to say, the inequality $\Omega < 0$ should be hold if the system (8) needs to be stable.

By use of Lemma 1, the condition of Theorem 1 is equality to $\Omega < 0$, this completes proof. ☐

Remark 2. The purpose of the introduction for the sufficiently small positive constant ε is to guarantee the strict negative definitiveness for LMI (12). That can avoid the case that LMI (12) is unsolvable caused by the case $\theta = 0$.

For the Theorem 1, the sufficient condition is established to ensure the stability of argument system (8) with both randomly occurring DoS attacks and randomly occurring FDI attacks. In order to estimate the system states, the following theorem is developed to obtain observer gain and controller gain.

Theorem 2. *For given positive parameters $\bar{\alpha}, \theta'$, the system (8) under diverse attacks is asymptotically stable, if there exist matrices $X > 0, Y > 0, T > 0$, such that the following matrix inequalities hold:*

$$
\begin{bmatrix}
-X & * & * & * & * & * & * \\
0 & -X & * & * & * & * & * \\
0 & 0 & 0 & * & * & * & * \\
AX + BY & \bar{\alpha}TC & \bar{\alpha}T & X & * & * & * \\
0 & AX - \bar{\alpha}TC & \bar{\alpha}T & 0 & X & * & * \\
0 & \theta'TC & \theta'T & 0 & 0 & \theta'X & * \\
0 & -\theta'TC & \theta'T & 0 & 0 & 0 & \theta'X
\end{bmatrix} < 0
\tag{14}
$$

In this case, the observer gain and controller gain are given by $L = TUSX_1^{-1}S^{-1}U^{-1}$ and $K = YX^{-1}$.

Proof: Set $P = diag\{\bar{P}, \bar{P}\}$ and define $X = \bar{P}^{-1}, Y = K\bar{P}^{-1}, T = L\bar{X}$. For $X = V \begin{bmatrix} X_1 & * \\ 0 & X_2 \end{bmatrix} V^T$, according to Lemma 2, there exists $\bar{X} = USX_1S^{-1}U^{-1}$ can let $CX = \bar{X}C$ where $\bar{X}^{-1} = USX_1^{-1}S^{-1}U^{-1}$. Then, pre post-multiplying (10) by $diag\{X, X, 0, X, X, X, X\}$, such that (14) can be obtained. This completes the proof. □

Remark 3. Similar to [15], we also assume that the output matrix C is common one with the constraint of full row rank, $rank(C) = n$. Then based Lemma 2, the SVD of C can be described as $C = U[S, 0]V^T$, where $U \cdot U^T = I$ and $V \cdot V^T = I$ in the derivation of Theorem 2.

4   Numerical Simulations

To illustrate the effectiveness of the proposed method, the DC motor control system based on networked is used in this section. The system is formed by concatenating a motor, a signal acquisition and conversion component, a personal computer via network. The signal acquisition and conversion component is used to transform control signal into pulse width modulation signal. Simultaneously, the measurements of motor are transmitted into controller by network. The discrete model of motor is represented as follows.

$$\begin{cases} x(k+1) = \begin{bmatrix} 1 & 1.0046 \\ 0.5 & 0.0002 \end{bmatrix} x(k) + \begin{bmatrix} 0.2719 \\ 0.00781 \end{bmatrix} u(k) \\ y(k) = \begin{bmatrix} 1 & 1 \\ 0 & 1 \end{bmatrix} x(k) \end{cases} \tag{15}$$

Setting the sampling period $T = 0.04\,$s, and the states are motor rotor angular displacement and angular velocity, respectively. Assume that the randomly occurring DoS attack probability is $\bar{\alpha} = 0.2$, the randomly occurring FDI attack $w(k)$ is a sequence containing a few non-zero, that is to say, the system is maliciously attacked when $w(k)$ is non zero. In terms of Theorem 2, by use of the LMI toolbox in MATLAB, we can obtain the desired parameters

$$L = \begin{bmatrix} 1.3930 & -0.4419 \\ -0.5189 & 1.7707 \end{bmatrix}, \quad K = [-3.8935, -3.4025]$$

Let the initial state $x(0) = [-1 \quad 0.8]$, consequently, the state responses are depicted in Fig. 2.

Firstly, Fig. 2 shows the situation of signal transmission, from which we can easily find the DoS attack time and the FDI attack time. When the signal value is 1, it represents the sensor signals are not attacked maliciously, that is to say, the signal transmission is normal. On the contrary, the signal is wrong when the value

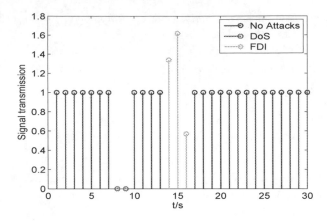

Fig. 2. The situation of signal transmission

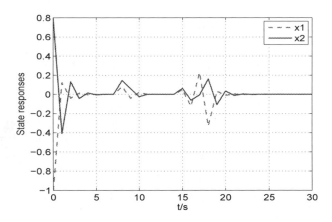

Fig. 3. State responses of the control system

is not 1. At $t = 8\,\text{s}, 9\,\text{s}$, the value is 0, it represents the sensors are destroyed by DoS attacks, and the sensors are destroyed by FDI attacks at $t = 14\,\text{s}, 15\,\text{s}, 16\,\text{s}$, the value represents the ratio between attack signal and actual signal value.

From Fig. 3, a conclusion is got that the observer-based controller can make the system mean-square stable even though the system is destroyed by DoS attacks at $t = 8\,\text{s}, 9\,\text{s}$ and destroyed by FDI attacks at $t = 14\,\text{s}, 15\,\text{s}, 16\,\text{s}$. Such that it illustrates the effectiveness of the proposed method.

5   Conclusion

An observer and an observer-based security controller design method have been proposed under randomly occurring DoS attacks and FDI attacks. The observer has been utilized to estimate the state destroyed by the malicious attacks, and the studied system under hybrid attacks has been modelled as a stochastic closed-loop system with an observer-based security controller. Then, two sufficient security stability and stabilization criteria are derived to ensure the asymptotically stable of the studied system in the mean-square sense. The practical example for networked DC motor control system has indicated the usefulness of proposed method.

Acknowledgments. This work was supported in part by the National Natural Science Foundation of China under Grants 61673255, 61633016 and 61533010, the International Corporation Project of Shanghai Science and Technology Commission under Grants 14510722500 and 15220710400, the Project of Shandong Province Higher Educational Science and Technology Program under Grant J17KA084.

References

1. Fawzi, H., Tabuada, P., Diggavi, S.: Secure estimation and control for cyber-physical systems under adversarial attacks. IEEE Trans. Autom. Control **59**(6), 1454–1467 (2014)
2. De Persis, C., Tesi, P.: Input-to-state stabilizing control under denial-of-service. IEEE Trans. Autom. Control **60**(11), 2930–2944 (2015)
3. Yu, Z.H., Chin, W.L.: Blind false data injection attack using PCA approximation method in smart grid. IEEE Trans. Smart Grid **6**(3), 1219–1226 (2015)
4. Amin, S., Litrico, X., Sastry, S., et al.: Cyber security of water SCADA systems Part I: analysis and experimentation of stealthy deception attacks. IEEE Trans. Control Syst. Technol. **21**(5), 1963–1970 (2013)
5. Zhu, M., Martnez, S.: On the performance analysis of resilient networked control systems under replay attacks. IEEE Trans. Autom. Control **59**(3), 804–808 (2014)
6. Ozay, M., Esnaola, I., Vural, F.T.Y., et al.: Sparse attack construction and state estimation in the smart grid: centralized and distributed models. IEEE J. Sel. Areas Commun. **31**(7), 1306–1318 (2013)
7. Kwon, C., Liu, W., Hwang, I.: Security analysis for cyber-physical systems against stealthy deception attacks. In: American Control Conference (ACC), pp. 3344–3349 (2013)
8. Manandhar, K., Cao, X., Hu, F., et al.: Detection of faults and attacks including false data injection attack in smart grid using kalman filter. IEEE Trans. Control Netw. Syst. **1**(4), 370–379 (2014)
9. Shoukry, Y., Tabuada, P.: Event-triggered projected Luenberger observer for linear systems under sparse sensor attacks. In: IEEE 53rd Annual Conference on Decision and Control (CDC), pp. 3548–3553 (2014)
10. Bi, S., Zhang, Y.J.: Graphical methods for defense against false-data injection attacks on power system state estimation. IEEE Trans. Smart Grid **5**(3), 1216–1227 (2014)
11. Shoukry, Y., Tabuada, P.: Event-triggered state observers for sparse sensor noise/attacks. IEEE Trans. Autom. Control **61**(8), 2079–2091 (2016)
12. Blumensath, T., Davies, M.E.: Normalized iterative hard thresholding: guaranteed stability and performance. IEEE J. Sel. Top. Sig. Process. **4**(2), 298–309 (2010)
13. Ding, D., Wang, Z., Shen, B., et al.: Event-triggered distributed H_∞ state estimation with packet dropouts through sensor networks. IET Control Theory Appl. **9**(13), 1948–1955 (2015)

14. Ding, D., Wang, Z., Wei, G., et al.: Event-based security control for discrete-time stochastic systems. IET Control Theory Appl. **10**(15), 1808–1815 (2016)
15. Peng, C., Ma, S., Xie, X.: Observer-based non-PDC control for networked TS fuzzy systems with an event-triggered communication. IEEE Trans. Cybern. (2017). doi:10.1109/TCYB.2017.2659698
16. Jahanshahi, N., Meskin, N., Abdollahi, F., et al.: An adaptive sliding mode observer for linear systems under malicious attack. In: 2016 IEEE International Conference on Systems, Man, and Cybernetics (SMC), pp. 001437–001442 (2016)

Hopf Bifurcation in a Delayed Two-Neuron Fractional Network with Incommensurate-Order

Lingzhi Zhao[1](✉), Beibei Shi[1], and Min Xiao[2]

[1] School of Information Engineering, Nanjing Xiaozhuang University,
Nanjing 211171, China
lzhzhao@163.com

[2] College of Automation, Nanjing University of Posts and Telecommunications,
Nanjing 210003, China

Abstract. In this paper, a delayed fractional two-neuron network with incommensurate-order is proposed. By analyzing the characteristic equation of the proposed network and using time delay as the bifurcation parameter, the conditions of stability and Hopf bifurcation are educed. And then, it is demonstrated that each order has important influence on the creation of bifurcation. Finally, a numerical example is given to illustrate the effectiveness of the proposed results.

Keywords: Stability · Hopf bifurcation · Incommensurate-order · Time delays · Two-neuron fractional network

1 Introduction

Fractional calculus is the theory of differential integral of any order. In recent decades, fractional derivative and integral have been widely found in scientific theory and many branches and engineering applications, such as colored noise, viscoelastic system, robotics, medical Science, biological systems, secure communication and so on [1,2]. Recently, the research on the dynamics properties of fractional-order system, including stability analysis [3], undamped oscillations [4], bifurcations and chaos [5], and synchronization [6], has become more and more interesting. The results show that fractional calculus has more advantages over traditional integer calculus in describing physical changes and viscoelastic materials with memory characteristics and historical dependence. The truth is, many real world problems usually or may be fractional order systems, but not integer order.

In recent decades, neural networks have been paid more and more attention by scientists and engineers. Fractional differentiation provides a basic and general computational power for neurons that facilitate efficient information processing, with oscillatory frequency independent phase changes in neuronal activity [7]. As everyone knows, neural network is a complex large-scale nonlinear dynamics, and the delay of dynamic neural network is even more abundant and complex [8]. In order to obtain a clear and profound understanding of the dynamic neural

© Springer Nature Singapore Pte Ltd. 2017
D. Yue et al. (Eds.): LSMS/ICSEE 2017, Part II, CCIS 762, pp. 477–487, 2017.
DOI: 10.1007/978-981-10-6373-2_48

network, the commonly used way is usually to explore the delayed neural network system with two neurons [9]. Some researchers have recently studied neural network formation of fractional order neural model, and found that can better characterise the dynamic behavior of neurons, such as "memory". In addition, the fractional recursive neural network in parameter estimation may plays an important role. Thence, our main purpose is to establishing the stability conditions and finding Hopf bifurcation point of the incommensurate fractional order two-neuron network with time delay.

Motivated by the above discussion, a delayed two-neuron model is extended to the fractional case with incommensurate-order. By Laplace transform, we mange to probe the capabilities of the fractional neural network model to demonstrate different dynamical properties, such as the stability switch and Hopf bifurcation point, where the delays are chosen as the bifurcation parameter. It is proved that there is a stable switch of time delay, the Hopf bifurcation occurs when the critical value is delayed and each order has important influence on the creation of Hopf bifurcation.

The organization of this paper is as follows. In Sect. 2, some preliminaries are addressed and the model is described. We analyze the stability conditions of delayed two-neuron fractional network with incommensurate-order and identify the Hopf bifurcation point in Sect. 3. In Sect. 4, the correctness of the obtained results is illustrated by a numerical example. In the last section, we draw some conclusions.

2   Preliminaries and Model Description

As we all know, fractional calculus has a variety of mathematical definitions, among which the three most common definitions are Riemann-Liouville fractional Grünwald-Letnikov fractional derivative and Caputo fractional derivative. In the present paper, we only use the well-known Caputo fractional derivative. In this paper, the main theoretical tools for qualitative analysis of fractional order dynamical systems are derived from [3,10].

First, we give the definition of Caputo fractional-order derivative as follows:

$$D_t^\alpha f(t) = \frac{1}{\Gamma(m-\alpha)} \int_0^t \frac{f^{(m)}(\tau)}{(t-\tau)^{\alpha-m+1}} d\tau, \tag{1}$$

where Γ denotes the Gamma function, and $m-1 \le \alpha < m$, $m \in N$. The symbol α is the value of the fractional order and the range of α is $(0,1)$.

The Laplace transform of the Caputo fractional-order derivative will be used:

$$L\{D_t^q f(t); s\} = s^q F(s) - \sum_{k=0}^{n-1} s^{q-k-1} f^{(k)}(0), \quad n-1 < q \le n. \tag{2}$$

when $f^{(k)}(0) = 0$, $k = 1, 2, \ldots, n$, then it follows $L\{D_t^q f(t); s\} = s^q F(s)$.

In [11], the following delayed two-neuron integer-order system was studied,

$$\begin{cases} \dot{x}(t) = -x(t) + b_{11}f(x(t - \tau_1)) + b_{12}f(y(t - \tau_2)), \\ \dot{y}(t) = -y(t) + b_{21}f(x(t - \tau_1)) + b_{22}f(y(t - \tau_2)), \end{cases} \tag{3}$$

where $x(t)$ and $y(t)$ are the activations of two neurons, $\mu_i > 0$ $(i = 1, 2)$ are the rate with which the neuron will reset its potential to the resetting state in isolation when disconnected from the network and external inputs; b_{ij} $(1 \leq i, j \leq 2)$ denote the synaptic weights, $f : R \to R$ denote the activation function; and $\tau_i(i = 1, 2)$ are the synaptic transmission delays.

In the present paper, the two-neuron network (3) will be extended to the fractional differential case with incommensurate-order as follows:

$$\begin{cases} D^{q_1}x(t) = -\mu_1 x(t) + b_{11}f(x(t - \tau_1)) + b_{12}f(y(t - \tau_2)), \\ D^{q_2}y(t) = -\mu_2 y(t) + b_{21}f(x(t - \tau_1)) + b_{22}f(y(t - \tau_2)), \end{cases} \tag{4}$$

where $q_i \in (0, 1], i = 1, 2$, and $\mu_i, i = 1, 2$, are the self-regulating parameters of the two-neuron. We should consider that neurons have self feedback and delayed signal transmission due to the limited switching speed of neurons. It is obvious that the system (4) is just (3) when $q_1 = q_2 = 1, \mu_i = \mu_2 = 1$.

In order to simplify the discussion, $\tau_1 = \tau_2 = \tau$ are assumed throughout this paper.

$$\begin{cases} D^{q_1}x(t) = -\mu_1 x(t) + b_{11}f(x(t - \tau)) + b_{12}f(y(t - \tau)), \\ D^{q_2}y(t) = -\mu_2 y(t) + b_{21}f(x(t - \tau)) + b_{22}f(y(t - \tau)), \end{cases} \tag{5}$$

To derive the main result, the following hypothesis in model (5) is necessary to be introduced.

$(\mathcal{H}_1)$ The activation function $f(\cdot)$ are Lipschitz continuous with $f(0) = 0$.

3   Analysis of Stability and Hopf Bifurcation

The stability conditions and Hopf bifurcation of incommensurate fractional two-neuron network (5) with time delay, will be investigated in this section and the basic theoretical method is based on literature [3]. It is obvious that $(0, 0)$ is the unique equilibrium point of system (5).

Linearizing system (5) around the equilibrium point $(0, 0)$, then the following system can be acquired:

$$\begin{cases} D^{q_1}x(t) = -\mu_1 x(t) + d_{11}x(t - \tau) + d_{12}y(t - \tau), \\ D^{q_2}y(t) = -\mu_2 y(t) + d_{21}x(t - \tau) + d_{22}y(t - \tau), \end{cases} \tag{6}$$

note that $d_{ij} = b_{ij}f'(0)(i, j = 1, 2)$.

By Laplace transform, we can get the characteristic equation immediately:

$$\begin{vmatrix} s^{q_1} + \mu_1 - d_{11}e^{-s\tau} & -d_{12}e^{-s\tau} \\ -d_{21}e^{-s\tau} & s^{q_2} + \mu_2 - d_{22}e^{-s\tau} \end{vmatrix} = 0, \tag{7}$$

thus, (7) is equivalent to

$$\mathcal{G}_1(s) + \mathcal{G}_2(s)e^{-s\tau} + \mathcal{G}_3(s)e^{-2s\tau} = 0, \tag{8}$$

and

$$\begin{aligned}
\mathcal{G}_1(s) &= s^{q_1+q_2} + \mu_1 s^{q_2} + \mu_2 s^{q_1} + \mu_1\mu_2, \\
\mathcal{G}_2(s) &= -[d_{11}s^{q_2} + d_{22}s^{q_1} + d_{11}\mu_2 + d_{22}\mu_1], \\
\mathcal{G}_3(s) &= d_{11}d_{22} - d_{12}d_{21}.
\end{aligned}$$

Multiplying $e^{s\tau}$ on both sides of (8), we can get

$$\mathcal{G}_1(s)e^{s\tau} + \mathcal{G}_2(s) + \mathcal{G}_3(s)e^{-s\tau} = 0. \tag{9}$$

Suppose $s = i\omega$ is a root of (9). Without losing generality, we can assume $\omega > 0$. Then it follows when we substitute s into (9) and separate the real and imaginary parts,

$$\begin{cases}
\mathcal{M}_1 \cos\omega\tau + \mathcal{M}_2 \sin\omega\tau = \mathcal{M}_3, \\
\mathcal{N}_1 \cos\omega\tau + \mathcal{N}_2 \sin\omega\tau = \mathcal{N}_3,
\end{cases} \tag{10}$$

where

$$\begin{aligned}
\mathcal{M}_1 &= \omega^{q_1+q_2} \cos\frac{(q_1+q_2)\pi}{2} + \mu_1\omega^{q_2} \cos\frac{q_2\pi}{2} + \mu_2\omega^{q_1} \cos\frac{q_1\pi}{2} + \mu_1\mu_2 \\
&\quad + (d_{11}d_{22} - d_{12}d_{21}), \\
\mathcal{M}_2 &= -[\omega^{q_1+q_2} \sin\frac{(q_1+q_2)\pi}{2} + \mu_1\omega^{q_2} \sin\frac{q_2\pi}{2} + \mu_2\omega^{q_1} \sin\frac{q_1\pi}{2}], \\
\mathcal{M}_3 &= d_{11}\omega^{q_2} \cos\frac{q_2\pi}{2} + d_{22}\omega^{q_1} \cos\frac{q_1\pi}{2} + d_{11}\mu_2 + d_{22}\mu_1, \\
\mathcal{N}_1 &= \omega^{q_1+q_2} \sin\frac{(q_1+q_2)\pi}{2} + \mu_1\omega^{q_2} \sin\frac{q_2\pi}{2} + \mu_2\omega^{q_1} \sin\frac{q_1\pi}{2}, \\
\mathcal{N}_2 &= \omega^{q_1+q_2} \cos\frac{(q_1+q_2)\pi}{2} + \mu_1\omega^{q_2} \cos\frac{q_2\pi}{2} + \mu_2\omega^{q_1} \cos\frac{q_1\pi}{2} + \mu_1\mu_2 \\
&\quad - (d_{11}d_{22} - d_{12}d_{21}), \\
\mathcal{N}_3 &= d_{11}\omega^{q_2} \sin\frac{q_2\pi}{2} + d_{22}\omega^{q_1} \sin\frac{q_1\pi}{2}.
\end{aligned}$$

Suppose that (10) has roots, the expression of $\cos\omega\tau$ and $\sin\omega\tau$ can be obtained as follows:

$$\begin{cases}
\cos\omega\tau = h_1(\omega), \\
\sin\omega\tau = h_2(\omega),
\end{cases} \tag{11}$$

where

$$h_1(\omega) = \frac{\mathcal{M}_3\mathcal{N}_2 - \mathcal{M}_2\mathcal{N}_3}{\mathcal{M}_1\mathcal{N}_2 - \mathcal{M}_2\mathcal{N}_1}, h_2(\omega) = \frac{\mathcal{M}_1\mathcal{N}_3 - \mathcal{M}_3\mathcal{N}_1}{\mathcal{M}_1\mathcal{N}_2 - \mathcal{M}_2\mathcal{N}_1}$$

are functions with respect to ω.

Then, we can have

$$h_1^2(\omega) + h_2^2(\omega) = 1. \tag{12}$$

From (12), it is derived

$$\tau_{(k)} = \frac{1}{\omega}[\arccos h_1(\omega) + 2k\pi], \quad k \in Z^+. \tag{13}$$

$(\mathcal{H}_2)$ $\mathcal{Q}_1 > 0$, $\mathcal{Q}_2 > 0$.

Lemma 1. *When $\tau = 0$, the zero equilibrium point of the fractional system (5) is asymptotically stable if $(\mathcal{H}_2)$ holds.*

Proof: When $\tau = 0$, then we can get

$$\lambda^2 + \mathcal{Q}_1\lambda + \mathcal{Q}_2 = 0, \tag{14}$$

where $\mathcal{Q}_1 = \mu_1 + \mu_2 - d_{11} - d_{22}$, $\mathcal{Q}_2 = \mu_1\mu_2 - d_{11}\mu_2 - d_{22}\mu_1 + d_{11}d_{22} - d_{12}b_{21}$.

When $\mathcal{Q}_1 > 0$, $\mathcal{Q}_2 > 0$ hold, then (14) has two roots with negative real parts. So, the positive equilibrium point $(0,0)$ of the fractional system (5) is asymptotically stable when $\tau = 0$. Then the proof is completed.

Remark 1. *The conditions $(\mathcal{H}_2)$ are only sufficient conditions, but not the necessary. They can guarantee the asymptotically stable of the incommensurate fractional neural network (5) when $\tau = 0$.*

We need the following additional assumption to get the transversality condition of the occurrence for Hopf bifurcation:

$(\mathcal{H}_3)$ $\mathrm{Re}\left(\frac{ds}{d\tau}\right)|_{\tau=\tau_0} \neq 0$.

Taking the derivative of s with respect to τ in (8), it can obtained

$$\frac{ds}{d\tau} = \frac{s[\mathcal{G}_2(s)e^{-s\tau} + 2\mathcal{G}_3(s)e^{-2s\tau}]}{\mathcal{G}_1'(s) + \mathcal{G}_2'(s)e^{-s\tau} - \tau\mathcal{G}_2(s)e^{-s\tau} + \mathcal{G}_3'(s)e^{-2s\tau} - 2\tau\mathcal{G}_3(s)e^{-2s\tau}}, \tag{15}$$

where $\mathcal{G}_1'(s)$, $\mathcal{G}_2'(s)$, $\mathcal{G}_3'(s)$ are the derivative of $\mathcal{G}_1(s)$, $\mathcal{G}_2(s)$, $\mathcal{G}_3(s)$ with respectively about to s.

Based on (15), we can deduce that

$$\mathrm{Re}\left(\frac{ds}{d\tau}\right)|_{\tau=\tau_0,\omega=\omega_0} = \frac{\mathcal{W}_1\mathcal{V}_1 + \mathcal{W}_2\mathcal{V}_2}{\mathcal{V}_1^2 + \mathcal{V}_2^2}, \tag{16}$$

where

$$\mathcal{W}_1 = -\omega_0^{q_1+q_2+1}\sin\left(\frac{q_1\pi + q_2\pi}{2} + \omega_0\tau_0\right) - \mu_2\omega_0^{\frac{q_1}{2}+1}\sin\left(\frac{q_1\pi}{2} + \omega_0\tau_0\right)$$
$$- \mu_1\omega_0^{\frac{q_2}{2}+1}\sin\left(\frac{q_2\pi}{2} + \omega_0\tau_0\right) - \omega_0\mu_1\mu_2\sin\omega_0\tau_0$$

$$+ \omega_0(d_{11}d_{22} - d_{12}d_{21})\sin\omega_0\tau_0,$$

$$\mathcal{W}_2 = \omega_0^{q_1+q_2+1}\cos\left(\frac{q_1\pi + q_2\pi}{2} + \omega_0\tau_0\right) + \mu_2\omega_0^{\frac{q_1}{2}+1}\cos\left(\frac{q_1\pi}{2} + \omega_0\tau_0\right)$$

$$+ \mu_1\omega_0^{\frac{q_2}{2}+1}\cos\left(\frac{q_2\pi}{2} + \omega_0\tau_0\right) + \omega_0\mu_1\mu_2\cos\omega_0\tau_0$$

$$+ \omega_0(d_{11}d_{22} - d_{12}d_{21})\sin\omega_0\tau_0,$$

$$\mathcal{V}_1 = (q_1 + q_2)\omega_0^{q_1+q_2-1}\cos\left(\frac{q_1+q_2-1}{2}\pi + \omega_0\tau_0\right) + q_1\omega_0^{q_1-1}\mu_2$$

$$\cos\left(\frac{q_1-1}{2}\pi + \omega_0\tau_0\right) + q_2\omega_0^{q_2-1}\mu_1\cos\left(\frac{q_2-1}{2}\pi + \omega_0\tau_0\right)$$

$$+ \tau_0\omega_0^{q_1+q_2}\cos\left(\frac{q_1\pi + q_2\pi}{2} + \omega_0\tau_0\right) + \tau_0\omega_0^{q_1}\mu_2\cos\left(\frac{q_1\pi}{2} + \omega_0\tau_0\right)$$

$$+ \tau_0\omega_0^{q_2}\mu_1\cos\left(\frac{q_2\pi}{2} + \omega_0\tau_0\right) + \tau_0\mu_1\mu_2\cos\omega_0\tau_0 - q_1d_{22}\omega_0^{q_1-1}\cos\frac{q_1-1}{2}\pi$$

$$- q_2d_{11}\omega_0^{q_2-1}\cos\frac{q_2-1}{2}\pi - \tau_0(d_{11}d_{22} - d_{12}d_{21})\cos\omega_0\tau_0,$$

$$\mathcal{V}_2 = (q_1 + q_2)\omega_0^{q_1+q_2-1}\sin\left(\frac{q_1+q_2-1}{2}\pi + \omega_0\tau_0\right) + q_1\omega_0^{q_1-1}\mu_2$$

$$\sin\left(\frac{q_1-1}{2}\pi + \omega_0\tau_0\right) + q_2\omega_0^{q_2-1}\mu_1\sin\left(\frac{q_2-1}{2}\pi + \omega_0\tau_0\right)$$

$$+ \tau_0\omega_0^{q_1+q_2}\sin\left(\frac{q_1\pi + q_2\pi}{2} + \omega_0\tau_0\right) + \tau_0\omega_0^{q_1}\mu_2\sin\left(\frac{q_1\pi}{2} + \omega_0\tau_0\right)$$

$$+ \tau_0\omega_0^{q_2}\mu_1\sin\left(\frac{q_2\pi}{2} + \omega_0\tau_0\right) + \tau_0\mu_1\mu_2\sin\omega_0\tau_0 - q_1d_{22}\omega_0^{q_1-1}\sin\frac{q_1-1}{2}\pi$$

$$- q_2d_{11}\omega_0^{q_2-1}\sin\frac{q_2-1}{2}\pi - \tau_0(d_{11}d_{22} - d_{12}d_{21})\sin\omega_0\tau_0, .$$

By the above deduction, the following theorem can be obtained immediately

Theorem 1. *If $(\mathcal{H}_1) - (\mathcal{H}_3)$ are hold for system (5), then we can get the following conclusion:*

(I) When $\tau \in [0, \tau_0)$, the zero equilibrium point is asymptotically stable.
(II) When $\tau = \tau_0$, the system (5) undergoes a Hopf bifurcation at the origin i.e., system (5) has a bifurcation of the zero equilibrium point of the bifurcation of the periodic solution near $\tau = \tau_0$.

Remark 2. *We select time delays as the bifurcation parameter to discuss the Hopf bifurcation situation of system (5) in this paper. Certainly, the fractional order or the other parameters of dynamic system also can influence the stability interval and Hopf bifurcation point of system (5). This will be one of the focuses of our future research work.*

Remark 3. *As we all know, many researchers have extensively studied and investigated the dynamical behaviors of two-neuron network and obtained many excellent results [11–13]. Unfortunately, there are very few research discussing*

the stability conditions, Hopf bifurcation of fractional neural network with incommensurate-order. As we all know, many real-world problems usually or most likely to be fractional order system, especially the incommensurate-order, rather than integer order. Therefore the extension and investigation are necessary and meaningful.

4   Illustrative Example

A numerical example will be provided to confirm our analysis about the delayed fractional two-neuron network with incommensurate-order in this Section. The simulation results all are based on Adama - CBashforth - CMoulton predictor - Ccorrector scheme [14] with step-length $h = 0.01$.

In this example, we consider the following case of the system (5) with the parameters: $b_{11} = -1$, $b_{12} = 2$, $b_{21} = -2$, $b_{22} = -3$, $\mu_1 = 0.8$, $\mu_2 = 0.6$, $f(x) = \tanh(x)$, and $q_1 = 0.95, q_2 = 0.98$, and initial values $(0.15, -0.15)$, then we can get the following system:

$$\begin{cases} D^{0.95}x(t) = -0.8x(t) - \tanh(t - \tau) + 2\tanh(t - \tau), \\ D^{0.98}y(t) = -0.6y(t) - 2\tanh(t - \tau) - 3\tanh(t - \tau). \end{cases} \tag{17}$$

By simple computation by means of Maple 13, we can get the critical value $\omega_0 = 2.6981$, and Hopf bifurcation point $\tau_0 = 0.4333$. We can easily verify that the condition $(\mathcal{H}_3)$ is satisfied and the equilibrium $(0,0)$ is asymptotically stable when $\tau = 0.42 < \tau_0 = 0.4333$, as shown in Figs. 1, 2 and 3. The equilibrium $(0,0)$ is unstable and the Hopf bifurcation occurs if $\tau = 0.45 > \tau_0 = 0.4333$, which is illustrated in Figs. 4, 5 and 6.

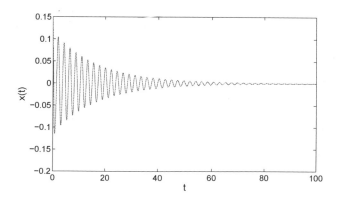

Fig. 1. State trajectories of the incommensurate-order fractional system (17). The zero equilibrium $(0,0)$ is asymptotically stable when $\tau = 0.42 < \tau_0 = 0.4333$.

When $q_1 = q_2 = 1$, the system (17) becomes the inter-order system, we can get that the integer-order system undergoes a Hopf bifurcation when τ passes

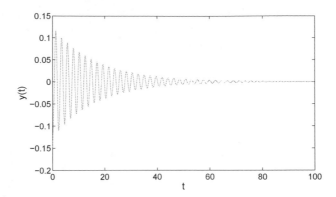

Fig. 2. State trajectories of the incommensurate fractional system (17). The zero equilibrium $(0,0)$ is asymptotically stable when $\tau = 0.42 < \tau_0 = 0.4333$.

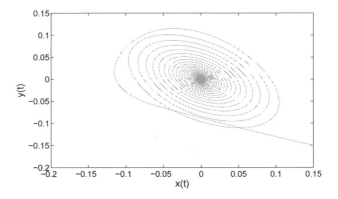

Fig. 3. Phase portrait of the incommensurate-order fractional system (17). The zero equilibrium $(0,0)$ is asymptotically stable when $\tau = 0.42 < \tau_0 = 0.4333$.

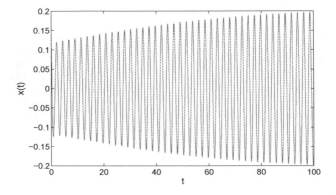

Fig. 4. State trajectories of the incommensurate-order fractional system (17). The zero equilibrium $(0,0)$ is not asymptotically stable when $\tau = 0.45 > \tau_0 = 0.4333$.

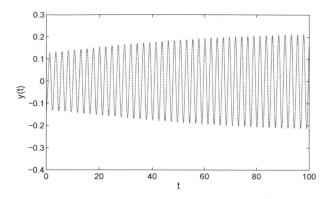

Fig. 5. State trajectories of the incommensurate-order fractional system (17). The zero equilibrium $(0,0)$ is not asymptotically stable when $\tau = 0.45 > \tau_0 = 0.4333$.

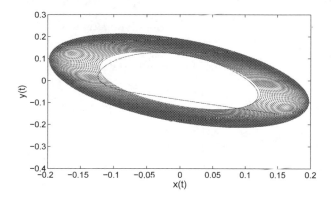

Fig. 6. Phase portrait of the incommensurate-order fractional system (17). The zero equilibrium $(0,0)$ of the system (17) is not asymptotically stable when $\tau = 0.45 > \tau_0 = 0.4333$.

through the critical value $\tau_0^\star = 0.4307$. It is Obvious that the fractional system can amplify the stability interval of the integer-order system (3) with $\tau_1 = \tau_2$.

In what follows, we shall discuss the influence of the different fractional order on Hopf bifurcation for system (17).

(I) Fix $q_2 = 0.98$, then observe the effect of q_1 on Hopf bifurcation for system (17). In this case, we easily compute the corresponding value ω_0 and τ_0 as q_1 varies, which is listed in Table 1.

(II) Fix $q_1 = 0.95$, then consider the impact of q_2 on bifurcation for system (17). It not hard to derive the corresponding value ω_0 and τ_0 as q_2 varies, which is listed in Table 2.

Table 1. The infulence of q_1 on Hopf bifurcation point for (17).

Fractional order q_1	Critical frequency ω_0	Bifurcation point τ_0
0.68	0.3937	4.3314
0.72	0.3797	4.2982
0.76	0.3693	4.2294
0.81	0.3595	4.1106
0.84	0.3549	4.0279
0.87	0.3513	3.9378
0.92	0.3466	3.7791
0.95	0.3446	3.6802
0.98	0.3431	3.5797
1	0.3423	3.5122

Table 2. The infulence of q_2 on Hopf bifurcation point for (17).

Fractional order q_2	Critical frequency ω_0	Bifurcation point τ_0
0.67	0.3564	3.6728
0.73	0.3542	3.6759
0.78	0.3523	3.6783
0.81	0.3511	3.6794
0.85	0.3495	3.6806
0.88	0.3483	3.6811
0.90	0.3475	3.6813
0.93	0.3463	3.6812
0.97	0.3446	3.6802
1	0.3434	3.6788

5   Conclusion

In present paper, we extend a integer-order two-neuron network to the fractional case with incommensurate-order. Then, we study the stability condition and Hopf bifurcation point for two-neuron incommensurate-order fractional network with time delay as the Hopf bifurcation parameter. Furthermore, we obtain the Hopf bifurcation point. Some explicit conditions for the stability interval and the Hopf bifurcation point are derived using fractional Laplace transform. And it is demonstrated that each order has important influence on the creation of bifurcation. The simulating example is exploited to verify the feasibility of obtained results.

Acknowledgments. The work was supported by the National Natural Science Foundation of China (Grant No. 61573194).

References

1. Reyes-Melo, E., Martinez-Vega, J., Guerrero-Salazar, C., Ortiz-Mendez, U.: Application of fractional calculus to the modeling of dielectric relaxation phenomena in poly meric materials. J. Appl. Polym. Sci. **98**(2), 923–935 (2005)
2. ÖZalp, N., Demirci, E.: A fractional order SEIR model with vertical transmission. Math. Comput. Model. **54**(1), 1–6 (2011)
3. Deng, W., Li, C., Lu, J.: Stability analysis of linear fractional differential system with multiple time delays. Nonlinear Dyn. **48**(4), 409–416 (2007)
4. Tavazoei, M.S., Haeri, M., Siami, M., Bolouki, S.: Maximum number of frequencies in oscillations generated by fractional order LTI systems. IEEE Trans. Sig. Process. **58**, 4003–4012 (2010)
5. Leung, A.Y.T., Yang, H., Zhu, P.: Periodic bifurcation of Duffing-van der Pol oscillators having fractional derivatives and time delay. Commum. Nonlin. Sci. Numer. Simulat. **19**, 1142–1155 (2014)
6. N'Doye, I., Voos, H., Darouach, M.: Observer-based approach for fractional-order chaotic synchronization and secure communication. IEEE J. Emerg. Sel. Top. Circ. Syst. **3**, 442–450 (2013)
7. Lundstrom, B., Higgs, M., Spain, W., Fairhall, A.: Fractional differentiation by neocortical pyramidal neurons. Nat. Neurosci. **11**, 1335–1342 (2008)
8. Wu, J.: Introduction to Neural Dynamics and Signal Transmission Delay. Walter de Gruyter, Berlin (2001)
9. Huang, C., Huang, L.: Existence and global exponential stability of periodic solutions of two-neuron networks with time-varying delays. Appl. Math. Lett. **19**, 126–134 (2006)
10. Podlubny, A., Srivastava, H., Trujillo, J.: Fractional Differential Equations. Acdemic Press, Cambridge (1999)
11. Olien, L., Bélair, J.: Bifurcations, stability, and monotonicity properties of a delayed neural network model. Phys. D **102**, 349–363 (1997)
12. Xiao, M., Zheng, W.X., Cao, J.D.: Frequency domain approach to computational analysis of bifurcation and periodic solution in a two-neuron network model with distributed delays and self-feedbacks. Neurocomputing **99**, 206–213 (2013)
13. Huang, C., Huang, L., Feng, J., Nai, M., He, Y.: Hopf bifurcation analysis for a two-neuron network with four delays. Caos Solitions Fractals **34**, 795–812 (2007)
14. Bhalekar, S., Varsha, D.: A predictor-corrector scheme for solving nonlinear delay differential equations of fractional order. J. Fract. Calc. Appl. **1**(5), 1–9 (2011)

Networked Control System Based on LQ Tracking and Response Strategy Under Data Injection Attack

Xinchun Jie[1,2], Minrui Fei[1(✉)], Dajun Du[1], and T.C. Yang[3]

[1] School of Mechanical Engineering and Automation,
Shanghai University, Shanghai 200072, China
mrfei@staff.shu.edu.cn
[2] School of Information and Engineering,
Inner Mongolia University of Science and Technology, Baotou 014010, China
[3] Department of Engineering and Design,
University of Sussex, Brighton BN1 9QJ, England

Abstract. It is one of the most important research topics in the field of automatic control to ensure stability of networked control system and keep controlled parameters unchanged in the presence of data injection attacks. On the basis of linear system state feedback, a linear quadratic (LQ) method keeping output error close to zero is presented. Stability condition of closed-loop system is given. Using integral control and LQ infinite time tracking strategy, a protective closed-loop control system is illustrated in detail. Simulation results show that the control strategy can reduce or remove the influence of illegal injecting data at sensor's output terminal in some degree. Controlled parameters are limited within small variation range. The control method has certain application prospect and popularization value.

Keywords: Data injection · LQ tracking control · Networked control system · Security control

1 Introduction

The development of control system has gone through several stages. Up to now many control system are constructed by large scale control network [1]. With the gradual extension to bottom layer of control network, intelligent instruments (such as actuators, controllers and sensors) have ability to exchange data directly with computers in upper management network [2]. The integration of control and management network brings hidden security problem to control system. Famous "Stuxnet" virus intrusion event took place in Iran nuclear power plant in 2010 [3] and attack event occurred in Ukraine power company in 2015 [4], which show that control system security is a very important problem [5, 6]. These two virus programs simulated one industrial configuration software's operation command and achieved the goal of destroying physical devices [7]. These events not only caused great damage to local production enterprises, but also gave rise to the inconvenient of local residents' daily life. The situation of multiple networks surviving together puts forward new challenge to keep control

© Springer Nature Singapore Pte Ltd. 2017
D. Yue et al. (Eds.): LSMS/ICSEE 2017, Part II, CCIS 762, pp. 488–496, 2017.
DOI: 10.1007/978-981-10-6373-2_49

system's stable operation. Traditional control strategy cannot meet the requirement of modern production process. It is an important and urgent problem for science workers to design a control system which can detect network intrusion behavior and have certain response strategy simultaneously.

In this paper, a controller with disturbance rejection capability is designed on the basis of state feedback and linear quadratic (LQ) tracking. The controller has ability to compensate for the influence of disturbance signals by adding integral section. By usage of attack detector and considering data injection action at sensor's output terminal, we also designed another protective controller to eliminate the impact of injected data. By setting up a general plant simulator and using iterative calculation, system's disturbance signal can be approximately estimated. The two kinds of controllers' switching strategies are designed simultaneously. To evaluate the proposed control strategy, it is employed to industrial MIMO control system.

2 Control System Based on Output Tracking and Integral Action

A closed-loop control system is implemented by a tracking controller and an integral section. The integral section enhances system's anti-interference ability [8]. System's block diagram is shown in Fig. 1. Where A, B and C are constant coefficient matrices. u_r

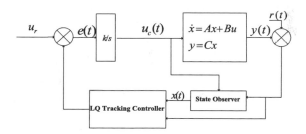

Fig. 1. Structure of control system in normal situation

is p dimension input constant vector, $y(t)$ is q dimension output vector. Input vector of LQ tracking controller (tracking vector) is approximately equal to the output vector of generalized plant. States' observation equation is

$$\dot{\hat{x}}(t) = (A - LC)\hat{x}(t) + Ly(t) + Bu_c(t), \hat{x}(0) = \hat{x}_0$$
$$L = \bar{K}^T \tag{1}$$

$\bar{K}$ is state feedback matrix satisfying $\bar{A} - \bar{B}\bar{K}(\bar{A} = A^T, \bar{B} = B^T)$ stability and desired poles. The LQ tracking controller is an infinite time tracking system, its performance index is denoted by

$$J = \frac{1}{2} \int_0^\infty [e^T(t)Qe(t) + u^T(t)Ru(t)]dt. \tag{2}$$

where Q, R is symmetric, positive definite weight coefficient matrix according to actual requirement [9], $e(t)$ is tracking error, $u(t)$ is output vector of the tracker. According to optimal control theory, approximate optimal control output of the tracker is

$$u^*(t) = -R^{-1}B^T Px(t) + R^{-1}B^T g. \tag{3}$$

where P is a symmetric and positive definite constant matrix, satisfy following algebraic Riccati equation [10], that is

$$PA + A^T P - PBR^{-1}B^T P + C^T QC = 0 \tag{4}$$

The g in Eq. (3) is adjoint vector, its value is related to tracking signal, where

$$\begin{aligned} g &= (PBR^{-1}B^T - A^T)^{-1}C^T Qy(t) \\ &= Mx(t) \end{aligned} \tag{5}$$

M is defined as adjoint matrix. Relationship of plant's p dimension input vector $u_c(t)$, setting input u_r and LQ tracker's output $\hat{u}(t)$ can be described as

$$\begin{aligned} u_c(t) &= k \int_0^t (u_r - \hat{u}(t))dt \\ &= k \int_0^t (u_r + R^{-1}B^T Px(t) - R^{-1}B^T g)dt \end{aligned} \tag{6}$$

where $k = diag\{k_1, k_2, ..., k_p\}$ is integral coefficient matrix. If system's initial states satisfies $\hat{x}(0) = 0$, then

$$\dot{u}_c(t) = k(u_r + R^{-1}B^T Px(t) - R^{-1}B^T Mx(t)) \tag{7}$$

Taking $u_c(t)$ as p dimension extended states, an augmented state equation can be described as

$$\begin{pmatrix} \dot{x} \\ \dot{u}_c \end{pmatrix} = \begin{pmatrix} A & B \\ kR^{-1}B^T P - kR^{-1}B^T M & o \end{pmatrix} \begin{pmatrix} x \\ u_c \end{pmatrix} + \begin{pmatrix} I_1 & o \\ o & I_2 \end{pmatrix} \begin{pmatrix} 0 \\ ku_r \end{pmatrix} \tag{8}$$

I_1 and I_2 denote n and p dimension unit matrix, respectively. In order to stabilize the closed-loop system, integral coefficient matrix k must be correctly selected. For infinite time tracking control strategy, followed values are considered as constants in a short time. It is difficult to achieve absolute tracking without bias in a certain time, there are some errors between actual output values and followed values until time reaches infinity. When followed value is constants, tracker's output value is

$$\hat{u}(t) = -R^{-1}B^T Px(t) + R^{-1}B^T g \tag{9}$$

State equation can be described as

$$\dot{x}(t) = (A - R^{-1}B^T P)x(t) + R^{-1}B^T g \tag{10}$$

If g takes a constant vector, state vector's steady error is

$$\lim_{t \to \infty} \Delta x = -A^{-1}Bu_r - (-A + BR^{-1}B^T P)^{-1}BR^{-1}B^T g \tag{11}$$

In order to make the error equal to 0, g must be selected correctly. By setting correction factor matrix the adjoint vector is expressed as

$$g = \lambda g_r \tag{12}$$

where

$$\lambda = diag(\lambda_1, \lambda_2, \ldots, \lambda_n) \tag{13}$$

$$g_r = (PBR^{-1}B^T - A^T)C^T Qy_r \tag{14}$$

$$y_r = -CA^{-1}Bu_r \tag{15}$$

If we do not consider traditional packet loss and communication delay problem, state observer adopts continuously sampling method, LQ tracker periodically reads observation state vector and gives out tracking output vector with fixed circle time T. The followed vector is considered as constant between two sampling instants. The actual output $\hat{u}(k)$ is

$$\hat{u}(k) = -R^{-1}B^T Px(k) + \lambda R^{-1}B^T g_r \tag{16}$$

3 Response Strategy Under Data Injection Attack

When a data injection behavior takes place at sensor's output terminal, we assume attack signal is periodic, average value of disturbance signal $r(t)$ does not change in a certain time T_r. T_r is much larger than attack signal's cycle time T_a and detector's analysis time T_s. For the injection behavior, a method of establishing plant simulator can be used to prevent the behavior's negative influence. Plant simulator is a mathematical function which is realized by MCU program in controller. It can be set up by plant's actual mathematical model. When plant is controllable and observable, a plant simulator of Linear Time-Invariant System is expressed by

$$y''(t) = C(e^{At}x_0 + \int_0^t e^{A(t-\tau)}Bu(\tau)d\tau). \tag{17}$$

where $y''(t)$ is l-dimensional output vector, $u(t)$ is q-dimensional input vector. A, B and C are coefficient matrix of actual plant. Attack detector is used to decide whether a data intrusion behavior has taken place by Euclidean distance $d(t)$.

$$d(t) = \sqrt{\sum_{i=1}^{l} (y_i(t) - y_i^0)^2}. \tag{18}$$

Where y_i^0 indicates the setting value of sensor's desired output. When average value of $d(t)$ within a certain time is greater than a specified value d_{Max}, we assume that an intrusion behavior has taken place. If external disturbance signals are considered, a statistical method based on recent data can be used to estimate average value of the disturbance signal. Once attack detector finds a data injection behavior, controller will replace observer and LQ tracker's input signal with simulator's output, estimated disturbance signal is used as simulator's disturbance signal to compensate actual disturbance signal. The block diagram of control system under data injection attack is described in Fig. 2. We assume controller's actual input signal $y'(t)$ is analyzed per T_S, disturbance signal $r(kT_S)$ remains unchanged during this period. Attack signal's circle time T_k, average difference value $(\overline{ar_{kT_s}})$ between $y'(t)$ and simulator's output $y''(t)$ can be got after this time(Eq. (19)). $\overline{ar_{kT_s}}$ represents the average sum of disturbance signal and attack signal from $(k-1)T_S$ to kT_S. We assume the disturbance signal at the beginning of attack action is represented by $r(0)$, it is obtained just before system's switching action from normal mode to protection mode. In first T_S, average value of attack signal and the disturbance signal can be estimated by Eqs. (20), (21), (22).

$$\overline{ar_{kT_s}} = \frac{1}{T_k} \sum_{T_k} (y'(t) - y''(t)) \tag{19}$$

$$\hat{r}_{T_s} \approx r_0 \tag{20}$$

$$\overline{a_{T_s}} \approx \overline{ar_{T_s}} - \hat{r}_{T_s} \tag{21}$$

$$\hat{r}_{2T_s} \approx \overline{ar_{2T_s}} - \overline{a_{T_s}} \tag{22}$$

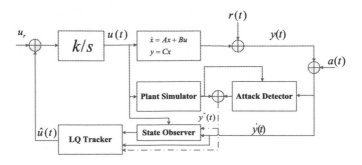

Fig. 2. Control system under data injection

Iterative calculation

$$\overline{a_{kT_s}} = \overline{ar_{kT_s}} - \hat{r}_{kT_s} \tag{23}$$

$$\hat{r}_{(k+1)T_s} \approx \overline{ar_{(k+1)T_s}} - \overline{a_{kT_s}} \tag{24}$$

In order to compensate for actual disturbance, $\hat{r}_{(k+1)T_s}$ can be considered as simulator's disturbance signal.

4 System Simulation and Result Analysis

Taking liquid level control system as a research object, general plant is made up of control valve, pipeline, tank and liquid sensor. Figure 3 is its mathematical description diagram. Because of an integral coefficient is contained in controller, we only consider the first three parts. Without considering constant K, general plant is described by state equation

$$\dot{x}(t) = Ax(t) + Bu(t)$$
$$y(t) = Cx(t) + \eta(t) + a(t) \tag{25}$$

Fig. 3. General plant of liquid level control system

where $\eta(t)$ denotes disturbance signal from sensor's input terminal, $a(t)$ is attack

$$A = \begin{pmatrix} -1/6 & 0 & 0 \\ 1/3 & -1/3 & 0 \\ 0 & 1/150 & -1/150 \end{pmatrix}, B = \begin{pmatrix} 1/6 \\ 0 \\ 0 \end{pmatrix}, C = (0, 0, 1)$$

data. Liquid level's setting value u_r is kept constant 20. Two weight coefficient R and Q are set to 1, respectively. Solution of corresponding Riccati equation is

$$P = \begin{pmatrix} 0.0941 & 0.0474 & 2.3437 \\ 0.0474 & 0.0246 & 1.2371 \\ 2.3437 & 1.2371 & 63.5562 \end{pmatrix}$$

Adding integral section, the augmented matrix is

$$
\bar{A} = \begin{pmatrix}
-1/6 & 0 & 0 & 1/6 \\
1/3 & -1/3 & 0 & 0 \\
0 & 1/150 & -1/150 & 0 \\
0.0157k & 0.0079k & -0.3165k & 0
\end{pmatrix}
$$

Setting integral constant $k = 0.001$, we know the control system is kept stable. Correction factor λ of adjoint vector is equal to 2 by corresponding computation. State feedback gain K is derived to (0.0157, 0.0079, 0.3906). If state observer's poles are configured to -1, observation vector L we got is $(260.4167, 254.1667, 2.4933)^{T}$. Setting sampling period as 1 s, under no injection data, system's step response curve is shown in Fig. 4a. In the case of a data injection action at sensor's output terminal, attack signal is expressed by Eq. (26), system's output response curve is

$$
a_1(t) = \begin{cases} 10\sin(\frac{\pi}{200}t) + 20, & t \in (6000, 14000) \\ 0, & t \notin (6000, 14000) \end{cases} \tag{26}
$$

shown in Fig. 4b (If control strategy is not changed under the data injection action). Figure 4c and d are system's curve under protection mode, injection signals are expressed in Eqs. (26) and (27), respectively.

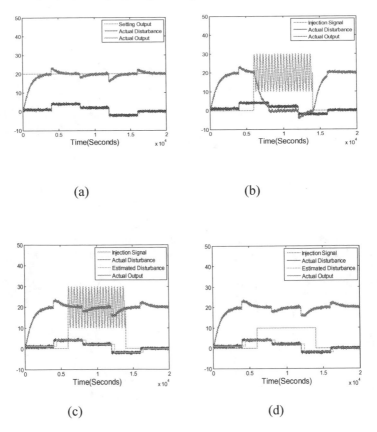

(a)   (b)

(c)   (d)

Fig. 4. Response curve of step input signal

$$a_2(t) = \begin{cases} 10, & t \in (6000, 14000) \\ 0, & t \notin (6000, 14000) \end{cases} \tag{27}$$

Under protection strategy, detector's analysis time T_S is set to 400 s, that is, after 400 s changing value of actual disturbance can be estimated by calculation. The maximum allowable circle time of attack signal is 400 s.

5 Conclusions

Taking liquid level control system as an example, based on LQ infinite time tracking control strategy, two control modes (with data injection and without data injection) are proposed, respectively. System's stability condition is put forward. Different from other networked control system, in the case of system plant is less affected by network-induced delay and data packet loss, controller with integral section can eliminate the effect of disturbance average changing value. Under data injection behavior taking place at sensor's output terminal, an anti data injection control strategy is designed based on LQ tracking. By constructing general plant simulator and estimating current disturbance signal's average value, the impact of data injection behavior can be completely eliminated. In the case of two different data injection actions, output curves of controlled parameters are individually obtained by simulation. The results show the control strategy can realize effective control of controlled parameters, and has some ability of anti-interference and anti data injection. The control system has certain value of applicability and popularization.

Acknowledgments. This work was supported by National Key Scientific Instrument and Equipment Development Project of China (2012YQ15008703), National Science Foundation of China (61633016) and Key Project of Science and Technology Commission of Shanghai Municipality (No. 15220710400).

References

1. Ge, X., Yang, F., Han, Q.-L.: Distributed networked control systems: a brief overview. Inf. Sci. **380**, 117–131 (2015)
2. Ji, X., He, G., Xu, J., Guo, Y.: Study on the mode of intelligent chemical industry based on cyber-physical system and its implementation. Adv. Eng. Softw. **99**, 18–26 (2016)
3. Ntalampiras, S.: Automatic identification of integrity attacks in cyber-physical systems. Expert Syst. Appl. **58**, 164–173 (2016)
4. Sullivan, J.E., Kamensky, D.: How cyber-attacks in ukraine show the vulnerability of the U. S. power grid. Electr. J. **30**(3), 30–35 (2017)
5. Morris, T.H., Gao, W.: Industrial control system cyber attacks. In: Proceedings of the 1st International Symposium on ICS & SCADA Cyber Security Research, BCS 2013, pp. 22–29 (2013)

6. Hashimoto, Y., Toyoshima, T., Yogo, S., Koike, M., Hamaguchi, T., Jing, S., Koshijima, I.: Safety securing approach against cyber-attacks for process control system. Comput. Chem. Eng. **57**(20), 181–186 (2013)
7. Falliere, N., Murchu, L.O., Chien, E.: W32.Stuxnet Dossier. White Pap. Symantec Corp. Secur. Response **5**, 6 (2011)
8. Han, J.: From PID to active disturbance rejection control. IEEE Trans. Ind. Electron. **56**(3), 900–906 (2009)
9. Modares, H., Lewis, F.L.: Linear quadratic tracking control of partially unknown continuous-time systems using reinforcement learning. IEEE Trans. Autom. Control **59** (11), 3051–3056 (2014)
10. Zdzislaw, B.: Modern control theory. Int. J. Robust Nonlinear Control **17**(1), 89–90 (2007)

Filtering for Stochastic Systems with Transmission Delays and Out-of-Order Packets

Li Liu[1(✉)], Aolei Yang[2], Wenju Zhou[1], Qiang Tao[3], Xiaowei Tu[2], and Jun Yue[1]

[1] School of Information Science and Electrical Engineering, Ludong University,
Yantai 264025, China
liulildu@163.com
[2] Shanghai Key Laboratory of Power Station Automation Technology,
School of Mechatronic Engineering and Automation, Shanghai University,
Shanghai 200072, China
[3] Department of Student Affairs, Shandong Commerce Vocational College,
Yantai 264003, China

Abstract. The robust filter is designed for a class of discrete-time stochastic systems with data random transmission delays and out-of-order packets in this paper. To drop packet disorders and improve system performance, the systems are modeled synthetically by utilizing the signal choosing scheme of logic zero-order-holder (ZOH). Moreover, a finite horizon robust Kalman-type filter is designed based on the established model, and minimizing error covariance matrices by the augmented state-space model are obtained from estimation variance constraints. And then, a linear delay compensation method is proposed to improve the filter performance by using the re-organized measurement. The simulation results are performed to show the effectiveness of the proposed method.

Keywords: Finite horizon filtering · Stochastic uncertain systems · Transmission delays · Out-of-order packets · Correlated noises

1 Introduction

The complex networked systems possess the successful applications, such as cyber-physical systems (CPSs) [1], smart grids [2], communication networks [3,4] and so on. Due to the limited capacity of the communication bandwidth deteriorate the system performance [5], it is reasonable to design the communication scheme, and lower installation and maintenance costs [1,6,7]. Therefore, it is significant to study the effects of network-induced phenomena.

L. Liu—This work was supported by Natural Science Foundation of China (61403244, 61633016, 61472172), Key Project of Science and Technology Commission of Shanghai Municipality (15220710400, 15411953502), Key Technical of Key Industries of Shandong (2016CYJS03A02-1), and Key Research and Development project of Shandong (2016ZDJS06A05).

© Springer Nature Singapore Pte Ltd. 2017
D. Yue et al. (Eds.): LSMS/ICSEE 2017, Part II, CCIS 762, pp. 497–506, 2017.
DOI: 10.1007/978-981-10-6373-2_50

The issue of filtering has attracted great interest. For data transmission over networks, the augmented state approach [8,9] applies the compensation scheme by one-step prediction to describe random delays. To transform the random delayed system into the delay-free one, the measurement re-organization approach [10–12] is an effective strategy. To describe packet dropouts, the system is transferred into random variables of Bernoulli distribution [5,8,13], and the state augmentation strategy is employed. For the finite-horizon filtering [11,14], due to the actual error covariance of the estimated state is less than the upper boundary, the finite-horizon filter has a better transient performance for filtering process in networked systems.

The typical signal choosing scheme of logic zero-order-holder (ZOH) is used for dropping the network-induced out-of-order packets. Since the logic ZOH only receives the latest time-stamped data packet [3,7,15–17], it has the capability of choosing the latest data packet, and the packet disorders are actively discarded. The logic ZOH is widely applied in networked control systems for the event-triggering mechanism. However, the analysis and design finite-horizon filter based on the signal choosing scheme are more complex.

Motivated by the above discussion, this paper focuses on designing a finite horizon robust Kalman-type filter for stochastic systems via the network-induced random transmission delays and out-of-order packets. The phenomena are modeled by the logic ZOH scheme.

The remainder of this paper is organized as follows. The stochastic system modeling is described in Sect. 2. Section 3 designs the finite horizon robust Kalman-type filtering using logic ZOH. Simulation results and analysis are given in Sect. 4 and the concluding remarks are outlined in Sect. 5.

2   Problem Formulation

2.1   System Description

The stochastic systems are described as following [13,18]:

$$x(k+1) = (A_k + \mathcal{F}_k F_k E_k) x(k) + B_k w_k, \quad k = 1, 2, \cdots \qquad (1)$$

$$z(k) = (C_k + \mathcal{H}_k F_k E_k) x(k) + v_k, \qquad (2)$$

where $x(k) \in \mathbb{R}^r$ represents the estimated state, $z(k) \in \mathbb{R}^m$ expresses the measurement output at the time instant of k. The multiplicative noise F_k denotes the parametric uncertainty, and $w_k \in \mathbb{R}$ and $v_k \in \mathbb{R}^m$ are zero-mean white noises with covariances Q_k and R_k, respectively. $A_k \in \mathbb{R}^{r \times r}$, $B_k \in \mathbb{R}^r$, $C_k \in \mathbb{R}^{m \times r}$, $\mathcal{F}_k$, $\mathcal{H}_k$ and E_k are known time-varying matrices. Note that the uncertainty F_k satisfies $F_k F_k^T \leq I$. The initial state $x(0)$ with mean μ_0 and covariance P_0, which is assumed to be uncorrelated with other noise signals.

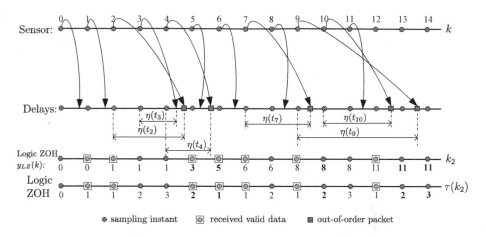

Fig. 1. Re-ordering for packet sequence with out-of-order data transmission.

2.2 Modeling Based on Signal Choosing Scheme

Figure 1 shows a typical scenario, set the constant sampling period as T, and the sampling time instant is $t \in \{kT, \ k \in \mathbb{N}\}$. Suppose that the largest delay is no more than N, and $N(k) \leq k$ at each time instant.

Set the upper boundary of time delay be $N = 5$, and $\eta(t_k)$ represent the transmission delay at k. An example of the sampled packets is given in Fig. 1. At the sampling time $9T$ and $10T$, the signals $z(8)$ and $z(7)$ generate the out-of-order packets in the transmission. $z(7)$ is dropped at the 10th instant using the logic ZOH; at the same time, the latest time-stamped data packet $z(8)$ is stored.

Remark 1. For the sampling time instant t, and the current time instant k, the transmission instant is denoted by k_2 as time-stamped using the logic ZOH. The network-induced transmission delay is represented as $\eta(k_2)$, and $\tau(k_2) \in \mathbb{N}$ denote the transmission delay, which satisfies:

$$k = \tau(k_2) + k_2 . \tag{3}$$

When the logic ZOH receives the arrived data packet $z(k_2)$, the stored signal $y_{LZ}(k)$ is modeled as

$$y_{LZ}(k) = z(k - \tau'(k)), \tag{4}$$

where $\tau'(k) = \tau(k_2)$. Note that the time-stamped data packet implies that the filter is able to obtain the knowledge of the data delays and dropout packets during the transmission [11].

3   Finite Horizon Robust Filtering for Logic ZOH

In this section, the received valid data packets are modeled with transmission delays and out-of-order packets by the signal choosing scheme of logic ZOH.

At the current sampling time instant k, when the stored data packet is $y_{LZ}(k)$, that is, for transmission delay $\tau'(k)$, the received data packet is $z(k - \tau'(k))$ before being transmitted. Set $r = k - \tau'(k)$, the stored measurement is then re-organized from (2) and (4):

$$y_{LZ}(k) = z(r) = (C_r + \mathcal{H}_r F_r E_r) x(r) + v_r. \tag{5}$$

The structure of the robust Kalman-type filtering is proposed:

$$\hat{x}_{LZ}(r|r) = \hat{x}_{LZ}(r|r-1) + K_{LZ,r}\left(z(r) - \hat{C}_{LZ,r}\hat{x}_{LZ}(r|r-1)\right), \tag{6}$$

$$\hat{x}_{LZ}(r+1|r) = \hat{A}_{LZ,r}\hat{x}_{LZ}(r|r-1) + L_{LZ,r}\left(z(r) - \hat{C}_{LZ,r}\hat{x}_{LZ}(r|r-1)\right), \tag{7}$$

where $\hat{C}_{LZ,r}$, $K_{LZ,r}$, $\hat{A}_{LZ,r}$ and $L_{LZ,r}$ are filter parameters.

The objective of the finite horizon robust Kalman-type filtering is to obtain a guaranteed upper boundary using the minimum estimation error covariance.

3.1   Upper Boundary for Estimation Covariance

To obtain the solution of the upper boundaries from the filtering and prediction covariance matrices, the augmented state vectors are defined as following:

$$\tilde{\Psi}_{LZ}(r) = \begin{bmatrix} \tilde{e}_{LZ}(r) \\ \hat{x}_{LZ}(r|r-1) \end{bmatrix}, \quad \Psi_{LZ}(r) = \begin{bmatrix} e_{LZ}(r) \\ \hat{x}_{LZ}(r|r) \end{bmatrix}, \tag{8}$$

and $\tilde{\Psi}_{LZ}(r+1) = \begin{bmatrix} \tilde{e}_{LZ}(r+1) \\ \hat{x}_{LZ}(r+1|r) \end{bmatrix}$. Furthermore, the augmented systems equations combining (1), (6)–(8) are defined as:

$$\Psi_{LZ}(r) = (A_{LZ,r1} + H_{LZ,r1} F_r E_{LZ,r1}) \tilde{\Psi}_{LZ}(r) + D_{LZ,r1} v_r, \tag{9}$$

$$\tilde{\Psi}_{LZ}(r+1) = (A_{LZ,r2} + H_{LZ,r2} F_r E_{LZ,r2}) \tilde{\Psi}_{LZ}(r) + B_{LZ,r2} w_r + D_{LZ,r2} v_r, \tag{10}$$

with

$$A_{LZ,r1} = \begin{bmatrix} I - K_{LZ,r}C_r & K_{LZ,r}\left(\hat{C}_{LZ,r} - C_r\right) \\ K_{LZ,r}C_r & I + K_{LZ,r}\left(C_r - \hat{C}_{LZ,r}\right) \end{bmatrix}, \quad H_{LZ,r1} = \begin{bmatrix} -K_{LZ,r}\mathcal{H}_r \\ K_{LZ,r}\mathcal{H}_r \end{bmatrix},$$

$$E_{LZ,r1} = [E_r \ \ E_r], \quad D_{LZ,r1} = \begin{bmatrix} -K_{LZ,r} \\ K_{LZ,r} \end{bmatrix}, \quad B_{LZ,r2} = \begin{bmatrix} B_r \\ 0 \end{bmatrix},$$

$$A_{LZ,r2} = \begin{bmatrix} A_r - L_{LZ,r}C_r & A_r - \hat{A}_{LZ,r} + L_{LZ,r}\left(\hat{C}_{LZ,r} - C_r\right) \\ L_{LZ,r}C_r & \hat{A}_{LZ,r} + L_{LZ,r}\left(C_r - \hat{C}_{LZ,r}\right) \end{bmatrix},$$

$$H_{LZ,r2} = \begin{bmatrix} \mathcal{F}_r - L_{LZ,r}\mathcal{H}_r \\ L_{LZ,r}\mathcal{H}_r \end{bmatrix}, \quad E_{LZ,r2} = [E_r \ \ E_r], \quad D_{LZ,r2} = \begin{bmatrix} -L_{LZ,r} \\ L_{LZ,r} \end{bmatrix}. \tag{11}$$

To minimize the filtering and prediction covariance matrices, denote $\tilde{\Sigma}_{LZ}(r) = E\left(\tilde{\Psi}_{LZ}(r)\tilde{\Psi}_{LZ}^T(r)\right)$ and $\tilde{\Theta}_{LZ}(r) = E\left(\Psi_{LZ}(r)\Psi_{LZ}^T(r)\right)$ based on vectors $\tilde{\Psi}_{LZ}(r)$ and $\Psi_{LZ}(r)$, respectively. And then, the upper boundaries of the estimation covariances are $\bar{\Sigma}_{LZ}(r)$ and $\bar{\Theta}_{LZ}(r)$. Furthermore, the optimal values of the proposed finite horizon robust Kalman-type filtering in (6) and (7) are derived from the following Theorem 1.

Theorem 1. *The current time instant is k, for the measurement $y_{LZ}(k)$ with transmission delay $\tau'(k)$, $z(r)$ with time-stamp $r = k - \tau'(k)$ is received before being transmitted. Let α_r be a positive scalar. $\bar{\Sigma}_{LZ}(r)$ and $P(r)$ are the positive definite solutions for the following discrete-time Riccati-like iterations:*

$$\bar{\Theta}_{LZ}(r) = \bar{\Sigma}_{LZ}(r) + \bar{\Sigma}_{LZ}(r)E_r^T\tilde{M}_{LZ,r}^{-1}E_r\bar{\Sigma}_{LZ}(r) - \Lambda_{LZ}(r)\Xi_{LZ}^{-1}(r)\Lambda_{LZ}^T(r),\tag{12}$$

$$\begin{aligned}\bar{\Sigma}_{LZ}(r+1) = {}& A_r\bar{\Sigma}_{LZ}(r)\left(I + E_r^T M_{LZ,r}^{-1}E_r\bar{\Sigma}_{LZ}(r)\right)A_r^T \\ & - \Delta_{LZ}(r)\Xi_{LZ}^{-1}(r)\Delta_{LZ}^T(r) + B_rQ_rB_r^T + \alpha_r^{-1}\mathcal{F}_r\mathcal{F}_r^T,\end{aligned}\tag{13}$$

$$P(r+1) = A_r\left(P^{-1}(r) - \alpha_r E_r^T E_r\right)^{-1}A_r^T + \alpha_r^{-1}\mathcal{F}_r\mathcal{F}_r^T + B_rQ_rB_r^T,\tag{14}$$

where $\Lambda_{LZ}(r) = \bar{\Sigma}_{LZ}(r)C_r^T + \bar{\Sigma}_{LZ}(r)E_r^T M_{LZ,r}^{-1}E_r\bar{\Sigma}_{LZ}(r)C_r^T$
and $\Delta_{LZ}(r) = A_r\bar{\Sigma}_{LZ}(r)\left(I + E_r^T M_{LZ,r}^{-1}E_r\bar{\Sigma}_{LZ}(r)\right)C_r^T + \alpha_r^{-1}\mathcal{F}_r\mathcal{H}_r^T + B_rS_r$,
satisfy $P^{-1}(r) \quad \alpha_r E_r^T E_r > 0$ *and* $M_{LZ,r} = \alpha_r^{-1}I - E_r\bar{\Sigma}_{LZ}(r)E_r^T > 0$. *Then, there is Kalman-like filtering (6)–(7) with parameters:*

$$\hat{C}_{LZ,r} = C_r\left(I + \bar{\Sigma}_{LZ}(r)E_r^T M_{LZ,r}^{-1}E_r\right),\tag{15}$$

$$K_{LZ,r} = \Lambda_{LZ}(r)\Xi_{LZ}^{-1}(r),\tag{16}$$

$$\hat{A}_{LZ,r} = A_r\left(I + \bar{\Sigma}_{LZ}(r)E_r^T M_{LZ,r}^{-1}E_r\right),\tag{17}$$

$$L_{LZ,r} = \Delta_{LZ}(r)\Xi_{LZ}^{-1}(r),\tag{18}$$

in which, $\Xi_{LZ}(r) = C_r\bar{\Sigma}_{LZ}(r)\left(I + E_r^T M_{LZ,r}^{-1}E_r\bar{\Sigma}_{LZ}(r)\right)C_r^T + \alpha_r^{-1}\mathcal{H}_r\mathcal{H}_r^T + R_r$
and $\tilde{M}_{LZ,r} = \alpha_r^{-1}I - E_rP(r)E_r^T$.

Proof. Referring to the inequalities holding on Lemma 1 and Lemma 2 in [11], the proof procedure is similar to the derivation from minimizing error covariance matrices.

3.2 Delay Compensation

The obtained optimal state estimation $\hat{x}(r|r)$ is used for compensating $\hat{x}(k|r)$ at k. To reduce the computational burden with transmission delay, the linear delay compensation method is proposed. It is assumed the largest delay is N, and the received data packet is $z(r)$ with delay $\tau'(k)$ at k, the estimated state value $\hat{x}_{LZ}(r|r)$ is used for compensating the estimation-based $\hat{x}_{LZ}(k|r)$, which is represented as following:

$$\hat{x}_{LZ}(k|r) = \left(1 - \frac{\tau'(k)-1}{N}\right)\hat{x}_{LZ}(r+1|r). \tag{19}$$

Remark 2. Filtering with transmission delays based on one-step prediction is an accurate estimation. However, the computational complexity is increased. Since the proposed linear compensation strategy is an approximate estimation, the estimation accuracy of the proposed strategy is lower than one-step prediction compensation. Note that the proposed strategy possess the significant advantage of suppressing the computational burden and improving the estimation efficiency.

Suppose that the arrived data is $y_{LZ}(k+1)$ with delay $\tau'(k+1)$, and the received measurement is $z(s)$ with time-stamped before being transmitted at $k+1$. Set $s = k+1-\tau(k+1)$ satisfy $s \geq r$. There are two cases for $\hat{x}_{LZ}(s|s)$:

Case 1. For $s = r$ or $s = r+1$, the state estimation $\hat{x}_{LZ}(s|s)$ is derived from (6), and the filter parameters are obtained by the recursive equations based on Theorem 1.

Case 2. If $s > r+1$, the estimated state $\hat{x}_{LZ}(s|s)$ will be compensated by one-step prediction of $\hat{x}_{LZ}(r+1|r+1)$, which is calculated from (6)–(7) with the artificial delay $\tau^{sr}(k) = s - r > 1$, and the re-organized compensated sequence is defined as:

$$\{\hat{x}_{LZ}(r+1|r+1), \cdots, \hat{x}_{LZ}(r+\tau^{sr}(k)|r+\tau^{sr}(k))\}. \tag{20}$$

Under the given system (1) and (2), the state to be compensated and the filter parameters are computed by the recursions in (12)–(18).

Note that the case of $s < r$ is nonexistence, the packet disorders are dropped actively via the logic ZOH [7,15,16]. Algorithm I summarizes the finite horizon robust Kalman-type filtering.

4   Numerical Simulation

The considered stochastic systems are described in [8,11,18,19]:

$$x(k+1) = \left(\begin{bmatrix} 0.9 & T & T^2/2 \\ 0 & 0.9 & T \\ 0 & 0 & 0.9 \end{bmatrix} + \mathcal{F}_k F_k E_k\right)x(k) + \begin{bmatrix} T^2/2 \\ T \\ T \end{bmatrix}w_k, \quad k=1,2,\cdots \tag{21}$$

$$z(k) = (C_k + \mathcal{H}_k F_k E_k)x(k) + v_k, \tag{22}$$

$$w_k = \eta_k, \quad v_k = \zeta w_k, \tag{23}$$

here, T is the sample period and set as 0.1s, the maximum of the transmission delay is $N = 5$, and the time-varying parametric uncertainties satisfy

Algorithm 1. Computational procedure of the finite horizon robust filtering

Input: $x(0)$, μ_0, P_0, $\bar{\Sigma}_{LZ}(0)$ and α_0.
Output: The filtering error covariance $\bar{\Sigma}_{LZ}(k+1)$ and $P(k+1)$.
  for $k = 1 \to iter$ **do**
    $r = k - \tau'(k)$;   /* $\tau'(k)$-step delays */
    if $\tau^{sr}(k) = 0$ or $\tau^{sr}(k) = 1$ **then**
      $\bar{\Theta}_{LZ}(r)$ in (12);   // the upper boundary of filtering error covariance
      $\hat{C}_{LZ,r}$, $K_{LZ,r}$, $\hat{A}_{LZ,r}$ and $L_{LZ,r}$ given in (15)-(18);
        /* the filter parameters derived from $\bar{\Sigma}_{LZ}(r)$ */
      $\hat{x}_{LZ}(r|r)$ from (6), and $\hat{x}_{LZ}(r+1|r)$ from (7); // the filter and predictor
      $\bar{\Sigma}_{LZ}(r+1)$ in (13), and $P(r+1)$ in (14);
        /* the filtering error covariance and state covariance */
    else
      if $\tau^{sr}(k) > 1$ **then**
        $\hat{x}_{LZ}(s|s)$ is compensated by $\hat{x}_{LZ}(r+1|r+1)$ calculated from (6)-(7);
      end if
    end if
    $\hat{x}_{LZ}(k|r)$ under (19);   /* the compensation of estimation-based state */
    $s = k + 1 - \tau'(k+1)$;   /* $\tau'(k+1)$-step delays */
    $\tau^{sr}(k) = s - r$;   /* the artificial delay */
  end for

$F_k = \sin(0.6k)$. The state $x(k) = \begin{pmatrix} s_k & \dot{s}_k & \ddot{s}_k \end{pmatrix}^T$ is composed of the position, velocity and acceleration. $\eta_k \subset \mathbb{R}$ is the zero mean white noise with variance $\upsilon_\eta^2 = 0.09$, the variable ζ in (23) determines the correlated strength and set $\zeta = 2$, and set $\mathcal{F}_k = [0.1\ 0.1\ 0.1]^T$, $E_k = [0.02\ 0.02\ 0.02]$, $C_k = [0.6\ 0.8\ 1]$, and $\mathcal{H}_k = 0.8$. Taking into account the correlation between process noise and measurement noise, the process noise w_k from (23) with unity covariance Q_k, and the covariance R_k is denoted as $R_k = \zeta Q_k \zeta^T$ and $S_k = Q_k \zeta^T$ given in (23).

The initial values are denoted as $\hat{x}(0|0) = \mu_0 = E(x(0)) = \begin{pmatrix} 1 & 1 & 1 \end{pmatrix}^T$ and $P(0|0) = 0.01 I_3$. Figures 2 compare the traces of the filtering error covariances and the estimated state $\hat{x}(k|k)$ using the improved robust finite-horizon Kalman filtering (IRFHKF) in [11] at k with delay-free. Note that the filtering error covariance upper boundary obtained by the proposed filter is remarkably less than IRFHKF. Owing to the appropriate filter of the proposed method, the dynamic tracking trajectory is more closer the state to be estimated.

To further illustrate the effectiveness performances, the corresponding filter results of the estimated states are demonstrated in Fig. 3. The simulation results are obtained from (6)–(7), which are calculated in Theorem 1 for the logic ZOH.

From Fig. 3(a)–(c) can be observed that the logic ZOH is able to discard out-of-order packets induced from random transmission delays, it possesses the better performances for target tacking and computational efficiency with the compensation strategy.

Depending on the simulation results and error covariance criteria, the comparison between the proposed method and IRFHKF implies that the proposed

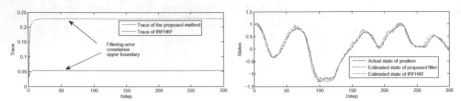

(a) The comparison of the filtering error co- (b) Estimated state for the position state.
variance upper boundary.

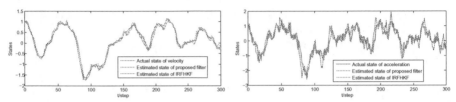

(c) Estimated state for the velocity state. (d) Estimated state for the acceleration s-
tate.

Fig. 2. The comparison of the proposed method and IRFHKF.

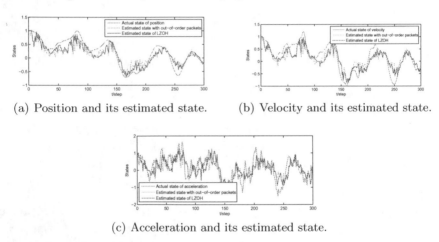

(a) Position and its estimated state. (b) Velocity and its estimated state.

(c) Acceleration and its estimated state.

Fig. 3. Comparison of filter results using logic ZOH.

filter has better accuracy than IRFHKF for the multi-step random delays. The
actual filtering error covariance below the upper boundaries, so that the proposed
filter with transmission delays and out-of-order packets provides the superiority
performances to rapidly converge to a steady-state.

5   Conclusion

The optimal state estimation based on finite horizon robust Kalman-type filtering is investigated. For the networked-induced phenomena, the system is modeled

by the logic ZOH scheme, and a finite horizon robust filter is designed, moreover, a linear delay compensation scheme is proposed. The proposed filtering possesses superior performance for dropping packet disorders, and the actual estimation error variances are less than their upper boundaries. The target tracking systems and numerical simulations are performed to demonstrate that the filter has the ability to track the actual state.

References

1. Reppa, V., Polycarpou, M.M., Panayiotou, C.G.: Distributed sensor fault diagnosis for a network of interconnected cyberphysical systems. IEEE Trans. Control Netw. Syst. **2**(1), 11–23 (2015)
2. Yu, L., Jiang, T., Cao, Y.: Energy cost minimization for distributed internet data centers in smart microgrids considering power outages. IEEE Trans. Parallel Distrib. Syst. **26**(1), 120–130 (2015)
3. Ge, X., Han, Q.-L.: Distributed event-triggered H_∞ filtering over sensor networks with communication delays. Inf. Sci. **291**, 128–142 (2015)
4. Liu, Q., Wang, Z., He, X., Zhou, D.: Event-based recursive distributed filtering over wireless sensor networks. IEEE Trans. Autom. Control **60**(9), 2470–2475 (2015)
5. Sun, S., Wang, G.: Modeling and estimation for networked systems with multiple random transmission delays and packet losses. Syst. Control Lett. **73**, 6–16 (2014)
6. Hu, J., Wang, Z., Chen, D., Alsaadi, F.E.: Estimation, filtering and fusion for networked systems with network-induced phenomena: new progress and prospects. Inf. Fusion **31**, 65–75 (2016)
7. Peng, C., Han, Q.-L., Yue, D.: To transmit or not to transmit: a discrete event-triggered communication scheme for networked Takagi-Sugeno fuzzy systems. IEEE Trans. Fuzzy Syst. **21**(1), 164–170 (2013)
8. Wang, S., Fang, H., Tian, X.: Recursive estimation for nonlinear stochastic systems with multi-step transmission delays, multiple packet dropouts and correlated noises. Sig. Process. **115**, 164–175 (2015)
9. Chen, B., Zhang, W.-A., Yu, L.: Distributed fusion estimation with missing measurements, random transmission delays and packet dropouts. IEEE Trans. Autom. Control **59**(7), 1961–1967 (2014)
10. García-Ligero, M., Hermoso-Carazo, A., Linares-Pérez, J.: Distributed fusion estimation in networked systems with uncertain observations and Markovian random delays. Sig. Process. **106**, 114–122 (2015)
11. Rezaei, H., Esfanjani, R.M., Sedaaghi, M.H.: Improved robust finite-horizon Kalman filtering for uncertain networked time-varying systems. Inf. Sci. **293**, 263–274 (2015)
12. Qi, W., Zhang, P., Deng, Z.: Robust weighted fusion Kalman filters for multisensor time-varying systems with uncertain noise variances. Sig. Process. **99**, 185–200 (2014)
13. Wang, S., Fang, H., Tian, X.: Minimum variance estimation for linear uncertain systems with one-step correlated noises and incomplete measurements. Digit. Sig. Proc. **49**, 126–136 (2016)
14. Chen, B., Zhang, W.-A., Yu, L.: Distributed finite-horizon fusion Kalman filtering for bandwidth and energy constrained wireless sensor networks. IEEE Trans. Sig. Process. **62**(4), 797–812 (2014)

15. Peng, C., Fei, M.-R., Tian, E., Guan, Y.P.: On hold or drop out-of-order packets in networked control systems. Inf. Sci. **268**, 436–446 (2014)
16. Zhang, X.-M., Han, Q.-L.: Network-based H_∞ filtering using a logic jumping-like trigger. Automatica **49**(5), 1428–1435 (2013)
17. Wang, H., Shi, P., Lim, C.C., Xue, Q.: Event-triggered control for networked Markovian jump systems. Int. J. Robust Nonlinear Control **25**(17), 3422–3438 (2015)
18. Tian, T., Sun, S., Li, N.: Multi-sensor information fusion estimators for stochastic uncertain systems with correlated noises. Inf. Fusion **27**, 126–137 (2016)
19. Feng, J., Wang, Z., Zeng, M.: Distributed weighted robust Kalman filter fusion for uncertain systems with autocorrelated and cross-correlated noises. Inf. Fusion **14**(1), 78–86 (2013)

Local Bifurcation Analysis of a Fractional-Order Dynamic Model of Genetic Regulatory Networks with Delays

Qingshan Sun[1], Min Xiao[1(✉)], Lingzhi Zhao[2], and Binbin Tao[1]

[1] College of Automation, Nanjing University of Posts and Telecommunications,
Nanjing 210003, China
candymanxm2003@aliyun.com
[2] College of Information Engineering, Nanjing Xiaozhuang University,
Nanjing 210017, China

Abstract. This paper proposes a mathematical model of gene networks, which includes the fractional derivative and delays. We obtain the conditions of the stability and Hopf bifurcation, and find that a Hopf bifurcation occurs when the sum of delays crosses the critical value, which can be calculated exactly. The fractional order can be used to effectively control the dynamics of such fractional-order model, and the stability domain can be changed by manipulated the order. Finally, a numerical example is presented to demonstrate the theoretical analysis.

Keywords: Fractional-order · Hopf bifurcation · Genetic regulatory networks · Time delays

1 Introduction

Numbers of genes and gene products are comprised of regulatory interactions in genetic regulatory networks. The genetic expression are extremely complicated because the interaction functions describes the biological reaction between DNAs, RNAs, proteins and other small molecules in an organism [1].

Fractional calculus was born in 1695 as an important branch of mathematics, almost simultaneously with classical calculus. In recent years, the theory of fractional calculus has been successfully applied to various fields, and it is gradually found that fractional calculus can describe some nonclassical phenomena in natural science and engineering applications such as neurons, finance systems, biological systems, and so on. A large number of examples show that fractional calculus is with more ambiguous universal meaning than the integer calculus ones.

The integer-order calculus is only determined by the local character of the function, while the fractional-order calculus can accumulate the global information of the function in the weighted form, which is also called the memory. The Hopf bifurcation analysis is an effective research method to get more useful information around the equilibrium point of complicated biological networks [2–4]. The time delay is indispensable in biochemical process when genes guiding the synthesis of proteins with

© Springer Nature Singapore Pte Ltd. 2017
D. Yue et al. (Eds.): LSMS/ICSEE 2017, Part II, CCIS 762, pp. 507–514, 2017.
DOI: 10.1007/978-981-10-6373-2_51

complex gene transcription, translation and transportation. In order to get insight to its mechanism, it is essential to research the dynamic behavior of the genetic regulatory networks with delays.

In recent years, there are many researches about the Hopf bifurcation analysis of genetic regulatory networks, and a great progress has been made. Though, most of these researches have only considered the condition of integer-order ones. In [5–7], it has been found that the fractional-order derivative is more appropriate when modeling its genetic regulatory mechanisms. The mathematical model based on the fractional-order differential equation can describe the more accurate dynamic behaviours of the studied system, and further improve the performance, stability, and for better control of the dynamical systems.

Until now, few researches regarding to the fractional-order genetic regulatory networks have been conducted. The existing researches pay little focus on the effect of time delays of the dynamics of fractional-order genetic regulatory networks. Motivated by those facts, we investigate the Hopf bifurcation of the delayed fractional-order genetic regulatory networks in this paper.

2   Preliminaries and Model Description

We briefly introduce the Caputo fractional derivative and the theoretical research method for the fractional-order genetic regulatory networks which are given in [8, 9].

Firstly, we give the definition of the Caputo fractional-order derivative:

$$
{}_a^C D_t^\alpha f(t) = \frac{1}{\Gamma(u-\alpha)} \int_a^t (t-\tau)^{u-\alpha-1} f^{(n)}(\tau) d\tau, \tag{1}
$$

where $u - 1 < \alpha < u$, $u \in N$, $0 < \alpha \le 1$ and $\Gamma(\cdot)$ is the Gamma function.

The definition of the Laplace transform of the Caputo fractional-order derivative is:

$$
L\{{}_0^C D_t^\alpha f(t)\} = s^\alpha F(s) - \sum_{l=0}^{m-1} s^{\alpha-l-1} f^{(l)}(0). \tag{2}
$$

If $f^{(l)}(0) = 0$, $l = 0, 1, \ldots, u - 1$, we get $L\{{}_0^C D_t^\alpha f(t)\} = s^\alpha F(s)$.

The single gene model is proposed by Lewis [10]:

$$
\begin{aligned}
\dot{m}(t) &= -cm(t) + g(p(t - \tau_1)), \\
\dot{p}(t) &= -bp(t) + am(t - \tau_2),
\end{aligned} \tag{3}
$$

where $p(t)$ represents the concentrations of the protein, $m(t)$ denotes the thickness of the mRNA, $b > 0$ and $c > 0$ stand for the depravation rates of protein and mRNA, and $a > 0$ represents the synthesis rate of protein. τ_1 and τ_2 are time delays in the processes of transcription and translation, respectively. $g(p(t))$ denotes the productive rate of mRNA, and $g(x)$ has the Hill form, $\sigma/(x^n + \in)$, where n is the Hill coefficient, and $\in\, > 0$, $\sigma > 0$.

In this paper, we investigate the delayed fractional-order genetic regulatory network which is as follows:

$$
\begin{aligned}
D^q m(t) &= -cm(t) + g(p(t - \tau_1)), \\
D^q p(t) &= -bp(t) + am(t - \tau_2),
\end{aligned}
\tag{4}
$$

where $q \in (0, 1], m(t), p(t), g(x), c, b, a, \tau_1$ and τ_2 have the same meanings as those defined in (3), and the notation D^q is chosen as the Caputo fractional derivative (1).

Obviously, when $q = 1$, network (4) degenerates to network (3). (m^*, p^*) is an equilibrium point of the fractional-order genetic regulatory network (4) if and only if

$$
\begin{cases}
-cm^* + g(p^*) = 0, \\
-bp^* + am^* = 0.
\end{cases}
$$

It is obvious that network (3) and (4) have the same equilibrium point.

3   The Stability and the Hopf Bifurcation Analysis

We study the stability of network (4), then some conditions of Hopf bifurcations are established in this section.

Let $x(t) = m(t) - m^*$, $y(t) = p(t) - p^*$. Then the (4) becomes:

$$
\begin{cases}
x^q(t) = -cx(t) + g'(p^*)y(t - \tau_1), \\
y^q(t) = -by(t) + ax(t - \tau_2),
\end{cases}
\tag{5}
$$

with the characteristic equation:

$$
\begin{vmatrix}
s^q + c & -g'(p^*)e^{-s\tau_1} \\
-ae^{-s\tau_2} & s^q + b
\end{vmatrix} = 0.
\tag{6}
$$

That is:

$$
s^{2q} + A_1 s^q + A_2 - A_3 e^{-s\tau} = 0,
\tag{7}
$$

where

$$
A_1 = b + c, A_2 = bc, A_3 = ag'(p^*), \tau = \tau_1 + \tau_2.
$$

In the following, we choose the total delay τ as the bifurcation parameter and analyze the characteristic Eq. (7).

Let $s = \omega(\cos\frac{\pi}{2} + i \sin\frac{\pi}{2})(\omega > 0)$. Then (7) becomes

$$
\omega^{2q} \cos q\pi + A_1 \omega^q \cos\frac{q\pi}{2} + A_2 - A_3 \cos \omega\tau
$$
$$
+ i(\omega^{2q} \sin q\pi + A_1 \omega^q \sin\frac{q\pi}{2} + A_3 \sin \omega\tau) = 0.
$$

It follows that:

$$\begin{cases} \phi_1 \cos \omega\tau = \mu_1, \\ -\phi_1 \sin \omega\tau = \eta_1, \end{cases} \tag{8}$$

where

$$\phi_1 = A_3, \mu_1 = \omega^{2q} \cos q\pi + A_1\omega^q \cos \frac{q\pi}{2} + A_2, \eta_1 = \omega^{2q} \sin q\pi + A_1\omega^q \sin \frac{q\pi}{2}.$$

Then,

$$\begin{cases} \cos \omega\tau = \mu_1/\phi_1, \\ \sin \omega\tau = -\eta_1/\phi_1. \end{cases} \tag{9}$$

Hence,

$$\omega^{4q} + D_1\omega^{3q} + D_2\omega^{2q} + D_3\omega^q + D_4 = 0, \tag{10}$$

where

$$D_1 = 2A_1 \cos \frac{q\pi}{2}, D_2 = A_1^2 + 2A_2 \cos q\pi,$$

$$D_3 = 2A_1A_2 \cos \frac{q\pi}{2}, D_4 = A_2^2 - A_3^2.$$

Denote

$$h(\omega) = \omega^{4q} + D_1\omega^{3q} + D_2\omega^{2q} + D_3\omega^q + D_4.$$

Lemma 3.1. *For (7), we get the following results:*

(i) If $D_k > 0$, $k = 1, 2, 3, 4$, $A_2 - A_3 \neq 0$, then there exists no zero real parts root for all $\tau \geq 0$.
(ii) If $D_4 < 0$, and $D_k > 0$, $k = 1, 2, 3$, then there exist a pair of purely imaginary roots $\pm j\omega_0$ as $\tau = \tau_j$, $j = 0, 1, \ldots$, where

$$\tau_j = \frac{1}{\omega_0} \arccos\left(\frac{\mu_1}{\phi_1} + 2j\pi\right), j = 0, 1, 2, \ldots, \tag{11}$$

in which ω_0 is the unique positive root of the function $h(\omega)$.

Proof: (i) From $D_k > 0$, $k = 1, 2, 3, 4$, it can be derived

$$h(0) = D_4 > 0,$$

and

$$h'(\omega) = 4q\omega^{4q-1} + D_1 3q\omega^{3q-1} + D_2 2q\omega^{2q-1} + D_3 q\omega^{q-1} > 0, \text{ for } \omega > 0.$$

Combining $q > 0$ and $D_k > 0$, $k = 1, 2, 3, 4$, we claim that there exists no real root for (10). Hence (7) has no purely imaginary root. Provided that $A_2 - A_3 \neq 0$, $\lambda = 0$ is not a root of (7).

(ii) If $D_4 < 0$, it is obvious that $h(0) = D_4 < 0$. From $\lim\limits_{\omega \to +\infty} h(\omega) = +\infty$, and $h'(\omega) > 0$ for $\omega > 0$, we conclude that a unique positive number ω_0 satisfies $h(\omega) = 0$. Then ω_0 is a root of (10). Hence, for τ_j as defined in (11), (ω_0, τ_j) is a root of (8). So, $\pm j\omega_0$ is a pair of purely imaginary roots of (7) when $\tau = \tau_j$, $j = 0, 1, \ldots$

Next, we make the following hypothesis to prove the transversality condition:

$$(T_1) \quad \frac{P_1 Q_1 + P_2 Q_2}{Q_1^2 + Q_2^2} > 0,$$

where

$$P_1 = -\omega_0 A_3 \sin \omega_0 \tau_0,$$
$$P_2 = -\omega_0 A_3 \cos \omega_0 \tau_0,$$
$$Q_1 = 2q\omega_0^{2q-1} \cos \frac{(2q-1)}{2}\pi + A_1 q\omega_0^{q-1} \cos \frac{(2q-1)}{2}\pi + A_3 \tau_0 \cos \omega_0 \tau_0,$$
$$Q_2 = 2q\omega_0^{2q-1} \sin \frac{(2q-1)}{2}\pi + A_1 q\omega_0^{q-1} \sin \frac{(2q-1)}{2}\pi - A_3 \tau_0 \sin \omega_0 \tau_0.$$

Lemma 3.2. *Let $s(\tau) = \varsigma(\tau) + i\omega(\tau)$ as the root of (7) around $\tau = \tau_j$ satisfying $\varsigma(\tau_j) = 0$, $\omega(\tau_j) = \omega_0$. If (T_1) holds, then we get:*

$$\mathrm{Re}[\frac{ds}{d\tau}]_{\omega=\omega_0, \tau=\tau_0} > 0.$$

Proof: Differentiating (7) implicitly regarding to τ, we have

$$\frac{ds}{d\tau} = \frac{-sA_3 e^{-s\tau}}{2qs^{2q-1} + qA_1 s^{q-1} + A_3 \tau e^{-s\tau}}. \tag{12}$$

Hence, we deduce that

$$\mathrm{Re}[\frac{ds}{d\tau}]_{\omega=\omega_0, \tau=\tau_0} = \frac{P_1 Q_1 + P_2 Q_2}{Q_1^2 + Q_2^2}.$$

If (T_1) holds, the conclusion follows immediately.

Theorem 3.3. *For network (4), we have the following results:*

(i) If $D_4 < 0$, $D_k > 0$, $k = 1, 2, 3, A_2 - A_3 > 0$, and $A_1 > 0$, then the equilibrium of network (4) is locally asymptotically stable for $\tau \in [0, \tau_0)$, and unstable when $\tau > \tau_0$. (ii) If all the conditions in (i) are satisfied, then a Hopf bifurcation occurs at (m^*, p^*) when $\tau = \tau_j$, $j = 0, 1, \ldots$, where $\tau = \tau_j$ defined in (11).

Proof: Observing that when $\tau = 0$, the characteristic Eq. (7) becomes:

$$s^{2q} + A_1 s^q + A_2 - A_3 = 0. \tag{13}$$

(i) It is easy to see from the fractional Routh-Hurwitz criterion that if $A_2 - A_3 > 0$, and $A_1 > 0$, all the roots of (13) have negative real parts. From Lemma 3.1, we conclude that (7) only have roots with negative real parts for $\tau \in [0, \tau_0)$. More-over, from Lemma 3.2, there exists at least a root with positive real parts for (7) when $\tau > \tau_0$. Here, we end the proof of the conclusion (i).

(ii) The proof of the conclusion (ii) follows directly from Lemma 3.2.

4   Simulation Examples

We present a numerical simulation to confirm our theoretical analysis in this section.

In this example, we choose the same parameters used in [11]: $a = 5$, $b = 2$, $c = 1.5$, $g(x) = 4/(1 + x^2)$, and choose the fractional order $q = 0.96$, then network (4) is as follows:

$$D^{0.96}m(t) = -1.5m(t) + 4/\left(1 + (p(t - \tau_1))^2\right),$$
$$D^{0.96}p(t) = -2p(t) + 5m(t - \tau_2). \tag{14}$$

We get a positive equilibrium $(m^*, p^*) = (0.6822, 1.7055)$. From (11), we can obtain $\tau_0 = 1.8709$. From Theorem 3.3, we can see the (m^*, p^*) of the fractional-order net-work (14) is asymptotically stable when $\tau = 1.6 < \tau_0 = 1.8709$ as illustrated in Figs. 1 and 2. When $\tau = 2.0 > \tau_0 = 1.8709$, the (m^*, p^*) of the fractional-order network (14) becomes unstable with a Hopf bifurcation occurring, as revealed in Figs. 3 and 4.

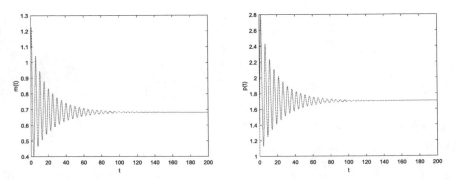

Fig. 1. Waveform plots of the fractional-order network (14) with the initial value (1, 1). The equilibrium (0.6822, 1.7055) is asymptotically stable when $\tau = 1.6 < \tau_0 = 1.8709$.

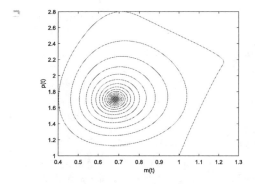

Fig. 2. Phase portrait of the fractional-order network (14) with the initial value (1, 1). The equilibrium (0.6822, 1.7055) is asymptotically stable when $\tau = 1.6 < \tau_0 = 1.8709$.

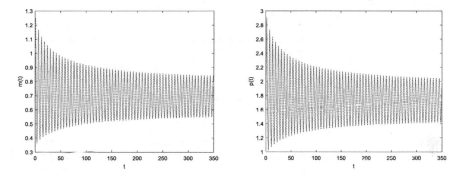

Fig. 3. Waveform plots of the fractional-order network (14) with the initial value (1, 1). The equilibrium (0.6822, 1.7055) is unstable when $\tau = 2.0 > \tau_0 = 1.8709$.

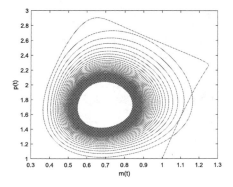

Fig. 4. Waveform plots of the fractional-order network (14) with the initial value (1, 1). The equilibrium (0.6822, 1.7055) is unstable when $\tau = 2.0 > \tau_0 = 1.8709$.

5 Conclusions

In present paper, we propose a delayed factional-order model of genetic regulatory networks, and study the stability and bifurcation. The delayed fractional-order genetic network model can generate a Hopf bifurcation when the total delay crosses the pre-calculated critical value. Thus we can choose proper fractional order to get desired stability domain of the delayed fractional-order genetic regulatory network and improve its performance better.

Acknowledgments. This paper is supported by National Natural Science Foundation of China (No. 61573194), Science Foundation of Nanjing University of Posts and Telecommunications (NY213095).

References

1. Hidde, D.J.: Modeling and simulation of genetic regulatory systems: a literature review. J. Comput. Biol. **9**(1), 67–103 (2002)
2. Verdugo, A., Rand, R.: Hopf bifurcation in a DDE model of gene expression. Commun. Nonlinear Sci. Numer. Simul. **13**(2), 235–242 (2008)
3. Wan, A.Y., Zou, X.F.: Hopf bifurcation analysis for a model of genetic regulatory system with delay. J. Math. Anal. Appl. **356**(2), 464–476 (2009)
4. Xu, C.J., Zhang, Q.M., Wu, Y.S.: Bifurcation analysis in a three-neuron artificial neural network model with distributed delays. Neural Process. Lett. **44**(2), 343–373 (2016)
5. Magin, R.L.: Fractional calculus models of complex dynamics in biological tissues. Comput. Math Appl. **59**(5), 1586–1593 (2010)
6. Ji, R.R., Ding, L., Yan, X.M., Xin, M.: Modelling gene regulatory network by fractional order differential equations. In: IEEE International Conference on BIC-TA, pp. 431–434 (2010)
7. Ren, F.L., Cao, F., Cao, J.D.: Mittag-Leffler stability and generalized Mittag-Leffler stability of fractional-order gene regulatory networks. Neurocomputing **160**, 185–190 (2015)
8. Deng, W., Li, C., Lu, J.: Stability analysis of linear fractional differential system with multiple time delays. Nonlinear Dyn. **48**(4), 409–416 (2007)
9. Podlubny, I.: Fractional differential equations. Academic Press, New York (1999)
10. Lewis, J.: Auto inhibition with transcriptional delay: a simple mechanism for the zebrafish somito genesis oscillator. Curr. Biol. **13**, 1398–1408 (2003)
11. Xiao, M., Cao, J.D.: Genetic oscillation deduced from Hopf bifurcation in a genetic regulatory network with delays. Math. Biosci. **215**, 55–63 (2008)

l_2/l_∞ Filtering for Wireless Networked Control Systems with Communication Constraints and Packet Losses

Li-sheng Wei$^{(\boxtimes)}$ and Yun-qiang Ma

School of Electrical Engineering, Anhui Polytechnic University,
Wuhu City 241000, Anhui Province, People's Republic of China
lshwei_11@163.com

Abstract. The issue of l_2/l_∞ filter designing for Wireless Networked Control System (WNCS) with both communication constraints and packet losses is discussed in this paper. By using the discrete Markov chain, the state of limited channel can be described. And the packet losses behavior is assumed to obey the Bernoulli random sequence. Then the WNCS is modeled as an Asynchronous Dynamic System (ADS) with random parameters and nonlinear term. The l_2/l_∞ filter design is also presented by using Linear Matrix Inequality (LMI) method. The sufficient condition of the closed-loop WNCS to be stable is obtained by using the ADS approach. Finally, a numerical example is presented to demonstrate the effectiveness of the proposed result.

Keywords: Wireless Networked Control System (WNCS) · Communication constraints · Packet losses · Linear Matrix Inequality (LMI) · Filter

1 Introduction

In the recent years, sensor network has been deployed for a variety of applications including manufacturing plants, automobiles, aircraft, and remote operation. Some processes are often connected to send the collected data by a real-time wireless network medium. Such systems are called Wireless Networked Control System (WNCS) [1]. WNCS has many advantages to the actual industrial control system and energy saving optimization [2]. However wireless sensor network has brought out new problems and difficulties when it is applied to in the process of industrial control system. Because wireless sensor network is an unstable shared channel, it can reduce the system control performance and make stability analysis difficultly [3]. Therefore, it is of great scientific significance and wide application value to research on the problem of filtering technique and controller design for WNCS.

In the last decade, the general theory for WNCS has been widely investigated. Many researchers have tried to solve the control performance and make stability with network-induced delay and packet-dropout in wireless NCS. For example, Lu *et al.* [4] based on upper and lower bounds of delay, studied the robust H_∞ filtering problem of interval time-varying delays. The sufficient conditions for the stability of the closed-loop WNCS using the average dwell time method were proposed. Zhang *et al.* [5] studied the

© Springer Nature Singapore Pte Ltd. 2017
D. Yue et al. (Eds.): LSMS/ICSEE 2017, Part II, CCIS 762, pp. 515–524, 2017.
DOI: 10.1007/978-981-10-6373-2_52

H_∞ filtering problem of network control system in the presence of multiple packet losses, multiple packet losses was described by Markov chain, Sufficient LMI conditions were derived for ensure exponentially stable, and the establishment of multi-channel packet loss probability and filter error system was established. Zhu and Guo [6] addressed integrated design of robust controller and dynamic scheduling for under consideration of communication constraints and quantization error. Summarizing the aforementioned discussion, most of the above research results focus on the issues of the delay and the packet losses. And the external noise disturbance and the output signal of the filtering is assumed energy bounded by using H_∞ filtering technology. On the basis of the above research results, we aim to investigate the problem of modeling, l_2/l_∞ filtering and stabilization of WNCS with both communication constraints and packet-dropout, where multiple packet losses is modeled by Bernoulli random binary distribution and channel communication constraints are described by discrete Markov chains in this paper,. Then the close-loop WNCS can be modeled as an asynchronous dynamic system.

The rest of paper is organized as follows. In Sect. 2, the problem and modeling of WNCS is formulated. In Sect. 3, we present sufficient conditions to make sure of the asymptotical stability of l_2/l_∞ filtering. Besides, the gain used in the l_2/l_∞ filtering can be derived by linear matrix inequalities. Then an illustrated example is given in Sect. 4 to demonstrate the effectiveness of proposed method. Finally, the conclusions are given in Sect. 5.

2 Problem Formulation

Considering the block diagram of WNCS with filter as shown in Fig. 1 [7]. We can know that wireless sensor nodes of WNCS comprise a fixed topology in advance and gather information from plants, then transfer data to filter nodes by quantized.

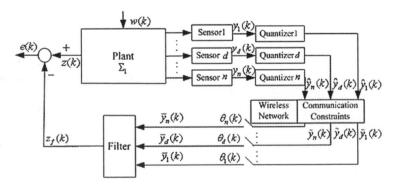

Fig. 1. Block diagram of WNCS with filter

The plant Σ_1 can be described by the following discrete equations:

$$\Sigma_1 : \begin{cases} x(k+1) = Ax(k) + B_1w(k) \\ y(k) = Cx(k) + B_2w(k) \\ z(k) = \Gamma_0 x(k) \end{cases} \tag{1}$$

where $x(k) = [x_1, x_2, \cdots, x_m]^T \in \mathbb{R}^m$ is the system state vector, $y(k) = [y_1, y_2, \cdots, y_n]^T \in \mathbb{R}^n$ is the measured output vector, $z(k) = [z_1, z_2, \cdots, z_p]^T \in \mathbb{R}^p$ is the estimated matrix of system and $w(k) \in l_2[0, \infty)$ is the disturbance noise with limited energy. A, B_1, B_2, C and Γ_0 are constant matrices with appropriate dimensions.

Due to limited bandwidth of wireless network channel, the sensor measured data requires be quantization processed before sending to the wireless network channel. The adverse effects of one hand, this process can get rid of the bandwidth limited of wireless network channel; on the other hand, it can reduce the resource consumption of wireless network channel. In general, multiple network channels are used to transmit data in Distributed WNCS. Therefore, the symmetry quantizer $q(\cdot)$ has been used. The quantizer $q(\cdot)$ can be described by the following equations:

$$q_d(y_d(k)) = \begin{cases} v_l^d & \text{if } \frac{1}{1+\alpha_d}v_l^d < y_d(k) \leq \frac{1}{1-\alpha_d}v_l^d, \ y_d(k) > 0 \\ 0 & \text{if } y_d(k) = 0 \\ -q_d(-y_d(k)) & \text{if } y_d(k) < 0 \end{cases} \tag{2}$$

where $\alpha_d = (1 - \beta_d)/(1 + \beta_d)$, v_l^d is the dth quantizer quantitative level, and $\beta_d(0 < \beta_d < 1)$ is the dth quantizer quantitative density. The value of parameter β_d directly affects the quantitative accuracy, $y_d(k)$ is the measured data of dth sensor nodes, $\hat{y}_d(k)$ is the quantitative output data of $y_d(k)$ by the dth quantizer, which can be described by Eq. (3).

$$\hat{y}_d(k) = q[y_d(k)] \tag{3}$$

Then the quantitative output data $\hat{y}(k)$ is written as the following matrix form:

$$\hat{y}(k) = q[y_1(k), y_2(k), \cdots, y_n(k)]^T \tag{4}$$

According to sector boundary method, Eq. (4) rewritten as:

$$\hat{y}(k) = (I + \Delta(k))y(k) \tag{5}$$

where $\Delta(k) = diag[\Delta_1(k), \Delta_2(k), \cdots, \Delta_n(k)]$ is quantization error. The bounded variable $\Delta_d(k)$ $(\Delta_d(k) \in [-\alpha_d, \alpha_d])$ is the diagonal element of $\Delta(k)$, namely $\Delta_d(k)$ is the quantization error of the dth quantizer.

Considering the limited wireless channel resources, parts of sensor nodes are only allowed to use through network channels. That is to say the value of wireless network channel n is greater than the value of effective channel $\bar{n}$ which take part in the competition. The modal of the wireless channel on-state is $N = C_n^{\bar{n}}$. The state of wireless network communication channel has the nature of random at any time. So we can use discrete Markov chain to describe the wireless network communication channel characteristics. In order to simplify the system description, the binary function $\varphi_d(k)$: $Z \mapsto \{0, 1\}, \forall d \in \{1, 2, \cdots, n\}$ is introduced to represent the state of wireless network communications channel. When $\varphi_d(k) = 1$ is represented that the state of wireless network communications channel is on-state, and the data of the dth sensor node is $\tilde{y}_d(k) = \hat{y}_d(k)$. When $\varphi_d(k) = 0$ is represented that the wireless network communications channel does not get through, and the data of the dth sensor node is $\tilde{y}_d(k) = 0$. Therefore the data $\tilde{y}(k)$ transmission from wireless network node with communication constraints can be expressed as:

$$\tilde{y}(k) = S_\varphi(k)\hat{y}(k) \tag{6}$$

Sending the Eq. (6) to Eq. (5), we have

$$\tilde{y}(k) = S_\varphi(k)(I + \Delta(k))y(k) \tag{7}$$

where $S_\varphi(k)$ is communication matrix, $S_\varphi(k) = diag[\varphi_1(k), \varphi_2(k), \cdots, \varphi_n(k)]$.

In order to further simplify the limited channel data transmission process, let $\varepsilon(k)$ express the Markov chain. The probability distribution is described below:

$$\begin{aligned} Pr[\theta_d(k) = 1] &= E[\theta_d(k)] = \theta_d \\ Pr[\theta_d(k) = 0] &= 1 - E[\theta_d(k)] = 1 - \theta_d = \bar{\theta}_d \\ Var[\theta_d(k)] &= \theta_d(1 - \theta_d) = \zeta_d^2 \end{aligned} \tag{8}$$

where θ_d is the no packet losses probability of d node. $\bar{\theta}_d$ is packet losses probability of d node. ζ_d is the variance of no packet losses. $\theta_d \in [0, 1]$ is the known constant. Then the input data of filter can be expressed as:

$$\begin{aligned} \bar{y}_d(k) &= \theta_d(k)\tilde{y}_d(k) + (1 - \theta_d(k))\bar{y}_d(k-1) \\ \bar{y}(k) &= N_\theta(k)\tilde{y}(k) + (I - N_\theta(k))\bar{y}(k-1) \\ \bar{y}(k) &= N_\theta(k)S_\varphi(k)(I + \Delta(k))y(k) + (I - N_\theta(k))\bar{y}(k-1) \end{aligned} \tag{9}$$

where $N_\theta(k)$ is the packet losses matrix, $N_\theta(k) = diag[\theta_1(k), \theta_2(k), \cdots, \theta_n(k)]$.

In order to deriving the sufficient conditions of l_2 / l_∞ filtering, we can use the following filter F,

$$F : \begin{cases} x_f(k+1) = A_{fi}x_f(k) + B_{fi}\bar{y}(k) \\ z_f(k) = C_{fi}x_f(k) \end{cases} \tag{10}$$

where $x_f(k) \in \mathbb{R}^m$ and $\bar{y}(k) \in \mathbb{R}^n$ is the state vector and the input vector of the filter F respectively. $z_f(k) \in \mathbb{R}^p$ is the estimation vector of the filter F. A_{fi}, B_{fi} and C_{fi} is constant matrices with appropriate dimensions of the filter F.

Combining with Eqs. (1), (9) and (10), and by augmenting, we have the following augmented filtering error system:

$$\begin{cases} X(k+1) = \Phi X(k) + Bw(k) \\ \quad e(k) = \Gamma X(k) \end{cases} \tag{11}$$

where $X(k)$ is the augmented state matrix $X(k) = \left[x^T(k) \quad x_f^T(k) \quad \bar{y}^T(k-1) \right]^T$. $e(k)$ is the filtering errors $e(k) = z(k) - z_f(k)$.

$$\Phi = \begin{bmatrix} A & 0 & 0 \\ B_{fi}N_\theta(k)S_\varphi(k)(I+\Delta(k))C & A_{fi} & B_{fi}(I - N_\theta(k)) \\ N_\theta(k)S_\varphi(k)(I+\Delta(k))C & 0 & (I - N_\theta(k)) \end{bmatrix}$$

$$B = \begin{bmatrix} B_1 \\ B_{fi}N_\theta(k)S_\varphi(k)(I+\Delta(k))B_2 \\ N_\theta(k)S_\varphi(k)(I+\Delta(k))B_2 \end{bmatrix}$$

$$\Gamma = \begin{bmatrix} \Gamma_0 & -C_{fi} & 0 \end{bmatrix}$$

Under consideration l_2 / l_∞ filter designing for WNCS, without loss of generality, we give the following two assumptions, which will be useful in our main results.

Assumption (1). When the external disturbance signal $w(k) = 0$, the filtering error system (12) of the close loop WNCS is stochastic stability.

$$lim \sum_0^\infty E\{x(k)^T x(k)\} < \infty \tag{12}$$

Assumption (2). In the condition of zero initial, for any given a scalar $\gamma > 0$, the filtering error system (12) can satisfy the following l_2 / l_∞ performance indicator

$$E\left\{ \|e(k)\|_\infty^2 \right\} \le \gamma^2 \|w(k)\|_2^2 \tag{13}$$

where $\|e(k)\|_\infty^2 = \underset{k}{sup}\ \{e(k)^T e(k)\}$, $\|w(k)\|_2^2 = \sum_{k=0}^\infty w(k)^T w(k)$.

So we call the filter is γ suppression level when the system (12) satisfy the above two conditions.

3   Main Results

The purpose of our work is to design the l_2 / l_∞ filter for WNCS, which has packet losses, combined with communication constraints. Before the development of the main results, some useful and important lemmas that will be used in deriving out results will be introduced in the following.

Lemma 1 [8]. Given any symmetric matrix $\prod = \prod^T$, and constant matrix M, N with appropriate dimension, if $F(t)$ is an uncertain matrix function with Lebesgue measurable elements and satisfies $F^T(k)F(k) \leq I$, in which I denotes the identity matrix of appropriate dimension. Then

$$\prod + MF(k)N + M^T F(k)^T N^T < 0$$

If and only if there exists positive constant $\varepsilon > 0$ such that

$$\prod + \varepsilon MM + \varepsilon^{-1} N^T N < 0$$

Lemma 2 (Schur complement [8]). Given any symmetric matrix $S = S^T$.

$$S = \begin{bmatrix} S_{11} & S_{12} \\ S_{21} & S_{22} \end{bmatrix}$$

where $S_{11} \in R^{r \times r}$, S_{12}, S_{21}, S_{22} are known real matrices with proper dimensions. The following three conditions are equivalent

(1) $S < 0$
(2) $S_{11} - S_{12} S_{22}^{-1} S_{12}^T < 0$ and $S_{22} < 0$
(3) $S_{22} - S_{12}^T S_{11}^{-1} S_{12} < 0$ and $S_{11} < 0$

In the following, the sufficient condition for convergence and the l_2 / l_∞ filter designing is given.

Theorem 1. Considering the WNCS (11), given positive constant $\gamma > 0$. Then the augmented system is asymptotical stable if there exist symmetric constant matrix $P_i > 0$, the filter meet l_2 / l_∞ performance requirements such that

$$\begin{bmatrix} -P_i & * & * & * \\ 0 & -I & * & * \\ \Phi & B & -\bar{P}_i^{-1} & * \\ \Phi_\zeta & B_\zeta & 0 & -\bar{P}_i^{-1} \end{bmatrix} < 0, \ g = diag[I \quad 0 \quad I \quad I] \tag{14}$$

$$\begin{bmatrix} -P_i & * \\ \Gamma & -\gamma^2 I \end{bmatrix} < 0 \tag{15}$$

where $*$ denotes the symmetric terms in a symmetric matrix and

$$\bar{\Phi} = \begin{bmatrix} A & 0 & 0 \\ 0 & A_{fi} & B_{fi} \\ 0 & 0 & I \end{bmatrix}, \bar{B} = \begin{bmatrix} B_1 \\ 0 \\ 0 \end{bmatrix}, \ \Phi_\zeta = \bar{\Phi}_1 \zeta \bar{\Phi}_2, \ B_\zeta = \bar{B}_1 \zeta \bar{B}_2$$

$$\bar{B}_1 = \begin{bmatrix} 0 \\ B_{fi} \\ I \end{bmatrix}, \bar{\Phi}_1 = \begin{bmatrix} 0 \\ B_{fi} \\ I \end{bmatrix}$$

$$\bar{B}_2 = [S_\varphi(k)(I + \Delta(k))B_2]$$

$$\bar{\Phi}_2 = [S_\varphi(k)(I + \Delta(k))C \quad 0 \quad -I]$$

Theorem 2. Considering the system (1) Σ_1, given a positive scalar $\gamma > 0$ and $\varepsilon > 0$, if there exist constant matrix $P_i > 0\,(i \in [1, \cdots, N])$, $R_s, > 0\,(s \in [1, \cdots, N])$, J_{11}, J_{12}, $J_{13}, J_{22}, J_{31}, J_{32}$ and J_{33} with proper dimensions such that the LMI (16) and (17) holds.

$$\begin{bmatrix} \Pi_1 & * & * & * & * & * \\ 0 & -I & * & * & * & * \\ \Pi_2 & \Pi_3 & \Pi_4 & * & * & * \\ \Pi_5 & \Pi_6 & 0 & \Pi_4 & * & * \\ 0 & 0 & 0 & \Pi_7 & -\varepsilon^{-1}I & * \\ \Pi_8 & \Pi_9 & 0 & 0 & 0 & -\varepsilon I \end{bmatrix} < 0 \tag{16}$$

$$\begin{bmatrix} \Pi_1 & * \\ \Pi_{10} & -\gamma^2 I \end{bmatrix} < 0 \tag{17}$$

Then the system (11) is asymptotical stable, and has the l_2 / l_∞ performance index. Where

$$\Pi_1 = -P_i,\ \Pi_2^T = \left[\underbrace{\overline{\Pi}_2^T \quad \cdots \quad \overline{\Pi}_2^T}_{N}\right],\ \Pi_3^T = \left[\underbrace{\overline{\Pi}_3^T \quad \cdots \quad \overline{\Pi}_3^T}_{N}\right]$$

$$\Pi_4 = diag\left[\underbrace{\frac{1}{\Lambda_{i1}}\left(R_1 - \overline{\Pi}_4\right) \quad \cdots \quad \frac{1}{\Lambda_{iN}}\left(R_N - \overline{\Pi}_4\right)}_{N}\right],\ \Pi_5^T = \left[\underbrace{\overline{\Pi}_5^T \quad \cdots \quad \overline{\Pi}_5^T}_{N}\right]$$

$$\Pi_6^T = \left[\underbrace{\overline{\Pi}_6^T \quad \cdots \quad \overline{\Pi}_6^T}_{N}\right],\ \Pi_7 = \left[\underbrace{\overline{\Pi}_7 \quad \cdots \quad \overline{\Pi}_7}_{N}\right]$$

$$\Pi_8 = [C\ \ 0\ \ 0],\ \Pi_9 = B_2,\ \Pi_{10} = [\Gamma_0 \ \ -W_i \ \ 0]$$

$$\overline{\Pi}_2 = \begin{bmatrix} J_{11}^T A & U_i & V_i + J_{31}^T \\ J_{12}^T A & U_i & V_i + J_{32}^T \\ J_{13}^T A & 0 & J_{33}^T \end{bmatrix},\ \overline{\Pi}_3 = \begin{bmatrix} J_{11}^T B_1 \\ J_{12}^T B_1 \\ J_{13}^T B_1 \end{bmatrix}$$

$$\overline{\Pi}_4 = \begin{bmatrix} J_{11} & J_{12} & J_{13} \\ J_{22} & J_{22} & 0 \\ J_{31} & J_{32} & J_{33} \end{bmatrix} + \begin{bmatrix} J_{11} & J_{12} & J_{13} \\ J_{22} & J_{22} & 0 \\ J_{31} & J_{32} & J_{33} \end{bmatrix}^T,\ \overline{\Pi}_6 = \begin{bmatrix} V_i\ \zeta S_\varphi(k) B_2 + J_{31}^T\ \zeta S_\varphi(k) B_2 \\ V_i\ \zeta S_\varphi(k) B_2 + J_{32}^T\ \zeta S_\varphi(k) B_2 \\ J_{33}^T\ \zeta S_\varphi(k) B_2 \end{bmatrix}$$

$$\overline{\Pi}_5 = \begin{bmatrix} V_i\ \zeta S_\varphi(k) C + J_{31}^T\ \zeta S_\varphi(k) C & 0 & -V_i \zeta - J_{31}^T \zeta \\ V_i\ \zeta S_\varphi(k) C + J_{32}^T\ \zeta S_\varphi(k) C & 0 & -V_i \zeta - J_{32}^T \zeta \\ J_{33}^T\ \zeta S_\varphi(k) C & 0 & -J_{33}^T \zeta \end{bmatrix}$$

$$\overline{\Pi}_7 = \left[\alpha^T S_\varphi(k)^T \zeta^T V_i^T + \alpha^T S_\varphi(k)^T \zeta^T J_{31} \quad \alpha^T S_\varphi(k)^T \zeta^T V_i^T + \alpha^T S_\varphi(k)^T \zeta^T J_{32} \quad \alpha^T S_\varphi(k)^T \zeta^T J_{33}\right]$$
$$\alpha = diag[\alpha_1, \alpha_2, \cdots, \alpha_n] \cdot \zeta = diag[\zeta_1, \zeta_2, \cdots, \zeta_n]$$

Remark: The optimal performance γ^* of filter l_2 / l_∞ can obtain by solving the convex optimization problem as follows:

$$min \quad \mu \quad subject\ to\ (16),\ (17)\ with \quad \mu = \gamma^2$$
$$J_{11} \sim J_{33}, P_i, R_s, U_i, V_i, W_i$$

So the optimal performance $\gamma^* = \sqrt{\mu_{min}}$.

4   Numerical Simulations

In this section, we present an illustrative example to demonstrate the effectiveness of
the proposed theorems. Consider the following discrete-time control system

$$x(k+1) = \begin{bmatrix} 0.5 & -0.7 \\ 0.4 & -0.32 \end{bmatrix} x(k) + \begin{bmatrix} -0.7 \\ 0.85 \end{bmatrix} w(k)$$

$$y(k) = \begin{bmatrix} 0.4 & 0.5 \\ -0.5 & 0.3 \end{bmatrix} x(k) + \begin{bmatrix} -0.4 \\ 0.6 \end{bmatrix} w(k)$$

$$z(k) = [\,0.8 \quad -0.5\,] x(k)$$

Assuming two channels of wireless network form Sensor node to Filter node in
WNCS, and choosing quantization density $\beta_1 = \beta_2 = 0.667$, the values of packet
losses probability is $\bar{\theta}_1 = \bar{\theta}_2 = 0.8$, and the values of variance is $\zeta_1 = \zeta_2 = 0.4$.
Because of the communication constraints of wireless network, only one channel can
be connected at any instant, that is $N = 2$. So there are two modals of Markov chain,
and the communication matrix have two values to choose, so

$$S_\varphi(k) \in \left\{ S_\varphi^1, S_\varphi^2 \right\}, S_\varphi^1 = \begin{bmatrix} 1 & 0 \\ 0 & 0 \end{bmatrix}, S_\varphi^2 = \begin{bmatrix} 0 & 0 \\ 0 & 1 \end{bmatrix}$$

Then we have the probability matrix for the Markov chain as follows:

$$\Lambda = \begin{bmatrix} 0.3 & 0.7 \\ 0.8 & 0.2 \end{bmatrix}$$

Setting the disturbance noise $w(k) = 2e^{-0.3k} \sin(0.5\pi k)$ and the performance level
of l_2 / l_∞ filter $\gamma^* = 1$, some parameters of filter can be acquired based on Theorems 1
and 2 and by using Matlab LMI Toolbox, we have

(1)   At the first modal, the parameters of filter are as follows:

$$A_{f1} = \begin{bmatrix} 0.0502 & -0.9477 \\ 0.0377 & -0.5993 \end{bmatrix}, B_{f1} = \begin{bmatrix} -0.7232 & 0.1794 \\ -0.4044 & 0.1861 \end{bmatrix}$$

$$C_{f1} = [\,-0.8159 \quad 0.5011\,]$$

(2) At the second modal, the parameters of filter are as follows:

$$A_{f2} = \begin{bmatrix} 0.1592 & -0.300 \\ 0.1432 & -0.1743 \end{bmatrix}, \; B_{f2} = \begin{bmatrix} 0.0389 & 1.6508 \\ 0.0022 & 0.9154 \end{bmatrix}$$

$$C_{f2} = \begin{bmatrix} -0.7752 & 0.5516 \end{bmatrix}$$

It is assumed that the initial values of control system $x(0) = \begin{bmatrix} 0.5 & -0.5 \end{bmatrix}^T$ and the initial values of filtering system $x_f(0) = \begin{bmatrix} 0 & 0 \end{bmatrix}^T$, it can be obtained the state tracking curves of system and the state tracking curves of filter that in Figs. 2 and 3 respectively. $x_i(k)$ is the state of plant and $x_{if}(k)$ is the state of filter. And we can get the error response of the filter $e(k)$ in Fig. 4 and the sequence of state transition for Markov chain in Fig. 5.

From Figs. 2 and 3, it can be clearly observed that the state of filter $x_{if}(k)$ can track the state of the state of plant $x_i(k)$ effectively in 15 time steps. So the state of control system can be accurately estimate by filter. From the Fig. 4, it is clear that the l_2 / l_∞

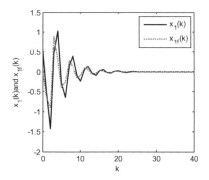

Fig. 2. The $x_1(k)$ and $x_{1f}(k)$ response

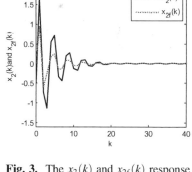

Fig. 3. The $x_2(k)$ and $x_{2f}(k)$ response

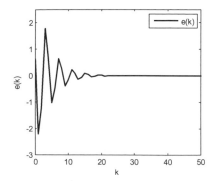

Fig. 4. The error response $e(k)$

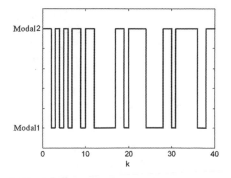

Fig. 5. The sequence of modal transition

filter error can convergence to zero with the increase of time. The sequences of modal transition for Markov chain are illustrated in Fig. 5. The modal 1 of the ordinate represents S_φ^1, and the modal 2 of the ordinate represents S_φ^2. The value of optimal performance γ^* is 0.2846 by using the proposed filter, and γ^* is 1.241 by using Ref. [9] filter, which confirms that the proposed l_2 / l_∞ filter can stabilize the system with communication constraints and packet losses.

5 Conclusion

In this paper, we have considered filtering problem for WNCS with communication constraints and packet losses. The l_2 / l_∞ filter has been designed such that the close loop WNCS is asymptotical stable, at the same time, the error $e(k)$ and the robust performances γ^* of filter is made as small as possible. Sufficient conditions have been derived by means of the feasibility of certain matrix inequality and asynchronous dynamic system method. Finally, the numerical example results show the effectiveness of proposed method.

Acknowledgments. All authors would like to thank anonymous reviewers and the editor for their valuable comments and helpful suggestions. This work was supported by the Natural Science Foundation of Anhui Province under grant 1608085MF146, the Natural Science Research Programme of Colleges and Universities of Anhui Province under grant KJ2016A062, the Visiting Study Foundation for outstanding young talent of Anhui Educational Committee under grant gxfxZD2016108, and the Foundation for talented young people of Anhui Polytechnic University under grant 2016BJRC008.

References

1. Kilinc, D., Ozger, M., Akan, O.B.: On the maximum coverage area of wireless networked control systems with maximum cost-efficiency under convergence constraint. IEEE Trans. Autom. Control **60**(7), 1910–1914 (2015)
2. Ji, K., Wei, D.: Resilient control for wireless networked control systems. Int. J. Control Autom. Syst. **9**(2), 285–293 (2011)
3. Makled, E.A., Halawa, H.H., Daoud, R.M., et al.: On the performability of hierarchical wireless networked control systems. Intell. Control Autom. **06**(2), 126–133 (2015)
4. Lu, R., Shu, J., Bai, J., Liu, S.: H_∞ control for a class of wireless networked control systems. In: 34th Chinese Control Conference (CCC), pp. 6805–6809 (2015)
5. Zhang, W.A., Yu, L., Song, H.: H_∞ filtering of networked discrete-time systems with random packet losses. Inf. Sci. **179**(22), 3944–3955 (2009)
6. Zhu, C., Guo, G.: Quantized feedback control of networked systems with constrained communication capacity. Sci. Sinica Inf. **44**(5), 633–646 (2014). (in Chinese)
7. Bai, J., Lu, R., Su, H., et al.: Modeling and control of wireless networked control system with both delay and packet loss. J. Frankl. Inst. **352**(10), 70–71 (2015)
8. Jing, Z.: Research on the robust filtering for network control system. Nanjing University of Science and Technology (2014). (in Chinese)
9. Song, H., Yu, L., Liu, A.: H_∞ filtering for network-based systems with communication constraints and packet dropouts. In: Proceedings of the 7th Asian Control Conference, Hong Kong, China, pp. 220–225 (2009)

Observer-Based H_∞ Output Feedback Control for Switched Systems with Sojourn Probability Method

Lei Wang, Juan Li, Engang Tian$^{(\boxtimes)}$, and Yinghui Hu

School of Electrical Engineering and Automation Engineering,
Nanjing Normal University, Nanjing 210042, China
teg@njnu.edu.cn

Abstract. This paper investigates the observer-based H_∞ output feedback control for a class of switched systems with time delay. Different from some existing methods, the switching rule in the considered systems is governed by the sojourn probability information (the probability of the switched system staying in one subsystem). In order to rebuild the switched systems and utilize those probability information, a set of random variables are introduced to represent the switching law of the switched systems. The expectation of the random variable is the sojourn probability of the subsystems. In such a way, new type of switched systems with random variables are built. The purpose of the addressed problem is to design the observer-based output feedback controller and to obtain sufficient conditions for the mean square stability of the system. By using a multiple Lyapunov functional method, one theorem is derived, and the controller and observer gains can be computed by solving a set of linear matrix inequalities. A simulation example is proposed to illustrate the effectiveness of the developed design method.

Keywords: Switched systems · Sojourn probability · Multiple Lyapunov functional method · Observer

1 Introduction

Switching systems consist of a set of subsystems with their own parameterizations subject to a rule orchestrating the switching rule between different subsystems, which can effectively describe the complex system such as complex industrial process, communication system, networked control systems and power systems [1, 2], thus have absorbed considerable attention in the past several decades [3]. Different from the single system, the stability of switched systems not only depend on the stability of each subsystem, but also closely related to the switching rate. In other words, the switching rules in the systems play a significant role in the stability and dynamic performance of the system [4].

Currently, the switching rules which have been widely employed can be classified into two categories, one is the deterministic switching law, such as time-dependent and state switching laws and arbitrary switching law, the other is stochastic switching law, such as Markovian switching law. By using these switching rules, many researchers

© Springer Nature Singapore Pte Ltd. 2017
D. Yue et al. (Eds.): LSMS/ICSEE 2017, Part II, CCIS 762, pp. 525–534, 2017.
DOI: 10.1007/978-981-10-6373-2_53

have made abundant research achievements. For example in [5], an output feedback controller which is based on state observer is devised by using the switching Lyapunov function method. The authors in [6] study the state dependent on switching rules which ensures the system asymptotically stable. In papers such as [7] the stabilization problem of a kind of neutral switched systems are studied. By giving the switching control scheme of each subsystem, the asymptotic stability of the whole system performance is ensured. The stochastically stable of the switched system is guaranteed in [8] through the design of a mode-dependent observer-based controller. As for the stochastic switching, a typical method is Markov jump systems (MJSs), wherein the Markov process is the switching law, which can be used to model many practical examples, such as networked control systems [9–12]. Therefore, the MJSs have drawn great attention over the past years.

However, for the MJSs, an important issue is to observe the transition probability of the subsystems. For a MJSs with n subsystems, there should be n * (n − 1)/2 transition probabilities to be determined, which is difficult in some practical examples especially when n is large. More recently, a sojourn-probability-dependent method is proposed in [13] to rebuild the switched systems. A group of random variables are introduced to represent the probability of the switched systems staying in the subsystems. In this model, only (n − 1) transition probabilities are needed, which is much easier to be measured. However, only the problem of state feedback control is studied in [13]. It is known that state variables are often difficult to obtain in many practical systems. Therefore, it is necessary and important to investigate the output feedback control for such systems.

On the other hand, time delay is encountered in practical systems frequently, which is one of the main issues to degrade the system performance. Switched systems with time delay have widespread adhibition in the engineering systems, such as the power electronics and networked control systems [14, 15]. Time delay makes the analysis and control synthesis for the switched systems more complicated. Switched systems with time delays have been studied in numerous existing literatures such as [3, 16–18]. However, when considering the observer-based output feedback control for switched systems with time delay, the sojourn-probability-based analysis and control method have not been fully considered, which is the main motivation of the current study.

In this paper, observer-based H_∞ output feedback controller design method is studied for the switched systems and a sojourn-probability-based method is introduced to design the observer as well as the output feedback gains. Sufficient conditions are obtained for the switched system by using Lyapunov functional and linear matrix inequality method. The observer gains, and the corresponding output feedback controller are also designed. Finally, one example is provided to illustrate the effectiveness of the presented method.

2   Problem Formulation

Consider the following discrete switched system with delay

$$\begin{cases} x(k+1) = A_{\sigma(k)}(k)x(k) + A_{d\sigma(k)}(k)x(k-d_k) + B_{\sigma(k)}u(k) + G_{\sigma(k)}\omega(k) \\ y(k) = C_{\sigma(k)}x(k) + C_{d\sigma(k)}x(k-d_k) \\ z(k) = D_{\sigma(k)}x(k), x(k) = \phi(k), k = -d^M, -d^M+1, \ldots, 0 \end{cases} \quad (1)$$

where $x(k) \in R^n$, $y(k) \in R^p$, $z(k) \in R^q$ are state vector, measured output and controlled output, respectively, $\omega(k) \in R^r$ is the disturbance input belonging to $l_2[0, +\infty)$. $\phi(k)$ is initial system value. The switching signal $\sigma(k)$ satisfies $\sigma(k) : Z^+ = \{0, 1, 2, \ldots\} \to \Omega = \{1, 2, \ldots, N\}$. d_k is the delay which satisfies $1 \le d_k \le d^M$, d^M is known. $A_i(k)$, $A_{di}(k)$, B_i, C_i, D_i, G_i, $(i \in \Omega)$ are the parameters of ith subsystems.

The output feedback controller is built as

$$\begin{cases} \tilde{x}(k+1) = A_{\sigma(k)}(k)\tilde{x}(k) + A_{d\sigma(k)}(k)\tilde{x}(k-d_k) + B_{\sigma(k)}u(k) + G_{\sigma(k)}\omega(k) \\ \quad + L_{\sigma(k)}(y(k) - \tilde{y}(k)) \\ \tilde{y}(k) = C_{\sigma(k)}\tilde{x}(k) + C_{d\sigma(k)}\tilde{x}(k-d_k) \\ u(k) = K_{\sigma(k)}\tilde{x}(k) \end{cases} \quad (2)$$

where $\tilde{x}(k)$ is state estimation, L_i, K_i are the gain matrices of observer and controller to be designed.

Assumption 1 [13]. The probability of the switched system staying in a particular subsystem is assumed to be known a prior such as

$$p_r\{\sigma(k) = i\} = \alpha_i, \ i \in \Omega, \ \sum_{i=1}^{N} a_i = 1. \quad (3)$$

where $\alpha_i \in (0, 1)$ is called the sojourn probability of the ith subsystem.

Remark 1. Switching rule based on sojourn probability is not dependent on time or current state, and the sojourn probabilities can be measured in a statistical way:

$$\alpha_i = \lim_{k \to \infty} \frac{k_i}{k}.$$

where k_i is number of times that $\sigma(k) = i$ belongs to $[1, k]$ ($k \in \Omega$ is big enough).

Definition 1. Define stochastic variables $\alpha_i(k) : Z^+ \to \{0, 1\}$:

$$\alpha_i(k) = \begin{cases} 1, \sigma(k) = i \\ 0, \sigma(k) \neq i \end{cases}, i \in \Omega, k \in Z^+. \quad (4)$$

$$E\{\alpha_i(k)\} = P_r\{\sigma(k) = i\} = \alpha_i. \quad (5)$$

where $\sum_{i=1}^{N} \alpha_i(k) = 1$, $\sum_{l=1}^{N} \alpha_i = 1$.

Through the above description, the system (1) and (2), respectively, can be rewritten as

$$\begin{cases} x(k+1) = \sum_{i=1}^{N} \alpha_i(k)\{A_i(k)x(k) + A_{di}(k)x(k-d_k) + B_iu(k) + G_i\omega(k)\} \\ y(k) = \sum_{i=1}^{N} \alpha_i(k)\{C_ix(k) + C_{di}x(k-d_k)\} \\ z(k) = \sum_{i=1}^{N} \alpha_i(k)\{D_ix(k)\}, x(k) = \phi(k), k = -d^M, -d^M + 1, \cdots, 0 \end{cases} \quad (6)$$

$$\begin{cases} \tilde{x}(k+1) = \sum_{i=1}^{N} \alpha_i(k)\{A_i(k)\tilde{x}(k) + A_{di}(k)\tilde{x}(k-d_k) + B_iu(k) + G_i\omega(k) + L_i(y(k) - \tilde{y}(k))\} \\ \tilde{y}(k) = \sum_{i=1}^{N} \alpha_i(k)\{C_i\tilde{x}(k) + C_{di}\tilde{x}(k-d_k)\} \\ u(k) = \sum_{i=1}^{N} \alpha_i(k)\{K_i\tilde{x}(k)\} \end{cases} \quad (7)$$

Define $\bar{x}(k) = \begin{bmatrix} x(k) \\ x(k) - \tilde{x}(k) \end{bmatrix}$, the augmented system can be obtained from (6) and (7)

$$\begin{cases} \bar{x}(k+1) = \sum_{i=1}^{N} \alpha_i(k)\{\bar{A}_i\bar{x}(k) + \bar{A}_{di}\bar{x}(k-d_k) + \bar{G}_i\omega(k)\} \\ \bar{z}(k) = \sum_{i=1}^{N} \alpha_i(k)\{\bar{D}_i\bar{x}(k)\} \\ x(k) = \varphi(k), k = -d^M, -d^M + 1, \ldots, 0 \end{cases} \quad (8)$$

where $\bar{A}_i = \begin{bmatrix} A_i + B_iK_i & -B_iK_i \\ 0 & A_i - L_iC_i \end{bmatrix}$, $\bar{A}_{di} = \begin{bmatrix} A_{di} & 0 \\ 0 & A_{di} - L_iC_{di} \end{bmatrix}$.

Next, we will give the definition of robust H_∞ mean square stability [19]:

Definition 2. Assuming that the system meets the following two conditions:

(1) If for $\omega(k) = 0$, there exists constants $c > 0$ such that

$$E\left\{\sum_{k=0}^{\infty} \|x(k)\|^2\right\} \le c \sup_{-d^M \le i \le 0} E\{\|\phi(i)\|\}^2,$$

(2) If for zero initial conditions, the controlled output $z(k)$ meets

$$E\left\{\sum_{k=0}^{\infty} \|z(k)\|^2\right\} \le \gamma^2 E\left\{\sum_{k=0}^{\infty} \|\omega(k)\|^2\right\}.$$

where $\omega(k) \in l_2 = \{\omega(k) : E\left\{\sum_{k=0}^{\infty} \|\omega(k)\|^2\right\} < \infty\}$, then the system (8) is robust mean square stable, and has the H_∞ performance level γ under zero initial conditions.

3   Main Results

Theorem 1. For given $\gamma > 0$, if there exist symmetric matrices $P_i > 0$, $Q > 0$, $R > 0$ and K_i, $L_i(i \in \Omega)$ with compatible dimensions such that the following inequalities hold

$$
\begin{bmatrix}
\Sigma_{11} & * & * & * \\
\Sigma_{21} & \Sigma_{22} & * & * \\
\Sigma_{31} & 0 & \Sigma_{33} & * \\
\Sigma_{41} & 0 & 0 & -I
\end{bmatrix} < 0,
\tag{9}
$$

where

$$
\Sigma_{11} =
\begin{bmatrix}
-\sum_{i=1}^{N} \alpha_i P_i + Q - R & * & * & * \\
R & -2R & * & * \\
0 & R & -Q - R & * \\
0 & 0 & 0 & -\gamma^2 I
\end{bmatrix},
$$

$$
\Sigma_{21} = d^M
\begin{bmatrix}
\sqrt{\alpha_1}(\bar{A}_1 - I) & \sqrt{\alpha_1}\bar{A}_{d1} & 0 & \sqrt{\alpha_1}\bar{G}_1 \\
\sqrt{\alpha_2}(\bar{A}_2 - I) & \sqrt{\alpha_2}\bar{A}_{d2} & 0 & \sqrt{\alpha_2}\bar{G}_2 \\
\vdots & \vdots & \vdots & \vdots \\
\sqrt{\alpha_N}(\bar{A}_N - I) & \sqrt{\alpha_N}\bar{A}_{dN} & 0 & \sqrt{\alpha_N}\bar{G}_N
\end{bmatrix},
$$

$$
\Sigma_{22} = diag\{-R^{-1}, -R^{-1}, \cdots, -R^{-1}\},
$$

$$
\Sigma_{31} =
\begin{bmatrix}
\Pi_1 \\
\Pi_2 \\
\vdots \\
\Pi_N
\end{bmatrix}, \quad
\Pi_i = \sqrt{\alpha_i}
\begin{bmatrix}
\sqrt{\alpha_1}\bar{A}_1 & \sqrt{\alpha_1}\bar{A}_{d1} & 0 & \sqrt{\alpha_1}\bar{G}_1 \\
\sqrt{\alpha_2}\bar{A}_2 & \sqrt{\alpha_2}\bar{A}_{d2} & 0 & \sqrt{\alpha_2}\bar{G}_2 \\
\vdots & \vdots & \vdots & \vdots \\
\sqrt{\alpha_N}\bar{A}_N & \sqrt{\alpha_N}\bar{A}_{dN} & 0 & \sqrt{\alpha_N}\bar{G}_N
\end{bmatrix},
$$

$$
\Sigma_{33} = diag\{\Lambda_1, \Lambda_2, \ldots, \Lambda_N\}, \quad \Lambda_i = diag\{-P_i^{-1}, -P_i^{-1}, \ldots, -P_i^{-1}\},
$$

$$
\Sigma_{41} =
\begin{bmatrix}
\sqrt{\alpha_1}\bar{D}_1 & 0 & 0 & 0 \\
\sqrt{\alpha_2}\bar{D}_2 & 0 & 0 & 0 \\
\vdots & \vdots & \vdots & \vdots \\
\sqrt{\alpha_N}\bar{D}_N & 0 & 0 & 0
\end{bmatrix}.
$$

then the system (8) is mean square stable, and possesses the H_∞ performance level γ under zero initial conditions.

Proof. Construct the following Lyapunov functional candidate for system (8):

$$V(k) = \bar{x}^T(k) \left(\sum_{i=1}^{N} \alpha_i(k)P_i \right) \bar{x}(k) + \sum_{s=k-d^M}^{k-1} \bar{x}^T(s)Q\bar{x}(s)$$

$$+ d^M \sum_{s=-d^M}^{-1} \sum_{\partial=k+s}^{k-1} y^T(\partial)Ry(\partial), \tag{10}$$

where $i \in \Omega$, $y(k) = \bar{x}(k+1) - \bar{x}(k)$, $E\{\Delta V(k)\} = E\{V(k+1) - V(k)\}$.

Because of

$$E\{\alpha_i(k)\alpha_j(k)\} = \begin{cases} \alpha_i, i = j \\ 0, i \neq j \end{cases}, \tag{11}$$

We obtain

$$E\{\Delta V(k) + \bar{z}^T(k)\bar{z}(k) - \gamma^2 \omega^T(k)\omega(k)\}$$

$$= E\left\{ \bar{x}^T(k+1) \left(\sum_{i=1}^{N} \alpha_i(k+1)P_i \right) \bar{x}(k+1) - \bar{x}^T(k) \left(\sum_{i=1}^{N} \alpha_i(k)P_i \right) \bar{x}(k) \right\}$$

$$+ E\{\bar{x}^T(k)Q\bar{x}(k) - \bar{x}^T(k-d^M)Q\bar{x}(k-d^M)\} \tag{12}$$

$$+ E\left\{ (d^M)^2 y^T(k)Ry(k) - d^M \sum_{\partial=k-d^M}^{k-1} y^T(\partial)Ry(\partial) \right\}$$

$$+ E\{\bar{z}^T(k)\bar{z}(k) - \gamma^2 \omega^T(k)\omega(k)\},$$

By using the Jensen inequality [20]

$$-d^M \sum_{\partial=k-d^M}^{k-1} y^T(\partial)Ry(\partial) \leq \begin{bmatrix} \bar{x}(k) \\ \bar{x}(k-d_k) \\ \bar{x}(k-d^M) \end{bmatrix}^T \begin{bmatrix} -R & R & 0 \\ R & -2R & R \\ 0 & R & -R \end{bmatrix} \begin{bmatrix} \bar{x}(k) \\ \bar{x}(k-d_k) \\ \bar{x}(k-d^M) \end{bmatrix}, \tag{13}$$

Then recalling condition (12), we obtain

$$E\{\Delta V(k) + \bar{z}^T(k)\bar{z}(k) - \gamma^2 \omega^T(k)\omega(k)\}$$

$$\leq E\left\{ \sum_{i=1}^{N} \alpha_i \xi^T(k)T_{1i}^T \left(\sum_{j=1}^{N} \alpha_j P_j \right) T_{1i}\xi(k) - \bar{x}^T(k) \left(\sum_{i=1}^{N} \alpha_i P_i \right) \bar{x}(k) \right\}$$

$$+ E\{\bar{x}^T(k)Q\bar{x}(k) - \bar{x}^T(k-d^M)Q\bar{x}(k-d^M)\}$$

$$+ E\left\{ (d^M)^2 \sum_{i=1}^{N} \alpha_i \xi^T(k)T_{2i}^T R T_{2i}\xi(k) + \xi^T(k)\Psi\xi(k) \right\} \tag{14}$$

$$+ E\left\{ \sum_{i=1}^{N} \alpha_i \xi^T(k)T_{3i}^T T_{3i}\xi(k) - \gamma^2 \omega^T(k)\omega(k) \right\}$$

$$\leq E\{\xi^T(k)\Xi\xi(k)\},$$

where

$$
\begin{aligned}
\xi^T(k) &= \begin{bmatrix} \bar{x}^T(k) & \bar{x}^T(k-d_k) & \bar{x}^T(k-d^M) & \omega^T(k) \end{bmatrix}, \\
T_{1i} &= \begin{bmatrix} \bar{A}_i & \bar{A}_{di} & 0 & \bar{G}_i \end{bmatrix}, \\
T_{2i} &= \begin{bmatrix} \bar{A}_i - I & \bar{A}_{di} & 0 & \bar{G}_i \end{bmatrix}, \\
T_{3i} &= \begin{bmatrix} \bar{D}_i & 0 & 0 & 0 \end{bmatrix}, \\
\Psi &= \begin{bmatrix} -R & R & 0 \\ R & -2R & R \\ 0 & R & -R \end{bmatrix},
\end{aligned}
$$

$$
\begin{aligned}
\Xi = \Xi_{11} &+ \sum_{i=1}^N \alpha_i \xi^T(k) T_{1i}^T (\alpha_1 P_1 + \alpha_2 P_2 + \cdots + \alpha_N P_N) T_{1i} \xi(k) \\
&+ (d^M)^2 \sum_{i=1}^N \alpha_i \xi^T(k) T_{2i}^T R T_{2i} \xi(k) + \sum_{i=1}^N \alpha_i T_{3i}^T T_{3i},
\end{aligned} \tag{15}
$$

By Schur complements, (15) is equivalent to (9), from (9) we can obtain constant $\lambda > 0$ such that

$$
E\{\Delta V(k)\} \leq -\lambda E\{x^T(k)x(k)\}. \tag{16}
$$

Then adding the equation above from $k = 0$ to $k = \infty$, we obtain

$$
E\left\{ \sum_{k=0}^\infty x^T(k)x(k) \right\} \leq \frac{1}{\lambda} E\{V(0)\}. \tag{17}
$$

According to $V(k)$, there exists μ such that

$$
E\{V(0)\} \leq \lambda\mu \sup_{-d^M \leq i \leq 0} E\{\phi^T(k)\phi(k)\}. \tag{18}
$$

From (17) and (18), we conclude that

$$
E\left\{ \sum_{k=0}^\infty x^T(k)x(k) \right\} \leq \mu \sup_{-d^M \leq i \leq 0} E\{\phi^T(k)\phi(k)\}. \tag{19}
$$

Then, by the Definition 2, we can complete the proof.

Remark 2. Because of the variable inverse form existing in the inequality, Eq. (9) is not a strict linear matrix inequality. So this paper will obtain the system gain K_i by adopting the cone complementary linearization method in Laurent EI [21].

4 Illustrative Example

Consider the following switched system (8) with two subsystems, the parameters are

$$A_1 = \begin{bmatrix} 0.82 & 0 \\ 0 & 0.9 \end{bmatrix}, A_2 = \begin{bmatrix} 1.18 & 1 \\ 0 & 1.02 \end{bmatrix},$$

$$A_{d1} = \begin{bmatrix} -0.0125 & -0.005 \\ 0 & 0 \end{bmatrix}, A_{d2} = \begin{bmatrix} -0.0125 & -0.23 \\ 0 & 0 \end{bmatrix},$$

$$B_1 = \begin{bmatrix} 0 \\ 1 \end{bmatrix}, B_2 = \begin{bmatrix} 1 \\ 0 \end{bmatrix}, I = \begin{bmatrix} 1 & 0 \\ 0 & 1 \end{bmatrix},$$

$$C_1 = [3 \ \ 1], C_2 = [1 \ \ 2], C_{d1} = [3 \ \ 1], C_{d2} = [0.2 \ \ 0],$$

$$G_1 = [0 \ \ 0.2], G_2 = [0.5 \ \ 0], D_1 = D_2 = 0.2.$$

In this example, the eigenvalues of A_1 and A_2 respectively are (0.82, 0.90) and (1.18, 1.02). Obviously, the subsystem 1 is stable and the subsystem 2 is unstable. For $d^M = 4, \alpha_1 = 0.8, \alpha_2 = 0.2$, using Theorem 1, the minimum $\gamma_{min} = 0.102$, the controller feedback gains and observer feedback gains are obtained as

$$K_1 = [0.0015 \ \ -0.5656], K_2 = [-1.1475 \ \ -0.8868],$$

$$L_1 = \begin{bmatrix} 0.0092 \\ 0.0127 \end{bmatrix}, L_2 = \begin{bmatrix} 0.5016 \\ 0.1924 \end{bmatrix}.$$

For disturbance $\omega(k) = e^{-k} \sin(0.2\pi k)$, initial condition $\phi(k) = [0.3, 0.1]^T$, by using the corresponding feedback gains in the above, the state error curve and the random switching sequence are displayed in Figs. 1 and 2. From these two figures, it can be found that by using the proposed design method, the computed controller feedback

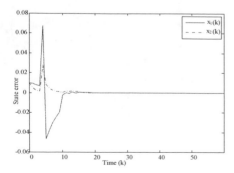

Fig. 1. The state error curve of the system

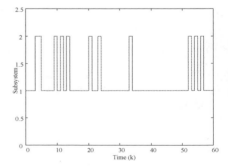

Fig. 2. A random switching sequence

gains and observer gains can stabilize the switched system while guarantee the H_∞ performance.

Next, we want to make clear that the effect of the sojourn probabilities on the system performance. To reach this purpose, we consider the following group of sojourn probability pairs (0.3, 0.7), (0.5, 0.5), (0.6, 0.4), (0.7, 0.3), (0.8, 0.2). The obtained minimum H_∞ performance indexes are different with various groups of sojourn probabilities, which are shown in Table 1. From Table 1, it can be concluded that with the increase of α_1, a better system performance can be obtained. Through this example, we can reach a conclusion that the proposed method can guarantee the mean square stable of the system with prescribed H_∞ performance.

Table 1. γ_{min} with different known sojourn probabilities

	α_1	α_2	γ_{min}
1	0.3	0.7	0.126
2	0.5	0.5	0.123
3	0.6	0.4	0.119
4	0.7	0.3	0.113
5	0.8	0.2	0.102

5 Conclusion

This paper investigates H_∞ control for a class of switched systems with state delay by adopting sojourn probability method. A new kind of switched system model is established with the sojourn probability information. The sufficient condition for H_∞ control with an H_∞ performance index for the switched system is proposed, and then the corresponding method of the output feedback controllers is obtained. Finally, the effectiveness of the developed approach has been illustrated by a simulation example.

Acknowledgements. This work was supported by the National Nature Science Foundation of China (61640313), the Natural Science Foundation of Jiangsu Province of China (No. BK20161561), and partly supported by Innovation Project of JiangSu Province and Six talent peaks project in Jiangsu Province.

References

1. Yu, L., Zhang, A.W.: Analysis and Design of Networked Control System: A Switched System Approach in Chinese. Science Press, Beijing (2012)
2. Hu, Y.H., Zhang, L.M., Tian, E.G.: Robust H_∞ control for discrete switched systems based on sojourn-probability-dependent method. Syst. Sci. Math. Sci. **4**, 372–384 (2015)
3. Perez, C., Benitez, F.: Convergence of switched linear systems with time-delay in detection of switching law. IET Control Theory Appl. **8**(8), 647–654 (2014)
4. Ke-You, Y., Li-Hua, X.: Survey of recent progress in networked control systems. Acta Autom. Sinica **39**(2), 101–117 (2003)

5. Ji, Z., Wang, L., Xie, G.M.: Stabilizing discrete-time switched systems via observer-based static output feedback. In: Proceedings of the IEEE International Conference on Systems, Man and Cybernetics, Washington, USA, pp. 2545–2550. IEEE Press (2003)
6. Scharlau, C.C., de Oliveira, M.C., Trofino, A.: Switching rule design for affine switched systems using a max-type composition rule. Syst. Control Lett. **68**, 1–8 (2014)
7. Jia, H., Li, T.F.: Feedback control of switched neutral systems via observer-based switching. In: 2014 International Conference on Mechatronics and Control (ICMC), pp. 1977–1982. IEEE Press (2014)
8. Zhao, F., Yao, X.M., Su, B.K.: Robust observer-based H_∞ control for a class of discrete-time Markovian jump systems. J. Jilin Univ. (Eng. Technol. Ed.) **40**(1), 136–142 (2010)
9. Yang, H., Zhang, L., Tao, G.: Observer-based robust switching control of switched fuzzy time-delay systems. In: 2016 Chinese Control and Decision Conference (CCDC), China, pp. 4079–4084 (2016)
10. Li, L.L., Shao, C.: Observer-based H∞ output tracking control for a class of switched Lipschitz nonlinear systems. Control Decis. **27**(2), 304–307 (2012)
11. Chaojie, Z., Xiaoli, L., Fei, L.: Observer-based finite-time controller for Markov jump systems with deterministic switches. In: 2015 34th Chinese Control Conference (CCC), China, pp. 1833–1838 (2015)
12. Chen, F., Luan, X., Liu, F.: Observer based finite-time stabilization for discrete-time Markov jump systems with Gaussian transition probabilities. Circuits Syst. Signal Process. **33**(10), 3019–3035 (2014)
13. Tian, E.G., Wong, W.K., Yue, D.: Robust control for switched systems with input delays: a sojourn-probability- dependent method. Inf. Sci. **283**, 22–35 (2014)
14. Meyer, C., Schroder, S., De Doncker, K.W.: Solid-state circuit breakers and current limiters for medium-voltage systems having distributed power systems. IEEE Trans. Power Electron. **19**(5), 1333–1340 (2004)
15. Kim, D.K., Park, P., Ko, J.W.: Output-feedback H∞ control of systems over communication networks using a deterministic switching system approach. Automatica **40**(7), 1205–1212 (2004)
16. Zong, G.D., Wang, R.H., Zheng, W.X.: Finite-time stabilization for a class of switched time-delay systems under asynchronous switching. Appl. Math. Comput. **219**(11), 5757–5771 (2013)
17. Selvi, S., Sakthivel, R., Mathiyalagan, K.: Delay-dependent robust reliable control for uncertain switched neutral systems. Complexity **21**(5), 224–237 (2016)
18. Gao, L.J., Cai, Y.Y.: Finite-time stability of time-delay switched systems with delayed impulse effects. Circuits Syst. Signal Process. **35**(9), 3135–3151 (2016)
19. Feng, X., Loparo, K., Ji, Y., et al.: Stochastic stability properties of jump linear systems. IEEE Trans. Autom. Control **37**(1), 38–53 (1992)
20. Sun, X.M., Zhao, J., David, J.H.: Stability and L2-gain analysis for switched delay systems: a delay-dependent method. IEEE Trans. Autom. Control **42**(10), 1769–1774 (2006)
21. Ghaoui, L.E., Oustry, F., Aitrami, M.: A cone complementarity linearization algorithm for static output-feedback and related problems. IEEE Trans. Autom. Control **42**(8), 1171–1176 (1997)

Event-Triggered Communication and H_∞ Filtering Co-design for Networked Control Systems

Weili Shen[1], Jingqi Fu[1(⊠)], Jie Wu[1], Weihua Bao[2], and Zhengming Gao[2]

[1] Department of Automation, College of Mechatronics Engineering and Automation, Shanghai University, No. 149, Yanchang Rd., Shanghai 200072, China
jqfu@staff.shu.edu.cn
[2] Shanghai Automation Instrumentation Co., Ltd., Shanghai, China

Abstract. In this paper, the issue of event-triggered H_∞ filtering for networked control systems (NCSs) with transmission delay is investigated. First of all, a strategy called event-triggered is introduced where tasks are generated only at the time that the event-triggering condition set before on the sampled measurements of the plant is satisfied. Then considering the double effects of the communication delay and the event-triggering technique, transform the filtering error system into a time-delay system the problem of which can be derived by the existing theory. A co-design method of event-triggered mechanism and H_∞ filtering which also guarantees the asymptotic stability of the NCSs is obtained by constructing a properly Lyapunov-Krasovskii functional and LMI technique based on the new model. Finally an example of verification is given to show the validity of the proposed method.

Keywords: H_∞ filtering design · Event-triggered communication scheme · LMI · NCSs · Lyapunov-Krasovskii functional

1 Introduction

In recent years, the networked control system (NCS) has a significant influence to control systems, especially in industrial process control and real-time control system, for its advantages [1]. However, it also brings a series of problems that reduce the performance of the system and even lead to the instability [2]. Therefore, it is necessary to take negative effects into account when design network-based systems with desired filtering performances. Kalman filtering is a useful way to solve the problem of filtering, but the external noise statistical information need to know in advance [3]. Different from the Kalman filtering approach, H_∞ filtering algorithm can successfully handle the uncertainties of external noises and minimize the infinity norm of the filtering error under bounded external noise interference.

For most NCSs, the measured outputs are sampled in a constant sampling period and all sampled signals will be sent to determine an H_∞ filtering, i.e., time-triggered. Modeling and analysis of NCSs based on this scheme are easy to implement. It is no

© Springer Nature Singapore Pte Ltd. 2017
D. Yue et al. (Eds.): LSMS/ICSEE 2017, Part II, CCIS 762, pp. 535–546, 2017.
DOI: 10.1007/978-981-10-6373-2_54

necessity to send a signal which carries almost no fluctuation information compared the last measurement output. So this kind of triggering method will send "redundant" sampling signals, what is unsuitable from the perspective of network resource utilization and network load reduction [5, 6]. Unlike the time triggering, the event-triggered transport cycle is not fixed and the task is executed only when a prescribed event condition is met, such as, a signal exceeds a given threshold. Accordingly, sampled-data packets are broadcast only when needed and the amount of corresponding tasks will be reduced, which can overcome the drawback of time-triggering [7, 8]. However, after introducing the event triggering mechanism, the difficulty of modeling and analysis of the system will be improved.

In [9], A convex optimization problem with some LMI constraints is formulated to design the H_∞ filtering but based on time-triggered method. In [10], the optimal event-triggered filtering approach has been proposed in linear discrete time systems but based on Kalman filtering method. In [4], the problem of event-based H_∞ filtering for linear continuous system which is exponential stability is studied without considering lower bound delay. In [14], event-based H_∞ filtering for sampled-data systems is developed by an improved inequality for the integral term while maintain satisfactory closed-loop performances. However, there are a few studies on consideration of the network-induced transmission delay, H_∞ filtering problems, and the output signal-dependent event-triggered communication scheme simultaneously up to now, which is the dominant motivation leading to the present research.

The main advantages of this paper will be epitomized as follows: (i) a discrete event-triggered mechanism is proposed which only needs the measured output information at the sampling instants. Consequently, it is convenient for software implementation and the additional hardware devices can be avoided. (ii) a Lyapunov-Krasovskii functional, which can provide less conservatism, is applied to get the event H_∞ filtering under which both the robust stability of the system and a specified H_∞ disturbance rejection attenuation level is met combining with LMI.

2   Problem Statement

2.1   System Description

Consider the following linear time-invariant continuous-time system:

$$\begin{cases} \dot{x}(t) = Ax(t) + B\omega(t) \\ y(t) = Cx(t) + D\omega(t) \\ z(t) = Lx(t) \\ x(0) = x_0 \end{cases} \tag{1}$$

where $x(t) \in R^n$ is the state vector, $y(t) \in R^m$ is the measured output, $\omega(t) \in R^l$ is the external input disturbance which belongs to $L_2[0, \infty)$, and $z(t) \in R^p$ is the signal to be estimated; A, B, C, D and L are constant matrices; $x(t_0) = x_0$ is the initial condition.

Construct the filter for NCSs based on event-triggered mechanism with transmission delay. The structure is shown in Fig. 1. There is an intelligent sensor in the NCSs.

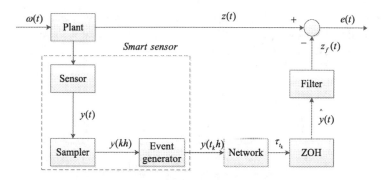

Fig. 1. The structure of event-triggered NCSs with time-varying and filter

The sensor and the sampler are time triggered. The controller and the ZOH are event-triggered. Once a signal data packet has been successfully sent over the network, it is will be continually hold in the ZOH until the next packet arrives. The signal transmission is a single packet, and no data packet loss or disorder. $\tau_{t_k} (k \in N)$ is network-induced delay, which is time-varying and bounded, i.e. $0 < \tau_m < \tau_{t_k} < \tau_M$. N denotes the natural number. The sampling period is h, the sampling instant is kh, and the sampled data $y(kh)$ is transmitted to the event generator directly. $y(t_k h)$ is a measurement signal which is transmitted successfully after the event generator.

The essence of the filtering problem is to estimate $z(t)$ through the system known measured outputs. Consider a full-order estimator, as following:

$$\begin{cases} \dot{x}_f(t) = \Lambda_f x_f(t) + B_f \hat{y}(t) \\ z_f(t) = C_f x_f(t) + D_f \hat{y}(t) \end{cases} \tag{2}$$

where $x_f(t)$ is the filter state vectors, $\hat{y}(t)$ is the filter input vectors, $z_f(t)$ is the estimation output of $z(t)$. A_f, B_f, C_f, D_f are matrices to be designed.

2.2 Event Trigger Mechanism

The event-triggered mechanism which transmits the signals on demand for NCSs with time-varying delay in Fig. 1 is designed as following:

$$\partial^T (t_k h + jh) \Omega \partial (t_k h + jh) \geq \sigma y^T (t_k h + jh) \Omega y(t_k h + jh) \tag{3}$$

where $y(t_k h + jh)$ is the current sampling data of $y(t)$; $y(t_k h)$ is the latest transmitted data of $y(t)$; $\partial(t_k h + jh)$ is the error between the current sampling data $y(t_k h + jh)$ and the latest transmitted sampling signal $y(t_k h)$, $j \in N$; Ω is a positive weighting matrix and enhances the feasibility of the linear matrix inequality compared by $\Omega = I$ [13]; σ is the threshold.

If the sampled data satisfies the given condition, it will be transmitted; otherwise, be neglected. This strategy does not require complex computing bounds of trigger interval and avoids Zeno phenomenon in principle [10]. The release instants of sampled data are $t_0h, t_1h, \ldots, t_kh \ldots$. And denote $\beta_k h = t_{k+1}h - t_k h$ is the transmission period of NCSs based on above event-triggered mechanism. The released sampled-data packets will reach the ZOH at the instants $t_0h + \tau_{t_0}, t_1h + \tau_{t_1}, \ldots, t_kh + \tau_{t_k}, \ldots$.

2.3   Filtering Error System

In combination with above analysis, take the bounded time-varying delay and the event-triggered mechanism (3) into consideration, the filter input can be converted to:

$$\hat{y}(t) = y(t_k h), \ t \in [t_k h + \tau_{t_k}, t_{k+1}h + \tau_{t_{k+1}}) \tag{4}$$

Combining (2) and (4), yields

$$\begin{cases} \dot{x}_f(t) = A_f x_f(t) + B_f y(t_k h) \\ z_f(t) = C_f x_f(t) + D_f y(t_k h) \\ t \in [t_k h + \tau_{t_k}, t_{k+1}h + \tau_{t_{k+1}}) \end{cases} \tag{5}$$

Consult the method in [4], and then analyze and discuss the interval $[t_k h + \tau_{t_k}, t_{k+1}h + \tau_{t_{k+1}})$. Two cases are discussed as follows.

(1) If $t_{k+1}h + \tau_{t_{k+1}} > t_k h + h + \tau_M$, there must be a positive integer d, such that

$$t_k h + dh + \tau_M \le t_{k+1}h + \tau_{t_{k+1}} \le t_k h + (d+1)h + \tau_M \tag{6}$$

Then the interval can be divided into $d + 1$ sub intervals and reconstructed as:

$$[t_k h + \tau_{t_k}, t_{k+1}h + \tau_{t_{k+1}}) = \beta_1 \cup \beta_2 \cup \beta_3 \tag{7}$$

where

$$\beta_1 = [t_k h + \tau_{t_k}, t_k h + h + \tau_M), \beta_2 = \{\cup_{i=1}^{d-1}[t_k h + ih + \tau_M, t_k h + (i+1)h + \tau_M\},$$
$$\beta_3 = [t_k h + dh + \tau_M, t_{k+1}h + \tau_{t_{k+1}})$$

Define a piecewise function $\tau(t)$:

$$\tau(t) = \begin{cases} t - t_k h, t \in \beta_1 \\ t - t_k h - ih, t \in \beta_2, i = 1, 2, \ldots, d - 1 \\ t - t_k h - dh, t \in \beta_3 \end{cases} \tag{8}$$

$\tau(t)$ satisfies $0 < \tau_m \le \tau(t) \le h + \tau_M$, $\dot{\tau}(t) = 1$. Define the error as

$$\partial_k(t) = \begin{cases} 0, t \in \beta_1 \\ y(t_k h + ih) - y(t_k h), t \in \beta_2, i = 1, 2, \ldots d - 1 \\ y(t_k h + dh) - y(t_k h), t \in \beta_3 \end{cases} \tag{9}$$

(2)   If $t_{k+1}h + \tau_{t_{k+1}} \leq t_k h + h + \tau_M$, define a function:

$$\tau(t) = t - t_k h, t \in [t_k h + \tau_{t_k}, t_{k+1} h + \tau_{t_{k+1}}) \qquad (10)$$

In this case, the error can be defined as

$$\partial_k(t) = 0 \qquad (11)$$

Combining (8) and (10), yields

$$\partial_k^T(t)\Omega\partial_k(t) \leq \sigma y^T(t - \tau(t))\Omega y(t - \tau(t)), t \in [t_k h + \tau_{t_k}, t_{k+1} h + \tau_{t_{k+1}}) \qquad (12)$$

Form (8), (9) and (10) together with (11), the state space of the filter in the formula (5) can be represented as:

$$\begin{cases} \dot{x}_f(t) = A_f x_f(t) + B_f y(t - \tau(t)) - B_f \partial_k(t) \\ z_f(t) = C_f x_f(t) + D_f y(t - \tau(t)) - D_f \partial_k(t) \\ t \in [t_k h + \tau_{t_k}, t_{k+1} h + \tau_{t_{k+1}}) \end{cases} \qquad (13)$$

Define $e(t) = z(t) - z_f(t)$, $\xi(t) = [x^T(t)\ x_f^T(t)]^T$, $v(t) = [\omega^T(t)\ \omega^T(t - \tau(t))]^T$, $\phi(t)$ is initial status of the resultant system. Combining (1) and (13), obtain the filtering error system model for NCSs based on event-triggered mechanism as following:

$$\begin{cases} \dot{\xi}(t) = \bar{A}\xi(t) + \bar{E}H\xi(t - \tau(t)) - \bar{B}_e\partial_k(t) + \bar{B}v(t) \\ t \in [t_k h + \tau_{t_k}, t_{k+1} h + \tau_{t_{k+1}}) \\ e(t) = \bar{C}\xi(t) + \bar{F}H\xi(t - \tau(t)) + D_f\partial_k(t) + \bar{D}v(t) \\ \xi(t) = \phi(t), t \in [t_0 - h_2, t_0 - h_1) \end{cases} \qquad (14)$$

where $\bar{A} = \begin{bmatrix} A & 0 \\ 0 & A_f \end{bmatrix}$, $\bar{E} = \begin{bmatrix} 0 \\ B_f C \end{bmatrix}$, $H = [I_n\ \ 0]$, $\bar{B}_e = \begin{bmatrix} 0 \\ B_f \end{bmatrix}$, $\bar{B} = \begin{bmatrix} B & 0 \\ 0 & B_f D \end{bmatrix}$, $\bar{C} = [L\ \ -C_f]$, $\bar{F} = -D_f C$, $\bar{D} = [0\ \ -D_f D]$, $h_1 = \tau_m$, $h_2 = \tau_M + h$.

3   Event-Triggered H_∞ Filtering Performance Analysis

In this section, assuming that the filter parameters are known, an H_∞ filtering analysis criterion for the filtering error system (14) is established by applying Lyapunov-Krasovskii functional approach and LMI method. The stability criterion for the resultant filtering error system (14) is presented in Theorem 1.

Theorem 1. For given positive parameters A_f, B_f, C_f, D_f, Ω, h_1, h_2, γ and threshold parameter σ, under the event-triggered communication scheme (3), the closed-loop system (14) is asymptotically stable with an H_∞ performance index γ for the disturbance attention, if there exist matrixes $P = P^T > 0$, $\Omega > 0$, $Q_i = Q_i^T > 0$, $R_i = R_i^T > 0$ $(i = 1, 2)$, $S = S^T > 0$ with appropriate dimensions, such that

$$\begin{bmatrix} \Phi_{11} & * \\ \Phi_{12}^T & \Phi_{22} \end{bmatrix} < 0 \tag{15}$$

where

$$\Phi_{11} = \begin{bmatrix} \Upsilon_1 & * & * & * & * & * \\ R_1^T H & \Upsilon_2 & * & * & * & * \\ R_2^T H & 0 & \Upsilon_3 & * & * & * \\ \bar{E}^T P & S^T & S^T & \Upsilon_4 & * & * \\ \bar{B}_e^T P & 0 & 0 & 0 & -\Omega & * \\ \bar{B}^T P & 0 & 0 & \sigma[0 \ \ D]^T \Omega C & 0 & \Upsilon_5 \end{bmatrix},$$

$$\Phi_{12}^T = \begin{bmatrix} h_1 R_1 H \bar{A} & 0 & 0 & h_1 R_1 H \bar{E} & -h_1 R_1 H \bar{B}_e & h_1 R_1 H \bar{B} \\ h_2 R_2 H \bar{A} & 0 & 0 & h_2 R_2 H \bar{E} & -h_2 R_2 H \bar{B}_e & h_2 R_1 H \bar{B} \\ \alpha S H \bar{A} & 0 & 0 & \alpha S H \bar{E} & -\alpha S H \bar{B}_e & \alpha S H \bar{B} \\ \bar{C} & 0 & 0 & \bar{F} & D_f & \bar{D} \end{bmatrix}$$

$\Upsilon_1 = P\bar{A} + \bar{A}^T P + H^T Q_1 H + H^T Q_2 H - H^T R_1 H - H^T R_2 H, \ \Upsilon_2 = -Q_1 - R_1 - S,$
$\Upsilon_3 = -Q_2 - R_2 - S, \ \Upsilon_4 = -2S + \sigma C^T \Omega C, \ \Upsilon_5 = \sigma_1 [0 \ \ D]^T \Omega[0 \ \ D] - \gamma^2 K^T K,$
$\Phi_{22} = diag\{-R_1, -R_2, -S, -I\}, \ K = [I_l \ \ 0], \ \alpha = h_2 - h_1$

The notation $X > 0$ denotes a real symmetric positive definite. Diag{} denotes the block-diagonal matrix. "*" is used as the ellipsis for terms induced by symmetry.

Proof. Select a Lyapunov-Krasovskii functional:

$$V(t, \xi(t)) = V_1(t, \xi(t)) + V_2(t, \xi(t)) + V_3(t, \xi(t)) \tag{16}$$

where

$V_1(t, \xi(t)) = \xi^T(t) P \xi(t)$

$V_2(t, \xi(t)) = \int_{t-h_1}^t \xi^T(s) H^T Q_1 H \xi(s) ds + \int_{t-h_2}^t \xi^T(s) H^T Q_2 H \xi(s) ds$

$V_3(t, \xi(t)) = h_1 \int_{-h_1}^0 \int_{t+s}^t \dot{\xi}^T(v) H^T R_1 H \dot{\xi}(v) dv ds + h_2 \int_{-h_2}^0 \int_{t+s}^t \dot{\xi}^T(v) H^T R_2 H \dot{\xi}(v) dv ds$

$\qquad\qquad + \alpha \int_{-h_2}^{-h_1} \int_{t+s}^t \dot{\xi}^T(v) H^T S H \dot{\xi}(v) dv ds$

Taking the derivative of $V(t, \xi(t))$ with respect to t along the trajectory of (14) obtains

$$\dot{V}(t, \xi(t)) = \dot{V}_1(t, \xi(t)) + \dot{V}_2(t, \xi(t)) + \dot{V}_3(t, \xi(t)) \tag{17}$$

where

$$\dot{V}_1(t, \xi(t)) = 2\xi^T(t)P\dot{\xi}(t)$$

$$\dot{V}_2(t, \xi(t)) = \xi^T(t)H^TQ_1H\xi(t) - \xi^T(t-h_1)H^TQ_1H\xi(t-h_1)$$
$$+ \xi^T(t)H^TQ_2H\xi(t) - \xi^T(t-h_2)H^TQ_2H\xi(t-h_2)$$

$$\dot{V}_3(t, \xi(t)) = \dot{\xi}(t)[h_1^2H^TR_1H + h_2^2H^TR_2H + \alpha^2H^TSH]\dot{\xi}(t)$$
$$- h_1\int_{t-h_1}^t \dot{\xi}^T(s)H^TR_1H\dot{\xi}(s)ds - h_2\int_{t-h_2}^t \dot{\xi}^T(s)H^TR_2H\dot{\xi}(s)ds$$
$$- \alpha\int_{t-h_2}^{t-h_1} \dot{\xi}^T(s)H^TSH\dot{\xi}(s)ds + \partial_k^T(t)\Omega\partial_k(t) - \partial_k^T(t)\Omega\partial_k(t)$$

Applying Jensen's inequality to deal with the integral items in (17), to obtain:

$$-\alpha\int_{t-h_2}^{t-h_1} \dot{\xi}^T(s)H^TSH\dot{\xi}(s)ds$$
$$= -\alpha[\int_{t-\tau(t)}^{t-h_1} \dot{\xi}^T(s)H^TSH\dot{\xi}(s)ds + \int_{t-h_2}^{t-\tau(t)} \dot{\xi}^T(s)H^TSH\dot{\xi}(s)ds]$$
$$\leq -(\xi^T(t-h_1)H^T \ \ \xi^T(t-\tau(t))H^T)\begin{pmatrix} S & -S \\ -S & S \end{pmatrix}\begin{pmatrix} H\xi(t-h_1) \\ H\xi(t-\tau(t)) \end{pmatrix}$$
$$- (\xi^T(t-\tau(t))H^T \ \ \xi^T(t-h_2)H^T)\begin{pmatrix} S & -S \\ -S & S \end{pmatrix}\begin{pmatrix} H\xi(t-\tau(t)) \\ H\xi(t-h_2) \end{pmatrix} \tag{18}$$

$$-h_1\int_{t-h_1}^t \dot{\xi}^T(s)H^TR_1H\dot{\xi}(s)ds$$
$$\leq -(\xi^T(t) \ \ \xi^T(t-h_1)H^T)\begin{pmatrix} H^TR_1H & -H^TR_1 \\ -R_1H & R_1 \end{pmatrix}\begin{pmatrix} \xi(t) \\ H\xi(t-h_1) \end{pmatrix} \tag{19}$$

$$-h_2\int_{t-h_2}^t \dot{\xi}^T(s)H^TR_2H\dot{\xi}(s)ds$$
$$\leq -(\xi^T(t) \ \ \xi^T(t-h_2)H^T)\begin{pmatrix} H^TR_2H & -H^TR_2 \\ -R_2H & R_2 \end{pmatrix}\begin{pmatrix} \xi(t) \\ H\xi(t-h_2) \end{pmatrix} \tag{20}$$

Define

$$\eta^T(t) = [\xi^T(t) \ \xi^T(t-h_1)H^T \ \xi^T(t-\tau(t))H^T \ \xi^T(t-h_2)H^T \ \partial_k(t) \ v^T(t)] \tag{21}$$

Combining (12) and (16–21), by Schur complements, then we can get:

$$\dot{V}(t) \leq \eta^T(t)\Phi\eta(t) - e^T(t)e(t) + \gamma^2\omega^T(t)\omega(t) \tag{22}$$

where $\omega(t) = Kv(t)$, $\Phi = \Phi_{11} - \Phi_{12}\Phi_{22}^{-1}\Phi_{12}^T$, Φ_{11}, Φ_{12}^T and Φ_{22} have been defined in Theorem 1. By Schur complements and using the Lyapunov-Krasovskii functional (16) guarantee that $\dot{V}(t, \xi(t)) < 0$ in (17); derive the closed-loop system (14) with $\omega(t) \equiv 0$ is asymptotically stable and $\|e(t)\|_2 \leq \gamma\|\omega(t)\|_2$ under the zero initial condition.

4   Co-design of Event-Triggered Communication and H_∞ Filter

In this section, for closed-loop system (5), an approach to the co-design of the reasonable filter parameters and the threshold parameter Ω under the event condition is proposed based on the Theorem 1.

Theorem 2. For given positive parameters h_1, h_2, γ and threshold parameter σ, under the event-trigged communication scheme (3), the closed-loop system (14) is asymptotically stable with an H_∞ performance index γ for the disturbance attention, if there exist matrices $P_1 > 0$, $\Omega > 0$, $Q_i = Q_i^T > 0$, $R_i = R_i^T > 0$ $(i = 1, 2)$, $S = S^T > 0$, $M > 0$, $\bar{A}_f$, $\bar{B}_f$, $\bar{C}_f$, $\bar{D}_f$ with appropriate dimensions, such that $P_1 - M > 0$ and the following matrix inequity holds

$$\begin{bmatrix} \Phi'_{11} & * \\ \Phi'^{T}_{12} & \Phi'_{22} \end{bmatrix} < 0 \tag{23}$$

Parameters of the filter can be designed as:

$$A_f = M^{-1}\bar{A}_f, \, B_f = M^{-1}\bar{B}_f, \, C_f = \bar{C}_f, \, D_f = \bar{D}_f$$

or

$$A_f = \bar{A}_f M^{-1}, \, B_f = \bar{B}_f, \, C_f = \bar{C}_f M^{-1}, \, D_f = \bar{D}_f$$

where

$$\Phi'^{T}_{12} = \begin{bmatrix} h_1 R_1 A & 0 & 0 & 0 & 0 & 0 & h_1 R_1 B & 0 \\ h_2 R_2 A & 0 & 0 & 0 & 0 & 0 & h_2 R_2 B & 0 \\ \alpha S A & 0 & 0 & 0 & 0 & 0 & \alpha S B & 0 \\ L & -\bar{C}_f & 0 & 0 & -\bar{D}_f C & \bar{D}_f & 0 & -\bar{D}_f D \end{bmatrix}$$

$$\Phi'_{11} = \begin{bmatrix} \bar{\Upsilon}_1 & * & * & * & * & * & * & * \\ MA + \bar{A}_f^T & \bar{A}_f + \bar{A}_f^T & * & * & * & * & * & * \\ R_1^T & 0 & \Upsilon_2 & * & * & * & * & * \\ R_2^T & 0 & 0 & \Upsilon_3 & * & * & * & * \\ C^T \bar{B}_f^T & C^T \bar{B}_f^T & S^T & S^T & \Upsilon_4 & * & * & * \\ \bar{B}_f^T & \bar{B}_f^T & 0 & 0 & 0 & -\Omega & * & * \\ B^T P_1 & B^T M & 0 & 0 & 0 & 0 & -\gamma^2 I_l & * \\ D^T \bar{B}_f^T & D^T \bar{B}_f^T & 0 & 0 & \sigma D^T \Omega C & 0 & 0 & \sigma D^T \Omega D \end{bmatrix}$$

$\Phi'_{22} = diag\{-R_1 \quad -R_2 \quad -S \quad -I\}$, $\bar{\Upsilon}_1 = P_1 A + A^T P_1 + Q_1 + Q_2 - R_1 - R_2$

Proof. Define $J_1 = diag\{I \quad P_2 P_3^{-1}\}$, $J_2 = diag\{J_1 \quad I \quad I \quad I \quad I \quad I \quad I\}$, pre and post multiplying both sides of (15) with J and its transpose respectively. Here we define $M = P_2 P_3^{-1} P_2^T$, $\bar{A}_f = P_2 A_f P_3^{-1} P_2^T$, $\bar{B}_f = P_2 B_f$, $\bar{C}_f = C_f P_3^{-1} P_2^T$, $\bar{D}_f = D_f$. It is easy to get (23) from (15). Consequently, system (14) is asymptotically stable and with an H_∞ performance index γ for the disturbance attention by Theorem 2.

$P = [P_{ij}]_{2 \times 2} > 0$ is equivalent to $P_1 - P_2 P_3^{-1} P_2^T = P_1 - M > 0$ by applying Schur complement. According to the definition of $\bar{A}_f$, $\bar{B}_f$, $\bar{C}_f$, $\bar{D}_f$, we can obtain:

$$
\begin{bmatrix} A_f & B_f \\ C_f & D_f \end{bmatrix} = \begin{bmatrix} P_2^{-1} & 0 \\ 0 & I \end{bmatrix} \begin{bmatrix} \bar{A}_f & \bar{B}_f \\ \bar{C}_f & \bar{D}_f \end{bmatrix} \begin{bmatrix} P_2^{-T} P_3 & 0 \\ 0 & I \end{bmatrix}
\tag{24}
$$

This completes the proof.

5   An Illustrative Example

In this section, a simulation example is given to show the effectiveness of the proposed filter design method developed in this paper. The simulation platform adopts MATLAB, and the related parameters can be solved through the LMI toolbox.

Consider a quarter-car model depicted in Fig. 2. The state space expression and parameters of the quarter-car model in this example are the same as [11]. The purpose here is to identify a filter to estimate $\dot{z}_s(t)$.

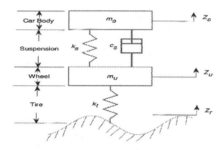

Fig. 2. The structure of active suspension system

Under the given performance index $\gamma = 0.2$, select the sampling period $h = 0.1$, $h_1 = 0.01$, $h_2 = 0.11$ and the threshold $\sigma = 0, 0.1, 0.2, 0.3, 0.4, 0.5$, respectively [4]. Applying Theorem 2 to get the different average transmission period $\bar{h}$ and the proportion of sensor sent data χ as shown in Table 1.

Table 1. Results of different σ_1 with given $\gamma = 0.2$

σ	0	0.1	0.2	0.3	0.4	0.5
Ω	53554	58.4531	32.7579	23.2908	17.7079	13.8569
$\bar{h}$	0.1	0.1406	0.1644	0.1803	0.2021	0.2256
χ	100%	69%	59%	53%	48%	43%

As shown in the Table 1, the event-triggered parameter Ω becomes smaller, the average transmission period h and the proportion of sensor sent data χ are larger when the threshold σ increases within certain range. Not all sampled signals are sent through a communication channel, so the event-triggering allows an effective reduction of the network burden and takes full advantage of the limited resources.

Then choose the parameters $\sigma = 0.2, \gamma = 0.9, h_1 = 0.01, h_2 = 0.11$ and obtain the event-triggered matrices and the filter parameter matrices by Theorem 2 as following:

$$A_f = \begin{bmatrix} 0.0 & 0.0 & -0.9 & 0.5 \\ 136.9 & -33.1 & -624.9 & 3391.1 \\ 44.0 & 0 & 2.8 & -1.6 \\ -368.5 & 887.0 & -57.7 & 196.3 \end{bmatrix}, \; B_f = [0.5 \quad -3213.8 \quad -1.4 \quad -161.0]^T$$

$$C_f = [-0.0003 \quad -0.0001 \quad 0.0017 \quad 0.0012], \; D_f = 0.1538, \; \Omega = 36.8407$$

Suppose there is an external disturbance input, choose $b = 0.2, d = 5m, h = 0.1s$.

$$\omega(t) = \begin{cases} \frac{b\pi v}{d}\sin(\frac{2\pi v}{d}t), & if \; 0 \le t < 10 \\ 0, & otherwise \end{cases} \tag{25}$$

The corresponding system estimation signal $z(t)$ and $zf(t)$ is clearly shown in Fig. 4. The time at which the estimation signal reaches equilibrium is less than in [12]. The system based on event-triggered method in this paper has good dynamic characteristics. A conclusion can be drawn that the H_∞ filter which has been designed is able to produce a good estimation on the signal $z(t)$ from Fig. 4.

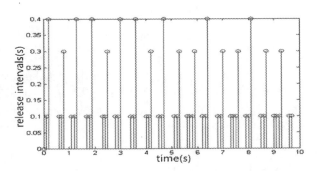

Fig. 3. The release instants and release intervals of sampling signals

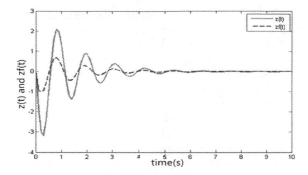

Fig. 4. The estimated signal $z(t)$ and $z_f(t)$

6 Conclusion Remarks

In this paper, the problem of event-triggered H_∞ filtering for NCSs has been studied. To save limited network resources, an event-triggered mechanism implemented by software is proposed through which the transmission data quantity can be reduced. Considering the influence of the time-varying transmission delay and the novel scheduling scheme, the filtering error system has been converted into an interval time-delay system. Based on the new model, the asymptotic stability of the NCSs filtering is studied by using Lyapunov stability theory and LMI technique. Since the proposed stability criterion, a cooperative design method of event-triggered mechanism and H_∞ filtering is obtained. However, there are other important research issues that need further study as well, such as the uncertainties or packet loss of the system (Fig. 3).

Acknowledgments. This work was financially supported by the Science and Technology Commission of Shanghai Municipality of China under Grant (No. 17511107002).

References

1. Yan, H.C., Yan, S., Zhang, H., Shi, H.B.: Event-triggered H_∞ control for networked control systems with time-varying delay. Math. Probl. Eng. **2014**(1), 1–7 (2014)
2. You, K.Y., Xie, L.H.: Survey of recent progress in studying networked control systems. Acta Autom. Sinica **39**(2), 101–117 (2013)
3. Song, H., Yu, L., Zhang, W.A.: H∞ filtering of network-based systems with random delay. Signal Process. **89**(4), 615–622 (2009)
4. Hu, S., Yue, D.: Event-based H ∞, filtering for networked system with communication delay. Signal Process. **92**(9), 2029–2039 (2012)
5. Donkers, M., Heemels, W.: Output-based event-triggered control with guaranteed L_∞ gain and improved event-triggering. In: Proceedings of the 49th IEEE Conference on Decision and Control, pp. 3246–3251 (2010)

6. Heemels, W., Donkers, M., Teel, A.: Periodic event-triggered control based on state feedback. In: Proceedings of the Joint 50th IEEE Conference on Decision and Control and 50th European Control Conference, pp. 2571–2576 (2011)
7. Arzen, K.: A simple event-based PID controller. In: Proceedings of the 14th IFAC World Congress, pp. 423–428 (1999)
8. Peng, C., Yang, T.C.: Event-triggered communication and control co-design for networked control system. Automatic **49**(5), 1326–1332 (2013)
9. Lien, C.H., Chen, J.D., Lee, C.T., et al.: Robust H∞ filter design for discrete-time switched systems with interval time-varying delay and linear fractional perturbations: LMI optimization approach. Appl. Math. Comput. **219**(24), 11395–11407 (2013)
10. Borgers, D.P., Heemels, W.P.M.H.: Event-separation properties of event-triggered control systems. IEEE Trans. Autom. Control **59**(10), 2644–2656 (2014)
11. Wu, J., Chen, X., Gao, H.: H_∞ filtering with stochastic sampling. Signal Process. **90**(4), 1131–1145 (2010)
12. Yan, S., Yan, H.C., Shi, H.B., et al.: Event-triggered H_∞ filtering for networked control systems with time-varying delay. In: Proceedings of the 33rd Chinese Control Conference, Nanjing, China, 28–30 July 2014, pp. 5869–5874 (2014)
13. Zhang, X.M., Han, Q.L.: Event-based H_∞ filtering for sampled-data systems. Automatica **51**, 55–69 (2015)

State Estimation for Discrete-Time Complex Dynamical Networks with Markovian Packet Losses

Shengnan Cao and Youhong Wan[✉]

College of Automation, Nanjing University of Posts and Telecommunications,
Nanjing 210023, China
wanyh@njupt.edu.cn

Abstract. In this paper, the state estimation problem is investigated for discrete-time output coupled complex networks with Markovian packet losses. Unlike the majority of emerging research on state estimation with Bernoulli packet dropout, the Markov chain is used to describe the random packet losses. In use of the Lyapunov functional theory and stochastic analysis method, the explicit description of the estimator gains is presented in the form of the solution to certain linear matrix inequalities (LMIs). At last, simulations are exploited to illustrate the proposed estimator design scheme is applicable.

Keywords: Complex networks · Markovian packet losses · State estimation

1 Introduction

Recently, the increasing interests have been attracted to the complexity of networks due to the successful research results in some practical fields such as biological, physical sciences, social and engineering [1]. With the presentation of small-world and scale-free characters of complex networks [2, 3], amount of efforts have been devoted to investigating the dynamical behaviours of complex networks in several different domains, mainly involving synchronization, state estimation, fault diagnosis and topology identification.

With the emergence of the large scale networks, it is common that merely partial information of nodes is accessible in the network outputs [4, 5]. It is imperative to estimate the unknown states of nodes via an effective state estimator. Lots of research achievements have been obtained for state estimation of complex networks [6–9]. For instance, state estimation of complex neural network with time delays was discussed in [6]. Moreover, state estimation of complex networks concerning the transmission channel with noise was studied in [8]. Also, state estimation for complex networks with random occurring delays was investigated in [9].

This work is supported by National Natural Science Foundation (NNSF) of China under Grant 61374180 and 61573194.

D. Yue et al. (Eds.): LSMS/ICSEE 2017, Part II, CCIS 762, pp. 547–556, 2017.
DOI: 10.1007/978-981-10-6373-2_55

In reality, transmission congestion probably lead to packet dropout in network linking, which has an influence on the performance of complex networks. There exists some research concerning Bernoulli packet dropout for complex networks [10–12].

The robust filtering for complex networks with Bernoulli packet dropout was studied in [10]. Similarly, the synchronization of complex networks with Bernoulli packet losses was investigated in [11]. In addition, state estimation for complex networks with stochastic packet dropout that described as a Bernoulli random variable was studied in [12].

In practical networked systems, especially in wireless communication networks, the random packet dropout is often regarded as a time-relevant Markov process. That is to say, the Markovian packet losses model would sufficiently utilize the temporal relevance of channel conditions in the process of transmission. As a result, some research achievements have been existed on Markovian packet dropout for the networked systems [13–16]. Minimum data rate stability in the mean square with Markovian packet losses was studied in [15]. Also, stabilization of uncertain systems with random packet losses which described as a Markov chain was investigated in [16]. However, the research considering Markovian packet losses for state estimation of complex dynamical networks is relatively scarce.

In the paper, we focus on the state estimation for discrete-time complex networks with Markovian packet losses, where the transition probability is known. The network is output coupled that could economize on the channel resource. An effective state estimator is established to ensure such the stability of the state error. By employing the Lyapunov stability approach plus stochastic analysis theory, we derive the criteria sufficiently in the form of LMIs.

The rest of this paper is arranged as follows. In Sect. 2, an output coupled complex network with Markovian packet losses and the corresponding state estimator are presented. In Sect. 3, a sufficient criteria is exploited in terms of LMIs and the desired estimator gain matrix is obtained. In Sect. 4, illustrative simulations are provided to testify the applicability of the results derived. In the end, conclusions are drawn in Sect. 5.

2   Problem Formulation

We consider the following discrete-time complex network consisting of N coupled nonlinear nodes:

$$\begin{cases} x_i(k+1) = A_i x_i(k) + f(x_i(k)) + \sum_{j=1}^{N} w_{ij} \Gamma y_j(k) \\ y_i(k) = C_i x_i(k) \quad (i = 1, 2, \ldots, N) \end{cases} \tag{1}$$

where $x_i(k) = (x_{i1}(k), x_{i2}(k), \ldots, x_{in}(k))^T \in R^n$ denote the state vector of the ith node, $y_i(k) \in R^m$ is the output vector of the ith node, $A_i \in R^{n \times n}$ denotes a constant matrix, $f(\cdot) : R^n \times R^n$ represents a nonlinear function with $f(0) \equiv 0$, $W = (w_{ij})_{N \times N}$ is the coupling configuration matrix which describes the topological structure of the network.

If there is a connection from node i to node $j (j \neq i)$, then $w_{ij} = 1$; otherwise $w_{ij} = 0$. As usual, matrix W satisfies $w_{ii} = -\sum_{j=1, j \neq i}^{N} w_{ij}$, $\Gamma \in R^{n \times n}$ is the inner coupling matrix, $C_i \in R^{m \times n}$ stands for the output matrix.

In fact, it is quite tough to access the states of some complex networks completely. In order to obtain the state variables of network (1), the output $y_i(k)$ is transmitted to the observer network. Actually, losing data such as packet dropout may occur in the process of transmission. So it is of great value to take the advantage of accessible state information to approximate the unknown information of nodes in network (1), regardless of packet losses.

In this paper, the network measurements from the transmission channel are of the following form:

$$\bar{y}_i(k) = r_i(k) y_i(k) \quad (i = 1, 2, \ldots, N) \tag{2}$$

where $\bar{y}_i(k) \in R^m$ is the actual measured output. The random variable $r_i(k) \in \{0, 1\}$ indicates the state of the packet at time k. If $r_i(k) = 0$ then the packet is lost; else it would succeed. The process of packet in the transmission channel is regarded as a Markov chain with two states: reception and loss. Furthermore, the transition probability matrix of the Markov chain is defined by

$$\Lambda_i = Prob(r_i(k+1) = c \mid r_i(k) = b)_{b,c \in \zeta} = \begin{bmatrix} 1 - q & q \\ p & 1 - p \end{bmatrix} \tag{3}$$

where $\zeta = \{0, 1\}$ is the state space of the Markov chain, p is the failure probability when the previous packet succeed, and q is the recovery probability from the loss state. To make the process $\{r_i(k)\}$ ergodic, we believe that $p, q \in (0, 1)$. Without loss of generality, the transmitted signal in the initial state is assumed received successfully, that is, $r_i(0) = 1$.

For the purpose of estimating the states of network (1), we construct a state estimator as follows:

$$\begin{cases} \hat{x}_i(k+1) = A_i \hat{x}_i(k) + f(\hat{x}_i(k)) + \sum_{j=1}^{N} w_{ij} \Gamma \hat{y}_j(k) + K_i(\bar{y}_i(k) - \hat{y}_i(k)) \\ \hat{y}_i(k) = C_i \hat{x}_i(k) \quad (i = 1, 2, \ldots, N) \end{cases} \tag{4}$$

where $\hat{x}_i(k) = (\hat{x}_{i1}(k), \hat{x}_{i2}(k), \ldots, \hat{x}_{in}(k))^T \in R^n$ represents the estimation states of the nodes in network (1). $\hat{y}_i(k) \in R^m$ denotes the output of the nodes in network (4), $K_i \in R^{n \times m}$ stands for the observer gain to be determined.

By applying the Kronecker product, networks (1), (2) and (4) can be expressed as the following concise form:

$$\begin{cases} x(k+1) = Ax(k) + f(x(k)) + (W \otimes \Gamma) y(k) \\ y(k) = Cx(k) \end{cases} \tag{5}$$

$$\bar{y}(k) = r(k)Cx(k) \tag{6}$$

$$\begin{cases} \hat{x}(k+1) = A\hat{x}(k) + f(\hat{x}(k)) + (W \otimes \Gamma)\hat{y}(k) + K[\bar{y}(k) - \hat{y}(k)] \\ \hat{y}(k) = C\hat{x}(k) \end{cases} \tag{7}$$

where

$x(k) = (x_1^T(k), x_2^T(k), \ldots, x_N^T(k))^T$, $\hat{x}(k) = (\hat{x}_1^T(k), \hat{x}_2^T(k), \ldots, \hat{x}_N^T(k))^T$,
$y(k) = (y_1^T(k), y_2^T(k), \ldots, y_N^T(k))^T$, $\hat{y}_i(k) = (\hat{y}_1^T(k), \hat{y}_2^T(k), \ldots, \hat{y}_N^T(k))^T$,
$\bar{y}_i(k) = (\bar{y}_1^T(k), \bar{y}_2^T(k), \ldots, \bar{y}_N^T(k))^T$,
$f(x(k)) = (f^T(x_1(k)), f^T(x_2(k)), \ldots, f^T(x_N(k)))^T$,
$f(\hat{x}(k)) = (f^T(\hat{x}_1(k)), f^T(\hat{x}_2(k)), \ldots, f^T(\hat{x}_N(k)))^T$, $A = diag\{A_1, A_2, \ldots, A_N\}$,
$C = diag\{C_1, C_2, \ldots, C_N\}$, $K = diag\{K_1, K_2, \ldots, K_N\}$,
$r(k) = (diag\{r_1(k), r_2(k), \ldots, r_N(k)\}) \otimes I_n$, I_n is the identical matrix of n
dimensions.

Letting the state error be

$$\tilde{x}(k+1) = x(k+1) - \hat{x}(k+1) \tag{8}$$

It follows from (5)–(7) that

$$\begin{aligned} \tilde{x}(k+1) &= A[x(k) - \hat{x}(k)] + [f(x(k)) - f(\hat{x}(k))] + (W \otimes \Gamma)C[x(k) - \hat{x}(k)] \\ &\quad - K[r(k)Cx(k) - C\hat{x}(k)] \\ &= A\tilde{x}(k) + \tilde{f}(x(k)) + (W \otimes \Gamma)C\tilde{x}(k) - K[r(k)Cx(k) - C\hat{x}(k)] \\ &= A\tilde{x}(k) + \tilde{f}(x(k)) + (W \otimes \Gamma)C\tilde{x}(k) - KC\tilde{x}(k) + K(I_{Nn} - r(k))Cx(k) \\ &= \tilde{f}(x(k)) + [(A - KC) + (W \otimes \Gamma)C]\tilde{x}(k) + K(I_{Nn} - r(k))Cx(k) \end{aligned}$$

where $\tilde{x}(k) = x(k) - \hat{x}(k)$, $\tilde{f}(x(k)) = f(x(k)) - f(\hat{x}(k))$. For the sake of concise expression, we could assume that $H = I_{Nn} - r(k)$ and $0 < H < I_{Nn}$, then

$$\tilde{x}(k+1) = [(A - KC) + (W \otimes \Gamma)C]\tilde{x}(k) + \tilde{f}(x(k)) + KHCx(k) \tag{9}$$

Since that $x(k)$ and $\tilde{x}(k)$ both exist in (9) at the same time, we take the augmented state vector to be

$$e(k) = \begin{bmatrix} x(k) \\ \tilde{x}(k) \end{bmatrix} \tag{10}$$

It follows from (5) and (9) that

$$e(k+1) = \begin{bmatrix} x(k+1) \\ \tilde{x}(k+1) \end{bmatrix}$$
$$= \begin{bmatrix} Ax(k) + f(x(k)) + (W \otimes \Gamma)Cx(k) \\ [(A-KC)+(W\otimes\Gamma)C]\tilde{x}(k) + \tilde{f}(x(k)) + KHCx(k) \end{bmatrix}$$
$$= \begin{bmatrix} f(x(k)) \\ \tilde{f}(x(k)) \end{bmatrix} + \begin{bmatrix} A+(W\otimes\Gamma)C & 0 \\ KHC & (A-KC)+(W\otimes\Gamma)C \end{bmatrix} \begin{bmatrix} x(k) \\ \tilde{x}(k) \end{bmatrix}$$
$$= \begin{bmatrix} f(x(k)) \\ \tilde{f}(x(k)) \end{bmatrix} + \begin{bmatrix} A+(W\otimes\Gamma)C & 0 \\ 0 & (A-KC)+(W\otimes\Gamma)C \end{bmatrix} \begin{bmatrix} x(k) \\ \tilde{x}(k) \end{bmatrix} + \begin{bmatrix} 0 & 0 \\ KHC & 0 \end{bmatrix} \begin{bmatrix} x(k) \\ \tilde{x}(k) \end{bmatrix}$$
$$= \begin{bmatrix} f(x(k)) \\ \tilde{f}(x(k)) \end{bmatrix} + \begin{bmatrix} A+(W\otimes\Gamma)C & 0 \\ 0 & (A-KC)+(W\otimes\Gamma)C \end{bmatrix} \begin{bmatrix} x(k) \\ \tilde{x}(k) \end{bmatrix} + \begin{bmatrix} 0 & 0 \\ 0 & K \end{bmatrix} \begin{bmatrix} 0 & 0 \\ HC & 0 \end{bmatrix} \begin{bmatrix} x(k) \\ \tilde{x}(k) \end{bmatrix}$$

suppose

$$B = \begin{bmatrix} A+(W\otimes\Gamma)C & 0 \\ 0 & (A-KC)+(W\otimes\Gamma)C \end{bmatrix}, \quad D_1 = \begin{bmatrix} 0 & 0 \\ 0 & K \end{bmatrix}, \quad D_2 = \begin{bmatrix} 0 & 0 \\ HC & 0 \end{bmatrix},$$
$$h(x(k), \hat{x}(k)) = \begin{bmatrix} f(x(k)) \\ \tilde{f}(x(k)) \end{bmatrix},$$

then

$$e(k+1) = Be(k) + D_1 D_2 e(k) + h(x(k), \hat{x}(k)) \tag{11}$$

Before deriving the main results, an available assumption and a useful lemma are given as follows throughout this paper.

Assumption 1: Suppose that $f(0) = 0$ and there exists a positive constant a such that

$$||f(u) - f(v)|| \leq a||u - v||, \forall u, v \in R^n.$$

Lemma 1 (Schur Complement): For a given real symmetric matrix $\Pi = \begin{bmatrix} \Pi_{11} & \Pi_{21} \\ \Pi_{12} & \Pi_{22} \end{bmatrix}$, where $\Pi_{11} = \Pi_{11}^T$, $\Pi_{12} = \Pi_{21}^T$, $\Pi_{22} = \Pi_{22}^T$, the condition $\Pi < 0$ is equivalent to

$$\begin{cases} \Pi_{22} < 0 \\ \Pi_{11} - \Pi_{12} \Pi_{22}^{-1} \Pi_{12}^T < 0 \end{cases}.$$

3   Main Results

In the section, the LMIs approach is applied to deal with the issue on state estimation of network (1), which was put forward previously.

Theorem 1: Under Assumption 1, network (4) becomes an effective state estimator of network (1) if there exist such matrixes $P = P_{r(k)} > 0$, $\bar{P} = P_{r(k+1)} = (\Lambda \otimes I_n)$ $P_{r(k)} > 0$, that $P = P^T = \begin{bmatrix} P_1 & 0 \\ 0 & P_2 \end{bmatrix}$, $\bar{P} = \bar{P}^T = \begin{bmatrix} \bar{P}_1 & 0 \\ 0 & \bar{P}_2 \end{bmatrix}$ and $\Lambda = diag$ $(\Lambda_1, \Lambda_2, \ldots, \Lambda_N)$, matrix K, scalar $\alpha > 0$ such that the LMI $\varphi < 0$ in (12) hold.

$$\varphi = \begin{bmatrix} \pi_1 & \pi_2 & A^T\bar{P}_1 + C^T(W \otimes \Gamma)^T\bar{P}_1 & C^T H^T K^T \bar{P}_2 & C^T H^T K^T \bar{P}_2 & 0 \\ * & \pi_3 - C^T K^T \bar{P}_2 KC & 0 & \pi_4 & -C^T K^T \bar{P}_2 & C^T K^T \bar{P}_2 \\ * & * & \bar{P}_1 - \alpha I & 0 & 0 & 0 \\ * & * & * & \bar{P}_2 - \alpha I & 0 & 0 \\ * & * & * & * & -\bar{P}_2 & 0 \\ * & * & * & * & * & -\bar{P}_2 \end{bmatrix} \quad (12)$$

where

$$\pi_1 = A^T\bar{P}_1 A + A^T\bar{P}_1(W \otimes \Gamma)C + C^T(W \otimes \Gamma)^T\bar{P}_1 A + C^T(W \otimes \Gamma)^T\bar{P}_1(W \otimes \Gamma)C - P_1 + \alpha a^2 I$$
$$\pi_2 = C^T H^T K^T \bar{P}_2 A + C^T H^T K^T \bar{P}_2(W \otimes \Gamma)C$$
$$\pi_3 = A^T\bar{P}_2 A - C^T K^T \bar{P}_2 A - A^T\bar{P}_2 KC + A^T\bar{P}_2(W \otimes \Gamma)C - C^T K^T \bar{P}_2(W \otimes \Gamma)C$$
$$\quad + C^T(W \otimes \Gamma)^T\bar{P}_2 A - C^T(W \otimes \Gamma)^T\bar{P}_2 KC + C^T(W \otimes \Gamma)^T\bar{P}_2(W \otimes \Gamma)C - P_2 + \alpha a^2 I$$
$$\pi_4 = A^T\bar{P}_2 - C^T K^T \bar{P}_2 + C^T(W \otimes \Gamma)^T\bar{P}_2.$$

Moreover, the state estimator gain can be determined by

$$K = \bar{P}_2^{-1} Y \quad (13)$$

Proof: Construct a Lyapunov functional candidate as follows:

$$V(k, r(k)) = e^T(k)P_{r(k)}e(k) \quad (14)$$

For calculating the difference of $V(k, r(k))$ along the trajectories of (11) and getting the mathematical expectation, one can obtain that

$$\begin{aligned} E\{\Delta V(k, r(k))\} &= E\{V(k+1, r(k+1)) - V(k, r(k))\} \\ &= E\{e^T(k+1)P_{r(k+1)}e(k+1) - e^T(k)P_{r(k)}e(k)\} \\ &= E\{[Be(k) + D_1 D_2 e(k) + h(x(k), \hat{x}(k))]^T \bar{P} \\ &\quad [Be(k) + D_1 D_2 e(k) + h(x(k), \hat{x}(k))] - e^T(k)Pe(k)\} \\ &= E\{e^T(k)B^T\bar{P}Be(k) + e^T(k)B^T\bar{P}D_1 D_2 e(k) \\ &\quad + e^T(k)B^T\bar{P}h(x(k), \hat{x}(k)) + e^T(k)D_2^T D_1^T \bar{P}Be(k) \\ &\quad + e^T(k)D_2^T D_1^T \bar{P}D_1 D_2 e(k) + e^T(k)D_2^T D_1^T \bar{P}h(x(k), \hat{x}(k)) \\ &\quad + h^T(x(k), \hat{x}(k))\bar{P}Be(k) + h^T(x(k), \hat{x}(k))\bar{P}D_1 D_2 e(k) \\ &\quad + h^T(x(k), \hat{x}(k))\bar{P}h(x(k), \hat{x}(k)) - e^T(k)Pe(k)\} \\ &= E\{\chi^T \varphi_1 \chi\} \end{aligned} \quad (15)$$

where

$$\chi = \begin{bmatrix} e(k) \\ h(x(k), \hat{x}(k)) \end{bmatrix}, \, P = P_{r(k)} > 0, \, \bar{P} = P_{r(k+1)} = (\Lambda \otimes I_n)P_{r(k)} > 0,$$

$$\varphi_1 = \begin{bmatrix} B^T \bar{P} B + B^T \bar{P} D_1 D_2 + D_2^T D_1^T \bar{P} B + D_2^T D_1^T \bar{P} D_1 D_2 - P & B^T \bar{P} + D_2^T D_1^T \bar{P} \\ \bar{P} B + \bar{P} D_1 D_2 & \bar{P} \end{bmatrix}.$$

From Assumption 1, it is easy to show that

$$\alpha h^T(x(k), \hat{x}(k)) h(x(k), \hat{x}(k)) \leq \alpha a^2 e^T(k) e(k). \tag{16}$$

From (15) and (16), we obtain that

$$E\{\Delta V(k, r(k))\} \leq E\{\chi^T \varphi_1 \chi + [\alpha a^2 e^T(k) e(k) - \alpha h^T(x(k), \hat{x}(k)) h(x(k), \hat{x}(k))]\}$$
$$= E\{\chi^T \varphi_2 \chi\}$$

$$\varphi_2 = \begin{bmatrix} B^T \bar{P} B + B^T \bar{P} D_1 D_2 + D_2^T D_1^T \bar{P} B + D_2^T D_1^T \bar{P} D_1 D_2 - P + \alpha a^2 I & B^T \bar{P} + D_2^T D_1^T \bar{P} \\ \bar{P} B + \bar{P} D_1 D_2 & \bar{P} - \alpha I \end{bmatrix}$$

$$= \begin{bmatrix} \pi_1 + C^T H^T K^T \bar{P}_2 KHC & \pi_2 - C^T H^T K^T \bar{P}_2 KC & A^T \bar{P}_1 + C^T (W \otimes \Gamma)^T \bar{P}_1 & C^T H^T K^T \bar{P}_2 \\ * & \pi_3 + C^T K^T \bar{P}_2 KC & 0 & \pi_4 \\ * & * & \bar{P}_1 - \alpha I & * \\ * & * & * & \bar{P}_2 - \alpha I \end{bmatrix}$$

By Lemma 1, we can obtain that $\varphi_2 < 0$ is equivalent to the inequality $\varphi < 0$. It can be derived that the estimation error network is asymptotically stable in the mean square by applying the Lyapunov functional approach. It means that network (4) is an effective state estimator of network (1).

4 Simulations

In the section, an example is given to justify the criteria proposed in the previous section. Considering an output coupled discrete-time complex network with 3 nodes. Following are the parameters for the network:

$$f(x_i(k)) = (-1.4x_{i1}(k) + 2.4 \tanh(x_{i1}(k)), -1.4x_{i2}(k) + 2.4 \tanh x_{i2}(k)), \\ -1.4x_{i3}(k) + 2.4 \tanh x_{i3}(k)))^T \qquad (i = 1, 2, 3)$$

$$A_i = \begin{bmatrix} 0.47 & 0 & 0 \\ 0 & 0.4 & 0 \\ 0 & 0 & 0.25 \end{bmatrix}, A = diag(A_1, A_2, A_3), C_i = \begin{bmatrix} 0.8 & 0 & 0 \\ 0 & 0.8 & 0 \\ 0 & 0 & 1 \end{bmatrix}, C = diag(C_1, C_2, C_3),$$

$$W = \begin{bmatrix} -2 & 1 & 1 \\ 1 & -1 & 0 \\ 1 & 1 & -2 \end{bmatrix}, \Gamma = \begin{bmatrix} 0.3 & -0.1 & 0.2 \\ 0 & -0.3 & 0.2 \\ -0.1 & -0.1 & -0.2 \end{bmatrix}, \Lambda_i = \begin{bmatrix} 0.1 & 0.9 \\ 0.2 & 0.8 \end{bmatrix}, \Lambda = diag(\Lambda_1, \Lambda_2, \Lambda_3),$$

$$r(k) = [b_{i1}, b_{i2}, b_{i3}]^T \quad (b_{i1}, b_{i2}, b_{i3} \in \{0, 1\} \ (i = 1, 2, 3)) \ H = I_9 - diag(r(k), r(k), r(k)),$$

then select $a = 0.4$ in (16). Applying the MATLAB LMI Toolbox, we obtain the equations including the gain matrix in Theorem 1 as follows:

$$\bar{P}_1 = diag(M, M, M) \quad M = \begin{bmatrix} 1.0021 & -0.0151 & 0.0079 \\ -0.0151 & 0.9576 & -0.0002 \\ 0.0079 & -0.0002 & 1.0246 \end{bmatrix},$$

$$\bar{P}_2 = diag(N, N, N) \quad N = \begin{bmatrix} 1.0117 & -0.0088 & 0.0061 \\ -0.0088 & 0.9834 & 0.0012 \\ 0.0038 & 0.0012 & 1.0255 \end{bmatrix},$$

$$K = diag(K_0, K_0, K_0) \quad K_0 = \begin{bmatrix} 0.1166 & 0.0458 & 0.0080 \\ 0.0384 & 0.1340 & 0.0150 \\ -0.0095 & 0.0007 & 0.0681 \end{bmatrix},$$

meanwhile, $\alpha = 1.9009$ is obtained in (16).

We choose the third state of each node to show the state trajectories of nodes, the simulations are presented in Fig. 1. Meanwhile, the simulations for all states of error system are shown in Fig. 2. From these simulations, we can conclude that the estimator (4) could effectively estimate the state of nodes in network (1), which exists Markovian packet losses. The proof is then verified.

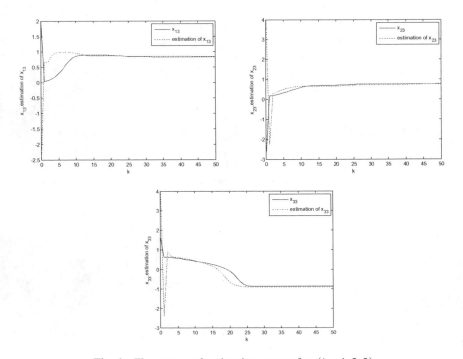

Fig. 1. The states and estimation states of $x_{i3}(i = 1, 2, 3)$

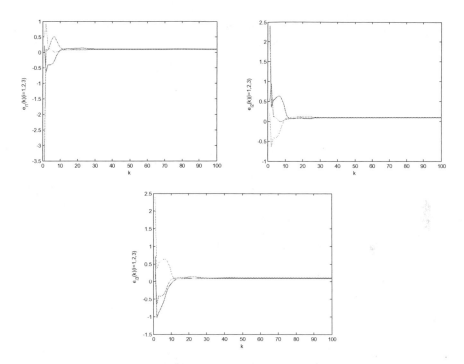

Fig. 2. The node states of error system

5   Conclusions

In the paper, we have dealt with the problem of state estimation for discrete-time directed complex networks with coupled outputs. It often occurs the packet losses in practical transmission channel. We describe it as a Markovian packet dropout and the transition probability is known. By employing the Lyapunov functional theory and stochastic analysis method, a state observer has been constructed to witness the estimation error to be asymptotically stable in the mean square. The criteria has been established to guarantee the existence of the desired estimator gain matrix. The simulations have been shown to illustrate the applicability of the criteria obtained.

References

1. Strogatz, S.H.: Exploring complex networks. Nature **410**(6825), 268–276 (2001)
2. Watts, D.J., Strogatz, S.H.: Collective dynamics of 'small-world' networks. Nature **393** (6684), 440–442 (1998)
3. Barabási, A.L., Albert, R.: Emergence of scaling in random networks. Science **286**(5439), 509–512 (1999)

4. Fan, C.X., Jiang, G.P., Jiang, F.H.: Synchronization between two complex dynamical networks using scalar signals under pinning control. IEEE Trans. Circuits Syst. **57**(11), 2991–2998 (2010)
5. Fan, C.X., Wan, Y.H., Jiang, G.P.: Topology identification for a class of complex dynamical networks using output variables. Chin. Phys. B **21**(2), 020510 (2012)
6. Wang, Z., Ho, D.W.C., Liu, X.: State estimation for delayed neural networks. IEEE Trans. Neural Netw. **16**(1), 279–284 (2005)
7. Liu, Y., Wang, Z., Liang, J., et al.: Synchronization and state estimation for discrete-time complex networks with distributed delays. IEEE Trans. Syst. Man Cybern. Part B **38**(5), 1314–1325 (2008)
8. Fan, C.X., Jiang, G.P.: State estimation of complex dynamical network under noisy transmission channel. In: 2012 IEEE International Symposium on Circuits and Systems (ISCAS), pp. 2107–2110 (2012)
9. Wang, L.C., Wei, G.L., Shu, H.S.: State estimation for complex network with randomly occurring coupling delays. Neurocomputing **122**, 513–520 (2013)
10. Zhang, J., Lyu, M., Karimi, H.R., Guo, P., Bo, Y.: Robust H_∞ filtering for a class of complex networks with stochastic packet dropouts and time delays. Sci. World J. (2014)
11. Yang, M., Wang, Y.W., Yi, J.W., Huang, Y.H.: Stability and synchronization of directed complex dynamical networks with random packet loss: the continuous-time case and the discrete-time case. Int. J. Circuit Theory Appl. **41**(12), 1272–1289 (2013)
12. Wu, X., Jiang, G.P.: State estimation for continuous-time directed complex dynamical network with random packet dropout. In: 2015 Chinese Control Conference (CCC), pp. 3696–3670 (2015)
13. Lv, B., Liang, J., Cao, J.: Robust distributed state estimation for genetic regulatory networks with Markovian jumping parameters. Commun. Nonlinear Sci. Numer. Simul. **16**(10), 4060–4078 (2011)
14. Huang, M., Dey, S.: Stability of Kalman filtering with Markovian packet losses. Automatica **43**(4), 598–607 (2007)
15. You, K., Xie, L.: Minimum data rate for mean square stability of linear systems with Markovian packet losses. IEEE Trans. Autom. Control **56**(4), 772–785 (2011)
16. Okano, K., Ishii, H.: Stabilization of uncertain systems with finite data rates and Markovian packet losses. In: Proceedings of European Control Conference, Zürich, Switzerland, pp. 2368–2373, June 2013

Coverage and Control of Diffusion Process in Cyber-Physical Systems

Ke-cai Cao[1,2(✉)], Fujiao Zhou[1], and Minglou Qian[1]

[1] Nanjing University of Posts and Telecommunications,
Nanjing 210003, People's Republic of China
caokc@njupt.edu.cn
[2] College of Automation Engineering,
Nanjing University of Aeronautics and Astronautics,
Nanjing 210003, People's Republic of China

Abstract. Coverage and control of a diffusion process using multiple robots have been studied in this paper. Two control strategies such as CVT (Centroidal Voronoi Tessellations)-Allocation-Motion Algorithm and CVT-Obstacles Avoidance-Motion Algorithm have been proposed for cooperative control of multiple robots in realizing the task of coverage and control of diffusion process that is modeled by parabolic partial differential equation. Reliability and transient performance have been improved based on the algorithms that is proposed in this paper. Simulation results using Diff-MAS2D for the diffusion process illustrate the effectiveness of the theoretical results.

Keywords: Diffusion process · Win-stay and lose-switch · Centroidal Voronoi Tessellations · Decision making · Obstacles Avoidance

1 Introduction

As robot technology is developing rapidly, more and more robots have been used to replace the role of human beings in many fields such as sensing and even control of poisonous material or tasks. But there is no agreement on the sensing and control of the above tasks even in the framework of Cyber-Physical System. Thus a lot of work has been conducted in recent years.

In [1,2], lose-shift, a strategy of win-stay has been provided. Although this algorithm is simple, the performance is not very good in application of the theoretical results due to the existence of uncertainty. A uniform coverage algorithm has also been considered in [3] for the coverage problem in distributed dynamic system and work of [3] has been further extended to nonuniform algorithms in [4] using cartograms. Simultaneous Coverage and Tracking Algorithm (SCAT) has been proposed in [5] where the problem of assignment, coverage and tracking has been solved based on local sensory measurements and neighbors information. Overall performance of multi robots systems has been enhanced using

© Springer Nature Singapore Pte Ltd. 2017
D. Yue et al. (Eds.): LSMS/ICSEE 2017, Part II, CCIS 762, pp. 557–565, 2017.
DOI: 10.1007/978-981-10-6373-2_56

dynamic task allocation mechanism [6] without requirement of explicit communications or global information while high computation ability of each robot is assumed. Although decentralized feed-back controllers have been proposed in [7] with obstacles in the workspace, it is not easy to apply the proposed method in large-scale system of robots due to its complexity. Computation burden and scalability have become the main bottleneck in dealing with the coverage and control problem of diffusion process using multiple robots.

In this paper, the pollution neutralization problem is the focus of this paper where dynamic diffusion on 2D plane has been studied for simplicity. The PDE has been used to model the dynamics of a diffusion process such as poisonous smog or gases. Control objective is to track the global evolution of poisonous gases and to neutralize its effect to the environment using multiple robots. There are not too much work on this topic due to the challenging problems such as:

- How to allocate different tasks for each robot to measure or neutralize the dynamic diffusion process?
- How to construct the coverage and control algorithms for the diffusion process which modeled using PDE?
- How about the performance when there are some obstacles and uncertainties in the environments and in the controlled system?

The rest of the paper is organized as follows. Section 2 discusses the formulation of our problem. CVT-Allocation-Motion Algorithm and CVT-Obstacles Avoidance-Motion Algorithm have been proposed in Sect. 3 where coverage and control of the diffusion of poisonous or dangerous material has been successfully solved. Simulation results based on the platform of Diff-2D that proposed in [8–10] have been presented to illustrate the effectiveness of theoretical results in Sect. 4. Finally, Sect. 5 concludes our paper.

2   Problem Formulation

Let Ω be an area in R^2, including its interior and $\rho(x, y)$: $\Omega \to R_+$ is a concentration function which represents the concentration of poison gas over Ω. The evolution of z with respect to time and position is governed by the following PDE system:

$$\frac{\partial u}{\partial t} = \frac{\partial}{\partial x}[k(x, y)\frac{\partial u}{\partial x}] + \frac{\partial}{\partial y}[k(x, y)\frac{\partial u}{\partial y}] + f(u, x, y, t), \qquad (1)$$

where $k(x, y) = c_1 + c_2 x + c_3 y$ and c_1, c_2, c_3 are nominal parameters and $f(u, x, y, t)$ is the source of the poisonous gas.

3   Centroidal Voronoi Tessellation Based Control

In order to monitor the dynamic process of the diffusion process, we use multiple sensors instead of one centralized sensor. How many sensors and where they should be put are interesting problems to be considered.

Assume there are N mobile robots in convex area Ω, and the position of the ith robot is given by $p_i \in \Omega$. Then $P = [p_1^T, p_2^T, \cdots, p_N^T]^T$ is a vector representing the configuration of the mobile sensor network. For each configuration, the following cost function is defined:

$$H(P) = \int_{\Omega} \min_{i \in \{1,2,\cdots,N\}} f(d(q, p_i))u(q)dq, \tag{2}$$

where $d(\cdot)$ is the distances between an interest point $q \in \Omega$ and the robot position p_i, $f(\cdot)$ is a strictly increasing function and $u(q)$ is the density of poisonous smog at point q. It is easy to see that the problem of covering the area Ω is an optimization problem that minimizing the above cost function (2). The technique of Voronoi Tessellation is adopted in our work to deal with the coverage problem.

3.1 CVT-Allocation Algorithm

In this subsection, we consider the sources are moving and do not limit the number of moving targets. Furthermore, the direction of movement and the time of appearance are unknown. The coverage is used to increase the probability of detecting new sources. For clearing the pollution which be leaked from sources, it is necessary to propose one allocation Algorithm. Let $L(t)$ is the number of sources at time t in the area Ω. Then there are $L(t)+1$ tasks ($L(t)$ tacking tasks and 1 coverage task). In early results, a distance R is given to measure which target can be obtained by robots. The R is called maximum tracking distance. That is to say, sources located at the distance lesser than R from V_i will be assigned to the robot i [5]. But in some actual cases, the diffusion rate of sources is different. If only use the distance to allocate tasks, the high-risk source will not be cleared timely. In our approach, we assume that each robot i can estimate the position and the diffusion rate of a source is located inside the corresponding Voronoi cell V_i and endow the source k with two wight values: W_k^1 and W_k^2, $k = 1, 2, \cdots, L(t)$. Next the CVT-Allocation Algorithm for allocation task will be given in Fig. 1:

3.2 CVT-Allocation-Motion Algorithm

The robots are modeled by the second order dynamic equation: $\ddot{p}_i = In_i(t)$ and $\dot{w}_i = m_i$, where In_i is the motion control input for robot i and m_i is the weight control input for robot i. $In_i(t)$ and $m_i(t)$ are given by

$$In_i = ae_i(t) + b\dot{e}_i(t), \tag{4}$$

$$m_i(t) = \frac{1}{N_i(t)}\left(\sum_{j \in N_i} u_{V_j}(t)\right) - u_{V_i}(t). \tag{5}$$

where a and b are two positive constants, $e_i(t)$ is the error from robot position p_i to the goal point at time t. $N_i(t)$ is the number of neighbors of the robot i and $u_{V_i}(t)$ is total quantity of poisonous in Voronioi cell $V_i(t)$ at time t.

$\mathcal{R}1$. Computation of the weights: denote the region within a certain radius R_k around the source k as a high-risk region S_k, $S_k \subset \Omega$. Let α_k be the number of robots in region S_k and β_k be the number of robots which closer to the source k, then we have

$$W_k^1 = 1 - \frac{\alpha_k}{M_k}; W_k^2 = 1 - \frac{\beta_k}{M_k}, \tag{3}$$

where M_k is the number of robots that should be assigned to the source k. The optimal sequel is $W_k^1 = 0$, that is to say the source k obtain a sufficient number of robots and the rest robots will not consider the source k. But in some cases the total number of robots is not enough for all targets, thus our goal of the task assignment is to make W_k^1 as low as possible.

$\mathcal{R}2$. Choosing the one with higher wight value: In each time step, the robot i which is not in high-risk region evaluates W_k^1 and W_k^2 for all sources. Then it identifies the source with maximum W_k^1 and with maximum W_k^2:

$$k_1 = \arg\max_k W_k^1; k_2 = \arg\max_k W_k^2.$$

If there are two or more sources with the same wight value, it chooses the closest one, and if there is still an ambiguity, it chooses one at random. This target k^* is called the most urgent event for robot i to clear, thus we allocate the target k^* to robot i. If a robot has no tracking target, it will execute the coverage task.

Fig. 1. CVT-Allocation Algorithm.

If the robot i performs coverage, then the Centroidal-Weighted Voronoi Tessellation Algorithm is to configure robot i to the centroid of the Voronoi cell V_i. That is to say, the centroid of Voronoi cell is our goal point. If the robot i executes the task of tracking moving targets, then the Task Assignment Algorithm computes two wight values and allocates the target k^* to the robot. The robot should move to the target immediately and the position of the target is our goal point:

$$e_i(t) = \begin{cases} a(q_i^* - p_i) & if \text{ robot } i \text{ chooses coverage} \\ a(q_{k^*} - p_i) & if \text{ robot } i \text{ chooses tracking} \end{cases}, \tag{6}$$

where q_i^* is the centroid of Voronoi cell V_i and q_{k^*} is the position of source k^*. The CVTA-Motion Algorithm can be simply described in Fig. 2:

$\mathcal{R}1$. The robot i chooses coverage: the robot will cover the area through Centroidal Voronoi Tessellation. That is to say

$$g_i = q_i^* \tag{7}$$

$\mathcal{R}2$. The robot i chooses tracking: the robot will go to the position of source k^*. That is to say

$$g_i = q_{k^*} \tag{8}$$

Fig. 2. CVT-Motion Algorithm.

3.3   CVT-Obstacles Avoidance-Motion Algorithm

For obstacles, we present a new approach for Voronoi coverage of a non-convex environment that builds on the Lloyd algorithm and Avoiding algorithm, a local path planner with obstacle avoidance behavior. The control strategy is composed of two layers of abstraction: (1) Lloyd algorithm provides virtual goal updates based on successive computation of Voronoi cells; (2) Avoiding algorithm plans the robot path to the next real goal position when the robot meets obstacles or holds. In our approach, we assume that each robot i can estimate the boundary ∂O of obstacle and hold that is located inside the corresponding Voronoi cell V_i.

Let p_i^{rl} be the actual position of robot i in the non-convex environment and p_i^{vl} be the desired position in disregard of the obstacles in the environment, as if we were dealing with a convex environment. In addition, we endow robot i two goals: real goal g_i^{rl} and virtual goal g_i^{vl}. The real goal g_i^{rl} is a position that the robot will go to next step in the real environment, whereas the virtual goal g_i^{vl} is the centroid of the current Voronoi region, which was computed based on p_i^{vl}. In some situations, the virtual and real points simply coincide.

The control strategy computes the Lloyd algorithm using the virtual points, which ignore the obstacles and holds. And each robot updates its Voronoi region and centroid based on the virtual position and its neighbors. All virtual robots are moving towards the centroid of the Voronoi regions. In parallel, the real robots are moving toward the real goals, while the robots approach the real goals in the real environment taking obstacles into account.

In other words, we can assume the non-convex environment is composed of convex Voronoi regions and obstacle boundary Voronoi regions. If V_i is an obstacle boundary Voronoi region, then we project g_i^{rl} to the point p_i^* on the boundary ∂S of obstacle. The CVT-Obstacles Avoidance-Motion Algorithm is intentionally kept in a rather theoretic description, for the purpose of generality and clarity, and needs for well engineered implementations. It is shown in Fig. 3

The control strategy is general and flexible. Obviously, when a robot encounters an obstacle, it can avoid the obstacle effectively and the non-convex environment is well covered.

4   Simulation Results

Diff-MAS2D is used as the simulation platform for our implementation. The area concerned is given by $\Omega = \{(x, y) \mid 0 \leq x \leq 1, 0 \leq y \leq 1\}$.

The system with control input is modeled as

$$\frac{\partial u}{\partial t} = \frac{\partial}{\partial x}[k\frac{\partial u}{\partial x}] + \frac{\partial}{\partial y}[k\frac{\partial u}{\partial y}] + f_c(x, y, t) + f_d(x, y, t), \tag{11}$$

where u is the variable we want to control (bring u to zero), k is a positive real constant related to system parameters. $f_c(x, y, t)$ is the control from the actuators and $f_d(x, y, t)$ is the disturbance. We use a number of sensors to measure u and moving actuators as controllers. Dirichlet boundary condition is given by

$\mathcal{R}1.$ real layer: the robot i computes their Voronoi region V_i and updates the centroid of V_i. Then the robot goes to the virtual goal point which computed in the virtual layer.

$$g_i^{rl} = g_i^{vl} \tag{9}$$

$\mathcal{R}2.$ virtual layer: the robot gets its position and Voronoi region V_i from the real layer. If V_i is a convex Voronoi region, that is to say the straight line $\overline{p_i^{vl} g_i^{vl}}$ do not pass through obstacles or holds, the virtual goal point of the robot is the centroid of V_i. Otherwise, the virtual goal point is the point in the boundary of obstacles.

$$g_i^{vl} = \begin{cases} q_i^* & \text{if } V_i \text{ is a convex region} \\ \partial O & \text{Otherwise} \end{cases} \tag{10}$$

where q_i^* is the centroid of V_i and ∂O is the boundary of obstacles.

Fig. 3. CVT-Obstacles Avoidance Motion Algorithm.

$u = 0$ and neumann boundary condition is given by $\frac{\partial u}{\partial n} = 0$, where n is the outward direction normal to the boundary.

In our simulation, we assume that once deployed, the sensors remain static. There are 29×29 sensors evenly distributed in a square area $(0, 1)^2$ and they form a mesh over the area. Nine robots are deployed with initial positions at $(0.33, 0.33)$, $(0.33, 0.5)$, $(0.33, 0.67)$, $(0.5, 0.33)$, $(0.5, 0.5)$, $(0.5, 0.67)$, $(0.67, 0.33)$, $(0.67, 0.5)$, $(0.67, 0.67)$. The pollution source is modeled as disturbance f_d to the PDE system (11). The system evolves under the effects of diffusion of pollutants and diffusion of neutralizing chemicals released by robots. And we assume that if the concentration of the pollution ranges in $0 \le u \le 0.025$, it is safe. We choose the simulation time step $\Delta t = 0.002\,\mathrm{s}$. To show how robots will control the diffusion of the pollution, the robots begin to react at $t = 0.2\,\mathrm{s}$.

Simulation Based on CVT-Allocation-Motion Algorithm
In this part, we consider two moving sources that diffusing at $(0.3, 0.7)$ and $(0.8, 0.2)$. The source 1 moves from $(0.3, 0.7)$ to $(0.5, 0.7)$ with diffusion rate of $10e^{-t}$ and the source 2 moves from $(0.8, 0.2)$ to $(0.8, 0.4)$ with diffusion rate of $2e^{-t}$. Then the disturbance over the area Ω is $f_d = 10e^{-t} + 2e^{-t}$. Because of the different diffusion rates, we assume that the high-risk region S_1 needs 4 robots and S_2 needs 2 robots.

Figure 4 also show the evolution of the diffusion process at $t = 0.5$, $t = 1.5$, $t = 2$, $t = 3$ after using CVT-Allocation-Motion Algorithm. The four robots in Fig. 4 are neutralizing poison gas and the rest are performing coverage. At the end we can see that all moving targets have been cleared.

Simulation Based on CVT-Obstacles Avoidance-Motion Algorithm
We consider two sources that diffusing at $(0.3, 0.7)$ with the diffusion rate of $2e^{-t}$ and diffuse at $(0.8, 0.2)$ with diffusion rate of $10e^{-t}$. Then the disturbance over the area Ω is $f_d = 10e^{-t} + 2e^{-t}$. There are two obstacles in the Ω. The first

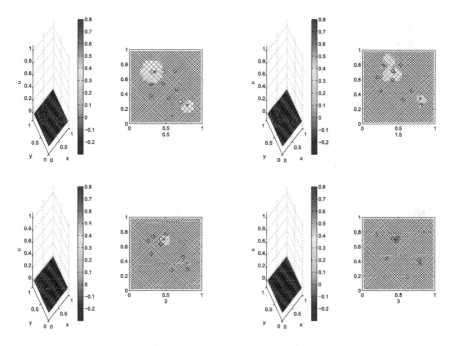

Fig. 4. Evolution of diffusion based on CVT-Allocation-Motion Algorithm

obstacle has the size 0.1×0.2 that locate in $(0.7, 0.25)$ and the second obstacle has the size 0.1×0.2 that locate in $(0.65, 0.75)$. Four robots are deployed with initial positions at $(0.4, 0.4)$, $(0.4, 0.6)$, $(0.6, 0.4)$, $(0.6, 0.6)$.

Figure 5 shows the trajectories of the robots for $t < 6$ s. The blue circles are robots and the red circles are sources of pollution while the black frames are obstacles. It can be seen that the robots move towards the pollution source to suppress the diffusion of the source. And then they move around to track the pollution that has already diffused and try to neutralize it. Dotted lines are the trajectories which are able to freely pass through obstacles and we call them virtual trajectories. Straight lines are the trajectories which take the obstacles into account and we call them real trajectories. It is easy to see that the robot 2 does not meet the obstacle and its real trajectory and virtual trajectory coincide. The virtual trajectories of robot 1, robot 3 and robot 4 pass through the obstacle 1. Using our methods, these robots avoid the obstacle successfully during the moving.

Figure 7 shows the evolution of the diffusion process at $t = 0.5$, $t = 2$, $t = 4$, $t = 6$, respectively. At $t = 0.5$ s, the robot 3 meet the obstacle 1 and begin to avoid the obstacle. At the same time, the robot 2 finds the source 1 and begins to clear the pollution. In SubFigure (2) of Fig. 7, the sources of pollution which located in $(0.3, 0.7)$ have been cleared. Form SubFigure (3) we can see that robot 1, robot 3 and robot 4 have avoided the obstacle 1 and begin to neutralize poison gas. At $t = 6$ s, all pollution sources have been cleared. There is no pollution

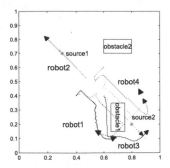

Fig. 5. Robots trajectories (real and virtual trajectories).

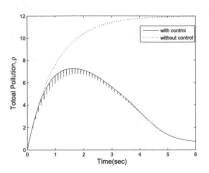

Fig. 6. Evolution of the amount of pollution.

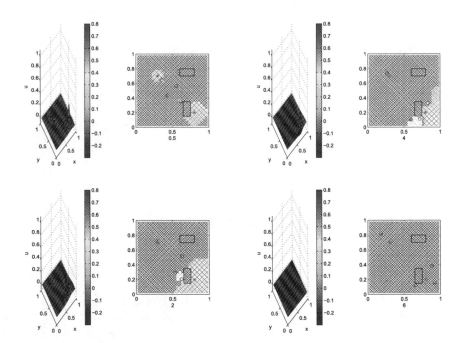

Fig. 7. The evolution of diffusion process based on CVT-Obstacles Avoidance-Motion Algorithm.

source in the area and the poison gas is well controlled. Figure 6 shows evolution of the amount of pollution respect to time.

5   Conclusion

In this paper, algorithms of coverage and control for robots and sensors in cooperative control of pollution have been considered in this paper. Two different algorithms have been considered and compared in this paper where simulation platform of Diff-MAS2D has been employed to illustrate the effectiveness of the proposed algorithms. In the future, sensing and control of fractional diffusion process where the diffusion of pollution is modeled using the framework of fractional calculus can be furthered studied based on the results of this paper.

References

1. Nowak, M., Sigmund, K.: A strategy of win-stay, lose-shift that outperforms tit-for-tat in the Prisoner's Dilemma game. Nature **364**(6432), 56–58 (1993)
2. Posch, M.: Win-stay, lose-shift strategies for repeated games-memory length, aspiration levels and noise. J. Theor. Biol. **198**, 183–195 (1999)
3. Cortes, J., Bullo, F.: Coordination and geometric optimization via distributed dynamical systems. SIAM J. Control Optim. **44**, 1543–1574 (2005)
4. Lekien, F., Leonard, N.: Nonuniform coverage and cartograms. SIAM J. Control Optim. **48**, 351–372 (2009)
5. Pimenta, L.C.A., Schwager, M., Lindsey, Q., Kumar, V., Rus, D., Mesquita, R.C., Pereira, G.A.S.: Simultaneous coverage and tracking (SCAT) of moving targets with robot networks. In: Chirikjian, G.S., Choset, H., Morales, M., Murphey, T. (eds.) Algorithmic Foundation of Robotics VIII. STAR, vol. 57, pp. 85–99. Springer, Heidelberg (2009). doi:10.1007/978-3-642-00312-7_6
6. Lerman, K., Galstyan, A.: Analysis of dynamic task allocation in multi-robot systems. Int. J. Robot. Res. **25**, 225–241 (2006)
7. Ayanian, N., Kumar, V.: Decentralized feedback controllers for multi-agent teams in environments with obstacles. In: IEEE Conference on Robotics and Automation (2008)
8. Liang, J., Chen, Y.: Diff-MAS2D (version 0.9) User's Manual-A simulation platform for controlling distributed parameter systems (diffusion) with networked movable actuators and sensors (MAS) in 2D domain. Utah State University, Technical report (2004)
9. Chen, Y., Moore, K.L.: Model-based approach to characterization of diffusion processes via distributed control of actuated sensor networks. Helsinki University of Technology Espoo, IFAC Symposium of Telemetries Applications in Automation and Robotics (2004)
10. Moore, K.L., Chen, Y.: Diffusion based path planning in mobile actuator-sensor networks (MAS-net) - some preliminary results. In: PIE Conference on Intelligent Computing: Theory and Applications II, Part of SPIE's Defense and Security (2004)

Jamming Attacks Against Control Systems: A Survey

Yanbo Dong and Peng Zhou[(⊠)]

School of Mechatronic Engineering and Automation, Shanghai University,
Shanghai 200072, China
dongyb@i.shu.edu.cn, pzhou@shu.edu.cn

Abstract. Modern control systems are now combining advanced network technology for control optimization and efficiency, but, on the other side, induce network attack as a new threat to control security. A typical network attack targeting control systems is Denial of Service (DoS) jamming attack. This attack can disable control operations by simply flooding network traffic to the control-network channels, and therefore is easy to deploy and hard to defend. In this paper, we conduct a comprehensive review on this attack and report our results in three aspects: the attacking strategies of jamming attack, the defending solutions to this attack and the arms race between them. To this end, we also discuss the potential research directions on this topic.

Keywords: Network control system · DoS · Jamming attack

1 Introduction

The control system is a management system that has its own objectives and functions, it is composed of the control subject, the control object and the control media. It can make the controlled object tend to a certain stable state. Now, the control system has been widely used in various fields of human society. In industry, a variety of physical quantities used in metallurgy [1], chemical [2], machinery manufacturing [3] and other production processes all have the corresponding control system. In military, the control system can be applied to various types of weapon control systems [4], fire control systems [5]. With the new control theory and control technology appearing, many advanced control systems such as cyber-physical system (CPS) [6], network control system (NCS) [7] have attracted more and more attention, many systems based on wireless sensor network (WSN) [8] have also been extensively studied. The structure of a typical CPS is shown in Fig. 1 and the evolution and development of CPS is described in Fig. 2. In each evolution of the CPS, the system has added new elements, which makes the system produce new features and brings a huge increase in productivity. At present, the application of these control systems is still expanding.

With the continuous development of the control system in the industrial, military, medical, biological and other fields, the security issues of control system pose threats to our daily life. Attack against the control system mainly threatens its physical security, functional security and system information security, it can damage the controller, communication equipment directly and tamper with the industrial parameters, it can

© Springer Nature Singapore Pte Ltd. 2017
D. Yue et al. (Eds.): LSMS/ICSEE 2017, Part II, CCIS 762, pp. 566–574, 2017.
DOI: 10.1007/978-981-10-6373-2_57

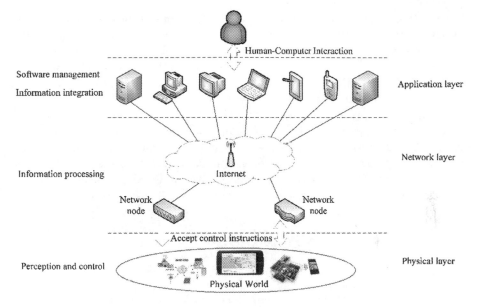

Fig. 1. The structure of a typical CPS

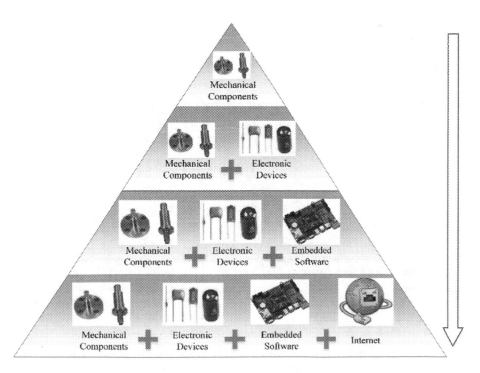

Fig. 2. The evolution and development of CPS

also invade the control system to damage the production equipment and access to business information [9]. As the Internet grows up, it is easier to attack the control system through the network. The security objectives of modern control system are availability, integrity and confidentiality. Denial of Service(DoS) attack aims at the control system availability. DoS attack is the commonly used network attack method, and now many research achievements have been gained [10–13].

Jamming attack is a kind of DoS attack which can denial the control service by purposely dropping packets. This attack is simple and effective. It only needs to obtain the communication band of the current network through monitoring passively, and then the attack can be launched rapidly. DoS attack can attack the server to exhaust the limited resources of CPU and memory of control system directly, it can also attack the communication channel directly to cause jamming. These attacks are shown in Fig. 3

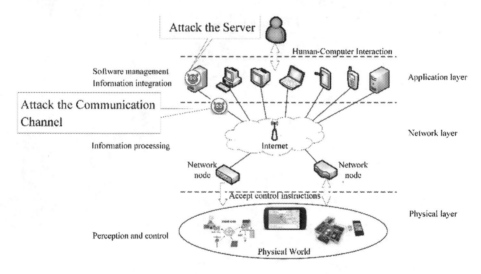

Fig. 3. DoS jamming attack

At present, a lot of work has been done on studying jamming attack against the communication channel of the control system. During the last decade, a number of papers about the jamming attack against control systems were reported, for instance, [14–37], which are listed in Table 1.

The remainder of this paper is organized as follows: some jamming attacking strategies on control system are reviewed in Sect. 2. Defense methods of jamming

Table 1. Papers about the jamming attack against control systems.

Years	Jamming attack	Defense of Jamming attack	Game of Jamming attack and defense
2005–2008	[20]	[21, 22]	
2009–2012	[15]	[25, 28–30]	[33, 34, 36, 37]
2013–2017	[14, 16–19]	[23, 24, 26, 27]	[31, 32, 35]

attack on control system are overviewed in Sect. 3. Arms Race between jamming attack and defense is discussed in Sect. 4. This paper is ended in Sect. 5 with the conclusion and some challenges on the future development.

2 Jamming Attack Against Control System

At the viewpoint of the attackers, they want the attack on the control system to be efficient and cannot be detected by the detector. If an attacker wants to do a jamming attack efficiently, it is important to consider energy constraints, because the energy constraints to a large extent affect the attacking strategy. The tools of optimal control theory are usually used to research on jamming attacks under energy constraints. For the security issues of Wireless Networked Control Systems (WNCS), an investigation was presented by [14] in 2014, which introduced the optimal jamming attack by maximizing the cost function of linear quadratic Gaussian (LQG) control under energy constraints from the standpoint of attacker. In [15], in order to solve the problem that the control and measurement packets transmitted through the communication network are jammed or compromised, a semi-definite programming (SDP) based solution has been investigated, which can minimize a given objective function suffer from security and power constraints. A research using Universal Software Radio Peripheral (USRP) to achieve wireless jamming attacks in [16], and through experiments to analyze the performance of different attacking strategy to find the best attacking strategy. In [17], the power system is modeled to study the effect of jamming attacks on load frequency control (LFC) at different times in smart grid.

In the cyber-physical system, there are two performance indicators: the expected terminal estimation error and the expected average estimation error. The jamming attack jams the communication channel between the sensor and the remote estimator, in [18] an attacking strategy that maximizes the two errors was presented, while avoiding being detected by the intrusion detection system (IDS). Another method to avoid detection by the intrusion detection system is proposed in [19], through the coordination of integrity attack and availability attack, cyclical switching false data injection attack and DoS attack to attack the communication channel, which has good application effect to avoid detection by IDS. Moreover, a layered jamming attack method for encrypted wireless network communication was proposed in [20].

3 Defense of Jamming Attack Against Control System

In some studies of early defense strategies for the jamming attack, an approach of checking consistency was used to detect whether a system is subject to jamming attacks. In [21], two schemes were proposed to detect the consistency, one is to detect by measuring the signal intensity, the other one is using the location information. There is also a method proposed in the early defense strategy of wireless sensor networks in [22], this method achieves the effect of defense by evading the DoS jamming and competing with the DoS jamming. Avoidance of DoS jamming can be done by changing the communication channel assignment, or moving the node away from the source of the DoS jamming. Competition with the interference can be achieved through error correction.

At present, some attacking defense strategies are given in many studies, the design of resilient control system is the most common method. The main idea of designing a resilient control system is to prevent and detect the jamming attacks and mitigate their harm to the control system. In [23], an algorithm is proposed for CPS by designing a resilient controller at the physical layer and designing an IDS configuration strategy at the cyber layer. This algorithm can calculate the best defense strategy. In a recent study, the predictor-based controller was designed to tolerate more DoS class signals in [24], which is also a way to achieve resilient control.

In addition to designing resilient control systems, more types of defense strategy of jamming attack have been proposed in recent years, such as updating control signals [25], delegating defense to Internet Service Providers (ISPs) [26], designing the transmission time [27], using more advanced machine learning methods [28] or distinguish whether the network traffic is legitimate [29].

1. Updating control signals

In [25], a method is proposed to solve the jamming attack which initialized periodically by the PWM jammer. This method discussed the sequence of the triggering time to cancel the effect of the jamming signal by updating the control signal, and finally the system achieves gradual stabilization.

2. Delegating defense to ISP

In [26], the jamming attack is defended by delegating to ISP, but using this method requires the path of the attacker to the attacked site, which is predicted employing Probabilistic Packet Marking.

3. Designing the transmission time

In [27], the stability of CPS under the jamming attack was discussed, which designed a reasonable transmission schedule to realize the Input-to-state stability (ISS) by explicitly expressing the jamming attack frequency and the duration.

4. Using machine learning methods

Many machine learning algorithms have made great contributions in detecting jamming attacks. Machine learning as the core of artificial intelligence has developed rapidly in recent years. Machine learning specializes in how computer simulates or realizes human learning behavior, and its application has spread all over the field. For example, in [28], the jamming attacks are detected on the MAC layer of WSN system using neural networks (NN) and support vector machines (SVM) respectively. The detection accuracy and the detection speed of the two algorithms is compared, which proved that SVM has higher accuracy and faster speed in DoS detection. This research improves the security of the WSN system.

5. Distinguish whether the network traffic is legitimate

Many defense solutions of the jamming attack for Home Automation System (HAS) are to distinguish between legitimate network traffic and the network traffic caused by jamming attacks, but the shortcomings of this approach is difficult to completely distinguish all network traffic. A defense strategy was proposed in [29] that designed a Virtual Home (VH) to mitigate the network traffic caused by jamming attacks directly to the HAS, which was achieved very good filtering effect through analyzing by Remote Home Server (RHS) and DoS Defense Server (DDS).

In addition, some papers do not provide the specific defense strategies directly, but provides some useful insights instead. Due to the communication methods of the Underwater Sensor Networks (UWSN) and the Wireless Sensor Network (WSN) on the ground are different, the validity of the jamming attack on UWSN has been confirmed in [30], which has contributed to the development of solutions for future researchers.

4 Arms Race Between Jamming Attacks and Their Defenses

Different from studying the attacking strategy and defense strategy of jamming attack against control systems independently, it is more meaningful to study the arms race between jamming attack and defense. Because the DoS attacker will change their own attacking strategy according to the defense strategy of control system that has been already set, which makes the research incomplete. It is very important to introduce the game theory into the security of control system. In this section, we review the arms race between jamming attack and defense respectively in CPS, NCS and WSN

For Cyber-physical systems, a game theory framework is proposed in [31] through the game of sensor sending time and attacker attack time. The optimal strategy achieves the Nash equilibrium of a zero-sum game. In order to reduce the computational complexity, the Markov chain theory can be used to simplify the calculation.

In the networked control system, the problem of resilient control problem is presented in [32], which uses the game theory to propose the optimal attack strategy and the optimal compensation strategy respectively. In [33], the equilibrium point of the dynamic zero-sum game is found by the game of the jammer and the controller in case of limited jamming actions, and it proved that the control strategy is based on the threshold.

In the wireless sensor network, limited work has been done on investigating the arms race between jamming attack and defense, but to the best of my knowledge, the research on optimal strategy of WSN intrusion detection using game theory has been very mature. For instance, a useful guide is proposed in [34] for IDS deployment. The optimal design scheme of IDS is obtained by the non-cooperative complete information static game of rational attacker and intrusion detection system. In [35], the Markovian intrusion detection system was proposed to design the best defense strategy by combining non-cooperative complete information static game with anomaly detection. Compared with the Markov decision process, this method improves the success rate of defense. In [36], a model between the jamming attacker and attacked network is established through a non-cooperative game, and when the game reaches the Nash equilibrium, a defensive strategy is achieved by increasing the energy consumption of the jamming attacker to cause its rapid death. In [37], the repeated game is used to establish a game model between the internal attack and the IDS, and the behaviors of the attacker is predicted by extending the general Nash equilibrium to the quantal response equilibrium.

5   Conclusion and Challenge

In this paper, we mainly focus on the jamming attacks against control system from three aspects: attack, defense and arms race between them, we have reviewed the existing methods of dealing with security issues. From the viewpoint of the attacker, the attacker wants the jamming attack to be efficiently under energy constraints and prevented from being detected by IDS. From the defender's point of view, the defender aims to improve the IDS to achieve a higher detection accuracy, or through the design of resilient controller and other methods (such as trust management systems [38, 39]) to reduce the risk of jamming attacks. We have also reviewed some existing strategies for the security of control systems by introducing game theory. In the future research, we can combine the machine learning algorithms and the game theory applied to the control system security issues, the attacker and the defender use the machine learning method simultaneously to confront and find the potential equilibrium in the arms race using some game theoretical methodologies.

Acknowledgement. This work was partially supported by the National Natural Science Foundation of China (Nos. 61502293, 61633016 and 61673255), the Shanghai Young Eastern Scholar Program (No. QD2016030), the Young Teachers' Training Program for Shanghai College and University, the Science and Technology Commission of Shanghai Municipality (Nos. 17511107002 and 15411953502) and the Shanghai Key Laboratory of Power Station Automation Technology.

References

1. Pieprzyca, J., Merder, T., Saternus, M., Kania, H.: The change of liquid steel flow control system in the tundish – modelling research/Zmiana Systemu Kontroli Przepływu Ciekłej Stali W Kadzi Pośredniej – Badania Modelowe. Arch. Metall. Mater. **59**, 1433–1440 (2015)
2. Chen, C.T., Peng, S.T.: Design of a sliding mode control system for chemical processes. J. Process Control **15**, 515–530 (2005)
3. Fan, H.M.: Design of flexiable manufacturing system based on practical application of engineering training. Appl. Mech. Mater. (2014)
4. Achanta, S.D.: Advanced submarine integrated weapon control system. Adv. Submar. Integr. Weapon Control Syst. **8**, 1–5 (2015)
5. Huang, F.: The design of the gateway based on arm and its application in the intelligent fire control system. Int. J. Digit. Content Technol. Appl. **6**, 275–282 (2012)
6. Cardenas, A.A., Amin, S., Sastry, S.: Secure control: towards survivable cyber-physical systems. In: The, International Conference on Distributed Computing Systems Workshops, pp. 495–500. IEEE Computer Society (2008)
7. Zhang, X., Han, Q.L., Yu, X.: Survey on recent advances in networked control systems. IEEE Tran. Ind. Inform. 1 (2015)

8. Butun, I., Morgera, S.D., Sankar, R.: A survey of intrusion detection systems in wireless sensor networks. IEEE Commun. Surv. Tutor. **16**, 266–282 (2014)
9. Farwell, J.P., Rohozinski, R.: Stuxnet and the future of cyber war. Survival **53**, 23–40 (2011)
10. Gao, Y., Feng, Y., Kawamoto, J., et al.: A machine learning based approach for detecting DRDoS attacks and its performance evaluation. In: Asia Joint Conference on Information Security, pp. 80–86. IEEE Computer Society (2016)
11. Vrat, B., Aggarwal, N., Venkatesan, S.: Anomaly detection in IPv4 and IPv6 networks using machine learning. In: IEEE India Conference, pp. 1–6. IEEE (2015)
12. Tsiatsikas, Z., Fakis, A., Papamartzivanos, D., et al.: Battling against DDoS in SIP is machine learning-based detection an effective weapon? In: The, International Conference on Security and Cryptography (2015)
13. Agarwal, M., Biswas, S., Nandi, S.: Detection of de-authentication DoS attacks in Wi-Fi networks: a machine learning approach. In: IEEE International Conference on Systems, Man, and Cybernetics, pp. 246–251. IEEE (2015)
14. Zhang, H., Cheng, P., Shi, L., et al.: Optimal denial-of-service attack scheduling against linear quadratic gaussian control. In: American Control Conference - ACC, pp. 3996–4001 (2014)
15. Amin, S., Cárdenas, A.A., Sastry, S.S.: Safe and secure networked control systems under denial-of-service attacks. In: Majumdar, R., Tabuada, P. (eds.) HSCC 2009. LNCS, vol. 5469, pp. 31–45. Springer, Heidelberg (2009). doi:10.1007/978-3-642-00602-9_3
16. Tang, H., Lu, Z., Zhang, L., et al.: LQG control under denial-of-service attacks: an experimental study. In: Conference on Emerging Technologies and Factory Automation, pp. 1–7. IEEE (2015)
17. Liu, S., Liu, X.P., Saddik, A.E.: Denial-of-service (dos) attacks on load frequency control in smart grids. In: Innovative Smart Grid Technologies, pp. 1–6. IEEE (2013)
18. Zhang, H., Cheng, P., Shi, L., et al.: Optimal DoS attack policy against remote state estimation. In: Decision and Control, pp. 5444–5449. IEEE (2013)
19. Anguluri, R., Gupta, V., Pasqualetti, F.: Periodic coordinated attacks against cyber-physical systems: detectability and performance bounds. In: 2016 IEEE 55th Conference on Decision and Control (CDC), pp. 5079–5084. IEEE (2016)
20. Brown, T.X., James, J.E., Sethi, A.: Jamming and sensing of encrypted wireless ad hoc networks. In: ACM International Symposium on Mobile Ad Hoc Networking and Computing, MOBIHOC 2006, Florence, Italy, May, pp. 120–130. DBLP (2006)
21. Xu, W., Trappe, W., Zhang, Y., et al.: The feasibility of launching and detecting jamming attacks in wireless networks. In: Proceedings of the 6th ACM International Symposium on Mobile Ad Hoc Networking and Computing, pp. 46–57. ACM (2005)
22. Xu, W., Ma, K., Trappe, W., et al.: Jamming sensor networks: attack and defense strategies. IEEE Netw. **20**, 41–47 (2006)
23. Yuan, Y., Zhu, Q., Sun, F., et al.: Resilient control of cyber-physical systems against denial-of-service attacks. In: International Symposium on Resilient Control Systems, pp. 54–59 (2013)
24. Feng, S., Tesi, P.: Resilient control under denial-of-service: robust design. Automatica **79**, 42–51 (2017)
25. Foroush, H.S., Martínez, S.: On event-triggered control of linear systems under periodic denial-of-service jamming attacks. In: Decision and Control, pp. 2551–2556. IEEE (2012)
26. Nur, A.Y., Tozal, M.E.: Defending cyber-physical systems against DoS attacks. In: IEEE International Conference on Smart Computing, pp. 1–3. IEEE Computer Society (2016)
27. De Persis, C., Tesi, P.: Input-to-state stabilizing control under denial-of-service. IEEE Trans. Autom. Control **60**, 2930–2944 (2015)

28. Raj, A.B., Ramesh, M.V., Kulkarni, R.V., et al.: Security enhancement in wireless sensor networks using machine learning. In: IEEE, International Conference on High Performance Computing and Communication and 2012 IEEE, International Conference on Embedded Software and Systems, pp. 1264–1269. IEEE (2012)
29. Gill, K., Yang, S.H., Wang, W.: Scheme for preventing low-level denial-of-service attacks on wireless sensor network-based home automation systems. Wirel. Sens. Syst. IET **2**, 361–368 (2012)
30. Zuba, M., Shi, Z., Peng, Z., et al.: Launching denial-of-service jamming attacks in underwater sensor networks. In: ACM International Workshop on Underwater Networks, p. 12. ACM (2011)
31. Li, Y., Shi, L., Cheng, P., et al.: Jamming attacks on remote state estimation in cyber-physical systems: a game-theoretic approach. IEEE Trans. Autom. Control **60**, 2831–2836 (2015)
32. Yuan, Y., Yuan, H., Guo, L., et al.: Resilient control of networked control system under DoS attacks: a unified game approach. IEEE Trans. Ind. Inform. (2016)
33. Gupta, A., Langbort, C., Başar, T.: Optimal control in the presence of an intelligent jammer with limited actions. In: Decision and Control, pp. 1096–1101. IEEE Xplore (2010)
34. Chen, L., Leneutre, J.: A game theoretical framework on intrusion detection in heterogeneous networks. IEEE Trans. Inf. Forensics Secur. **4**, 165–178 (2009)
35. Huang, J.Y., Liao, I.E., Chung, Y.F., et al.: Shielding wireless sensor network using Markovian intrusion detection system with attack pattern mining. Inf. Sci. **231**, 32–44 (2013)
36. Chen, L., Leneutre, J.: Fight jamming with jamming – a game theoretic analysis of jamming attack in wireless networks and defense strategy. Comput. Netw. **55**, 2259–2270 (2011)
37. Kantzavelou, I., Katsikas, S.: A game-based intrusion detection mechanism to confront internal attackers. Comput. Secur. **29**, 859–874 (2010)
38. Zhou, P., Jiang, S., Irissappane, A., et al.: Toward energy-efficient trust system through watchdog optimization for WSNs. IEEE Trans. Inf. Forensics Secur. **10**(3), 613–625 (2015)
39. Zhou, P., Gu, X., Zhang, J., et al.: A priori trust inference with context-aware stereotypical deep learning. Knowl.-Based Syst. **88**, 97–106 (2015)

State Estimation for Complex Network with One Step Induced Delay Based on Structural Controllability and Pinning Control

Wei Wang, Youhong Wan[(⊠)], and Xinyuan Liang

College of Automation, Nanjing University of Posts and Telecommunications,
Nanjing 210023, China
wanyh@njupt.edu.cn

Abstract. In this paper, the design of state estimation for the complex network with one-step induced delay are studied that only need a part of the network node's output measurement, based on structural controllability. Firstly, vwe selected the driver nodes according to the maximum matching method instead of the topological degree's size, and then estimated all nodes' information with these driver node's measurement output. By using the Lyapunov stability theory and the stochastic analysis method, the conditions for the existence of the gain matrix of the state estimator are presented in the form of linear inequalities. Finally, the simulation example is given to verify the present theoretical analysis in this study.

Keywords: Complex network · Maximum matching · Pinning control · One-step delay · State estimation

1 Introduction

In our life, complex networks are almost everywhere, such as the World Wide Web, power networks, and so on. These networks are related to our lives. So the studies of complex networks will not only promote the development of certain branches of science but also change the life of mankind greatly [1–3]. In many cases, it is great interest to use the corresponding state system for estimating the state of the source network, that is state estimation [4, 5]. Nowadays, there are many papers study the state estimation for different style networks by controlling each node [6]. In [7], by means of Lyapunov stability theory, designing the global states observer for complex network with short time-delay under white noise. In [8], the problem of state estimation about the complex networks with different delay is studied. The state estimator network system is achieved by applying a controller to each node.

However, it is well known that there are many nodes in a complex network and it is literally impossible to obtain all the nodes' information by controlling each node. To

This work is supported by National Natural Science Foundation (NNSF) of China under Grant 61374180 and 61573194.

D. Yue et al. (Eds.): LSMS/ICSEE 2017, Part II, CCIS 762, pp. 575–584, 2017.
DOI: 10.1007/978-981-10-6373-2_58

save cost, we just control some nodes, that is pinning control [9, 10]. In [9], the problem about the external synchronization of nonlinear coupled discrete-time network without delay via pinning controlling is discussed. In [10], the idea of pinning control is used to achieve the external synchronization of discrete-time complex dynamic networks with internal coupling delay. In these documents, the pinning nodes are selected according to the topological degree's size of the networks. Since 2011, Liu published article about the controllability of complex networks in Natural [10], which studied the way to select drive nodes according to the maximum matching method.

Now, the problem about achieving synchronization based on pinning control is discussed by many scholars, otherwise not involve the state estimation. Until 2014, Yu et al. [12] proposed the pinning observability in complex networks to acquire the nodes' information firstly. But in [12], the network model is idealized without considering delay. And Yu assumed that the state information of some nodes in network is known, but only the output information of nodes can be measured in actual network. So motivated by the above articles, in this paper, we will study the discrete-time complex network with one-step induced delay and the state estimator are designed based on structural controllability and pinning observability which based on the output information of nodes.

The rest of this paper is organized as follows. In Sect. 2, the theorem about maximal matching is introduced. In Sect. 3, the model formulation of one-step induced delay and the state estimation with pinning controller will be given. In Sect. 4, some estimation criteria and the minimum number of pinned nodes will be given. In Sect. 5, an illustrative example of complex dynamic network is given to verify the effectiveness of the proposed method. Section 6, summarizes the paper and gives concluding remarks.

2   Preliminry

Liu analyzed the structural controllability based on the graph theory, and proposed the maximum matching method by the following minimum input theorem.

Theorem 1 [11]**: Minimal Input Theorem.** If the network is perfectly matched, the drive nodes set is any node in the network; otherwise, the minimum set of drive nodes N_D equals the set of nodes that are not matched after the "maximum matching". That is: $|N_D| = \max\{1, N - |M^*|\}$. Where $|M^*|$ is the "maximum matching" nodes in the directed network.

We used the Hopcroft & Krap algorithm, where the basic idea is to transform a directed network into the form of bipartite graphs and then find the augmented paths P from any matching M. There exists a greater match M' than M in the networks when having an augmented path. So the "maximum matching" sets will be found until such an augmented path does not exist. Specific steps are as follows:

(1) First, we transform Figs. 1 to 2 and then choose a matching edge $e_{12'}$. We set the nodes that matched as the matching nodes.

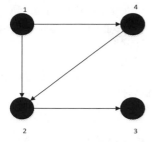

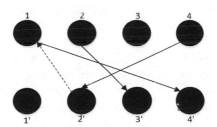

Fig. 1. Describe the network with four nodes.

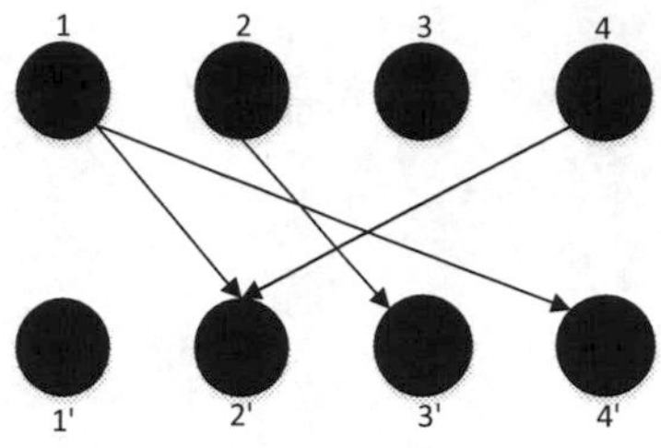

Fig. 2. Transform the Fig. 2 to the form of bipartite graphs.

(2) Second, selecting any unmatched node in the upper part of the bipartite graph and take it as the starting point to find the augmented path. An augmented path is a path consisting of alternate edges and unmatched edges. The number of edges in a augmented path must be odd, and the starting and ending points are unmatched, and the rest points are already matched. Therefore, according to the above principles, we can obtain the augmented path just from Fig. 3 and then invert the edges of the augmented path, that is, the matching edges become unmatched edges and the unmatched edges become matching edges. So that the number of matching edges can be increased.

Fig. 3. Look for the augmented path

(3) Finally, repeat the above steps, finding the unmatched nodes in the bipartite graph and taking this node as the starting node to find out its augmentation path. In the graph C, only node 2 and path $e_{23'}$ can be found. Therefore, the maximum matching sets e_{14}, e_{42}, e_{23} can be obtained, and the minimum number of driver node is 1 (Fig. 4).

According to theory of controllability, the driving node set is a non-matching node in the maximum matching edge set. In the above example, only node 1 is the node with no edge to pointed in the maximum matching edge set, so the node 1 is the unmatched node, that is, the driver node.

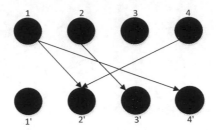

Fig. 4. Maximum match set path diagram

3   Estimator Design Based on Structural Properties and Pinning Control

In this paper, we consider a discrete complex network consisting of N identical nodes. Each node of the network is an n-dimensional dynamical system. The state equations of the entire network are described as follows:

$$\begin{cases} x_i(k+1) = f(x_i(k)) + a \sum_{j=1}^{N} w_{ij} \Gamma x_j(k) \\ y_i(k) = C_i x_i(k) \end{cases}, i = 1, 2, .., N \qquad (1)$$

Where $x_i(k) = (x_{i1}(k), x_{i2}(k), \ldots, x_{in}(k))^T \in R^n$ is the state vector of the ith node. $y_i(k) \in R^m(m \leq n)$ is the output vector of the node. $f(\cdot) : R^n \to R^n$ is a continuously linear function.

And $f(\cdot)$ satisfies: $f(x_i(k)) = A_i x_i(k), A_i \in R^{n \times n}, A = diag(A_1, A_2, \ldots, A_N)$. $\Gamma \in R^{n \times n}$ is the inner connection matrix between two connected node; $W = (w_{ij}) \in R^{N \times N}$ represents the outer-coupling configurations of the network, whose entries are defined as follows: if there is a link from node i to j, then set $w_{ij} = w_{ji} = 1(1 \leq i, j \leq N, i \neq j)$, otherwise $w_{ij} = w_{ji} = 0$. So the diagonal elements of matrix are defined by $w_{ii} = - \sum_{j=1, j \neq i}^{N} w_{ij} (i = 1, 2, \ldots, N)$, which ensures the diffusion that $\sum_{j=0}^{N} w_{ij} = 0$. So we can calculate the minimum number of driver nodes according to the matrix W.

$C_i \in R^{m \times n}(i = 1, 2, .., N)$, $C = diag(C_1, C_2, \ldots, C_N)$ is the output matrix of each node.

Considering the one-step induced delay in the process of network transmission, the observer node from the source network to receive the information can be expressed as Eq. (2):

$$\bar{y}_i(k) = C_i x_i(k-1), i = 1, 2, .., N \qquad (2)$$

In this paper, we only control the first l nodes of the state estimator network as shown in Eq. (3), and the first l nodes are the unmatched nodes in "maximum matching" set. So to reconstruct all the states in Eq. (1), the following observer is presented:

$$\begin{cases} \hat{x}_i(k+1) = f(\hat{x}_i(k)) + a \sum_{j=1}^{N} w_{ij} \Gamma \hat{x}_j(k) + u_i(k), 1 \le i \le l \\ \hat{x}_i(k+1) = f(\hat{x}_i(k)) + a \sum_{j=1}^{N} w_{ij} \Gamma \hat{x}_j(k), l+1 \le i \le N \end{cases} \quad (3)$$

$$\hat{y}_i(k) = C_i \hat{x}_i(k-1)$$

Where $i = 1, 2, .., N$, $\hat{x}_i(k) = (\hat{x}_{i1}(k), \hat{x}_{i2}(k), \ldots, \hat{x}_{in}(k))^T$ is the state vector of the ith node, $\hat{y}_i(k) \in R^m$ is the output vector of node. $u_i(k)$ is the output-feedback controllers that can be designed as:

$$u_i(k) = -K_i(\hat{y}_i(k) - y_i(k)) \quad (4)$$

Where $K_i = (K_{i1}, K_{i2}, \ldots, K_{im})^T$ is the gain of the pinning controller.

Then define the state errors: $e_i(k) = x_i(k) - \hat{x}_i(k)$, where $i = 1, 2, \ldots, N$. So we can obtain the following equality from (1), (3) and (4):

$$\begin{cases} e_i(k+1) = A_i e_i(k) + a \sum_{j=1}^{N} w_{ij} \Gamma e_j(k) - K_i \cdot C_i e_i(k-1), 1 \le i \le l \\ e_i(k+1) = A_i e_i(k) + a \sum_{j=1}^{N} w_{ij} \Gamma e_j(k), l+1 \le i \le N \end{cases} \quad (5)$$

Then we will drive the gain matrix K to guarantee $e_i(k)$ being convergent to zeros. So the following assumptions and lemmas will be used for demonstrating.

Lemma 1: For any vectors $x, y \in R^n$, the inequality holds:

$$2x^T y \le x^T Q x + y^T Q^{-1} y \quad (6)$$

where $Q \in R^{n \times n}$ is the positive definite matrix.

Lemma 2: For any vector $x \in R^n$, if $P \in R^{n \times n}$ is a positive definite matrix, $Q \in R^{n \times n}$ is a symmetric matrix, the following inequality holds:

$$\lambda_{\min}(P^{-1}Q)x^T P x \le x^T Q x \le \lambda_{\max}(P^{-1}Q)x^T P x \quad (7)$$

where $\lambda_{\min}(P)$ and $\lambda_{\max}(P)$ denote the smallest and the largest eigenvalues of the matrix P respectively.

4   Main Conclusion

Theorem 2: If there exist matrix $K = [K_1, K_2, \ldots, K_m]^T$, the following inequalities hold $\lambda_{\max}(a(W \otimes \Gamma)^T A - aC^T K^T (W \otimes \Gamma)) \le 0$ and $\lambda_{\max}(A^T KC - a(W \otimes \Gamma)^T KC \le 0$.

Determine the number l based on the Theorem 1 and exits $K_i \in R^{n \times n}$ that satisfies:

$$\lambda_{\max}(A^T A) - 1 + \lambda_{\max}(\bar{M}_i) + \lambda_{\max}(\bar{W}) < 0 (1 \leq i \leq l)$$

$\bar{M}_i = (A_i^T K_i C_i + C_i^T K_i^T A_i + C_i^T K_i^T KC)$ and $\lambda_{\max}(A^T A) - 1 + \lambda_{\max}(\bar{W}) < 0$. $\bar{W}$ is the matrix that the w_{ij} elements of W is replaced by $a^2 \lambda_{\max}(\Gamma^T \Gamma) w_{ij}^2$. Then the state estimator system (3) under the action of the pinning controller (4) can effectively estimate the state of the discrete complex network system (1).

Proof: Define a Lyapunov function as follows: $V(k) = v_1(k) + v_2(k)$, where

$$v_1(k) = \sum_{i=1}^{N} e_i^T(k) e_i(k), v_2(k) = \sum_{i=1}^{N} e_i^T(k-1) P e_i(k-1)$$

Then combining the Lyapunov theorem and Lemma 1–2, we can get:

$$\Delta v_1(k) = v_1(k+1) - v_1(k)$$
$$\leq \sum_{i=1}^{N} e_i^T(k) A_i^T A_i e_i(k) + \sum_{i=1}^{N} \sum_{j=1}^{N} [e_i^T(k) A_i^T a w_{ij} \Gamma e_j(k) + \sum_{i=1}^{l} \lambda_{\max}(C_i^T K_i^T K_i C_i) e_i^T(k-1) e_i(k-1)$$
$$+ \sum_{i=1}^{l} \sum_{j=1}^{N} e_i^T(k) [A_i^T K_i C_i + C_i^T K_i^T A_i - a w_{ij} C_i^T K_i^T \Gamma - a w_{ij} \Gamma K_i C_i] e_i(k)$$
$$+ \sum_{i=1}^{l} \sum_{j=1}^{N} e_j^T(k-1) [A_i^T K_i C_i + C_i^T K_i^T A_i - a w_{ij} C_i^T K_i^T \Gamma$$
$$- a w_{ij} \Gamma^T K_i C_i] e_j(k-1) - \sum_{i=1}^{N} e_i^T(k) e_i(k)$$
$$\leq e^T(k)(\lambda_{\max}(A^T A) I_N + R - I_N + \bar{W}) e(k) + \lambda_{\max}(a A^T(W \otimes \Gamma) - a C^T K^T(W \otimes \Gamma)) e1^T(k) e1(k)$$
$$+ \lambda_{\max}(a(W \otimes \Gamma)^T A - a(W \otimes \Gamma)^T KC) e1^T(k) e1(k)$$
$$+ \lambda_{\max}(A^T KC - a C^T K^T(W \otimes \Gamma)) e1^T(k-1) e1(k-1) e1^T(k-1) e1(k-1)$$

$$\tag{8}$$

Due to $\lambda_{\max}(a(W \otimes \Gamma)^T A - a C^T K^T(W \otimes \Gamma)) \leq 0$ and $\lambda_{\max}(A^T KC - a(W \otimes \Gamma)^T KC) \leq 0$, so the inequality (8) can be reduced to:

$$\Delta v_1(k) = v_1(k+1) - v_1(k) \leq e^T(k)(\lambda_{\max}(A^T A) I_N + R + \bar{W} - I_N) e(k)$$
$$+ \lambda_{\max}(C^T K^T KC) e^T(k-1) e(k-1)$$

Where, I_N is the unit matrix of $N \times N$, $e(k) = (e_1(k), e_2(k), \ldots, e_N(k))$

$$e(k-1) = (e_1(k-1), e_2(k-1), \ldots, e_N(k-1)),$$

$$e1(k) = (\underbrace{e_{11}(k), \ldots, e_{1n}(k)}_{n}, \ldots, \underbrace{e_{N1}(k), \ldots, e_{Nn}(k)}_{n})^T$$

with the nN brace over the full expression.

$$R = diag(\underbrace{\lambda_{\max}(M_1), \ldots, \lambda_{\max}(M_l)}_{l}, \underbrace{0, \ldots, 0}_{N-l}), M_i = A_i^T K_i C_i + C_i^T K_i^T A_i \ (i = 1, 2, \ldots, l)$$

$$\Delta v_2(k) = v_2(k+1) - v_2(k) = \sum_{i=1}^{N} e_i^T(k) P e_i(k) - \sum_{i=1}^{N} e_i^T(k-1) P e_i(k-1).$$

Since the matrix P is the positive definite matrix, so it can be assumed:
$P = \lambda_{\max}(C^T K^T K C) I_N$, so

$$\begin{aligned} \Delta V(k) &\le e^T(k)(\lambda_{\max}(A^T A) I_N + R + \bar{W} + \lambda_{\max}(C^T K^T K C) I_N - I_N) e(k) \\ &= e^T(k)(\lambda_{\max}(A^T A) I_N + \bar{M}_i + \bar{W} - I_N) e(k) \end{aligned} \tag{9}$$

Thus it is possible to make:

$$\bar{M}_i = A_i^T K_i C_i + C_i^T K_i^T A_i + C_i^T K_i^T K C \ (i = 1, 2, .., l).$$

Because of $\bar{W}$ is a real symmetric matrix, so there is orthogonal matrix Q to meet:

$$\bar{W} = Q^T diag(\lambda_1(\bar{W}), \lambda_2(\bar{W}), \ldots, \lambda_N(\bar{W})) Q.$$

Where $\lambda_i(\bar{W})$ represent the ith eigenvalues of the real symmetric matrices $\bar{W}$, and the eigenvalues are arranged in ascending order, i.e.: $\lambda_1(\bar{W}) \ge \lambda_2(\bar{W}) \ge \ldots \ge \lambda_N(W)$.
So the inequality (9) can be also expressed as:

$$\Delta V(k) \le (Qe(k))^T Z(Qe(k)), Z = diag(z_1, z_2, \ldots, z_N)$$

where:

$$z_i = \begin{cases} \lambda_{\max}(A^T A) - 1 + \lambda_{\max}(\bar{M}_i) + \lambda_i(\bar{W}), 1 \le i \le l \\ \lambda_{\max}(A^T A) - 1 + \lambda_i(\bar{W}), l+1 \le i \le N \end{cases} < 0 \tag{10}$$

Because of

$$\lambda_1(\bar{W}) \ge \lambda_2(\bar{W}) \ge \ldots \ge \lambda_N(\bar{W}), \text{ so } z_i < \begin{cases} \lambda_{\max}(A^T A) - 1 + \lambda_{\max}(\bar{M}_i) + \lambda_1(\bar{W}), 1 \le i \le l \\ \lambda_{\max}(A^T A) - 1 + \lambda_1(\bar{W}) \end{cases} < 0$$

Firstly, according to Theorem 1 and the network topology W, we can compute the number l of pinned nodes. Then, we set the gain matrix K of state estimation system according to the inequality (10) and the number l. So when $k \to \infty$, the estimation error vector can be convergent to zeros under the condition of the above, such as:

$$(e_1(k), e_2(k), \ldots, e_N(k))^T \to 0.$$

Finally we can get the conclusion that the state estimator system, as shown in the expression (3), can estimate the state of the complex network system, as shown in the expression (1), under the action of the pinning controller effectively, as shown in the expression (4).

5   Simulation

Consider a complex dynamical network model with 20 identical nodes, where each node has three states: $x_i = (x_{i1}, x_{i2}, x_{i3})^T$, $i = 1, 2, 3, \ldots, 20$. And the topology of this network is shown in Fig. 5.

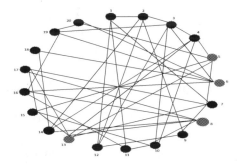

Fig. 5. The topology of the source network (Color figure online)

And $f(\cdot)$ satisfies: $f(x_i(k)) = A_i x_i(k), A_i \in R^{n \times n}, A = diag(A_1, A_2, \ldots, A_N)$. Then the parameters about the complex network system (1) can be set:

$$A_i = \begin{bmatrix} 0.6 & 0.3 & 0.1 \\ 0.2 & 0.5 & 0.3 \\ 0.6 & -0.6 & 1 \end{bmatrix}, C_i = \begin{bmatrix} 0.8 & 0 & 0 \\ 0 & 0.8 & 0 \\ 0 & 0 & 0.8 \end{bmatrix}, a = 0.08, \Gamma = \begin{bmatrix} 1 & 0 & 0 \\ 0 & 1 & 0 \\ 0 & 0 & 1 \end{bmatrix}$$

According to the Theorem 1, we get the conclusion that 4 nodes should be controlled, which are shown as the red nodes in Fig. 5. However, if the pinned nodes are selected by the size of the degree, we should control 8 nodes by simulation [8, 9]. Then according to the Theorem 2, one can get the gain matrix:

$$K_i = diag(0.9, 0.9, 0.9), i = 1, \ldots, 4.$$

Then the simulation results are shown in Fig. 6, 7 and 8. Figures 6, 7 and 8 are described the three components of error state changes over time for the 20 nodes in the network. From the figures, one can see that the error estimation converges to zero.

Finally, from the results of simulation, we can get the conclusion that the state estimator system can estimate the state of the complex network system effectively under the designed pinning observer.

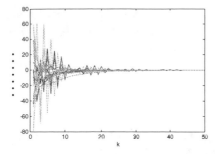

Fig. 6. The change curve of estimated error $e_{i1}(k)(i = 1, 2, \ldots, 20)$

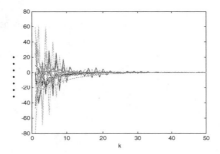

Fig. 7. The change curve of estimated error $e_{i2}(k)(i = 1, 2, \ldots, 20)$

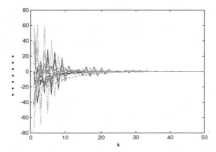

Fig. 8. The change curve of estimated error $e_{i3}(k)(i = 1, 2, \ldots, 20)$

6   Conclusion

In this paper, we studied the state estimation of a discrete complex network with one-step induced delay based on the pinning observability. By controlling only a fraction of the nodes selected according to maximum matching method, this paper designed a kind of output-feedback pinning observer, which is more practical for the engineering applications in contrast to existing methods. The condition for state estimation is derived by using Lapunov stability theory. Finally, the simulation results showed the effectiveness of the state estimator by applying the designed output-feedback pinning observer.

References

1. Gardillo, A., Scellato, S., Latora, V., et al.: Structural properties of planar graphs of urban street patterns. Phys. Rev. E **73**(6), 066–072 (2006)
2. Jeong, H., Tombor, B., et al.: The large-scale organization of metabolic networks. Nature **407**(6804), 65154–65164 (2000)
3. Wang, X., Li, X., Chen, G.: Complex network theory and its application. Tsinghua University Press, Beijing
4. Zhu, Z., Zhou, C., Hu, W.: Design of robust states observer for networked control systems with short time-delay. Control Decis. **20**(3), 66–73 (2005)
5. Roy, R., Murphy Jr., T.W., Maier, T.D., et al.: Dynamical control of a chaotic laser: experiment stabilization of a globally coupled system. Phys. Rev. Lett. **68**(9), 1259–1262 (1992)
6. Fan, C.X., Jiang, G.P., Jiang, F.H.: Synchronization between two complex dynamical network using scalar signals under pinning control. IEEE Trans. Circ. Syst. Pap. **57**(11), 2991–2998 (2010)
7. Zhu, Z., Zhou, C., Hu, W.: Design of robust states observer for networked control systems with short time-delay. Control Decis. **20**(3), 103–108 (2005)
8. Du, D., Qi, B., Fei, M.: Quantized control for networked control systems with multi-channel hybrid network-induced delay constraints. Syst. Sci. Math Sci. **35**(4), 397–406 (2015)
9. Liu, X., Chen, T.: Synchronization of nonlinear coupled networks via aperiodically intermittent pinning control. IEEE Trans. Neural Netw. Learn. Syst. **26**(1), 113–125 (2015)
10. Xu, C.-G., Guo, W.-H., Yang, C.-H.: Synchronous control of singular discrete time-delay complex dynamic network. J. Syst. Eng. **12**(25), 115–120 (2010)
11. Liu, Y.Y., Slotine, J.J., Barabrási, A.L.: Controllability of complex networks. Nature **473**(167), 100–105 (2011)
12. Yu, W., Wen, G., Lu, J., et al.: Pinning observability in complex networks. IET Control Theory Appl. **8**(18), 2136–2144 (2014)
13. Liu, X., Chen, T.: Synchronization of nonlinear coupled networks via aperiodically intermittent pinning control. IEEE Trans. Neural Netw. Learn. Syst. **07**(26), 45–60 (2015)
14. Wang, L., Wei, G., Shu, H.: State estimation for complex networks with randomly occurring coupling delays. Neuro Comput. **122**(4), 513–520 (2013)

Design of Output Feedback Controller for Networked Control Systems with Delay and Packet Dropout

Jun Xiang Dai$^{(\boxtimes)}$, Ying Zhou, Chao Sun, and Jin Xing Lin

College of Automation, Nanjing University of Posts and Telecommunications,
Nanjing 210023, China
junxiang.dai0@gamil.com

Abstract. The design problem of controller for a dynamic output feedback networked control system with uncertain short time delay and packet dropout is studied. The data packet dropout is assumed to be satisfied with the Bernoulli distribution sequence with known probability. The dynamic output feedback networked control system is modeled as a discrete time-varying system with uncertaintics. Sufficient conditions for the existence of the controller are given by the linear matrix inequality (LMI) method and the Lyapunov principle. And the controller design problem is transformed into solving the feasible solution of LMI. Finally, a simulation example is given to prove the effectiveness and feasibility of the design method.

Keywords: Networked control systems · Output feedback · Time delay · Packet dropout · Linear matrix inequality

1 Introduction

Over the past decade, with the rapid development of computer technology and communication technology, the networked control systems (NCSs) has attracted more and more attention [1–6]. However, the network as an unstable medium, due to its bandwidth and the physical limitations of service capacity, the packet in network transmission inevitably exists network induction delay, packet dropout and disorder and other issues [7], these problems can easily lead to the instability of NCSs, so it has been widely concerned.

There have been significant research efforts on the design of controllers for NCSs with time delay and packet dropout. The paper [8] discusses a class of NCSs with stochastic short delay, using binary sequences satisfying the Bernoulli distribution to describe the stochastic delay of data transmission, and design the controller with H_∞ performance. In [9], for short time delay NCSs with white noise disturbance, the influence of stochastic delay on the system is transformed into unknown bounded uncertainties by matrix decomposition. In [10], for discrete time NCSs with random

This work is supported by National Natural Science Foundation (NNSF) of China under Grant 61104103, 61473158 and the Natural Science Foundation of Jiangsu Province under Grant BK20141430.

© Springer Nature Singapore Pte Ltd. 2017
D. Yue et al. (Eds.): LSMS/ICSEE 2017, Part II, CCIS 762, pp. 585–595, 2017.
DOI: 10.1007/978-981-10-6373-2_59

long delays, two Markov chains are used to describe the network induced delay of feedback and forward channel. The closed-loop system is modeled into a Markov stochastic time delay system. In [11], for the NCSs with packet dropout, which is described as a switching system model, and the fault-tolerant controller design is carried out on the stochastic packet dropout process. In [12], the controller design of linear NCSs with stochastic packet dropout is discussed. A binary switching sequence satisfying the Bernoulli distribution is used to describe the random packet dropout.

So far, most existing results are mainly for NCSs with time delay or packet dropout, and the design of the state feedback controller, such as paper [13]. But the state of the system is often unable to detect completely. In this paper, the output feedback control system of NCSs with time-varying delays and packet dropout is considered. Not only considering the situation of uncertain time delay and packet dropout, but also considering the fact that the system state is not easily all observed. Compared with the previous study, the conditions considered in this paper are more reasonable and realistic. Based on the above conditions, we establish an output feedback network control system model, which transforms the time delay into system uncertain parameters. The packet dropout is described by Bernoulli random sequence, and the robustness of the system is studied by Lyapunov stability principle and LMI tools. The design method of the controller is given, and the validity of the results is verified by simulation.

2   Problem Formulation

The structure of the output feedback networked control system with delay and packet dropout is shown in Fig. 1.

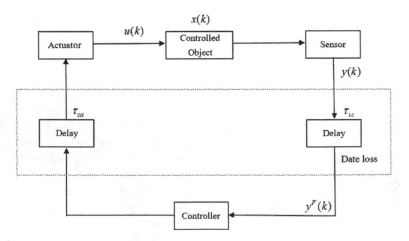

Fig. 1. System structure diagram.

where τ_{ca} represents the delay between the controller and the actuator channel, τ_{sc} represents the delay between the sensor and the controller channel. We make the following assumptions about the NCSs:

Assumption 1: The sensor is clock driven and the sampling period is constant T.
Assumption 2: The controller and actuator are the event-driven, i.e. receiving the data signal for immediate correspondence operation.
Assumption 3: The data are transmitted in a single packet. Assume that the packet dropout occurs between sensors and controllers. Packet dropout satisfies Bernoulli random sequence and probability are known.
Assumption 4: The total time-induced delay of the k periodic network of the closed loop is τ_k ($\tau_k = \tau_{ca} + \tau_{sc}$). In this paper the delay is uncertain short delay, i.e. $\tau_k \in [0, T]$.

Based on the above conditions, the state variables $y^F(k)$ received by the controller can be expressed as:

$$y^F(k) = \alpha(k)y(k) \tag{1}$$

where $\alpha(k)$ is a Bernoulli random sequence. Its value can be 0 and 1, satisfying the following probability:

$$\begin{aligned} prob\{\alpha(k) = 1\} &= E\{\alpha(k)\} = \alpha \\ prob\{\alpha(k) = 0\} &= 1 - E\{\alpha(k)\} = 1 - \alpha \end{aligned} \tag{2}$$

When $\alpha(k) = 1$, the controller can completely receive data, that means no packet dropout; When $\alpha(k) = 0$, the data is lost. α is a known integer real number.

Consider the following linear time-invariant system

$$\begin{cases} \dot{x}(t) = Ax(t) + Bu(t) \\ y(t) = Cx(t) \end{cases} \tag{3}$$

where $x(t) \in R^n$, $u(t) \in R^r$ and $y(t) \in R^m$ represents the state of the system, control inputs and measurement outputs respectively. A, B, C are constant matrices with corresponding dimensions.

Based on the assumption 1–4 above, the linear time invariant system can be discretized into

$$\begin{cases} x(k+1) = A_d x(k) + (B_0 + DF(\tau_k)E)u(k) + (B_1 - DF(\tau_k)E)u(k-1) \\ y(k) = Cx(k) \end{cases} \tag{4}$$

where $A_d = e^{AT}$, B_0, B_1, D and E are constant matrices, $F(\tau_k)$ is a time-varying matrix which contains uncertainties.

$$\begin{aligned} B_0 &= \Lambda diag(-\frac{1}{\lambda_1}, \cdots, -\frac{1}{\lambda_n})\Lambda^{-1}B \\ B_1 &= \Lambda diag(-\frac{1}{\lambda_1}e^{-\lambda_1 T}, \cdots, -\frac{1}{\lambda_n}e^{-\lambda_n T})\Lambda^{-1}B \\ D &= \Lambda diag(-\frac{1}{\lambda_1}e^{-\lambda_1 \alpha_1}, \cdots, -\frac{1}{\lambda_n}e^{-\lambda_n \alpha_n}) \\ F(\tau_k) &= diag(e^{\lambda_1(T-\tau_k-\alpha_1)}, \cdots, e^{\lambda_n(T-\tau_k-\alpha_n)}) \\ E &= \Lambda^{-1}B \end{aligned} \tag{5}$$

where $\lambda_1, \lambda_2, \cdots, \lambda_n$ are the n different eigenvalues of the matrix A, $\Lambda_1, \cdots, \Lambda_n$ are the eigenvectors of the matrix A. $F(\tau_k)$ satisfies the following conditions

$$F^T(\tau_k)F(\tau_k) \le I \tag{6}$$

In order to improve the control performance, the controller adopts the dynamic output feedback controller with time delay compensation

$$\begin{cases} x_c(k+1) = A_c x_c(k) + B_c y^F(k) \\ u(k) = C_c x_c(k) \end{cases} \tag{7}$$

where x_c is the controller state, A_c, B_c, C_c are constant matrices with corresponding dimensions.

Connecting Eqs. (4) and (7), substituting $u(k) = C_c x_c(k)$ into the Eq. (3), we can obtain the following:

$$\begin{cases} x(k+1) = A_d x(k) + (B_0 + DF(\tau_k)E)C_c x_c(k) + (B_1 - DF(\tau_k)E)C_c x_c(k-1) \\ y(k) = Cx(k) \end{cases} \tag{8}$$

Choose the augmented vector as $z(k) = [x^T(k) \quad x_c^T(k)]^T$, the closed loop NCSs model is

$$z(k+1) = \Phi_1 z(k) + \Phi_2 z(k-1) \tag{9}$$

where

$$\Phi_1 = \begin{bmatrix} A_d & (B_0 + DF(\tau_k)E)C_c \\ \alpha(k)B_c C & A_c \end{bmatrix},$$

$$\Phi_2 = \begin{bmatrix} 0 & (B_1 - DF(\tau_k)E)C_c \\ 0 & 0 \end{bmatrix}$$

It can be seen that the output feedback NCSs with uncertain delay and packet dropout can be transformed into a class of discrete time-varying systems with uncertain terms.

The following are the lemmas to prove the stability of the closed-loop system (9):

Lemma 1 [14]. (Schur complement) For symmetric matrix A, symmetric positive definite matrix B, matrix C, thus $A + B^T CB < 0$ is equivalent to

$$\begin{bmatrix} A & B^T \\ B & -C^{-1} \end{bmatrix} < 0 \text{ or } \begin{bmatrix} -C^{-1} & B \\ B^T & A \end{bmatrix} < 0$$

Lemma 2 [15]. Let $W, M, N, F(k)$ be the real matrices of appropriate dimensions such that $W > 0$ and $F^T(\tau_k)F(\tau_k) \le I$. Then, for any scalar $\varepsilon > 0$ such that $W + MF(k)N + N^T F^T(K)M^T < 0$, we have $W + \varepsilon MM^T + \varepsilon^{-1}N^T N < 0$.

3 Main Result

Theorem 1. For NCSs (3) with uncertain time delay and packet dropout delay, where $\tau_k \in [0, T]$ satisfy constraints $F^T(\tau_k)F(\tau_k) \leq I$, and the packet dropout satisfies the Bernoulli stochastic sequence (2). If there exist symmetric positive definite matrices $\bar{P}, \bar{R} \in R^{n \times n}$, $\bar{Q}, \bar{S} \in R^{p \times p}$, matrices $W \in R^{r \times p}$, $N \in R^{p \times p}$, $Y \in R^{r \times n}$, and scalar $\varepsilon > 0$ satisfying

$$
\begin{bmatrix}
\bar{R} - \bar{P} & 0 & 0 & 0 & \bar{P}A_d^T & 0 & \alpha V^T & \beta V^T \\
0 & \bar{S} - \bar{Q} & 0 & 0 & W^T B_0^T & W^T E^T & U^T & 0 \\
0 & 0 & -\bar{R} & 0 & 0 & 0 & 0 & 0 \\
0 & 0 & 0 & -\bar{S} & W^T B_1^T & -W^T F^T & 0 & 0 \\
A_d P & B_0 W & 0 & B_1 W & \varepsilon DD^T - \bar{P} & 0 & 0 & 0 \\
0 & EW & 0 & -EW & 0 & -\varepsilon I & 0 & 0 \\
\alpha V & U & 0 & 0 & 0 & 0 & -\bar{Q} & 0 \\
\beta V & 0 & 0 & 0 & 0 & 0 & 0 & -\bar{Q}
\end{bmatrix} < 0 \quad (10)
$$

where α, β are given constants. Then the control law exists, which makes the closed-loop system (9) asymptotic stability.

When the matrix inequality (10) has a feasible solution, the control law is

$$
\begin{cases}
x_c(k+1) = U\bar{Q}^{-1}x_c(k) + V(C\bar{P})^{-1}\alpha(k)y(k) \\
u(k) = W\bar{Q}^{-1}x_c(k)
\end{cases}
\quad (11)
$$

Proof: Choose a Lyapunov functional candidate for the system (9) as follows

$$
V(k) = x^T(k)Px(k) + x_c^T(k)Qx_c(k) + x^T(k-1)Rx(k-1) + x_c^T(k-1)Sx_c(k-1)
\quad (12)
$$

where $P, R \in R^{n \times x}$, $Q, S \in R^{p \times p}$ are symmetric positive definite matrices.

Then along the solution of system (9) we have

$$
\begin{aligned}
\Delta V(k) &= V(k+1) - V(k) \\
&= x^T(k)(A_d P A_d + (\alpha(k)B_c C)^T Q(\alpha(k)B_c C) + R - P)x(k) \\
&\quad + x^T(k)(A_d^T P M_1 + (\alpha(k)B_c C)^T Q A_c)x_c(k) \\
&\quad + x^T(k)(A_d^T P M_2)x_c(k-1) + x_c^T(k)(M_1^T P A_d + A_c^T Q\alpha(k)B_c C)x(k) \\
&\quad + x_c^T(k)(M_1^T P M_1 + A_c^T Q A_c + S - Q)x_c(k) + x_c^T(k)(M_1 P M_2)x_c(k-1) \\
&\quad + x^T(-R)x(k-1) + x_c^T(k-1)(M_2^T P A_d)x(k) + x_c^T(k-1)(M_2 P M_1)x_c(k) \\
&\quad + x_c^T(k-1)(M_2 P M_2 - S)x_c(k-1)
\end{aligned}
$$

where $F = F(\tau_k)$, $M_1 = (B_0 + DFE)C_c$, $M_2 = (B_1 - DFE)C_c$.

For $E\{\alpha(k) - \alpha\} = 0$, $E\{(\alpha(k) - \alpha)^2\} = (1 - \alpha)\alpha \triangleq \beta^2$, we obtain

$$
\begin{aligned}
&E\{V(x(k+1)|x(k))\} - V(x(k))\\
=&x^T(k)(A_dPA_d + ((\alpha(k) - a)B_cC + aB_cC)^TQ((\alpha(k) - a)B_cC + aB_cC) + R - P)x(k)\\
&+ x^T(k)(A_d^TPM_1 + ((\alpha(k) - a)B_cC + aB_cC)^TQA_c)x_c(k) + x^T(k)(A_d^TPM_2)x_c(k-1)\\
&+ x_c^T(k)(M_1^TPA_d + A_c^TQ((\alpha(k) - a)B_cC + aB_cC))x(k)\\
&+ x_c^T(k)(M_1^TPM_1 + A_c^TQA_c + S - Q)x_c(k) + x_c^T(k)(M_1PM_2)x_c(k-1)\\
&+ x^T(-R)x(k-1) + x_c^T(k-1)(M_2^TPA_d)x(k) + x_c^T(k-1)(M_2PM_1)x_c(k)\\
&+ x_c^T(k-1)(M_2PM_2 - S)x_c(k-1)\\
=&x^T(k)(A_dPA_d + a(B_cC)^TQ(B_cC) + R - P)x(k) + x^T(k)(A_d^TPM_1 + a(B_cC)^TQA_c)x_c(k)\\
&+ x^T(k)(A_d^TPM_2)x_c(k-1) + x_c^T(k)(M_1^TPA_d + aA_c^TQ(B_cC))x(k)\\
&+ x_c^T(k)(M_1^TPM_1 + A_c^TQA_c + S - Q)x_c(k) + x_c^T(k)(M_1PM_2)x_c(k-1)\\
&+ x^T(-R)x(k-1) + x_c^T(k-1)(M_2^TPA_d)x(k) + x_c^T(k-1)(M_2PM_1)x_c(k)\\
&+ x_c^T(k-1)(M_2PM_2 - S)x_c(k-1)\\
\triangleq&\bar{z}^TM\bar{z}
\end{aligned}
$$

where $\bar{z} = \begin{bmatrix} x^T(k) & x_c^T(k) & x^T(k-1) & x_c^T(k-1) \end{bmatrix}$,

$$
M = \begin{bmatrix}
A_d^TPA_d + \alpha(B_cC)^TQ(B_cC) + R - P & A_d^TPM_1 + \alpha(B_cC)^TQA_c & 0 & A_d^TPM_2\\
M_1^TPA_d + \alpha A_c^TQB_cC & M_1^TPM_1 + A_c^TQA_c + S - Q & 0 & M_1PM_2\\
0 & 0 & -R & 0\\
M_2^TPA_d & M_2PM_1 & 0 & M_2PM_2 - S
\end{bmatrix}
$$

$$(13)$$

By the above conditions, $\Delta V(k) < 0$ is equivalent to $M < 0$, then consider

$$
M = \begin{bmatrix}
A_d^TPA_d + \alpha(B_cC)^TQ(B_cC) + R - P & A_d^TPM_1 + \alpha(B_cC)^TQA_c & 0 & 0\\
M_1^TPA_d + \alpha A_c^TQB_cC & M_1^TPM_1 + A_c^TQA_c + S - Q & 0 & 0\\
0 & 0 & -R & 0\\
0 & 0 & 0 & -S
\end{bmatrix}
$$

$$
+ \begin{bmatrix} A_d^T\\ M_1^T\\ 0\\ M_2^T \end{bmatrix} P[A_d \quad M_1 \quad 0 \quad M_2]
$$

$$(14)$$

Based on Schur complement, and consider the definition of M_1, M_2, define

$$
H = \begin{bmatrix}
\alpha(B_cC)^TQ(B_cC)+R-P & \alpha(B_cC)^TQA_c & 0 & 0 & A_d^T \\
\alpha A_c^TQB_cC & A_c^TQA_c+S-Q & 0 & 0 & (B_0C_c)^T \\
0 & 0 & -R & 0 & 0 \\
0 & 0 & 0 & -S & (B_1C_c)^T \\
A_d & B_0C_c & 0 & B_1C_c & -P^{-1}
\end{bmatrix}
$$

Then

$$
M = H + \begin{bmatrix} 0 \\ 0 \\ 0 \\ 0 \\ D \end{bmatrix} F[0\ \ EC_c\ \ 0\ \ -EC_c\ \ 0] + [0\ \ EC_c\ \ 0\ \ -EC_c\ \ 0]^T F^T \begin{bmatrix} 0 \\ 0 \\ 0 \\ 0 \\ D \end{bmatrix}^T < 0 \quad (15)
$$

According to Lemma 2, for any scalar $\varepsilon > 0$ such that Eq. (15) was established, we have

$$
H + \varepsilon \begin{bmatrix} 0 \\ 0 \\ 0 \\ 0 \\ D^T \end{bmatrix} [0\ \ 0\ \ 0\ \ 0\ \ D] + \varepsilon^{-1} \begin{bmatrix} 0 \\ (EC_c)^T \\ 0 \\ -(EC_c)^T \\ 0 \end{bmatrix} [0\ \ EC_c\ \ 0\ \ -EC_c\ \ 0] < 0
$$

By Schur complement, we obtain

$$
\begin{bmatrix}
\alpha(B_cC)^TQ(B_cC)+R-P & \alpha(B_cC)^TQA_c & 0 & 0 & A_d^T & 0 \\
\alpha A_c^TQB_cC & A_c^TQA_c+S-Q & 0 & 0 & (B_0C_c)^T & (EC_c)^T \\
0 & 0 & -R & 0 & 0 & 0 \\
0 & 0 & 0 & -S & (B_1C_c)^T & -(EC_c)^T \\
A_d & B_0C_c & 0 & B_1C_c & \varepsilon DD^T-P^{-1} & 0 \\
0 & EC_c & 0 & -EC_c & 0 & -\varepsilon I
\end{bmatrix} < 0
$$

By the same method as before, we get (16)

$$
\begin{bmatrix}
R-P & 0 & 0 & 0 & A_d^T & 0 & \alpha(B_cC)^T & \beta(B_cC)^T \\
0 & S-Q & 0 & 0 & (B_0C_c)^T & (EC_c)^T & A_c^T & 0 \\
0 & 0 & -R & 0 & 0 & 0 & 0 & 0 \\
0 & 0 & 0 & -S & (B_1C_c)^T & -(EC_c)^T & 0 & 0 \\
A_d & B_0C_c & 0 & B_1C_c & \varepsilon DD^T-P^{-1} & 0 & 0 & 0 \\
0 & EC_c & 0 & -EC_c & 0 & -\varepsilon I & 0 & 0 \\
\alpha B_cC & A_c & 0 & 0 & 0 & 0 & -Q^{-1} & 0 \\
\beta B_cC & 0 & 0 & 0 & 0 & 0 & 0 & -Q^{-1}
\end{bmatrix} < 0
$$

$$(16)$$

It should be noted that matrix inequality (16) is not a linear matrix inequality and difficult to be solved. For this, we have following method.

Through left-and-right multiplying by $diag\{P^{-1} \quad Q^{-1} \quad P^{-1} \quad Q^{-1} \quad I \quad I \quad I\}$, and make $\bar{P} = P^{-1}$, $\bar{Q} = Q^{-1}$, $\bar{R} = P^{-1}RP^{-1}$, $\bar{S} = Q^{-1}SQ^{-1}$, we obtain

$$
\begin{bmatrix}
\bar{R} - \bar{P} & 0 & 0 & 0 & \bar{P}A_d^T & 0 & \alpha\bar{P}(B_cC)^T & \beta\bar{P}(B_cC)^T \\
0 & \bar{S} - \bar{Q} & 0 & 0 & \bar{Q}(B_0C_c)^T & \bar{Q}(EC_c)^T & \bar{Q}A_c^T & 0 \\
0 & 0 & -\bar{R} & 0 & 0 & 0 & 0 & 0 \\
0 & 0 & 0 & -\bar{S} & \bar{Q}(B_1C_c)^T & -\bar{Q}(EC_c)^T & 0 & 0 \\
A_d\bar{P} & B_0C_c\bar{Q} & 0 & B_1C_c\bar{Q} & \varepsilon DD^T - P^{-1} & 0 & 0 & 0 \\
0 & EC_c\bar{Q} & 0 & -EC_c\bar{Q} & 0 & -\varepsilon I & 0 & 0 \\
\alpha B_c C\bar{P} & A_c\bar{Q} & 0 & 0 & 0 & 0 & -\bar{Q} & 0 \\
\beta B_c C\bar{P} & 0 & 0 & 0 & 0 & 0 & 0 & -\bar{Q}
\end{bmatrix} < 0
$$

(17)

Define $U = A_c\bar{Q}$, $V = B_cC\bar{P}$, $W = C_c\bar{Q}$, then (17) can be transformed to (10). If (10) has the feasible solution, then figure out A_c, B_c, C_c, and substitute the results into (7). The dynamic output feedback controller can be obtained.

For Theorem 1, the feasibility of solving linear matrix inequalities with $\bar{P}, \bar{Q}, \bar{R}, \bar{S}, U, V, W, \varepsilon$ as a variable can be solved by using the LMI toolbox of Matlab.

4 Simulation Example

Consider the NCSs in the form of (3)

$$
\begin{cases}
\dot{x}(t) = \begin{bmatrix} 0 & 1 \\ -2 & -3 \end{bmatrix} x(t) + \begin{bmatrix} 0 \\ 1 \end{bmatrix} u(t) \\
y(k) = \begin{bmatrix} 1 & 0 \end{bmatrix} x(k)
\end{cases}
$$

(18)

If the sampling period $T = 0.1$ s, the eigenvalues of A are $\lambda_1 = -1, \lambda_2 = -2$. The eigenvector of A is $\Lambda = [\Lambda_1, \Lambda_2] = \begin{bmatrix} 1 & 1 \\ -1 & -2 \end{bmatrix}$. Define $\alpha_1 = -1$, $\alpha_2 = -1$ in $F(\tau_k)$, then we can obtain

$$
A_d = \begin{bmatrix} 0.9909 & 0.0861 \\ -0.1722 & 0.7326 \end{bmatrix}, B_0 = \begin{bmatrix} 0.5 \\ 0 \end{bmatrix}, B_1 = \begin{bmatrix} 0.4945 \\ 0.1162 \end{bmatrix}, E = \begin{bmatrix} 1 \\ -1 \end{bmatrix},
$$

$$
D = \begin{bmatrix} 0.3679 & 0.0677 \\ -0.3679 & -0.1353 \end{bmatrix}
$$

Assume that the packet dropout rate is $1 - E\{\alpha(k)\} = 1 - \alpha = 0.1$. Solving the linear matrix inequality (10) by the LMI tool in Matlab, we can obtain

$$P = \begin{bmatrix} 18.0142 & -17.8291 \\ -17.8291 & 37.9709 \end{bmatrix}, Q = \begin{bmatrix} 8.4977 & -2.7666 \\ -2.7666 & 5.1184 \end{bmatrix}, R = \begin{bmatrix} 1.7230 & -2.7039 \\ -2.7039 & 8.0404 \end{bmatrix},$$

$$S = \begin{bmatrix} 4.5788 & -0.3343 \\ -0.3343 & 1.0004 \end{bmatrix}, U = \begin{bmatrix} -2.7666 & 5.1184 \\ -0.5731 & -0.2352 \end{bmatrix}, V = \begin{bmatrix} 0 & 0 \\ -1.4411 & 1.4263 \end{bmatrix},$$

$$W = [0.1423 \quad -0.0041], \varepsilon = 0.721,$$

Thus, the controller parameters can be obtained

$$\begin{cases} x_c(k+1) = \begin{bmatrix} 0 & 0.98 \\ -0.11 & -0.11 \end{bmatrix} x_c(k) + \begin{bmatrix} 0 \\ -0.01 \end{bmatrix} \alpha(k)y(k) \\ u(k) = [0.02 \quad 0.01] x_c(k) \end{cases} \tag{19}$$

Under the action of this control law, the initial state of the closed-loop system is $\begin{bmatrix} x_1 \\ x_2 \end{bmatrix} = \begin{bmatrix} 4 \\ 1 \end{bmatrix}$. The state response diagram of a closed-loop system can be obtained by Matlab simulation tool as shown in Fig. 2, It can be seen from the figure that the state of closed-loop system has bounded and finally tends to 0, the system is stable, so the method is feasible (Fig. 3).

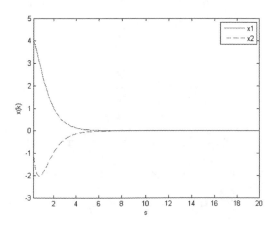

Fig. 2. State response of closed-loop system.

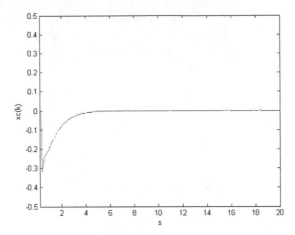

Fig. 3. State response of controller.

5 Conclusion

In the case where the system sensor sampling period is constant, the controller and actuator are event driven, the data are transmitted in a single packet and the noise are not considered. In this paper, for the networked control system with both uncertain delay and packet dropout, the system is modeled as a discrete time-varying system with uncertain items, the existence condition of controller is given by the Lypunov stability principle and method of LMI. The design method of control law is given. The final simulation example proves that the designed controller is effective.

References

1. Xia, Y.Q., Gao, Y.L., Yan, L.P., Fu, M.Y.: Recent progress in networked control systems - a survey. Int. J. Autom. Comput. **04**, 343–367 (2015)
2. Li, H.B., Sun, Q.Z., Sun, F.C.: Networked control systems: an overview of state-of-the-art and the prospect in future research. Control Theory Appl. **02**, 238–243 (2010)
3. Yang, T.C.: Networked control system: a brief survey. IET Proc. Control Theory Appl. **153**(4), 403–412 (2006)
4. You, Y.K., Xie, L.H.: Survey of recent progress in networked control systems. Acta Autom. Sinica **02**, 101–118 (2013)
5. Antsaklis, P., Baillieul, J.: Special issue on technology of networked control systems. Proc. IEEE **95**(1), 5–8 (2007)
6. Hespanha, J.P., Naghshtabrizi, P., Xu, Y.G.: A survey of recent results in networked control systems. Proc. IEEE **95**(1), 138–162 (2007)
7. Chen, Z.P., Liu, L., Zhang, J.F.: Observer based networked control systems with networked-induced time delay. In: International Conference on Systems, pp. 3333–3337 (2004)
8. Wu, W., Lin, Q.B., Cai, F.H., Yang, F.W.: Design of H-infinity output feedback controller for networked control system with random delays. Control Theory Appl. **05**, 920–924 (2008)

9. Zhu, Z.Q., Zhou, C., Hu, W.L.: Design of robust H2/H∞ states observer for networked control systems with short time-delay. Control Decis. **03**, 280–284 (2005)
10. Yu, L., Wu, Y.S., Song, H.B.: Guaranteed cost control for networked control systems with random long time-delay. Control Theory Appl. **08**, 985–990 (2010)
11. Zhao, M.Y., Liu, H.P., Li, Z.J., Sun, D.H.: Fault tolerant control for networked control systems with packet loss and time delay. Int. J. Autom. Comput. **02**, 244–253 (2011)
12. Li, J.G., Jiang, Y., Lu, L.: Controller design for networked control systems with random packet losses. Comput. Simul. **09**, 302–305 (2013)
13. Ma, J.T., Bu, X.H., Cheng, Z.H., Han, X.J.: Two-dimensional state feedback control with missing measurement. Control Eng. China **07**, 1080–1084 (2016)
14. Yue, D., Han, Q.L., Peng, C.: State feedback controller design of networked control systems. IEEE Trans. Circ. Syst. **51**, 640–644 (2004)
15. Yu, L.: Optimal guaranteed cost control of linear uncertain system: an LMI approach. Control Theory Appl. **03**, 423–428 (2000)

Distributed Economic Dispatch Based on Consensus Algorithm Under Event-Triggered Mechanism

Shengxuan Weng$^{(\boxtimes)}$, Dong Yue, and Chongxin Huang

Institute of Advanced Technology,
Nanjing University of Posts and Telecommunications, Nanjing 210023, China
shxweng@gmail.com

Abstract. This paper investigates the problem of distributed event-triggered economic dispatch method for generators in power system. Considering the issue of limited bandwidth of communication network in practical application, the novel distributed event-triggered mechanism are introduced to reduce the information transmission pressure, and the distributed economic dispatch method is constructed based on the triggering schemes. Under the designed method, the economic dispatch problem can be solved and the generation-demand equality constraint is satisfied. Simulation results show the effectiveness of the proposed method.

1 Introduction

Economic dispatch is a fundamental problem in the research and application areas of power system. It aims at reducing the total cost of power generation by optimization algorithms while facing the constraints of total load demand as well as respecting individual resource capacity limits [4,6,13]. Traditionally, the economic dispatch method usually be executed in a centralized architecture [1,8,12,13]. In this architecture, the centralized control center is needed to collect the global information of power system, calculate the optimization values by the designed optimization algorithm, and send these values to all the generators in system globally to achieve the goal of economic dispatch. However, this traditional economic dispatch method based on centralized architecture is difficult to implement for the future power system which contains a lot of distributed generators. This can be reflected in the following aspects: Firstly, the centralized control center is under an arduous calculation task and costly. Secondly, the robustness is inferior since all the calculation tasks are implemented at the centralized control center, which may face the single-point failure. Finally, because of the widespread use of distributed generators and the plug-and-play technology in future power system, it is difficult to obtain the topology of power network, which makes it difficult to get the global information of power system for the

---

C. Huang—This work was sponsored by National Natural Science Foundation of China (Grant Nos. 61503193, 61533010, 51507085 and 61374055).

D. Yue et al. (Eds.): LSMS/ICSEE 2017, Part II, CCIS 762, pp. 596–603, 2017.
DOI: 10.1007/978-981-10-6373-2_60

centralized control center. Therefore, the economic dispatch method based on distributed architecture will emerge as required.

For the distributed economic dispatch, the generators require only neighbor-to-neighbor interaction and calculate the incremental cost based on the designed consensus algorithm locally to make the incremental costs of all generators achieve consensus. Based on the consensus incremental cost, the generator can obtain the optimal output power in order to minimize the total cost of generator [2,3,10,14,17,18]. Compared to the centralized economic dispatch, the tasks of optimization algorithm are assigned to all the generators in power system in the distributed one, then the costly centralized control center is not required. Furthermore, the robustness is enhanced and the plug-and play function can be implemented well since the calculation tasks are interspersed. Therefore, the distributed economic dispatch is especially suitable for the future power system. In addition, the implementation of distributed economic dispatch is based on local neighbor-to-neighbor interaction, which saves the cost of communication network construction.

As mentioned before, each generator in power system needs to communication with its neighbors to execute the distributed economic dispatch. The existing distributed economic dispatch method assumes that the information of each generator can be transmitted through the communication network continuously. However, for the practical communication network with band-width constraint, it would be desirable to reduce the communication burdens between generators. To solve this problem, the event-triggered mechanism, which is used in networked control system and multi-agent system recently, maybe a feasible scheme [5,7,9,15,19]. Under the event-triggered mechanism, the unnecessary redundant communication can be mitigated since it emphasizes that the information broadcasting is executed only when it is needed.

This paper focuses on the distributed economic dispatch method under event-triggered mechanism. In order to reduce the communication burdens, the distributed event-triggered mechanism is introduced in the economic dispatch algorithm design. The information broadcasting time of each generator is determined by the constructed event-triggered conditions. This method can reduce the amount of information transmission, which implies that less pressure in communication network can be expected. Moreover, either the implementation of the designed event-triggered mechanism or optimisation algorithm needs only the local information and discrete triggered information broadcasted from neighbors. This means that the novel event-triggered economic dispatch method can be executed in a distributed architecture, which can avoid the shortcomings of centralized strategy as mentioned before.

The paper is organized as follows. Section 2 presents the problem formulation and preliminaries. The main theoretic result is given in Sect. 3 and the simulation result is shown in Sect. 4. The conclusion and our future works are located in Sect. 5.

2   Problem Formulation and Preliminaries

Consider a power system contained n generators. The cost functions of generator $i(i = 1, \ldots, n)$ is usually approximated by a quadratic function as follows

$$C_i(P_i) = \alpha_i + \beta_i P_i + \gamma_i P_i^2 \tag{1}$$

where the constants α_i, β_i and γ_i are the cost coefficients, and P_i denotes the output power of generator i.

The aim of economic dispatch problem is to schedule the power output of each generator such that the total cost of generation is minimized while satisfying the power balance requirements. It can be expressed as

$$\min \sum_{i=1}^{n} C_i(P_i) \tag{2}$$

subject to the generation-demand equality constraint

$$\sum_{i=1}^{n} P_i = P_D \tag{3}$$

where P_D represents the total power demand in the power system.

In this paper, the distributed economic dispatch method is considered because it can avoid the disadvantages of the centralized one as mentioned before. This implies that each generator needs to communicate with its neighbors. An undirected fixed graph $G \triangleq \{\mathcal{V}, \mathcal{E}, A\}$ is used to describe the communication network topology among all the generators by graph theory. $\mathcal{V} \triangleq \{v_1, \ldots, v_n\}$ is the node set where v_i signifies generator i. $\mathcal{E} \triangleq \{(v_j, v_i), \; if \; j \to i\}$ is the edge set in which $j \to i$ represents that the information of the jth generator can be transmitted to the ith one. $A \triangleq \{a_{ij}\} \in R^{n \times n}$ is the weighted adjacency matrix of graph G, where $a_{ij} = 1$ if and only if $(v_i, v_j) \in \mathcal{E}$, otherwise $a_{ij} = 0$, and it is assumed that $a_{ii} = 0$. The neighbouring set of node v_i is denoted by $N_i \triangleq \{v_j \in \mathcal{V} | (v_j, v_i) \in \mathcal{E}\}$, and the cardinal number of N_i is represented as $|N_i|$. The 'undirected' means that $(v_i, v_j) \in \mathcal{E}$ if and only if $(v_j, v_i) \in \mathcal{E}$, and the 'fixed' means all elements in $\mathcal{E}$ are constant. A sequence of edges (v_1, v_2), $(v_2, v_3), \ldots, (v_{k-1}, v_k)$ with $(v_{j-1}, v_j) \in \mathcal{E}$ for all $j \in \{2, \ldots, k\}$ is called a path from v_1 to v_k. The graph G is assumed to be connected, which means that there is a path between any two nodes in G. Defining the matrix $D \triangleq diag\{d_1, \ldots, d_n\}$ where $d_i = \sum_{j \in N_i} a_{ij}$, the Laplacian matrix of graph G is given as $L = D - A$. Since the graph G is undirected connected, the Laplacian matrix L is semi-positive definite and the eigenvector corresponding to the zero eigenvalue is unit vector based on [11].

Assuming that all the generators are operating within their generation constraints, the distributed economic dispatch method can be designed based on the distributed incremental cost consensus algorithm [20]. The incremental cost of generator $i(i = 1, 2, \ldots, n)$ is defined as

$$\lambda_i = \frac{\partial C_i(P_i)}{\partial P_i} = \beta_i + 2\gamma_i P_i \tag{4}$$

However, the existing method assume that the information of incremental cost of each generator (4) can be transmitted through the communication network continuously, which is impractical for practical network as mentioned in Sect. 1. In order to reduce the information transmission pressure, the event-triggered mechanism will be introduced in the economic dispatch method design. Each generator only transmits its own information to its neighbors at the triggering time when the corresponding designed triggering condition is satisfied.

3   Distributed Event-Triggered Economic Dispatch

In order to satisfy the generation-demand equality constraint (3), the following dynamical system is established

$$\frac{d}{dt}\lambda_0(t) = K \cdot sign(P_D - \sum_{i=1}^{n} P_i(t)) \tag{5}$$

where K is a positive constant and $\lambda_0(t)$ is defined as the desired incremental cost. It is stipulated that $a_{i0} = 1$ if and only if generator i can receive the information of desired incremental cost $\lambda_0(t)$, otherwise $a_{i0} = 0$.

Define the incremental cost measurement error for generator i as

$$e_i(t) = \lambda_i(t) - \lambda_i(t_k^i), \qquad t \in [t_k^i, t_{k+1}^i) \tag{6}$$

where t_k^i is the kth triggering time for $\lambda_i(t)$ of generator i. The event-triggered mechanism for generator i is designed as follows.

Event-Triggered Mechanism: For generator i, suppose the last triggering times for $\lambda_i(t)$ is t_k^i. At time t, if the triggering condition

$$|e_i(t)| > \frac{a \cdot c \cdot g_i^2(t)}{\sum_{j=1}^{n} a_{ij}h_j(t) + (a_{i0} + |N_i|)h_i(t)} \tag{7}$$

is satisfied, where

$$g_i(t) \triangleq a_{i0}\big(\lambda_i(t_k^i) - \alpha_P^0(t)\big) + \sum_{j=1}^{n} a_{ij}(\lambda_i(t_k^i) - \lambda_j(t_{k'(t)}^j)) \tag{8}$$

$$h_i(t) \triangleq |a \cdot g_i(t) + b \cdot sign(g_i(t))| + K \tag{9}$$

$t_{k'(t)}^j$ is the latest triggering time corresponding to incremental cost of generator j at time t, and the constants $a > 0$, $b > K$, $0 < c < 1$, then the incremental cost $\lambda_i(t)$ of generator i will be sampled and transmitted to its neighbours in N_i and denote the time t as t_{k+1}^i.

Based on the event-triggered mechanism, construct the following distributed economic dispatch method for generator i.

$$\frac{d}{dt}\lambda_i(t) = -a \cdot g_i(t) - b \cdot sign(g_i(t)) \tag{10}$$

where $sign(\cdot)$ denotes the sign function.

Theorem 1. *Assume that at least one a_{i0} equals to 1 for $i = 1, \ldots, n$, then under the distributed event-triggered economic dispatch method (5) and (10) with event-triggered mechanism (7), the economic dispatch problem (2) can be solved and the generation-demand equality constraint (3) is satisfied. The inter-event time intervals of the triggering condition (7) is lower bounded as follows*

$$t_{k+1}^i - t_k^i > \frac{a \cdot c \cdot g_i^2(t_{k+1}^i)}{M_i\left(\sum_{j=1}^n a_{ij} h_j(t_{k+1}^i) + (a_{i0} + |N_i|) h_i(t_{k+1}^i)\right)} \tag{11}$$

where M_i is some positive constant. Moreover, the Zeno behavior can be excluded.

The proof of Theorem 1 is similar in our paper [16], and we omit it here.

Remark 1. The execution of the designed event-triggered mechanism 1 only requires the information of the generator i's one-hoop and two-hoop neighbors. This implies that the event-triggered mechanism can be implemented in a distributed architecture. Moreover, for each generator in the power system, either the execution of event-triggered mechanism (7) or the distributed economic dispatch method (10) only needs the discrete triggered information of its neighbors, and the Zeno behavior can be excluded as shown in Theorem 1, which indicates that the information transmission pressure of the communication network can be sharply reduced compared with the conventional controllers based on continuous information transmission.

4   Simulation

The simulation results will be presented to demonstrate the effectiveness of the event-triggered economic dispatch method designed in Sects. 3. Considering a power system contained six generators with the communication network topology as shown in Fig. 1. We assume that only the generator 1 can receive the desired incremental cost.

The total power demand is set as $P_D = 1050\,\mathrm{MW}$. The cost coefficients of six generators are shown in Table 1. The parameters of the distributed economic dispatch method (5)(10) and the triggering condition (7) are set as $a = 10$, $b = 2$, $c = 0.9$ and $K = 1$.

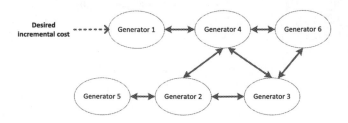

Fig. 1. Communication topology with six generators

Table 1. Cost coefficients

Generator	α_i	β_i	γ_i
1	561	7.92	0.001561
2	310	7.85	0.00194
3	78	7.8	0.00482
4	561	7.92	0.001562
5	78	7.8	0.00482
6	100	7.9	0.00204

The simulation results are shown in Figs. 2, 3 and 4. Figure 2 shows the variations of the incremental costs of all the six generators with respect to time. It can be seen that the incremental costs achieve consensus, which implies that the economic dispatch problem (2) is solved. Figure 3 shows that the total power supply by the six generators converges to the power demand in the system, i.e., 1050 MW, which means the generation-demand equality constraint (3) is satisfied under the designed distribute event-triggered economic dispatch method. The broadcast period of the incremental cost of generator 5 is given in Fig. 4, where the x-coordinates of circles signify the triggering times, and the y-coordinates of them denote the elapsed times since the last event triggering. This figure indicates that the information of generator is transmitted discretely only when 'needed' instead of being transmitted continually in the traditional economic dispatch method, which implies that the unnecessary redundant communication is mitigated in the context of ensuring the optimization purpose. Moreover, Fig. 4 shows that the broadcast periods under event-triggered strategy are not equivalent, which demonstrates the ability of event triggering in adjusting broadcast periods in response to variations of the system's states.

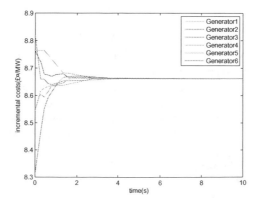

Fig. 2. Incremental costs

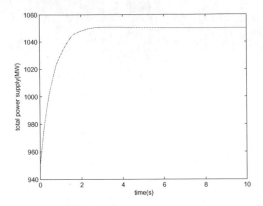

Fig. 3. Total power supply

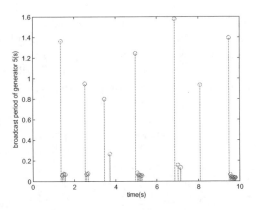

Fig. 4. Broadcast period of generator 5

5   Conclusion

The problem of distributed economic dispatch method for generators in power system has been investigated in this paper. The main contribution is that the distributed event-triggered mechanism has been introduced in order to reduce the information transmission pressure in communication network. Under the designed method, the economic dispatch problem can be solved and the generation-demand equality constraint is satisfied. Non-ideal signal transfer in practical communication networks, such as time-delay, packet-loss, and so on, is to be considered in our future works. Moreover, research is also planned for the distributed economic dispatch problem with power generation constraints.

References

1. Abido, M.: Multiobjective particle swarm optimization for environmental/economic dispatch problem. Electr. Power Syst. Res. **79**(7), 1105–1113 (2009)

2. Binetti, G., Davoudi, A., Lewis, F.L., Naso, D., Turchiano, B.: Distributed consensus-based economic dispatch with transmission losses. IEEE Trans. Power Syst. **29**(4), 1711–1720 (2014)
3. Chen, G., Lewis, F.L., Feng, E.N., Song, Y.: Distributed optimal active power control of multiple generation systems. IEEE Trans. Ind. Electron. **62**(11), 7079–7090 (2015)
4. Chen, G., Ren, J., Feng, E.N.: Distributed finite-time economic dispatch of a network of energy resources. IEEE Trans. Smart Grid **8**(2), 822–832 (2017)
5. Dimarogonas, D.V., Frazzoli, E., Johansson, K.H.: Distributed event-triggered control for multi-agent systems. IEEE Trans. Autom. Control **57**(5), 1291–1297 (2012)
6. El-Keib, A.A., Ma, H., Hart, J.L.: Environmentally constrained economic dispatch using the lagrangian relaxation method. IEEE Trans. Power Syst. **9**(4), 1723–1729 (1994)
7. Fan, Y., Feng, G., Wang, Y., Song, C.: Distributed event-triggered control of multi-agent systems with combinational measurements. Automatica **49**(2), 671–675 (2013)
8. Gaing, Z.L.: Particle swarm optimization to solving the economic dispatch considering the generator constraints. IEEE Trans. Power Syst. **18**(3), 1187–1195 (2003)
9. Garcia, E., Cao, Y., Casbeer, D.W.: Decentralized event-triggered consensus with general linear dynamics. Automatica **50**(10), 2633–2640 (2014)
10. Guo, F., Wen, C., Mao, J., Song, Y.D.: Distributed economic dispatch for smart grids with random wind power. IEEE Trans. Smart Grid **7**(3), 1572–1583 (2016)
11. Olfati-Saber, R., Murray, R.M.: Consensus problems in networks of agents with switching topology and time-delays. IEEE Trans. Autom. Control **49**(9), 1520–1533 (2004)
12. Park, J.B., Jeong, Y.W., Shin, J.R., Lee, K.Y.: An improved particle swarm optimization for nonconvex economic dispatch problems. IEEE Trans. Power Syst. **25**(1), 156–166 (2010)
13. Sashirekha, A., Pasupuleti, J., Moin, N., Tan, C.: Combined heat and power (CHP) economic dispatch solved using lagrangian relaxation with surrogate subgradient multiplier updates. Int. J. Electr. Power Energy Syst. **44**(1), 421–430 (2013)
14. Somarakis, C., Baras, J.S.: Distributed solution of the economic dispatch problem in smart grid power systems framework with delays. In: 2015 54th IEEE Conference on Decision and Control (CDC), pp. 6577–6582, December 2015
15. Wang, X., Lemmon, M.D.: Event-triggering in distributed networked control systems. IEEE Trans. Autom. Control **56**(3), 586–601 (2011)
16. Weng, S., Yue, D., Shi, J.: Distributed cooperative control for multiple photovoltaic generators in distribution power system under event-triggered mechanism. J. Franklin Inst. **353**(14), 3407–3427 (2016)
17. Yang, S., Tan, S., Xu, J.X.: Consensus based approach for economic dispatch problem in a smart grid. IEEE Trans. Power Syst. **28**(4), 4416–4426 (2013)
18. Yang, Z., Xiang, J., Li, Y.: Distributed consensus based supply-demand balance algorithm for economic dispatch problem in a smart grid with switching graph. IEEE Trans. Ind. Electron. **64**(2), 1600–1610 (2017)
19. Yue, D., Tian, E., Han, Q.L.: A delay system method for designing event-triggered controllers of networked control systems. IEEE Trans. Autom. Control **58**(2), 475–481 (2013)
20. Zhang, Z., Chow, M.Y.: Convergence analysis of the incremental cost consensus algorithm under different communication network topologies in a smart grid. IEEE Trans. Power Syst. **27**(4), 1761–1768 (2012)

Control and Analysis of Transportation Systems

MTMDs-Based Noise Control for Box-Girder Bridge of High Speed Railway

Xiaoan Zhang[1,2(✉)], Guangtian Shi[1], Jianjin Yang[2], and Xiaoyun Zhang[1]

[1] School of Mechanical Engineering,
Lanzhou Jiaotong University, Lanzhou 730070, China
zhangxa@mail.lzjtu.cn
[2] State Key Laboratory of Traction Power, Train and Track Research Institute,
Southwest Jiaotong University, Chengdu 610031, China

Abstract. The environmental issues induced by the high speed railway become more and more serious with its rapid development. In order to control the low-frequency structure noise of the box-girder bridge of high speed railway, this paper proposes a new idea that the multi-mass-dampers (MTMDs) may be used. A sound radiation analysis model of the box-girder bridge is developed to validate the idea and to evaluate the control effect. Firstly, a vehicle-track-bridge coupled dynamic model is established to obtain the dynamic responses of the box-girder bridge induced by the excitation of German railway spectra of low irregularity. Then the sound radiation analysis model of the box-girder bridge is established using boundary element method and the dynamic responses are used as the boundary condition to solve the acoustic radiation characteristics of the box-girder bridge. The mechanism of noise radiation of the box-girder bridge is analyzed combined the acoustic radiation efficiency, the vibration response and the vibration distribution. Finally, the MTMDs are using to control the noise radiated by the box-girder bridge based on its mechanism of noise radiation and the control effect is evaluated.

Keywords: High speed railway · Box-girder bridge · Structure noise · Radiation mechanism · Vibration and noise reduction · MTMDs

1 Introduction

The proportion of elevated bridge is very large in high-speed railway. The box-girder bridge can generate secondary structure noise radiation which will worsen the noise radiation problem of the high speed railway. The noise radiated by the box-girder bridge structure mainly falls in the low frequency which has the characteristics of large energy, slow decay, strong penetrating power, far propagation distance and so on. What's more, the natural frequencies of human organs are also mainly in low frequency band, and so the structure noise of low frequency has more serious impact on the human body. Some measures must be used to control the low-frequency noise radiated by the box-girder bridge [1, 2].

© Springer Nature Singapore Pte Ltd. 2017
D. Yue et al. (Eds.): LSMS/ICSEE 2017, Part II, CCIS 762, pp. 607–617, 2017.
DOI: 10.1007/978-981-10-6373-2_61

The research on the noise radiated by the railway bridge structure has attracted the attention of scholars and even became a hot issue since the Japan's Shinkansen caused a serious noise problem. At present, the prediction methods for noise radiation of the bridge structure mainly include the finite element-boundary element method (FEM-BEM), the statistical energy analysis (SEA), the modal acoustic transfer vector method (MATV) and 2.5 dimensional method. Institute of Sound and Vibration Research (ISVR), University of Southampton mainly used the SEA to predict the bridge-born noise. The SEA divides the research object into multiple sub-systems, the power flows between the sub-systems are used to implement the analysis. After many years of research, ISVR had programed and improved introduced a software for the bridge-born noise prediction induced by the passing train, NORBERT 2.0 [3–5]. However, the BEM can more accurately predict the low frequency structural noise of the concrete bridge [6]. After many years of development, the BEM has generated a lot of research results and many scholars have applied it to study the theory of noise radiation of the bridge structure. Ghimire et al. applied the FEM and the three-dimensional acoustic BEM to analyze the acoustic radiation characteristics of the bridge induced by the harmonic unit force [7]. Li et al. analyzed the noise radiation of the 32 m railway box-girder bridge by combining the theory of train-bridge dynamic interaction and 3D boundary element method [8]. Then he proposed an approach to predict the structural noise of the bridge in the whole frequency band. In the approach, the direct/indirect boundary element method was used to analyze the low-frequency structural noise and the SEA was used to analyze the mid-high frequency structural noise [6]. In addition, Li et al. used the MATV to predict the structural noise of U-shaped bridge in time domain and frequency domain [9]. This method includes some technical means, such as modal superposition, acoustic vector based on boundary element method, Fourier transform and Inverse Fourier transform and so on. On this basis, Song et al. further proposed a 2.5D method based on the infinite element method [10]. On the basis of the above researches, some research scholars have also studied the influence factors and the noise and vibration reduction measures of the structural noise of the bridge [11–13]. Besides theoretical researches, the field tests were also conducted [14, 15].

Compared to the vibration mechanism, the noise radiation mechanism of a structure is more complicated. The radiation noise of the bridge structure is not only related to the vibration amplitude, and the type of the bridge, the mode acoustic radiation efficiency and the vibration distribution will also affect its low-frequency structural noise radiation. So the noise reduction of the bridge is extremely difficult. As a commonly used device for vibration control, the tuned mass damper (TMD) belongs to the passive vibration control system and is composed of mass block, spring and damper. By changing the spring stiffness or the mass of the mass block, the natural frequency of the TMD is close to the frequency of the controlled vibration mode of the structure. Therefore, the TMD will produce an inertial force opposite to the vibration of the controlled structure as the controlled structure vibrates, and the vibration response of the controlled structure is attenuated. The existing research results show that the TMD can effectively reduce the vibration of the bridge structure [16, 17]. In order to reduce the frequency sensitivity of TMD and improve the robustness of TMD, Igusa and Xu developed the MTMDs in 1991 [18]. The MTMDs are applied to control the vibration of the bridge structure induced by the passing train and the theoretical results have shown that MTMDs have obvious effect on the vertical vibration of bridge structure [19–21]. However, there is little research on whether the MTMDs can effectively reduce the noise radiation of the bridge [13]. Therefore, this paper put focus on the influences of the MTMDs on the noise radiation characteristics of the bridge. The simply supported concrete box-girder bridge of China high-speed railway is taken as the controlled structure.

The research ideas of this paper are as follows. A vehicle-track-bridge coupled dynamic model is established to obtain the dynamic responses of the bridge. Then the dynamic responses are used as the boundary condition in the sound radiation analysis model of the bridge which is developed using the boundary element method. The mechanism of noise radiation of the bridge is analyzed combined the acoustic radiation efficiency, the vibration response and the vibration distribution, in order to determine the optimal installation location of MTMDs. Finally, the parameters of the MTMDs are designed and the control effect of noise radiation of the bridge is analyzed.

2 Numerical Calculation and Mechanism of Noise Radiation

The theory and field test of vehicle-track-bridge were shown in literatures [22–24], and the literature [25] gave the detailedsolvingprocesses. In this paper, the 32 m dual-line railway simply supported box-girder bridge of China high-speed railway, which is commonly used in high-speed railway in China, is selected as the research object. The track is CRTSI ballastless slab track and the excitation is German railway spectra of low irregularity. The structural noise of the bridge is solved using the above proposed analysis model and the mechanism of noise radiation is also further studied. The cross-section of the bridge is shown in Fig. 1.

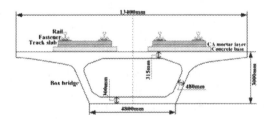

Fig. 1. Sketch of 32 m box-girder bridge

Figure 2 shows the vibration acceleration and the radiated sound power of the box-girder bridge. It can be seen from Fig. 2(a) that the vibration of the box-girder bridge is mainly concentrated in 0–100 Hz, which reached the maximum in 80–100 Hz, and in 0–40 Hz the vibration amplitude is small. From Fig. 2(b), we can find that the box-girder bridge can radiate much structural noise 80–100 Hz. The reason is that in this frequency range the vibration of the bridge is severe, shown in Fig. 2(a). The Fig. 2(b) also shows that in 0–30 Hz the box bridge also radiate much structural noise which is even more than that in 80–100 Hz. Comparing with Fig. 2(a), we can find than in the lower frequency band, the vibration of the bridge is weak but the radiated structural noise is much more serious. This phenomenon may be closely related to the acoustic radiation characteristics of the box-girder bridge, so the following will put focus on the acoustic radiation characteristics of the bridge (Table 1).

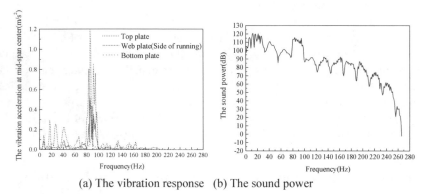

(a) The vibration response   (b) The sound power

Fig. 2. The vibration noise of box-girder bridge

Table 1. Dynamic parameters of track and box bridge

Dynamic parameters	Parameter values	Dynamic parameters	Parameter values
Modulus of elasticity of rail/(N m^{-2})	2.1×10^{11}	Adjust the layer stiffness under the track plate/(N m^{-1})	9.375×10^9
Moment of inertia of rail cross section/(m^4)	3.215×10^{-5}	Adjust the layer damping under the track plate/(N s m^{-1})	7.5×10^5
Poisson's ratio of rail	0.3	Elastic modulus of base/(N m^{-2})	3.3×10^{10}
Linear density of rail/ (kg m^{-1})	60.64	Poisson ratio of base	0.2
Rigidity of fastener/ (N m^{-1})	4×10^7	Density of base/(kg m^{-3})	2500
Damping of fastener/ (N s m^{-1})	2.2656×10^4	Elastic modulus of bridge/(N m^{-2})	3.8×10^{10}
Elastic modulus of track plate/(N m^{-2})	3.6×10^{10}	Poisson ratio of bridge	0.25
Poisson ratio of track plate	0.2	Density of bridge/(kg m^{-3})	2500
Density of track plate/ (kg m^{-3})	2500		

The mechanism of structural noise radiation is mainly related to the acoustical radiation efficiency, vibration response and vibration distribution of the structure. Figure 3 shows some typical modal shape of the bridge and Fig. 4 shows the acoustical

Fig. 3. The vibration characteristics of box-girder bridge (a. The second order mode shape (mm)-7.0 Hz, b Vibration acceleration cloud chart (m/s²)-7.9 Hz, c. The sixth order mode shape (mm)-15.8 Hz, d. Vibration acceleration cloud chart (m/s²)-15.8 Hz)

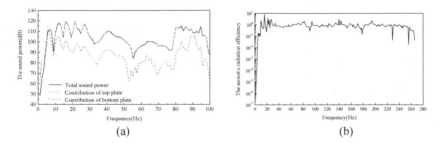

Fig. 4. The acoustical radiation characteristics of box-girder bridge

radiation characteristics of the box-girder bridge. It can be see that, for the top plate of the box-girder bridge, the local vibration characteristics are very obviously, and its sound power contribution is also larger than other plates. Therefore, the mechanism of acoustic radiation of the box-girder bridge can be studied using the theory of sound radiation of ideal thin plate.

According to the modal acoustical radiation efficiency theory of the rectangular thin plate has following characteristics, the mode of the lower order generally has larger acoustic radiation efficiency. If the frequency of the same mode is higher, the corresponding acoustic wavelength is shorter leading to the larger acoustic radiation efficiency. If a mode shape of the rectangular thin plate is expressed as (m, n) in low frequency, the odd-odd mode has a larger acoustic radiation efficiency than that of the odd-even mode and even-even mode [26].

The low order modes of the rectangular thin plate have high acoustic radiation efficiencies, which indicate that the corresponding sound radiation power is very strong. Figure 3 shows that in 0–30 Hz the main vibration forms of the box-girder bridge are the vertical vibrations of the top plate and there are the corresponding mode shapes. Similar to the characteristics of thin plate, in this frequency the box-girder bridge has the high acoustic radiation efficiency and the strong ability to radiate noise. The acoustical radiation efficiency of the box-girder bridge shown as Fig. 4(b). Additionally, the top plate is easy to occur resonance. Therefore, in the frequency range of 0–30 Hz, even the slight vibration of the box-girder bridge will radiate the large structure noise. It can thus be drawn a conclusion that it may reduce the structural noise of the box-girder bridge to suppress its radiation ability by lessening its low-frequency acoustical radiation efficiencies.

In summary, the structural noise of the box-girder bridge is closely related to its top plate and its top plate is the main contributor to its structural noise. Therefore, for the design of reducing noise and vibration of the box-girder bridge, it's reasonable to take its top plate as the main control object. In the following, the control effects of the MTMDs installed on the top plate of the box-girder bridge on the structural noise of the box-girder bridge is studied. In the 80–100 Hz, the vibration response of the box girder bridge is large, but the acoustical radiation efficiency is not significant, so in this frequency range the structural noise can be reduced by decreasing its vibration. However, in the 0–30 Hz, its acoustic radiation efficiency is large and the slight vibration even can induce the larger structural noise radiation. So in this frequency range, both reducing its vibration and lessening its acoustical radiation efficiency must be implemented to reduce its structural noise. It should be pointed out that the design of the vibration and noise reduction is just aimed at the mechanism of noise radiation of the box-girder bridge structure. It is difficult to accurately judge the influence of the box-girder bridge on the sound field by taking the influence of the ground reflection into consideration. So the effect of the ground reflection is ignored in the follow analysis.

3   Multiple Tuned Mass Dampers (MTMDs)

3.1   The Differential Equation of Motion of Box-Grider Bridge-MTMDs

According to the d'Alembert principle, the differential equation of motion of the ith TMD is:

$$m_i \ddot{u}_i + c_i(\dot{u}_i - \dot{u}_q) - k_i(u_i - u_q) = 0; (i = 1, 2, \ldots, n) \qquad (1)$$

m_i, c_i and k_i are the mass, damping and stiffness of the ith TMD, respectively. x_i is the vertical displacement of the ith TMD. And x_q is the vertical displacement of bridge at the installation position of the ith TMD.

The differential equation of motion of the box-girder bridge is:

$$M_b \ddot{u}_t + C_b \dot{u}_b + K_b u_b - \sum_{i=1}^{n} c_i(\dot{u}_i - \dot{u}_q) - \sum_{i=1}^{n} k_i(u_i - u_q) = R_b \qquad (2)$$

3.2   Parameter Design of MTMDs

Involving the study on the control of noise radiation of the bridge by using MTMDs, the literature 13] used a constrained nonlinear programming model to search the optimal control parameters, but the noise reduction effect of the drawn design scheme is not satisfactory. The reason is that the acoustical principle is more complicated than the vibration principle and it is difficult to find the effective installation position of MTMDs. The literature [19] used the finite element method to determine the controlled modes of the bridge and the mass ratio and the installation location of MTMDs and a preferable scheme of vibration reduction were achieved. Therefore, if the mechanism of noise radiation of the box-girder bridge is availably used, the installation location and design parameters of MTMDs can be reasonably chosen to achieve the purpose of vibration and noise reduction in the aspects of the vibration and the characteristics of noise radiation of the box-girder bridge.

(1) Installing positions of MTMDs

Since the box-girder bridge is a cavity structure, the MTMDs can be installed in its cavity. In general, the more compactly the TMDs is installed, the stronger the control effect of the MTMDs. So a series of TMDs was often installed in the longitudinal direction of the box-girder bridge. Based on the mechanism of noise radiation of the box-girder bridge in Sect. 2, the design scheme of TMDs mainly plays a role in the control of the vertical vibration of the bridge. Additionally, the space of the cavity and the project cost are fully considered. In order to a more effective design of the installation of TMDs, TMDs will be mainly installed in the mid-span section and the ends of the box-girder bridge, and there are four columns of TMDs in the lateral direction.

In the design, the natural frequency of the TMD is tuned slightly below the controlled frequency of the bridge. The TMDs are arranged at the ends and mid-span section of the bridge and are symmetrical about its mid-span section. TMDs 1–3 arranged at the mid-span section of the bridge are designed for 7.9 Hz. The ends of the bridge vibrate fiercely at 15.8 Hz and 27.1 Hz, so the controlled frequencies of the TMDs arranged at the ends of the bridge are 15.8 Hz and 27.1 Hz. TMDs 4 and 5 arranged at the end of the bridge are designed for 15.8 Hz. TMDs 6 and 7 arranged at another end of the bridge are designed for 27.1 Hz. The lateral spacing of TMDs has to consider the space size of the cavity. The specific installation diagram is shown in Fig. 5.

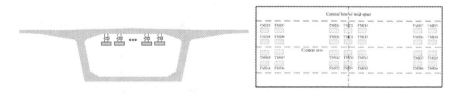

Fig. 5. Sketch of installation positions of MTMDs on box-girder bridge

(2) Selection of the damping ratio

The damping of TMDs can suppress the vibrations of TMDs themselves, which weakens the control over the controlled structure. So the smaller damping of TMDs will produce better control effect. However, due to the limits of the space size of the cavity and the vibration displacement of MTMDs themselves, TMDs need a certain damping. But the damping ratio should be controlled within 5%.

(3) Selection of the mass ratio

According to the theory of structural control, the larger the mass of the mass blocks is, the better the effect of vibration reduction is. But the mass blocks also increase the static load of the controlled structure, which will cause some negative effects. The ideal quality ratio should be between 1% and 2%. Since the top plate of the box-girder bridge is the main controlled object, the mass of the top plate rather than the mass of the whole bridge is taken as the total mass of the mass ratio. The quality ratio is selected as 0.01 based on comprehensive consideration (Table 2).

Table 2. Design parameters of the MTMDs

Orientation	Numbers of TMDs	Mass ratio	Damping ratio	Frequency bandwidth
Vertical	28	0.01	0.03	0.10

3.3   Comparison of Control Effect

It can be seen from Table 3 that the design scheme can reduce the structural noise of the bridge to some extent in the vicinity of the controlled frequencies, which indicates that the scheme has proper effectiveness in reducing the structural noise of the box-girder bridge. The main reasons are as follows.

Table 3. Comparison of sound pressure at bridge bottom of distant 18 m

Sound pressure (dB)	Frequency (Hz)		
	7.9	15.8	27.1
Without MTMDs	79.0	83.4	81.8
With MTMDs	78.2	84.6	66.3

(1) The installation of MTMDs changes the vibration mode of the box-girder bridge and also lessens the modal acoustic radiation efficiency of the box-girder bridge, which leads to a weaker sound radiation power of the box-girder bridge.

(2) The vibration amplitude of the box-girder bridge at the installation positions of the MTMDs is weakened by MTMDs, so the vibration distribution of the top plate is also changed (Fig. 6).

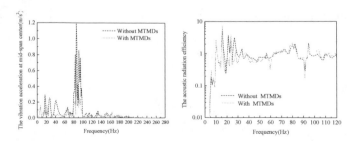

Fig. 6. Comparison of the vibration noise control effect

Due to the above two reasons, at 27.1 Hz the structural noise of the box-girder bridge of is relieved obviously. However, at 15.8 Hz, the MTMDs have distinctly suppressed the vibration of the bridge but the structural noise of the bridge is not lessened. By comparing the acoustic radiation efficiency, the reason turns out to be that the acoustic radiation efficiency is not decreased at 15.8 Hz. This phenomenon indicates that in the low frequency range it can't be achieved that the structural noise of the box-girder bridge is reduced by only weakening its vibration. So in order to reduce the low-frequency structural noise of the box-girder bridge, both reducing its vibration and lessening its acoustical radiation efficiency must be implemented together.

4 Conclusion

The reasonable installation of MTMDs has an obvious effect of reducing the vibration of the box-girder bridge, which has been widely recognized. However, how to use MTMDs to reduce the structural noise of the bridge is rarely studied. Therefore, this paper presents a way to reduce the structural noise of the box-girder bridge by using MTMDs. The research results are as follows.

The top plate has the greatest contribution to the structural noise of the box-girder bridge. The main vibration forms of the top plate are the vertical vibrations and there are the corresponding mode shapes. Therefore, the top plate can be used as the main controlled object and the structural noise of the box-girder bridge would be reduced by installing MTMDs on the top plate. The structural noise of the box-girder bridge may not be lessened by only decreasing its vibration, and its acoustical radiation efficiency must also be lessened together. In the low frequency range, the acoustic radiation efficiency of the box-girder bridge structure is the main influence factor of its structural noise radiation, and even the slight vibration will lead to a large structure noise radiation. Therefore, only based on the comprehensive consideration of the vibration modes, the vibration response and the vibration distribution of the box-girder bridge, the installation positions and the design parameters of MTMDs can be reasonably determined to reduce the structural noise radiation of the box-girder bridge by lessening the acoustic radiation efficiency and weakening the sound radiation power.

By comparing the acoustic radiation characteristics of the box-girder bridge whether the MTMDs are installed, it turns out to be of proper effectiveness and reasonability that the proposed design scheme of installing MTMDs for the purpose of reducing the structural noise of the box-girder bridge.

Acknowledgements. This research was supported by the National Key Basic Research Program of China (973 Program) (Grant No. 2013CB036200); the Program of Introducing Talents of Discipline to Universities (111 Project) (Grant No. B16041); Open Project of State Key Laboratory of Traction Power, Southwest Jiaotong University (TPL1604); Young Fund of Lanzhou Jiaotong University (2015025).

References

1. Rasmussen, G.: Human body vibration exposure and its measurement, Technical review no. 1-1982. Brüel&Kjær, Denmark (1982)
2. Guo, Q., Yang, Y.C., Zhao, S.Q.: Simulation experiment research of human healthy effected by environment infrasound. Noise Vib. Control **S2**, 22–25 (2009)
3. Thompson, D.J., Jones, C.J.: Thameslink 2000 metropolitan junction to London bridge noise and vibration studies. Institute of Sound and Vibration Research (ISVR), Southampton (1997)
4. Bewes, O.G.: The calculation of noise from railway bridge and viaducts. University of Southampton, Southampton (2005)
5. Thompson, D.J., Jones, C.J., Bewes, O.G.: NORBERT-Software for predicting the noise of railway bridges and elevated structures-Version 2.0. Institute of Sound and Vibration Research (ISVR), Southampton (2005)
6. Li, X.Z., Zhang, X., Liu, Q.M., et al.: Prediction of structure-borne noise of high-speed railway bridges in whole frequency bands (part I): theoretical model. J. China Railway Soc. **35**(1), 101–107 (2013)
7. Ghimire, J.P., Matsumoto, Y., Yamaguchi, H., et al.: Numerical investigation of noise generation and radiation from an existing modular expansion joint between prestressed concrete bridges. J. Sound Vib. **328**(1/2), 129–147 (2009)
8. Li, X.Z., Zhang, X., Li, Y.D.: Application of boundary element method in study of noise from simply-supported box girder in high speed railway. China Civil Eng. J. **44**(S1), 95–101 (2011)
9. Li, Q., Xu, Y.L., Wu, D.J.: Concrete bridge-borne low-frequency noise simulation based on train-track-bridge dynamic interaction. J. Sound Vib. **331**(10), 2457–2470 (2012)
10. Song, X.D., Wu, D.J., Li, Q., Botteldooren, D.: Structure-borne low-frequency noise from multi-span bridges: a prediction method and spatial distribution. J. Sound Vib. **376**, 114–128 (2016)
11. Zhang, X., Li, X.Z., Liu, Q.M., et al.: Structure-born noise of concrete box-grider and its influence factors. J. Southwest Jiaotong Univ. **48**(3), 409–414 (2013)
12. Shi, G.T., Zhang, X.A., Yang, X.W., Wang, P.: Influences of the material properties of cement asphalt mortar on box bridge structure vibration-born noise. In: The Fifth International Conference on Transportation Engineering, Dalian, China, September 2015
13. Zhang, X., Li, X.Z., Liu, Q.M., et al.: Structure-borne noise control with MTMDs for a high-speed railway simply supported box-girder bridge. J. Vib. Shock **32**(13), 194–200 (2013)
14. Ngai, K.W., Ng, C.F.: Structure-borne noise and vibration of concrete box structure and rail viaduct. J. Sound Vib. **255**(2), 281–297 (2002)
15. Zhang, X., Li, X.Z., Hong, H., et al.: A case study of interior low-frequency noise from box-shaped bridge girders induced by running trains: its mechanism, prediction and countermeasures. J. Sound Vib. **367**, 129–144 (2016)
16. Kwon, H.C., Kim, M.C., Lee, I.W.: Vibration control of bridges under moving loads. Comput. Struct. **66**(4), 473–480 (1998)
17. Wang, J.F., Lin, C.C., Chen, B.L.: Vibration suppression for high-speed railway bridges using tuned mass dampers. Int. J. Solids Struct. **40**(2), 465–491 (2003)
18. Igusa, T., Xu, K.: Vibration reduction characteristics of distributed tuned mass dampers. In: Proceedings of the 4th International Conference on Recent Advances in Structural Dynamics, Southampton, UK, pp. 596–605 (1991)

19. Han, X., Li, L., Zhong, L., Liu, J.B.: Study on parameter of MTMD for controlling vertical of arch bridge. J. Vib. Shock **27**(3), 104–107+135 (2008)
20. Yau, J., Yang, Y.B.: Vibration reduction for cable-stayed bridges traveled by high-speed trains. Finite Elem. Anal. Des. **40**(3), 341–359 (2004)
21. Lin, C.C., Wang, J.F., Chen, B.L.: Train-induced vibration control of high-speed railway bridges equipped with multiple tuned mass dampers. J. Bridge Eng. **10**(4), 398–414 (2005)
22. Zhai, W.M., Xia, H.: Train-Track-Bridge Dynamic Interaction: Theory and Engineering Applicatin. Science Press, Beijing (2011)
23. Zhai, W.M., Xia, H., Cai, C.B., et al.: High-speed train-track-bridge dynamic interactions-part I: theoretical model and numerical simulation. Int. J. Rail Transp. **1**(1–2), 3–24 (2013)
24. Zhai, W.M., Wang, S.L., Zhang, N., et al.: High speed train-track-bridge dynamic interactions-part II: experimental validation and engineering application. Int. J. Rail Transp. **1**(1–2), 25–41 (2013)
25. George, C.H., Wolfgang, L.W.: Boundary Integral Equations. Springer, Heidelberg (2008)
26. Nilsson, A., Liu, B.: Vibro-Acoustics: Volume II. Science Press, Beijing (2014)

Influences of Stiffness of Rail Pads on System Dynamic Performances of Heavy Haul Railway

Guangtian Shi[1(✉)], Kaiyun Wang[2], Qianxing Huang[1],
and Xiaoyun Zhang[1,2]

[1] Lanzhou Jiaotong University, Lanzhou 730070, China
zxa_lzjtu@163.com
[2] Southwest Jiaotong University, Chengdu 610031, China

Abstract. In order to solve the problem that the track structure is oversimplified in the dynamics study of heavy haul railway, a wagon vehicle-track coupled dynamic model is proposed in this paper. The track structure is more detailed and is modelled by a composite double-layer dynamic model. The upper layer is composed of two rails and the lower layer is composed of many sleepers. The rails are connected with sleepers by the rail pads. This more detailed model is then used to study the influences of the stiffness of the rail pads on the system dynamic performances of heavy haul railway. The results reveal that the proposed model is more practical to study the dynamic problems of heavy haul railway, and the model is able to subtly analyze the dynamic influences of local structure on the wagon vehicle-track coupled dynamic system. The results also shows that the stiffness of the rail pads has a great impact on the vertical wheel/rail force, the dynamic responses of the wagon and the vertical displacement of the rail. The smaller stiffness of the rail pads will worsen the wear process of the rail and aggravate the vibration displacement amplitude of the fasteners by increasing the vibration of the rail. Therefore, an appropriate stiffness of the rail pads is of great significance to extend the service life of the track and to reduce the maintenance and operation cost.

Keywords: Composite double-layer dynamic model · Wagon vehicle-track coupled dynamics · Track structure · Stiffness of rail pad · Heavy haul railway

1 Introduction

The rail pad is an important elastic component of the ballast track and also plays an important role in vibration and noise reduction of the wheel/rail coupled dynamic system. In order to meet the needs of the freight transportation, the axle load of the heavy-haul wagon is more and more heavy and the train velocity is also speeded up. This has greatly worsened the load conditions of the track structure, which will aggravate the aging rate of the rail pads, intensify the damage of the track structure, increase the railway maintenance and even endanger the running safety [1].

The existing research results show that the failure coefficient of track structure is proportional to the square root of the stiffness of the rail pads, and the provision of elastic the rail pads can effectively reduce the wheel/rail interaction, slow down the

© Springer Nature Singapore Pte Ltd. 2017
D. Yue et al. (Eds.): LSMS/ICSEE 2017, Part II, CCIS 762, pp. 618–628, 2017.
DOI: 10.1007/978-981-10-6373-2_62

pulverization of the ballast and decrease the railway maintenance. So an appropriate stiffness of the rail pad is of great significance to improve dynamic performances of the train and the track structure. It is necessary to study the influence of the stiffness of the rail pad on dynamic performances of the vehicle and the track. Shi et al. used the NUCARS software to establish a wagon vehicle-track coupled dynamics model, in which the rail and the sleeper were modelled by the discretely supported Euler-Bernoulli beam, and the track bed and the subgrade were simplified as many parallel damping-spring units. This model reduces the computational complexity and also has high accuracy [2]. Xu and Zhai analyzed the influence of different stiffness of the rail foundation on vibration and noise of the wheel/rail system induced by the wheel/rail surface roughness [3]. Tu used the vertical vehicle-track coupled dynamic model to demonstrate the impact of fasteners and the rail pads on the dynamic response of the wheel/rail system [4]. Luo et al. established a finite element model of the rail pad using Abaqus software to analyze its dynamic response and fatigue performance [5, 6]. Chang developed a finite element model of the track structure of the heavy haul railway using ANSYS software. In the model, the rail pads were simplified as spring-damping units and the concrete sleepers were discreted as beam elements. He focused his research on influences of the rail type, the stiffness of the rail pads and the state of the track bed on the static performance of track structure [7]. Xu and Cai proposed a spatial train-ballast track-subgrade coupled dynamic model which considered the dynamic properties of the rail pads, sleepers and the subgrade. Using the model, they obtained the dynamic responses characteristics of the track and the dynamic characteristics of the deformation and stress of the track bed surface [8]. Lundqvist used the finite element method to establish a dynamic analysis model of the track considering the aging deformation of the rail pads and the hanged sleepers. The model is used to study the effect of the stiffness of the rail pads and the hanged sleepers on the dynamic vehicle-track interaction [9]. Shu et al. proposed a new infiltrated wheel/rail contact model considering the deformation of wheel/rail contact, which led to a more realistic vehicle-track coupled dynamic model [10]. By the numerical simulation and the test of the track of hundreds of kilometers, Li and Berggren studied influences of the vertical stiffness of the components of the track on the dynamic performances of the track system and investigated the global matching problem of the vertical stiffness of the components of the track [11]. Huang established the dynamic simulation model of the heavy-haul wagon using SIMPACK software to analyze influences on the dynamic wheel/rail interaction by the dynamic parameters of the wagon and the track, such as the wheel/rail friction coefficient, the stiffness of the rail pads and the rail cant [12]. Based on the theory of vehicle-track coupled dynamics, Wang used the large-scale computer simulation soft TTSIM to studied influences of the key parameters of the track and the vertical and lateral support stiffness of the rails on dynamic performances of the wheel/rail interaction of curve track [13]. Based on the theory of vehicle-track coupled dynamics, Zhai took into account the impact of three aspects of the vehicle, the track, wheel and the wheel/rail interaction interface the orbital structure of the dynamic response to study the dynamic responses of the track, which broke through the limitations of the simplify of the traditional methods [14].

In the above studies, the model of the track is often too simplified to accurately reflect the dynamic performances of the heavy haul railway. Additionally, most of the studies involving the stiffness of the rail pads put focus on its influences on the dynamic responses of the track structure, and rarely studied its effect on the dynamic performances of the whole vehicle-track coupled system. Aiming at the shortcomings of the above researches, this paper proposes a more practical wagon vehicle-track coupled dynamic model in which the track structure is more detailed and is modelled by a composite double-layer dynamic model. The wagon of 30t axle load is token as the study object to study the influences of the stiffness of the rail pads on the dynamic performances of the whole heavy haul wagon vehicle-track coupled dynamic system.

2   Composite Double-Layer Dynamic Model of Track

In most of existing researches, the track structure is often simplified as a single-layer structural model, as shown in Fig. 1. The main idea of this model is that all of the rails, sleeper, track bed, subgrade and other structures are regarded as a rigid body (called as integrated track in Fig. 1) and the stiffness and damping of the structure and all elastic components are integrated as the spring-damping units supporting the integrated track. So this model can be regarded as a single-layer structural model. The actual track is very complicated and each component of the track has stiffness and damping. But the single-layer structural model uses lumped parameterization for all the structural components such as rails, sleepers, track bed and subgrade and all the elastic damping components such as fasteners and the rail pads. This simplification can't reflect the practical dynamic performances of the track, especially for the heavy haul railway.

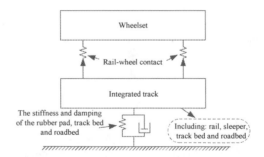

Fig. 1. The single-layer structural model of the track structure

In this paper, the track structure is more detailed and is modelled by a composite double-layer dynamic model. Then a more practical wagon vehicle-track coupled dynamic model is proposed based on the theory of vehicle-track coupled dynamics. Lastly the wagon vehicle-track coupled dynamic model is used to study the influences of the stiffness of the rail pads on the dynamic performances of the whole heavy haul wagon vehicle-track coupled dynamic system.

The composite double-layer dynamic model of the track structure is developed on the basis of the single-layer structural model, as shown in Figs. 2 and 3. The basic idea is that the track structure is more detailed and is modelled by a composite double-layer

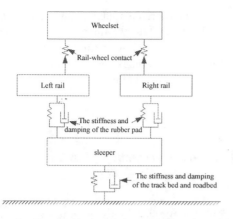

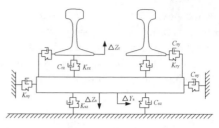

Fig. 3. Composite double-layer dynamic model of the track structure of the track structure

Fig. 2. Composite double-layer structural model

dynamic model. The upper layer is composed of two rails and the lower layer is composed of many sleepers. The rails are connected with sleepers by the rail pads and fasteners. The track bed and the subgrade are integrated as the elastic foundation under the sleepers. So in the double-layer dynamic model, the rail is separated from the sleeper and the interaction between the rail and the sleepers are more practical which is able to accurately simulate the role of the rail pads. Meanwhile the wheel/rail contacts also need to be modified in new model.

3   Rang of the Stiffness of the Rail Pads

As the existing railway lines is generally the mixed passenger and freight railway, therefore, the stiffness of the pads is generally in the range of 55–80 MN/m [16]. For the Daqin line of the largest annual transport capacity in China, according to the field test in the Datong line [17], the relationship between the stiffness of the rail pads and the total transport volume is as shown in Fig. 4.

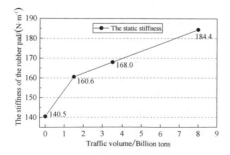

Fig. 4. Observation data of static stiffness of rail pads

In view of the above, considering the development trends of axle load and running speed creasing and in order to more comprehensive study of the influences of the stiffness of the rail pads on the dynamic performances of the whole heavy haul wagon vehicle-track coupled dynamic system, the range of the stiffness of the rail pads is 40–200 MN/m, and the velocity of the wagon vehicle is 100 km/h.

4   Numerical Analysis

4.1   Influences of the Stiffness of the Rail Pads on Dynamic Performances of Car Body

In China, the specification, *railway vehicles—Specification for evaluation the dynamic performance and accreditation test* (GB 5599-85), provides the vibration acceleration limit and the stability index level of the vehicle [18]. The vertical and lateral stationarity of the car body use the evaluation scale and the value less than 4.25 is the qualified level. The vibration acceleration limits of the car body are defined as: the vertical and lateral vibration are not more than 0.7 g and 0.5 g.

It can be seen from Fig. 5 that the stiffness of the rail pads has little effect on the vertical vibration acceleration and the stationarity of the car body. With the stiffness of the rail pads increasing, the maximum value of the vertical vibration acceleration of the car body varies in the range of 3.03–3.18 m/s^2, and the maximum value of the stationarity of the car body is in the range of 3.65–3.68. The maximum value of both change in a small range.

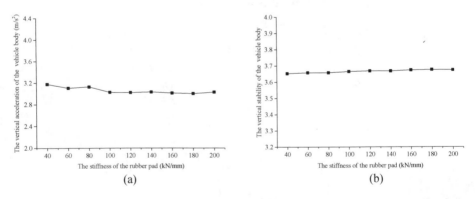

Fig. 5. Influences of the stiffness of the rail pads on the vertical acceleration of the vehicle body

Figure 6 shows that with the stiffness of the rail pads increasing, the maximum value of the lateral vibration acceleration and the stationarity of the car body don't obviously change. The maximum value of the lateral vibration acceleration of the car body varies in the range of 4.36 m/s^2–4.52 m/s^2, and the maximum value of the stationarity of the car body is in the range of 3.58–3.62. So the stiffness of the rail pads has little influences on the lateral vibration acceleration and the stationarity of the car body.

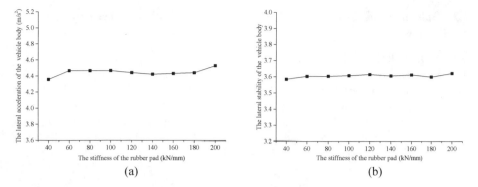

Fig. 6. Influences of the stiffness of the rail pads on the lateral acceleration of the vehicle body

4.2 Influences of the Stiffness of the Rail Pads on Vertical Wheel/Rail Forces

It can be seen from Fig. 7 that with the stiffness of the rail pads increasing, the maximal vertical wheel/rail force gradually stabilized after the initial increase. Figure 7(a) shows the comparison of the vertical wheel/rail force in time-domain when the stiffness of the rail pads are 40 MN/m and 200 MN/m and the maximal values are 214.357 kN and 220.463 kN respectively. Although both are less than the limit value 322 kN, but the vertical wheel/rail force increasing will aggravate the wheel/rail impact and the wheel/rail wear and also will lead to that the sleepers and track bed seriously vibrate and make the track structure vulnerable to damage and even affect the running safety of the wagon vehicle. Therefore, it is favorable that the stiffness of the rail pads is not too high in the heavy haul railway. It should be noted that the stiffness of the rail pads will increase with its aging, so it is need to regularly sample the rail pads and timely replace the aged rail pads.

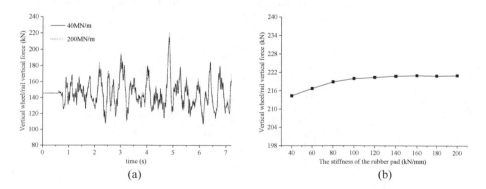

Fig. 7. Influences of the stiffness of the rail pads on vertical wheel/rail forces

4.3   Influences of the Stiffness of the Rail Pads on Lateral Wheel/Rail Forces

According to the field testes of the heavy haul railway in Europe and the United States, the allowable limit value of the lateral wheel/rail force is generally 0.4 times of the axle load [14]. In this paper, the static axle load is 300 kN. So the lateral wheel/rail force should be less than 120 kN. As can be seen from Fig. 8, there was no regular changes of the maximal lateral wheel/rail force with the stiffness of the rail pads increasing. The maximum value fluctuates between 26.67 kN and 31.18 kN, which can meet the safety requirements.

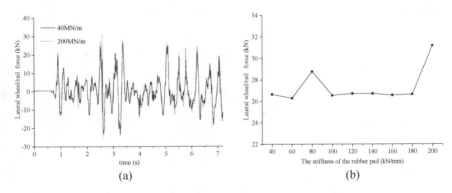

Fig. 8.   Influences of the stiffness of the rail pads on lateral wheel/rail forces

The derailment factor is the ratio of the lateral wheel/rail force to the vertical wheel/rail force. According to the standard, *dynamic performance test methods and assessment criteria of railway locomotive* (TB/T2360-93), provides that the derailment coefficient can't be greater than 0.9 [19]. It can be seen from Fig. 9 that the maximal derailment factor fluctuates between 0.188 and 0.220 with the stiffness increase of the

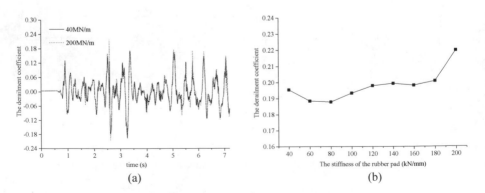

Fig. 9.   Influences of the stiffness of the rail pads on derailment factor

rail pads when the vehicle speed is 100 km/h. In general, the fluctuation range of the maximal derailment factor is very small and the overall level is much lower than the limit value. It can be seen that the stiffness of the rail pads has little effect on the derailment factor.

4.4   Influences of the Stiffness of the Rail Pads on Vertical Displacement of Rail

It can be seen from Fig. 10, the stiffness of the rail pads has obvious effects on the vertical displacement of the rail. When the vehicle speed is 100 km/h, the vertical displacement of the rail is greatly reduced with the stiffness increase of the rail pads and the decreasing range becomes smaller. When the pad stiffness is increased from 40 MN/m to 200 MN/m, the vertical displacement of the rail is reduced from 2.070 mm to 0.749 mm and the descend range is 63.8%. Therefore, the vertical displacement of the rail is very sensitive to the stiffness change of the rail pads. For the heavy haul railway, the use of high elastic rail pads will increase the vertical displacement of the rail which is easy to cause the crushing failure of the rail pads and the durability of the rail pads can't be guaranteed resulting in the uneven stiffness of the track structure. Additionally, the vertical displacement of the rail increasing aggravates the vibration of the fastener which is harmful to the life of the fastener and the stability of the connection with the rail and even affects the running safety.

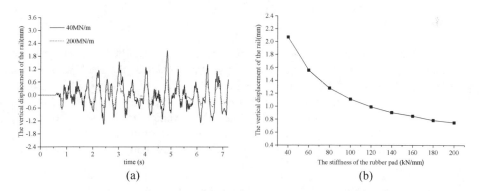

Fig. 10. Influences of the stiffness of the rail pads on vertical displacement of rail

From the above analysis, we can see that the stiffness of the rail pads has a great influence on the vertical displacement of the rail, which can cause many problems. Therefore, the stiffness of the rail pads should be not too low for heavy haul railway.

4.5   Influences of the Stiffness of the Rail Pads on Wheel/Rail Wear

Wheel/rail wear is an important basis for evaluating the running quality of the vehicle and the type of the track. There are rolling friction and sliding friction on the wheel/rail contact surface which will cause the wear of the wheel and rail. The sliding friction between the wheel flange and the rail is an important reason for the side wear of the rail. It can be seen from Fig. 11, wheel/rail wear increases with the stiffness of the rail pads increasing. When the stiffness of the rail pads is increased from 40 MN/m to 200 MN/m, the wheel/rail wear is increased from 0.086 kN/mm to 0.111 kN/mm and the growth rate is 29%. Therefore, the effect of the stiffness of the rail pads on the wheel/rail wear is obvious, reducing the running of the vehicle and the life of the rail.

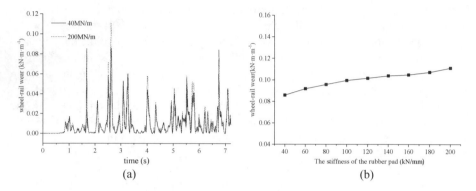

Fig. 11. Influences of the stiffness of the rail pads on wheel/rail wear

5 Conclusions

In most of existing researches, the track structure is often simplified as a single-layer structural model. A composite double-layer dynamic model of the track structure is proposed on the basis of the single-layer structural model in this paper. Then a more practical wagon vehicle-track coupled dynamic model is proposed based on the theory of vehicle-track coupled dynamics. Lastly the wagon vehicle-track coupled dynamic model is used to study the influences of the stiffness of the rail pads on the dynamic performances of the whole heavy haul wagon vehicle-track coupled dynamic system. The results are as follows.

(1) The proposed model is more practical to study the dynamic problems of heavy haul railway and it can analyze the influence of the local structure of the track on the dynamic performance of the whole system.
(2) The primary and secondary suspension system of the wagon vehicle can eliminate the impact of the stiffness change of the rail pads on the dynamic responses of the car body. In the choice of rail pads, the impact of its stiffness on the dynamic response of the car body can be ignored.
(3) The stiffness of the rail pads has obvious effects on the maximal vertical wheel/rail force. For the heavy haul railway, the stiffness of the rail pads should be not too high. Additionally, the stiffness of the rail pads will increase with its aging, so it is need to regularly sample the rail pads and timely replace the aged rail pads. The stiffness of the rail pads has little effects on the lateral wheel/rail force and the

derailment factor which meet the safety requirements. However, the effect of the stiffness of the rail pads on the wheel/rail wear is obvious, reducing the running of the vehicle and the life of the rail.

(4) The stiffness of the rail pads has a great influence on the vertical displacement of the rail, which can cause many problems. Therefore, the stiffness of the rail pads should be not too low for heavy haul railway.

To sum up, it is of great significance for improving the fatigue performance of the elastic rail pads, prolonging the service life of the sleeper, the ballast and the rail and reducing the maintenance and operation cost to reasonably set the stiffness of the rail pads.

References

1. Xue, J.L.: Experimental study on strengthening method of track structure for 30t axle load in shenchi-huanghua railway. J. China Railway Soc. **2**, 70–77 (2015)
2. Shi, X.F., Liang, S.N., Sun, J.L.: Reasonable track stiffness for heavy haul railway under the action of freight car with 32.5t axle load. China Railway Sci. **2**, 24–29 (2015)
3. Xu, Z.S., Zhai, W.M.: Influence of track stiffness on vibration and noise of high-speed wheel/rail system. Noise Vib. Control **4**, 15–18 (2004)
4. Tu, G.J.: Dynamic Response of Wheel-Rail System. Southwest Jiaotong University, Chengdu (2012)
5. Luo, R.K., Mortel, W.J., Wu, X.P.: Fatigue failure investigation on anti-vibration spring. Eng. Fail. Anal. **16**(5), 1366–1378 (2009)
6. Luo, R.K., Mortel, W.J., Cook, P.W., et al.: Computer simulation and experimental investigation of offset sandwich mount. Plast. Rubber Compos. **40**(4), 155–160 (2011)
7. Chang, W.H.: Study on key parameters of heavy haul railway track under 35.7t axle load. Railway Stand. Des. **8**, 47–50+54 (2015)
8. Xu, P., Cai, C.B.: Spatial dynamic model of train-ballast track-subgrade coupled system. Eng. Mech. **3**, 191–197 (2011)
9. Lundqvist, A.: Dynamic train/track interaction including model for track settlement evolvement. Veh. Syst. Dyn. **41**(Suppl.), 667–676 (2004)
10. Shu, X., Wilson, N., Elkins, C.S.J.: Development of a real-time wheel/rail contact model in NUCARS and application to diamond crossing and turnout design simulations **44**(Suppl.), 251–260 (2006)
11. Li, M.X.D., Berggren, E.G.: A study of the effect of global track stiffness and its variations on track performance: Simulation and measurement. J. Rail Rapid Transit **1**(5), 1–7 (2007)
12. Huang, X.C.: Research on Influence of Wheel/Rail Interaction Force for Heavy Haul Wagon. Southwest Jiaotong University, Chengdu (2013)
13. Wang, K.Y.: Study on Performance Matching of Wheel-Rail Dynamic Interaction on Curved Track of Speed-Raised and High-Speed Railways. Southwest Jiaotong University, Chengdu (2013)
14. Zhai, W.M.: Vehicle-Track Coupled Dynamics, 4th edn. Science Press, Beijing (2015)
15. Miu, B.R., Fang, X.H., Fu, X.T.: SIMPACK Fundamentals of Dynamic Analysis. Southwest Jiaotong University Press, Chengdu (2008)
16. Li, G.B., Zhang, J.F.: Discussion on the use of thermoplastic elastomer track under heavy rail in China. Railway Eng. **10**, 82–84 (2007)

17. Xiao, J.H., Fang, H.W., Liu, W.B., et al.: Study on performance of under-slab for heavy haul railway in China. In: The Collection of Railway Heavy-haul Transportation Technology Symposium. China Railway Society, vol. 4 (2014)
18. GB5599-85: Code for qualification evaluation and test qualification of railway vehicle. China Planning Press, Beijing (1985)
19. TB/T2360-93: Identification method and evaluation standard for dynamic performance test of railway locomotive. China Railway Press, Beijing (1993)

Passing Control Between Driver and Highly Automated Driving Functions

Niko Maas[1](✉), Frédéric Etienne Kracht[1], Mira Schüller[1], Weiyan Hou[2], and Dieter Schramm[1]

[1] Universität Duisburg-Essen, Lotharstr. 1, 47057 Duisburg, Germany
niko.maas@uni-due.de
[2] School of Information Engineering, Zhengzhou University,
Zhengzhou 450001, Henan, China

Abstract. In this paper challenges to face in "taking over control from highly automated driving mode" are derived from human driving patterns and a technological analysis of the vehicle state. On the same basis, an automated driving model (driver model) is generated and used for studies in a driving simulator. Finally, strategies, which support the driver in taking over control from highly automated driving are designed in three different levels, implemented and tested in a driving simulator.

Keywords: Taking over control · Highly automated driving · Autonomous driving · Driving simulator · Driver modelling

1 Problem Description

The introduction of automated vehicles into road traffic is expected to be gradual in the upcoming decades. While today's partially automated driver functions are used in standard vehicles, the next development stage is a complete automation of the driving task for limited time and situations [1]. In this intermediate stage on the way to fully automated driving, a vehicle is supposed to take over the entire task itself in defined situations and for a restricted time (SAE Level 3, [2]). As soon as a system limit is detected or reached, the driver acts as fallback level and is requested by the vehicle to take over the control of the driving task again.

The transfer of the driving task from a highly-automated driving operation presents drivers with a unprecedented challenge [3]. First, a completely distracted driver [4] is to be released from his secondary activity. Subsequently, he must capture the current traffic situation, whereupon the control of the vehicle is to be taken over. This process, which, in addition to the situation-related difficulty, also represents an unfamiliar situation, can quickly overwhelm drivers. In this phase, drivers should be supported as much as possible.

2 Transitions from Highly Automated Driving

The transition problem is described in the following from the vehicles and the drivers perspective.

© Springer Nature Singapore Pte Ltd. 2017
D. Yue et al. (Eds.): LSMS/ICSEE 2017, Part II, CCIS 762, pp. 629–638, 2017.
DOI: 10.1007/978-981-10-6373-2_63

2.1   Vehicle

For the description of the vehicle-side processes, the preconditions which must be fulfilled to initiate a transfer of the driver's task to the driver are first described. The first specification results from the classification according to [1], which means that the driver must be provided with a time reserve that is sufficient to take over the driving task. After [3–5], this time reserve can be limited to a range of less than 10 s. Thus, for a vehicle operating in the "highly-automated driving" state, it must be ensured that the automated system is capable to execute control over the vehicle during the time of a handover phase to the driver for at least 10 s. Since the possibility must be considered that a driver is not available for the takeover, a "safe state" (or "risk-minimized condition") must also be achieved independently of the driver. However, according to [6], the latter results in a considerable technological effort, which is the reason that the transfer to the driver should always be preferred.

The transfer of control to the driver can take place under the circumstances described for two obvious reasons. On the one hand, a system limit can be detected by the vehicle sensor system. An example of this cause is the approach to a motorway exit for a highway pilot system. On the other hand, the prediction horizon can fall below a critical value, which means that automated driving can only be ensured for the observable time range. This situation can occur, for example, in a narrow curve, which can possibly not be completely detected by the vehicle sensor system.

2.2   Driver

In addition to the technological aspects of handing over the driving task, psychological aspects must also be considered. For this purpose, a hypothetical transfer situation (see Fig. 1) can be used to describe the processes from the driver's point of view.

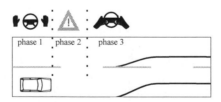

Fig. 1. Fragmentation of the take over situation

In the shown situation, a vehicle with an activated, highly-automated driving function is displayed on a two-lane highway. First, the driver must be reactivated in this transfer situation from his secondary task (phase 1). The system is therefore dependent on a reaction of the driver. How well a driver can be extracted from the situation depends on the currently executed secondary task.

The diverted driver then must capture the traffic situation completely (phase 2). The (incremental) process of perception must therefore be performed in the shortest time possible. Furthermore, feasible action alternatives have to be played over in a short time and a variant selected. Finally, the manual control of the vehicle must be recovered and the driving task has to be executed again manually (phase 3). In addition to the directly recognizable challenges arising from the perception and the limited time available, the latter point is also a negligible influence factor. Since this situation cannot be trained frequently (at least in the introductory scenario), the behavioral model of Rasmussen [7] can be characterized by at least rule-based behavior, which leads to an increased mental stress. In addition, an increased stress in the overall situation according to [8] is expected to result in a decrease in performance due to increased workload. These losses in performance can influence both the takeover of the driving task and the perception, for example by slowing down the speed or by overlooking individual objects in the surrounding area. Since the automated assistance system has information about the environment in such a situation (even if only for the next seconds), this is a great opportunity to support the driver.

3 Design of Assistance Functions

3.1 Design Criteria

From the considerations presented above regarding the challenges of taking over the driving task from the driver's point of view, the following design criteria and the resulting areas of investigation for an assistance function, which is intended to assist the driver before, during and after the transfer of the driving task from highly-automated driving mode, are derived:

- The takeover request must release the driver from the secondary activity
  According to [9], a design with a high degree of coverage is capable of strongly influencing the driver. This is also necessary to increase the likelihood of a takeover by the driver. As a basis for the examinations of this contribution, an attempt is therefore made to keep the driving state within a defined range and to check how well and rapidly the driver can be released from the corresponding secondary task. The sensory channel is varied in the investigations for this article from purely auditory warnings to visual-auditive warnings, including switching off secondary tasks.
- A transition assistance system should support perception
  A perception support in the context of the takeover situations can also lead to an additional burden next to the supporting effect. For example, a visual presentation of additional information may, on the one hand, represent a whole situation compressed, on the other hand, additional objects to be perceived are created. The effect of additional information on the longitudinal guidance behavior is investigated in this article.
- The transition assistance system is intended to assist the driver in the execution of the driving task

Within the framework of the present paper, the effect of an active lateral-guiding assist on the manual execution of the driving task is examined. The resulting steering angles are compared with a stored driver model. Depending on the present traffic situation, different effects are produced by the lateral-guiding assistance on the lateral guidance behavior of the driver.

3.2 Driver Model

Within the scope of this article, a driving simulator has to be operated with an automated system (virtual driver) as well as from a human driver. For this purpose, a driver model was developed and integrated into the driving simu-lator, which allows automated vehicle guidance. This driver model also serves as a basis for the implementation of the assistance functions described in the following chapter. The implementation in the driving simulator leads to a strong simplification of the perception level since all relevant objects and parameters are already present within a simulation environment. In the following, the focus is thus placed on the planning and execution level of the developed driving model.

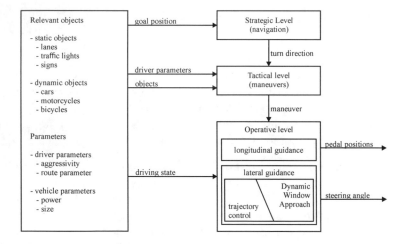

Fig. 2. Structure of the driver model

Figure 2 shows the structure of the driver model schematically. This is closely related to the levels according to [7] and shows the different planning and exe-cution tasks sorted according to the temporary relevance. The strategic level describes planning tasks, in particular from the area of navigation and route guidance. This includes start and end points as well as all intersections between these waypoints. Furthermore, it is determined at this level which lanes are to be selected before the respective intersections in order to follow the predetermined route.

The tactical level is then responsible for the areas between intersections. At this level, it is determined by means of various evaluation criteria which maneuver (e.g., lane keep or lane change, Fig. 3) is most appropriate in the context of time, travel and cooperative parameters. The assessment is context-sensitive by extrapolating the current situation, consisting of all relevant objects and traffic rules of the current traffic situation, for each possible maneuver. In this extrapolation, it is assumed that all vehicles (except the EGO vehicle) follow their own track unchanged.

Using the example of a motorway situation where the next departure is to be taken, the assessment of the maneuvers "lane change" and "lane keep" is shown in Fig. 3. It is assumed that the vehicle is on the right one of two lanes and is traveling at a constant speed. The route evaluation shows that with a shorter distance to the intersection a higher value for the route evaluation of the maneuver "lane change" occurs. The rating for "lane keep" remains constant, however, until the exit ramp is reached. When the exit ramp is reached, the evaluation of the maneuver "lane keep" also increases because the target state no longer leads to the route determined in the navigation plane, but the exit lane is to be selected according to this specification. It should be noted here that a lower value of the "evaluation route" marks the preferred maneuver (minimization problem). In this way, a complete maneuver catalog is compared with further evaluation criteria, which can be used in accordance with [11] to completely describe the task of the vehicle.

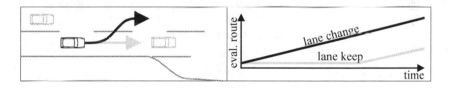

Fig. 3. evaluation of lane change and lane keep

In addition to the determination of various possible target states and the selection of a suitable maneuver, the target speed is also determined at this level and passed on to the subsequent operative level. The operational level therefore includes the longitudinal and transverse regulation. The longitudinal regulation is implemented as an acceleration controller, divided into a virtual throttle and brake pedal position, with driving resistances being regarded as a disturbance variable. The corresponding equations of the PI controller are

$$p_g = \begin{cases} K_{gP}(a_{soll} - a) + K_{gI} \int (a_{soll} - a)dt & \text{for } a > 0 \\ 0 & \text{for } a \leq 0 \end{cases} \text{ with } p_g \in [0, 1] \quad (1)$$

for the accelerator pedal and similarly for the brake pedal, where a is the current acceleration, a_{soll} is the target acceleration and K_i are the respective controller constants. For the transverse control, a steering controller according to

[12] was used which operates with a lookahead-point and a planned trajectory. This lookahead-point is achieved by shifting the center of gravity by the advance distance d_{BP} along the vehicle longitudinal axis. The deviation of this advance point (from the planned trajectory) is used as the controller input for a corresponding steering control. With this representation, the deviation of the predicted point is a function of both the current transverse deviation, the angular difference between the vehicle longitudinal axis and the target trajectory, as well as of the target trajectory geometry itself. The corresponding control equation is obtained by

$$\delta_{SW} = -K_{LF}y_{lat}, \tag{2}$$

where y_{lat} is the lateral deviation of the viewpoint to the desired lane, K_{LF} is the controller gain and δ_{sw} is the steering angle. The deviation of the lookahead-point (shifted by d_{BP} along the longitudinal axis of the vehicle) can also be determined by the angle deviation $\Delta\psi_S$ and the actual lateral deviation of the center of gravity T (according to [12]) of the vehicle in the simple case of a straight target trajectory

$$y_{lat} = \sin(\Delta\psi_S)d_{BP} + T \tag{3}$$

which leads to

$$\delta_{SW} = -K_{LF}(\sin(\Delta\psi_S)d_{BP} + T). \tag{4}$$

Whereby, in addition to the purely lateral deviation, the influence of the angle deviation becomes clear. The driver model generated in this way serves as a basis for the assistance functions for taking over the driving task.

3.3   Implementation

Based on the considerations of human behavior as well as the findings of previous studies on the assumption of the driving task (e.g., [10]), it can be concluded that an ideal takeover request must be able to solve the driver from a secondary occupation. For this purpose, a secondary task (in automated driving mode) was offered in the test environment driving simulator on an existing control panel (touchscreen), which can be superimposed by the takeover request. In addition, the examinations for this system allow the subjects to use secondary occupations only on the touch screen. In this combination, the takeover request obtains a maximum possible cover rate by allowing the subject to be released by directly deactivating the secondary task. In the case of a planned takeover of the driving task by the driver, the control panel is superimposed by the red message "Take over now" and the touch function is deactivated. During an automated journey, media can be used on this touch screen or vehicle functions can be controlled. In addition to a visual warning, an audible warning was also implemented. The signal is composed of a fundamental frequency of approx. 900 Hz and three saw teeth of length 0.6 s and resembles a typical signal of the seat belt reminder. This auditive signal has been selected because it is already associated with a request for a manual reaction. The information presentation serves to support perception based on the relevant objects and parameters represented in the driver model (Sect. 3.2). This system has already been tested for the first time in the investigations of [5]. The perception is to be supported with the help of this system, by displaying relevant elements of the traffic situation in the instrument cluster. This was done in two different forms (see Fig. 4). The evaluation showed that the majority of the test persons interviewed preferred an abstracted variant of the presentation. It was concluded from the objective criteria that the take-over time (time between the takeover request and the manual take-over of vehicle control) could increase if additional perceptible objects were presented. Furthermore, no effect could be detected by the representation in relation to the speed behavior.

Fig. 4. Information presentation, left: detailed, right abstract

In the course of the work on this article, the information presentation was subjected to an extended investigation in order to examine both the cause for the difference in the transfer time recognized in [5] and the objective effect with a larger number of subjects.

The support of the driving task is implemented in the above-mentioned assistance system by active lateral guidance. The basis for the calculation of a support torque in this case is the driver model (the steering controller), which is used in the "highly-automated driving" state for the whole vehicle guidance. With the model assumption of a virtual spring between the (drivers) steering angle and the steering angle which results from the driver model, a support torque M_{assist} which moves the driver's steering angle δ_{drv} in the direction of the driver model steering angle δ_{dm} arises due to the formula

$$M_{assist} = K_{assist}\Delta\delta_{SW} = K_{assist}(\delta_{drv} - \delta_{dm}), \tag{5}$$

with the proportional scaling factor K_{assist}. The spring constant of the virtual spring can in this case be used as a scaling factor. In order, not to pat the driver with regard to a maneuver selection, the assist torque is deactivated as soon as the turn signal is activated in order to initiate a lane change or turn. In order to enable the driver to override the assist torque, the assist torque is limited whenever the sum of the driving-state dependent torque, the power steering and the assisting torque (M_{veh}, M_{servo} and M_{assist}) exceeds 3 Nm. The permissible dynamic interval for the supporting torque thus results in

$$M_{assist} \in [-3 - M_{servo} - M_{veh}, 3 - M_{servo} - M_{veh}]. \tag{6}$$

During the first phase of the manual driving for highly automated driving operation, the lateral guiding assistance is used to reduce the difficulty of the driving task. In particular, during and shortly after the transfer, it is to be assumed that the necessary environmental information is present which is the basis of this function.

4   Results

The conceptualized and designed assistance system for handing over the driving task was examined in different simulator studies. Overall, the system was tested with 75 subjects aged 18 to 73 years. The takeover situations were also separated into obvious situations and situations which cannot be foreseen by the driver even if the vehicle environment is actively perceived. In a time frame of 2 to 8 s before the respective situation was reached, the subjects were either warned, audibly, visually or visually-audibly or then supported with varying elements of the assistance function in the takeover of the driving task. In the following, the study results are divided into the elements of the assistant function.

4.1   Takeover Request

The characteristic of the takeover request differs in particular in the addressed warning channel. In the course of the investigations, it was examined whether the warning channel and the possibility of deactivating the secondary task exerts an influence on the takeover of the driving task. It could be determined that switching off the secondary task leads to fewer errors and a combined warning over several channels can have an additional positive effect.

Figure 5 (left) shows the relative rate of the take over mistakes for the individual variants of the takeover request. In this case, a too late takeover is shown in light gray, and a never happened takeover of the driving task in dark gray.

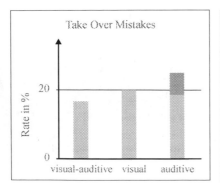 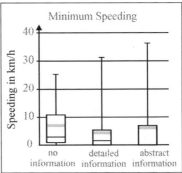

Fig. 5. Left: Rate of Take Over Mistakes; right: Speeding after Take Over Situations

4.2   Information System

Each of the presented situations was approached with increased speed. The task of the drivers was therefore to reduce the speed within the framework of the take-over of the driving task so far that the illustrated speed is maintained. Figure 5 (right) shows the minimum speeding after the takeover request, in the presence of the different information systems (detailed information, abstract information, no information).

Here, it is shown which minimum speeding was set by the subjects. There is a tendency to recognize that a representation of the permitted speed in the context of the transfer situation can lead to the speed being adjusted, but no significant difference could be detected from a statistical point of view (variance analysis F = 0.5, p = 0.61).

4.3   Lateral Guidance Assistance

The third support function of the presented assistance system is active lateral-guide assistance. In the evaluation of the simulator study, the mean difference between the steering angles of the automated steering controller and the actual steering angle δ_{SW} was used as a comparison value and compared in seconds. With the aid of the resulting characteristic values, a check is made as to whether the lateral guidance assistance influences the set steering angle. As an example, the distributions of the average steering angle differences after the takeover for the situation "construction site in the city" are shown in Fig. 6 with and without activated lateral-guiding assistance.

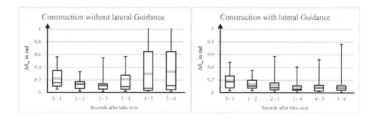

Fig. 6. Steering angle differences after take over situations

For this situation, it can be concluded that the cross-guide assistance can positively influence drivers.

5   Conclusion

On the basis of the studies, the suitability of the designed functions could thus be assessed. First, it could be seen that the take-over time (the time between warning and manual take-over of the driving task) can be significantly reduced by a warning, which is able to deactivate secondary occupations. In particular, very low transfer times could be determined compared to previous studies (e.g., [3,4]). Compared to studies on the sensory channel (for example, [10]), a deviating result could be observed, as a visual prompt can also lead to low transfer times. Furthermore, it could be shown that additional information in the phase can lead in some cases to positive effects with regard to the vehicle guidance behavior. A supportive effect on the steering behavior can be exercised, which can, however, be differently specific to the situation. Overall, subjects were positively influenced by the consistent support in the three phases of taking over the driving task from highly automated driving mode.

References

1. Gasser, T.M., Schmidt, E.A., Bengler, K., Chiellino, U., Diederichs, F., Eckstein, L., Zeeb, E.: Bericht zum Forschungsbedarf: Runder Tisch Automatisiertes Fahren-AG Forschung. Bundesanstalt für Straßenwesen, Germany (2015)
2. SAE: Taxonomy and Definitions for Terms Related to On-Road Motor Vehicle Automated Driving Systems. Berlin, Beuth (2014)
3. Damböck, D., Farid, M., Tönert, L., Bengler, K.: Übernahmezeiten beim hochautomatisierten Autofahren. 5. Tagung Fahrerassistenz, München, Germany (2012)
4. Petermann-Stock, I., Hackenberg, L., Muhr, T., Mergl, C.: Wie lange braucht der Fahrer? Eine Analyse zu Übernahmezeiten aus verschiedenen Nebentätigkeiten während einer hochautomatisierten Staufahrt 6. Tagung Fahrerassistenz, München, Germany (2013)
5. Maas, N., Schramm, D.: Lösungsansätze zur Problematik der Übergabe der Fahraufgabe an den Fahrer aus automatisiertem Fahrbetrieb. In: GMM-Fachbericht-AmE 2016 Automotive meets Electronics (2016)
6. Maurer, M., Gerdes, J.C., Lenz, B., Winner, H.: Autonomes Fahren: Technische, rechtliche und gesellschaftliche Aspekte. Springer, Heidelberg (2015)
7. Rasmussen, J.: Skill, rules and knowledge; signals, signs, and symbols, and other distinctions in human performance models. IEEE Trans. Syst. Man Cybern. **SMC–13**(3), 257–266 (1983)
8. de Waard, D.: The measurement of drivers? Mental workload. Ph.D. thesis, University of Groningen (1996)
9. Fecher, N., Hoffmann, J.: Fahrerwarnelemente. In: Winner, H., Hakuli, S., Lotz, F., Singer, C. (eds.) Handbuch Fahrerassistenzsysteme. ATZ/MTZ-Fachbuch, pp. 675–685. Springer, Wiesbaden (2015). doi:10.1007/978-3-658-05734-3_37
10. Naujoks, F., Mai, C., Neukum, A.: The effect of urgency of take-over requests during highly automated driving under distraction conditions. In: Advances in Human Aspects of Transportation (2014)
11. Nagel, H.-H., Enkelmann, W., Struck, G.: FhG-Co-Driver: from map-guided automatic driving by machine vision to a cooperative driver support. Math. Comput. Model. **22**, 185–222 (1995)
12. Fiala, E.: Mensch und Fahrzeug - Fahrzeugführung und sanfte Technik. Vieweg, Wiesbaden (2006)

Advanced Sliding Mode Control and Applications

Noise Observer Based Sliding Mode Control for Time-Varying Delay Systems

Yanliang Cui[1]([✉]), Guangtian Shi[1], Lanlan Xu[2], Xiaoan Zhang[1], and Xue Li[1]

[1] School of Mechanical Engineering, Lanzhou Jiaotong University,
Lanzhou 730070, Gansu, China
cyl1600@126.com
[2] School of Civil Engineering, Lanzhou Jiaotong University,
Lanzhou 730070, Gansu, China

Abstract. This paper investigates the control issue for noise-perturbed time-varying delay systems. A novel state and noise observer (SNO) based sliding mode control (SMC) law is designed, meanwhile, a weighted energy-to-energy performance (WEEP) is proposed for reducing the negative influence of the observer-induced complex exogenous noises. By a novel free-weight matrix method, the stability condition is conveniently obtained. By the proposed method, the exponential stability of close-loop system can be guaranteed while a WEEP is simultaneously achieved, moreover, the exponential convergence rate can be pre-specified. Numerical examples are provided to demonstrate the effectiveness of the proposed methods.

Keywords: Noise observer · Integral sliding mode control · Time-varying delay · Energy-to-energy performance

1 Introduction

Time-varying delays are universally encountered in many practical control systems because the physical process usually requires some period of time for occurring. Typical time-varying delays are mostly induced by the communication network [1], data sampling mechanism [2] and intrinsic process [3].

Generally, the main purpose of controlling time-delayed systems is to probe effective controller for guaranteeing system stability, meanwhile, reducing the conservative as much as possible. The main purpose of reducing conservative is to allow larger time-varying delays for avoiding controller over-design. For reducing the conservative, the following three methodologies are fundamental: (i) partitioning the time-delay as some smaller time-intervals or introducing many high order integral items into the LKFs [4,5]; (ii) the free-weight matrix method [6]; (iii) some inequality-based techniques including the Jensens' inequality [7]; and the Wirtinger's inequality [8,9]. Although the conservative of time-varying delay control systems can only be furthermore reduced, it is barely impossible

© Springer Nature Singapore Pte Ltd. 2017
D. Yue et al. (Eds.): LSMS/ICSEE 2017, Part II, CCIS 762, pp. 641–651, 2017.
DOI: 10.1007/978-981-10-6373-2_64

to be completely overcome. In this sense, as far as time-varying delay control systems are concerned, the conservative reduction plays an important role.

On the other hand, the exogenous noise is another considerable issue [10]. For suppressing the negative influences, some noise suppression methods are gradually proposed. For example, the traditional Kalman method is adapted and employed to suppress white noise in [11]. An H_∞ control scheme is proposed for alleviating network congestion in [12]. A distributed H_∞ cooperative control laws are advocated for guaranteeing group consensus of large-scale systems in [13]. A distributed H_∞ control scheme is proposed for guaranteeing consensus of multi-agent systems in [14]. Considering the energy-bounded disturbances, H_∞ filtering methods are proposed in [15,16]. In the aforementioned literatures, the considered exogenous noises are commonly regarded as uncontrollable components. However, if the noises can be accurately estimated, it will provide a feasible method to improve system performance.

With the motivations mentioned above, this paper further investigates an effective control scheme for exogenous noise-perturbed time-varying delay systems. The contributions of this work are listed as follows. (i) A novel time-delayed SNO is designed for accurately estimating the exogenous noise. (ii) Base on the SNO, a SMC law is designed meanwhile a WEEP is proposed. (iii) A novel free-weight equation is designed to reduce the conservative, moreover, the exponential convergence rate of close-looped system can be pre-specified.

The remainder of the paper is organized as follows. Problem is formulated in Sect. 2. Main result is presented in Sect. 3. Section 4 gives a simulation example. Conclusion remarks are outlined in Sect. 5.

The following notations will be used throughout the literature. Let $\mathscr{R}$ and $\mathscr{N}$ denote the real numbers and the integer numbers, respectively. The notation $\mathscr{R}^n$ is the n-dimensional Euclidean space and $\mathscr{R}^{n_1 \times n_2}$ is the set of $n_1 \times n_2$ real matrices. For a given square matrix A, $\lambda_{max}(A)$ and $\lambda_{min}(A)$ represent its maximum and minimum eigenvalue, respectively. The script '*' denotes the corresponding transposed matrix item. The functions $\| \cdot \|$ and $E(\cdot)$ denote the Euclidean norm and the mathematical expectation, respectively. The notations $I_n \in \mathscr{R}^{n \times n}$ and '0' denote a n-dimensional identity matrix and any appropriate dimensional zero matrix, respectively.

2   Problem Formulation

The considered time-varying delay system is described as:

$$\begin{cases} \dot{x}(t) = A_1 x(t) + A_2 x(t - \tau(t)) + Bu(t) + B_\omega \omega(t), \\ x(\theta) = \phi(\theta), \theta \in [-\tau, 0], \end{cases} \tag{1}$$

where $x(t), \omega(t) \in \mathscr{R}^n$ and $u(t) \in \mathscr{R}^p$ denote the system state, process noise, and control input; $A_1, A_2, B_\omega \in \mathscr{R}^{n \times n}$ and $B \in \mathscr{R}^{n \times p}$ are the constant matrices with appropriate dimensions. The notation $\phi(\theta)$ is a continuous vector-valued initial function.

Without loss generality, $\omega(t)$ is supposed as:

$$\|\omega(t)\| \leq \omega_1, \|\dot{\omega}(t)\| \leq \omega_2, \tag{2}$$

where ω_1 and ω_2 are upper boundaries of amplitude and change rate, respectively. The time-delay is given as:

$$0 \leq \tau(t) \leq \tau, 0 \leq \tau_l \leq \dot{\tau}(t) \leq \tau_d < 1, \tag{3}$$

where $\tau(t)$ is the data transmission time-varying delay; τ_1, τ_2, τ_l and τ_d are constant positive real numbers.

2.1 SNO

For acquiring estimation of state and noise, a SNO is designed as:

$$
\begin{aligned}
\begin{pmatrix} \dot{\hat{x}}(t) \\ \dot{\hat{\omega}}(t) \end{pmatrix} &= \begin{pmatrix} A_1 & B_\omega \\ 0 & 0 \end{pmatrix} \begin{pmatrix} \hat{x}(t) \\ \hat{\omega}(t) \end{pmatrix} + \begin{pmatrix} A_2 & 0 \\ 0 & 0 \end{pmatrix} \begin{pmatrix} \hat{x}(t - \tau(t)) \\ \hat{\omega}(t - \tau(t)) \end{pmatrix} \\
&+ \begin{pmatrix} B \\ 0 \end{pmatrix} u(t) - \begin{pmatrix} L_1 \\ L_2 \end{pmatrix} (\hat{x}(t)) - x(t)) - \begin{pmatrix} 0 \\ L_3 \end{pmatrix} \hat{\omega}(t),
\end{aligned}
\tag{4}
$$

where $\hat{x}(t)$ and $\hat{\omega}(t)$ are the observed state and noise; $L_1, L_2, L_3 \in \mathscr{R}^{n \times n}$ are the observer gains.

Defining observer errors as $\tilde{x}(t) = \hat{x}(t) - x(t)$ and $\tilde{\omega}(t) = \hat{\omega}(t) - \omega(t)$; by (1) and (4), the error system is obtained as:

$$
\begin{pmatrix} \dot{\tilde{x}}(t) \\ \dot{\tilde{\omega}}(t) \end{pmatrix} = \begin{pmatrix} A_1 - L_1 & B_\omega \\ -L_2 & -L_3 \end{pmatrix} \begin{pmatrix} \tilde{x}(t) \\ \tilde{\omega}(t) \end{pmatrix} + \begin{pmatrix} A_2 & 0 \\ 0 & 0 \end{pmatrix} \begin{pmatrix} \tilde{x}(t - \tau(t)) \\ \tilde{\omega}(t - \tau(t)) \end{pmatrix} + \begin{pmatrix} B_\omega \omega(t) \\ -L_3 \omega(t) - \dot{\omega}(t) \end{pmatrix}.
\tag{5}
$$

By choosing appropriate matrices L_i, $i = 1, 2, 3, 4$, system (5) can be stabilized.

Remark 1. In some literatures [17–19], the observers are employed only for acquiring the system state $\hat{x}(t)$. Different with the above works, the proposed SNO (4) is designed for obtaining an extra observed noise $\hat{\omega}(t)$. Since a helpful noise information $\hat{\omega}(t)$ can be directly controlled, the SNO (4) provides a chance to form a robust control law for reducing the influence of noise.

Defining $\eta(t) = (x^T(t), \tilde{x}^T(t), \tilde{\omega}^T(t))^T$, by yielding (1) and (5) gives:

$$\dot{\eta}(t) = \hat{A}_1 \eta(t) + \tilde{A}_2 \eta(t - \tau(t)) + \tilde{B}u(t) + \tilde{f}(t), \tag{6}$$

where $\hat{A}_1 = \begin{pmatrix} A_1 & 0 & 0 \\ 0 & A_1 - L_1 & B_\omega \\ 0 & -L_2 & -L_3 \end{pmatrix}$, $\tilde{A}_2 = \begin{pmatrix} A_2 & 0 & 0 \\ 0 & A_2 & 0 \\ 0 & 0 & 0 \end{pmatrix}$, $\tilde{B} = \begin{pmatrix} B \\ 0 \\ 0 \end{pmatrix}$ and $\tilde{f}(t) = \begin{pmatrix} B_\omega \omega(t) \\ -B_\omega \omega(t) \\ -L_3 \omega(t) - \dot{\omega}(t) \end{pmatrix}$.

2.2 SMC

For further reducing the noise influence while maintaining the stability, a SMC is chosen because it has an excellent virtue of insensitivity to the system uncertainties and the nonlinear variants. Therefore, a time-delay integral sliding function is designed for (6) as:

$$s(t) = \tilde{G}\eta(t) - \int_0^t \tilde{G}(\hat{A}_1 + \tilde{B}K)\eta(s)ds - \int_0^t \tilde{G}\tilde{A}_2\eta(s - \tau(s))ds, \qquad (7)$$

where $\tilde{G}$ and K are appropriate dimension matrix variables.

Based on the sliding function $s(t)$, a sliding surface is designed as:

$$s(t) = 0, \dot{s}(t) = 0, \qquad (8)$$

The main idea of SMC is to drive and attract the trajectory of system state towards the sliding surface and maintain sliding on it by designing a suitable SMC law. For achieving the above objective, the following steps are fundamental: (i) designing a SML law; (ii) proving that the trajectory of (6) can be attracted to the sliding surface in finite time (for avoiding an asymptotical approaching).

(i) The SML law design.

By (6), (6) and (7) gives:

$$\dot{s}(t) = \tilde{G}\dot{\eta}(t) - \tilde{G}(\hat{A}_1 + \tilde{B}K)\eta(t) - \tilde{G}\tilde{A}_2\eta(t - \tau(t)) = \tilde{G}\tilde{B}u(t) - \tilde{G}\tilde{B}K\eta(t) + \tilde{G}\tilde{f}(t).$$

Therefore, when the trajectory of (6) has been attracted on the sliding surface (8), the SML law will be changed as:

$$u_s(t) = K\eta(t) - (\tilde{G}\tilde{B})^{-1}\tilde{G}\tilde{f}(t). \qquad (9)$$

Before the trajectory of (6) reaches the sliding surface, a SML law is designed as:

$$u(t) = u_s(t) - (\kappa + \zeta(t))(GB)^{-1}sgn(s(t)) - \mu(GB)^{-1}s(t), \qquad (10)$$

where $\zeta(t)$ is an adaptive item which will be designed later; $G \in \mathscr{R}^{p \times n}$ satisfies: (1) GB is invertible; (2) $\tilde{G}$ can be divided as $\tilde{G} = (G, \bullet, \bullet)$, where $\bullet$ denotes any matrix belong $\mathscr{R}^{p \times n}$.

(ii) Reaching the sliding surface within finite time.

By (7) and (10), one has $\dot{s}(t) = -(\kappa + \zeta(t))sgn(s(t)) - \mu s(t)$. A Lyapunov functional is designed as $V_s(t) = \|s(t)\|$. Calculate the differential of $V_s(t)$ along the trajectory of $s(t)$ with respect to t gives $\dot{V}_s(t) = \dfrac{s^T(t)\dot{s}(t)}{\|s(t)\|} \leq \dfrac{1}{\|s(t)\|}(\tilde{s}^T(t)G\tilde{f}(t) - (\kappa + \zeta(t))\|s(t)\|_1 - \mu\|s(t)\|)$. If the following equality can be hold $\zeta(t) = \zeta + \|\tilde{G}\|F$, where ζ is a positive real number. Accordingly, one obtains $\dot{V}_s(t) \leq -(\kappa + \zeta) - \mu\|s(t)\|$.

According to the well-known Comparison Theorem, one obtains $V_s(t) \leq (V_s(0) + \frac{\kappa + \zeta}{\mu})e^{-\mu t} - \frac{\kappa + \zeta}{\mu}$. From the above inequality, it can be discovered that when $t \geq t^* = \mu^{-1} \ln \frac{\mu \|s(0)\| + \kappa + \zeta}{\kappa + \zeta}$, $V(t) \leq 0$. Therefore, the trajectory of (6) can be attracted to the sliding surface in finite time by the SML law (10).

2.3   Close-Looped Control System

When the trajectory reaches the sliding surface, the SMC law turns as:

$$u(t) = u_s(t) = K_1 \hat{x}(t) + K_2 \hat{w}(t) - (\tilde{G}\tilde{B})^{-1}\tilde{G}\tilde{f}(t), \tag{11}$$

where $K_1, K_2 \in \mathscr{R}^{p \times n}$ are control gain matrices.

By (6) and (11), the close-looped control system is obtained as:

$$\dot{\eta}(t) = \tilde{A}_1 \eta(t) + \tilde{A}_2 \eta(t - \tau(t)) + \tilde{B}_\omega \Omega(t), \tag{12}$$

where $\tilde{A}_1 = \begin{pmatrix} A + BK_1 & BK_1 & BK_2 \\ 0 & A - L_1 & B_\omega \\ 0 & -L_2 & -L_3 \end{pmatrix}$, $\tilde{B}_\omega = \begin{pmatrix} B_\omega - B(GB)^{-1}G & BK_2 & 0 \\ 0 & -B_\omega & 0 \\ 0 & -L_3 & -I \end{pmatrix}$

and $\Omega(t) = (\omega^T(t), \omega^T(t), \dot{\omega}^T(t))^T$.

Before presenting the main result, the following definitions are fundamental.

Definition 1. [20,21] Consider the time-varying system (12), if there exist positive constants $\alpha > 0$ and $\sigma \geq 1$ such that $\|\eta(t)\| \leq \sigma \sup_{-\tau \leq \theta \leq 0} \|\eta(\theta)\| e^{-\alpha t}, \forall t > 0$, then the system (12) is exponential stable, where α is called the exponential convergence rate (decay rate).

Given an positive real number $0 < \gamma < 1$, a weighted energy-to-energy performance (WEEP) is defined as:

$$\eta^T(t)\Phi\eta(t) \leq \gamma^2 \Omega^T(t)\Phi\Omega(t), \tag{13}$$

where Φ and γ is the positive definite matrix and noise suppression performance.

3   Main Result

Theorem 1. Given a positive number $\alpha > 0$, if there exist a positive scalar $\beta > 0$, positive definite matrices $\bar{P} = diag(\hat{P}, \hat{P}, \hat{P})$ and $\bar{\Phi}$, semi-positive definite matrices Q_i, R_i, S_i, $i = 1, 2$; and any matrices M_j, N_j, $j = 1, 2, 3$; if:

$$\bar{\Gamma} = \begin{pmatrix} \bar{\Gamma}_{11} & \bar{\Gamma}_{12} & \bar{\Gamma}_{13} & \bar{B}_\omega & \bar{A}_1^T & \bar{M}_1 & \bar{N}_1 & \bar{M}_1 & \bar{N}_1 \\ * & \bar{\Gamma}_{22} & \bar{\Gamma}_{23} & 0 & 0 & \bar{M}_2 & \bar{N}_2 & \bar{M}_2 & \bar{N}_2 \\ * & * & \bar{\Gamma}_{33} & 0 & \bar{A}_2^T & \bar{M}_3 & \bar{N}_3 & \bar{M}_3 & \bar{N}_3 \\ * & * & * & -\gamma^2\bar{\Phi} & \bar{B}_\omega^T & 0 & 0 & 0 & 0 \\ * & * & * & * & \bar{\Gamma}_{44} & 0 & 0 & 0 & 0 \\ * & * & * & * & * & -\zeta_2 \bar{R}_1 & 0 & 0 & 0 \\ * & * & * & * & * & * & -\zeta_2 \bar{\tau}_l \bar{R}_2 & 0 & 0 \\ * & * & * & * & * & * & * & -\zeta_3 \bar{S}_1 & 0 \\ * & * & * & * & * & * & * & * & -\zeta_3 \bar{\tau}_l \bar{S}_2 \end{pmatrix} < 0,$$

then, system (12) is exponential stable with γ performance under SML law (11); the gain matrices are given as $K_k = \bar{K}_k \hat{P}_k^{-1}$, $k = 1, 2$; $L_l = \bar{L}_l \hat{P}_1^{-1}$, and $l = 1, 2, 3$.
Where:

$$\bar{\Gamma}_{11} = \alpha\bar{P} + \Phi + \bar{A}_1 + \bar{A}_1^T + \bar{Q}_1 + \bar{Q}_2 + \tau\bar{R}_1 + \tau\bar{R}_2 - \bar{M}_1 - \bar{M}_1^T - \bar{N}_1 - \bar{N}_1^T,$$
$$\bar{\Gamma}_{12} = \zeta_1\bar{M}_1 - \bar{M}_2^T - \bar{N}_2^T, \bar{\Gamma}_{13} = \bar{A}_2 - \bar{M}_3^T + \zeta_1\bar{N}_1 - \bar{N}_3^T, \bar{\Gamma}_{22} = -\zeta_1\bar{Q}_1 + \zeta_1(\bar{M}_2 + \bar{M}_2^T),$$

$$\bar{\Gamma}_{23} = \zeta_1\bar{M}_3^T + \zeta_1\bar{N}_2, \bar{\Gamma}_{33} = -(1 - \tau_d)\zeta_1\bar{Q}_2 + \zeta_1(\bar{N}_3 + \bar{N}_3^T), \bar{\Gamma}_{44} = \tau\beta^2(S_1 + S_2) - 2\beta\bar{P},$$
$$\bar{\tau}_l = \frac{1}{1 - \tau_l}, \zeta_1 = e^{-\alpha\tau}, \zeta_2 = \frac{1}{\alpha(1 - \zeta_1)}, \zeta_3 = \frac{\alpha}{(1 - \zeta_1)},$$
$$\bar{A}_1 = \begin{pmatrix} A_1\hat{P} + B\bar{K}_1 & B\bar{K}_1 & B\bar{K}_2 \\ 0 & A_1\hat{P} - \bar{L}_1 & B_\omega\hat{P} \\ 0 & -\bar{L}_2 & -\bar{L}_3 \end{pmatrix}, \bar{A}_2 = \begin{pmatrix} A_2\hat{P} & 0 & 0 \\ 0 & A_2\hat{P} & 0 \\ 0 & 0 & 0 \end{pmatrix},$$
$$\bar{B}_\omega = \begin{pmatrix} B_\omega\bar{P} - B(GB)^{-1}G\bar{P} & B\bar{K}_2 & 0 \\ 0 & -B_\omega\bar{P} & 0 \\ 0 & -\bar{L}_3 & -\bar{P} \end{pmatrix}.$$

Remark 2. It worth to point out that actual decay rate of (12) usually can not exactly equal to $-\frac{1}{2}\alpha$ due to real variant values of time-varying delay $\tau(t)$ and exogenous noise $\omega(t)$. For obtaining the desired decay rate, a feasible method is to perform some numerical experiments to seek an acceptable value of α.

Proof: A Lyapunov-Krasovskii functional is designed for (12) as:

$$V(t) = e^{\alpha t}\eta^T(t)P\eta(t) + \int_{t-\tau}^{t} e^{\alpha s}\eta^T(s)Q_1\eta(s)ds + \int_{t-\tau(t)}^{t} e^{\alpha s}\eta^T(s)Q_2\eta(s)ds$$
$$+ \int_{-\tau}^{0}\int_{t+\phi}^{t} e^{\alpha s}\eta^T(s)R_1\eta(s)dsd\phi + \int_{-\tau(t)}^{0}\int_{t+\phi}^{t} e^{\alpha s}\eta^T(s)R_2\eta(s)dsd\phi$$
$$+ \int_{-\tau}^{0}\int_{t+\phi}^{t} e^{\alpha s}\dot{\eta}^T(s)S_1\dot{\eta}(s)dsd\phi + \int_{-\tau(t)}^{0}\int_{t+\phi}^{t} e^{\alpha s}\dot{\eta}^T(s)S_2\dot{\eta}(s)dsd\phi,$$

where $P \in \mathcal{R}^{n \times n}$ is a positive definite symmetric matrix, $Q_i, R_i, S_i \in \mathcal{R}^{n \times n}$, $i = 1, 2$ are semi-positive definite symmetric matrices.
    Calculating the differential of $V(t)$ along the trajectory of (12) gives:

$$\dot{V}(t) = \alpha e^{\alpha t}\eta^T(t)P\eta(t) + 2e^{\alpha t}\eta^T(t)P\dot{\eta}(t) + e^{\alpha t}\eta^T(t)Q_1\eta(t) + e^{\alpha t}\eta^T(t)Q_2\eta(t)$$
$$- e^{\alpha(t-\tau)}\eta^T(t-\tau)Q_1\eta(t-\tau) - (1 - \dot{\tau}(t))e^{\alpha(t-\tau(t))}\eta^T(t-\tau(t))Q_2\eta(t-\tau(t))$$
$$+ \tau e^{\alpha t}\eta^T(t)R_1\eta(t) - \int_{t-\tau}^{t} e^{\alpha s}\eta^T(s)R_1\eta(s)ds + \dot{\tau}(t)\int_{t-\tau(t)}^{t} e^{\alpha s}\eta^T(s)R_2\eta(s)ds$$
$$+ \tau(t)e^{\alpha t}\eta^T(t)R_2\eta(t) - \int_{t-\tau(t)}^{t} e^{\alpha s}\eta^T(s)R_2\eta(s)ds + \tau e^{\alpha t}\dot{\eta}^T(t)S_1\dot{\eta}(t)$$
$$- \int_{t-\tau}^{t} e^{\alpha s}\dot{\eta}^T(s)S_1\dot{\eta}(s)ds + \dot{\tau}(t)\int_{t-\tau(t)}^{t} e^{\alpha s}\dot{\eta}^T(s)S_2\dot{\eta}(s)ds$$
$$+ \tau(t)e^{\alpha t}\dot{\eta}^T(t)S_2\dot{\eta}(t) - \int_{t-\tau(t)}^{t} e^{\alpha s}\dot{\eta}^T(s)S_2\dot{\eta}(s)ds$$

Define an augment vector as $\xi^T(t) = (\eta^T(t), \eta^T(t - \tau), \eta^T(t - \tau(t)))$, the following two zero items will be appended in $\dot{V}(t)$:

$$2\xi^T M \left(-e^{\alpha t}\eta(t) + e^{\alpha(t-\tau)}\eta(t - \tau) + \int_{t-\tau}^{t} (\alpha e^{\alpha s}\eta(s) + e^{\alpha s}\dot{\eta}(s))\, ds \right),$$

$$2\xi^T N \left(-e^{\alpha t}\eta(t) + e^{\alpha(t-\tau(t))}\eta(t - \tau(t)) + \int_{t-\tau(t)}^{t} (\alpha e^{\alpha s}\eta(s) + e^{\alpha s}\dot{\eta}(s))\, ds \right),$$

where $M = (M_1^T, M_2^T, M_3^T)^T$ and $N = (N_1^T, N_2^T, N_3^T)^T$; $M_i, N_i \in \mathscr{R}^{n \times n}$, $i = 1, 2, 3$, are any matrices.

Given any appropriate dimension positive definite matrix R and vectors a, b, the following inequality always holds $2ab \leq aRa^T + b^T R^{-1} b$. Define $\bar{\xi}(t) = (\xi^T(t), \Omega^T(t))^T$, then one has $\dot{V}(t) \leq e^{\alpha t}\bar{\xi}^T(t)\Gamma\bar{\xi}(t)$. Therefore, the inequality $\Gamma + \eta^T(t)\Phi\eta(t) - \gamma^2\Omega^T(t)\Phi\Omega(t) < 0$ guarantees the desired stability with γ performance of (12). By the well-known Schur Lemma, the above inequality is equivalent as $\hat{\Gamma} < 0$, where :

$$\hat{\Gamma} = \begin{pmatrix} \Gamma_{11} & \Gamma_{12} & \Gamma_{13} & P\tilde{B}_\omega & A_1^T P & M_1 & N_1 & M_1 & N_1 \\ * & \Gamma_{22} & \Gamma_{23} & 0 & 0 & M_2 & N_2 & M_2 & N_2 \\ * & * & \Gamma_{33} & 0 & A_2^T P & M_3 & N_3 & M_3 & N_3 \\ * & * & * & -\gamma^2\Phi & \bar{B}_\omega^T P & 0 & 0 & 0 & 0 \\ * & * & * & * & -(\tau S_1 + \tau S_2)^{-1} & 0 & 0 & 0 & 0 \\ * & * & * & * & * & -\zeta_2 R_1 & 0 & 0 & 0 \\ * & * & * & * & * & * & -\zeta_2\tau_l R_2 & 0 & 0 \\ * & * & * & * & * & * & * & -\zeta_3 S_1 & 0 \\ * & * & * & * & * & * & * & * & -\zeta_3\bar{\tau}_l S_2 \end{pmatrix},$$

$\Gamma_{11} = \alpha P + \Phi + PA_1 + A_1^T P + Q_1 + Q_2 + \tau R_1 + \tau R_2 - M_1 - M_1^T - N_1 - N_1^T$,
$\Gamma_{12} = \zeta_1 M_1 - M_2^T - N_2^T$, $\Gamma_{13} = PA_2 - M_3^T + \zeta_1 N_1 - N_3^T$,
$\Gamma_{22} = -\zeta_1 Q_1 + \zeta_1(M_2 + M_2^T)$, $\Gamma_{23} = \zeta_1 M_3^T + \zeta_1 N_2$, $\Gamma_{33} = -(1 - \tau_d)\zeta_1 Q_2 + \zeta_1(N_3 + N_3^T)$,
$\bar{\tau}_l = \dfrac{1}{1 - \tau_l}$, $\zeta_1 = e^{-\alpha\tau}$, $\zeta_2 = \dfrac{1}{\alpha(1 - \zeta_1)}$, $\zeta_3 = \dfrac{\alpha}{(1 - \zeta_1)}$.

If $\hat{\Gamma} < 0$, one knows that the asymptotical stability of (12) can be guaranteed. Therefore, from the definition of $V(t)$, one has $e^{\alpha t}\lambda_{min}(P)\|\eta(t)\|^2 \leq V(t) \leq V(0) + \int_0^t e^{\alpha s}\xi^T(s)\Gamma\xi(s)ds$. Since $\Gamma < 0$, one obtains $V(t) \leq V(0)$.

Note that $\|\eta(0)\|^2 \leq \sup_{-\tau \leq s \leq 0} \|\eta(s)\|^2$, one obtains $\int_{t-\tau}^{t} e^{\alpha s}\eta^T(s)Q_1\eta(s)ds \leq$

$\tau\lambda_{max}(Q_1)(\sup_{-\tau \leq s \leq 0} \|\eta(s)\|)^2$, $\int_{-\tau}^{0}\int_{t+\phi}^{t} e^{\alpha s}\eta^T(s)R_1\eta(s)dsd\phi \leq \dfrac{\tau^2}{2}\lambda_{max}(R_1)$

$(\sup_{-\tau \leq s \leq 0} \|\eta(s)\|)^2$ and $\int_{-\tau}^{0}\int_{t+\phi}^{t} e^{\alpha s}\dot{\eta}^T(s)S_1\dot{\eta}(s)dsd\phi \leq \dfrac{\tau^2}{2}\lambda_{max}(S_1)\|\tilde{A}_1 + \tilde{A}_2\|^2(\sup_{-\tau \leq s \leq 0} \|\eta(s)\|)^2$.

Accordingly, one has $V(0) \leq \Upsilon(\sup_{-\tau \leq s \leq 0} \|\eta(s)\|)^2$, where $\Upsilon = \lambda_{max}(P) +$

$\tau(\lambda_{max}(Q_1) + \lambda_{max}(Q_2)) + \dfrac{\tau^2}{2}(\lambda_{max}(R_1) + \lambda_{max}(R_2)) + \dfrac{\tau^2}{2}(\lambda_{max}(S_1) +$

$\lambda_{max}(S_2))\|\tilde{A}_1+\tilde{A}_2\|^2$. Therefore, $\|\eta(t)\| \leq \sqrt{\dfrac{\varUpsilon}{\lambda_{min}(P)}}\,e^{-\frac{1}{2}\alpha t}\ \sup_{-\tau\leq s\leq 0}\ \|\eta(s)\|$. Note

that $\sqrt{\dfrac{\varUpsilon}{\lambda_{min}(P)}} > 1$, and according to Definition 1, the above inequality implies

the close-looped system has a convergence rate $-\frac{1}{2}\alpha$.

Regulate $\bar{P} = P^{-1} = diag(\hat{P}, \hat{P}, \hat{P})$, perform congruence transformations to $\varGamma < 0$ by $diag(\underbrace{\bar{P}, ..., \bar{P}}_{8})$ thus completes the Theorem 1.

4   Numerical Examples

Given system matrices as $A_1 = \begin{pmatrix} 1.2 & 0.4 \\ 0 & 2.3 \end{pmatrix}$, $A_2 = \begin{pmatrix} -1.1 & 0.5 \\ 0 & -0.7 \end{pmatrix}$ and $B = \begin{pmatrix} 1.0 \\ 1.0 \end{pmatrix}$; set $\alpha = 1$, $\tau = 0.15$, $\tau_l = 0.05$, $\tau_d = 0.10$, $\gamma = 0.5$ and $\beta = 20$; by Theorem 1, the gain matrices are obtained as: $K_1 = \begin{pmatrix} 24.8084 & -37.4546 \end{pmatrix}$, $K_2 = \begin{pmatrix} 0.1936 & -0.2749 \end{pmatrix}$, $L_1 = \begin{pmatrix} -7.9403 & 29.9224 \\ -35.2565 & 60.8960 \end{pmatrix}$, $L_2 = \begin{pmatrix} 2.3028 & 1.6342 \\ -0.7649 & 4.6069 \end{pmatrix}$ and $L_3 = \begin{pmatrix} 4.3658 & -1.5906 \\ -0.3652 & 3.4912 \end{pmatrix}$.

Accordingly, the minimal eigenvalue of $\tilde{A}_1$ in (12) is -0.5778. Since the pre-scheduled convergence rate of (12) is -0.5, it indicates that practical convenance rate can be approximately regulated by the proposed method.

The sampling period is set as $T = 0.05$. The noise $w(t) = \begin{pmatrix} w_1(t) & w_2(t) \end{pmatrix}^T$ is substituted as $w_1(t) = \varphi_1 \sin(\vartheta_1 kT)$ and $w_2(t) = \varphi_2 \sin(\vartheta_2 kT)$, where φ_1, φ_2 are two independent scalars and they randomly take values in $[0.1, 0.5]$; ϑ_1, ϑ_2 are two independent scalars in $[0.1, 2.0]$; $k = 1, 2, ...$.

The profile of time-varying delay $\tau(t)$ is shown in Fig. 1.

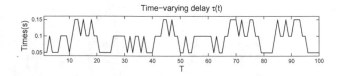

Fig. 1. Time-varying delay $\tau(t)$

The parameters of sliding function are set as $\mu = 20$, $\kappa = 0.01$, $\zeta = 0.01$, $G = \begin{pmatrix} 1 & 1 \end{pmatrix}$, and the initial values are set as $s(0) = 0.1$, $x(0) = \begin{pmatrix} 1 & 1 \end{pmatrix}^T$. By Theorem 1 and according to the above-all parameters, the noise $w(t) = (w_1^T(t), w_2^T(t))^T$ and observed noise $\hat{w}(t) = (\hat{w}_1^T(t), \hat{w}_2^T(t))^T$ are shown in Figs. 2(a) and (b), respectively. The system state $x(t) = (x_1^T(t), x_2^T(t))^T$ and observed state

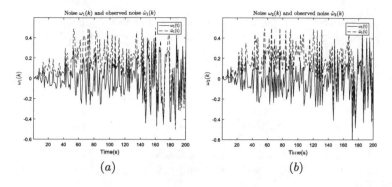

Fig. 2. Trajectories of $\omega(t)$ and observed noise $\hat{\omega}(t)$

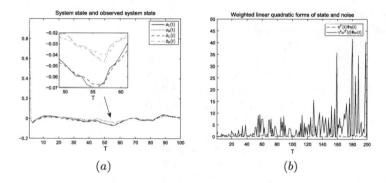

Fig. 3. Trajectories system states and weighted states

$\hat{x}(t) = (\hat{x}_1^T(t), \hat{x}_2^T(t))^T$ are illustrated in Fig. 3(a). Meanwhile, the trajectories of $\eta^T(t)\Phi\eta(t)$ and $\gamma^2\Omega^T(t)\Phi\Omega(t)$ are illustrated as Fig. 3(b).

One can intuitively see from Fig. 2(a) and (b) that the red curve and black curve fluctuate synchronously. It implies that the noise $\omega(t)$ can be accurately estimated by the proposed SNO.

In Fig. 3(a), the trajectories are reduced down and converge close to the equilibrium point quickly. From Fig. 3(b), one can observed that the dash curve is always under the black curve. It explains that the desired WEEP is achieved.

5 Conclusion

This paper addresses the control issue for exogenous noise-perturbed time-varying delay systems. By a novel time-delayed SNO, the system state as well as the exogenous noise can be accurately estimated. Base on the SNO, a SMC law is designed and a WEEP is proposed. By the proposed method, the exponential stability of the close-looped control systems can be guaranteed and the convergence rate is also pre-specifiable.

Acknowledgments. This work was supported by the Open Project of State Key Laboratory of Traction Power, Southwest Jiaotong University (TPL1604).

References

1. Pang, Z.H., Liu, G.P., Zhou, D.H., Sun, D.H.: Data-based predictive control for networked nonlinear systems with network-induced delay and packet dropout. IEEE Trans. Ind. Electron. **63**(2), 1249–1257 (2016)
2. Peng, C., Zhang, J.: Event-triggered output-feedback H_∞ control for networked control systems with time-varying sampling. IET Control Theory Appl. **9**(9), 1384–1391 (2015)
3. Zhu, J., Chen, J.: Stability of systems with time-varying delays: an L_1 small-gain perspective. Automatica **52**, 260–265 (2015)
4. Wen, S.P., Zeng, Z.G., Huang, T.W., Yu, X.H., Xiao, M.Q.: New criteria of passivity analysis for fuzzy time-delay systems with parameter uncertainties. IEEE Trans. Fuzzy Syst. **23**(6), 2284–2301 (2015)
5. Wang, Z.S., Liu, L., Shan, Q.H., Zhang, H.G.: Stability criteria for recurrent neural networks with time-varying delay based on secondary delay partitioning method. IEEE Trans. Nerual Netw. Learn. Syst. **26**(10), 2589–2595 (2015)
6. Zeng, H.B., He, Y., Wu, M., She, J.H.: Free-matrix-based integral inequality for stability analysis of systems with time-varying delay. IEEE Trans. Autom. Control **60**(10), 2768–2772 (2015)
7. Rakkiyappan, R., Sakthivel, N.: Pinning sampled-data control for synchronization of complex networks with probabilitic time-varying delays using quadratic convex approach. Neurocomputing **162**, 26–40 (2016)
8. Zhang, X.M., Han, Q.L.: Event-based H_∞ filtering for sampled-data systems. Automatica **51**, 55–69 (2015)
9. Park, M., Kown, O.M., Park, J.H., Lee, S.M., Cha, E.J.: Stability of time-delay systems via Wirtinger-based double integral inequality. Automatica **55**, 204–208 (2015)
10. Yan, H., Qian, F., Zhang, H., Yang, F., Guo, G.: H_∞ fault detection for networked mechanical spring-mass systems with incomplete information. IEEE Trans. Ind. Electron. **63**(9), 5622–5631 (2016)
11. Chen, B., Zhang, W.A., Li, Y.: Distributed fusion estimation with missing measurement, random transmission delays and packet dropouts. IEEE Trans. Autom. Control **59**(7), 1961–1967 (2014)
12. Cui, Y.L., Fei, M.R., Du, D.J.: Design of a robust observer-based memoryless H_∞ control for internet congestion. Int. J. Robust Nonlinear Control **26**, 1732–1747 (2016)
13. Cui, Y.L., Fei, M.R., Du, D.J.: Event-triggered H_∞ Markovian switching pinning control for group consensus of large-scale systems. IET Gener. Transm. Distrib. **10**(11), 2565–2575 (2016)
14. Cui, Y.L., Fei, M.R., Du, D.J.: Improved H_∞ consensus of multi-agent systems under network constraints within multiple disturbances. Int. J. Control **89**(10), 2107–2120 (2016)
15. Zhang, H., Zheng, X., Yan, H., Peng, C., Wang, Z., Chen, Q.: Codesign of event-triggered and distributed H filtering for active semi-vehicle suspension systems. IEEE Trans. Mechatron. **22**(2), 1047–1058 (2017)

16. Yan, H.C., Qian, F.F., Yang, F.W., Shi, H.B.: H_∞ filtering for nonlinear networked systems with randomly occurring distributed delays, missing measurements and sensor saturation. Inf. Sci. **370–371**, 772–782 (2016)
17. Chu, H.J., Yuan, J.Q., Zhang, W.D.: Observer-based adaptive consensus tracking for linear multi-agent systems with input saturation. IET Control Theory Appl. **9**(14), 2124–2131 (2015)
18. Wang, Y.L., Han, Q.L.: Modelling and observer-based H_∞ controller design for networked control systems. IET Control Theory Appl. **8**(15), 1478–1486 (2014)
19. Zhang, J.H., Shi, P., Qiu, J.Q., Nguang, S.K.: A novel observer-based output feedback controller design for discrete-time fuzzy systems. IEEE Trans. Fuzzy Syst. **23**(1), 223–229 (2015)
20. Li, Z.Y., Zhou, B., Lin, Z.L.: On exponential stability of integral delay systems. Automatica **49**, 3368–3376 (2013)
21. Zhang, H., Wu, Z.J., Xia, Y.Q.: Exponential stability of stochastic systems with hysteresis switching. Automatica **50**, 599–606 (2014)

Research on Speed Identification of Induction Motor Based on Sliding Mode Observer

Qiwei Xu[✉], Meng Zhao, Xiaoxiao Luo, Xiaobiao Jiang,
Yunqi Mao, Weidong Chen, and Yiming Su

Chongqing University, Chongqing 400044, China
xuqw@cqu.edu.cn

Abstract. An improved integral sliding mode observer in this paper is proposed for speed identification in induction motor, compared with traditional sliding mode observer, the steady-state error and buffeting of the control system are reduced, and the integral saturation is effectively suppressed. Based on the phase-locked loop decoding technique, the rotor position angle is calculated. The system has a good performance in speed tracking and has a satisfied accuracy of identified speed in full speed range. Finally, the correctness of the speed identification strategy proposed in this paper is verified by simulation and experimental study.

Keywords: Induction motor · Speed identification · Sliding mode observer · Integral sliding surface

1 Introduction

In the high-performance motor dynamic control, the speed is a very important parameter, vector control and direct torque control need the speed feedback signal to achieve closed-loop control. Normally, the acquisition of speed depends on the speed sensor for detecting. However, the speed sensor increases the installation volume and control system costs, but also reduces the reliability of motor control system applied in the harsh working environment. Therefore, the identification of motor speed has practical application significance. At present, the commonly used motor speed identification methods are direct calculation method, model reference adaptive method, adaptive observer method, sliding mode observer method and high frequency injection method [1, 2].

In the induction motor control system with high dynamic response, the speed changes quickly, it is required that the dynamic response of the speed identification is fast enough and the precision is high enough. It is difficult for the traditional motor speed identification strategy such as model reference adaptation and observer to meet the dynamic requirements of speed identification. The sliding mode observer has the advantages of strong robustness to system parameters and external disturbances, fast response speed, no need for on-line parameter identification, easier for digital realization, high dynamic precision and steady-state accuracy. The high speed switching and non-linear control characteristics of the sliding mode observer are very suitable for complex control objects with high order, nonlinear, strong coupling and time varying such as induction motor [3]. Therefore, this paper uses the sliding mode observer to identify the induction motor speed.

© Springer Nature Singapore Pte Ltd. 2017
D. Yue et al. (Eds.): LSMS/ICSEE 2017, Part II, CCIS 762, pp. 652–662, 2017.
DOI: 10.1007/978-981-10-6373-2_65

The paper firstly analyzes the soft commutation function and the improved integral sliding mode in the sliding mode observer, and then the sliding mode observer is designed based on the improved integral sliding mode to identify the rotational speed of the induction motor. The rotor position angle calculation in the rotational speed identification system is analyzed, and the rotor position angle is calculated by the phase locked loop decoding technique.

2 Soft Switching Function and Improved Integral Sliding Mode in Sliding Mode Observer

In the quasi-sliding mode system, the symbol function in the traditional sliding mode algorithm is usually transformed into a symmetric saturated linear transfer function (satlins), a hyperbolic tangent S-type function(tansig) or a symmetrical saturated sinusoidal function(satsin), carrying out soft switching continuous sliding mode control [4], three switching functions are shown in Fig. 1.

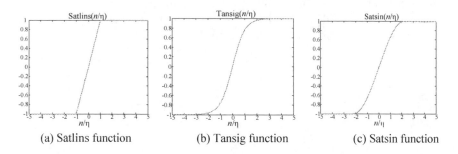

(a) Satlins function   (b) Tansig function   (c) Satsin function

Fig. 1. The soft switch functions of sliding mode observer

By setting the boundary layer of the quasi-sliding mode, a continuous function is used to control the interior of the control boundary layer for feedback control, the sliding mode observer outputs a smaller amplitude signal in the unsaturated region according to the error input, reducing the shaking of the sliding mode observer. For example, the satlins function is used as the soft handoff function to reduce the chattering of the sliding mode observer, the mathematical expression of the satlins function is given in Eq. (1):

$$
\text{satlins}(n/\eta) \begin{cases} -1 & n < -\eta \\ n & -\eta \le n \le +\eta \\ +1 & n > +\eta \end{cases} \tag{1}
$$

where η – the extended domain constant.

Sliding mode control using boundary layer can converge the system state to the boundary layer centered on the slip surface, and reduce the buffering to the control of the boundary layer. However, in the boundary layer, the system buffering still exists.

Moreover, the sliding mode control based on the boundary layer cannot guarantee the robustness of the control in the boundary layer, resulting in the increase of the steady-state error. Therefore, the integral term is added in the sliding mode to reduce the system chattering and the steady state error, improving control accuracy [5]. However, in the case of large load disturbance or initial error, the integral adjustment of the sliding mode surface will saturate, resulting in overshoot of the control system, slowing down the adjustment time and even affecting the stability of the system [6]. Therefore, this paper presents an improved integral sliding surface design, as shown in Eq. (2):

$$s = k_p x + k_i \int_0^t \frac{c_i(e^x - 1)}{e^x + 1} dt \tag{2}$$

According to Eq. (2), the integral function is shown in Fig. 2, and the adjustment function is weakened with the input error in integral sliding surface increasing, the degree of weakening can be measured by the size of the error input, which can effectively prevent the integral adjustment saturation, avoiding overshoot caused by integral saturation or system instability. By adjusting the parameter c_i, the range of the integral sliding mode could be determined. When the adjustment error approaches zero, the integral of the error also approaches zero.

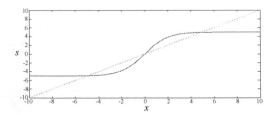

Fig. 2. The improved integral layer of sliding mode observer

3   Design of Improved Integral Sliding Mode Observer

In order to improve the performance of the sliding mode observer, the feedback gain coefficient h of the sliding mode observer is introduced, and the output of the sliding mode observer is fed back to the input terminal so that the oscillation of the sliding mode observer becomes smaller [7]. The feedback gain coefficient h of sliding mode observer is added to the sliding mode observer equation:

$$P\tilde{I}_s = A\tilde{I}_s + C^* h^* \hat{e}_s - C^* e_s - C^* u(t) \tag{3}$$

where $u(t)$—the control input of sliding mode observer.

The dynamic error Eq. (3) of the sliding mode observer could be written into the component form as follows,

$$\begin{cases} \frac{d\tilde{i}_{s\alpha}}{dt} = a_1\tilde{i}_{s\alpha} + C^*h^*\hat{e}_{s\alpha} - C^*e_{s\alpha} - C^*u_\alpha(t) \\ \frac{d\tilde{i}_{s\beta}}{dt} = a_1\tilde{i}_{s\beta} + C^*h^*\hat{e}_{s\beta} - C^*e_{s\beta} - C^*u_\beta(t) \end{cases} \tag{4}$$

where $\tilde{i}_{s\alpha} = \hat{i}_{s\alpha} - i_{s\alpha}, \tilde{i}_{s\beta} = \hat{i}_{s\beta} - i_{s\beta}$.

If the cut-off frequency of the first-order low-pass filter satisfies the $\omega_0 \gg \omega$ condition, the Eq. (5) can be established:

$$\hat{e}_s = u_{eq}(t) \tag{5}$$

where $u_{eq}(t)$—the low frequency component of the output signal in the sliding mode observer.

According to the above analysis, the Eq. (6) can be obtained by calculating.

$$\hat{e}_s \approx \frac{1}{h-1}e_s \tag{6}$$

The coefficients can be adjusted in the sliding mode observer by changing the parameter h. When the speed is low, e_s is very small, so it is difficult to accurately identify e_s, adjusting the coefficient h, increasing $\hat{e}_s$ and making identified $\hat{e}_s$ greater than the actual e_s can improve the low-speed identification performance and expand the minimum speed of sensor speed. At high speed, e_s is large, the convergence time of the system is long, so after adjusting the coefficient h and decreasing $\hat{e}_s$, the convergence time of sliding mode observer will be reduced.

Selecting $\tilde{I}_s = \hat{I}_s - I_s$ as the error input for the sliding mode observer, the improved integral sliding mode in this paper is shown as follows:

$$\begin{cases} S = k_p\tilde{I}_s + k_i\chi \\ \chi' = \frac{c_i(e^{\tilde{I}_s} - 1)}{e^{\tilde{I}_s} + 1} \end{cases} \tag{7}$$

The derivation of the sliding surface S is shown as Eq. (8),

$$S' = \begin{bmatrix} k_p(\hat{i}'_{s\alpha} - i'_{s\alpha}) + \dfrac{k_ic_i(e^{(\widehat{i_{s\alpha}-i_{s\alpha}})} - 1)}{e^{(\widehat{i_{s\alpha}-i_{s\alpha}})} + 1} \\ k_p(\hat{i}'_{s\beta} - i'_{s\beta}) + \dfrac{k_ic_i(e^{(\widehat{i_{s\beta}-i_{s\beta}})} - 1)}{e^{(\widehat{i_{s\beta}-i_{s\beta}})} + 1} \end{bmatrix} \tag{8}$$

According to the sliding surface, the Lyapunov equation is defined as follows:

$$V = \frac{1}{2}S^{\mathrm{T}}S > 0 \tag{9}$$

Derivation of Eq. (8) is shown as Eq. (10):

$$V' = S^{\mathrm{T}}S' = S^{\mathrm{T}}\begin{bmatrix} k_p\big(\hat{i}'_{s\alpha} - i'_{s\alpha}\big) + \dfrac{k_i c_i\big(e^{(\widehat{i_{s\alpha} - i_{s\alpha}})} - 1\big)}{e^{(\widehat{i_{s\alpha} - i_{s\alpha}})} + 1} \\[3mm] k_p\big(\hat{i}'_{s\beta} - i'_{s\beta}\big) + \dfrac{k_i c_i\big(e^{(\widehat{i_{s\beta} - i_{s\beta}})} - 1\big)}{e^{(\widehat{i_{s\beta} - i_{s\beta}})} + 1} \end{bmatrix} \tag{10}$$

If the formula (11) and (12) is right, the dynamic error equation is asymptotically stable.

$$S_\alpha S'_\alpha \le 0 \tag{11}$$

$$S_\beta S'_\beta \le 0 \tag{12}$$

Substituting Eq. (7) into Eq. (11), the Eq. (13) could be obtained,

$$S_\alpha S'_\alpha = S_\alpha [k_p\big(\hat{i}'_{s\alpha} - i'_{s\alpha}\big) + \frac{k_i c_i\big(e^{(\widehat{i_{s\alpha} - i_{s\alpha}})} - 1\big)}{e^{(\widehat{i_{s\alpha} - i_{s\alpha}})} + 1}]$$

$$= S_\alpha [k_p(a_1 \tilde{i}_{s\alpha} + Ch\hat{e}_{s\alpha} - Ce_{s\alpha} - C*u_\alpha) + \frac{k_i c_i\big(e^{(\widehat{i_{s\alpha} - i_{s\alpha}})} - 1\big)}{e^{(\widehat{i_{s\alpha} - i_{s\alpha}})} + 1}] \tag{13}$$

The control input of the sliding mode observer in α axis could be designed as Eq. (14),

$$u_a(t) = u_{a\_eq}(t) + u_{a\_n}(t) \tag{14}$$

where

$u_{\alpha\_eq}(t)$—equivalent control item in α axis based on motor model;

$u_{\alpha\_n}(t)$—switching control term in α axis suppressing parameter variations and external disturbances;

$u_{\alpha\_eq}(t)$ is designed based on equation (15):

$$u_{\alpha\_eq}(t) = -\frac{a_1}{C}\tilde{i}_{s\alpha} - \frac{k_i c_i\big(e^{(\widehat{i_{s\alpha} - i_{s\alpha}})} - 1\big)}{k_p\big(e^{(\widehat{i_{s\alpha} - i_{s\alpha}})} + 1\big)} \tag{15}$$

$u_{\alpha\_n}(t)$ is designed based on equation (16):

$$u_{\alpha\_n}(t) = M_\alpha \text{sgn}(S_\alpha) \tag{16}$$

Substituting Eqs. (15) and (16) into Eq. (13), the following equation could be obtained:

$$
\begin{aligned}
S_\alpha * S'_\alpha &= S_\alpha * [C * k_p(h\hat{e}_{s\alpha} - e_{s\alpha} - M_\alpha \text{sgn}(S_\alpha))] \\
&= \begin{cases} S_\alpha * C * k_p(\frac{2-h}{h-1}e_{s\alpha} - M_\alpha) & S_\alpha > 0 \\ S_\alpha * C * k_p(\frac{2-h}{h-1}e_{s\alpha} + M_\alpha) & S_\alpha < 0 \end{cases}
\end{aligned} \tag{17}
$$

therefore:

$$
\begin{cases} S_\alpha > 0 & \frac{2-h}{h-1}e_{s\alpha} - M_\alpha < 0 \Rightarrow M_\alpha > \frac{2-h}{h-1}e_{s\alpha} \\ S_\alpha < 0 & \frac{2-h}{h-1}e_{s\alpha} + M_\alpha > 0 \Rightarrow M_\alpha > -\frac{2-h}{h-1}e_{s\alpha} \end{cases} \tag{18}
$$

Similarly, the control input in β axis of the sliding mode observer is designed as shown in Eq. (19):

$$u_b(t) = u_{b\_eq}(t) + u_{b\_n}(t) \tag{19}$$

where

$u_{\beta\_eq}(t)$—equivalent control item in β axis based on motor model;
$u_{\beta\_n}(t)$—switching control term in β axis suppressing parameter variations and external disturbances.

$u_{\beta\_eq}(t)$ is designed based on Eq. (20):

$$u_{\beta\_eq}(t) = -\frac{a_1}{C}\tilde{i}_{s\beta} - \frac{k_i c_i(e^{(\widehat{i_{s\beta}} - i_{s\beta})} - 1)}{k_p(e^{(\widehat{i_{s\beta}} - i_{s\beta})} + 1)} \tag{20}$$

$u_{\beta\_n}(t)$ is designed based on Eq. (21):

$$u_{\beta\_n}(t) = M_\beta \text{sgn}(S_\beta) \tag{21}$$

According to the derivation, the following equation can be obtained:

$$
\begin{cases} S_\beta > 0 & \frac{2-h}{h-1}e_{s\beta} - M_\beta < 0 \Rightarrow M_\alpha > \frac{2-h}{h-1}e_{s\beta} \\ S_\beta < 0 & \frac{2-h}{h-1}e_{s\beta} + M_\beta > 0 \Rightarrow M_\alpha > -\frac{2-h}{h-1}e_{s\beta} \end{cases} \tag{22}
$$

Let $M_\alpha = M_\beta = M$, therefore, according to Eqs. (18) and (22), the conditions that meet equitation Eqs. (11) and (12) can be derived as shown in Eq. (23).

$$M > \max\left(\left|\frac{2-h}{h-1}e_{s\alpha}\right|, \left|\frac{2-h}{h-1}e_{s\beta}\right|\right) \tag{23}$$

That is, if the Eq. (23) is satisfied, the sliding mode motion can be generated, and the dynamic error Eq. (3) will be stabilized [8]. When the control system reaches the slip surface, which is $S = [0\ 0]^T$, the α-axis component and the β-axis component observing current converge to the actual current, and the recognition error of the sliding mode observer converges to zero at the same time.

Generally, the switching gain M is designed as a constant value to ensure convergence over the entire motor speed range. This will cause it that when the motor runs at low speed, the switch gain M is too large, the identification error is large, the system oscillation is serious. If the sliding mode switch gain M is reduced when the motor runs at low speed, the oscillation will be significantly reduced.

Therefore, the switching gain M can be adjusted in the motor running speed range, the switching gain M can be changed according to the target speed as shown in Eq. (24):

$$M_\omega = K_0 + K_1 |\omega_{ref}| \tag{24}$$

where K_0, K_1—positive coefficients.

According to the above analysis, the construction of the sliding mode observer is shown in Eq. (25):

$$\begin{cases} \frac{d\hat{i}_s}{dt} = A\hat{I}_s + Bu_s + C^*h^*\hat{e}_s - C^*u(t) \\ u(t) = u_{eq}(t) + u_n(t) \\ \frac{d\hat{e}_s}{dt} = -\omega_0\hat{e}_s + \omega_0 u(t) \end{cases} \tag{25}$$

Therefore, the improved sliding mode observer structure designed in this paper is shown in Fig. 3.

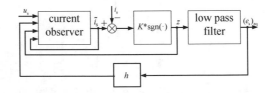

Fig. 3. The structure diagram of improved sliding mode observer

According to the sliding mode observer designed in this paper, the motor speed could be analyzed and calculated by Eq. (26).

$$\begin{pmatrix} \dfrac{d\psi_{r\alpha}}{dt} \\ \dfrac{d\psi_{r\alpha}}{dt} \end{pmatrix} = \begin{pmatrix} -\frac{1}{T_r} & -\omega_r \\ \omega_r & -\frac{1}{T_r} \end{pmatrix} \begin{pmatrix} \psi_{r\alpha} \\ \psi_{r\beta} \end{pmatrix} + \begin{pmatrix} \dfrac{L_m}{T_r} \\ \dfrac{L_m}{T_r} \end{pmatrix} \begin{pmatrix} i_{s\alpha} \\ i_{s\beta} \end{pmatrix} \tag{26}$$

Therefore, with the initial definition, after derivation the Eq. (27) can be drawn:

$$\hat{\omega}_r = \frac{\hat{e}_{s\alpha}\psi_{r\beta} - \hat{e}_{s\beta}\psi_{r\alpha}}{\psi_{r\alpha}^2 + \psi_{r\beta}^2} \qquad (27)$$

In the theoretical sense, the sliding mode control is mainly used in the continuous control system, because only the continuous sliding mode control with variable structures has equivalent control functions generated by variable structure control. However, in practical engineering applications, the system using digital signal processor is discrete, the discrete sliding mode control of system is a "quasi-sliding mode", and the switching action cannot be carried out precisely on the sliding surface [9]. Since the sliding mode observer contains non-linear links, the Eq. (25) can only be discretized by using the forward difference method with self-starting characteristics:

$$\begin{cases} \hat{I}_s(n+1) = \hat{I}_s(n) + T_s[A\hat{I}_s(n) + Bu_s(n) + C^*h^*\hat{e}_s(n) - C^*u_s(n)] \\ u(n) = u_{eq}(n) + u_n(n) \\ \hat{e}_s(n+1) = \hat{e}_s(n) + T_s[-\omega_0\hat{e}_s(n) + \omega_0 u(n)] \end{cases} \qquad (28)$$

where T_s—the sampling period (s).

4   System Modelling and Simulation Analyzing

The simulation model in Matlab/Simulink which is based on improved integral sliding mode observer proposed in this passage is shown in Fig. 4:

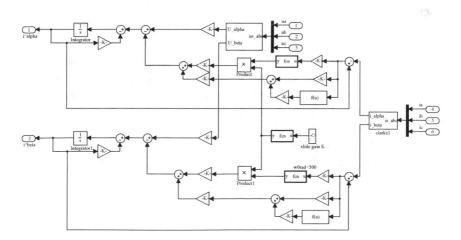

Fig. 4. The simulation model of improved sliding mode observer

In the process of simulating, sampling frequency is set to 20 kHz, the gain factor of feedback $h = 0.5$ and the speed given is 50 rad/s, the cut-off frequency of low pass filter is set to 500 Hz. The improved integral sliding observer is used and the simulation wave forms are shown in Figs. 5 and 6.

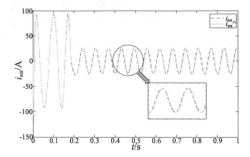

Fig. 5. The comparison between the real value of $i_{s\alpha}$ and observation value using improved sliding mode observer

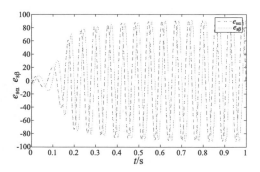

Fig. 6. The $e_{s\alpha}$ and $e_{s\beta}$ waveforms of improved sliding mode observer

From Fig. 5, it could be seen that the fluctuation on observed value of stator current $i_{s\alpha}$ is very small with the improved integral sliding mode observer, and the wave form of $e_{s\alpha}$ and $e_{s\beta}$ which output from sliding mode observer is well enough to fit sine.

According to $e_{s\alpha}$ and $e_{s\beta}$ which output from sliding mode observer, the speed identification could be processed, through the identification of the speed a closed loop control could be constituted. From the speed identification simulation wave form in Fig. 7 it could be seen that identification speed follows the given speed very well and the error is small in the identification progress.

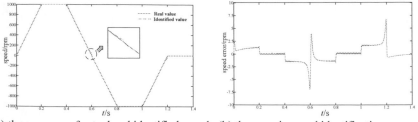

(a) the compare of actual and identified speed   (b) the error in speed identification progress

Fig. 7. The simulation waveform of estimated speed

5 Speed Identification Analysis

In the experiment with no speed sensor, the interruption frequency of PWM is set to 10 kHz, and the compute of sliding mode observer is finished in the interruption subroutine of PWM. In order to compare the performance of speed observer, photo-electric encoder using 2048 channels is used to take the real-time sampling motor speed, which is then compared with identified speed.

In the experiment, Fig. 8 shows the actual speed and identified speed at 10 rpm, the actual rotor position angle and the identified position angle of the experimental waveform.

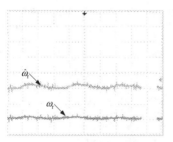 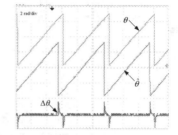

(a) The actual speed and identified speed   (b)The actual location and identified location

Fig. 8. Experiment waveforms of sensorless control at 10 rpm

Figure 9 shows the experimental waveforms of the actual speed and the identified speed at 1200 rpm, the actual rotor position angle and the identified position angle.

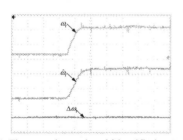 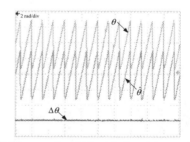

(a) The actual speed and identified speed   (b) The actual and identified position angle

Fig. 9. Experiment waveforms of sensorless control at 1200 rpm

6 Conclusion

In this paper, the speed identification strategy of induction motor is analyzed, and a speed identification strategy is proposed, the improved integral type sliding mode observer is used to reduce the steady-state error and buffeting of the control system, effectively suppressing the integral saturation. The proposed speed identification strategy is small and easy to implement digitally.

References

1. Bojoi, R., Guglielmi, P., Pellegrino, G.-M.: Sensorless direct field oriented control of three phase induction motor drives for low cost applications. IEEE Trans. Ind. Appl. **44**(2), 475–481 (2008)
2. Shanshan, W., Yongdong, L.: New Method of Speed sensorless Control of IM at Very Low Speed. Electr. Drive **38**(9), 39–42 (2008)
3. Salamci, M.U., Tombul, G.S.: Sliding mode control design with time varying sliding surfaces for a class of nonlinear system. In: Proceedings of IEEE Conference on Control Applications, pp. 996–1001 (2006)
4. Limin, H., Huaguang, Z., Xiuchong, L., Enhui, C., Qiang, W.: Adaptive fuzzy sliding mode soft switch of speed sensorless for PMSM based on robust passivity-based control. Control Decis. **25**(5), 686–694 (2010)
5. Peng, L., Weimeng, S., Wenqiang, L., Zhiqiang, Z.: Application of improved integral sliding surface to flight control system. Control Eng. China **17**(3), 269–271 (2010)
6. Barambones, O., Garrido, A.J., Maseda, F.J.: Intrgral sliding-mode control for induction motor based on field-oriented control theory. IET Control Theory Appl. **1**(3), 786–794 (2007)
7. Chi, S., Zhang, Z., Xu, L.: Sliding-mode sensorless control of direct-driven PM synchronous motor for washing mashines applications. IEEE Trans. Ind. Appl. 582–590 (2009)
8. Derdiyok, A., Guven, M.K., Rehman, H., Xu, L.: Design and implementation of a new sliding-mode observer for speed-sensorless control of induction machine. IEEE Trans. Ind. Electron. **49**, 1177–1182 (2002)
9. Xiaoguang, Z., Li, S., Ke, Z.: Sliding mode control of PMSM based on a novel load torque sliding mode observer. Proc. CSEE **32**(3), 112–116 (2012)

Integral Sliding Mode Based Precision Motion Control for PMLM

Yang Liu[1(⊠)], Hao Luo[1], Zhile Yang[2], Zhenxian Fu[1],
and Xiaofeng Yang[2]

[1] Department of Control Science and Engineering,
Harbin Institute of Technology, Harbin 150001, China
hitlg@hit.edu.cn
[2] School of Microelectronics, Fudan University, Shanghai 200433, China

Abstract. In ultra-precision fabrication, permanent magnet linear motor (PMLM) is generally applied thanks to its excellent performance. Thus, it is expected to meet high accuracy and high speed simultaneously. However, it is difficult to reach the goal using the tradition control strategies. In this paper, a novel method is proposed to improve response speed and tracking accuracy, which employs an integral sliding mode controller that switches between PD control and PID control according to the value of tracking errors. Based on the modeling of PMLM, an integral sliding mode controller is constructed, taking the advantages of both PD and PID control. Thus, the closed-loop system could respond rapidly and ideally reduce state error. To optimize the performance of the proposed control strategy, its parameters are adjusted using particle swarm optimization (PSO) algorithm. The validity of the method is verified by simulation under different inputs and constant disturbance in a 1DOF precision stage.

Keywords: Integral sliding mode control · PMLM · PSO · Ultra precision

1 Introduction

In ultra-precision fabrication, such as integrated circuits production, rapidity is required for the whole system to improve the throughput. Linear motor has the advantages of high speed and large acceleration; therefore, it is commonly used as actuator in linear motion control system. However, it is difficult to achieve high speed and high accuracy simultaneously with the traditional control strategy, such as PID. It is urgent to find a novel approach to reach both objectives for precision stage.

To address this issue, several researches are carried out. Peng adopted a PID to reach required nanometer scale position precision, but could not guarantee high speed response [1]. Tang proposed a 2DOF PID, which is used in a dual linear motor cooperative control system [2]. Moreover, the controller could be adjusted independently to obtain good performance in terms of both robustness and tracking ability. Wang used particle swarm optimization to optimize a PID online for permanent magnet synchronous linear motor [3], which could improve the robustness in loading disturbance and accuracy in tracking position. Sun proposed a fuzzy PID controller for permanent magnet linear synchronous motor [4]. It combines PID and fuzzy control to

D. Yue et al. (Eds.): LSMS/ICSEE 2017, Part II, CCIS 762, pp. 663–673, 2017.
DOI: 10.1007/978-981-10-6373-2_66

improve precision in a complex control system and a high precision servo system. Several adaptive and robust control methods were compared in experiments for improvement of the positioning accuracy [5]. However, these methods can not achieve the rapid response required of the linear motors. Cu presented an approach combining a linear PID controller and a nonlinear neural network [6]. The nonlinear part of the controller is introduced to improve the tracking performance of the system and is trained online by a compact genetic algorithm, which requires less memory and can be implemented in a low capacity microcontroller. However, this method is complex and hard to implement in system.

To achieve the high speed response of a linear motor, various methods have been investigated. Xiao proposed an adaptive fuzzy PID control strategy to improve the dynamic characteristic of PMLM and to reject disturbance under different load levels [7], but without giving the parameter designing method. Zhu designed a novel fuzzy controller to promote the speed performance of PMLM. However, it cannot achieve high static performance, since fuzzy controllers have no integral part [8]. In [9], a controller with learning control component was proposed to achieve tracking control with high speed and high precision. However, the controller with learning control subsystem is so complex that it can only be used under some particular conditions. Moreover, the learning control process sometimes diverges. Huang and Zhao designed a sliding mode controller for linear synchronous motors to improve the non-linear character, raise response speed and reduce tracking errors [10, 11]. In [12], fuzzy sliding mode control based on mode reference adaptive control for PMSLM was proposed to improve tracking characteristic and robustness. Sliding mode control (SMC) is an effective method for PMLM to meet the high speed response and high accuracy synchronously. However, these papers have not mentioned the method to optimize or calculate the parameters, which are important for SMC. Marcel proposed an integral sliding mode control method, which used Levenberg–Marquardt algorithm to optimize the parameters of integral sliding mode control (ISMC) [13], but the convergence of the proposed algorithm is not fast.

In this paper, a new method of ISMC combining PD and PID control is proposed to meet the requirements of high speed and high precision simultaneously for linear motors. The approach could utilize the rapidity of PD and non-error characteristic of PID. By simulation, the effectiveness of the method proposed is verified.

2   Modeling of Permanent Magnet Linear Motor

In this paper, the model of the PMLM is identified using sinusoidal sweep frequency response. A series of sinusoidal input signals with different frequencies are applied to the system, and the frequency responses are measured in a sweep experiment. The sweep experiment is done in a closed-loop with a PI controller. The close-loop system for sweep frequency is as shown in Fig. 1. The increment was different in different frequency range so as to achieve accurate and rapid measurement. In a low frequency range, such as one below 1 Hz, the input sweep frequency increases at intervals of 0.05 Hz; in a middle frequency range, such as one between 1 Hz and 100 Hz, it is done at internals 0.5 Hz; in a high frequency range, such as one above 100 Hz, it increases at intervals of 5 Hz. The PMLM is identified in the frequency range from 0.1 Hz to 300 Hz. The model of the PMLM can be obtained by comparing the discrete Fourier transforms of output y(t) of the close-loop system and input u(t) of the plant in terms of amplitude gain and phase shift which are both measured in sweep frequency experiment [14–16].

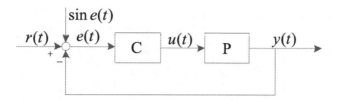

Fig. 1. The close-loop structure of sweep frequency identification

The response of the sweep frequency experiment is shown in Fig. 2. It can be seen that, at meddle frequencies, the frequency response of the PMLM can be approximated by a double integrator. However, at high frequencies, such as those beyond 150 Hz, the dynamic response becomes increasingly more complex for higher frequencies, causing difficulty in modeling the PMLM.

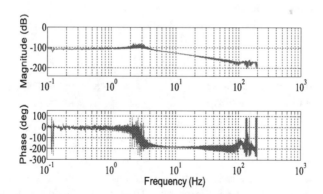

Fig. 2. Frequency response of PMLM

3   Integral Sliding Mode Control for PMLM

In this paper, integral sliding mode control, or ISMC, is applied. An ISMC is as shown in Fig. 3, in which the module of the PMLM is denoted by P, which is subjected indirectly to output disturbances denoted by d and subjected directly to input disturbances denoted by f_d.

A result of fast response and less error is anticipated for the PMLM using ISMC. Thus, the ISMC designed and the plant controlled are comprised of three parts: a feedforward control part, with the controller c_{ff} and the feedforward output u_{ff}; a linear

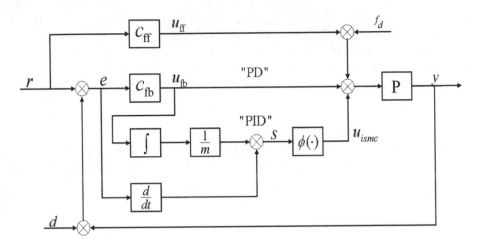

Fig. 3. Block diagram of the ISMC

feedback control part, with the controller c_{fb} and the feedback output u_{fb}; and a robustness feedback control part, which contains a saturation function and produces an output u_{ismc}.

For feedforward control, a second order differential model is adopted as the feedforward controller. That is

$$u_{ff}(t) = m\frac{d^2r(t)}{dt^2} \tag{1}$$

To obtain high speed response, the linear feedback controller adopts a PD controller, which can be described as

$$u_{fb}(t) = k_p e(t) + k_d \frac{de(t)}{dt} \tag{2}$$

For robustness, sliding mode control is adopted to switch control states under different state vectors. Therefore, the output of the robust feedback controller can be described as

$$u_{ismc}(t) = \phi(s(t)) = k sign(s(t)) \tag{3}$$

where $k > 0$ is the gain of the controller, and $s(t)$ is the switch function related to the error denoted by e in Fig. 3.

However, the control output $u_{ismc}(t)$ will make the system chattering, also called chattering of SMC, because it has only two output states (k or $-k$) and is not continuous in switch point. A solution is to replace the sign function with a continuous saturation function. The saturation function satisfies [17]

$$sat(s(t)) \overset{def}{=} \begin{cases} \frac{s(t)}{\varepsilon} & |s(t)| \leq \varepsilon \\ sign(s(t)) & |s(t)| > \varepsilon \end{cases} \tag{4}$$

where $\varepsilon > 0$ is saturation length.

Thus, we have the robust feedback controller modified as below

$$u_{ismc}(t) = \phi(s(t)) = ksat(s(t)) \tag{5}$$

The output of $u_{ismc}(t)$ is related to the switching function $s(t)$. From Fig. 3, it can be obtained by

$$s(t) = \frac{de(t)}{dt} + \frac{1}{m} \int_0^t u_{fb}(\tau)d\tau \tag{6}$$

where m is the total mass of the rotor of the PMLM and the loads (when present), e is the error, defined as

$$e(t) = r(t) - y(t) - d(t) \tag{7}$$

where r is the input signal to be tracked. Next, a second order integral model can be employed to approximate the PMLM, which means that p is a double integrator plant. It can be described using

$$y(t) = \frac{1}{m} \iint_R u(\tau)d\tau \tag{8}$$

where R is an integral interval with dimension $[0, t] \times [0, t]$.

From Fig. 3, the transfer function from the error e to the output u_{fb} can be derived as

$$\frac{U_{fb}(s)}{E(s)} = C_{fb}(s) \tag{9}$$

Suppose $|s(t)| \leq \varepsilon, t \in [0, \infty)$, Eqs. (4)–(6) yields

$$\frac{U_{ismc}(s)}{E(s)} = \frac{k}{\varepsilon} \left(\frac{ms^2 + C_{fb}(s)}{ms} \right) \tag{10}$$

Next, let $r = f_d = d = 0$, then the integral sliding mode controller can be seen as two linear controllers in the transfer from the error e to u, the input to the plant in Fig. 3. When $u_{fb}(t) \gg k, t \in [0, \infty)$, the output of the first linear controller can be approximated as the output u_{fb} of linear feedback controller. In other words, the system adopts PD control which achieves a speedy response at the price of a large control error. If $|s(t)| \leq \varepsilon, t \in [0, \infty)$, the output of second linear controller is consisted of two parts, u_{fb} and u_{ismc}. Therefore, PID control is adopted for the system, which can reduce the steady state error of the system. So, the transfer function from error e to the output u is given as

$$\frac{U(s)}{E(s)} = \begin{cases} C_{fb}(s), |u_{fb}(t)| \gg k \\ C_{fb}(s) + \frac{\kappa}{\varepsilon} \left(\frac{ms^2 + C_{fb}(s)}{ms} \right), |s(t)| \le \varepsilon \end{cases} \tag{11}$$

From Eq. (11), it can be concluded that the control is switched between PD and PID, achieving both high speed and high accuracy.

Next, the Lyapunov criteria is employed to prove the stability of the system. For simplicity, let $e(0) = \dot{e}(0) = 0$, which will not affect the result of the proof.

According to Eq. (2) and Fig. 3, we have

$$s(t) = \frac{k_p}{m} \int_0^t e(\tau) d\tau + \frac{k_d}{m} e(t) + \frac{de(t)}{dt} \tag{12}$$

Substitution of (8) in (6) and taking derivatives yields

$$u(t) = u_{ff}(t) + u_{fb}(t) + u_{sat}(t) + f_d(t) \tag{13}$$

Next,

$$\frac{ds(t)}{dt} = -\frac{1}{m} sat(s(t)) - \frac{d^2 d(t)}{dt^2} - \frac{1}{m} f_d(t) \tag{14}$$

where d is a white noise process.

Construct Lyapunov function

$$V(t) = s^2(t) \tag{15}$$

which is positive definite $s(t) \ne 0$. It follows that

$$\begin{aligned} \frac{dV(t)}{dt} &= 2\frac{ds(t)}{dt} s(t) = -\frac{2k}{m} sat(s(t)) s(t) \\ &- 2(\frac{d^2 d(t)}{dt^2} + \frac{1}{m} f_d(t)) s(t) \end{aligned} \tag{16}$$

if the disturbances to the system are uniformly bounded, that is,

$$\left| \frac{d^2 d(t)}{dt^2} + \frac{1}{m} f_d(t) \right| < \frac{k}{m}, t \in [0, \infty) \tag{17}$$

The gain k needs to be large enough to suppress these disturbances. If $|s(t)| > \varepsilon$, Eq. (16) produces

$$\frac{dV(t)}{dt} \le -\frac{k}{m} |s(t)| + \left| \left(\frac{d^2 d(t)}{dt^2} + \frac{1}{m} f_d(t) \right) \right| |s(t)| < 0 \tag{18}$$

For now, $\dot{V}(t)$ is negative definite. When $|s(t)| \leq \varepsilon$, Nyquist diagram can be used to prove that the system is stable [13].

When system works under closed-loop condition, the parameters of the ISMC have to be optimized using different input signals. That is to say, optimization (or tuning) of the parameters is based on the input tracking performance. In this paper, the two parameters to be optimized are the gain k and saturation length ε. Particle Swarm Optimization is adopted for the optimization, whose goal is to find the best value $p_{opt} = [k_{opt} \, \varepsilon_{opt}]$ from a series of parameters to minimize a performance cost function J(t) which is constructed using the error e (possibly filtered) in the time interval $t \in [t_1 \, t_2]$. That is,

$$p_{opt} \overset{\text{def}}{=} \arg \min_{p_g} J(t), J(t) = \int_{t_1}^{t_2} e_n^2(\tau) d\tau \tag{19}$$

where n is the iteration number, and $p_g = [k_g \, \varepsilon_g]$ is global optimal values in the all iterations. The time t_1 (or t_2) is the time start (or end) point to be optimized to track the input, which much determines the cost function.

The usage of PSO to find the optimal parameters is given below. Suppose the particle swarm has m members. Let $X_i = (k_{xi}, \varepsilon_{xi}), V_i = (k_{vi}, \varepsilon_{vi}), p_i = (k_i, \varepsilon_i), p_g = (k_g, \varepsilon_g)$ where X_i and V_i are the position and velocity of the i_{th} particle respectively, p_i and p_{gi} are the updated optimal values of the i_{th} particle and the whole particle swarm respectively.

From the n_{th} iteration to the $n + 1_{th}$, the velocity and position of every particle can be modified using [18]

$$\begin{aligned} V_i^{n+1} &= \omega V_i^n + c_1 \xi (p_i^n - X_i^n) + c_2 \eta (p_g^n - X_i^n) \\ X_i^{n+1} &= X_i^n + \gamma V_i^{n+1} \end{aligned} \tag{20}$$

where ω is the inertia weight, c_1 and c_2 are the learning factors for oneself and the particle swarm respectively, ξ, η are random numbers in the range of [0,1], and γ is a weight factor of velocity.

4   Simulation Results and Analysis

Simulation is performed to check the effectiveness of the method. First, step input is adopted to test ISMC and compare its results with those using PD and PID. The magnitude of the step input is set as 0.1 m. In ISMC using PSO optimization, the results are $k = 5.32, \varepsilon = 0.0015$. The step responses using different control strategies are shown in Fig. 4, from which it is obvious that ISMC has a speedier response than both PD and PID control. Moreover, it has a smaller overshoot than PID.

When systems reach stable state, a constant disturbance is added to system. The responses of different control strategies are shown in Fig. 5, which shows that PD control has a constant tracking error, PID control has overshoot and oscillation before the steady state is reached, and ISMC control achieves smooth transition to the stable state and has requires shorter dynamic time than PID control.

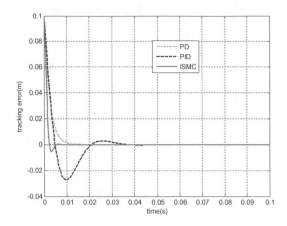

Fig. 4. Tracking error contrast with step response

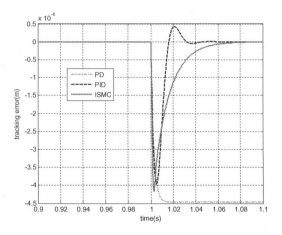

Fig. 5. Tracking error contrast with constant disturbance

However, the trajectory is not a step position signal for PMLM at most times. Instead, S curve has been applied generally as input signal in ultra-precision field. Thus, simulation using an S curve as the input will be more meaningful. Let the position magnitude be 0.1 m, the maximal velocity be 0.25 m/s, the maximal acceleration be 5 m/s^2, and the differential of acceleration be 500 m/s^3. The S curve is plotted as in Fig. 6.

Using PSO to optimize the parameters of ISMC yields $k = 10, \varepsilon = 0.1$. The responses using other control strategies with S curve input are shown in Fig. 7, which demonstrates that ISMC has smaller tracking error than both PD and PID control and requires shorter transient time to reach stable state during acceleration and deceleration. In addition, in the process of uniform motion, ISMC has a smaller state error than PID and PD whose errors are both obvious as seen from Fig. 7. Therefore, ISMC is an effective method in improving response speed and reducing tracking error.

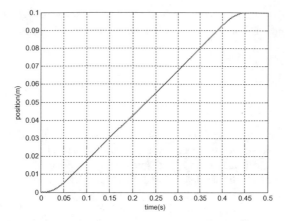

Fig. 6. S curve for input

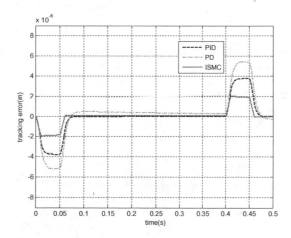

Fig. 7. Tracking error contrast with S curve input

5 Conclusion

In this paper, a novel integral sliding mode control combining PD and PID control is proposed. The simulation results show that the proposed method can significantly reduce the error, compared with PD and PID control under the same conditions. Meanwhile, the method enables the parameters of the controller to be optimized for variant input to track it more accurately. In addition, the method achieves high speed response for PMLM. Comparison of simulation results using different inputs and different control strategies illustrates the effectiveness of the method to obtain high accuracy and high speed simultaneously.

Acknowledgments. This work was supported by the State Key Program of National Natural Science of China under Grant 51537002, and Chinese National Science Foundation under Grant 51405097.

References

1. Peng, W.F.: Linear motor velocity and acceleration motion control study based on PID + velocity and acceleration feedforward parameters adjustment, pp. 239–243 (2011)
2. Tang, J., Dong, F., Zhao, J., et al.: Disturbance suppression research in parallel dual permanent synchronous linear motors based on 2DOF PID controller. In: IEEE Conference on Industrial Electronics and Applications, pp. 1475–1478. IEEE (2016)
3. Wang, X., Xia, T., Xu, X., et al.: Design of the particle swarm optimized PID for permanent magnet synchronous linear motor. In: International Conference on Electrical Machines and Systems, pp. 2289–2293. IEEE (2014)
4. Hua, S., Dai, Y.: Fuzzy PID control and simulation experiment on permanent magnet linear synchronous motors. In: International Conference on Electrical and Control Engineering, pp. 1047–1049. IEEE Xplore (2010)
5. Cupertino, F., Naso, D.: An experimental comparison of adaptive and robust control methods for precise positioning with tubular linear motors. In: IECON 2010, Conference on IEEE Industrial Electronics Society, pp. 71–76. IEEE Xplore (2010)
6. Cupertino, F., Naso, D., Turchiano, B.: Precision motion control of tubular linear motors with neural networks and compact genetic algorithms. In: ASME 2009 Inter-national Design Engineering Technical Conferences and Computers and Information in Engineering Conference, pp. 143–149 (2009)
7. Xiao, J.F., Zhu, F.H., Xiao, Q.M.: Research on high precision linear motor control system based on adaptive fuzzy-PID control. In: Advances in Engineering Materials and Applied Mechanics, pp. 279–289 (2015)
8. Zhu, L., Tang, Y., Zhang, D.: Application of fuzzy controller in the speed control of permanent magnet linear motors. In: Chinese Control Conference, pp. 242–245 (2007)
9. Hama, T., Sato, K.: High-speed and high-precision tracking control of ultrahigh-acceleration moving-permanent-magnet linear synchronous motor. Precis. Eng. **40**, 151–159 (2015)
10. Huang, Y.S., Sung, C.C.: Implementation of sliding mode controller for linear synchronous motors based on direct thrust control theory. IET Control Theory Appl. **4**(3), 326–338 (2010)
11. Zhao, X., Zhao, J.: Complementary sliding mode variable structure control for permanent magnet linear synchronous motor. Zhongguo, Dianji, Gongcheng, Xuebao Proc. Chinese Soc. Electr. Eng. **35**(10), 2552–2557 (2015)
12. Zhao, Y., Wang, Q., Jinxue, X.U., et al.: A fuzzy sliding mode control based on model reference adaptive control for permanent magnet synchronous linear motor. In: ICIEA 2007 IEEE Conference on Industrial Electronics and Applications, pp. 980–984. IEEE Xplore (2007)
13. Heertjes, M., Verstappen, R.: Self-tuning in integral sliding mode control with a Levenberg–Marquardt algorithm. J Mechatron. **24**(4), 385–393 (2014)
14. Stearns, H.M.: Iterative methods for high precision motion control with application to a wafer scanner system. Dissertations & theses – Gradworks (2011)
15. Amer, A.F., Sallam, E.A., Elawady, W.M.: Adaptive fuzzy sliding mode control using supervisory fuzzy control for 3 DOF planar robot manipulators. J. Appl. Soft Comput. **11**(8), 4943–4953 (2011)

16. Tsuruta, K., Sato, K., Ushimi, N., et al.: High-speed and high-precision position control using a sliding mode compensator. Electr. Eng. Jpn. **174**(2), 65–71 (2011)
17. Nonaka, K., Sugizaki, H.: Integral sliding mode altitude control for a small model helicopter with ground effect compensation. In: American Control Conference, pp. 202–207. IEEE (2011)
18. Yi, L.: Study on an improved PSO algorithm and its application for solving function problem. Int. J. Smart Home **10**, 51–62 (2016)

Advanced Analysis of New Materials and Devices

Magnetic Field Measurement Instrument Based on Asymmetric Giant Magneto-Impedance Effect

Feng Jiang[1,2(✉)] and Shulin Liu[1]

[1] School of Mechatronics Engineering and Automation, Shanghai University,
Shanghai 200072, China
jf_415@126.com
[2] School of Mechatronics Engineering,
Jiangsu College of Information Technology, Wuxi 214153, China

Abstract. A magnetic field measurement instrument based on asymmetric giant magneto-impedance effect is developed by using $Co_{66.3}Fe_{3.7}Si_{12}B_{18}$ amorphous ribbon. The signal processing circuit of the sensor and the hardware circuit of the measurement instrument are designed, and the experiment result is given. The result shows that this instrument can measure the weak magnetic field ranging from -260 to $+260$ A/m. The sensitivity is 0.01 A/m and measurement accuracy is $\pm0.55\%$ because of applying sensor nonlinear compensation technique through microcontroller. The instrument has high sensitivity, high repeatability, high frequency response characteristic, which is widely used in aerospace, aviation, national defense and other fields.

Keywords: Giant magneto-impedance effect · Asymmetric characteristic · Magnetic measurement instrument · Microcontroller

1 Introduction

Earth's magnetic field is related to human life as a kind of important natural resources. It has important applications such as aerospace, earth science, resources exploration, earthquake prediction and other fields. The measurement of the magnetic field has become a hot research topic because of the important application value of earth's magnetic field. The geomagnetic field which is about 40 A/m, is difficult to be measured accurately. The common methods to measure geomagnetic field include optical pump magnetic resonance, hall sensors, tangent galvanometer [1–3]. Giant magneto-impedance (GMI) effect is refers to, when the material directly into the high frequency current, the impedance change with magnetic field [4]. This phenomenon is very sensitive, suitable for weak field of geomagnetic field and environmental magnetic field detection. Comparing with the traditional magnetic flux sensor and magnetic resistance sensor, GMI effect sensor has the advantages of small size, fast response. Some of GMI effect in magnetic sensors, current sensors and magnetic encoder are reported in abroad [5–8].

© Springer Nature Singapore Pte Ltd. 2017
D. Yue et al. (Eds.): LSMS/ICSEE 2017, Part II, CCIS 762, pp. 677–685, 2017.
DOI: 10.1007/978-981-10-6373-2_67

On the basis of the author's research on GMI effect and sensor application in recent years, a kind of magnetic field sensor is developed based on GMI effect of asymmetric feature. GMI asymmetric feature is a very effective way to enhance the linearity and sensitivity of sensitive element. The traditional open-loop system is changed, and the negative feedback circuit is added to improve the sensor performance. The correction system is developed by using VB software and the performance indexes of the instrument, such as nonlinear error, temperature stability and frequency bandwidth are obviously improved. We also developed a digital measuring instrument by combining the sensor with single-chip microcomputer and display circuit, which can be easily applied to the detection of weak magnetic field.

2 GMI Asymmetric Features

This experiment adopts the 25 mm length, 1.5 mm width, 34 μm thickness $Co_{66.3}$ $Fe_{3.7}Si_{12}B_{18}$ amorphous alloy as the sensitive element. Co-based amorphous material is an excellent soft magnetic material which is an important premise of GMI effect. Amorphous ribbon is annealed by pulsed current with pulse width 1 s, pulse frequency 1 Hz and 50 s of annealing time. GMI rate is defined as:

$$GMI(Z) = \Delta Z/Z = [Z(H) - Z(0)]/Z(0) \times 100\%, \qquad (1)$$

which Z(0), Z(H) is impedance under external magnetic field of zero and H respectively.

As shown in Fig. 1 (unbiased magnetic field), with the increase of the magnetic field, the GMI(Z) increases abruptly, then slowly decrease with the increase of magnetic field further. The similar change will happen if we apply opposite direction magnetic field. It is a typical GMI symmetry behavior.

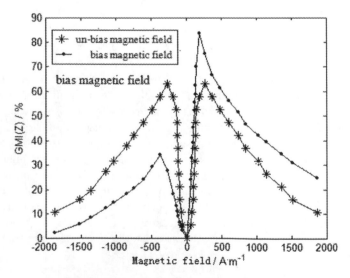

Fig. 1. GMI properties of amorphous ribbon

Due to the impedance change with the external magnetic field symmetry, the sensor based on GMI effect is not very sensitive. In order to improve the GMI effect sensor near the zero field characteristics, we set a solenoid on the amorphous ribbon which produces a parallel to the amorphous with axial bias magnetic field. By changing the bias coil current to adjust the operating point of amorphous material, so as to achieve GMI asymmetric features, as shown in Fig. 1 (bias magnetic field). Amorphous ribbon impedance curve along with the change of magnetic field is not symmetrical behavior. The peak is strengthened (positive direction magnetic field) on one side and the peak is weakened (negative direction of the magnetic field) on the other side. Experiments show that GMI asymmetric characteristics can be used to improve the linearity and sensitivity of GMI sensor. It can meet the requirements of sensor for detecting weak magnetic field.

3   Sensor Circuit

3.1   Working Principle

Working principle of the magnetic field measuring instrument is shown in Fig. 2. The impedance of amorphous ribbon changes when the applied magnetic field passes through the amorphous ribbon. After amplified, the voltage is detected by detector circuit of its peak. Through a low-pass filter smoothing, and difference operation and voltage reference, voltage value with applied magnetic field is received. Using V/I conversion circuit, differential circuit output voltage signal is changed into current signal. Then output current is delivered to the feedback of the coil as shown in Fig. 2. The magnetic field H_f produced by feedback coil and the measured magnetic field H are in opposite directions. If V/I conversion coefficient is very large, amorphous ribbon can work at close to zero magnetic field. This can greatly improve the magnetic field detection range.

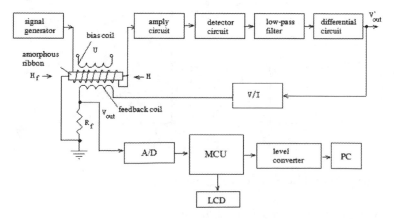

Fig. 2. Schematic diagram of magnetic field measuring instrument

3.2   Signal Processing Circuit

The output voltage of amorphous ribbon is very weak which must been enlarged to the signal processing circuit. Amplifier circuits are composed of two amplifiers. The former amplifier has high input impedance and low output impedance. The negative dc signal becomes a positive signal after the later inverse proportion amplifier. The output voltage of amorphous ribbon is magnetic field modulation signal. Peak detection circuit is used to the signal demodulation. Peak detection circuit is composed of diodes and RC low-pass filter. It is simple and easy to implement. The noise generated in the circuit components and the interference of external electromagnetic field will cause some unnecessary high frequency signal of the output signal. Voltage-controlled voltage source type 4th-order Butterworth low-pass filter has high input impedance, low output impedance and stable performances.

3.3   V/I Conversion Circuit

As shown in Fig. 3 V/I conversion circuit is composed of operational amplifier, resistance, capacity and other elements. Output voltage V_1 is obtained from A_1 by compared with the feedback voltage V_f and input voltage V'_{out}. V_1 control the output voltage of the operational amplifier A_2, which changes the output current of the transistor T_1. Output current $i_L = V'_{out}/(R_w + R_7)$, which is proportional to the input voltage, and has nothing to do with the load resistance R_L. The output of differential circuit is connected to the V/I conversion circuit input V'_{out}. The output of the V/I conversion circuit is connected to feedback coil as shown in Fig. 2. The output of the closed-loop sensor is taken from resistor R_f. When the closed loop gain is high enough, the sensor output voltage only depends on the feedback loop and has a linear relation with the measured magnetic field. It is not influenced by outside factors and improves the measuring accuracy of the sensor.

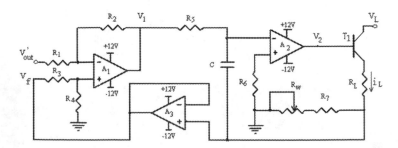

Fig. 3. V/I conversion circuit

4   Display Circuit and Linear Correction

The hardware circuit of magnetic field measuring instrument is composed of sensor circuit, STC12C5A60S2, A/D conversion circuit and LCD display as shown Fig. 4. Sensor is responsible for data collection, measurement, and transmits the collected data

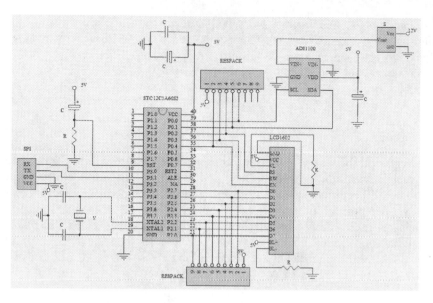

Fig. 4. Hardware circuit

to the A/D conversion circuit. A/D conversion circuit converts analog signals to the corresponding digital quantity and takes the digital signal to the single chip micro-computer for processing. STC12C5A60S2 is the control center of system and responsible for receiving measurement data, magnetic field calculation, display and control process. LCD display measuring magnetic field values visually.

4.1 A/D Converter

The ADS1100 is a precision, self-calibrating A/D converter with differential inputs and up to 16 bits of resolution. Conversions are performed ratio metrically, using the power supply as the reference voltage. The ADS1100 uses an I_2C-compatible serial interface and operates from a single power supply ranging from 2.7 V to 5.5 V. The ADS1100 can perform conversions at rates of 8, 16, 32, or 128 samples per second. The ADS1100 is designed for applications requiring high-resolution measurement. Because ADS1100 will produce a brief spike pulse current when switching off the power and, so you need to add bypass capacitor on the power supply.

4.2 Microprocessor

STC12C5A60S2 is a single-chip microcontroller based on a high performance 1T architecture 80C51 CPU. With the enhanced kernel, STC12C5A60S2 executes instructions in 1–6 clock cycles which is about 6–7 times the standard 8051 device, and has a fully compatible instruction set with industrial-standard 80C51 series microcon-troller. In-System-Programming (ISP) and In-Application-Programming (IAP) support the users to upgrade the program and data in system. The STC12C5A60S2 retains all features of the standard 80C51. In addition, the STC12C5A60S2 has two extra I/O ports (P4 and P5), a 10-source, 4-priority-level interrupt structure, 10-bit ADC, two UARTs, on-chip crystal oscillator, a 2-channel PCA and PWM, SPI, a one-time enabled watchdog timer.

4.3   Display

Liquid crystal display with low energy consumption, small heat, fiber thin light and many other advantages, has been widely used in various field. LCD1602 is a type of dot-matrix LCD dedicating to display letters, numbers, symbols and so on. Considering economy and practice in this regard, adopting LCD1602 is enough to meet the requirements of character displaying on the LCD. According to the design of the analysis, the hardware circuitry of single-chip electronic is shown in the Fig. 4. P2 port connects LCD1602 8-bit data bus and connected to the resistances. P0.2, P0.3 and P0.4 respectively connect the RS, RW, E-port of the LCD1602.

4.4   Linear Correction

The magnetic field sensor can measure weak magnetic field and display the results in effective range. The problem is the external magnetic field and display values are not consistent within the whole measuring range. When the actual magnetic field is larger, display value is less than the actual value. Display values are in conformity with the actual value only in the middle section. The main reason is the linearity of the sensor. Output voltage on both ends of resistor R_f is $V_{out} = I_f R_f = \frac{KG_1 GHR_f}{1 + KG_1 Gn}$, where K is magnetoelectricity conversion coefficient, G_1 is open-loop gain, G is the voltage current conversion coefficient. As seen from the formula, the output voltage V_{out} keep linear relationship with measured magnetic field H only when parameter K, G_1, G, R_f are constant. From Fig. 1, amorphous ribbon impedance changes with magnetic field is not a straight line, namely the magnetoelectricity conversion coefficient K is not constant. Several other parameters also influence the sensor output voltage. Therefore, display value is not consistent with the actual data after A/D conversion.

The solution to this problem can be considered from hardware and software. The nonlinear of hardware circuit can be processed through software to reduce the error. The amount of numbers collected by A/D conversion circuit is not measured itself, but rather has relationship with measured data. It cannot be directly used to display, but need to be converted. Assumes that digital quantity acquired by A/D conversion circuit have linear relationship with the measured magnetic field, results are obtained by the A/D conversion digital quantity multiplied by a factor M. It is only for magnetic field sensor with good linearity because M is a fixed amount. In the case of linearity is not good, using the similar method above can make the results as much as possible close to the actual value. The smaller the M is divided, the more accurate results are. This kind of method to realize sensor linear correction by the software needs to communicate with the MCU and PC. This measuring instrument communication part is that MCU send data by USB serial port and receive data by the PC microcomputer. Microcomputer communicates with single-chip using custom interface written by Visual Basic software, as shown in Fig. 5. Sensor nonlinear correction by software can further improve the sensor measurement accuracy.

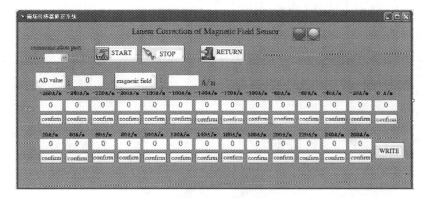

Fig. 5. VB linear correction

5 Experimental Results and Analysis

Measuring instrument is placed in the center of the Helmholtz coil position, and the direction should be perpendicular to the earth's magnetic field and magnetic field direction. Helmholtz coil is connected to the regulated power supply and produces dc magnetic field. The value of magnetic field is calculated by the formula $H = 1600 \times I$. The actual value of the magnetic field is measured by digital gauss meter which accuracy is 0.1%. We change the Helmholtz coil current, and write down the corresponding gauss meter measured the magnetic field and LCD display voltage value. The experimental results are shown in Table 1.

We set the range of the magnetic field measurement instrument is ± 260 A/m. Through actual measurement and calculation, the performance indicators of instrument are: resolution 0.01 A/m, repeatability $\delta_R = 0.38\%$ and accuracy $\delta = \pm 0.55\%$. Let's compare this measurement instrument with a superior performance magnetic field measuring instrument on currently markets. Magnetic field resolution of HM-101 (single axis) based on Hall effect is very high (0.001 GS or 0.08 A/m). Its effective measurement range is $0 -\pm 2$ GS (about $0 -\pm 160$ A/m) and the basic error is $\pm 0.5\%$. But its price is very high, about 5500 RMB. The result shows that the measuring instrument is suitable for weak magnetic field detection especially under the room temperature environment. By introducing a negative feedback and linear correction, performance indicators such as nonlinear error of instrument, temperature stability, linear range and frequency band get obvious improvement.

Table 1. Measurement data

Helmholtz coil current (A)	Magnetic field converted by current (A/m)	Gauss meter measured magnetic field (A/m)	Digital display (A/m)
−0.165	−264	−263.75	−263.32
−0.145	−232	−231.81	−231.17
−0.125	−200	−199.83	−199.03
−0.105	−168	−167.89	−167.08
−0.085	−136	−135.78	−135.34
−0.065	−104	−103.87	−103.21
−0.045	−72	−71.83	−71.25
−0.025	−40	−39.95	−39.39
−0.015	−24	−23.86	−23.21
0	0	−0.12	−0.26
0.015	24	23.87	23.41
0.025	40	39.78	39.25
0.045	72	71.88	71.36
0.065	104	103.86	103.27
0.085	136	135.85	135.22
0.105	168	167.79	167.34
0.125	200	199.87	199.29
0.145	232	231.82	231.10
0.165	264	263.87	263.08

6   Conclusion

On the basis of sensor sensitive element annealing treatment and the optimization design of structure, we developed a magnetic field measuring instrument based on GMI effect of asymmetric feature. We also analyzed the working principle of the magnetic field measuring instrument and designed the signal processing circuit using negative feedback technology to improve the measurement range and precision of the measuring instrument. Making clear the relation between output voltage and input field, the modification of software for measuring data realize digital display measured magnetic field. The instrument can meet the digital detection of weak magnetic field.

Acknowledgements. The authors gratefully acknowledge the financial supports by the National Science Foundation of China under Grant numbers 51575331 and 51175316.

References

1. Gokemeijer, N.J., Clinton, T.W., Crawford, T.M., Crawford, T.M., Johnson, M.: Direct measurement of the field from a magnetic recording head using an inas hall sensor on a contact write/read tester. J. Magn. Magn. Mater. **290**, 254–256 (2005)

2. Kubota, M., Tokunaga, Y., Kanazawa, N., Kagawa, F., Tokura, Y., Kawasaki, M.: Miniature hall sensor integrated on a magnetic thin film for detecting domain wall motion. J. Appl. Phys. **114**, 053909–053912 (2013)
3. Laurinavičius, L.: Helicon resonator based strong magnetic field sensor. Meas. Sci. Rev. **11**, 149–153 (2011)
4. Mohri, K., Kohsawa, T., Kawashima, K., Yoshida, H., Panina, L.V.: Magneto-inductive effect (MI effect) in amorphous wires. IEEE Trans. Magn. **28**, 3150–3152 (1992)
5. Chiriac, H., Tibu, M., Moga, A.E., Herea, D.D.: Magnetic GMI sensor for detection of biomolecules. J. Magn. Magn. Mater. **293**, 671–676 (2005)
6. Kurlyandskaya, G., Levit, V.: Magnetic dynabeads detection by sensitive element based on giant magneto-impedance. Sens. Actuat. A-Phys. **20**, 1611–1616 (2005)
7. Kudo, T., Tsuji, N., Asada, T., Sugiyama, S., Wakui, S.: Development of a small and wide-range three-phase current sensor using an MI element. IEEE Trans. Magn. **42**, 3362–3364 (2006)
8. Geliang, Y., Xiongzhu, B., Chao, X., Hong, X.: Design of a GMI magnetic sensor based on the longitudinal excitation. Sens. Actuat. A-Phys. **161**, 72–77 (2010)

Analysis of Effective Transmission Distance of Double Transmitters in Magnetic Coupled Resonant WPT System

Nenghong Xia[✉], Menglin Tian, Haisheng Lian, and Yimin Zhu

Shanghai University of Electric Power, Shanghai 200090, China
xia_nh@shiep.edu.cn

Abstract. The coupling coefficient between the transmitters and receivers is a key factor of power transfer efficiency for magnetic resonant coupling wireless power transfer system. Firstly, the equivalent circuit model of double-transmitter (DT) structure is established. The correlation between the transmission power and coupling coefficient of both single-transmitter (ST) and DT structure is compared and analyzed. The result shows that the critical coupling coefficient of DT structure is reduced to 0.707 times of the ST structure, when there are peak transfer power. And it means that the former can increase the transmission distance. In this paper, the effective transmission area is defined, and the effective transmission areas of DT structure can be obtained in two cases of symmetric and asymmetric structures, respectively. Finally the numerical simulation analysis is conducted and a conclusion is drawn that the effective transmission area in over-coupling area can be significantly enlarged with frequency tracking measures, which validates the correctness of the aforesaid theoretical analysis.

Keywords: Wireless transmission · Double transmitters · Transmission distance · Effective transmission area

1 Introduction

Magnetic resonant coupling WPT(MRC-WPT) utilizes the resonance of magnetic fields to realize power transmission. It has moderate transmission distance in comparison with inductive power transfer (IPT) and has become the focus of current research [1].

Current researches focus on the expansion of transmission distance [2]. Hamam proposed adding a relay coil between the transmitter and receiver coil [3]. Another possible approach is to optimize coil structure. The magnetic fields of spiral, transposition parallel coil and disc shaped parallel coil were measured and a conclusion was drawn that disc shaped parallel winding has better magnetic aggregation, higher quality factor and longer transmission distance in [7]. As mentioned in [8], a method of replacing the original coil with the Hilbert fractal coil was proposed and validated with experiments. As shown in [9–11], based on the original coil structure, performance of transmission can be improved by increasing the number of turns and the radius of the coil, while this method is limited by the actual size.

© Springer Nature Singapore Pte Ltd. 2017
D. Yue et al. (Eds.): LSMS/ICSEE 2017, Part II, CCIS 762, pp. 686–694, 2017.
DOI: 10.1007/978-981-10-6373-2_68

As shown in [12–14], multi-transmitter structure can obtain a stable magnetic field in the center region of two transmitting coils which are placed vertically. [15] analyzed DT structure, and validated that the structure can extend the transmission distance; In [16], a four coil excitation WPT system was proposed, which extends the transmission distance and weakens the sensitivity in transmission direction. Up to now, there are few researches on the quantitative analyses in the view of specific circuit theory.

In this paper, a DT structure WPT system is proposed to analyze the superiority over the ST structure in effective transmission distance. First of all, this paper discusses the little influence that coupling coefficient has on the load power of DT structure. What's more, the structure can decrease the critical coupling coefficient to 0.707 times that of the ST structure. The effective transmission area is defined by the maximum load power in a ST structure, two cases of $M_{12} = M_{23}$ and $M_{12} \neq M_{23}$ are analyzed respectively. A numerical simulation analysis is conducted and a conclusion is drawn that the effective transmission area in over-coupling area can be significantly enlarged with frequency tracking measures and the correctness of the aforesaid theoretical analysis is validated.

2 Model and Theoretical Analysis

The configuration of DT WPT system is shown in Fig. 1. There are two transmitter coils and one receiver coil, which is placed between the two transmitter coils. The equivalent circuit is shown in Fig. 2. The transmitters 1 and 3 are connected to the voltage source, U_S, and the receiver coil is connected to the load resistor, R_L. R_1 and R_3 are resistances of transmitter 1 and 3, respectively (including the internal resistance of the source and the equivalent resistance of the coil in the high frequency) and R_2 is equivalent resistance of receiver coil which is small enough to be neglected; L_1, L_2 and L_3 are the equivalent inductance of the coils respectively; k_{12} and k_{23} are the coupling coefficient between the receiver coil and transmitter 1 and 3, respectively; k_{13} is the coupling coefficient between the transmitter 1 and transmitter 3. C_1, C_2 and C_3 are the coils' equivalent capacitance (including parasitic capacitance and compensation capacitance), which meet $\omega_0 = 1/\sqrt{L_i C_i}(i = 1, 2, 3)$, where ω_0 is the resonant frequency of the system.

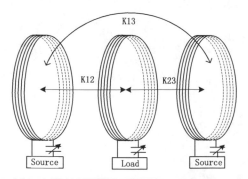

Fig. 1. Schematic diagram of double-transmitter

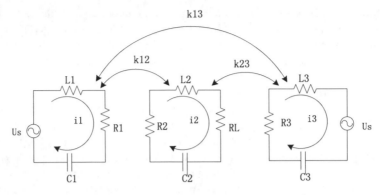

Fig. 2. Equivalent circuit of double-transmitter

As shown in Fig. 2, i_1, i_2 and i_3 are the instantaneous value of currents in coil1, coil2 and coil3. Since the coils parameters are constant and $k_{ij} = M_{ij}/\sqrt{L_i L_j}, M_{ij}$ is proportional to k_{ij}. In order to facilitate research, the following study is done by studying M_{ij} instead of k_{ij}. According to Kirchhoff's voltage law (KVL), we can obtain

$$\begin{cases} (R_1 + j\omega L_1 + 1/j\omega C_1)\dot{I}_1 + j\omega M_{12}\dot{I}_2 = \dot{U}_S \\ (R_3 + j\omega L_3 + 1/j\omega C_3)\dot{I}_3 + j\omega M_{23}\dot{I}_2 = \dot{U}_S \\ (R_2 + R_L + j\omega L_2 + 1/j\omega C_2)\dot{I}_2 + j\omega M_{12}\dot{I}_1 + j\omega M_{23}\dot{I}_3 = 0 \end{cases} \quad (1)$$

When the system is operating at the resonant frequency, i.e. $j\omega L_i + 1/j\omega C_i = 0$, the current can be expressed as:

$$\begin{cases} \dot{I}_1 = \dfrac{\omega^2 M_{23}^2 U_s + R_3(R_2 + R_L)U_s - \omega^2 M_{12}M_{23}U_s}{\omega^2 M_{12}^2 R_3 + \omega^2 M_{23}^2 R_1 + R_1 R_3(R_2 + R_L)} \\[3mm] \dot{I}_2 = \dfrac{j\omega M_{12}R_3 U_s + j\omega M_{23}R_1 U_s}{\omega^2 M_{12}^2 R_3 + \omega^2 M_{23}^2 R_1 + R_1 R_3(R_2 + R_L)} \\[3mm] \dot{I}_3 = \dfrac{\omega^2 M_{12}^2 U_s + R_1(R_2 + R_L)U_s - \omega^2 M_{12}M_{23}U_s}{\omega^2 M_{12}^2 R_3 + \omega^2 M_{23}^2 R_1 + R_1 R_3(R_2 + R_L)} \end{cases} \quad (2)$$

And output power can be calculated as

$$P_{\mathrm{m}} = |I_2|^2 R_L = \frac{\omega^2 (M_{12}R_3 + M_{23}R_1)^2 U_s^2 R_L}{[\omega^2 M_{12}^2 R_3 + \omega^2 M_{23}^2 R_1 + R_1 R_3(R_2 + R_L)]^2} \quad (3)$$

By the same token, it can be easily drawn that the output power of ST structure can be calculated as

$$P_{\mathrm{s}} = \frac{\omega^2 M_{12}^2 U_s^2 R_L}{[\omega^2 M_{12}^2 + R_1(R_2 + R_L)]^2} \quad (4)$$

3   Analysis of Effective Transmission Area

3.1   Symmetric Structure

For the two transmitter coils and sources are identical and load matching is satisfied, we can assume that $R_1 = R_3 = R_2 + R_L = R$, the partial derivative (3) of M_{12}, M_{23} and load power of the DT structure can be respectively expressed as

$$\frac{dP_m}{dM} = \frac{8\omega^2 M U_s^2 R^3 - 16\omega^4 M^3 U_s^2 R}{[R^2 + 2\omega^2 M^2]^3} \tag{5}$$

When $\frac{dP_m}{dM} = 0$, we can obtain

$$M_m = \frac{R}{\sqrt{2}\omega} \tag{6}$$

By substituting (6) into (4)

$$P_{m-max} = \frac{U_S^2}{2R} \tag{7}$$

(6) shows that the DT system has only one maximum output power. The system can be divided into three different regions according to the Mutual inductance in analogy with ST structure [17].

- $\omega M/R > \sqrt{2}/2$, system is in the over-coupling region. Frequency splitting will appear in this region.
- $\omega M/R = \sqrt{2}/2$, system is in the critical coupling region.
- $\omega M/R < \sqrt{2}/2$, system is in the under-coupling region. In this area, maximum output power can only be achieved at the intrinsic frequency.

In order to compare the transmission distance, the partial derivative of (4) with respect to M and $dP_s/dM_{12} = 0$, we can obtain $M_{12} = M_c = R/\omega$, the system achieves maximum power $P_{s-max} = U_s^2/4R$, Since $M_c = \sqrt{2}M_m$ and M decreases as the distance between the transmitter and the receiver coil increases, the DT structure can enlarge the transmission distance compared to the ST structure.

Effective transmission area of DT structure is defined by $P > P_{S-max}$, thus $P_m \geq P_{S-max}$ must be satisfied, applying $P_m \geq P_{S-max}$ to (3), we can obtain

$$\left(M - \frac{R}{\omega}\right)^2 \leq \frac{R^2}{2\omega^2} \tag{8}$$

It can be seen from (8) that the effective transmission area meets $P_m \geq P_{S-max}$ with $(\sqrt{2} - 1)/\sqrt{2} \leq \omega M/R \leq (\sqrt{2}+1)/\sqrt{2}$, when $(\sqrt{2}+1)/\sqrt{2} \geq \omega M/R \geq \sqrt{2}/2$, the system is in a condition of over-coupling, although the frequency splitting phenomenon occurs, the maximum power P_m which is larger than that of the ST structure can be obtained at the intrinsic frequency point.

3.2   Asymmetric Structure

When $M_{12} \neq M_{23}$, applying $P_m \geq P_{s-\max}$ to (3), we can obtain

$$(M_{12} - \frac{R}{\omega})^2 + (M_{23} - \frac{R}{\omega})^2 \leq \frac{R^2}{\omega^2} \tag{9}$$

It can be drawn that the effective transmission area which meets $P_m \geq P_{s-\max}$ is circular with a center of $(R/\omega, R/\omega)$ and a radius of R/ω.

4   Experimental Verification

The WPT model in HFSS is shown in Fig. 3. The transmitter and receiver coils both adopt the spiral coil structure and have the same sizes and parameters, as shown in Table 1.

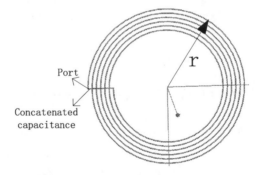

Fig. 3.   The model of transmitter and receiver coil

Table 1.   System parameters

Parameters	Design value	Parameters	Design value
Line width	w = 1 mm	Coil inductance	L = 15.76 μH
Number of turns	n = 6	Capacitance	C = 3.547 pF
Line spacing	g = 5 mm	Series capacitor	C_S = 50 PF
Maximum radius	r = 9.25 cm	Port impedance	Z_P = 50 Ω
Resonant frequency	14.5 MHz		

The transmitter and receiver coils are placed in parallel and coaxial, as shown in Fig. 4, where D represents the distance between the transmitter and receiver coils.

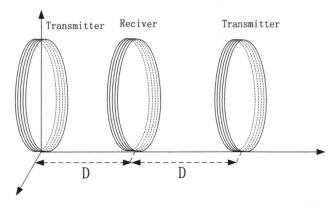

Fig. 4. Schematic diagram of double-transmitter

Varying the transmission distance D while keeping the distance between the receiver coil and the two transmitters constant, i.e. $M_{12} = M_{23}$. It can be seen from Fig. 5 that in the under-coupling region and critical coupling region, i.e. D $\geq$ 33 cm, S21 and S23 completely overlap and both have only one extreme point and no frequency splitting phenomenon. The maximum value of the under-coupling region is obviously lower than that of the critical coupling region. when the transmission distance is D < 29 cm, there is a obvious frequency splitting phenomenon, where transmission coefficient S21 coincides with S23 completely and they both cannot reach the maximum value at the intrinsic frequency of 14.5 MHz and two maximum points on both sides. When 28 cm < D < 33 cm, the frequency splitting phenomenon is weakened, S21 and S23 have only one extreme point that appear on the different side of the intrinsic frequency. Therefore, the higher transmission coefficient can be obtained by changing the system frequency in the over-coupling region. As shown in Fig. 6, the transmission power that obtained with the frequency tracking in the over-coupling region.

As shown in Fig. 6, the load power increased gradually with the transmission distance when system operating frequency is identical to the intrinsic frequency of the

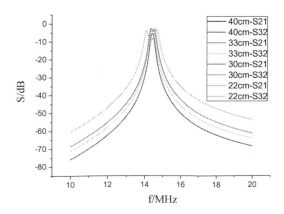

Fig. 5. The transmission coefficient in the under-coupling, critical-coupling and over-coupling region

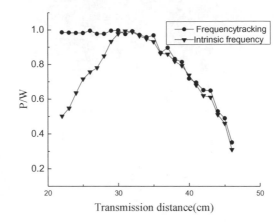

Fig. 6. The transmission power with the frequency tracking

coil in the over-coupling region. When D = 33 cm and $M = M_c$, the system enters the critical coupling region, the transmission power reaches the maximum. However, when the frequency tracking is carried out in this process, the transmission power will remain a high value and almost equal to the transmission coefficient at critical coupling, thus ensuring the effective transmission in the over-coupling region.

Varying the transmission distance D gradually and recording the value of $\omega M/R$ every 1 cm, the simulation results are shown in Fig. 7. When D > 29 cm, the ST structure is already in under-coupling region which is beyond the scope of effective transmission. When D ≤ 33 cm, the DT structure meets $\omega M/R > \sqrt{2}/2 = 0.707$ and enters the over-coupling or critical coupling region, the effective transmission range of DT structure is expanded to 33 cm, which is 1.18 times that of the ST structure. Therefore, the DT structure has obvious advantages over ST structure in improving the transmission distance.

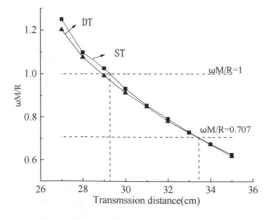

Fig. 7. The effective transmission range of the two structures

As shown in Fig. 8, the transmission distance will be expanded to $D \leq 47$ cm, in the range of 33 cm $\leq D \leq 47$ cm, the mutual inductance satisfies $(\sqrt{2}-1)/\sqrt{2} \leq \omega M/R \leq \sqrt{2}/2$ and load power meets $P_{s-\max} \leq P_m \leq P_{m-\max}$; In the range of $D \leq 33$ cm, $\omega M/R \geq \sqrt{2}/2$ is satisfied and when the frequency tracking method is adopted, the load power can be kept as $P_{m-\max}$. As shown in Fig. 7, the effective transmission distance of ST structure is 29 cm, so in order to meet the transmission power under the condition of $P_m \geq P_{s-\max}$, DT structure can extend the transmission distance by 19 cm, which can improve the effective transmission distance and enlarge its application field.

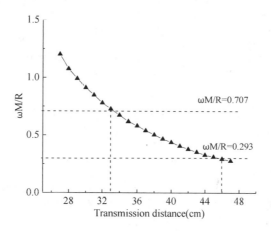

Fig. 8. Effective transmission area of DT structure

5   Conclusion

In this paper, the equivalent circuit method is utilized to establish the mutual inductance equivalent circuit model of DT structure and analyze the influence of coupling coefficient on the transmission power and the effective transmission distance of the DT structure. Based on theoretical analysis and numerical verification, the conclusions can be drawn as follows:

(1) The coupling coefficient has little influence on DT structure compared with ST structure, which can intrinsically extend the transmission distance;
(2) The critical coupling coefficient of DT structure can be reduced to 0. 707 times that of the ST structure;
(3) The effective transmission areas of DT structure in both cases of symmetric and asymmetric are given.
(4) DT structure can significantly expand the effective transmission area in the over-coupled region by utilizing frequency tracking measure.

Acknowledgments. The work leading to this paper was supported by the National Natural Science Foundation of China (Project No. 51607110) and Natural Science Foundation of Shanghai (Project No. 14ZR1417600).

References

1. Kurs, A., Karalis, A., Moffatt, R., et al.: Wireless power transfer via strongly coupled magnetic resonances. Science **317**(5834), 83–86 (2007)
2. Huang, X., Tan, L., Chen, Z., et al.: Review and research progress on wireless power transfer technology. Trans. China Electrotech. Soc. **28**(10), 1–11 (2013)
3. Hamam, R.E., Karalis, A., Joannopoulos, J.D., et al.: Efficient weakly-radiative wireless energy transfer: an EIT-like approach. Ann. Phys. **324**, 1783–1795 (2009)
4. Lu, Y.: Magnetic coupled resonant wireless energy transmission characteristics. Harbin Institute of Technology (2014)
5. Luo, B., Sheng, M., Wu, S., et al.: Modeling and analysis of magnetic resonance coupling wireless relay power transfer system with single intermediate coil resonator. Proc. CSEE **21**, 170–177 (2013)
6. Kim, J.W., Son, H.C., Kim, K.H., et al.: Efficiency analysis of magnetic resonance wireless power transfer with intermediate resonant coil. IEEE Antennas Wirel. Propag. Lett. **10**(3), 389–392 (2011)
7. Zhang, X., Yang, Q., Cui, Y., et al.: Design, optimization and verification of energy transmitting coil for high power radio energy transmission system. trans. China Electrotech. Soc. **10**(10), 12–18 (2013)
8. Ren, D.: Study on transmission characteristics of magnetically coupled resonant wireless power transmission system. Zhengzhou University, Zhengzhou
9. Tan, L., Huang, X., et al.: Optimal control of transmission efficiency for magnetically coupled resonant wireless power transmission system based on frequency control. Chin. Sci. **41**(7), 913–919 (2011)
10. Zhai, Y., Sun, Y., Dai, X., et al.: Modeling and analysis of the power transmission system of magnetic resonance model. Proc. Chin. Electr. Eng. **32**(12), 155–160 (2012)
11. Sun, Y., Xia, C.Y., Dai, X., et al.: Analysis and optimization of mutual inductance for inductively coupled power transmission system. China CSEE **30**(33), 44–50 (2010)
12. Uchida, A., Shimokawa, S., Kawano, H., et al.: Phase and intensity control of multiple coil currents in resonant magnetic coupling. In: Microwave Workshop Series on Innovative Wireless Power Transmission: Technologies, Systems, and Applications, pp. 53–56. IEEE (2012)
13. Uchida, A., Shimokawa, S., Kawano, H., et al.: Phase and intensity control of multiple coil currents in mid-range wireless power transfer. IET Microw. Antennas Propag. **8**(7), 498–505 (2014)
14. Ishizaki, T., Nojiri, S., Ishida, T., et al.: 3-D free-access WPT system for charging movable terminals. In: 2012 IEEE MTT-S International Microwave Workshop Series on Innovative Wireless Power Transmission: Technologies, Systems, and Applications (IMWS), pp. 219–222. IEEE (2012)
15. Lee, K., Cho, D.H.: Diversity analysis of multiple transmitters in wireless power transfer system. IEEE Trans. Magn. **49**(6), 2946–2952 (2013)
16. Huang, J., Chen, Q., et al.: Four coil excited resonant radio energy transmission system and its analysis. Autom. Electr. Power Syst.16 (2015)
17. Xue, M., Yang, Q., et al.: Research of frequency characteristics in wireless power transfer system via magnetic resonance coupling under interference factors. Adv. Technol. Electr. Eng. Energy **34**(4), 24–30 (2015)

Analysis on Al-Cu Dissimilar Materials Friction Stir Welding Butt Joint Based on J Integral Model

Hongyu Sun[1], Jun Zhu[2], Shun Guo[1], Yong Peng[1], Qi Zhou[1](✉),
Jun Huang[1], and Yushan Chen[1]

[1] School of Materials Science and Engineering,
Nanjing University of Science and Technology, Nanjing 210094, China
cheezhou@njust.edu.cn
[2] Nanjing Institute of Technology, Nanjing 211167, China

Abstract. The fracture J Integral Model was build on the actual Al-Cu dissimilar materials Friction Stir Welding joint to investigate the microdefects ont properties of the joint. The calculation results showed that the severe stress concentration emerged at the tip of crack in interface, the pack stress could reach up to 379 MPa, which was higher than the strength of the base metal, and resulted in the joint fracture. Further, the x-direction stress was much higher than the y-direction stress. In the J Integral Model, the x-direction stress would lead to the opening fracture and the y direction stress would lead to the shearing fracture, thus the opening fracture with small shearing fracture was the character of the Al-Cu joint.

Keywords: J Integral Model · Friction stir welding · Al-Cu joint · Stress concentration

1 Introduce

Al-Cu dissimilar metal welding has been found wide application in special fields like energy source, electric power and so on, while there are great differences in the properties of melting point, thermal conductivity and thermal expansion between aluminum and copper, leading to the difficulty of welding Al and Cu to a certain extent [1–4]. When conventional fusion welding is adopted, a large amount of intermetallic compounds form between aluminum and copper due to excessive heat input, weakening the properties of joints and resulting in heat cracking when it is serious. Therefore, Al-Cu dissimilar metal joining has been a puzzle in the field of welding for long [5–7].

Friction stir welding (FSW) is an emerging solid-state joining technology, invented by the Welding Institute (TWI) in 1991, which was mainly used to join nonferrous metals like aluminum alloy, titanium alloy, copper alloy and so on [8–11]. Weld heat input can be reduced greatly through generating heat by friction between the tool and workpiece. Meanwhile, FSW can overcome the hot crack that is more likelyto come into being in the process of conventional fusion welding, thus FSW was employed to

© Springer Nature Singapore Pte Ltd. 2017
D. Yue et al. (Eds.): LSMS/ICSEE 2017, Part II, CCIS 762, pp. 695–704, 2017.
DOI: 10.1007/978-981-10-6373-2_69

join dissimilar metals and has been utilized to join numerous dissimilar metals including Al-Cu, Mg-Al and Al-Fe and so on [12–16].

Despite of the excellent ability of the FSW for joining Al-Cu dissimilar metals, the microdefects are not completely avoided, because of the great difference in the properties between aluminum and copper, which would influence the mechanical properties of the joints. Thus, some scholars investigated the effect of microdefects on the properties of the joints. Liu et al. [17] adopted three kinds of the tools with different pins to join 6082-T6 aluminum alloy and obtained three joints, and the test results showed that its tensile strength was minimum when the joint was incomplete weld. Wang et al. [18] investigated the mechanical properties of the 6061-T4 aluminum alloy T joints and discovered the weak-link appeared in the joint, which resulted in the fracture of joint along the rib plate. Moghadam and Farhangdoost et al. [19] studied the effect of parameters on the fracture toughness and growth rate of the fatigue crack of the joints, and revealed that the fracture toughness and growth rate of the fatigue crack were influenced by the rotation rate and travel speed. In the Al-Cu welding process, the tunnel defects, voids and weak-link were easy to form, leading to the properties reduction of the joints [20–22]. In this paper, the effect of microdefects on the tensile strength of the Al-Cu joint will be investigated by a J Integral Model.

2   Modeling

2.1   Fracture Model of J Integral

Based on mechanics of fracture, fracture mode was classified into three types: opening mode, shearing mode and tearing mode. Actual fracture is usually depicted by three modes comprehensively. Fracture Theory shows that the fracture of linear elastic and nonlinear elastic plastic material can be described by J Integral. J Integral can be defined as:

$$J = \lim_{\Gamma \to 0} \int [(\omega + \mathrm{T})\delta_{ij} - \sigma_{ij}\frac{\partial u_j}{\partial x_i}]n_i d\Gamma \tag{1}$$

where ω is strain energy density, T is kinetic energy density, σ is stress, u is displacement vector, and Γ is integral boundary. To crack in linear elastic material, J integral stands for energy release rate. To nonlinear elastic material, J integral means stress amplitude and displacement field at the crack tip. Nonlinear elastic plastic deformation appeared in Al-Cu lap joint in the process of stretching, thus stress concentration of crack tip in Al-Cu lap joint can be attained by J Integral. On the basis of J Integral depiction of nonlinear elastic material crack tip field deduced by Hutchinson Rice and Rosengren independently, there is an exponential relationship between stress and strain:

$$\frac{\varepsilon}{\varepsilon_0} = \frac{\sigma}{\sigma_0} + \alpha(\frac{\sigma}{\sigma_0})^n \tag{2}$$

where σ_0 is material yield, $\varepsilon_0 = \sigma_0/E$, α is zero dimension constant, and n is hardening component. When the area was very close to the crack tip, which was in the complete plastic zone, the stress and strain of crack tip can be expressed as:

$$\sigma_{ij} = f(\theta)(\frac{J}{r})^{\frac{1}{n}} \tag{3}$$

$$\varepsilon_{ij} = g(\theta)(\frac{J}{r})^{\frac{n}{n+1}} \tag{4}$$

2.2 Building Model

To optimize welding conditions, predict the effect of microdefects on the properties of the joints, the actual joint must be used in conjunction with the model [23]. Thus a Al –Cu dissimilar material joint was carried out. In the experiment, 6061-T4 aluminum alloy and T2 commercially pure copper with the thickness of 5 mm and the size of 100 mm × 50 mm were used. The chemical compositions and mechanical properties of two materials are given in Tables 1 and 2. The tool used in this study had a shoulder 16 mm in diameter and a pin 4.5 mm in length. And the welding tool titled 2.5° forward during welding process. The experiment was conducted at the rotation rate of 1100 r/min and welding speed of 30 mm/min (the parameters in this experiment were optimized).

Table 1. Chemical compositions of materials

Materials	Elements (wt%)				
Copper(T2)	Cu + Ag	Bi	Fe	Zn	Pb
	99.9	0.001	0.005	0.002	0.005
6061 Al-T4	Al	Si	Cu	Fe	Mg
	99.39	0.20	0.05	0.25	0.05

Table 2. Mechanical properties of materials

	Elastic Modulus $(10^{-12}Pa)$	Yield strength (MPa)	Shear modulus $(10^{-12}Pa)$	Poisson's ratio
Copper (T2)	110	300	40	0.32
6061 Al-T4	7	250	27	0.3

Figure 1 shows the macro-morphology of the Al-Cu joint, which is the macro-defects-free joint. However, to ensure a good contact between the shoulder and workpiece, the shoulder inserted the workpiece to a certain depth, so the thinning appeared in the joint, which would be considered in the modeling process. Amplify the area near the interface, the micro-voids could be seen. The micro-void near the interface was likely to become a crack source and resulted in the interfacial cracking.

Based on the principle of J integral and the actual characteristics of the Al-Cu joint, the J integral model was built, which used the PLANE183 attribute cell. The position of the voids was set as singularity element and refined the grid of the tip position. The results are shown as Fig. 2.

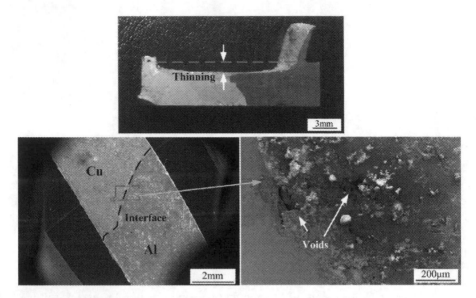

Fig. 1. The macrostructure and microstructure of the Al-Cu joint

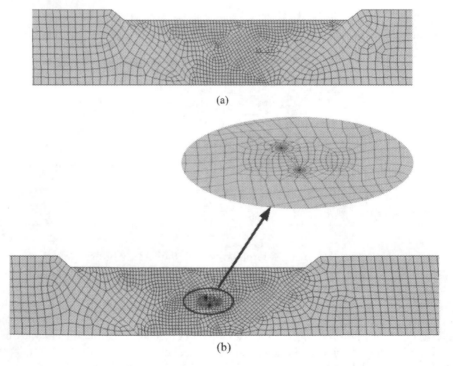

Fig. 2. Finite element Mesh of the workpieces. (a) The grid without microdefects; (b) The grid with voids

2.3   Computing

In the computing process, the load applied to the model was determined according to the results of the tensile test. The average tension of the joint was 4.95KN, which would be applied to the model. The calculation of the J integral was based on two-dimensional space, so the calculation path depended on the plastic strain, the J integral could be expressed as:

$$J = \int [\sigma_{ij} \frac{\partial \mu_j}{\partial x_i} - w\delta_{ij}] \frac{\partial q}{\partial x_i} dA \tag{5}$$

where q was the extended vector of the crack and the node of q vector was 0 along the boundary of Γ.

3   Modeling

The J integral model based on actual Al-Cu butt joint was applied to investigate the effect of microdefects on mechanical properties of the joint.

3.1   Stress Distribution Without Microdefects

Figure 3 was the stress distribution of the defect-free joint, it can be seen that the high stress area appeared in the Stir Zone (SZ) and the corner between surface of SZ and stress concentration existed in base metal (BM). As shown in Fig. 1, the thinning existed in the joint, which was determined by the principle of the FSW. From the calculation results, the existence of the thinning would have effect on the joints, it can be conclude that the two factors influence the properties of the joint. Primarily, the thinning reduced the effective thickness of the joint, so the stress of the SZ was higher than the stress of the BM under the same tensile force, which can be reflected in the calculation results in Fig. 3. Secondly, the thinning leaded to the emergence of the corner, which was easy to cause the stress concentration.

Fig. 3. Stress distribution without microdefects

3.2   Stress Distribution with Microdefects

Previous works [20, 22] show that the microdefects have influence on the properties of the joint. By observing the Al-Cu interface, the microvoids were found that they would become crack source in the tensile test. So the J integral model was used to investigate the effect of voids on the joint, and the results is shown in Figs. 4 and 5. The crack extension occurred in the tensile test, and the severe stress concentration emerged at the tip of crack. Figure 5 showed the stress curve along the crack and the peak stress has reached 379 MPa, which was higher than the strength of Cu. In order to find which

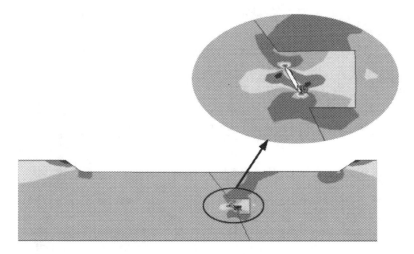

Fig. 4. Stress distribution with microdefects

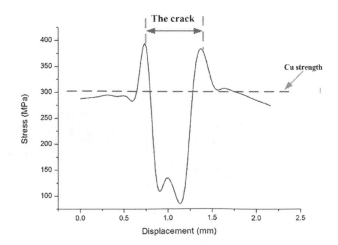

Fig. 5. The stress curve along the crack

kind of stress played a major role in the growth of crack, the stress of x-direction and y-direction was shown in Fig. 6. Andit can be found that the x-direction stress in the crack tip was much higher than the y-direction stress according to Fig. 6.

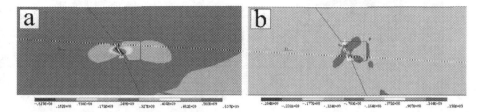

Fig. 6. The stress distribution (a) the x-component of stress; (b) the y-component of stress

According to calculation result, the stress of the crack tip was higher than the strength of the BM, which would lead to the growth of the crack along the crack direction and caused the joint fracture. An angle was formed between the crack direction and the tensile force direction, so a part of the stress on the crack would converted into normal stress and the other converted into shear stress. From the Fig. 6 itcan concluded that the normal stress was the main stress, which would result in the opening mode, meanwhile, the shearing model also existed. So the joint fracture was a mixture of the opening model and the shearing model, which was a mixed fracture.

4 Modeling

The model was compared with the experimental result in order to verify the accuracy of the model. Figures 7 and 8 show the tensile sample and fracture morphology. The fracture of the tensile sample occurred along the interface, which can be further confirmed from the fracture morphology. In Fig. 8, it can observed that the copper interface scattered in the aluminum interface. The voids can also be found in the fracture morphology, which might be the crack source of the joint.

Fig. 7. The tensile sample

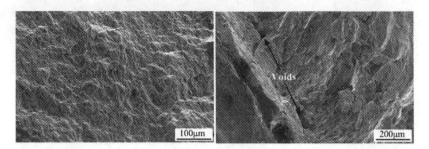

Fig. 8. The fracture morphology

5 Conclusions

In this work, the effect of microdefects on the mechanical properties of the joint was investigated by a J integral model. The following conclusion were derived from the result and discussion.

(1) The J integral model was built based on the actual Al-Cu butt joint. The calculation results show that the thinning existing in the joint reduced the effective thickness, leading to appearance of high stress area in the SZ, and the stress concentration occurred to the corner between the surface of SZ and BM.

(2) The tip of the crack produced severe stress concentration, the pack stress could reach 379 MPa, which is higher than the strength of the BM, and caused the joint fracture.

(3) The x-direction stress and y-direction stress was also calculated and the results showed that the x- direction stress was much higher than the y-direction stress. The x-direction stress would lead to the opening fracture and the y-direction would lead to the shearing fracture, thus the opening fracture with small shearing fracture was the character of the joint.

(4) The tensile test results showed that the joint fracture along the Al-Cu interface and microdefects like the voids has been found on the fracture, which was in agreement with the calculation results by the J integral model.

References

1. Carlone, P., Astarita, A., Palazzo, G.S., Paradiso, V., Squillace, A.: Microstructural aspects in Al–Cu dissimilar joining by FSW. Int. J. Adv. Manuf. Tech. **79**(5), 1109–1116 (2015)
2. Abnar, B., Kazeminezhad, M., Kokabi, A., Mater, J.: The effect of premixed Al-Cu powder on the stir zone in friction stir welding of AA3003-H18. J. Mater. Eng. Perfor. **24**(2), 1086–1093 (2015)
3. Muthu, M.F.X., Jayabalan, V.: Effect of pin profile and process parameters on microstructure and mechanical properties of friction stir welded Al-Cu joints. T. Nonferr. Metal. Soc. **26**(4), 984–993 (2016)

4. Wang, D., Xiao, B.L., Wang, Q.Z., Ma, Z.Y.: Evolution of the microstructure and strength in the nugget zone of friction stir welded SiCp/Al–Cu–Mg composite. J. Mater. Sci. Technol. **30**(1), 54–60 (2014)

5. Huang, Y.X., Wan, L., Lv, Z.L., Lv, S.X., Zhou, L., Feng, J.C.: Microstructure and microhardness of aluminium alloy friction stir welds with heat treatment. Sci. Technol. Weld. Joi. **21**, 638–644 (2016)

6. Jolu, T.L., Morgeneyer, T.F., Denquin, A., Sennour, M., Laurent, A., Besson, J., Lorenzon, A.F.G.: Microstructural characterization of internal welding defects and their effect on the tensile behavior of FSW joints of AA2198 Al-Cu-Li alloy. Metall. Mater. Trans. A. **45**(12), 5531–5544 (2014)

7. Barekatain, H., Kazeminezhad, M., Kokabi, A.H.: Microstructure and mechanical properties in dissimilar butt friction stir welding of severely plastic deformed aluminum AA 1050 and commercially pure copper sheets. J. Mater. Sci. Technol. **30**(8), 826–834 (2014)

8. Radisavljevic, I., Zivkovic, A., Radovic, N., Grabulov, V.: Influence of FSW parameters on formation quality and mechanical properties of Al 2024-T351 butt welded joints. T. Nonferr. Metal. Soc. **23**(12), 3525–3539 (2013)

9. Sungook, Y., Rintaro, U., Hidetoshi, F.: Microstructure and texture distribution of Ti–6Al–4V alloy joints friction stir welded below β-transus temperature. J. Mater. Process. Tec. **229**, 390–397 (2016)

10. Buffa, G., Fratini, L., Micari, F.: Mechanical and microstructural properties prediction by artificial neural networks in FSW processes of dual phase titanium alloys. J. Manuf. Process. **14**(3), 289–296 (2012)

11. Naghibi, H.D., Shakeri, M., Hosseinzadeh, M.: Neural network and genetic algorithm based modeling and optimization of tensile properties in FSW of AA 5052 to AISI 304 dissimilar joints. T. Indian. I. Metals. **69**(4), 891–900 (2016)

12. Kasai, H., Morisada, Y., Fujii, H.: Dissimilar FSW of immiscible materials: steel/magnesium. Mater. Sci. Eng., A **624**, 250–255 (2015)

13. Liang, Z.Y., Chen, K., Wang, X.N., Yao, J.H., Yang, Q., Zhang, L.T., Shan, A.D.: Effect of tool offset and tool rotational speed on enhancing mechanical property of Al/Mg dissimilar FSW joints. Metall. Mater. Trans. A. **44**(8), 3721–3731 (2013)

14. Woo, W., Choo, H.: Softening behaviour of friction stir welded Al 6061-T6 and Mg AZ31B alloys. Sci. Technol. Weld. Joi. **16**(3), 267–272 (2011)

15. Liu, X., Lan, S.H., Ni, J.: Electrically assisted friction stir welding for joining Al 6061 to TRIP 780 steel. J. Mater. Process. Tech. **219**, 112–123 (2015)

16. Abnar, B., Kazeminezhad, M., Kokabi, A.H.: Effects of heat input in friction stir welding on microstructure and mechanical properties of AA3003-H18 plates. T. Nonferr. Metal. Soc. **25**(7), 2147–2155 (2015)

17. Liu, H.J., Liu, X.Q., Hu, Y.Y.: Effects of weld characteristics on tensile properties and fracture morphologies of friction stir welded joints. Chin. J. Mech. Eng. **51**(22), 29–34 (2015)

18. Wang, Z.B., Song, H.P., Fu, D.H., Ji, J.M., Cui, L., Yang, X.Q.: Experimental investigation on tensile fracture behavior of friction stir welded t-joints of 6061-T4 aluminum alloy. J. Tianjin. Univ. **8**, 728–733 (2015)

19. Moghadam, D.G., Farhangdoost, K.: Influence of welding parameters on fracture toughness and fatigue crack growth rate in friction stir welded nugget of 2024-T351 aluminum alloy joints. T. Nonferr. Metal. Soc. **26**(10), 2567–2585 (2016)

20. Al-Roubaiy, A.O., Nabet, S.M., Batako, A.D.L.: Experimental and theoretical analysis of frictionstir welding of Al–Cu joints. Int. J. Adv. Manuf. Tech. **71**(9), 1631–1642 (2014)

21. Kuang, B.B., Shen, Y.F., Chen, W.H., Yao, X., Xu, H.S., Gao, J.C., Zhang, J.Q.: The dissimilar friction stir lap welding of 1A99 Al to pure Cu using Zn as filler metal with "pinless" tool configuration. Mater. Design. **68**, 54–62 (2015)
22. Vahid, F., Sindol, K.: Al-to-cu friction stir lap welding. Metall. Mater. Trans. A. **43**(1), 303–315 (2012)
23. Heurtier, P., Jones, M., Desrayaud, C., Driver, J.H., Montheillet, F., Allehaux, D.: Mechanical and thermal modelling of friction stir welding. J. Mater. Process. Tech. **171**(3), 348–357 (2006)

Pinched Hysteresis Loop Characteristics of a Fractional-Order HP TiO$_2$ memristor

Min Shi[1,2]($\boxtimes$) and Songlin Hu[1,2]

[1] Institute of Advanced Technology,
Nanjing University of Posts and Telecommunications,
Nanjing 210023, People's Republic of China
15996301586@163.com
[2] Hubei Province Collaborative Innovation Center for New Energy Microgrid,
China Three Gorges University, Yichang 443002, People's Republic of China

Abstract. A memristor is a nonlinear resistor with time memory. Usually, the memory without any loss is an ideal case. Recent studies show that there is a memory loss of the classic HP TiO$_2$ linear model, which has memory effect between no memory and ideal memory (complete memory). To describe the memory property, we propose a fractional-order HP TiO$_2$ memristor model with the order α between 0 and 1, and the pinched hysteresis loop characteristics are studied as the fractional-order model under periodic external excitation. Compared with the classic integer-order memristor model, numerical simulations show that the fractional-order derivative α is also an important paramcter effects the pinched hysteresis loop area, the memristor value and the output voltage amplitude evidently and regularly.

Keywords: Fractional calculus · Memory · Fractional-order memristor · Pinched hysteresis loop

1 Introduction

The memristor is a pure nonlinear circuit element with memory feature, called the fourth passive two terminal memory circuit element [1]. In the past decades, the existence of the memristor has been extended to memristive systems [2]. However, the theoretical research has not been attracted much attention due to relevant physical device has not been produced for a long time. In 2008, the Hewlett-Packard (HP) laboratory team developed such memristor element with typical resistance features successfully [3]. Motivated by the realization of this new circuit element, the classic capacitor and transistor circuits can be replaced

This work was sponsored by NSF of China under Grant 11402125, 61673223, NSF of Jiangsu Province of China under Grant BK20140861, NSF of Jiangsu Higher Education Institutions of China under Grant 14KJB130003, and the Nanjing University of Posts and Telecommunications Talent Introduction Foundation under Grant NY213107.

© Springer Nature Singapore Pte Ltd. 2017
D. Yue et al. (Eds.): LSMS/ICSEE 2017, Part II, CCIS 762, pp. 705–713, 2017.
DOI: 10.1007/978-981-10-6373-2_70

by the memristor due to the non-volatile memory effect, in other words, its memory function is relevant to its previous state [4,5]. Many novel fundamentals in the analogy circuit design, described by the time-varying property of the memristor resistance, a typical case is memristor-based oscillators [6]. Recently, the modeling, design and analysis of memristor-based application circuits play an important role in artificial intelligence, new type of storage, complex neural network and so on [7–9], due to its unique electrical performance and memory effect.

Relevant research shows that the amplitude of variation of the memristor value reflects memory effect [10] is equal to the time integration of the currents cross through the memristor before the time instant. Different from the traditional circuit system, the memory feature still retained in the case of a closed state, for instance, the non-volatile memory property can maintain the status before shutdown, as the computer is turned on [11,12]. Recently, more and more memristor models are studied as relevant theory improved gradually [13–15]. The linear HP TiO$_2$ linear memristor is one of the most studied model. it will lead to memory loss and can not remember the device boundary effect of the element [3]. That is to say, the memory effect of the linear HP TiO$_2$ memristor is between no memory and ideal memory (complete memory). To describe this property, the most effective tool is the fractional-order derivative [16]. Hence, it is reasonable to construct a fractional-order HP TiO$_2$ linear memristor model.

Compared with the integer-order systems, fractional-order models have more superiority to describe many physical phenomena relevant to non-locality, history memory, frequency dependency, power law and weak singularity [17–19]. In addition, fractional calculus are suitable to describe the physical and chemical properties of the real materials, many research related to the fields of signal analysis and processing, circuits and systems, and chaotic control systems [20–22]. The application of fractional calculus to design and analyze the memristor is more challenge and only a few of fractional-order model have been studied [23–26]. From the physical sense, one of the most important property of the memristors and memristive systems is the existence of a pinched hysteresis effect [27]. Motivated by the above discussions, in this paper, our proposal is to construct a fractional-order HP TiO$_2$ linear memristor model and analyze the pinched hysteresis loop characteristics of such new model.

The rest of this paper is organized as follows. In Sect. 2, preliminary knowledge is prepared, including the mathematical theory of fractional calculus, and some useful fractional-order trigonometric functions based on the Mittag-Leffler function which plays a key role for the solutions of the fractional-order differential equations (FDE). Then, we construct a fractional-order memritstor in Sect. 3. In Sect. 4, we discuss the pinched hysteresis loop properties of the fractional-order memristor model, and numerical simulations show the relationship between voltage and current, and the variety of memristor of this model with different value of fractional-order derivative in Sect. 5. Finally, some concluding remarks are drawn in Sect. 6.

2   Preliminaries

The frequently used fractional-order derivatives are the Riemann-Liouville and the Caputo definition [16,18]. The initial conditions for the FDE with the Riemann-Liouville derivative have no clear physical significance, but in the sense of Caputo derivative, it has the same form as that for the integer-order differential equations, and also has definite physical meaning. Hence, we will use the fractional-order derivative with Caputo definition in this paper.

2.1   Fractional Calculus

The Caputo fractional-order derivative [16] is defined as

$$\,_0^C D_t^\alpha f(t) = \frac{1}{\Gamma(n-\alpha)} \int_0^t \frac{f^{(n)}(\tau)}{(t-\tau)^{\alpha-n+1}} d\tau,$$

where n is the integer satisfying $n-1 < \alpha \leq n$, and the Gamma function $\Gamma(z)$ satisfying $\Gamma(z+1) = z\Gamma(z)$ for $z > 0$. The definition of fractional-order integral [16] is

$$\,_0 I_t^\alpha f(t) = \frac{1}{\Gamma(\alpha)} \int_0^t \frac{f(\tau)}{(t-\tau)^{1-\alpha}} d\tau,$$

and satisfies the following formula $\,_0^C D_t^\alpha(\,_0 I_t^\alpha f(t)) = f(t)$. In this paper, we consider the case of $0 < \alpha \leq 1$. The Mittag-Leffler function which is fundamental solutions of the FDE. The one-parameter Mittag-Leffler function $E_\alpha(t)$ is

$$E_\alpha(t) = \sum_{n=0}^\infty \frac{t^n}{\Gamma(n\alpha+1)},$$

for $\lambda > 0$, the fractional-order derivative of $E_\alpha(t)$ with Caputo definition is

$$\,_0^C D_t^\alpha E_\alpha(\lambda t^\alpha) = \lambda E_\alpha(\lambda t^\alpha).$$

2.2   Fractional Trigonometric Functions

Similar to the classic trigonometric functions, the fractional trigonometric functions has been stated, but these functions are not periodic [17,18]. The classic trigonometric functions formula are also not hold, for example, $\,_0^C D_t^\alpha \sin\omega t = \omega^\alpha \sin(\omega t + \frac{\alpha\pi}{2})$. Now, we introduce the new fractional trigonometric functions which are periodic with the period $2\pi_\alpha \approx 2\pi$. The formula of the fractional trigonometric functions are [28]:

$$\sin_\alpha(t^\alpha) = \frac{E_\alpha((it)^\alpha) - E_\alpha((-it)^\alpha)}{2i}, \quad \cos_\alpha(t^\alpha) = \frac{E_\alpha((it)^\alpha) + E_\alpha((-it)^\alpha)}{2},$$

where

$$E_\alpha((it)^\alpha) = \cos_\alpha(t^\alpha) + i\sin_\alpha(t^\alpha), \quad E_\alpha((-it)^\alpha) = \cos_\alpha(t^\alpha) - i\sin_\alpha(t^\alpha).$$

Some properties of the fractional trigonometric functions are presented as follows [28]:

$$\sin_\alpha(-t)^\alpha = -\sin_\alpha(t^\alpha), \quad \cos_\alpha(-t)^\alpha = \cos_\alpha(t^\alpha),$$

$${}_0^C D_t^\alpha \sin_\alpha(\omega^\alpha t^\alpha) = \omega^\alpha i^{\alpha-1} \cos_\alpha(\omega^\alpha t^\alpha), \quad {}_0^C D_t^\alpha \cos_\alpha(\omega^\alpha t^\alpha) = \omega^\alpha i^{\alpha+1} \sin_\alpha(\omega^\alpha t^\alpha).$$

Figure 1 shows that $\sin_\alpha(t^\alpha)$ is periodic with period $2\pi_\alpha \approx 2\pi$, the case of $\cos_\alpha(t^\alpha)$ is similar.

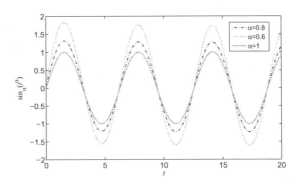

Fig. 1. The trajectory of $\sin_\alpha(t^\alpha)$ with respect to t.

3   Fractional-Order HP TiO$_2$ memristor

The classic current controlled HP TiO$_2$ memristor model [2] is described mathematically by

$$\begin{cases} v(t) = M(x)i(t), \\ M(x) = R_{ON}x + R_{OFF}(1 - x), \\ \dot{x}(t) = ki(t), \end{cases} \tag{1}$$

where $i(t)$ is the input current, $v(t)$ is the output voltage, R_{ON} and R_{OFF} are the allowable low and high resistances of the memristor ($R_{ON} \ll R_{OFF}$) respectively, The memristor value $M(x)$ depends on its internal state variable $x(t)$ continuously, and $x(t) \in [0, 1]$. Consider the time memory effect of $x(t)$, the relationship between $i(t)$ and $x(t)$ is

$$x(t) = k \int_0^t K(t - \tau)i(\tau)d\tau,$$

when $K(t)$ is Dirac function, $x(t) = ki(t)$, it means $x(t)$ has no memory effect; when $K(t)$ is Heaviside function, $x(t) = k \int_0^t i(t)dt$, it means $x(t)$ has ideal memory effect, i.e., there is no memory loss before the time t. But in fact, the memory effect is usually between no memory and ideal memory. Due to the

Laplace transform of Dirac function and Heaviside function is $1/s^0 = 1$ and $1/s^1 = 1/s$, we can denote the Laplace transform of $K(t)$ is $1/s^\alpha (0 < \alpha < 1)$, which means the memory effect is between no memory and ideal memory. With the inverse Laplace transform, we have $K(t) = \frac{t^{\alpha-1}}{\Gamma(\alpha)}$, then,

$$x(t) = k \int_0^t \frac{(t-\tau)^{\alpha-1}}{\Gamma(\alpha)} i(\tau) \mathrm{d}\tau$$

$$= \frac{k}{\Gamma(\alpha)} \int_0^t \frac{i(\tau)}{(t-\tau)^{1-\alpha}} \mathrm{d}\tau = k \cdot {}_0 I_t^\alpha i(t).$$

Hence, ${}_0^C D_t^\alpha x(t) = {}_0^C D_t^\alpha ({}_0 I_t^\alpha k i(t)) = k i(t)$. Similarly, we can construct a fractional-order HP TiO_2 memristor model as follows,

$$\begin{cases} v(t) = M_\alpha(x) i(t), \\ M_\alpha(x) = R_{ON} x + R_{OFF}(1-x), \\ {}_0^C D_t^\alpha x(t) = k i(t). \end{cases} \quad (2)$$

To the classic memristor model (1), three fingerprints of the pinched hysteresis loop are given [29]: (i) Pinched hysteresis loop of memristor is a double-valued Lissajous curve, whose $i - v$ trajectories always pinch at the origin of the coordinates; (ii) The pinched hysteresis loop shrinks when the excitation frequency of the input current increases; (iii) If the frequency increases to infinity, then the shape of the pinched hysteresis of a memristor tends to a single-valued function line. In the following section, we will investigate the pinched hysteresis loop characteristics of fractional-order memristor model (2).

4 Pinched Hysteresis Loop of the Fractional-Order HP TiO_2 memristor

Consider the fractional-order HP TiO_2 memristor system excited by the variable $i(t)$ in the form of harmonic signal $i(t) = A \sin_\alpha(\omega^\alpha t^\alpha)$, A is the amplitude and ω is the excitation frequency. Substitute the harmonic signal $i(t)$ into the equation ${}_0^C D_t^\alpha x(t) = k i(t)$, then $x(t)$ is deriving by

$$x(t) = x(0) + \frac{kA}{\omega^\alpha \mathrm{j}^{3+\alpha}} (1 - \cos_\alpha(\omega^\alpha t^\alpha)), \quad (3)$$

where $x(0)$ is the initial state at $t = 0$. Combine (3) to equation $M_\alpha(x) = R_{ON} x + R_{OFF}(1-x)$ has

$$M_\alpha(x) = (R_{ON} - R_{OFF})\left(x(0) + \frac{kA}{\omega^\alpha \mathrm{j}^{3+\alpha}}\right) + R_{OFF}$$

$$- (R_{ON} - R_{OFF})\frac{kA}{\omega^\alpha \mathrm{j}^{3+\alpha}} \cos_\alpha(\omega^\alpha t^\alpha). \quad (4)$$

Substituting (4) into $v(t) = M_\alpha(x)i(t)$, we have

$$v(t) = B_1(\omega)\sin_\alpha(\omega^\alpha t^\alpha) + B_2(\omega)\sin_\alpha(\omega^\alpha t^\alpha)\cos_\alpha(\omega^\alpha t^\alpha), \tag{5}$$

where

$$B_1(\omega) = \left[(R_{ON} - R_{OFF})\left(x(0) + \frac{kA}{\omega^\alpha i^{3+\alpha}}\right) + R_{OFF}\right]A,$$

$$B_2(\omega) = (R_{OFF} - R_{ON})\frac{kA^2}{\omega^\alpha i^{3+\alpha}}.$$

Next, numerical simulations show the characteristics of the pinched hysteresis loop of fractional-order HP TiO$_2$ memristor (2). In this model, we will give the relevant parameters as follows: $k = 10^4$, $R_{ON} = 100\,\Omega$, $R_{OFF} = 10\,\text{K}\Omega$, $A = 0.1\text{mA}$ and the initial value $x(0) = 0.01$.

Obviously, $v(t)$ is a periodic function due to $\sin_\alpha(t^\alpha)$ and $\cos_\alpha(t^\alpha)$ are periodic. Given $\omega = 2$, Fig. 2(a) shows that the pinched hysteresis loop of fractional-order memristor is also a double-valued Lissajous curve, whose trajectories always pinch at the origin of the coordinates. It is similar to the case of integer-order model as $\alpha = 1$. Moreover, the area of the pinched hysteresis loop increases as the value of α decreases. Figure 2(b) shows that the pinched hysteresis loop shrinks when the excitation frequency increases, and if the frequency increases to infinity, then the shape of the pinched hysteresis loop of a memristor trends to a single-valued function line.

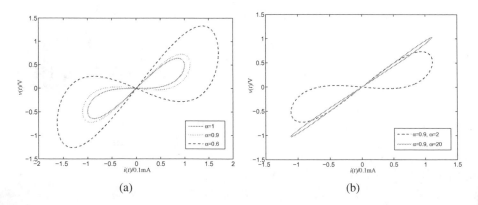

(a)   (b)

Fig. 2. (a): The effect of fractional-order α to the pinched hysteresis loop and (b): The effect of excitation frequency ω to the pinched hysteresis loop.

5   Analysis of the Fractional-Order Memristor Value $M_\alpha(x)$

The memristor value $M_\alpha(x)$ has the same dimension with the resistance [1], which is equal to the time integration of the currents cross through the memristor before the time instant. The dynamic range of the memristor value reflects the memory effect. According to (2),

$$_0^C D_t^\alpha M_\alpha(x) = -kR_d i(t),$$

where $R_d = R_{OFF} - R_{ON}$. Then, we have

$$M_\alpha(x)_0^C D_t^\alpha M_\alpha(x) = -kR_d v(t). \tag{6}$$

Applying the fractional-order integral to both side of (6), and if the memristor value changes from its initial value $M_\alpha(x_0)$ to $M_\alpha(x)$, the memristor value as a function of the input voltage and the time can be obtained by

$$\frac{[M_\alpha(x)]^{\alpha+1} - [M_\alpha(x_0)]^{\alpha+1}}{\Gamma(\alpha+2)} = \frac{-kR_d}{\Gamma(\alpha)} \int_0^t \frac{v(\tau)}{(t-\tau)^{1-\alpha}} d\tau.$$

Figure 3(a) shows that the wave shape of $M_\alpha(x)$ at time domain. As the value α decreases, the amplitude of the memristor value increases, it implies that the memory effect is stronger than the classic case as $\alpha = 1$. Figure 3(b) shows the wave shape of $v(t)$ at time domain. Similarly, the output voltage amplitude increases as the value α decreases.

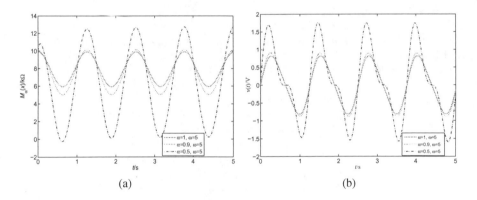

(a)   (b)

Fig. 3. (a): The effect of fractional-order α to the wave shape of $M_\alpha(x)$ at time domain and (b): The effect of fractional-order α to the wave shape of $v(t)$ at time domain.

6   Conclusion

The memory of linear HP TiO$_2$ memristor is not ideal, the doped layer width of the element is between zero and total width of the element, it will lead to memory loss. Based on this property, we introduced a fractional-order HP TiO$_2$ linear memristor model, and verified the pinched hysteresis loop existence of such new type of memristor model. Three essential properties of the pinched hysteresis loop is the same as classic model as $\alpha = 1$. In addition, the fractional-order derivative α with different value affects the pinched hysteresis loop area, the memristor value and the output voltage amplitude evidently and regularly. Hence, the fractional-order HP TiO_2 linear memristor model is a more general model to describe the dynamic change properties of the memristor. In our future work, we will concern on how to realize the best memory ability of the fractional-order memristor and the design and simulation of analog fractional-order circuits.

References

1. Chua, L.O.: Memristor-the missing circuit element. IEEE Trans. Circuit Theory **18**(5), 507–519 (1971)
2. Chua, L.O., Kang, S.M.: Memristive devices and systems. Proc. IEEE **64**(2), 209–223 (1976)
3. Strukov, D.B., Snider, G.S., Stewart, D.R., Williams, R.S.: The missing memristor found. Nature **453**(7191), 80–83 (2008)
4. Chua, L.O.: Nonlinear circuit foundations for nanodevices. I. The four-element torus. Proc. IEEE **91**(11), 1830–1859 (2003)
5. Adhikari, S.P., Sah, M.P., Kim, H., Chua, L.O.: Three fingerprints of memristor. IEEE Trans. Circ. Syst. I, Reg. Pap. **60**(11), 3008–3021 (2013)
6. Corinto, F., Ascoli, A.: Memristive diode bridge with LCR filter. Electron. Lett. **48**(14), 824–825 (2012)
7. Di Ventra, M., Pershin, Y.V.: On the physical properties of memristive, memcapacitive and meminductive systems. Nanotechnology **24** (2013). Article no. 255201
8. Ebong, I.E., Mazumder, P.: CMOS and memristor-based neural network design for position detection. Proc. IEEE **100**(6), 2050–2060 (2012)
9. Crupi, M., Pradhan, L., Tozer, S.: Modelling neural plasticity with memristors. IEEE Can. Rev. **68**, 10–14 (2012)
10. Di Ventra, M., Pershin, Y.V., Chua, L.O.: Circuit elements with memory: memristors, memcapacitors, and meminductors. Proc. IEEE **97**(10), 1717–1723 (2009)
11. Niu, D., Chen, Y., Xie, Y.: Low-power dual-element memristor based memory design. In: Proceedings of the 16th ACM/IEEE International Symposium on Low Power Electronics and Design, pp. 25–30 (2010)
12. Ho, Y., Huang, G.M., Li, P.: Nonvolatile memristor memory: device characteristics and design implications. In: Proceedings of the 2009 International Conference on Computer-Aided Design, pp. 485–490 (2009)
13. Itoh, M., Chua, L.O.: Memristor oscillators. Int. J. Bifurcat. Chaos **18**(11), 3183–3206 (2008)
14. Muthuswamy, B., Kokate, P.P.: Memristor-based chaotic circuits. IEEE Tech. Rev. **26**(6), 415–426 (2009)
15. Bao, B., Ma, Z., Xu, J., Liu, Z., Xu, Q.: A simple memristor chaotic circuit with complex dynamics. Int. J. Bifurcat. Chaos **21**(9), 2629–2645 (2011)
16. Podlubny, I.: Fractional Differential Equations: An Introduction to Fractional Derivatives, Fractional Differential Equations, to Methods of Their Solution and Some of Their Applications. Academic, San Diego (1998)
17. Oldham, K.B., Spanier, J.: The Fractional Calculus: Theory and Applications of Differentiation and Integration to Arbitrary Order. Academic, New York (1974)

18. Butzer, P.L.: An introduction to fractional calculus. In: Butzer, P.L., Westphal, U. (eds.) Applications of Fractional Calculus in Physics. World Scientific, Singapore (2000)
19. Caponetto, R., Dongola, G., Luigi, F., Ivo, P.: Fractional order systems: modeling and control applications. Academic, World Scientific, New Jersey (2010)
20. Chen, Y., Vinagre, B.M.: A new IIR-type digital fractional order differentiator. Sign. Process. **83**(11), 2359–2365 (2011)
21. Elwakil, A.S.: Fractional-order circuits and systems: an emerging interdisciplinary research area. IEEE Circ. Syst. Mag. **10**(4), 40–50 (2010)
22. Freeborn, T.J.: A survey of fractional-order circuit models for biology and biomedicine. IEEE J. Emerg. Sel. Topics Circ. Syst. **3**(3), 416–424 (2013)
23. Radwan, A.G., Moaddy, K., Hashim, I.: Amplitude modulation and synchronization of fractional-order memristor-based Chua's circuit. Abstract Appl. Anal. (2013). Article no. 758676
24. Machado, J.T.: Fractional generalization of memristor and higher order elements. Commun. Nonlinear Sci. Numer. Simul. **18**(2), 264–275 (2013)
25. Abdelouahab, M.S., Lozi, R., Chua, L.: Memfractance: a mathematical paradigm for circuit elements with memory. Int. J. Bifurcation Chaos **24** (2014). Article no. 1430023
26. Pu, Y.F., Yuan, X.: Fracmemristor: fractional-order memristor. IEEE Access **4**, 1872–1888 (2016)
27. Pershin, Y.V., Di Ventra, M.: Memory effects in complex materials and nanoscale systems. Adv. Phys. **60**(2), 145–227 (2011)
28. Rezazadeh, H., Aminikhah, H., Sheikhani, A.H.R.: Analytical studies for linear periodic systems of fractional order. Math. Sci. **10**(1–2), 13–21 (2016)
29. Sun, J., Yao, L., Zhang, X., Wang, Y., Cui, G.: Generalised mathematical model of memristor. IET Circ. Devices Syst. **10**(3), 244–249 (2016)

Author Index